MIDNIGHT AGAIN

For Helen's family –
then and now

MIDNIGHT AGAIN

THE WARTIME LETTERS OF HELEN RAMSEY TURTLE

Edited by
John Wilson Foster

Foreword by
Julie Turtle Mackie

MAHEE
ISLAND

Published 2021
by Turtle Mackie of Mahee

ISBN 978-1-5272-9411-0

Printed by W&G Baird Ltd
Design and production by Wendy Dunbar, Dunbar Design

CONTENTS

FOREWORD

To read through anyone's letters is an unusual kind of journey; to read through my mother's even more so. She died before I got to know her and yet I have got to know myself through her letters, as reading them is to travel inside one's own personal history seen from a very different yet very intimate perspective. I'm inclined to think that as we get older we become more like our younger selves, so I have been able to pay particular attention to my childhood and to see if I'm coming full circle, thereby meeting myself coming back. Little did I know how well I would get to know her and what a wonderful journey I would have.

Every waking moment of Helen's three girls' lives and the life she was living during the Second World War years were meticulously recorded for her mother and sister. The long wartime separation from her Colorado family was extremely hard to bear, so writing these extraordinary and revealing letters became the solace she needed then and have become a joy for us now.

She was living in Northern Ireland, cut off from her native city of Denver, because she had married a Northern Irishman. How Helen Ramsey from Denver Colorado and Lancelot Turtle from Belfast met is the question I am invariably asked when my American parentage comes up and it's a pleasure to recount the love story that spans two continents and forms the background and backbone of this book.

The story begins in Virginia, USA in 1879 when Lee Ramsey, a young lawyer of 27 and suffering from tuberculosis, decided that the dry climate and high altitude of Colorado might aid his recovery. In Colorado he met Augustus Turtle, a young man from County Down in the north of Ireland whose ambition to be a cowboy had inspired him to "Go West". It was in the West, in Denver, that these two young men became friends. Lee Ramsey recovered from TB and Gus Turtle, having achieved his ambition, returned to his family linen business in County Down where he married.

I don't know precisely how or when Lee Ramsey met Grace and Margaret Bradley from Philadelphia but meet they did. These young women were teachers who had come to Colorado in 1899 in the hope that Margaret would recover from her debilitating tuberculosis and it was thanks to Grace's dedicated determination to make their move that Margaret made a complete recovery. When in 1906 Lee and Grace married, they asked Margaret to live with them. Lee Ramsey Jr was born in 1908, Helen in 1911 and Virginia (Ginna) in 1912.

Margaret continued her teaching career until 1925 when she retired and decided to fulfil a long held ambition to go to Europe. Lee Ramsey suggested that his sister-in-law might go to Ireland to visit his friend of so long ago whom he referred to as "Turtle". Gus Turtle whose wife Beatrix had died welcomed this unexpected visitor who brought him news from Denver. A year later in 1926, Gus travelled to Denver to marry Margaret and they both returned to Lisburn in County Down.

In 1927 Grace Ramsey with Helen (16) and Ginna (15) visited Gus and Margaret. Gus had asked a young cousin to meet their train in Belfast which Lancelot Turtle duly did.

A month later Grace and Ginna returned to Denver and Helen entered Smith College in Massachusetts. A prolific correspondence between Helen and Lancelot began and continued until their marriage in 1933 after which Helen moved to Belfast. Her letters back to Denver became the continuation of this Irish-American story.

My father's meeting Helen in 1927 wasn't his first association with America, as he had actually been born there in 1905. In 1900 his father Herbert Turtle had gone to New York City to join two of his brothers who were already there, having opened an American office for Turtle Bros., the family linen firm in County Armagh. On a trip back to Belfast for the wedding of another brother, he met Emily Turtle, a distant cousin. On his return to New York Herbert wrote to Emily to continue the friendship that had begun at the wedding, and in this way the first of the family's romances by correspondence began and continued until in 1904 Herbert returned to Belfast for his own wedding.

The Turtles lived in Montclair, New Jersey until Herbert's ill health brought them back to Ireland where he died in 1916. Lancelot was 11 and his sister Arabella 10.

Lancelot's maternal grandfather was an active member of the renowned Belfast Naturalists' Field Club and it was through him that Lancelot's life-long ornithological interest was nurtured. At his Quaker boarding school in Reading, England Lancelot built bird boxes with a map of their locations which was still in existence and being referred to when another generation of the Turtle family with the same interest went to the same school in the 1950s.

Following school and now at Cambridge, Lancelot met a fellow bird enthusiast with whom he travelled on several ambitious ornithological quests. This was Marquis Masauji Hachisuka from Tokyo whose future publications, *A Handbook of the Birds of Iceland* (1927) and *The Birds of the Philippine Islands* (1931), as well as his research into the extinction of the Dodo, ensured his reputation in ornithological circles. When my parents got married in 1933, the first part of their honeymoon was spent birding in Colorado, the rest was a continuation in England where one of the highlights was finding a stone curlew's nest in a remote part of Cambridgeshire! This was to become a regular pattern of their happy marriage as evidenced by my mother's 1942 wartime broadcast.

Living "virtually" through the Second World War by reading these historic descriptions of the war-torn world – so many of which were written from Mahee Island where I now live – I was profoundly struck by the similarities of those years with the impact of this year's Covid 19 pandemic. This realisation began for me when engineering companies were asked to start making ventilators instead of their usual production lines – in 1940 it was Spitfires. Gas masks compare to anti-virus masks, rationing was threatened this year as witnessed by unbecoming runs on supplies, hoarding and over-loaded trolleys.

There was during World War Two a "digging for Britain" ethos as front gardens became vegetable plots and the Minister of Food Lord Woolton's words echoed back over 80 years as we have been encouraged in 2020 to go back to "simpler living" when we too bought packets of seeds. Likewise, this year there were barely any other topics of conversation amongst friends and neighbours. The Glendinning and Browne families, whose company my parents so often enjoyed during the 1940s, are now my own friends and neighbours, two generations on and we too are consumed with our restricted lives. And how interesting to read in my mother's letters that the days were "slipping by like magic – every Sunday it seems that it has only been a minute since last Sunday". Many people have remarked similarly this year, as they have also about the unpredictability of the future.

It seems many more minutes since I started reading, learning and thinking about my mother. She never lost her joint loyalty and enthusiasm for both the country of her birth and that of her adoption. She has enabled us to join her on her journey as she picked up her pen again and again to record, now for posterity, the life so lovingly and bravely lived.

It has been said that letters are the most significant memorial that a person can leave, and thanks to the foresight of my mother's family in Denver Colorado who kept each and every one she wrote from 1933 until 1945, her legacy has been assured.

That most of the wartime letters survived the Battle of the North Atlantic is something of a miracle. The censor's scissors occasionally and by necessity had to be wielded but their return journey was a peaceful one and made possible by the thoughtfulness of Helen's nephew Penn Hughes whose late mother, Ginna had made a start on editing the wartime letters with a view to a publication. It was clear to Penn that the project should now be continued and in Ireland. In 1991 my son-in-law Martin Hamilton was in Los Angeles on business and with Penn living in California, in Oakland, it was arranged that they should meet and the box of valuable cargo be handed over. Thank you, Penn and Martin.

My sister Gay Firth, who became the next custodian, lived in London where she was Letter's Editor for the *Financial Times*. It was therefore a seamless transition to treat this archive with the professional expertise required. Gay read every letter and a précis was written. Each letter with its envelope was then put in a file appropriate to its year with the word "Use" on the ones she thought necessary for the book *The Wartime Letters of Helen Ramsey Turtle* which she was planning to edit. Very sadly this was not to be. Diagnosed with a rare lymphoma in 2004 Gay died a year later.

Now and very unexpectedly I had become the next custodian. My husband, realising their fragility, photocopied the many hundreds of tightly written letters which was another dedicated task for which, Paddy, your entire family is in your debt.

Enter Joan Cowdy with her word processing skills who typed each letter from these photocopies and with whom I had many conversations as to how to proceed. Sincere thanks, Joan: you made the next stage of the journey possible.

The last stage was as unexpected as was my custodianship, and it began when I had the great and good fortune to meet John Wilson Foster. That was in 2014 and his interest then and his invaluable professional editorial skills, advice, guidance and untold patience since then has brought this wartime story to its ultimate and historic destination.

To you, Jack, my continuing and grateful thanks.

MAHEE ISLAND, DECEMBER 2020

1939

A Czechoslovakian friend warns
   of German aggression

A feast of Shakespeare on a Belfast stage

Germany invades Poland;
   Britain and France declare war

The British government imposes a
   sunset-to-sunrise blackout

Helen relents on her pacifism

Louis MacNeice lectures to the
   Drawing Room Circle

27th Jan.
88 Belmont Road,
Belfast

Dear Mother and Ginna,

It is a lovely sunny day and it, the sun, is blazing in on me at my desk which looks so business like and which is such a comfort because I always have loved everything to do with a desk – especially notebooks! Gay is asleep in her bed where she sleeps every morning now because she is too big for her pram and only talks and disturbs Julie who is sound asleep on the porch. They are both fine. ...

2nd Feb.

Here it is a week later and this letter hasn't been sent because I have been brooding on Ginna's love life and there hasn't been much news anyway. ... No cable yet so I know that you aren't engaged – I hesitate strongly to say anything about your marrying Lloyd because I don't know enough about the whole situation, but if you do get engaged to him I would be delighted to have him for a brother-in-law and it seems to me that the drawbacks are relative unimportant – his family, lack of intellectual curiosity (too much of which would be wearing to live with I think). If you do decide to marry him I should think you would get along very well because knowing his limitations you would have to exercise your own gumption to keep yourself up to your own abilities – just offhand he seems to have lots of Lancelot's qualities and if he hasn't that extra glamour that L. has, it is probably because his background is more like ours was whereas L.'s seems enchanted by merit of Auntie's cracking him up and the undoubted romantic element of being British with a good accent and a Cambridge background – both superficial things in the last analysis. To make up for L.'s "grand manner" or whatever it is that he undeniably has Lloyd has an equally attractive casualness and ease of manner and a devil-may-care cheerfulness that would be very easy to live with – in fact I can work up a good case for Lloyd with no trouble at all but you know all his good points better than I do and it naturally rests with you. ...

Lunch is announced – spaghetti on toast Ma, how do you spell (spaghetti) quick – Herbert Morowitz [sic] and his brother were here for lunch on Tuesday and gave us the low-down on Czecho-Slovakia England sure done her wrong[1] – more later but I want this to catch the Queen.[2] Julie and Gay are both fine and too cute for words. Gay says that any glamorous looking girls in a magazine is "Zis" (Ginna) so she hasn't forgotten her glamorous Auntie.

Love,
Helen

10th Feb.
Belmont

Dear Mother and Ginna,

I am all ready to go to town to do some "messages" as errands are always called here, and I see where there is a mail to catch the *Aquitania*, hence my haste.[3]

In your letters I was delighted to hear that something stopped Ginna's marrying Lloyd next Wednesday because your motives seemed more of desperation to get settled than anything else, and although I fully realize and sympathize with your great uncertainty of mind I think it would be fatal to marry in such a desperate spirit – which you no doubt realized yourself. I regret now having written the letter making out such a good case for Lloyd because although it is all true I could

---

[1] The Munich Agreement of late September 1938, to which the United Kingdom was a co-signatory, permitted Nazi Germany to annex portions of Czechoslovakia. The remainder of Czechoslovakia was occupied by Spring 1939. Herbert Morawetz, whose family bought machinery from Mackies, an important Belfast foundry, was from Czechoslovakia. Herbert and his family arrived as Jewish refugees in Belfast where he worked in the foundry until he and his sister Sonja emigrated to Canada on 22nd December 1939. See Linda Wang, "Herbert Morawetz", *c & en* 96: 4, 22nd January, 2018: https://cen.acs.org; "Herbert Morawetz," Wikipedia.

[2] Royal Mail Steamer *Queen Mary*, a Cunard liner whose maiden voyage was in May 1936; she became a troopship for the duration of the war.

[3] RMS *Aquitania* ("the Ship Beautiful"), launched in 1913, served the Cunard Line between England and the United States from 1914 until 1950. In the Great War the ship became a troop transport, resumed passenger and mail service in 1920, but once again became a troopship when the Second World War broke out.

make out an equally convincing case for all your beaux ... I read somewhere once that women have the peculiar ability to shut their eyes to any obstacle in the way and I am particularly prone to self-delusion almost to the point of an unbalanced mind. ...

[We are going to] Mahee in May[4] and I am hoping America in September – depending on getting a good nurse, how the children are and L.'s business, the war-scare, Ginna's wedding *and all.*

We are leading a very social life at the moment and I'll write you a long letter again soon –

G'bye now

Love,
Helen

Per S.S. *Ile de France* – Mrs. Lee Ramsey, Miss Virginal Ramsey[5], 757 Williams Street, DENVER, Colorado, U.S.A.

11th Feb.
Belmont.

Dear Mother and Ginna,

Having just waked up from a nap in a chair I feel as fresh as the proverbial daisy although it is going on for eleven. I was just up to see Julie who was stretched out on Nanny's knee looking very big and fine; she rolled her eyes sideways to see me and they are *colossal.* Sometimes the likeness to Ginna is so striking that I think it is Ginna sitting there (on her pot!) It is the shape of her eyes and eye-lids as much as the expression which definitely is all Ramsey and sometimes like Lee. Her hair isn't really red yet although her complexion is such that her hair can only be red because when her cheeks get red they are orange colored and she would have to use a Tangee lipstick.[6] She gained four ounces from Tuesday to Friday, but I told you that.

---

[4] Helen and Lancelot had bought a cottage on Mahee Island that juts out into Strangford Lough, County Down.

[5] Helen played a number of ironic variations on her sister Virginia's name.

[6] During the Second World War, American best-selling Tangee lipstick (unavailable in the UK until after the war) was marketed as a female morale-booster and showed a woman pilot the more confident through its application.

Lancelot is still at Mahee and I went to the Classic [picturehouse] with Mrs. Turtle at 1.45 to see mainly *The Cheat* with Sacha Guitry (French and excellent) and *The Amazing Dr. Clutterhouse* [sic] which was just fair. I am glad that you have a chance to see foreign films too because they are so interesting. We had *Carnet de Bal* at the last Film Society show and it is good all right.[7] The jazz that was coming from all the English stations was so awful that I had to change to Paris (I think) and now it is quite good. We hardly ever play the radio[8] – why you should "play" it I don't know. While I am on the subject of films – movies to you – (I'm afraid that films just came off my pen as naturally as off any British subject's, but I was thinking about the fillum society) be sure to see *The Lady Vanishes*, if you haven't already; believe it or not *it's British and it's good* – produced by Alfred Hitchcock and of the spy-thriller type that he does so well. ...

We had Isabel and Billy Noble, Jack and Elaine and a cousin of Jack's, Miss Armerod, and John Carr[9] to dinner on Wednesday and the dinner was so good although the conversation, or swing of the party I thought was slow but L. thought that it was all right. Isabel Noble gave a masterpiece at the D. R. Circle the last time on Somerset Maugham.[10]

[7] The Belfast Film Society held its first season in 1937–38 and by its second season had close to 600 members. It rented suitable cinemas for its showings of five foreign films per season. See Tom Hughes, *How Belfast Saw the Light: A Cinematic History* (Belfast: Tom Hughes, 2014), p. 511. (Helen later uses the two-syllable Belfast pronunciation of film, "fillum", when referring to the Film Society.) *Un Carnet de Bal* (1937) is a French romantic drama. *Confessions of a Cheat* (1936) was directed by Sacha Guitry and adapted from his 1935 novel, *Les Mémoires d'un Tricheur*. *The Amazing Dr. Clitterhouse* is an American crime film (1938) starring Edward G. Robinson and Humphrey Bogart.

[8] This changed once the war began; like many, Helen became addicted to the BBC, both to news bulletins and the art and entertainment programmes that helped to lift the spirits.

[9] Isabel Noble was a Belfast friend of Helen's. Jack (later Sir John) Andrews (1903–86) was to become a Unionist MP in the Northern Ireland parliament 1953–64, then a senator until the Stormont parliament was prorogued in 1972. He was the son of John M. Andrews (1871–1956), Prime Minister of Northern Ireland, 1940–43. Jack's wife Elaine (née Maynard James), from Newport, Wales, died in 1980. Since Jane Ormrod married James Andrews in 1922, Helen is almost certainly referring to a Miss Ormrod. John Carr (b. 1908) was a brother of the artist Tom Carr who will appear often in the letters. Their father was a stockbroker and their mother was a member of the Workman family that recurs in Helen's letters. The brothers were friends of the Turtles.

[10] The Belfast Drawing Room Circle was begun in 1926 by an American woman, Mary Elizabeth Morwood (née Bell), b. 1872 in New Orleans and who died in Belfast on 3rd August 1939 before war broke out. *Cont'd overleaf*

She is engaged to an American widower and is going to live in Connecticut; she hasn't told me yet but it seems to be generally known ...

Herbert and Rosemary Bryson[11] are adopting a Jewish refugee for whom they are going to be responsible until he or she is 18, if necessary.[12] L. and I talked about taking a little boy of 3 or 4 years old for a short period but from what we hear you are likely to be stuck and I wouldn't want to have him always but we are making enquiries. John Carr was so optimistic about the situation and said that Germany would be completely broke before this year is out and that Hitler's sanity couldn't last much longer according to Freud who says that he is a megalomaniac – how John knows I don't know, but he is positive.[13]

Cont'd She arrived in Ireland in 1919 with her five children and husband, James Morwood (b. 1862, Co. Londonderry, d.1946 Belfast) and whom she had met on a ship sailing to India where as Lt. Col. James Morwood MD he was Chief Surgeon of the British Army in India, and whom she had married in Calcutta in 1907. The Circle of women met every other Monday afternoon in the homes of members where in large drawing-rooms they heard a paper by a member or invited speaker. Membership was by invitation and there were some forty members. Each year there was a printed Report by the Committee. (See Afterword.) Mary Morwood's obituary is in the *Northern Whig*, 5th August 1939.

[11] Herbert Bryson was a member of a Portadown linen-manufacturing family, now living in the Malone neighbourhood of Belfast. In 1891, the Brysons amalgamated with the Spences, to form Spence Bryson Ltd to produce fine linen products, and is still doing so. See Kathleen Rankin, *The Linen Houses of the Bann Valley: The Story of their Families* (Belfast: Ulster Historical Foundation, 2012), p. 198. In 1965, Herbert Bryson was appointed Chairman of the new Northern Ireland Housing Trust. See *Belfast Gazette* 12th February 1965, p. 49. Rosemary Bryson was Rosemary Sinton before her marriage. Huntley House in Dunmurry on the outskirts of Belfast became the Bryson family home in 1932, its name deriving from the intermarriage of the distinguished Charley and Hunter families in 1817.

[12] The Kindertransport operation, rescuing Jewish children from Germany, Austria and Czechoslovakia, began in December 1938 when 206 children arrived in England; eventually around 10,000 unaccompanied children were allowed into the United Kingdom. A few were taken into foster homes such as the Brysons offered. In Northern Ireland, older refugee children went to a hostel in Cliftonpark Avenue, Belfast. In the summer of 1939 a resettlement farm was created at Millisle, County Down where the children lived, worked, played and attended local schools. Most of the children left the farm at the end of the war though some remained until 1948 when it closed. See Marilyn Taylor, "Millisle, County Down – Haven from Nazi Terror," *History Ireland* vol. 9, no. 4 (Winter 2001); Taylor had written a novel on the subject: *Faraway Home* (1999).

[13] Hitler was analysed remotely by Freudians in the 1940s but I have found no record of Freud himself making observations about Hitler. Their lives overlapped to the extent that they both lived in Vienna before the Great War.

He said that he had a letter from Ginna that he finally made out, all but one word.

Next Wednesday I am breaking down and having a luncheon ostensibly for a new American girl who lives in one of the Moat flats[14] but really to pay a few long-standing debts... Mrs. Sloan is married to some Scotsman in the air force and is a divorcée and has lived in England for the last ten years and has been home 26 times or maybe 18 voyages. She is blonde and pretty glamorous but a nit-wit, I'm afraid – we are going there for supper tomorrow night. ...

We are working up to going to Paris for Easter and we are going to make the stable at Mahee into a bedroom and plan to go for May, June, July and August. The snowdrops are all in bloom at Mahee and [they] look so cute. I have the little red girl out sprinkling our snowdrops and crocuses and she looks so natural. ...

L. just arrived and so to bed.

Love,
Helen

16th Feb.
Belmont

Dear Mother and Ginna,

... Yesterday I gave a luncheon for seven which while not a flop was not a success, and decided me against giving any more luncheons – it was too much of a rush for Mary [the maid] and nothing looked very nice although it tasted good and between the babies both bawling it wasn't worth it... We had corn soup, creamed lobster on the shells, ham, baked bananas, peas new potatoes and super lemon meringue pie but everything looked like those pictures "How she thought she

---

[14] The Moat, Strandtown, Belfast was one of the "many sumptuous mansions ordered by the linen lords", Jonathan Bardon, *Belfast An Illustrated History* (1982; Belfast: Blackstaff Press, 1990), p. 107. The Moat was built in 1862 for Thomas Valentine. It came into the possession of the titled McConnell family (Terence McConnell was a friend of the Turtles) and in 1907 was bought by Frank Workman of Workman, Clark, the well-known Belfast shipbuilders. The Moat was converted into apartments in 1938. See "The McConnell Baronets" in Lord Belmont in Northern Ireland, a website maintained by Timothy Ferres.

looked" – the lobster was supposed to have fins on top for decoration, the ham was supposed to be sliced down the big platter with the bananas peas and potatoes around it instead of which each thing was passed separately looking as plain as possible ... – however it's over now and will be forgotten long before you read this. Mrs. Sloan, the American, I like better than I thought I would – she looked so pretty and although blondined[15] is otherwise conservative and snappy and although she isn't bursting with brains she is a rock of sense and has character, I think...

We went to hear Pouissnoff [sic] on Tuesday night playing all Chopin with two by Bach and the *Liebstraume* [sic] for encores.[16] Jack and Elaine took us and at the last minute Elaine ate something that upset her and couldn't go. Tomorrow night we are going to the theatre and dinner with Esmé – it is *The Scarlet Pimpernel*.[17] Saturday night we are going to dinner with Jimmy and Molly Cunningham.[18] I wear my pink topped dinner dress to all these dinners – it will almost fasten at the side and the gap that doesn't fasten is covered by the blousing of the pink top, so my "meat" doesn't show. ...

---

[15] Her bleached hair suggests to Helen that Mrs Sloan is a "dumb blonde"; bleached blonde hair would have been a rarity in 1930s Belfast, a predominantly conservative and religious society. That she was a divorcée in monogamous Northern Ireland would also have burnished her apparently dangerous glamour.

[16] Leff Pouishnoff performed a Chopin recital in the Ulster Hall, Belfast on the evening of 14th February. Pouishnoff (1891–1959), born in the Ukraine into a Russian aristocratic family, was a pianist renowned for his performances of Chopin and Liszt. (*Liebestraum* is 3 piano solo works by Liszt.) He lived in Britain from 1920. His recital on 2BE (the call sign of the Belfast station of the BBC) on 17th October, 1925 was in the same year as Pouishnoff first broadcast for the BBC in England at the old Savoy Hill station. He gave concerts in Britain to workers and during the Second World War to Forces personnel in the Middle East.

[17] Emma Orczy's play, set amidst the Reign of Terror during the French Revolution, was first staged in 1903 in Nottingham before moving to the London's West End and great popular acclaim. The novel followed two years later. (Esmé Mitchell will reappear.)

[18] Jimmy (James) Glencairn Cunningham OBE (1903–1996) was the son of Samuel Cunningham (1862–1946, stockbroker and businessman and Unionist Party senator in the first Stormont parliament), and Janet Knox McCosh (1875–1941) from Scotland. He lived in Glencairn, northwest Belfast. Jimmy was to serve with the British Army in Burma during the Second World War. After the war he inherited ownership of the *Northern Whig* newspaper. He like his father became a Unionist senator in the Northern Ireland parliament. Jimmy married Mollie Barbour Pears (1907–1998).

There are three yaller parrot tulips bursting in front of me in Ginna's Swedish bowl and they are wonderful. I bought 2 dozen yesterday for 2/- a dozen.

I had the house to myself this afternoon while Nanny and Julie and Gay were out for a walk and it was so pleasant. Mrs. Sloan rang up to say how nice the luncheon was and Eggie dropped in.[19] He is going to America in May – going straight to Chicago where he is going to have an exhibit of pictures – then to Denver and then to the Canadian Rockies – Banff and Lake Louise and then to Vancouver and home by Honolulu and Japan. ...

I still wear my hair up though often I am reminded of what Orson Welles said about ladies who wear their hair up – either they look like a lady or a washwoman depending on the woman and sometimes I think mine looks like the wash all right alright. ...

Auntie lent me the biography of Franklin which I am disappointed in from glancing at it but when I have time to read it I may be equal to it.[20] Now we lead such a hectic life that my reading is confined to *The New Yorker.* ...

As I explained in my last, it is much better for me to keep out of your love-life Ginna because my advice is unreliable on the spot and with full knowledge of the situation much less from a 5000 mile distance and a "foreign" perspective – Ma! I'm a foreigner!

Love,
Helen

[19] Eggy (or Eggie) was Francis (Frank) Egginton (1908–1990), the landscape painter who was born in Cheshire but as a water-colourist spent increasing amounts of time in Ireland, especially Donegal. He regularly exhibited with the Fine Art Society in London.

[20] Almost certainly *Benjamin Franklin* for which Carl van Doren won the 1938 Pulitzer Prize.

21st Feb.
[*Written from L's office, Belfast*]

Dear Mother and Ginna,

While I wait for L. to come back from the S. Exchange I may as well write to you...[21]

Last night we went to see *Pygmalion* with Leslie Howard[22] – it is so good. Tonight we are going to Maureen's sherry party and this afternoon I am going to pick up Mrs. Barr[23] and go sign my name at Government House in Hillsborough[24] under the supposition that then I will be invited to things that might be worth going to – such as a party when the Duke and Duchess of Kent come – I'm not keen but I suppose it won't hurt anything to go.

Tomorrow is the film society and Friday we are going to the theatre with Percy and Doreen to see Yvonne Arnaud in *A Plan for a Hostess*.[25]

Frances our house-maid gave notice yesterday – she has to go home because her mother can't open her eyes in the morning and won't go to a doctor – so now I don't know what to do – whether to get another maid and keep Mary – fire Mary or what. A man and wife would be

[21] The Belfast Stock Exchange was established in 1895 (though a second source gives 1897). A founding member of the Belfast Stock Exchange was James (later Sir James) Craig, first Prime Minister of Northern Ireland.

[22] A 1938 British film version of George Bernard Shaw's play of the same name.

[23] Maureen Topping was married to Walter W. B. (Ken) Topping QC, who later became a Unionist politician: see the footnote to the letter of 21st April 1945. Mrs Barr was a member of the Ulster Unionist Council since 1919. During the gun-running days of unionist resistance to Home Rule, she acted as postmistress to the Ulster Volunteer Force. In 1901 she married Ainsworth Barr, a well-known Belfast stockbroker and Irish rugby international. She was awarded the CBE in 1920 in recognition of her work with the Ulster Women's Gift Fund during the Great War, work she was soon to resume in the Second World War. See *Belfast Telegraph*, 19th September 1947 and *Belfast News-Letter*, 3rd November 1947.

[24] The official residence of the Governor of Northern Ireland until with the proroguing of the Stormont parliament in 1972 it became the residence of the Secretary of State for Northern Ireland and referred to as Hillsborough Castle.

[25] Before marriage to Doreen, Percy Metcalfe had been Ginna's "beau" earlier in the decade; Doreen (née Hind) was the daughter of Nina (Eliza) Hind, née Andrews and sister of Thomas Andrews, co-designer of RMS *Titanic* who went down with the ship; see the footnote for the letter of 4th May 1939. *Plan for a Hostess* by Thomas Browne premièred in Edinburgh on 7th February before travelling to Belfast (where it was staged in the Grand Opera House) and then London's West End in March. The cast also included the young William Douglas Home who had written only the first of what would become fifty stage plays.

so good at Mahee but there are snags to that too. Frances doesn't want to go.

I got Gay two of the cutest peasant dresses yesterday – they are just in at Anderson and McAuley's from America[26] – one has a white blouse and a peasant skirt and one is all horizontally striped and sticks out all around. ...

Here comes Pa.

Love,
Helen

Via S. S. Queen Mary postmarked envelope 17 MCH 1939 to Mrs. Lee Ramsey – Miss Virginia Ramsey 757 Williams Street, Denver, Colorado, U.S.A.

13th March
Belmont

Dear Mother and Ginna,

... I stayed at home all week except for Wed. Fri. and Sat. nights when I went to three Shakespeare plays. *As you Like It, Macbeth,* and *Much Ado about Nothing.* – all wonderful. The Company was the best I've ever seen – they are from Stratford or did play at Stratford, but don't any more – the leading man was Donald Wolfit and the leading lady was Rosalinde Fuller.[27] Janet Boyd[28] went to 7 of the 8 performances

---

[26] Anderson and McAuley was a major Belfast department store that was in business from 1861 until 1994. It called itself the Shopping Centre of Ulster.

[27] The Donald Wolfit Shakespeare Company toured the United Kingdom between 1937 and 1952. Besides the plays Helen watched, the Company also staged *Hamlet, Othello, The Merchant of Venice* and *Romeo and Juliet,* all in the Grand Opera House, Belfast between 6th and 11th of March. Rosalinde Fuller (1892–1982) was Wolfit's leading lady, and she had played Ophelia to John Barrymore's Hamlet on Broadway in 1922.

[28] Janet Dempster Boyd, née Wiles, was born in 1904 in Rhode Island. Her father was Thomas Wiles, an engineer and inventor. She met Austen Boyd, an Ulsterman, while on a world cruise. After marriage they lived in Cultra, County Down in a house called Skibbereen. Janet was a member of the DRC and the Ulster-American Friendship Committee which in 1947 founded in Helen's memory the Helen Ramsey Turtle Scholarship at Queen's University Belfast. In 1953, in memory of her father, Janet established the prestigious Wiles Lectures at Queen's University. She herself was awarded an honorary M.A. from Queen's in 1959. In 1994 she wrote an unpublished memoir, *Grandma Remembers,* to which the Belfast author Alf McCreary wrote the Foreword and Gay Firth (née Turtle) the Introduction. She died in 2000.

and I certainly wish that I had. Even after three the lines rang in my head like music.

16th Mar.

We are going to Paris on the Wednesday before Easter and will be in Paris from Thursday night until Monday morning – London Monday afternoon until Tuesday evening and home on Wednesday morning. We are going to dinner and the theatre with Arabella on Monday evening. I am so pleased about going – Nursy Long is coming Tuesday and will stay until the following Thursday –

It is so too bad about Czecho-Slovakia. The day that Herbert Morowitz was here and told us about it I felt life was a husk.[29] However he said that one of his friends asked him what he was living for and he said "the next two years because things happen and change so quickly that there is hope of a big bust up". All the cheerful people here say that Hitler cannot last longer than this year because Germany is so bankrupt and there are so many dissenting spirits within. I prefer to agree with the rumour that Hitler is dead – don't you. ...

L. and I went to Mahee last evening to see the lambs – there are 18 now – the cutest things you ever saw. Mahee looked so nice – the garden is going to be a dream this year – we had forty rose plants in as well as lots of flowers and flowering shrubs. The daffodils are all in bloom now and the snowdrops were so pretty...

Did you see the new advertisement for Chryslers in the *New Yorker* saying that you never feel tired in Denver? ...

I am bearing in mind that this should reach you in time to wish Ginna many happy returns. ...

If I see something in Paris that will do as a present I will send it otherwise I can only send love and best wishes for an early marriage – but if denied you best wishes anyway.

Love,
Helen

[29] Morawetz told Helen about the threat to Czechoslovakia on 31st January. German occupation of the remainder of Czechoslovakia began early on the 15th March.

24th Mar.
Belmont

Dear Mother and Ginna,

... The inevitable has happened and Mary and I gave each other notice last Friday – it is the entertaining that bothers her and throws her clear cock eyed. Even with another maid. She was in a black mood over the weekend but has recovered and is all right again, but if I tell her that there will be even one extra she is furious so I am again ringing up agencies. ...

Last night we went to Spence's[30] for supper and then to the last movie of the Film society – which was just fair – called *L'Orage* [sic] and was a passionate love story.[31] We have no other engagements this week but are going to hear Paul Robeson[32] on Monday – L.'s birthday. We went to *Boys' Town* on Monday night and enjoyed it – especially Micky [sic] Rooney[33].

... So far we are still optimistic about the International Situation – even Lancelot!

Love,
Helen

---

[30] Kathleen Forbes Morehouse Spence, always referred to by Helen as "Spence", was born in 1904 in New Jersey but grew up in Berkeley, CA. Much later she wrote an unpublished auto- and family biography for her grandchildren. She married Toby Spence, for whom see the footnote to Helen's letter of 13th January, 1940. Besides being an artist, Toby Spence alternated chairmanship with Herbert Bryson of the two-family firm of Spence Bryson Ltd.

[31] *Orage* is a 1938 French drama based on Henri Bernstein's play, *Le Venin* (*Venom*), and starring Charles Boyer and Michèle Morgan – "the story of the mistress of an engineer who has a pregnant wife": not the stuff of mainstream UK cinema release in those days.

[32] The American singer, actor and political activist Paul Robeson, a Belfast favourite, performed in the Ulster Hall, Belfast on 27th March 1939 where he sang "Songs of the Folk". He had already performed at the same venue on 18th February 1935 and 6th February in 1936, and was to do so in the Grosvenor Hall, Belfast on 2nd March, 1949.

[33] *Boys Town* (1938), starring Mickey Rooney and Spencer Tracy, won Tracy rather than Rooney an Oscar.

30th Mar.
Belmont

Dear Mother and Ginna,

It is a nice, sunny, spring morning and the birds are singing and the flowers are growing and it is hard to think that we may have war within six months as your today's cable prophesies. The position here is that until war is closer we won't leave – that is Gay, Julie and I; but we are negotiating right now with Mr. Beverstock, the consul, to have an American passport made for me, Gay and Julie and on the strength of L.'s being born in America and on the excuse of not knowing exactly how to register Gay and Julie here with the consulate (whether L. is purely British or whether he has some claim to American citizenship).[34] We are asking at Washington exactly what status L. has in America. Mr. Beverstock once said that the U.S. was very reluctant to give up on anyone born in America so we have a slight hope of getting L. an American passport of some kind. Not that he would use it in the event of war and escape to America because although the common sense thing – it plain just would never satisfy him to think he ran away – but if there is no war – which I still hold out there won't be – I think that some day if things go haywire here – which they will sooner or later (and in America too) we may move to America – meaning a social revolution, labor uprising, Communism or what you will – it is coming as sure as eggs is eggs.

There are as usual two schools of thought here – one for war and one against war at any price. The optimists say that Germany will be its own end either through bankruptcy or the assimilation of so many anti-Nazi peoples[35] – the pessimists think either that there will be war when the Germans start to take British possessions and/or the desperate women think that they would give in to Hitler lying down rather than see a shot fired. Goodness knows things are far from rosy and rest

---

[34] Roswell C. Beverstock arrived in Belfast in April 1937 to become U.S. Vice-consul. He left Belfast for the United States in July 1941 after his wife became pregnant, and was soon after reassigned elsewhere. His career in Belfast is noted in Francis M. Carroll's book, *The American Presence in Ulster: A Diplomatic History, 1796–1996* (2012), which also narrates the Northern Ireland-United States relationship during the years of Helen Turtle's letters.

[35] Helen is presumably referring to non-Teutonic peoples recently annexed by Germany.

assured that when it really looks bad I will cheese it for home as fast as I can. ...

Love,
Helen

27th Apl
Belmont

Dear Mother and Ginna,

Now it is Thursday the 27th of April and I am sorry that it has been so long since I have written to you. I have not been as busy as all that but busy enough to want to relax with a book in my free time. ...

We have hardly done anything lately ... we went to the theatre to see a funny Irish play called *Spring Meeting*[36] and to a movie and of course now and then to Mahee. I stay home most afternoons – in fact every afternoon to be with Gay who is really one of the funniest children and the best company you ever saw – she is so interested in her books and her gramophone and she knows what the records are by looking at them – awful bright! ...

Mrs. Turtle arrived at the Midland[37] last Saturday and was here for Sunday supper and lunch on Monday ... Spence gave a paper on Mary Ellen Chase[38] at the D.R.C. on Monday – I was chairman and Auntie

[36] *Spring Meeting* was written by M.J. Farrell and John Perry; it premiered in London in 1938 with its Irish premiere in 1939. It was staged in the Grand Opera House Belfast in mid-to-late April. Farrell (1904–1996) was born Mary Nesta Skrine in Co. Kildare; her mother was the famous Irish-Canadian poet of the Antrim glens, Moira O'Neill (1864–1955) who had married an Alberta rancher called Walter Skrine. Farrell's married name was Molly Keane, under which she published acclaimed novels. She took the pseudonym M.J. Farrell for her plays and some of her early novels. John Perry (1906–1995) from Tipperary was an actor, playwright and theatrical agent who worked with the legendary "Binkie" Beaumont. *Spring Meeting* was directed by John Gielgud and established the stage career of Margaret Rutherford who performed in the Belfast production. (It was adapted for film in 1941 starring Michael Wilding.)

[37] The Midland Hotel stood beside the York Road Railway station, Belfast, which was acquired in 1903 by Midland Railway. The hotel was destroyed in April 1941 during the Nazi Blitz.

[38] Mary Ellen Chase (1887–1973) was an educator and writer. She was one of Helen's tutors at Smith College, Massachusetts. Her novels, set in her native Maine, include *Mary Peters* (1934) and *The Edge of Darkness* (1957). She visited Helen in Mahee in the 1930s but according to Helen's daughter Julie, her former student did not warm to her.

proposed the vote of thanks – such a good one too. Elaine is going to have the next D.R.C. in their bedroom! It is the biggest room in the house and she is going to take the bed out. ...

Mahee is coming along – the new room is finished all but the inside door. I have ordered the cutest wallpaper you ever saw for the hall and bathroom – it is Swiss and guaranteed washable. It is a red butterfly on a white ground with red and yaller scallops. Hard to describe much less for me to draw but [drawing here] it went to my head like wine.

... I dream about being home almost every night – goodness knows what will happen here – things look bad all right and I may be home sooner than I think but until it is necessary I don't want to bring Gay and Julie and leave L. here alone for a year or so but I am prepared to come at once if war breaks out. ... Monday is our wedding anniversary and we are going out to dinner and to the theatre – Hotcha! ...

Love,
Helen

I read a good book called *Flamingo* by Mary Borden. Also *The Buccaneers* by Edith Wharton is good.[39]

Sat. 29th Apl
Belmont

Dear Mary Lou,[40]

I am spending a quiet Saturday afternoon minding the baby who is playing in her pram beside me and kicking her heels in the sunshine

---

[39] Mary Borden (1886–1968) was an American novelist and poet who married a Scottish missionary and moved to England. If Borden's American-British connections appealed to Helen, so must the theme of her fourth book, *Flamingo* (1927), a novel set in New York and London and very much concerned with the two transatlantic cultures, the old and the new. It is one of the best novels written about New York. *The Buccaneers* was published, unfinished, in 1938, a year after Wharton's death.

[40] Mary Louise Gurd (née Moore) was born in 1910 on a cattle ranch in eastern Colorado but was brought up in Denver where she became a childhood friend of Helen's. (The Moores emigrated from Cootehill, Co. Cavan in the 19th century.) On a ship she met a Montrealer, Fraser N. Gurd (1914–1995); they married in 1938 and moved to Montreal. Her husband was from a family of distinguished physicians who over three generations, "changed the face of surgery in Canada": "Fraser Gurd Biography for Trauma Association of Canada": www.traumacanada.org) *Cont'd overleaf*

and giving little squeals now and again. It is a lovely, sunny day, not hot, although I'll bet the Irish are complaining of the heat wave, but very pleasant and peaceful. Lancelot is at Mahee paring his lambs' toes and Gay is out for a walk with Miss Robson, her governess and/or my Mother's Help – which accounts for the whole family.

While on the subject of babies I wanted to tell you how delighted I am that you are going to have one – what's more I think you are lucky to be having it so soon unexpected and all as it is. We waited a year, but since, I have always regarded that year as a waste of good time. In fact my enthusiasm for having many children early has been unbounded up until this last month when we have suffered reverses and encountered problems with our two but when they blow over my self-deceptive optimism will no doubt spring again. ... Of course the great advantage over here is the fact that maids and nurses are so cheap by comparison and certainly we have a much easier time of it from that point of view...

Your wedding sounded so nice and from what you say Montreal must be foreign enough to be quite interesting. I recognize the conservative people that you mention because there is the same type here and they are both funny and pathetic and yet in their own way quite admirable from a Denver or Brush point of view[41].

The thing that living in Ireland has done for me is to give me a rabid interest in America amounting almost to an obsession – I dream about it nights. My present conclusion is that Americans are pleasantly haywire – but quite definitely haywire – maybe the *New Yorker* has a lot to do with my outlook. Anyway I'm glad I'm haywire, aren't you?

We lead a quiet and at the moment very domestic life. Lancelot is so interested in Gay and next to Gay, Mahee. We spent all last summer at Mahee leading a completely rural life and are going to do the same this summer. We put in a bathroom, slapped on some paint and cleaned it

---

[40] *Cont'd* (The Gurds had emigrated from Ireland to Quebec in 1847 during the Great Famine.) In an interview, Gurd acknowledged the help of his wife, Mary Louise. "Her sagacious counsel and cheerful equanimity clearly helped shape the career of this giant among Canadian surgeons": Douglas Waugh, "Fraser N. Gurd," *CMAJ*, 134 (1986): 1410.

[41] Brush is a small town about a hundred miles from Denver. Mary Lou, who was born there, seems to have been chafing against the conservative Catholic society that Quebec then composed. It isn't clear why conservatives from Belfast or Northern Ireland are admirable from a Denver or Brush perspective: perhaps both were, like Montreal, conservative places.

up a little and it really is cute. This year we have made the stable that was next to the living room (so Irish!) into a bedroom and Lancelot has made a lovely garden and it will be nicer than ever. Lancelot is interested in the farming side – we have bullocks, sheep, two horses, a donkey, and the farmer's wife has hens and turkeys so you can imagine that it is a real farmyard. I don't do a thing but pick flowers and moon around but it is very pleasant. Last summer I had the excuse of my condition but this summer I may have to be a little more active – but not very much. ...

I still think that something will prevent a war but it looks as if it will have to be a miracle at this stage. I don't know about coming home this year – I would love to and so would Lancelot but the outlook is so uncertain and the question of bringing Gay and Julie too makes planning indefinite. Will you be going to Denver at all? ...

Ginna and Mother are erratic correspondents but I manage to keep fairly well informed by them on what is going on in Denver. ... Monday is our 6th wedding anniversary and it just plain don't seem possible.

It makes me sad when I think how long it has been and may be until we see each other again but it may be sooner than we think – anyway I think of you and your new baby oftener than you would believe and I am both *pleathed*,[42] surprised and flattered to be told so "early on". If Lancelot knew that I was writing he would send his love and so do I.

Helen

P.S. Remembering my birthday was a downright touching gesture and I appreciate it more than I can say.

---

[42] The origin of the in-joke, "pleathed", is unknown. Could it have originated in Dickens's novel, *Hard Times* in which Mr Sleary the circus-man speaks with an extraordinary lisp? It occurs again in a letter to her mother 11th Dec 1940.

4th May
Belmont

Dear Mother and Ginna,

This letter should smell of nutmeg because this rhododendron leaf is from one that Jack Mackie[43] gave us – the loveliest thing you ever saw and it smells the whole house of nutmeg!

It is a rainy cold evening and Lancelot and Eggy have just gone to the Flow Dam beyond Comber to look at a bird's nest or something. I have had Gay and Julie on my hands this afternoon but it wasn't wearing because Gay takes a nap in the afternoon too. On nice days she goes out but today was not nice. ...

I went to see Bodo and Edie's baby on Wednesday ... she, Elizabeth, has almost as much hair as Gay had and more than Julie has now though Julie has a lot sticking straight up on top. Edie is fine and only had about five hours of bad labor. Bodo[44] is already a devoted father and has forgotten that he wanted a boy.

Monday being our anniversary we went to the theatre to see *Under Suspicion* a thriller which was pretty good[45]. Last night Mrs. Bingham and Arabella came to dinner and we went to Mahee afterwards and then called on Jack and Elaine. Mrs. Bingham was so full of war talk – all English people are.

---

[43] John Pringle (Jack) Mackie, b. 1897, was one of five sons of James Mackie Jnr (b.1864), then head of the industrial Mackie family, the others being James, b.1895, Frazer, b. 1899, Grenville, b. 1902 and Lavens, b. 1905. There was one daughter, Isobel, b. 1901.

[44] Redmond Thibeaudeau (hence "Bodo") Taggart (1903–1987), a family friend, was a prominent Belfast architect who practised into the 1980s. He was educated at Rugby School and earned a degree in chemistry from the University of Oxford before being persuaded to join his father's architectural and engineering practice; he took another degree in architecture and engineering in order to do so. He joined the Royal Naval Volunteer Reserve in the mid-1930s and was a lieutenant-commander when war broke out. (Redmond Taggart, son, personal communication.) His wife was Edith Hind, sister of Doreen Metcalfe (née Hind) and daughter of Nina Hind (née Andrews): see the letter of 21st February 1939. Nina's mother was the sister of W.J. (Viscount) Pirrie, the presiding genius of Harland & Wolff that built *Titanic* and other liners.

[45] *Under Suspicion*, a comedy thriller written by Basil Dearden and Leslie Harcourt, was a huge hit at the Playhouse Theatre London in 1938. It went directly from the Playhouse to the Grand Opera House in Belfast in early May 1939.

10th May

Summer seems to be nearly here and we are making a big effort to get to Mahee as soon as possible. ...

Last night we went to the theatre with Arabella to see *Whiteoaks* the play of Jalna and it was so good.[46] Arabella and I are going to a sherry party at Mrs. Beath's[47] today to meet the leading lady who was Gran in the play aged 101 and she was wonderful. She lectured at the Alpha Club yesterday – I wasn't there but Arabella was breathless with excitement about the whole thing.[48]

15th May

The weather for the past week has been almost hot and all the trees and hedges are out. We are moving to Mahee on Friday, I think, and I can hardly wait. ...

Arabella leaves tonight to go back to London and won't be over again until Christmas if she goes to America in August as she is thinking of doing – or else she is going to the Highlands of Scotland. She is only half-hearted about going to America.

Eggie is going all right – sailing on the 27th and he expects to be in Denver around the 15th–20th of June. I told him that he could stay with you for a few days until he finds a place in the mountains to make his headquarters. He is going to have an exhibit in N.Y. or Boston, he thinks and one in Denver of Irish and Colorado paintings combined. I told him that you would try to find out about where he could exhibit

---

[46] *Whiteoaks of Jalna* was first staged in London in 1936 and was an adaptation of Mazo de la Roche's 1927 novel of the same name; it was performed at the Grand Opera House, Belfast.

[47] Mrs Beath was the wife of Dr R.M. Beath, a radiologist at the Royal Victoria Hospital.

[48] Nancy Price (1880–1970) was the English actress who took the leading role in *Whiteoaks*. She lectured on "The Theatre and Its Magic" to the women of the Belfast Alpha Club at a luncheon on 9th May. Among her claims was that the theatre recuperated the mind ("the theatre was a hospital for the mind"): "Belfast Alpha Club: The Theatre and its Magic", *Belfast News-Letter*, 10th May, 1939. In the afternoon, Price lectured from the set of the play on audiences and the theatre. Price was honorary director of the People's National Theatre, in London, which she co-founded in 1930. Alpha Club events were reported in the *Belfast News-Letter* in the "Mainly for Women" column. They were usually held in the Carlton Hall Belfast, presumably in the spacious restaurant of the Carlton, 25 Donegall Street.

in Denver – either Chappell House or Kendricks or wherever people do exhibit paintings.[49] He is so nice and will be very easy to have around and will need no entertaining. He is sociable and shy at the same time but I think you will like him – he is very blunt but has natural good manners – not much smoothness but a kindly feeling and he gets so much fun out of everything. He is going to buy a car either in N.Y. or Denver, and he does everything as cheaply as possible. ...

Friday night we took a trailer load to Mahee and Saturday spent the day there working. ...

Mrs. Turtle is thinking of going to a Psycho-Analyst and if he is good I think it might do her a lot of good.[50] She is still at the Midland and has a nurse nights to read her to sleep. She is better on the whole but I think A. will be just as glad to go back to London. A. is so devoted to us and to Gay and Julie – a strong family feeling. She has another beau in London, a young 34 or so doctor and she is holding Gordon [Freeman] off to see if this other one will propose. ...

I still lie awake *nights* (not for long) thinking about Ginna's love life. I think I will have to come to America in September no matter what to see you both because I can't stay away much longer – I will probably bring Gay and Lancelot if it is humanly possible and it will kill me to leave Julie ... but it would nearly kill me to bring her. ...

Love,
Helen

Per S.S. *Queen Mary* – date stamped 15 MAY 1939

---

[49] Chappell House was a brownstone mansion which in the 1930s housed the Denver University School of Art and the Denver Art Museum. Helen is also in all likelihood referring to Kendrick-Bellamy Company, a large bookshop on 16th Street.

[50] Mrs Turtle lived mostly in Eire which the Irish Free State became in 1937. Helen's reference to a psychoanalyst strikes a surprisingly modern note for 1930s Ireland. See the letter of 20th September 1942 for a footnote on psychoanalysis in Ireland. Lancelot's mother suffered chronically from what was then called "nerves". According to Julie Mackie, her grandmother, Mrs Turtle, had an alcoholic mother and she lost her husband when he was 49 after which she spent years moving between guesthouses and hotels.

22nd May
Mahee Island
County Down

Dear Mother and Ginna,

We are all moved in – have had a week-end guest and have another guest asleep in Gay's room so the summer season has started! What's more we are having simply glorious weather – hot sun and no rain today! The guest was Eggy and is Janet Webb[51] who arrived tonight with Lancelot to stay until a week from day after tomorrow. Janet was so excited that her hand shook while she was having her supper and Gay has been talking for two hours! They are both quiet now – if this happens again we will put Janet in our room. ...

I love this house so that I feel a different person here and just like to sit and look around – I like every bit of it and the bathroom and hall look so nice with their new paper – we have a wonderful new anthracite stove in the bathroom that goes day and night and makes the room like an oven. We have fires in the living room, kitchen, bathroom and Miss Robson's and Julie's room and the house is so comfortable. In our room we have an oil stove to help dry it out. It isn't dry yet and although it is all right to sleep in we don't put any clothes in it yet but keep them all in the bathroom.

I will write more later –

25th May
Mahee

Dear Mother and Ginna,

We will have been here a week tomorrow and it seems like only a day. The weather has been lovely all but yesterday morning when it drizzled.

---

[51] Janet Webb, aged four, was the youngest of the three daughters of Patrick and Rosemary Webb. The eldest daughter was Joan Webb (later Cowdy) who became a friend of Julie Mackie's and word-processed Helen's handwritten letters; she answered the queries of the present editor most helpfully; she died in January 2020 at the age of ninety-one. Joan's daughter Belinda married Philip Haas, the American film-maker who directed the movie *Angels and Insects* (1995) which was co-written by Haas and Belinda, with help on production from A.S. Byatt from whose novella the plot derived.

... There is a yacht going by with the sun on it and it is a perfect picture – the boat is red the water blue, and the sail so white. Here comes another one. ...

We have a day old baby duck in on top of the bathroom stove trying to get it revived – Miss R[obson] is in watching it – *so* pathetic it is because it can't hold its head up and the head keeps going over to the side – it has nine brothers and sisters (shoveller ducks) and we have five baby Pintails (the first L. knows of to be bred in captivity in Ireland)[52]...

The duck has revived! and is cheeping away like mad. ...

Mrs. T. has moved to a new place as a paying guest and is under a new Psycho-Analyst. ...

The garden will be so pretty now we only have lupins and double poppies and pyrethrums and double narcissi – the last of our 1000 bulbs. Isabel sent me a huge bunch of lilies of the valley – maybe to make up for our having their four old geese which waddle around the yard and are a general nuisance.

War news and Talk seems to have died down or maybe it is because we are out of touch here. Of course the news which we are listening to now is full of war news and planes –

We have our gas masks!

Love,
Helen

---

[52] Lance Turtle as an experienced ornithologist was in a position to know. He was the first to report a pintail duck nest on Strangford Lough, the large body of tidal water that the causeway island of Mahee juts out into. See C. Douglas Deane, *Birds of Northern Ireland* (Belfast: Belfast Museum and Art Gallery, 1954), p. 133. Lance's contributions to the book are acknowledged.

29th June
Mahee

Dear Mother,

I hope this letter makes the grade and catches you on the *Laconia* and that you have a smooth and pleasant crossing.[53] This is your 11th crossing!![54]

There isn't anything new to tell you – Gay and Julie are both asleep and it is a peaceful, quiet summer's day with not a sound except the crackle of the fire and the tick of the clock, and the hum of bees and flies. It rained all day yesterday for the first time in six weeks and I hope that it will only rain at night while you are here. It is such a good time for you to come because the gardens are all so lovely and the countryside is a joy to behold. ...

I haven't budged from here for almost two weeks but tonight we are going to the Sloan's to dinner – in evening dress by cracky! ...

Why aren't you coming? Where are you? [illegible] just told me Gay is going to have her tonsils out on Tuesday. She is fine. This is in the car.

Love,
Helen

---

[53] Three years later the passenger liner RMS *Laconia* was torpedoed and sunk by a German U-boat off the coast of west Africa on 12th September 1942. During the U-boat crew's rescue operation, the vessel was attacked by an American bomber, killing dozens of survivors from the sunken liner. As a result, the German navy issued the "*Laconia* Order" forbidding the rescue of Allied seamen.

[54] On Thursday 22nd June Helen got the thrilling news that her mother would visit from Denver. In the letter of that date, and of Sunday 25th June, Helen excitedly listed what her mother could bring her from the United States: this included any new slim volumes of Robert Frost poems coming after his *Collected Poems* (1930) and a new critical book on Frost. A hasty postscript to this letter written in a car in a shaky hand asks why the visit is off. (The answer is unknown.)

11th July
Miss Wallace's Nursing Home[55]

Dear Mother and Aunt Ethel,

Gay is asleep so I have time to write to you to tell you that her operation is very successfully over – yesterday morning at about 9.15 and she was back here before 9.30. Her tonsils were very big and they said that there was no doubt they were better out.

12th July

Now it is 10.30 at night and we are back at Mahee and believe it or not there are 30 boys swimming outside our gate! They are camping in one of our fields over the 12th week.[56] Gay is still fine and we are so glad to be home again…

Two letters from Mother were here and one from Ginna from Pennsylvania . .…

I am glad that you liked Eggy so well. I hoped you would because he is such a nice little soul and so easy to have around. He must have liked you quite well if he is going to give you a picture because he doesn't give many away to anyone. I knew he would love the prairie and Colorado generally. … He is one of the most original people I know in his attitude toward everything and he always makes me laugh – both with him and at him. …

We have done nothing lately but mill around here looking after Gay and Julie – principally Gay. We had visitors for the weekend – the Tuckers from Oxford – Mr. Tucker is a don at Oxford[57] and one of the

---

[55] A Miss Wallace ran a nursing home at 7 Upper Crescent, Belfast from the late 1920s until the 1970s. See the 17th February 2018 posting on the Lord Belmont in Northern Ireland website: "Upper Crescent, Belfast". Upper Crescent is an elegant curved terrace in Regency-style. The father of the Belfast writer and scholar C.S. Lewis died in Miss Wallace's nursing home in 1929: Sandy Smith, "Surprised by Belfast: Significant Sites in the Life of C.S. Lewis". Part 4: "Queen's University Belfast and Surrounding Area," Knowing & Doing: C.S. Lewis Institute (online) Winter 2016.

[56] The public holiday week straddling The Twelfth (12th July), the ostentatious commemoration of the Battle of the Boyne, 1690.

[57] Bernard Tucker (1901–1950) was a lecturer in zoology at Oxford University and a distinguished British ornithologist, editor of *British Birds* journal and one of the authors of the authoritative *Handbook to British Birds* (Witherby et al., 1938–41).

best bird men in England and with them was a lady don from Oxford who was only here one night – the Tuckers visited us before the summer we were married [1933]. Mrs. Tucker was bats on Julie and wanted to take her home. ...

I will try to get this on the Clipper[58] to reach you for your birthday – many happy returns and much love. I'm sorry you won't be here for it – our garden is a dream now – roses, big Shasta daisies, white lilies, sweet pea, and about twenty or thirty other things – you know Lancelot – he does things so well and the lawn is like velvet ...

This letter is a mess and quite uninspired but I am pole-axed and am going to bed. Love and kisses to you and Aunt Ethel – A special birthday kiss

Helen

14th July
Mahee

Dear Ginna and Mother,

... I spent yesterday mostly in bed reading *Listen! The Wind* which I think is wonderful and it, in my glandy frame of mind, made me so mad to think that Mrs. Lindbergh can write books like that and I don't – I say don't instead of can't because you know I really think I could! – that's what makes me so mad. And Sis! Am I mad! I just took a holiver-oil pill[59] in my effort to build up and get going writing something. I even think that Mrs. Lindbergh, Anne to me, and I have the same kind of minds – poetic and full of word images, and fairly detailed in descriptions. Have you read this book by the way? It even made the *New Yorker* cheap in my eyes because Anne Lindbergh seems to me to be really somebody, and somebody who has a very good idea

---

[58] Pan-American Airways with its Boeing B-314 flying boat (Yankee Clipper) inaugurated regular transatlantic flights in early 1939. In July a New York-Southampton route was begun and it is presumably via that route that Helen and her mother and sister sent and received letters.

[59] Haliver oil was a nutritional supplement derived from halibut liver.

of what her life is all about. There is no humor in it but it does very well without it – the book I mean[60] …

18th July

I have just been reading *Antony* and if you haven't read it you should – it is a collection of his letters edited by his father, Lord Lytton and they are wonderful. Antony was killed in 1933 in an airplane crash and his father published these letters.[61] Another very good book about China is *The House of Exile* by Nora Waln.[62] I read *All This and Heaven Too* in the nursing Home but it wasn't a bit good – did you read it?[63] …

Helen

27th July
Mahee

Dear Mother and Ginna,

I know so many people who are going away for their "holidays" today and I wish you could see the day! The only good thing is that it isn't cold – everything else is bad – rain and wind both beating against the

---

[60] Anne Morrow Lindbergh published *Listen! The Wind* in 1938 and it won the American National Book Award for Nonfiction. She had already won the National Book Award for *North to the Orient* (1935). Both books recount pioneering transoceanic flights she took with her husband Charles Lindbergh. "She is Anne to me", remarks Helen, because the women overlapped as B.A. majors at Smith College from which Lindbergh graduated in 1928, Helen in 1930.

[61] *Antony: A Record of Youth* (1935) was written by the Earl of Lytton, father of the book's subject, Antony Bulwer-Lytton, who died young in 1933 when the plane he was piloting crashed. J.M. Barrie provided a Foreword to the book.

[62] *The House of Exile* – a neglected classic – is a memoir of twelve years of life in China (1920–32) by the American writer and journalist Nora Waln (1895–1964), intrigued by China from childhood. While Helen was reading *The House of Exile*, Waln had just left Germany, having lived there from 1934; in 1939 she published *Reaching for the Stars*, in which her fondness for Germans and Germany is sabotaged by the chilling nature of what she sees under an increasingly totalitarian Hitlerism. Waln returned to Germany after the war to attend the Nuremberg Trials.

[63] *All This and Heaven Too* (1938) is a novel by Rachel Field (1894–1942), a best-seller set in nineteenth-century France and described as a "thrilling historical romance, full of passion, mystery and intrigue". It was turned into a movie in 1940, directed by Anatole Litvak and starring Bette Davis.

house and swirling around the garden. It was like this last night too until about 10.30. After that L. and I went for a walk over the wet fields in the moonlight and it was such fun because it was warm and the air was so soft that it was like a caress and it made even my hair feel soft and fine! At 11.30 I went down and looked at the tide which was right in and up to the gate and believe it or not *I bathed*! It was really fun because the moon was shining on the water and the waves were making little splashy noises and it was so calm and peaceful. Wednesday morning I bathed before breakfast too so I am coming along in my British love of the elements. My love won't be so strong in a little while when I have to go out and pick peas with everything dripping wet – just now it is well-nigh impossible because the rain is making a noise on the tin roof like rice thrown on it – coming down in stair-rods they say here. ...

I went to see Isabel Noble to ask her to come down to stay. She is coming around the middle of August and she is going to America in September to marry a widower named Roscoe Whitney who has a 16 year old daughter.[64] I had a letter from Mary Morwood who is in America with James – having a field day. Elizabeth is at home running the house.[65] ... Mrs. Turtle has gone to London for a while – she is so much better since having treatments from the Psycho-Analyst. Arabella is coming over to stay with us some time in August I think. ...

I weighed on Wednesday and I only weigh 114 with all my clothes on! Ma! It's wonderful! I lost about five pounds a time with each of Gay's illnesses and now I eat like a horse and am still so nice and thin – my fanny needs exercise and reduction and then my figure will be almost as good as ever...

---

[64] For Roscoe Whitney, see Helen's letter of 4th September.

[65] For Mary Morwood's mother, also Mary, see the letter of 11th February above. Mary *fille* was born in Allahbad, India in 1913. (www.myheritage.com). She was educated at Victoria College, Belfast and the University of Oxford from which she graduated with an honours B.A. in 1936. She became honorary secretary of the Northern Ireland Peace Council associated with the International Peace Campaign promoting international peace through collective security. Her letter to the *Belfast News-Letter*, Monday 26th June 1939 promoting the cause of the International Peace Campaign, was followed by a questionnaire that was to be given to all Northern Ireland MPs at Westminster seeking their cooperation in the cause of peace. Her brother James was born in India in 1911; he followed his father into medicine and became James Bryan Morwood M.D. For sister Elizabeth, see the letter of 18th October below.

They are playing "Surrecho" or Little Surrecho on the radio – it is the rage here now. "Sir Echo" I suppose it is[66] ...

I was glad to hear that Eggy likes the west because I cracked it up so – he almost didn't go and I'll bet he is so glad that he did. Do you think he is selling many pictures and how much is he charging for them? We had a letter from him from above Estes[67] saying how much he enjoyed being in Denver and how nice you both were to him. He is such an individual that he is fun to talk to because he has such an original viewpoint. ...

I just plain don't know whether I will or can come to Denver this year or not – I will allright, you can bet your life, if I can – but there are three things –

1　The war scare
2　Lancelot probably won't come
3　I don't want to bring Gay and Julie
4　Who to leave them with here if I do come.

However I should know by September and I'll come if I can ...

Love,
Helen

Posted "Via *Queen Mary*" – date stamped 3 – PM 31 JLY 1939.

14th August
Mahee

Dear Mother and Aunt Ethel and Ginna,

It is another heat wave and I am sitting here outside actually sweating. Gay is asleep. Julie is asleep. Janet Webb is making sand pies in front of me and L. is weeding and digging in the garden. Rock and Sambo (our new pup) are stretched out pole-axed beside me. Lancelot has this week off and is just going to stay around here. ...

I took Gay to see Dr. Allen last Wednesday because she still has a temperature and I wanted to know why... In view of this and in view

---

[66] It was "Little Sir Echo," a song written by Fearis and Smith in 1917 but a hit in 1939 for Guy Lombardo & his Royal Canadians and also for Bing Crosby.

[67] Estes Park is a resort town in northern Colorado and a gateway to the Rocky Mountain National Park. Presumably Egginton was painting in the Colorado outdoors.

of Julie being difficult to feed I would not like to leave either Gay or Julie to come to Denver this autumn – much as I would *love* to come.
...

Another drawback is whether there will be war – I would hate to be there and have war break out here so I must postpone my visit but maybe I could bring them both in the spring – who knows? And maybe Lancelot too.

We both went to supper at Bodo and Edie's at Whiterock[68] last night on L.'s motor bicycle – it was a riot! I was sitting on a cushion behind. It was so pleasant and airy bowling along – it is half bike and half motor cycle and like that thing that the Kennedys used to have – a Smith motor wheel or I forget what they called it.[69] I could ride it myself with practice. ...

Ginna will remember Penn Hughes,[70] that attractive friend of Lancelot's who came to dinner the last time she was over – we just heard that he was killed in an airplane crash – he had his own plane.

I wish that you would write oftener – I so enjoy hearing your news about everybody in Denver. Tell Eggy we are sorry that we can't come.
...

Love,
Helen

---

[68] Whiterock is a small village on the scenic western shore of Strangford Lough, about a mile from Mahee Island as the crow flies, but about nine miles by car.

[69] The Wall Auto Wheel was invented by a young Englishman in 1910 by which a one-horsepower engine propelled the bicycle. It went on the market in 1914 and in the same year the A.O. Smith company bought the U.S. rights, made some modifications and called it the Smith Motor Wheel. The idea was further developed, and Lance probably had a motorised bicycle with a two-stroke engine which was popular before the Second World War.

[70] Clifton Penn-Hughes (1905–1939) was a sports pilot and race-car driver. He was killed when the plane he was piloting crashed as he was returning from a business trip to Paris. In 1933 he and Pat Driscoll in an Aston Martin were 5th overall in the 1933 24-hour Le Mans, but second in the Biennial Cup awarded to the smaller cars. He also raced in the well-known Ards Tourist Trophy car race (Northern Ireland); there is a photograph of him at the wheel of a Frazer Nash in the 1931 race in John S. Moore, *The Ulster Vintage Car Club Book of the Ards T.T.* (Belfast: Blackstaff Press, 1978), p. 43. In 1934 Penn-Hughes married a Dubliner, Heather Seymour "Judy" Guinness who fenced for Great Britain. She won a silver medal in the 1932 Olympics; she had in fact won the gold medal but in the cause of fair play informed the judges that they had miscounted the hits of her Austrian opponent.

17th Aug.

Mahee

Dear Mother and Ginna and Aunt Ethel,

We are in the middle of another heat wave and it is divine – boiling hot all day long. It is so nice for Lancelot on his week off to have such good weather and we are never in the house – morning, noon or night.

Yesterday Janet, Gay, L. and I went to Elaine's to lunch and Rosemary, Joan and Mary were there and then we all went in their boat and landed on Chapel Island[71] and had tea. ... John Andrews[72] is such a handsome, attractive boy now and he and Heather are so wild and fight so but won't go any place without each other.

I think I forgot to tell you in my last that I went to the horseshow last Thursday with Betty Haselden and Joy.[73] I got up here at 6.30 bathed (!!!) and got all dressed up in my fox cape and blue pleated sleeve suit and my 2/11 "boater" hat and called for Betty and Joy in Comber and we caught an 8.10 special for Dublin – breakfast on the train. The Show was such fun because of the people – the clothes were sensational – to give you an idea there were lots of doll hats which were conservative compared to the other hats. The really snappy people could have been counted on one hand but every other person was something to stare at openmouthed. ... The horses and jumping were as wonderful as ever – we missed the finals of the international jumping which were on Friday but we saw them all – the Germans were leading when we left. What impressed me most were the adorable children in

[71] Chapel Island is one of the bigger of the many islands in Strangford Lough, County Down, though uninhabited save for sheep.

[72] John Andrews (1929–2014), son of Jack and Elaine Andrews, was the great-nephew of Thomas Andrews, co-designer of RMS *Titanic* who lost his life during the sinking; For the last few years of his life, John was President of the Belfast Titanic Society. The Andrews family of Comber (near Mahee Island and on the shores of Strangford Lough) has been engaged in flax spinning and linen production since the eighteenth century. Heather, John's sister, later married Trevor Boyd, son of Janet and Austen Boyd.

[73] Betty Haselden (née Harris) was the first wife of Cyril Ormrod (Micky) Haselden (b. 1910). Joy is Joyce, Micky's sister and step-daughter of Sir James Andrews (1877-1951), Lord Chief Justice of Northern Ireland and brother of John Miller Andrews (1871-1956), second Prime Minister of Northern Ireland, and Thomas Andrews (1873-1912) of *Titanic* fame. Joy's mother, Jane Lawson Haselden (née Ormrod, b. England 1878), widow of Captain Haselden, married Sir James Andrews. Jane's sister Jessie Ormrod married John Miller Andrews.

their little bowler hats riding as if they had been born on horses. ...[74]

Gay and Julie are fine – Hope you are too. I really feel better having decided against coming to Denver in Sept. ... but I know it's better for me to stay here.

Must go

Love,
Helen

20th Aug.
Mahee

Dear Mother and Ginna,

... This week should decide whether there will be a war or no – although it is so much a matter of chance that it is impossible to say but I do think if we could get September over we are safe for a while.[75] It is awful to have that big black cloud always hanging over us and to feel this awful insecurity from year to year. People have stopped talking about it here almost entirely but not from thinking about it – and now it seems to me close for the first time but I have always felt that our generation instead of Earnest Hemmingway's [sic] is lost[76] – that is doomed to something and whether it is war or not I still think that

---

[74] The first Dublin Horse Show was mounted in 1864 and soon became an internationally famous week-long show-jumping competition with a strong social and fashion dimension, an Irish Royal Ascot, complete with a Ladies' Day.

[75] Tripartite talks among the United Kingdom, France and the Soviet Union began in mid-August. While these were going on, The Soviets on 19th August entered into economic talks with Nazi Germany, and on 21st August suspended their discussions with France and Great Britain. On 24th August – during the week Helen is anticipating – Germany and the Soviet Union signed a ten-year non-aggression pact (the Molotov-Ribbentrop Pact), which had the effect of giving Germany free rein in large parts of Europe. Helen is alluding presumably to public knowledge that the Tripartite talks were foundering. In any case, the military situation was heating up: one newspaper headline for events on 18th August ran "German soldiers Grab Slovakia" and for 19th August "German Press Sends Warning to Rumania". The British did not get September over them, and Great Britain declared war on Germany in the early hours of 3rd September.

[76] Hemingway used Gertrude Stein's remark about the lost generation as an epigraph to his 1926 novel, *The Sun Also Rises*. It can refer to the generation that came of age just after 1900 or, more specifically, the generation of expatriate Americans in Europe in the 1920s. Despite her declaration, only a decade separated Hemingway's from Helen's generation.

from now on things aren't going to be too rosy anyplace – a gloomy outlook but I'm convinced of it.

We were just talking, Lancelot and I, about what we might or could do to Mahee in the future – even as far ahead as when Gay and Julie are young ladies and somehow there is a day-dream quality about anything as far ahead as that which to us now seems impossible – how things ever can be straightened out goodness only knows but maybe it will all be so gradual that we will just slip into it without a war, or anything. Anyway life is far from a husk yet! ...

24th Aug.

It certainly looks black tonight and by the time this reaches you heaven knows what will have happened – the worst, I'm afraid.

We have been hanging on the radio all day – now it is 11.30 and things look worse than ever.

I still don't want to come unless I have to – only on account of Lancelot who hasn't joined anything yet but will probably try the navy again if he has to.[77] I would come now except that I wouldn't know when I would ever see Lancelot again which is too grim to contemplate. However if Lancelot is sent away someplace I will come at once with Gay and Julie because if I'm going to be stuck without him I would twice as rather be with you than here.

25th Aug.

This is Friday morning and the 10.30 bulletin just told about President Roosevelt's messages to Hitler and Poland.[78] I am going to Donaghadee [Co. Down] to lunch with Maureen – and maybe to have tea with Spence. Spence's mother is here trying to get Spence to go tomorrow if she can. ...

Lancelot isn't as depressed as he was during the last crisis and says that no one is as worked up as they were then. I am much more worked

---

[77] Lancelot Turtle was born (in the United States) in 1905 and so was in his mid-thirties when war broke out.

[78] Franklin D. Roosevelt's "Message to Adolf Hitler on the Poland Crisis", addressed to Chancellor Adolf Hitler in Berlin, was dated 24th August, 1939. In it he appealed for negotiation, arbitration or conciliation between Poland and Germany.

up but then I was calm last year. Everyone here is resigned to their fate because they know that Hitler must be stopped and they have let so much slide by. Viscount Halifax made a very cool and reasonable speech last night – you probably heard it.[79]

All the reservists have been called up – Bodo was sent to Hong Kong, but got out of it because his father isn't well and Bodo has the whole business on his shoulders. He will be sent someplace of course, if war comes.

This will all be ancient history by the time you get it but if war has broken you can rest assured that I'll come if I can and if not, Mahee is probably as safe a place as there is in the British Isles. I haven't talked to anybody much since the crisis started – John Carr and Stella and Tommy[80] called on Tuesday night and were very flippant about the whole thing.

It is just like last year the same calm announcing, the same suspense, the same dread – only worse. ...

Well – I may be seeing you –

Love,
Helen

---

[79] Lord Halifax, Secretary of State for Foreign Affairs, delivered a lengthy and analytical speech to the House of Lords on 24th August. In it he identified an attempt by Germany to impose its will on certain European countries and "the imminent peril of war"; summarised the counter-measures His Majesty's Government was taking (including compulsory military service); deplored the Soviet-Nazi Pact; reiterated Britain's defence obligations to Poland; and restated British policy: determination to resist force and the pursuit of peace.

[80] Tom Carr (1909–1999), the landscape painter, brother of John, was born into a family involved in stockbroking, banking, linen manufacture and shipping: the familiar Ulster commercial-industrial spectrum. In 1927 he was accepted into the Slade School of Fine Art in London where his teachers included Henry Tonks and Philip Wilson Steer. When he returned to Northern Ireland in 1939 he settled in Newcastle, Co. Down. During the war he was commissioned to depict the manufacture of parachutes for the Sunderland flying-boats built by Short Brothers of Belfast. After the war he taught at the Belfast College of Art and lived in Belfast. His wife Stella Robbins, a Londoner, died in 1995 and on her death Carr moved to Norfolk. He was appointed OBE in 1993. See Tom Carr's obituary in *The Independent*, 18th March, 1999 and Wikipedia entries.

4th Sept.
Mahee

Dear Mother and Ginna,

Lancelot is putting up a curtain rod over our big window preparatory to hanging our Belmont Road dining room curtains because the sunset to sunrise blackout caught us without a single curtain here and we have been hanging a tarpaulin outside to obscure the light.[81]

So far down here ... the war has made no difference to us apart from blacking out our house and car lights. Every time I seriously think of it I can't believe it and it makes me clear sick to think about it. I can't imagine anyone I know having to drop bombs to fight anyone and I still think that it would be equally as good, if not better to give in and let Hitler take everything although I realize that that is impossible. ...

Isabel was sailing on the 23rd to marry a New Englander named Roscoe Whitney, who lives in Luminster, Mass – a divorced widower with a daughter sixteen.[82] Isabel, to use a trite expression, is delightful. She had her aunt's book about the theory with her in its type-written stage – it has been refused by a publisher and Isabel is trying to improve it and we talked an awful lot about it because we were all so interested. I have a copy of the main points which I am sending you.[83] When I say Isabel was sailing I mean that I don't know what she will do now – she has had endless trouble in trying to become an American citizen – apparently so many people marry Americans just to get to America that the regulations are terribly rigid and she hasn't her papers ready yet even if there is away to get there.

I listened to the news at 7-0 this morning after I had given Julie her bottle and heard about the *Athenia* which shook me to the core – and

---

[81] Germany invaded Poland on 1st September, Britain and France declaring war two days later. The British government imposed a sunset to sunrise blackout on the population.

[82] "The name Whitney has been associated with New England history from its earliest days": *Encyclopedia of Massachusetts*, vol. 3. There was a Roscoe Johnson Whitney born in Leominster, MA – there is no Luminster – in 1898, making him 41 at the time of this letter. Roscoe J. Whitney published *The Rare Alkalis in New England* (Washington D.C., 1943).

[83] Isabel Noble's aunt's theory of human personality and Helen's synopsis of it remain unlocated.

Mother's cable to stay here came today.[84] On Saturday I went to town, or rather Friday, and filled out a card at the American Consulate asking to be evacuated if L. goes to war and if Honey Roseveldt[85] sends ships over for us. Meantime I feel perfectly safe – Northern Ireland is the only place that is allowed to keep movies open which is a very good indication that air-raids are not expected here.

We haven't decided yet where to live – Mahee is obviously safer but if petrol is very limited and food is very much rationed we will be very cut off not only from supplies but from our friends.[86] We also have to consider taking refugees if Belfast is evacuated – that is school-children – our quota is 14 people![87] – we have 7 rooms not counting the bathroom and there are supposed to be 2 per room. If there was a possibility of our having to take people I would try to fill up with mothers and children I know – such as Roberta[88] and anyone else that I felt I could stand in such close and marooned proximity.

I naturally can do no war-work even if I wanted to because of Gay and Julie. I don't know what Miss Robson will do – she would much prefer to stay here, but duty may call her to nursing or something and I won't be one bit sorry. I like her extremely well as a person but she is not a bit good with Gay and much too fond of Julie – however I have left it up to her in the meantime. ...

The curtains are up now and look quite nice – we have brown paper over the little window and brown paper over the kitchen window – not that we fear an air attack but it is the law, city or country. I haven't been to town at night yet to see everything dimmed – tram windows are blue and the curbings are black and white striped.

[84] SS *Athenia* was an Anchor-Donaldson passenger liner en route to Montreal from Glasgow via Liverpool and Belfast when on 3rd September, 200 nautical miles north-west of Ireland, it was sighted by a German U-boat and torpedoed. It was the first British ship sunk by Germany in World War Two. Of the 1418 passengers and crew, 117 were lost, including 28 American citizens and some Canadian crew members. Helen's profound shock was shared by many.

[85] Helen's play on President Franklin Delano Roosevelt's name may derive from the name of the popular American blues musician, Roosevelt Sykes (1906–1983), who was known as the Honeydripper.

[86] In the early stages of the war, rationing was less stringent in Northern Ireland than in the rest of the United Kingdom.

[87] After the Blitz of 1941, over 60% of children in Belfast were evacuated. "Evacuation of Civilians during World War II", Wikipedia.

[88] Roberta McMullan, married to Harry McMullan, for whom see the letter of 7th September.

I didn't give up hope until we heard at noon on Thursday that they were evacuating London and then I knew or pretty well knew that the jig was up. Miss Robson broke down at the lunch table when Arabella said that if I went to America they might never see us again. Miss Robson wasn't going on her holiday because she was so afraid that I would go to America in the meantime and she wouldn't be here to say goodbye to Julie. When I went to the Consulate I found that it would be weeks away before I could go so she was reassured.

We are now listening as usual to the radio which contained strings of announcements. There is no conscription in Ulster and so far L. hasn't joined anything. He applied in the spring to the Caroline[89] but they refused him because they said he was too old! Bodo and all the Caroline people have gone. ...

Spence is the only person I know who has gone home. I could perhaps have rushed to get a passage when she did – at two day's notice but I couldn't bear to leave then not knowing whether there would be war or not, if there was war whether I would ever see L. again and generally I just plain waited to see and here I am! I went to see Spence the day before she sailed and I didn't see how she could leave Toby like that. At times when I think only of Gay and Julie I am sorry that I didn't come long ago but mostly I am glad I'm here because we are not in danger the way English and Scotch people are and although I fully realize that there may be nightmare days ahead we can only hope for the best and I may come later. I am beginning to think that our peace of mind here at Mahee will be worth the loneliness and inconvenience because we are so near the airport in Belfast that those constant planes would have us jittery day and night – however we can only wait and see. ...

What we should have done but didn't and what everyone talked of or at least thought about, was clearing out when they realized that Europe not only smelled bad but stank – not original – E. B. White

---

[89] HMS *Caroline*, a Great War cruiser, sailed in 1924 to Belfast where she became the stationary floating headquarters of the newly created Ulster Division of the Royal Naval Volunteer Reserve. Bodo Taggart was trained aboard *Caroline*. Soon after war commenced, *Caroline* became a depot ship for anti-submarine patrol vessels, and when war ended resumed her Reserve duties until 2009. Decommissioned in 2011, this sole surviving cruiser of the Battle of Jutland (31st May–1st June 1916) is still afloat and having undergone conservation is now a visitor attraction.

moved out of New York because it just didn't smell good to him.[90] However here we are and we will soon know exactly how bad it is to be living in a country at war. I hope that my idea that nothing is ever as bad as you think it is going to be will come true this time.

You can think of us, meanwhile, quite comfortably installed and doing fine, thank you. If Lancelot goes away I will certainly cheese it to you if possible – if Lancelot stays here and farms I will stay here too if things are not unbearable for Gay and Julie – food etc. and we seem to be safe. There is of course no hope of L.'s coming to America which is a great pity. Time will tell and meanwhile we live from day to day – we have no future – I have more than most with my possible "scoot hole" as our neighbor, Mr. Chamberlain, calls it. I am not afraid to be killed but don't expect to be and I will be very interested to see what happens at the end. ...

This is the worst all right but I always was an optimist and believe that we will all smile again someday together. International marriages have their disadvantages but this is the biggest drawback yet.

Letters are being censored we are told hence the address at the top of every page – one of our many instructions. I would like you to send an occasional newspaper if you would please so we can see what America thinks and we will send you some too.

Enough for now, I'll keep you posted on how we're doin'!

Love,
Helen

[*(Censors have decreed that all letters should now have recipient's address on every page)*]

7th Sept.
Mahee

Dear Mother and Ginna,

Mother's Clipper letter arrived today making not such good time as Lancelot's 3 days and one hour which seems incredible. It is nice to

---

[90] E.B. White (1899-1985) was an American writer and journalist born in New York State. Helen would have known his work chiefly through *The New Yorker* for which he wrote for at least fifty years, starting in 1925. He wrote *Charlotte's Web* (1952). White later lived in Maine instead of New York.

think that I could, if necessary, be home in four days but it would certainly be a last resort to go on the Clipper – Miss Robson says that she wouldn't let Julie go on it. …

The 9 o'clock news is now on. Germans only 20 miles from Warsaw! The poor Poles! Time out while I listened. There are news bulletins at 8- 12- 4- 6- 9- and midnight and announcement bulletins at 7.30–10.30.

We have decided to move back to town a week from tomorrow. Miss Robson will be back a week from today. She went home and has to get a permit both to go and come. Everybody does anyplace in the British Isles. The petrol rationing goes into effect a week from Saturday – we with a 12 horsepower car will be allowed 6 gallons a week. If there are any air raids over Belfast we will tear down here but everyone thinks that Belfast is the safest place in the British Isles – City, that is. Of course you never know. Our windows present a problem because our living room, dining room and bedroom are the only three rooms with curtains heavy enough to keep out the light – or rather keep it in. We are going to paint some of the windows – we think. Jack Andrews said to L. today that they have already spent £200 in curtain material for their mill. …

Harry and Roberta are staying in town after all because Harry [McMullan] was called back to the B.B.C. and works twelve hours a day![91] …

After the petrol restrictions go on we will be sorely limited and will have to walk to the Astoria and the Strand for our amusements.[92]

Lancelot bought us both bicycles today! …

Lancelot has his name in for 3 things, the Caroline, some tank thing and a new anti-aircraft searchlight thing.[93] Most people we know who

---

[91] Henry Wallace (Harry) McMullan OBE (1909–1988) had joined the BBC in 1931. As a broadcaster, he covered the coronation of George VI in 1937 and was later to cover the surrender of the German Atlantic Fleet in 1945 and the arrival of survivors of the *Princess Victoria* ferry disaster in the Irish sea in 1953. He joined the Royal Navy during the war and afterwards became Programme Director, BBC Northern Ireland (1945–1969). Roberta, née Gardiner (d. 1988) was his wife. Peter McMullan, son, pers. comm.

[92] Two Belfast cinemas, roughly a mile and half a mile respectively from The Turtles' Belmont Road home in Belfast.

[93] The 3rd Anti-Aircraft Brigade was formed in Belfast in December 1938 and the 3rd (Ulster) Searchlight Regiment in 1939. The "tank thing" remains unidentified.

aren't on the Caroline and are in anything are in the Searchlight's thing, but lots aren't in anything.

I listen to the news but I don't read the papers much – no point. ...
I still plan to come to America

1   When Lancelot goes away.
2   "   it is perfectly safe.
3   "   bombing or food problems or anything affecting Gay
          and Julie start here.

But meantime we really do feel reasonably safe and here at Mahee it is remote enough and new enough that it just seems unreal but I'm afraid the cold reality of living in a country at war will net us all too soon. ...

Love,
Helen

12th Sept.
Mahee

Dear Mother and Ginna,

I am in the midst of packing up to go home but since it is such a lovely day I have taken time out (very willingly because my efforts so far are only half-hearted) to sit out here and write. Since last writing the weather has been beautiful – all but Sunday – The garden has begun to go over but there are still masses of flowers but they have become bedraggled and autumnal looking. The lough is sparkling in the sun, the birds are singing, the sun is shining and it is hard to believe that we are at war! Having been here since it started the town is going to burst on me as a bomb shell – the blackness at night, I mean. No one is allowed to have even a crack of light and we will just plain have to live in the dark for a day or two until we get our curtains fixed. L. has ordered cheap black material from someone he knows who is cutting it (same linen firm) and we will just baste it on the outside of all our curtains and it will look like deep mourning. Our car was fixed by the garage yesterday to comply with the regulations – bumpers painted white and the headlights are covered with black metal all except a tiny slit and big black visors are put over the lights. L. says we won't be able to see anything at all at night – anyway we only have 6 gallons of petrol a month so we won't be able to go far anyway except by train or bicycle. I am sure that we will come down here every Sunday afternoon anyway.

We called on the Glendinnings[94] the other night. They will just be stuck here except for occasional sprees into town. Mary Glendinning went to a movie at night the other night and said it was like a bad dream – the city so black that you literally had to feel your way across the street and an usher held a tiny torch for the people to come down the outside stairs. The trams are so dark too that people don't know where to get off and spend the whole time running back and forth in the tram trying to see where they are. ...

We will only come back here if Belfast is bombed or if L. decides to farm instead of joining anything. He applied yesterday for the pay corps – Charlie Mitchell[95] is in that and there is no active fighting although you may be sent anyplace. Charlie said that for every man in the front line there are five people behind him making arrangements, transport, food, clothes etc. ...

If you want to read some funny light English novels read *Wild Strawberries* or *August Folly* by Angela Thirkell – I laughed myself sick

---

[94] The Glendinnings were near neighbours of the Turtles on Reagh Island, near Mahee Island. Acheson Harden Glendinning, a prominent linen manufacturer, and his wife Elizabeth (Bess) were the parents of Margery, Harden, Joan, Barbara and Mary who will appear in the letters. In the context of Northern Ireland's post-war manufacturing woes, A.H. and Elizabeth appear in Francis M. Carroll's *The American Presence in Ulster*, p. 166.

[95] Charlie Mitchell, married to Nancy, was the brother of Dunsmuir Mitchell. The brothers were cousins to Armstrong and Esmé Mitchell. In 1965, Esmé was to establish the well-known Esmé Mitchell Trust for a variety of charitable purposes and of which the editor of these letters has been a beneficiary. On 31st October 1939 Dunsmuir Mitchell wrote to his friend Lancelot Turtle from Inchkeith, the strategically important island in the Firth of Forth. A lieutenant in the Royal Naval Volunteer Reserve, he explained how, working alongside the Royal Artillery which was in charge of the island's defences, his job was to keep tabs on all of His Majesty's vessels moving in and out of the Firth and examining all merchant ships. However, there had been recent excitement when German planes ("raiders") came up the Firth on 16th October endeavouring to sink cruisers anchored near the Forth Bridge and were engaged both by the cruisers and by the Auxiliary Air Force ("A.A.F." in the letter). These were the opening shots in the air war above Britain and Mitchell credited the AAF with victory over the raiding Junkers. Mitchell was on watch at the time and though nine miles from the bridge had a grandstand view of the action. The letter is in the possession of Julie Mackie. See "Battle of the River Forth", Wikipedia.

at *August Folly*.[96] Ginna would like *Civilization* by Clive Bell, too. Have you read *The Grapes of Wrath*. I tried to read that one of William Faulkner's *Wild Palms* – it was a dilly allright![97] …

You will know to address all mail from now on the Belmont Road again. I will write often and hope that you will too.

Love,
Helen

Thank you very much for the can opener, fish nets, shoes and socks and cellophane mats which have all arrived and are much appreciated. H.

16th Sept.
Belmont

Dear Mother and Ginna,

We are home again having moved yesterday and I am positively delighted to be here – mainly because of the intense isolation of Mahee for the last two weeks while Miss R. was away. The house looks so nice and so does the garden and we had an intensive moving in and rearranging yesterday including our blacking out which was the last straw to pole-axing us.

18th Sept.

Now I am at Rottgers[98] having a much needed wave. I am still well-nigh breathlessly glad to be back in town – I didn't realize how glad until we got home and now even without the war I am ecstatic …

[96] Angela Thirkell (1890–1961) was born in Scotland, her father J.W. Mackail the Oxford Professor of Poetry, 1906–1911, her mother Margaret the daughter of Edward Burne-Jones the Pre-Raphaelite painter, her godfather J.M. Barrie, the Scottish creator of Peter Pan. Her early novels, including *Wild Strawberries* (1934) and *August Folly* (1936), have been described as displaying satiric exuberance. She went on to write novels set during the Second World War.

[97] Despite Helen's advanced liberal education, the "dilly" quality of Faulkner's *The Wild Palms* (1939) may be due less to the familiar challenges of Faulkner's prose than to the story elements of adultery and a botched abortion.

[98] Rottgers hairdressing salon was in Belfast city centre and was still in business in the 1960s, though re-located

Anyway now I feel emancipated and the petrol rationing has been postponed a week so I have this whole week to go around to my heart's content night and day I intend to be *on the Go*.

… This morning I have to go buy more stuff for our black out – we have had A.R.P. (Air Raid Precaution) wardens at our house every night telling us about lights they can see. Any crack at all or glow must be blotted out – as it is we have black curtains hanging nakedly everyplace looking just like funeral [sic] bunting.

We went to a movie Saturday night and it just don't seem possible when you are outside at night – not a single light any place except the stars and the searchlights which are beautiful. There are 15 around Belfast scanning the skies and crossing each other in geometric patterns and when they light up a cloud from behind it is really lovely to see. I expect to break both my feet in the first month because of stumbling around in the dark. All I can think of when we go past the rows of black houses is:

> "Now o'er the one half world nature seems dead
> And wicked dreams abuse the curtained sleep".[99]

Everyone is agreed that [we] will be lucky to have our underwear left at the end of this war – we will be the poor Turtles and you will be the rich Ramseys even without striking oil or gold! Everyone just enjoys what they have now and it gives an added zest to living – for me fresh from Mahee everything looks so pretty in our house, the silver, china, glass etc. and it will make me at last take care of my things when I know that we won't have any more.

I am glad to know that Gay and Julie are too young to know that their lives are going to be so different – I think England will be just like Russia by the end of this war but I've thought so for years and never dreamed of putting them down for schools or planning for their debuts or anything[100] and I think that they will be just as happy anyway – if we are all spared as Mrs. Watson is wont to say. – or Toots if nuffin

---

[99] *Macbeth*, Act 2, i.

[100] See Helen's letter of 30th March. Helen assumes a post-War future shorn of English public (i.e. private) schools (enrolment for which takes place while the future pupil is a child) and debutantes' presentation at court ("coming out"). Interestingly, George Orwell thought much the same thing, believing that England could not win the war without a very English socialist rebirth which he thought inevitable (and would see the end of the public schools): see *The Lion and the Unicorn: Socialism and the English Genius* (1941).

happens but this time it has happened. My big book *Technique's and Civilization* [sic][101] told all about it and any prophetic history did too.

Do you think Honey Rosenfeldt has changed his policy or what?[102] I would like to know your views.

So far here it is only exciting and not grim but the grimness is creeping up on us all right all right and my ink is going –

Love,
Helen

21st Sept.
Belmont

Dear Mother and Ginna,

We are having the most wonderful spell of weather – hot and sunny and no rain for weeks. ...

Tomorrow I have to go to a hospital meeting and then to a sherry party Mrs. Noble is giving as a farewell to Isabel – Isabel is sailing on a Dutch boat a week from Tuesday. ...

Arabella and Mrs. T. were here for dinner last night – A. got over 50 letters about her engagement – all so nice. ... A. doesn't intend to be married for a year anyway and is going to do nursing. The girls who are doing things are driving ambulances or driving anything, being land girls (ploughing etc.) nurses or cooks for the army. Most men we know who aren't on the Caroline are in the anti-aircraft searchlight things – L. applied for a commission in one but wasn't chosen for which I was thankful – it was a case of knowing a friend in to get in or maybe they thought he would be more useful in some naval job. Anyway everything is full at the moment and he isn't rushing into anything.

Everyone thinks it is awful that Spence left Toby in the lurch the way she did. I don't think it is so awful but I couldn't have done it.

Harry McMullan is in London on some wonderfully exciting (so he says) secret job – Dick Pim lives in Churchill's house and does

[101] *Technics and Civilization* (1934) by Lewis Mumford saw war as a social release from mechanised life.

[102] President Franklin Delano Roosevelt was an ambivalent isolationist but was respectful of the various Neutrality Acts the U.S. Congress had passed. By the autumn of 1939, in the light of events in Europe, FDR was having some success in causing the American isolationist stance to sway.

something big and he got Harry his job I think.[103] ... T. McConnell is on the *Iron Duke*, nobody knows where[104]. ... Joe and Ken Topping are in the Searchlight thing – they are in camp in Ulster for a few months anyway, and then may be sent anyplace. John Carr is at Croydon doing some managing of airplanes but no flying – he is supposed to be in a dangerous place. Bodo is on the east coast of England inspecting ships that pass ... – Patrick, Jack Andrews etc. are staying home managing their mills in what are called reserved industries – the Mackies are making munitions 24 hours a day.[105] ...

Everyone has bought bicycles. Imagine having only 6 gallons a month! Anyway we live on the tram lines and have bicycles.

Rosemary [Webb] was saying on Monday night that the worst part of this war is the herding and she is right – so many people have in-laws of all kinds living with them – mainly married daughters and daughters-in-law from Eng. who have rushed over with their children and the fighting, rearranging, cooks and maids leaving because of extra

---

[103] Dick Pim – later Captain Sir Richard Pike Pim KBE (1900–1987), civil servant and naval officer – indeed did something big: he was in charge of the Map Room of Winston Churchill, First Lord of the Admiralty. He was a district inspector in the Royal Irish Constabulary before entering the Northern Ireland civil service where he was on the staff of the Prime Minister. He oversaw air raid precautions in 1938, and in the month Helen is writing he was promoted to Commander and transferred to the Operations Division of the Admiralty in London. At war's end he became Inspector-General of the Royal Ulster Constabulary. As well as Harry McMullan, Pim also got Jack Sayers into the Map Room; Sayers was later editor of the *Belfast Telegraph*. See *Dictionary of Irish Biography* (Royal Irish Academy, online); "Richard Pim", Wikipedia.

[104] *Iron Duke* was a Great War battleship that later became a gunnery training ship. In September 1939 she was moved and became a harbour defence ship in Scapa Flow. Presumably its movement was not widely publicised. The modestly referred to T. McConnell was Robert Melville Terence McConnell (1902–1987), son of Sir Joseph McConnell of The Moat, Strandtown, Belfast. Terence, who later became 3rd baronet, was Commander of the Royal Naval Reserve. His first wife, Rosie Reade, later married Micky Haselden: see the letter of 17th August above; his second wife was Alice Glendinning, cousin to the Reagh Island Glendinnings.

[105] "Mackies" (James Mackie & Sons), whose textile machinery-engineering plant had operated since 1858. During the war, it became an industrial powerhouse, with 12,000 employees when it turned to designing and manufacturing armour-piercing shells that proved highly effective in the North African campaign and for which Winston Churchill later sent a telegram of congratulations. They produced 75 million projectiles during the course of the war. See Gordon Mackie, "Third Generation Mackies: Textile Engineers to the World, 1897–1988", in Professor Sir Bernard Crossland (ed.), *The Lives of the Great Engineers of Ulster* (Belfast: NE Consultancy, n.d.), p. 85. Helen's daughter Julie married Patrick ("Paddy") Mackie of that firm. In the 1970s Mackies became a workers' cooperative.

people and general confusion is one of the unheard of heroic sacrifices of a war – not to mention having slum kids or pregnant women billeted on you! Wives whose husbands have gone (sister-in-law etc.) are moving together to pool petrol, food, coal etc. none that I know of yet but there is talk of it. Isabel [sic] is moving in with Molly Cunningham maybe![106]

Anyway as I said before we have felt no inconvenience yet except for the black-out – next week it will be petrol – I doubt if coal will be rationed for a long time or electricity – food will be pretty soon – butter and bacon first.

Much as I don't think any war is worth it and much as I've talked about giving all Europe to Hitler instead I realize that it is inevitable and that his regime must be stopped but at what a price! ...

No use in our cabling you yet – you will hear when Belfast is bombed (no one thinks that it will be until the B. Empire is crumbling) and then we will start cabling – if L. goes off I still have it in mind to come and spare myself my living with in-laws ...

Love,

Helen

We have 8 wonderful new movies of our summer holiday –

27th Sept.
Belmont

Dear Mother and Ginna,

We are still having the most heavenly weather – sunny and warm every day – it hasn't rained for weeks. I have been trying to get collectors for a district for the Maternity Hospital Flag Day on the 20th of October – I am supposed to get 50 and I can only rake up about ten – it is a nightmare. I got into it by mistake and do I wish I were out of it! So far I haven't been hooked for any war work but have skated on thin ice over it and am bound to get hooked in the end. The more I think of

---

[106] Helen is probably referring to Isobel Mackie's moving in with her sister-in-law Molly Cunningham (née Pears). Isobel (b. 1901) was married to Joe (Josias) Cunningham, a stockbroker. Molly married Jimmy Cunningham, who inherited ownership of the *Northern Whig* newspaper. The Cunninghams were a stockbroker family whose firm became Cunningham Coates in 1991.

it the crazier I think it is – the war, I mean and I am a pacifist full of good arguments. L. can raise no enthusiasm at all for it either – he is waiting now until the Admiralty wants him and isn't trying to get into anything. The navy is full now so I hope it stays full. ...

L. is giving notice on this house today – whether we can give it up inside 6 months I don't know but anyway 6 months from now it will be April and we can move to Mahee if we have no other place to go. The reason we are giving it up is the high rent for one thing and its position in the town isn't too good if there are air-raids – we are too near the ship yards and the airport – although not very near as you know. People reckon that this is the 5th most likely spot in the British Isles to be bombed but no one expects it to be bombed because of the distance the Germans have to travel over England. No one has a trench or a basement shelter except Dunlop Cunningham[107] and all the public johns are sand bagged and are supposed to be air-raid shelters. L. is an A.R.P. warden since last night – to arrange for cripples and invalids and to know where fire hydrants are etc. ...

Mother's letter came today. I know you are more worried about us because I would be too but even if I never get home until the war is over I think that you needn't worry – we can move around the country here – Free State[108] if we have to, to some isolated place and I don't think England can be blockaded as to food. I know that we aren't as well off by any means as we would be in Denver but we are reasonably safe. No American but Spence has left and none of them is thinking of going, even those whose husbands have gone.

2nd Oct.

This is Monday the 2nd now and it is Arabella's birthday. Gordon is up for the weekend and A. or Gordon is taking us to the Grand

[107] Dunlop McCosh Cunningham (1901–1984), son of Samuel Cunningham (see the letter of 16th February above), inherited ownership of Murray and Sons, the tobacco firm. His three brothers included Joe, Jimmy and Knox (later Sir Knox Cunningham, barrister and Unionist Party MP). When his brothers joined up, Dunlop took charge of their businesses during the Second World War. In the 1920s Dunlop built a home, Garnock Hill, in the leafy Dunmurry district of Belfast, the house Helen refers to. Garnock Hill is now a suburban housing development.

[108] The south of Ireland ceased being the Irish Free State in 1937 but the name remained in popular usage for several decades.

Central[109] for dinner tonight and Auntie is having a dinner party for G. and A. tomorrow night. I am going to Elinor [sic] Nicholson's for lunch today so life is a whirl[110] ...

We found out that any petrol pump still sells petrol – a thing not generally known so we are using the car again after I used the train all last week! ...

We went to Randalstown on Saturday or rather Shane's Park – L., Armstrong [Mitchell] and Patrick [Webb] were shooting and then to Rosemary's to supper. Shane's Park was a dream – it is the prettiest place anyway and it was such a lovely day.[111] Armstrong tried to get in the Air-arm service – he went to London to be examined and he said that after keeping him standing naked for two hours they decided he had a divergent squint and wouldn't take him. All of which cheers me up because Lancelot's color blindness may keep him out until they are desperate and I hope the war will be over before then. ...

Ma! It's wonderful! All my bras, girdles and everything hang on me – I don't know how I have got so thin because I eat like a horse – twice as much as L. eats, but you can imagine how I love it. My waist is still two inches bigger than it should be but otherwise my figure is almost as good as ever – hips a bit wide too, I'm afraid.

... Kenneth [Pringle] just arrived from New York on the Washington – there were 800 passengers and they are taking 1800 home – three layers of them in the swimming pool![112]

---

[109] The Grand Central Hotel (1893–1972) in Belfast city centre was indeed both central and grand, a synonym for opulence in the city devoted to industry and business.

[110] Eleanor Nicholson (née Caffrey) was a friend of Helen's who was also a member of the Drawing Room Circle. After Helen's death she was one of her women friends responsible for setting up the Helen Ramsey Turtle Scholarship at Queen's University Belfast. In 1928 she married Cyril Anthony de Lacy Nicholson KC, who was a captain in the army by 1940 and who became High Sheriff of County Londonderry in 1946 and whose family seat was Beech Hill House, Londonderry, occupied by the U.S. Marines in 1942. See *Belfast Gazette*, 4th January 1946; "The Nicholson Family Crest," www.myfamily silver.com; "Beech Hill House," Lord Belmont in Northern Ireland website.

[111] The 2600-acre demesne near Randalstown, County Antrim. Its 14th century castle was built by the O'Neill dynasty and its name changed to Shane's Castle in 1722 by Shane O'Neill.

[112] Kenneth Pringle was a close friend of Lance Turtle's; he married Katie Batch of Dublin. The luxury liner SS *Washington* was, at 24,000 tons, the largest ever U.S.-built liner when it was launched in 1932. It became a troopship in 1941 and carried British troops to Singapore.

Did Eggy come to see you again and is he coming home? Is Raymond Gram Swing considered good in America?[113] I haven't had any mail except Mother's Clipper letter for a long time – no *N. Yorkers* either so it must be the confusion of shipping.

Nobody talks about anything here but the war and everybody is so philosophical about it – even accepting the 7/6 on the income tax without a murmur – Everyone is buying now but will stop shortly when they have their stocks in and prices go up.[114] I bought two ugly pairs of shoes (American) and am going to get a fleece lined pair of boots. ...

Love,
Helen

5th Oct.
Belmont

Dear Mother and Ginna,

I am huddled in front of the drawing-room fire just out of bed at 5 p.m. recovering from a stinker of a cold – the gramophone upstairs in the nursery (guest-room to you) is playing "I'm going to wander all over God's Heaven."[115] And it is downright gay. Our good weather sure busted with equinoctial gales yesterday and driving rain today. The "girls" are playing with Miss Robson and are being so good that my yesterday's decision from bed to fire Miss Robson is fading – yells all day from Gaysie but no yells at all today. I had it all worked out

---

[113] Raymond Swing (1887–1968) was an American journalist and broadcaster. He worked in Berlin for the *Chicago Daily News* before and during the Great War and it was through his German experience he was later chosen as a war-time commentator back in the United States where he had become a strong opponent of Hitler and American isolationism. His broadcast commentaries were heard worldwide, hence Helen's question. Swing had married the feminist Betty Gram who insisted he adopt her name if she did his, and he was known as Raymond Gram Swing until his divorce in 1944.

[114] A war budget in the United Kingdom introduced on 28th September raised income tax to 7s 6d in the pound (20 shillings) – the highest rate ever in the country. Also, a pint of beer was to cost 1d more, 20 cigarettes also 1d more. At the time the average wage was £6 a week.

[115] "I'm Going to Walk (sometimes "Wander" or "Shout") all over God's Heaven" is a "Negro spiritual" attributed to Thomas A. Dorsey. Helen's recording may have been by Mahalia Jackson.

yesterday that I was going to fire the lot and get a cook-general and nurse-maid – one thing the war has done is to glut the maid market – there are some even offering to work for their board and keep and the papers are full of ads for places instead of for maids ... The reasons that there are so many maids are

1 All the ones who were in England have rushed home for safety and because so many people have left London and don't need maids.

2 So many people here are cutting down their staffs for economical reasons and because there is no entertaining to speak of...

We have plenty of petrol this month but the pinch will come later. Food rationing hasn't started yet here – but we will eat our margarine and like it I suppose. I have a big supply of baby vegetables and glucose and soap and we have supplies at Mahee.

There are so many weddings – and all so sad. I am a fierce pacifist because I don't think *anything* is worth war – when I say to give all Europe to Hitler people think I'm coo-coo but I think in the long run it would be better though certainly not pleasant now –

I still take the *New Yorker* which I love and I would love getting clippings from you. Are you a socialist or a communist?

Love,
Helen

... I was trying to think of what would be of interest to you from our "Home-front". Half the people are furious with America for not coming in and thinks if America had come in earlier there would have been no war and half don't blame her. It depends on whether you regard this war as a crusade against Hitlerism and as a salvation of the world or whether you think of it as England saving her skin – the diplomats seem to use both arguments with a leaning toward idealism.
...

I had lunch at the Nicholson's on Monday and such good conversation with Elinor Nicholson and Maureen. Cyril Nicholson who is in one of the new anti-aircraft units came home to lunch and said "How's your war?" I said it was fine – I still had L. and the children, could go to America when I wanted (maybe) and had petrol for another week. He said their's [sic] was terrible – he hates being a soldier, they have to rent their house to keep solvent, their kids are in Londonderry with his mother. Elinor doesn't know what to do – they can't afford to keep a maid – she said there was always a bed in her own family's house, or she could go live in purgatory with her ma-in-law or she could take a job –

Luckily L. and I are of one mind on this war – we don't believe in it and there isn't that false pride or patriotism or whatever it is that makes most men rather die than stay at home and not join up – when I say most I don't really know because there are lots we know who are waiting until the last ditch and they are called.

Everyone expects Hitler to make a gigantic attack when his peace plans are rejected and then we'll know we are at war. No one carries gas masks here except the police and the soldiers but everyone does in England. People half suspect the I.R.A to rise but so far so good.[116] ...

Do you still take the *New Yorker*? I just love it so. I am now about to read The Mind in Chains – Socialism or communism?[117]

Helen

We had a card from Eggy from Belfast, Maine. He said "What's this I hear about war?" Did you see him on his way east? Did he leave some pictures in Denver? Did he sell any? Did he give you one?

16th Oct.
Belmont

Dear Mother and Ginna,

On our return from Dublin last night we found a letter from each of you and if we hadn't I would have blown up from disappointment and

[116] The Irish Republican Army Council, unreconciled to an Ireland partitioned into two countries from 1922, had declared war on Britain in January 1939, and it was thought the illegal force would seize the opportunity of the war to disrupt Britain and Northern Ireland. Indeed, the IRA drew up a plan ("Plan Kathleen") to invade Northern Ireland but they were discovered by the southern Irish authorities. Nonetheless, The IRA began an armed campaign in Northern Ireland in 1942 though both Irish governments took measures against the illegal force and introduced internment (preventive detention).

[117] Helen refers to the book published in 1937 and edited by Cecil Day-Lewis: *The Mind in Chains: Socialism and the Cultural Revolution*. Its contributors were well-known British Marxists and socialists, including Anthony Blunt, Charles Madge, Rex Warner, Edward Upward and Edgell Rickword.

sorrow. Today I have that unsettled "back home" feeling – our trip having interrupted my annual burst of good housekeeping. However, I think my enthusiasm or more accurately determination will carry me over and I can renew my efforts at organization.

It is a lovely, sunny day but there was a heavy frost and winter has come – I am almost sweating sitting here at the desk in a new green sweater and worst of all a wool shirt! However, my feet in their new ground-gripper shoes are like two long thin lumps of ice which no degree of warmth seems to thaw out. Gosh! Am I hot, Ma!

… We went to Dublin Friday afternoon – Arabella, L. and I and Gordon met us and took us straight out to his house where we spent a not bad, chilly, weekend every minute of which we both wished we were home and when we got in the car to come home L. couldn't wipe the smile off his face! He said if it was like that for two days away, what would it be like if he had to go to war – away from me too – he would hate it as much if not more than anyone I know. …

18th Oct.

Now it is Wednesday evening and I have just come in from posting some letters and was it dark. I had a flashlight but even so it was scary because you can hear footsteps but you can't see anybody until they are right beside you. L. is reading *The Stars Look Down*[118] and has taken one of our black shades off a light to read and from the outside the glow is much too bright for an A.R.P. warden's house but when I told him he just said "Aw, to hell". …

Now we are having tea and L. is twiddling the radio – he listens to the German broadcasts in German and it drives me bugs or "crackers" as the latest British slang would have us say. We get America direct almost every night but only once have heard a news bulletin.

Everyone is so disgusted with the news bulletins here and the dearth of information – as the Letter from London says, everyone is fed up with something and I am fed with it all.[119]… We are actually invited

---

[118] *The Stars Look Down* is a 1935 novel by A.J. Cronin, set in the north-country mining district of England.

[119] Having told readers of *The New Yorker* of the negative economic and social impact of the war so far, Mollie Panter-Downes in her 7th October "Letter from London" observes: "Criticism is in the air these days. … Everyone is slightly fed up with something or other."

out to dinner on Friday and Saturday nights – Friday at the Chamberlain's and Sat. at the Sloan's. Gay and I are going to lunch at Elizabeth Morwood's to meet some Spanish refugee mothers and their babies.[120]

Mrs. Marshall's tap dancing class has started again. It is such fun even if she is a Panic From Panicville. There is ice-skating too now at Balmoral – the King's Hall – we haven't been yet. I was going today with Maureen but she was in bed with a cold.

… Everything is going up so in price and this is only the beginning. Petrol is up another tuppence and is now 1/8 a gallon. We are very lucky there and have almost plenty – 6 gallons allowance with the car, 8 gallons for running Mahee as a farm (3 trips a week supposedly) 4 gallons for the 2 motorcycles and 5 gallons for pumping water at Mahee! – 17 extra a month which makes us in an excellent position and spares me any more 40 minute tram trips for a cup of tea with Mrs. Dolan![121]

The town is full of soldiers in uniform and occasional women who look awful usually.

Again so far the war really hasn't affected us except for the black-out, higher prices, shortage of groceries in some shops and of course the general depression and endless discussions, but people aren't half so downcast as you would think though everyone is full of pessimism but there is a general attitude of "Well, this is the worst, all right, but what can we do?" and it is quite true that the sense of humor or esprit de muddling through or whatever you call it is in the British people to

---

[120] Elizabeth Morwood was born in 1908 in India, daughter of James and Mary Morwood, the American founder of the Drawing Room Circle in Belfast, and sister of Mary: see the letters of 11th February and 27th July above. Morwood had become a social campaigner and civil libertarian. She supported the Spanish republicans opposed to Franco and during the Spanish Civil War (1936–39) she persuaded her father to take in refugee children from the Basque region. Almost 4000 Spanish children had arrived in Southampton in May 1937. The plan was to distribute them in "colonies" (*colonias*) throughout the UK. Most were repatriated even before the end of the Spanish Civil War in April 1939 but many stayed on beyond that date. See "Refugee History", http://refugeehistory.org.;, "Evacuation of children in the Spanish Civil War," Wikipedia. The Belfast poet John Hewitt and his wife Roberta also took in Basque refugee children: see Connal Parr, "Honouring Belfast men who died for democracy of Spain," *Belfast Telegraph* , 9th November, 2015.

[121] Mrs Dolan was the American wife of Major Francis Dolan: see the letter of 22nd May 1941.

the extent that they can almost laugh and can smile over the 7/6 on the income tax.

I broke down and bought *The Grapes of Wrath* which is gripping and good though not as good as other people seem to think – and it seems to me that the philosophizing is labored and dragged in and the extreme coarseness unnecessary but if that book's message is true, America don't smell like no rose. Have you read it?

I got William Lyons Phelps's *Autobiography with Letters* [1939] and was very disappointed in it – his conceit and trivial way of writing got me down.[122] A good book about the servant problem in England – very funny and readable is called *One Pair of Hands* by Monica Dickens.[123]

… We are going to give notice for this house for the 1st of May – not the 1st of February – by that time we should know a little more what the score is…

Must go to bed

Love
Helen

Did you ever get that theory of Isabel Noble's? I sent it early in September.

31st October
i.e. Hallowe'en
Belmont

Dear Mommer and Gin,

I am an A.R.P. widow tonight and I hate it. Lancelot has to be out until midnight alternately patrolling and sitting by a telephone. …

Auntie has called up twice thinking that she heard an air-raid in this direction – I have been out both times but I think that she was pretty excited about it. The only excitement in that line is the fact that there was what they call an Air-raid warning yellow last Saturday. That just means that wardens are told by telephone to stand by for air-raid

---

[122] William Lyons Phelps (1865–1943) was a high-profile American scholar and critic who also wrote newspaper columns and presented radio programmes.

[123] *One Pair of Hands* (1939) by Monica Dickens (1915–1992) has never been out of print. It recounts her experiences in domestic service, even though her London family was upper middle-class. Her great-grandfather was Charles Dickens.

warning red which is when the sirens are sounded and everyone is supposed to take shelter. …

No one here thinks that the Germans will bother to run the risk of coming all this way even to bomb Harland and Wolff's and the air-port and even the people who think that they might come to bomb don't think that they will bring gas which is very heavy to travel with. However, if the industrial towns in England or Glasgow are attacked we are moving to Mahee at once. We are all ready to go – the place is stocked with food and fires are lighted in the bathroom and living room every week-end. … What with winter coming on and all I really don't expect raids here unless Hitler just sends everything over and doesn't care what happens to them.

There is a variety of opinion as to what to do in an air-raid – I think that the A.R.P. advises rolling yourself in a blanket and lying against an inside wall away from any windows with your gas mask on and a pencil between your teeth to keep you ear drums from getting the shock of noise or something like that – what a picture! Some people are going outside to watch it and to keep away from falling buildings – some are going to stay in bed and some are going to lie under the dining room table and a very few have sand-bagged and water filled trenches in their gardens and Dunlop Cunningham has a concrete trench 30 feet deep for his family and they have drills and all.

The public johns are the only shelters in town although they are building more and lots of places are sand bagged. The black-outs on the houses are all so good and the trams now have blue lights and they have taken the blue paint off the windows. …

Most people's lives are the same as ever except for the sissys who don't budge out at night it certainly is no fun driving with practically no light in the pitch dark. I have only done it once and then I wore my glasses and simply crawled along. There were 1000 more people killed on the roads last month than usual in England and Ireland and there is furious correspondence in the papers about the crazy pedestrians and bicycles with no rear lights.

When day light savings goes off I think there will be a big change because the town will be black by about 4.30 and at the rush hour going home at 6. I'll bet the confusion at the junction will be frantic. The night that we came home from Dublin was the only night I have been at the junction but it was bedlam because all the people waiting for trams stand in the middle of the street in a solid and seething black mass. It is pie for bag snatchers I should think although I haven't heard of many cases but is awfully scary on quiet roads walking along and it is reputedly hard to get maids unless you live on a tram line. ...

The autumn here this year is the prettiest one I've seen but nothing like America's for brilliance. – however, there is a grayed or subdued haze over the colors here that is hard to beat in its own Irish way.

I went to Eggie's exhibit today – Irish pictures that he did before he went to America and they *are* good – I would have bought several gladly. L. heard from Eggie who is home again and waiting to be asked for rather than applying for anything. He is hard at work on his sketches from America – making them into big pictures. They said at Rodman's[124] today that he is going to have a big exhibition in America in December. ... The man at Rodman's said that there is no one to touch him in his line and that he is such a hard worker. He is not coming over here until after Christmas because he has no car and couldn't get around to paint. ...

Mrs. Chamberlain just rang me up to see if I would help at some naval canteen – every other Friday afternoon and every other Tuesday evening – to give food to naval officers and men who are on destroyers that come in. Almost everyone I know is either in a sewing depot or a canteen. I have lain low so far except for volunteering to help Esmé [Mitchell] who is doing soldiers' and sailors' wives and children – more social work and more in my line than sewing.

We don't know anyone who has been killed yet –T. McConnell is at Scapa Flow which was bombed but he is all right[125]. ...

Lancelot is still just waiting to be called by the Admiralty. ... All the people in the linen business are still here because it is a reserved industry and we know lots of people who aren't in anything because there is no need yet.

Lots of people say that the war will be over by Christmas and less optimistic ones say by the summer. ...

---

[124] Rodman's art gallery, Donegall Place, Belfast.

[125] On 14th October 1939, the supposedly safe Royal Naval base in Scapa Flow, Orkney Islands, in which there were 51 ships anchored, was penetrated by a U-boat. It torpedoed HMS *Royal Oak* which quickly sank; 834 sailors lost their lives. See Scapa Flow Historic Wreck Site: www.scapaflowwrecks.com

Since it is [now] the 1st of November and I have had no cable I'm supposed, I suppose, to offer condolences, but I won't because I'm a firm believer despite everything in [Isabel Noble's] theory that everything happens for the best.

L. came in a while back with his tin helmet and special gas mask. I will send you photos soon of us arrayed to meet mustard gas!

I have been reading *John Brown's Body* by Benét[126] – the invocation is worth getting the book to read –

Here it is "Midnight again" –

It always is these nights –

Be sure to write often and at length – I WANT TO KNOW!

Love,

Helen

10th Nov.

Belmont

Dear Mother and Ginna,

... If you hadn't sent the clipping about the $225 gloves I wouldn't have believed it – no wonder that books like *The Grapes of Wrath* are written and *The New Yorker* says to watch for the Revolution. I read in *The New Statesman* tonight that there is a social change going on behind the black out only equaled by that that went on before the French Revolution.[127] Things look bad again here after the long lull on the home front and almost as big a lull on the Western Front. We are still ready to move to Mahee at any time.

There was an air raid warning siren rehearsal the other morning which was scary enough to listen to – sirens going up and down like an American ambulance siren only not so shrill and more of them a more "holocaustic"[128] sounding noise, but you couldn't have heard it if you had been talking inside with the windows shut.

Lancelot is sitting on the couch with his feet on the coffee table

---

126 The 15,000-line poem, *John Brown's Body*, by Stephen Vincent Benét (or Benet), set during the American Civil War, won the Pulitzer Prize in 1929.

127 Helen was persuaded by the claim that the social disruptions on the home front disguised more serious social realignments which would survive the war.

128 Knowing nothing of the secret Shoah under way, Helen by "holocaustic" must mean "intimating of major destruction".

reading (of all things!) *Mein Kampf*[129] and I am closer to the fire under a 100 watt reading light – I decided that we were living in a twilight that was making us blind and I was right. When the time changes a week from Sunday this blackout will be on about 4.30 or so and it will be *awful*...

The biggest excitement of the week was Julie's birthday party on Wednesday – a roaring success since none of the nine babies roared and Julie looked every inch the birthday child in her white organdie dress ... with a pink bow on her topknot and her hair curled (with Nestol)[130] fit to kill. The babies all came except Simon Haselden and Colin Shillington[131] and they were all so good. Tom Andrews cried pretty steadily before tea but only a shy cry and he had a swell time after tea.[132] Ours were without doubt the cutest ...

We are going to Shane's Park tomorrow ferreting rabbits and Sunday Mrs. Turtle, Arabella and Mrs. Noble are coming to lunch and we will go to Mahee. Monday, Tuesday and Wednesday afternoons next week I have to play bridge!

15th Nov. Wednesday Morning:

It is really afternoon having just struck 12 – and I have just come in from an hour's walk with Gay half in the pram and half walking. It is

[129] Adolf Hitler's *Mein Kampf*, first published 1925–26, was published in English translation (*My Struggle*) in London by Hurst & Blackett in 1938. A different translation, by the Irish priest James Murphy at the request of the Nazi propaganda ministry, and co-published by Hutchinson & Co. and Hurst & Blackett, appeared in 1939. (Murphy ran afoul of the Nazis and was ordered to leave Germany before his translation was published.) An American translation also appeared in 1939. See "James Vincent Murphy": Wikipedia; "*Mein Kampf*": Wikipedia; and John Murphy, "Why did my grandfather translate Mein Kampf," BBC online News Magazine, 14th January, 2015.

[130] Nestol – "makes baby's hair grow curly" – a hair product from Nestle & Co., London.

[131] Colin Shillington (b. 1939) would later be educated at Stowe and Trinity College Dublin where he broke the college half-mile and mile records and ran what was then the season's second fastest half mile in Europe. (See *Trinity News*, 8th June, 1961, p.4.) He represented Northern Ireland at the Commonwealth Games in 1958. Simon Haselden (b. 1938), son of Micky and Betty Haselden, likewise would attend Stowe public school; he later went on to work in the linen industry in Belfast.

[132] Tom Andrews (b. 1938) grew up to become Managing Director of John Andrews & Co. (famous producers of fine linen) until the Comber Co. Down mill shut down in 1997. He and his wife Dianne were the UK Flying 15 champions at Cowes in 1971.

a lovely, sunny day. I am now contemplating putting an egg on my face against this afternoon's bridge party in the Grand Central – 200 women all glaring at each other to see who is where and with whom and how they look! This afternoon's party is for the East Belfast Supply Depot or some war thing . ... My past two bridge afternoons have been financially successful having won 5 bob [five shillings, then worth $1] in the two days – yesterday I ups and bid 6 spades and it was doubled and I made it – whoops dearie! ...

Did you happen to hear Churchill's speech on Sunday – "Ten weeks of war" – it was a masterpiece for a war speech and he has a superb choice of words.[133] Herbert Bryson was saying that he has a reputation for what is known as "the telling phrase" – this time it was "leather-lunged" and he painted a wonderful picture of Hitler and his cronies looking out over the world at night and not seeing one friendly eye in the whole world – Russia returns their look with a flinty glare and Italy averts her gaze – if these speeches are broadcast to you he is well worth listening to. Did you hear the Queen? Her speech was very disappointing I thought though it has been explained by everyone that she purposely and rightfully plays the rôle of simplicity but I thought her speech was simple to the point of dullness – her voice sounds so young.[134]

The second news bulletin from the Pacific arrived yesterday – eagerly clutched and read but I am still waiting tense with anticipation for the denouement. ...

Mary Morwood is being married on the 23rd of December. She is on her way over from America now. Elizabeth and the two Isaacs girls[135] were here to play bridge yesterday and I hadn't had anyone for

---

[133] Readers can assess the justice of Helen's opinion by listening to Churchill's 12th November 1939 speech broadcast on the BBC, "Ten Weeks of War", on YouTube. It is a rallying cry to boost the national morale, a girding of loins on behalf of his compatriots. Although he claims to avoid saying anything of "an unduly sanguine nature," Churchill's real (or feigned) confidence was embodied in his magniloquence.

[134] Queen Elizabeth's 7½ minute Armistice Day address to women listeners was broadcast by the BBC. She expressed sympathy for the women of Poland, the first female victims of the war, and paid tribute to "the gallant womanhood of France" before rallying the women of Britain and the Empire.

[135] Melanie and Joan Isaacs. The Isaacs family lived in Malone Park, Belfast where Helen and Lance would later live. B. Isaacs is listed in the 1932 Belfast street directory as an outfitter with Hyam's of North Street, a large store opened in High Street in 1896 as a "men's and boys' clothiers" but in 1933 added women's departments. It was still going strong in 1960.

so long that I couldn't find the cards for ages – Elizabeth has a knack of telling things so vividly too – she said that it was so hard on husbands when they came home and found the "drawing room full of women in diamonds and furs" – a good description of the pampered rich woman and her friends. Will mail this.

Love,
Helen

21st Nov.
Belmont

Dear Mother and Ginna,

It is nearly six and there are sounds coming down to me from the nursery upstairs where Gay is sitting in Julie's bed reading and Julie is having supper. I gave Gay a bath and put her in under the nom de plume of "Jane". Lately she has been calling herself Jane because one day when she climbed in Julie's pram and lay down I asked her if she was our new baby and if her name was Jane so now every so often she is Jane. Today we went to tea at the Toppings and it was Jane who went because Jane said that Gay was a bad girl because she pulled down all the books off the couch and Jane had to smack her and put her to bed. The minute we came home Jane went upstairs to wake Gay up … we were home at 5 – on account [of] the black-out which since Sunday is an hour earlier and it is pitch black at 5 – and by the middle of December it will be dark by about 4 and on dull days about 3.30.
…
The news is now on announcing that the British will seize German exports on the high seas – because ten ships have been sunk in the last 3 days – 6 of them neutral –

All of which makes our latest war news so much worse because last week the worst happened and Lancelot got a letter from the Admiralty asking him to send in his age and how much sea training he has had – this is because L. applied even before war broke out to the Admiralty and they said that that didn't need him then, but would let him know. The letter said that when they know his experience an appointment will be considered. L. thinks that he has not had enough sea-training to qualify for a job on a boat but I'll bet anything that he will be hooked for some dull and maybe dangerous land job. He replied on Friday and so far hasn't heard anything. I wanted him not to reply but he did anyway. So at any moment I expect to be a war-widow to the extent of having to live alone (but not like it!). But we might be lucky yet and they might not want him! He would rather be in the navy than in the army and would have his commission (that is be an officer) which if he waited until later to enlist or be drafted he would not have – that is he would have to go as a private because no further commissions are being given – they all have to rise from the ranks.

If he gets a land job in a safe place I would go live with him if possible, but we haven't heard anything yet and maybe nothing will happen!

22nd Nov.

We are in the midst of too great a wave of popularity – making me long for the peace and quiet of Mahee – but not in this weather. It is now Wednesday morning and simply pouring with rain. ...

Last night we were at the Sloans to dinner and the night before Joe and Isobel [Cunningham] were here and we went to the Mikado.[136] Tomorrow I am going to be home all day and Friday only have to go see Bodo sometime in the afternoon – he is home for 48 hour's leave and sent a list of everyone he wanted to see and we were on the head of the list according to Tory Taggart[137]. ...

Did you ever read any of Archibald McLeish's poems? Some of them are lovely. ...

Elizabeth Morwood gave the paper at the D.R.C. on Pushkin and Mary [Morwood] was there fresh home from N.Y. after an awful crossing. She had paid £15 extra to sail on the *Washington* and at the last minute the *Washington* didn't sail and the passengers were

---

[136] Joe Cunningham, a stockbroker who married Isobel Mackie, was the brother of Jimmy: see the letter of 16th February above. *The Mikado*, a 1939 British movie adaptation of the Gilbert and Sullivan comic opera, played at the Astoria picture-house, Belfast.

[137] Tory Taggart was Bodo's mother said to be a colourful figure. Her grandson Redmond tells me (pers. comm.) that she was once becalmed in the Irish Sea on a yacht skippered by her brother; she prayed for wind and a dangerous gale ensued; she then was forced to pray for calm.

transferred to the British *Scythia* which was the first boat to sail after the embargo act business and they had £1,000,000 worth of guns etc. on board and *no* convoy – their sole protection being one little gun.[138] The ocean was rough which was some reassurance of safety, but even so I think that they were all nearly white-headed with anxiety. She is going to be married either at Christmas or at Easter to an Englishman – a professor at some small college – everyone who has met him thinks he is charming.[139] I like Elizabeth so much better than I used to – if you get behind her way of talking she is so nice although she has an awful bee in her bonnet about the present state of the world – a real reactionary or revolutionary outlook. She does a lot of work with the Spanish refugees. If you just sit down and think what the continent of Europe must be like it would drive you bugs – Czechs, Austrians, Poles and Spaniards – all with nothing and all refugees wandering around and whole populations on the move – sisters, it certainly stinks!! …

Did you see that the Ionides have published their book?[140] It was briefly mentioned in the *N. Yorker* and I got a postcard about it from the Eng. Publisher – I am going to get it for Mrs. Turtle for Christmas. …

Julie crawls like the wind now and sometimes from sheer delight she bucks just like a horse and then crawls on. Her idea of heaven is to see a floor stretching in front of her to be crawled on…

Must go – Love,
Helen

---

[138] During the war, RMS *Scythia*, a Cunard liner, became a troop carrier. At war's end, she carried many American troops home, along with many war brides. This 1939 sailing took advantage of the American Neutrality Act passed on 4th November 1939. The Act allowed for an arms trade with Great Britain and France (on a cash-and-carry basis), although they were belligerent nations, thus ending the arms embargo.

[139] Percival Rogers (1913–2001) was from Essex; the wedding in Belfast on New Year's Day was recorded in the *Belfast News-Letter* of 2 January, 1940 and noticed, with photograph, in the *Northern Whig* of 13 January 1940.

[140] Stephen A. Ionides and his daughter Margaret L. Ionides were the authors of *Stars and Men* (Bobbs-Merrill, 1939). This history of the human relationship with the heavens is described as an authoritative if idiosyncratic engagement with its subject. See a review in *Publications of the Astronomical Society of the Pacific*, vol. 52, no. 303 (1940): 51–52. The authors summered in the mountains of Helen's home state of Colorado, and Margaret had visited Lance and Helen: see the letter of 10th March 1943.

4th Dec.
Belmont

Dear Mother and Ginna,

... L. has just gone out with his flashlight and gasmask to his gas lectures.

It has been an awful day except for an hour or two when it snowed and it was lovely – the rest cold, gray and rainy. Julie and Gay loved the big flakes of snow. I went to the last D.R.C. meeting until the end of January today and it was wonderful. It was Louis MacNeice in person. He is the Bishop of Down's son, one of the best young poets in England (one about 28 I think) and one of the "new" school of poets – known as Auden, Spender and MacNeice School.[141] He was so natural and simple and coherent and at the end he read a few of his poems which were not only lovely but so good and had so much in and behind them. He just talked about his way of writing poetry (and Auden's and Spender's) and was defending it. He is, I gathered from his poems both a socialist and a pacifist and as you can gather I was completely won by him. Elaine [Andrews], who sat next to me, and had never heard of him, was too and will be in a daze for a week, I should think. ...

Lancelot hasn't heard anything from the Admiralty yet and I hope against hope that he won't. The broken home doesn't hold any appeal for me.

To show you how normal our life is – I was out for lunch every day last week and we went dancing twice and to a Thanksgiving dinner party and that's all but it was enough – too much if the truth be known. The lunches were – Monday – "fork" lunch and bridge for a canteen

[141] Louis MacNeice, who was born in Belfast and grew up in Carrickfergus, was thirty-two when Helen saw him and was living in London. He had recently published *Autumn Journal*, one of his major works, concerned among other things with the Spanish Civil War and what seemed like Britain's impending war with Germany. In the autumn of 1939, he was staying in Belfast, at the Bishops' House on the Malone Road (his father was Bishop of Down, Connor and Dromore), later to house the Arts Council of Northern Ireland and currently the Chinese Embassy. He gave a talk at Queen's University, Belfast on 12th December and sailed for the United States in January 1940. See *Letters of Louis MacNeice*, ed. Jonathan Allison (London; Faber, 2010), pp. xx, 355–373. MacNeice was one of a high-profile group of 1930s British poets referred to by the portmanteau coinage MacSpaunday (MacNeice, Stephen Spender, W.H. Auden and Cecil Day-Lewis).

at Billy's Mother's house (Billy Stephens).[142] Tuesday Mrs. Turtle and A. gave a lunch-party Wednesday to lunch with Nancy Mitchell, Thursday to lunch with Roberta, Friday lunch in town after our tap class with Maureen. The dances were a big [International] Red Cross one at the Plaza on Tuesday in Maureen's party and Sat. at the G. Central dinner dance with Maureen again – both fun. The Thanksgiving party was at Marcia's for the new American Consul, Mr. Randolph,[143] and to get Betty Carr out after losing her baby. We took Betty and Maurice Shillington[144] on account of the petrol shortage and I nearly came to blows with Betty over (1) Roosevelt. (2) Isolation. (3) Socialism – she is a snob of the first water as Ginna discovered when you talked to her about *With Malice Toward Some*. I was talking to her about that (*With Malice Toward Some*) once and she was saying to someone else at the bridge table that it, the book, was just pathetic because the poor little thing (Margaret Halsey) had never been anyplace.[145] Sister, did we fight and Sister, did I back her up to the wall when she said the only reason America was staying out of the war was to make money out if it! Are most people you know isolationist? Anyone with any sense here thinks that the U.S. is just lucky to be in a position to stay out but most people hope that she will come in (naturally enough). ...

[142] William (Billy) Stephens will reappear in Helen's letters as the war progresses.

[143] Marcia Mackie (neé Hopkins) was the American wife of James (Jim) Mackie, chairman of James Mackie & Sons. John Randolph arrived in Belfast as U.S. consul in July 1939 from Quebec City (Canada) and lived in the Grand Central Hotel. He was transferred from Northern Ireland in December 1941 and as he left he described his post to his superiors in Washington as a diplomatic as well as consular post, because of the complicated Irish situation. See Francis M. Carroll, *The American Presence in Ulster*, pp. 142–44.

[144] Maurice Shillington of the well-known family was a BBC radio newsreader in Belfast. Later he became the first reader of the news on BBC Northern Ireland television.

[145] The American Halsey spent a year in Exeter in the mid-1930s. She found the English exasperating and deftly skewered them on scathing witticisms and lethal similes ("Englishwomen's shoes look as if they had been made by someone who had often heard shoes described, but had never seen any. ...") There are parallels between Halsey's life and Helen's. Like Helen, Halsey (1910–1997) attended a women's only college (Skidmore College, New York) and like Helen she lived in the United Kingdom after marriage. Halsey's letters from England to her American friends and relatives evolved into *With Malice Toward Some* (the title a witty rewrite of Lincoln), a book that sold hugely and was voted the Most Original Book of 1938. Had she lived, Helen may well have adapted her own letters to literary purpose.

People are home on leave now and the G. C. Hotel is the most warlike in atmosphere of anyplace in town. On Sat. night L. and I arrived about 8.45 and tried to get into the cocktail lounge to sit down – it is now a big double ball room fully as big as the Cosmopolitan or Brown ball rooms[146] and it was jammed and they were standing 6 deep around the bar and every other person was in uniform. Everyone had said that it is *the* place in town and jammed morning, noon and night...

Wuthering Heights is here this week – maybe we can go tomorrow. I loved *Mr. Chips* – I remember you liked it so well months ago.[147]

Mary Morwood is being married on New Year's Day. [Her brother, Dr] James's American wife was at the D.R.C. today – too much rouge but very good looking and with one of those snood hats or whatever you call the ones with a gathered curtain at the back. ...

I am so sleepy so must go to bed because it's always "midnight again"

Love,
Helen

17th Dec.
Belmont

Dear Ginna,

Mrs. Noble was just here and we were discussing people and the "theory" and odds and ends and she was saying what she thinks Gay and Julie are and we somehow got onto you and your love life and I was telling her about Lloyd and Charles. She said for me to cable you *at once* to marry Lloyd! I told her how interesting Charles [Graham] was, how uncertain, how attractive etc. and she said that he was probably suave-animal and more fond of himself than anyone else and a very unsatisfactory person to think about marrying. She said that

---

[146] The Cosmopolitan Hotel stood on 18th Street in Denver from 1926. YouTube has dramatic 20-second footage of its controlled implosion in 1984. The Brown Palace Hotel on 17th Street was built in 1892 and is still in business.

[147] Laurence Olivier played Heathcliff and Merle Oberon played Catherine in the 1939 Hollywood movie directed by William Wyler and produced by Samuel Goldwyn. It was nominated for eight Academy Awards. *Goodbye, Mr Chips* was an acclaimed British movie of the same year.

what those people (suave animal) want to find is someone to marry who can make them forget themselves and then they are delightful – gentle, considerate and charming but if they don't get exactly the right type they are such difficult husbands. ...

She said for me to tell you that your type, simple suave, is the very type that needs someone to push them into matrimony because you will never make up your mind until it is too late – her sister is that type and never got married and wishes she had. She said, Mrs. Noble, that the type of man who doesn't appeal to you strongly at the time is the type you would like later and she said to be sure to tell you to marry him quickly.

Lancelot is taking her home now and you can see how quickly I am writing this to you. A minute ago, I was going to cable you – I may yet! Lancelot thought he, Lloyd was very good looking from his picture and Nurse Long thought he was a film actor! If I cable I'd say "I'd marry Lloyd if I were you!" ...

I am convinced that I was glamour-blinded when I got married for the main reason of our and especially my "on the make" philosophy mostly absorbed from mother because Daddy didn't have any e.g. Daddy wouldn't join the Country Club because he didn't like the atmosphere and how wise he was. I only found out years later. Daddy wouldn't stump up for us to go to Kent[148]

Auntie gave L. a good write-up of "glamour-boy" years before we met him or at least one year – Cambridge, yacht (Bodo's – which to my middle-western mind spelt Vanderbilt) trips to Iceland, North Africa, Norway, Renault car, Anglo-phobia, English accent, name, (Lancelot Turtle), wealth and general desirability –

After nearly seven years of marriage I am in a clear position to discredit all of that glamorous set-up and it is only my luck and some guiding instinct (yours) that got me to make the grade. I know as well as anything that if he were a beau of mine now at my present age that I probably wouldn't marry him and I would be wrong. As I have proved – by our successful marriage –

We haven't a taste in common though we have a common point of view if you see the difference – to be more explicit he likes birds (I

---

[148] Presumably Kent School for Girls, a small, independent (or private) school in Denver founded in 1922 and which offered a college preparatory curriculum and which presumably charged substantial fees.

don't), he likes shooting, badminton, sports, and talk about such. I like books, movies, the theatre, intellectual or pseudo arty talk and arty people. L. is shyly interested in arty people too – because he is interested in everything. He likes practical people – this is general or rather specialized because we both like people.

If he had married a less worldly and pushing wife and had a less worldly and pushing mother his friends wouldn't be near "society" or if so by accident – not purposely away from society or in it because he plain doesn't bother much if at all ... or am I clear? ...

This all sounds traitorous and awful but I am trying to get at what holds you back with Lloyd ...

The main message is Mrs. Noble's – to marry him at once...

I would be glad to see you married to Lloyd – even if my dream of diplomats, cabinet ministers etc. that I had for you dies hard – from a romantic schoolgirl I have become an hard headed woman but still I see the real romance – a happy married life with a kind and good man because when the trappings of wealth and position are gone (and they're slipping, sister) you want to be sure to like to live in the same house in any circumstances with your husband. ...

Love,
Helen

Boxing Day
Belmont

Dear Mother and Ginna,

Miss Robson and Gay have just gone out for a walk and Gay has on her Red Riding Hood cape because it looks like rain. Bertha is roaring around upstairs with the Hoover, Julie is asleep on the porch, Rock is asleep on the hearthrug and the pussy is playing on the window seat. It is 11.15 a.m. and there are awful English ballads on the radio ...

Mother's three Clipper letters arrived during Christmas week – the first took three weeks, the second and third about nine days respectively – the third arriving at noon on Christmas Day which was very lucky and I was delighted to get all three and also the $25 – for which thank you both very much... I will probably buy books with your money – probably poetry – I am going to try to send you two books that have delighted me more than any I've seen in years – one called *Pillar to Post* and the other *Homes, Sweet Homes*. They are by Osbert Lancaster and are both the wittiest and soundest architectural and interior decorating books respectively that I have seen.[149] ...

We had the whole family to dinner yesterday – Auntie and Uncle Gus. Mrs. T. and Arabella and Gordon and with us and Miss Robson and Gay and Julie we were ten around the festive board which was a mass of holly in the middle and the red glasses making it look extra festive (we had cider in the wine size.) The dinner was good clear soup, turkey done to a turn, peas, turnips, potatoes, celery, nuts, plum pudding, Manhattan pudding which is orange ice and ice-cream with nuts in a two layer brick, dessert and coffee...

Saturday night Lancelot gave a party for Arabella and Gordon at the Grand Central dinner dance. It was lots of fun and we had A. and Gordon, Maureen and Ken, Patrick and Rosemary and Jack and Elaine. I bought A. the green orchids and we had cocktails first and champagne and the band and crowd were lively and we did The Lambeth Walk, Boomps a Daisy, Palais Glide, Chestnut Tree and the Military Two-step and it was *real* gay. ...

We had Gay all primed with stories of Santa Claus and she hung up one of L's shooting stockings over the foot of her bed and we filled the other one. In the morning she was so pleased and excited and she said that she saw Santa when he came down the chimley.[150] I asked her what he looked like and she said that he was so old and had a long beard and a Red Riding Hood cape. Then we had breakfast and then we looked at the other presents from Santa which were all around the tree. ...The presents just flew around and Gay sat in the middle so bewildered and saying "how lovely"! because she had heard Mrs. T. and A. saying it. ...

Fred Eves and John Carr came to call and Fred stayed to supper.[151] John is over for only three days from Croydon where he loves his work

---

[149] Osbert Lancaster (1908–1986), an English cartoonist, architecture critic and satirist, and stage designer. *Pillar to Post: The Pocket Lamp of Architecture* appeared in 1938, *Homes Sweet Homes* in 1939.

[150] Helen, presumably consciously, is using the Ulster-Scots word for chimney.

[151] Fred Eves was a shooting friend of Lance's; he was a member of the Plymouth Brethren, a Christian movement or network (rather than denomination) that started in Dublin in the 1820s.

which seems to be the reorganization of an air-line. He says that everybody in Croydon says that the war will be over in a few months because there will be a "palace revolution" in Germany that is, the tops of things will revolt – the rich people who are powerful and not with Hitler – heads of the army, navy, banks, big corporations etc. I just hope it's true and it can't be over too soon. I am counting on L.'s color-blindness to keep him out of the navy – several people have been sent home because of it and there is a new test now that you can't cheat at.

Edith and her baby had just lived ten days in the house in Wales with Bodo when Bodo was transferred to Whale island[152] to take a Gunnery Course – so she had another awful train journey of 10 or so hours with the baby to spend Christmas with an aunt ... and from what we hear traveling is a nightmare even without a baby what with red-tape, permits, passports, standing for hours in queues, blacked out trains and general delays and no food. Everyone has to hold a life belt in his hand crossing from Larne to Stranraer. Everyone also says that the Belfast black-out is so bad compared to Scotland and England and everyone there carried his gas mask constantly while here no one but the police, all men in uniform, Dunlop Cunningham and Janet Boyd carry theirs – also school children.

The war songs are so weak – do you have "Runledoff Run" which is the best – "I'm going to Hang out the Washing on the Seigfried [sic] Line", "Kiss me goodnight Sergeant Major" (awful). The best dance tune here now is "Franklin D. Roosevelt Jones" – is it old there? [153]

---

[152] Whale Island is in Portsmouth harbour and home to a long-established Royal naval gunnery school on shore and on board HMS *Excellent*; the school closed in 1985 and *Excellent* decommissioned.

[153] Helen must have misheard "Run, Adolf, Run," a parody of "Run, Rabbit, Run," a song sung by the British comic duo (Bud) Flanagan and (Chesney) Allen in the London Palladium show *The Little Dog Laughed* (October 1939). After Germans allegedly killed two rabbits on a bombing raid in November, the original lyrics by Ralph Butler were changed by Flanagan and Allen to scorn the bad aim of Luftwaffe pilots and express humorous contempt for Hitler and British Pathé showed a cartoon that accompanied the new words, watchable on YouTube. "Franklin D. Roosevelt Jones" is a clever song from the same show, celebrating the baptism of a black baby in Harlem destined for great things because of his name. Flanagan and Allen's rendition is available on YouTube. The morale-boosting "We're Going to Hang out the Washing on the Siegfried Line" was a hit written by the Ulster songwriter Jimmy Kennedy (music by Michael Carr); Kennedy, who wrote the song early in the war while he was a captain in the British Expeditionary Force, also wrote "South of the Border (Down Mexico Way)" and "Red Sails in the Sunset". The music-hall humour of "Kiss Me Goodnight Sergeant Major" *Cont'd overleaf*

Everyone feels better here since the scuttling of the *Graf Spee* and the *Columbus*[154] because before that every news bulletin told of two or three more British ships which had been mined – not to mention the poor neutrals. The radio speeches here seem to be trying to make the people realize how serious the situation is financially and how many sacrifices we will be called on to make which everyone suspects means 10/6 on the income tax. Everyone with two cars is putting up one because of the tax and the high price of petrol which makes motor travel cost 1/6 or 2/6 a mile, I forget which. In Italy, Lavens said[155], petrol is 5/0 gallon and there are no private cars on the roads and all the Italians are so depressed. Linen here is up 100% – that is the new linen, the old stocks in the shops are up 12½%. ...

No one is saving because they think that the gov't will take it anyway and although we aren't splurging we aren't scrimping though the gov't advises thrift. It is the uncertainty of everything that gives everyone that "eat, drink and be merry" attitude.

There goes the lunch gong and the radio is back to ballads again so I will go eat a turkey leg and then devote the afternoon to my daughters and I will mail this when I am out with Gay and Julie.

Happy New Year and love
Helen

Ma, I get so wound up!

[153] *Cont'd* would not have been to Helen's taste but Arthur Askey, the song's populariser (his performance of the song is on YouTube), had a demotic appeal that helped raise British morale during the war.

[154] *Admiral Graf Spee* was a German pocket battleship that sank more than 50,000 tons of merchant shipping before being challenged by three Royal Navy cruisers. The ensuing engagement inflicted damage on three of the four ships. Taking his wounded ship to Montevideo and believing a massive British naval force was impending, the German captain ordered his ship scuttled on 18th December before shooting himself two days later in a Buenos Aires hotel room. SS *Columbus* was a German liner that became an enemy target on the outbreak of war. When confronted by HMS *Hyperion* off the Virginia coast on 19th December, the crew of the SS *Columbus* scuttled the 32,000 ton liner rather that surrender her.

[155] Lavens Mackie (1905–1966) was a member of the famous industrial family, one of the six children of James Mackie Jnr (1864–1943) who managed James Mackie and Sons. Lavens joined the firm in 1925 and later became a joint director. He travelled abroad on firm's business. See Gordon Mackie's chapter in Professor Sir Bernard Crossland (ed.), *The Lives of Great Engineers of Ulster*, pp. 82, 86, 90.

1940

Helen visits neutral Dublin

Ploughing for Victory at Mahee Island

Friends Dick and Harry in Churchill's War Rooms

Germany invades Denmark, Belgium and the Netherlands

France falls

"Never in the field of human conflict ..."

11th Jan.
Belmont Rd.

Dear Mother and Ginna,

... As for us, we are getting along famously – this war makes you value what you have so much more than normally, that it gives that zeal to life that you only get in times of stress and probably impending catastrophe. The two nights a month that I work at the canteen from 5.30–10.30 seem endless and I race home as if I were a week old bride instead of a seven years married woman ...

Love,
Helen

13th Jan.
Belmont

Dear Mother and Ginna,

Now this is a Saturday forenoon and I am so close to the fire as I can get wearing a wool shirt, a sweater and a suit and feet and hands are like ice. Lancelot is shooting at Shane's Park and I nearly went! I did go two weeks ago today and it was almost a co-ed – and it was fun. We, the women and children helped to beat and ploughing through the underbrush kept us warm. I only did it half a day and then went home and lunch with Rosemary, Joan and Mary. ...

What do you think is standing in the corner of the bookcase on an easel? A portrait of me half done in oils by Toby Spence. It is a riot and is pretty good although it makes me look so old. I have only had two sittings but he is so interested that he works away for hours. The poor soul comes on the tram (40 minutes each way) every Sunday and Thursday nights and it is a mutual benefit arrangement. He wanted someone to sit and I always have wanted my portrait painted so we are both very happy.

I have on a blue sweater and that bright red wool coat – which will make a pretty picture. I have my right hand up holding a cigarette – Toby's idea of a characteristic pose which has been much admired as characteristic and although L and I were against the cigarette it is typical and has character and brings in a hand which makes it more interesting than just a bust especially when I fancy that I am graceful with my hands – even my stubby right one. ... both L and I have given up smoking too![1] ... I am not having another baby – I just saw the light again and decided I would rather spend that money on something else – I have a typewriter in mind. I have given it up since the 2nd of January – twelve days and I'm doing nicely thank you. ...

I meant to give it up on New Year's Day, but we went to Mary Morwood's Wedding which was such a whooping, hollering success that I thought 'to hell' what's one day in 365 so I went strong (the news is now on – such a sissy voiced announcer telling us that the RAF flights to Austria are a "marvelous show" and that a German plane has been shot down on the East Coast. These reconnaissance flights sound ominous to me – one and two planes roaming around at random. If this war doesn't stop before wholesale bombing starts it will be *the worst*.)

Esme had me to lunch on Wed. to fight with Silva Harrison about America's neutrality and did we fight![2] She is quite bright and in the end after about 2 hours of spluttering argument we decided that we were on the same side almost, but she said that for the last 4 months she has been ashamed that she is an American because she thinks that America could have stopped this war in July when congress met and didn't do a thing for the international situation. Did you read Anne Lindbergh's article in the January *Reader's Digest* "A prayer for Peace"?[3]

---

[1] Thomas Everard (Toby) Spence (1899–1992) was a Belfast artist and collector. Whereas his portrait of Helen came to naught (cigarette or no cigarette, as her daughter Julie has remarked, since Spence tried a later version of the portrait sans cigarette), his successful portraits of elderly inmates of Clifton House (run by the Belfast Charitable Society of which Spence later became President, 1987–1989) recently turned up.

[2] Silva Harrison was an American living in Northern Ireland, otherwise unidentified.

[3] The article is summarised in Beverly Gherman's *Anne Morrow Lindbergh: Between the Sea and the Stars* (Minneapolis: Twenty-First Century Books, 2007), pp. 111–112. Lindbergh rehearsed the justice in German grievances after the Great War settlement, though this did not pardon German aggression; she hoped the United States would not enter the war but pursue peace internationally.

I think it is the best article I have read in years except that there isn't much construction in her letting women to become better informed – the idea is good, but to most people something more definite is required. I think more American people should think about saving Europe from this war – in other words – think out some peace plans and keep sending peace propaganda over here instead of building so many airplanes. We are told that the U.S. is spending £1,000,000 a day on armaments – what for?

Now it is after lunch and my belligerent mood has changed. I started to tell you about Mary's wedding.[4] It really started the night before with a buffet supper at the Topping's and then a party at the Isaac's – New Years Eve – and it was a good party and made for me by the bridegroom's little brother aged 19 who is an undergraduate at the University of London evacuated to Cambridge. He was a 'jitter bug' and the best dancer in the wildest way and he took the steps so seriously and had the right name for everything e.g. chasse, glide, follow through, step and change. Black out shade etc and we did everything from the tango to trucking.[5] He danced with me most of the evening and sometimes when I couldn't make the grade he just let me go and went wild by himself. The second brother of the three was so nice too – he is an air-plane pilot and the oldest one is a school master and he was the groom. Lancelot had to do his ARP warden stuff that Sunday night and didn't arrive until after midnight which was a pity but I don't think he would have liked it terribly anyway...

We are trying to find a cheaper house to live in and it is such a discouraging job because they all look awful – especially the cheap ones. Lancelot is toying with the idea of farming at Mahee for the duration of the war. I hope that he will because he feels it will be a national service and it will ease what conscience he has for not being a soldier. So far the admiralty is still silent, but we never know when the blow will fall. If L is at Mahee all the time, I won't mind staying there, although I doubt if we will ever live there in the winter. ... I dream about pretty houses at night and look at ugly ones by day.

---

[4] See the letter of 22nd November 1939.
[5] Chasse, glide, follow-through, and step and change were steps in the swing dances of the 1920s and 1930s, two of which were the jitterbug and truckin'. Those who danced the former were, as Helen calls the London undergraduate, jitter bugs. There is vintage footage of dancers truckin' on YouTube, see for example *Truckin Jumbo 70*, as well as revival footage.

The rationing isn't a bit bad – we have been on butter rationing 4oz each a week for officially a week, but actually about three or four weeks. We mix our 28oz of butter (7 persons) with an equal amount of the best margarine and make butter balls and you honestly wouldn't know that there was any margarine in it except in an occasional ball which must be 4/5 or so margarine. We don't use even so much sugar as our ration allows us because Gay and Julie use glucose which I have hoarded. The meat rationing starts on Monday, but so long as the shooting season lasts we will be hard put to use all of ours because we always have pheasants, woodcock, snipe and ducks hanging around. I am still buying up things like toilet paper, soap, baby vegetables, syrup, olive oil, haliver oil etc. ...

Well girls, I do run on so but now I must beat it – won't it be awful if we don't see each other soon – a year or two anyway? But I always was an optimist and this war is so apathetic that maybe something will stop it soon – otherwise we are a doomed generation —

If it once stops I am going to try to get L to come to Canada to live. Why I didn't think of it before, I don't know, but he wouldn't have come anyway —— but afterward I think he will ————

Love,
Helen
We both take haliver oil and feel dandy!

[undated: 14/15th Jan.?]
The Gables, Rathgar,
Dublin

Dear Mother and Ginna,

Surprise! Surprise! Who would have thought that we'd be here so soon and having the best time and staying in the prettiest house in a neutral country!

It started last Monday night at about 6.15 when Philip Scanlan an old school friend of L's rang up from the G[rand]. Central to ask us to lunch the next day with him and his wife [Kathleen]. ... They are so nice – she is English and they have only moved to Dublin from Nottingham. ...

We were invited this weekend especially for the races but they were postponed on account of the cold weather.

It has been the coldest here and in Belfast for about 60 years – only about 20 above zero at the coldest but in this damp and with an east wind it well nigh kill you dead. L has chilblains on his feet and I nearly have them on my hands and it is awful. It seems warmer tonight. ...

This house has 3 bathrooms as well as central heating and is olde Englishe and just like a stage setting for an English comedy of manners or what Osburt (sic) Lancaster calls 'Stockbroker Tudor'. It is the nearest like an American house in comfort to any I've seen in Ireland and in very good British taste on the luxurious side. ... It is more wealthy than arty, but quite good. The children are named Bridget, Maureen and Bryan. Kathleen, the mother is 32 and *so* pretty and terribly nice and so is Philsy, the husband. He is a Quaker pacifist and she is a pacifist. ...

My paper is running out – I left m'book downstairs so I'll go to bed. It is so nice to be here and she is such a good housekeeper – everything *shines*. That's all for now – Nighty night –

Helen

23rd Jan.
Belmont

Dear Mother and Ginna,

... I was skating yesterday and today at Ballydrain – a great big lake and it was such fun.[6] I bought some new skates yesterday – white boots too. ...

On Saturday we went skating in Phoenix Park [Dublin] – $1.25 each to skate and so there were only about 20 or 30 people there. In the

---

6 Ballydrain lake is a twenty-acre body of water, formerly part of the estate of Ballydrain House, Dunmurry on the southern outskirts of Belfast, owned successively by the well-known Stewart and Montgomery families originally from Scotland until it was sold in 1918 to the Director of the Ulster Spinning Company (the estate house had a linen-making history from the late 18th century). Ballydrain House was inhabited until the year of Helen's letter when it was occupied by the British Army during the Second World War. It became the Malone Golf Club in 1960. See Eileen Black, "Ballydrain, Dunmurry: An Estate through the Ages," *Lisburn Historical Society Journal*, vol. 5 (1984): http://lisburn.com; "Ballydrain House", Lord Belmont in Northern Ireland.

afternoon we went to the movies *Juarez* – not so hot[7] and the evening we went dancing at the Gresham – it was so gay.[8] Eire is neutral! You know and there is no blackout, no rationing and no uniforms. It is divine.

No one in a British army uniform is allowed into Eire, there is no war news in the news reels, they won't allow any British or German propaganda – for instance they wouldn't let "I was a Nazi spy" be shown.[9] It is here this week and we will try to go. ...

I am learning Bob Crosby's band on records from America and is it low down and blue![10] Do you know a song called "Scatterbrain". It is so cute and is very popular here now and very new because I tried to get a record of it and it isn't to be released until Feb 1st![11]

We had a concert at our canteen on Tuesday night and served 120 meals! – mostly teas but some eggs etc.[12] ...

I wish we lived in the Free State – the atmosphere gets me every time I go there. I just like to be there and I always expect that I am full of Irish blood.

Well – nighty-night!

Love,
Helen

[7] *Juarez* is a 1939 American historical drama set in the 1860s and depicting the struggle for supremacy between Napoleon III's surrogate in Mexico (Maximilian I) and the Mexican President (Benito Juarez). It starred Brian Aherne, Claude Rains, Paul Muni and Bette Davis. Despite its ambition, critics considered it, all in all, "not so hot".

[8] The Gresham Hotel, then Dublin's most notable and opulent hotel, and once known as a hotel hospitable to Irish nationalism, plays a climactic role in the great story, "The Dead", that closes James Joyce's volume of stories, *Dubliners* (1914).

[9] *Confessions of a Nazi Spy* (1939), claimed to be the first clearly anti-Nazi Hollywood film. It starred Edward G. Robinson, George Sanders, and numbers of German actors, including some who had fled Nazi Germany. It failed at the box office but succeeded with critics. It was banned in Germany, Japan, certain South American countries – as well as in the Irish Free State on grounds that its showing would violate Irish neutrality. The plot is generated by the activities of American Nazis and based on actual events.

[10] Bob Crosby (1913–93) was an American jazz singer and band-leader, and brother of Bing Crosby. Crosby spent eighteen months in the U.S. Marines during the Second World War, touring with musicians in the Pacific theatre.

[11] "Scatter-Brain" was a Frankie Masters song played by his orchestra that was in the Hit Parade at the end of 1939 and start of 1940; it was also made famous by the Freddy Martin Orchestra.

[12] The canteen, known as the Pollock Club because it was beside Pollock Dock on the River Lagan, was opened on 1st January, 1940 for use by sailors of the Royal Navy; Helen volunteered there.

29th Jan.
Belmont

Dear Mother and Ginna,

If there is anything I like better than anything else it is a good sharp pencil and I just couldn't resist writing with it after I sharpened it. Gay got the sharpener in a cracker at Mark's birthday party and I have been having a field day with it. I always have loved pencils, notebooks, rubber-bands, paper clips and erasers with an inordinate fondness for showing a neatness of mine connected with desks that is sadly lacking in my personal life!

The lunch gong sounded before this letter was started and now lunch is over and I am back in front of the fire looking out at the cold and snow. The D.R circle is this afternoon but I'm not going on account of still being convalescent from flu. I have that weakly feeling following it, and some depression of mind which isn't bad and only comes out in bad temper and impatience. Gaysie is sitting beside me on the floor drawing – she just made quite a good T and now said 'I want a dance Mama' so she is up whipping around the room. The radio is playing Marches and their history – a programme for schools – I think the programs for schools are the best of all the BBC programs. The poor BBC is taking an awful beating for their terrible programs, but apart from their so called funny and variety programs to cheer up the troops, I think that the programs are better than ever. The news is usually so dull that when I am trying to tell L. what happened I never can remember anything. Raymond swung in on every other Saturday night telling us what is going on in America and he [Raymond Swing] is so good. ...

Toby came over again last night to paint me ... Toby said that Kathleen [Spence] is so homesick and wishes that she hadn't gone [to the United States], but as I said to him she may laugh last yet. If they don't get this war stopped soon, I don't think anyone will laugh much, but even if worst comes to worst we can dodge around Ireland especially the Free State which will stay neutral as long as it possibly can.

Everything here is white and it is getting colder and colder with a few cold looking flakes falling. There will be Ice Skating again after this. I should be knitting comforts for the troops, but instead I am knitting a pale blue sweater for Gaysie. ...

Gay and Miss R are going out for a walk, so I will tell them to mail this effusion.

Love, Helen

4th Mar.
Belmont

Dear Mother,

... I am gladder that Ginna is finally married to Lloyd than I have been in years, because he is so nice and will be such a nice husband and she will be such a good wife. I just made a list of eleven of Ginna's beaux and without even wishful thinking I think that Lloyd is the best of them all for Ginna to have married.

Gay is dancing around the room to "My Rubber Dolly" with an umbrella hoisted.[13] She is growing so tall and looks *such* a big girl. ...

We have a sign on our gate and a sticker on our bedroom window announcing 'House to Let' so the chances are that we will be moving on the first of May. Lancelot's last offer was that we could take the house for another year at the reduced rent of £125, but Mrs. Morrow wanted us to take it for another three years and L. rightly said that we can't look three years ahead. So we are moving to Mahee on the 1st of May or a little before with Molly and Bertha but not Miss Robson. I have told Miss Robson that since I am just going to sit all summer at Mahee because there is no petrol to go anyplace I would rather look after my two children than do housework and I will have to have something to do. Molly and Bertha will do their laundry and can look after them the once a month or less that I will have to go to town. ... We are going to have a telephone this summer so we won't be so cut off. I can hardly wait to go down there again. We were there all day on Saturday with Bertha sort of house-dreaming for Eggy and his bride [Hilary Middleton] who are going there for two weeks on Saturday. Eggy is giving one of his American pictures instead of rent. He told me

---

[13] Despite its title, "My Wubba Dolly" is an adult song, released by Ella Fitzgerald in 1939.

that he is going to send you one Mother and that he hasn't forgotten that he promised you one.

We saw [Hilary's] picture and she looks so pretty – she is nearly my age and dark with very pretty eyes, but she looks much younger in the photograph. They are going to stay around water for a while and then are going to live in a caravan in Belmullet, Co. Mayo!

Lancelot says that Mahee in March will be heaven compared to a caravan in Mayo and for most people Mahee at any time except midsummer is far from tempting.

We have some Eggy movies and pictures and talked to him twice. He said that he would rather live in America than England, but he would rather live in Belmullet than America! ...

We are going on a spree to the Free State at Easter. We are given 24 gallons of petrol by the Free State and maybe more, and are going to a place called Waterville near Dingle Bay and to Cong a huge estate and castle that used to belong to the Guinness's but now is a hotel.[14] We have asked Philip and Kathleen Scanlan to come along but haven't heard yet whether they can. ...

I can hardly wait to go to Mahee because I really do love being there so and this summer will be more fun than ever because Gay and Zoo will be at an age where they will enjoy it so much. We were there again yesterday and it was divine and all the snowdrops are in bloom. I picked two enormous bunches as big as two fists each. All the daffodils and narcissus are coming up and it looks so springy and fresh and pale green. ...

We have ploughed so much land over thirteen acres – known on the home front as 'ploughing for victory'.[15] We are sowing beans and corn (not Indian corn.) ...

[14] Ashford Castle, Cong, Co. Galway, now a luxury hotel, was a medieval castle purchased in 1852 and extended by the Guinness family before the family gifted the building to the Irish government the year before Helen's letter. It was then opened as a hotel and the Turtles must have been among the earliest guests. In Waterville, Co. Kerry it is likely that the Turtles were to stay in the Butler Arms Hotel which in 1917 was bought by the Huggard family that were to acquire Ashford Castle and open it as a hotel.

[15] Ploughing for Victory was the British government's plan to plough grassland for cultivation: the target for 1940 was 2 million acres beyond the average annual planting. *Ploughing for Victory* (1940) was the short British Pathé film introducing the programme in which the Minister of Food, Sir Reginald Dorrian-Smith, explains its aims and benefits; the film is available on YouTube.

I don't know if Auntie told you about the awful tragedy that happened our canteen last Thursday when a car with five women went into the harbour and they were all drowned! It was during the black-out and it is a mystery how it happened because the road is as straight as a die to the canteen and wide enough for about 10 cars and away from it but the driver must have got confused with so many women in the car and she just plain drove in![16]

The women were the last to leave at night around 11 and they weren't missed until about 3 when one of the husbands woke up to find his wife not home and rang up the police to see if any accidents had been reported and they hadn't. I think they found them where marks on the road going to the edge of the water that night and at daylight they found the petrol and oil floating on the water and got a crane and hauled up the car – a tiny little sedan. I knew two of them quite well – one has three children aged 11, 7, 5 and the other one daughter, 19. You needn't start cabling me not to go there any more because I am through at the end of this month and after this I'll bet they will have the place floodlit, war or no war.

You won't believe it when I say that it is a safe place after that happened but it is and no one can see how such an awful thing could happen. It has completely stunned the whole city – the bodies were only recovered at 8 o'clock in the morning and the whole town was buzzing with it by ten o'clock and it wasn't in any paper until that evening.

What is so lamentable is that it seems so unnecessary – I mean no skidding, no speeding, no accident with another car, just a freak thing that no one ever dreamed of or even thought could ever happen.

I hardly ever drive at night but when I do I wear my glasses and crawl.

Both Harry [McMullan] and Bodo [Taggart] are home on leave now – They were here on Friday with Roberta and Edith. Harry is still at the heart of things, one of six people working in Churchill's private holy of holies. It is about the best job any one ever heard of except that it is such hard work and long hours and everyone in town is mad that Harry got it – not that anyone blames Harry because he was just offered the job by Dick Pim and everyone would have jumped at it, but

---

[16] The five women were leaving the "Pollock Club" canteen and heading for home when their car plunged into the water off Pollock Dock. The deaths had a huge impact on Belfast despite the preoccupation with the war.

Harry wasn't very high up in the RNVR and had resigned when he got married. Bodo and lots of others should have been asked first by rights. Harry as good as says that it was just his wonderful brain that got him there and he may have some special qualifications for that particular job that we don't know about. Anyway we are pleased and proud to know someone who sees Churchill at 3AM going to bed with a cigar in his mouth and is sitting up again in bed at 7AM. having had his night's sleep with another cigar in his mouth. Harry refers to him affectionately as 'Winnie'.[17]

Bodo has just finished a course and now is gunnery officer on a boat or will be when he goes to sea again.[18] You have no idea how very careful both Bodo and Harry and for that matter everyone is about giving away information – none of the wives who have husbands in France or at sea have any idea where they are – they don't even know what boats they are on or near what towns in France. Everything is 'somewhere in France', 'somewhere in water', or just 'at sea'.

So far we can still say that the war isn't inconveniencing us in the slightest – apart from petrol and that doesn't even bother us much because we have extra every week. We have more sugar than we can use and the meat hasn't come in yet – I mean rationing.

Our life socially has been terrific lately with four dances in two weeks – two of them balls! I wore my good lace twice, my purple taffeta (stepped up by a dressmaker) once and my black with orange confetti painted on it once. ...

---

[17] In the May following Helen's letter, Pim was promoted to Captain and followed Churchill to Downing Street to the Cabinet War Rooms in Whitehall. He worked alongside Anthony Eden and Lord Beaverbrook. I am grateful to Harry's son Peter for drawing my attention to John Potter's *Pim and Churchill's Map Room: Based on the Papers of Captain Richard Pim RNVR, Supervisor of Churchill's War Room, 1939–1945* (Belfast: Northern Ireland War Memorial, 2014). This book is out of print but there is an informative review by the historian Andrew Roberts, "'Pim and Churchill's Map Room' – by John Potter", The Churchill Project, Hillsdale College, 24th July 2016: https://winstonchurchill.hillsdale.edu/pim-churchills-map-room-john-potter/ from which I have drawn some of my information. Pim's papers are in the Public Record Office of Northern Ireland. For Harry McMullan and Dick Pim, see also the letters of 7th and 21st September, 1939.

[18] During the war, "Bodo" Taggart (see the letter of 4th May, 1939) served aboard HMS *Foylebank*, HMS *Queen Elizabeth* and HMS *Saker*. After the war Taggart wrote the Admiralty manual on 15" guns.

On Ginna's wedding day Toby came to paint me – so at 8 o'clock here he, Miss Robson, Lancelot and I opened the only bottle of champagne we have ever had and drank to Ginna and Lloyd – it was real sentimental and I could have bawled if I'd let myself. I did bawl when we sent the first cable thinking up sentimental things to say – but not for long because as L. said 'what was there to bawl about?'

I hope you aren't too lonely – console yourself with the thought that Ginna might have married a Chinese missionary or an Alaskan trapper or a Finn and also pat yourself on the back that you have got both of your daughters married off!! And look how well married we both are too!

Love,
Helen

5th Mar.
88 Belmont

Dear Mary Lou [Gurd],

... Sitting here as I am in the sunshine in a terribly warm room looking out on a semi-circle of crocuses under the tree life seems rosy enough. It is my birthday and I am having my godson and his mother[19] to tea and two good friends of ours to dinner.

We have been to four dances in the last two weeks; we have plenty to eat and drink even if our butter is half margarine; the friends of ours who are in the fighting forces are safe, so far and are merely bored stiff; there is no desperation or urgency about what war work we women do; and apart from the growing consciousness of a changing world and the four daily news bulletins of war news our lives are peaceful enough.

But the one thing that we completely lack is security. For instance we are leaving this house on the 1st of May and are moving to Mahee and storing our furniture 'until we see' – we don't know whether we will want a house in September. Lancelot may be called up, bombing may have started, anything might happen. However we are so used to this feeling that it isn't a new one with the war because literally since 1937 or before we have not been able to look 6 months ahead.

---

[19] Mark Topping and his mother Maureen.

Lancelot is the realist and pessimist and I am the optimist or rather I used to be and I still don't expect the worst which for us would be a 'blitz kreig' I suppose. ...

What do you think of this war? I don't know what to think because I don't know enough but I hope I live long enough to find out why it had to start.

I preached my pacifist propaganda for a long time, but it became inextricably interwoven with anti-British propaganda and the people who retaliated with anti-American arguments usually backed me against a wall so I shut up being handicapped in explaining just why America is staying out.

I still love living here but not if it means never coming home again and if the taxes go up and up and if we have any money after the holocaust I will agitate to move to Canada – the cost isn't worth it over here.

I have no idea where you are – Baltimore was your last stand, I know but this will have to go via Denver. I don't deserve a letter but if you would like to send a 'cheery greeting to your old friend now marooned in a war-torn country' I would write right back – or maybe that isn't so good. ...

Love,
Helen

16th Mar.
Belmont

Dear Mother,

We are on the point of going to Mahee and I will finish this there probably but now I am waiting for L. to dig up a few more plants from the garden. Here he is now. Eggie and Hilary, his wife are at Mahee now.

Mahee –

Here we are now and I am parked in front of a good fire for the morning. We met Eggie along the way and he and Hilary have gone painting. ...

Next Saturday we will be in the Free State – either Kerry or Mayo I don't know which. …

Lancelot is digging in the garden and just handed me in two iris stilosa in bloom – lovely purple irises that bloom in the winter.

I have been rushing down to look for mail every morning for a week and so far have only got the announcement which is so nice and made me feel more than anything that Ginna is Mrs. Hughes. I hope we aren't both Grandmothers before we meet again – sometimes the outlook is pretty discouraging but maybe something unexpected will turn up. Anyway you can imagine that I can hardly wait to hear all about it and see the pictures.

We had Jack and Kay. Eggie and Hilary. Bessie (Eggie's sister) and her husband and Paddy to dinner last Friday night to welcome Hilary who had arrived on Thursday … She smokes and wears a lot of lipstick but otherwise is not what you expect of the conventional young English girl because she just goes her own way and you can see doesn't give two hoots for anyone. She's not the sort of person that you take to at once, but she grows on you and seems ideal for Eggy which is what counts…

Last night we went to the Astoria to *Love Affair* - you have probably seen it months ago.[20] …

The wind is whistling and the sea is gray. The double daffodils are out and the thousand dutch bulbs are on the point of coming out. …

[17th Mar.]   This is Sunday evening now – …

Have you got the pictures that Eggie sent you yet? He sent one to you and one to Ginna and I chose them for you so I hope that you like them. I loved them both and couldn't decide which I liked the best. He gave us one too – one of his American ones for two weeks rent for Mahee and I chose one of the Grand Teton range in Wyoming. A mountain of rock with some water in the foreground and a few pine trees. …

I liked Hilary better yesterday and she is most amusing to talk to and quite fun. She is lovely from the side when she looks down … Eggie

---

[20] *Love Affair* (1939) is a romantic drama starring Charles Boyer and Irene Dunne.

has painted three big pictures and two little ones in a week there – the prettiest is painted from just outside the shore gate looking at the grove of trees on the right.

They have been down to see about the telephone and it will take 17 or 27 poles (L. forgets which) to reach us from the nearest phone on Mahee [Island]. It will be so nice to have it and unless they tack on a lot of extras it will only cost $3.00 to install apart from the yearly rental which is $20. How much is your phone a year? ...

We are invited to one more dance – at Craigavon on the 29th for 'comforts' for the Searchlight Battery from here that is in France. They went to France in December, have been sitting there ever since and are just beginning to get leave unless it is postponed. The present news says that there is some holdup. Robin Henry, Jimmy Cunningham, Archie Carr and a few others we know are in that but the majority of people we know aren't in anything. All the linen people are doing important war work – so linen is known as a 'reserved occupation'.

The meat ration has been on for a week – the ration for adults is 1/10 a week or 46c and for children 11d or 22cents. This week we had bacon and eggs on Monday and Thursday and Friday – chicken on Wednesday, ground steak pie with tomatoes and macaroni last night and our usual roast beef today. The three bacon and eggs touch was an accident – Monday I had the D.R.C here, 40 for tea no less so I had no time to think about anything else – Tuesday we were out – Wednesday 8 for dinner. Thursday L. had a Quaker meeting at 6.30 (what a time!) and Friday I was supposed to bring fish and didn't![21] "Lord Haw Haw" the humbug from Hamburg is on now. I love listening to him and we hear him at 9.15 and 10.15 every night that we are in. Do you ever hear him? He is the talk of the war and in every English skit and reverie – he is the German propaganda agent – news in English and he has what is called a devastating 'microphone personality'. He has such a nasty incriminating voice that some people froth at the mouth when they hear him and of course he cracks everything English right and left and tells awful insidious lies about life in England.[22]

[21] Lance's paternal grandparents were Quakers; he himself attended Friends' School, a Quaker grammar school in Lisburn, Co. Down and then Leighton Park, another Quaker school in Reading. It was at Leighton that he met Philip Scanlan.

[22] The American-born William Joyce (Lord Haw-Haw), b. 1906, was cordially detested by British listeners to his Nazi propaganda radio broadcasts from Germany. He was hanged for treason in January 1946.

Auntie has "days of our years" out now but I will get it when she turns it in again.[23] If you want to read a typically English light book about a typical English woman read *Mrs Miniver* by Jan Struther[24]. ... Goodnight and much love,

Helen.

P.S. If you save these letters for Ginna it would oblige because it is too soon to write to her – I saw in the *N.Y. Times* that the *President Taft* sailed that Saturday for Honolulu did they go on it?[25]

25th Mar.
Club House Hotel, Kilkenny[26]

Dear Mother,

Do you remember this place? Here we are again having just arrived at 9. And having just finished supper now at 10. There is a priest sitting here lapping whisky and two platinum blondes in silver gloves with their husbands who are drinking with the priest. One of the blondes has a bad toothache.

---

[23] *Days of Our Years* (1939) is the autobiography of Pierre van Paassen (1895–1968), an adventurous, anti-Fascist Dutch-born Canadian-American foreign correspondent. It expanded on his newspaper reports from Palestine, Germany and elsewhere. It was a best-seller in the U.S., as *Kirkus Review* of 30th January 1939 predicted in its warm commendation. Van Paassen's first book was *Nazism: An Assault on Civilization* (1934). See also "Pierre van Paassen", Wikipedia.

[24] Jan Struther (Joyce Anstruther, 1901–1953) was an English writer most celebrated for her fact-based fiction, *Mrs. Miniver* (1939) which began life as *Times* columns in 1937. The book's huge success in the United States is credited with helping to deflect the tide of American non-interventionism. The MGM movie was released in 1942 with Greer Garson in the title role, and it too played its part in drawing the United States into the war. (The film won six Oscars.)

[25] SS *President Taft* was a liner launched (as *Buckeye State*) in 1920 and renamed two years later. After acquisition by the U.S. Maritime Commission in 1938 the ship was assigned to the New York-Pacific Coast-Asiatic service. It was requisitioned by the U.S. War Department eighteen months after Helen's letter and renamed *Willard A. Holbrook*. It had a distinguished career as a troopship in the Pacific theatre of war. Throughout its life it often visited Honolulu.

[26] The Kilkenny Foxhunters' Club (est. 1797) became the Hibernian Hotel and Foxhunting Club in 1817. By Helen's time it was, and still is, known by its alternative name, the Club House Hotel Kilkenny.

We are talking about going to bed, but our bedrooms are so far away that the prospect is discouraging. Philip and Kathleen are afraid that the beds haven't been slept in for twenty years and will be so damp ... – Those are the perils of travelling in Ireland for you!

This is the morning and we are going sightseeing in a minute or two to see the Cathedral and to buy Gay and Zoozie each a Kilkenny cat. We have to go now.

Love,
Helen

Poem about Kilkenny cats:

Kilkenny Cats[27]
There once were two cats of Kilkenny,
Each thought there was one cat too many;
So they fought and they fit,
And they scratched and they bit,
Till, excepting their nails
And the tips of their tails,
Instead of two cats there weren't any

28th Mar.
Belmont[28]

[Dear Ginna,]

... We had such a good time on our holiday – we were away five nights and six days. The first night we spent in Dublin at the Scanlan's. We like them both so well – he is Irish and she is English, but they both act *so* English – that is to say he isn't at all the 'Happy-go-lucky' Irish type. They are quite funny together and she rags him terribly, because he is such a fuss-pot. The next three nights we spent at a place in the south and west of Co. Kerry called Waterville at a fishing hotel where we were the only guests, except a 72 year old lady from here who was slightly bats and fished all day every day.

[27] This unattributed modified limerick commemorates these legendary creatures that have served through the centuries many allegorical purposes, often political. The application to the war in Helen's mind is possible.

[28] The first two pages of this letter to Ginna on her birthday are missing.

... We motored the first day to Parknasilla for lunch which was packed with such gay and snappy people mostly from Cork and so fashionable they are. It is the place that is semi-tropical and has mimosa trees in full bloom in the drive!

The daffodils were in full bloom everyplace – you know how they plant them in clumps in the lawns. Then we went to Killarney for tea – I love it. The next day was Easter Sunday and we went for a long walk around the lake in the morning and sun-bathed! In the afternoon we went to the Island of Valencia (only about five minutes in a motor boat) and took a jaunting car all around the island and it was such fun. All the Transatlantic commercial cables come in on Valencia. The Western Union ones come in someplace else.

Sunday night, we went to a local dance pronounced a "Kayley" and spelled "Ceilidh" or something like that in Gaelic. It was held in a little tin shed and was a real example of local color. The band was three accordions and a drum and you could barely recognise tunes like "run rabbit run" and the "the Lambeth walk" because the playing was so minor and off key.

None of the Irish people danced anything, but square dances and only one kind – called "set" which was pretty shuffly and repeated itself for about eight goes, by which time the eight dancers per set were well nigh spent.

A middle aged jockey asked me to dance and I did – much to Philip and Kathleen's surprise and secret horror. The jockey smelled of Poteen and was a good dancer with big flat feet which he used like a duck would and we got along quite well considering. ...

We are going to a big dance tomorrow night at Craigavad and to dinner first with Janet Boyd who not having any maids is having a chef and two waitresses from the Midland Hotel.

She never has any maids, but has a house closer to an American one than anyone there so gets along pretty well.

She has an Aga Cooker, automatic central heating, an electric dishwasher, ice-box, electric floor polish and vacuum cleaner, so she manages quite well and has a char in every day to cook the noon meal, so it isn't so bad. She is 'simple-pleasing'[29] though, the type that never lets a detail pass and during the maidless months she cooks three

[29] Perhaps a term from Mrs Noble's Theory.

breakfasts per morning – her own, next the children and nurses and finally Austen's!...

The war drags on – since the Finland tragedy, I haven't taken much notice, I got all stirred up at the end about Finland and read everything about it, but since then I only know what somebody tells me.[30] I have stopped my canteen with no regrets whatsoever and will devote myself to my two amusing daughters. ...

[unfinished, unsigned]

31st Mar.
Belmont

Dear Mother,

It is Sunday night and we have spent the last two days at Mahee and slept there last night. ...

Lancelot has just turned on the radio to hear 'Horace the Humbug from Hamburg' or 'Lord Haw-Haw'. He Haw Haw will be so mad tonight on account of Churchill's speech last night.[31]

Friday night we went to the dance at Craigavad which was fun.[32] I wore my red piquet dress that was $10.50 three years ago and still looks so nice. The Boyd's house is so super – we were in their newest

---

[30] After years of tension between the two countries, the Soviet Union invaded Finland on 30th November 1939; after a gallant struggle against a much larger foe during what was called the Winter War, Finland suffered losses in lives and territory; a peace agreement was signed on 13th March 1940 and its terms on the Finnish side were harsh.

[31] In his speech of 30th March, known as the "Sterner war" speech, Winston Churchill (First Lord of the Admiralty) was eloquently defiant. At a time "when spring is caressing the land", Britons' thoughts must turn away from nature's regeneration to "the sterner war". He deplored and defied Nazi violence and brutality. Luxembourg, Belgium and Holland stood at risk of an imminent "avalanche of steel and fire" from a million German soldiers poised on their borders; "the decision rests in the hands of a haunted, morbid being who to their eternal shame the German people in their bewilderment have worshipped as a god". Corroboration of Churchill's last claim can be found in a portrait of 1930s Germany, *Reaching for the Stars* (1939) by Nora Waln, author of *The House of Exile* (1933), earlier admired by Helen.

[32] The dance, in aid of the Third Searchlight Regiment R.A. Comforts' Fund, was held in the clubhouse of the Royal Belfast Golf Club (Craigavad). Guests included Lady Mairi Stewart, daughter of Lord and Lady Londonderry, and Lady Dufferin of Clandeboye.

bathroom – their 5th – it has a specially low scientific john and a sink tub and is in pale pink tiles about a foot square and a special little tooth basin like they have on trains! And she has had no maids for months! She is such a character and goes her own way regardless of anything or anybody. She and Austen and the children are going to emigrate to New Zealand or someplace with a good climate at the end of the war, because they think it is not worth living here. I have my eye on Canada and that is my main reason for not wanting to buy a house here. L. never has wanted to buy a house, but if we saw one we liked we would buy it as an investment on account of inflation. L. could get into Canada I think, but hardly America – though of course I would rather live in America.

Thank you ever so much for our birthday presents – we are going to subscribe to *Life* – and will we be popular with our friends![33] ...

L. is now listening to a play in German-English propaganda for Germany.

The Scanlans had a stateroom reserved on the *Queen Elizabeth* for her maiden voyage and were so disappointed not to be able to go.[34] We had such a good time with them although we motored so much that it wasn't much of a rest, though it was a nice change.

Dublin looked so pretty because all the prunus trees were in bloom and all the forsythia was out. ...

Love,
Helen

2nd Apr.
Belmont

Dear Mother,

I am just about to take the girls for a walk – my first day with them without Miss Robson and we are coming along swimmingly.[35]

---

[33] *Life,* owned by Henry Luce from 1936, included weekly coverage of all the major theatres of war and would therefore have been prized by Britons hungry for war news.

[34] The Cunard liner RMS *Queen Elizabeth*, launched in September 1938, was meant to enter passenger service on the transatlantic route but the war supervened and she became a troop carrier instead; it was not until October 1946 that she assumed her intended role.

[35] Miss Robson had left Helen to go to work for Isabel Noble.

Enclosed [newspaper photograph] is your glamorous daughter – no 1 is Betty Shillington. No.2 is the Marchioness of Dufferin and Ava whom Ginna will remember we stood behind on the *Aquitania* and no.3 is me with Cyril Nicholson, whom Ginna will remember too – he has a white- haired wife and their house is the one with the housekeeping so much worse than mine. No.4 is Betsy Henry's young sister and no.5 is Michael Prynne an ornithologist friend of L's and a regular army man.[36] Their dress uniform is navy blue with a red stripe down the pants and it is wonderful looking – but not worth it. ...

Love,
Helen.

9th Apr.
Belmont

Dear Ginna,

You really are the limit! To think that your first communication after you are Mrs. Hughes – and how long after?

Only twenty eight days – is only half a postcard or less from San Francisco – which was so cryptic, that it was nearly worse than nothing, but not quite. However, I really didn't expect a letter yet – I know it is too soon, but I do hope that now that you are home again if you have time you will settle down and write me a real letter telling me all about your wedding from the word go and ending with your present moment. ...

I heard from Rosie [Reade][37] whom I called on this morning, that Hitler has taken Denmark, so things will probably be in a pretty pickle

---

[36] Maureen Guinness, Marchioness of Dufferin and Ava (1907–1998) lived in Clandeboye, the family seat. In 1930 she married her cousin, Basil Hamilton-Temple-Blackwood who succeeded as 4th Marquess of Dufferin and Ava. Her husband died in action in Burma in 1945; the Marchioness married twice more and outlived both husbands. For Cyril Nicholson see the letter of 27th September 1939. Betsy Henry was the wife of Robin Henry, both Belfast friends of the Turtles'. Major G.M.F. Prynne in 1939 represented the GOC (General Officer Commanding), Northern Ireland at a Grand Opera House show: "A 'Services' Matinee," *Belfast News-Letter*, 9th November, 1939. He was later the author of *Egg-Shells* (London, 1963), an authoritative guide to all aspects of birds' eggs.

[37] Rosie Reade was the first wife of Terence McConnell (see the letter of 21st September, 1939).

by the time you get this.[38] Hell certainly seems to have chosen this time in the history of events to let loose. What life in Poland must be like is simply unimaginable.[39] Both T [Terence McConnell] and Bodo are gunnery officers now and in full command of the anti-aircraft guns on their ships – neither is at sea yet, but they will be at any moment. ...

We haven't a house yet. We have just started looking seriously at night, but we will wait now until September to move and will store our furniture – at Mahee if the other places are full...

Mahee is the apple of our eyes and great activity will be under way soon there in the painting line – floors etc. We will be moving in about two weeks, but I don't even think about it.

Arabella has bought a house in Deramore Park[40] – A is still at Newcastle with her ma, I have given A up as hopeless – I used to try to help her and generally befriend her against her ma, but it was a mistake because A is too 'unaware' altogether and says one thing one minute and the opposite the next – she has a mind like a blotter – soaks up somebody else's ideas and gives them up backwards. ... – however she is happy and that's the main thing. ...

How is Mother making out on her own?

Just rang up L. – he says he has just got another letter from the Admiralty saying to come for an interview – I will try to get him not to go – Bombers fly over here all day long – Must go take the babes for a walk.

Love,
Helen

---

[38] Germany invaded neutral Denmark in the early hours of 9th April 1940 in order to establish a forward position for an invasion of Norway.

[39] Germany invaded Poland on 1st September 1939 and (following the Hitler-Stalin non-aggression pact) by the Soviet Union on 17th September. Millions of Poles died during the dual invasions and occupations. After the summer of 1941 Nazi Germany became the sole occupier and ethnic Poles and Jews were persecuted and murdered.

[40] In the leafy Malone neighbourhood of south Belfast to which the Turtles would soon move.

12th Apr.
Belmont

Dear Mother,

Just a short note to thank you for your lovely Easter box that arrived yesterday and was a tremendous success. ...

At the rate things are moving in the war world now we would be well advised to wait over the summer to see what goes on – the uncertainty takes the heart out of everything – including househunting. ...

Eggy has gone to Connemara – we househunt every night. Lancelot had another letter from the Admiralty this time saying to come for an interview but he is going to tell them that he can't come now – I hope – he hasn't fully decided yet.

[14th Apr.]

This is Sunday night and L. is taking Toby and Mr. Randolph in to town. Mr. Randolph is the American consul-general and is so nice – he was here for lunch and supper and we went to Mahee for tea. Toby just came over to shellac my portrait. It is an *awful* night – wind and rain and cold.

Mr. Randolph's wife and three children are parked in Iowa – not allowed to come and I think it kills him because he is fairly old and they are young – 12, 7, and 5. He has been in Spain, Russia during the Revolution, Roumania, Quebec, Africa and a few other places and he is a lamb. ...

T and Rosie were here for dinner on Friday and T. gave us the low-down on Scapa Flow and the navy there – Last night we were at a bottle party at Elizabeth Morwood's[41] – very Bohemian with people all sitting on the floor talking about LIFE and being *very* intelligent and highbrow and arty. ...

Will you please send me about 4 or more slips while the sending is good? About 6 pairs of silk stockings size 10 and about 2 satin nighties. Silk is prohibitive here and it is well worth it to pay the duty.

---

[41] At bottle parties, guests brought their own drinks.

Here comes L. so we had better go to beddy-bye.

Nighty-night and love from a war-torn country. It isn't bad yet.

Helen

10th May
Mahee

Dear Mother,

... We are carefully blacked out tonight, for the first time since coming here – Today's events in Holland and Belgium being enough to make one feel jittery even here.[42] We have all of our black curtains from town here and can put two on each window if necessary. Things are certainly bad now and this is only the beginning and by the time this reaches you – goodness only knows what may have happened. Lancelot thinks that Hitler is desperate and I certainly hope he is right. ...

Lancelot bought me an anniversary present today. Surprise surprise! A new car! It is a small Ford and from the looks of things the last one we will ever buy. We still have the Austin too and the little one is partially an investment and partly to save our meagre petrol ration – it does 35 miles to the gallon. He got it through sheer good luck because he had tried a while ago and they weren't to be had for love nor money and they had orders back-dated for months and very limited production – mostly for export trade. ...

[12th May]

The new Ford is quite snappy with red leather upholstery and white wheels. I will take the kids up to town on Tuesday to have their second diphtheria inoculation. ...

We have some new photos, but haven't duplicates yet, but will send some along. I wish that you could take more of yourselves and Ginna's house and all, because I'm so interested and so far away – not to

---

[42] Despite their declared neutrality, Belgium and the Netherlands were invaded by Nazi Germany on the day Helen wrote this letter: 10th May, 1940. The invasions ended the so-called Phoney War.

mention being in a war-torn country and I get so little news from both of you – it's a shame so it is!

On which sad note I will again say Nighty–night and love

Helen

16th May
Mahee

Dear Mother,

Thank you for your cable and letter which L. brought home yesterday. As for coming home, I'm afraid it is not only improbable, but impossible. The Consulate here long ago said that there was only one way for American citizens to go to America and still be within the law – that is from Italy on an Italian boat. It is against the law for an A. Citizen to sail from a belligerent country and/or on a belligerent boat – I would be put into jail on arrival or fined $10,000, so I'm afraid I'm stuck.

However, they can't kill everybody and we are in as good a place as we can be, although there isn't any place that you could call rosy or even healthy! ...

Love,
Helen

The situation is bad all right, but by the time you get this it will probably be worse!

I meant that letter to be posted by L. this morning, but forgot to give it to him, so I will try to catch the postman. The letter of yours that came yesterday took over a month to come. The things from California never did come, nor the photographs – at least not yet.

It has been pouring all day, but the kids were remarkably good considering. I am getting along fine with Roberta [McMullan] who is staying a week from last Monday to this.

She is writing to Harry now and all the children are resting. ...

Now it is Sunday night [19th May] and we haven't been too cheerful since hearing the Churchill's speech – it's the Blitz Krieg this time all right.[43]

Fred, Roberta's brother, has been here since Thursday. He is in the Air Force and on leave and he is the nicest boy – 22 and very quiet. Roberta says that he has never taken a girl out in his life, which drives them crazy because he is so good looking. He has just been appointed to some engineer's job in England, so he is safe for a while anyway. [44]

Peter and Roberta and Fred are leaving tomorrow, which is too bad, because we have had fun. Peter is the life and soul of the house and is incredibly funny.[45] The first morning at breakfast he looked at Julie and said to me "so she long born"? One day he was put in his room for hitting Gay and he was half crying and said "Mommy, I'm wasting time". Another time he was so taken with a salad, that Molly had fixed with hard boiled eggs and tomato laid around on top of lettuce so carefully and he said "Hasn't she tidied it up lovely"!

---

[43] This is not the famous speech – his first since becoming Prime Minister – offering his compatriots only "blood, toil, tears and sweat" and anticipating "an ordeal of the most grievous kind" which was delivered six days before in the House of Commons. He broadcast a follow-up speech on the radio on 19th May to which Helen has just listened. No wonder it cast a gloom over her. It contained a tacit admission that France might well fall and the battle for Britain commence. It ended with a rallying quotation worthy of Shakespeare's Henry V but from the Apocrypha: "Arm yourselves, and be ye men of valour and be in readiness for the conflict".

[44] Fred Gardiner was born in Belfast in 1917; he studied engineering at Cambridge University where he joined the university air squadron and was mobilised at the outbreak of war. For this and other information on Gardiner, see the obituary article in the (Toronto) *Globe & Mail*, 30th January, 2004: Tom Hawthorn, "Fighter pilot had many close calls". This is accessible on the Royal Air Force Commands website.

[45] Peter is Roberta and Harry's son (and Fred Gardiner's nephew), born in 1935 and educated at Elm Park School and Stowe School in England. He later became a rugby and fishing reporter for the *Belfast Telegraph* before emigrating to British Columbia, Canada in 1971 where he became editor of the *Nanaimo Free Press*. He thereafter became Manager of Corporate Communications for BC Hydro and Power Authority, 1981–1996, while serving unpaid in the same capacity for the Canadian rugby team, before being appointed to the International Rugby Board (now World Rugby), 1996–2000. Among his books is a recent professional and leisure-time autobiography, *Casting Back: Sixty Years of Fishing and Writing* (2016).

L. is turning the light out on me, so I must go – more later. Everyone laughs over parts of the news and it is lucky they can – just as Mr. Churchill started tonight Roberta said that she wished he would get some new teeth and I giggled away.

The weather is divine and the kids are as brown as berries. L. is holding a flashlight so g'bye.

Love,
Helen

21st May
Mahee

Dear Mother,

Just because I am restless and know that you don't mind the dearth of news – excepting war news! – I will pop off a letter though goodness knows there is no news here – but plenty on the radio. However we have just had Mr. Duff Cooper soothing us down in the 9 o'clock news after the French Prime Minister's speech was reported in the 6 o'clock news and were we depressed![46]

We used to say that we never knew whether it was *really* a crisis or not unless we had a cable from you – we still say that – and expect another tomorrow! But now the acid test has been reached because today L. bought a cow!

We talked about it at the beginning of the war, but never did anything about it and we have been working up to it since the invasion of the Low Countries and now, by gum she is here and the vet from Comber is giving her a T.B. test right now.

[46] Duff Cooper, 1st Viscount Norwich (1890–1954), had accepted the inevitability of war with Germany and resigned from the cabinet in repudiation of the Munich Agreement. Churchill when he became Prime Minister appointed Cooper as Minister of Information, the role in which Helen heard him speak. Two days after Churchill's ominous speech to the nation on 13th May, Paul Reynaud (1878–1966), briefly Prime Minister of France (March-June, 1940), contacted Churchill to inform him of France's defeat. On 21st May he described to the French parliament the military disaster. Reynaud resigned soon after rather than support an armistice with Germany (Churchill's epithet for Reynaud, "indomitable", was a prescient one). He later tried to leave France, was arrested by Philippe Petain's pro-armistice administration in 1942 and imprisoned in Germany. He was released after the war and resumed his political life in France.

We won't use the milk until she is really tested (two or three shots) and then Mrs. Middleton will milk her and do the dairy work and we will just have the bother of scalding pans etc...

The object of course is to be independent in case of food shortage or transport breakdown or any other emergency that may arise. We also have a goat who had a kid at teatime yesterday. ...

[27th May?]

This as you can see is written at another time – Monday morning to be exact and it is the beginning of a hot day after a more or less rainy weekend. ...

We went to Jack and Elaine's to supper last night ... Herbert Malcolmson and Major Prynne were here yesterday afternoon and L. went birdnesting with them.[47] Just when they came in Dorothy and Scotty Sloan arrived – Dorothy is going home on the *President Roosevelt* next week and came to say goodbye.[48] Betty Carr is also going – she is having another baby – her first one died in November and [husband] Archie is in France[49]. ...

We talked very seriously about my going and L. said it was up to me, but I decided not to go for a number of reasons – chief one of course is that it would kill L. and me too to be separated under these conditions with maybe no chance of seeing each other again for years or maybe never. L. would join up at once if we left – in anything. We are reasonably safe here from bombing, parachutists and gas and can

---

[47] Herbert (H.T.) Malcolmson was a stockbroker and distinguished Northern Irish ornithologist whose collection of birds' eggs and stuffed specimens are in the Ulster Museum; he is warmly acknowledged in C.D. Deane's *Birds of Northern Ireland* (1954).

[48] In October 1940 SS *President Roosevelt* passed into War Department ownership and became a busy troopship and transporter under the name USS *Joseph T. Dickman*. The ship took part in the D-Day landings. It was decommissioned in 1946 after action in the Pacific theatre in the latter years of the war.

[49] Archibald Carr was made second lieutenant in the 3rd Ulster Anti-Aircraft Brigade in April 1939. "3rd Anti-Aircraft Brigade (3AABde) was a Supplementary Reserve air defence formation of the British Army formed in Northern Ireland in 1938. On the outbreak of World War II it saw active service with the British Expeditionary Force during the Battle of France and Operation Aerial. It then returned to Northern Ireland and defended the Province for the next two years": "3rd Anti-Aircraft Brigade (United Kingdom)", Wikipedia. Carr's wife Betty was American.

cope with food shortage better than most people – having a big supply of potatoes, vegetables, eggs, milk, meat, fish and cod liver oil concentrates, glucose, concentrated Vitamin A pills, honey, golden syrup, etc...

Another thing is that I'm not at all happy about the [liner] Roosevelt getting here and back safely at a time like this, anything might happen and it will be crammed to overflowing. I would have sent Gay and Zoo but L. wouldn't – and if it had come to it I probably wouldn't have either.

From what we hear, even lethargic Belfast is thoroughly roused by now – machine guns at both ends of the Queens and Albert bridges – you know those that you go over from our house 88 Belmont Road to town. 1500 soldiers sleeping on the airdrome and general restrained excitement everyplace. ...

We are getting practically no news on the radio now about the battle in France, because they don't want the Germans to know how their units are doing. Everyone is surprisingly calm considering that everyone expects England to get it next. It would be exciting if it weren't so *awful*. The only bad possibility here is of 5th column treachery in the Neutral Free State – I think America should send all the help they can free *at once* – short of men – but they are crazy if they don't send material help.

The wives of Ulster soldiers in France are clear wild – as well they might be. So far I haven't known anyone killed, but L. has known a few. There are 6,000 Dutch and Belgian refugees in Belfast now, I think. They are all parked on straw mattresses in empty warehouses and public buildings.[50]

The talks on the radio are really superb now – and they make you take off your hat to the British again and again and I don't think it is

---

[50] On 18th May, many hundreds of Belgian refugees arrived at a southern English port. A refugee crisis was caused by the German onslaught of Rotterdam in which 100,000 were reported killed. The Northern Ireland Ministry of Home Affairs appealed for households to billet refugees for a weekly allowance. (There was also an appeal for Belgian and Dutch speakers to volunteer as interpreters and 150 bilingual or trilingual speakers quickly responded in Belfast.) Refugees were at first to be billeted in buildings requisitioned by the Ministry, including the Floral Hall, Bellevue (Belfast), Belfast Castle, the Ulster Hall (Belfast), some vacant factories, and church halls volunteered by congregations. See, however, the following letter in which Helen reports the non-appearance of the 6000 refugees.

just "smoothness" either. We are both reading *Failure of a Mission* and it is so good.[51] L. is reading it now – it is night now after such a lovely day.

We just sit outside all day long and enjoy ourselves – seeing the baby ducks, the baby goat, the moo cows, the baa lambs etc. and the peacefulness of it all is beyond belief when you think of that terrible struggle going on across the channel.

Once it starts here we will cable occasionally, so there is no good you're worrying yourself sick over us. We are fine and enjoying ourselves enormously. This can't last for ever and we would be darned unlucky not to live through it and no one ever thinks that England won't win! But no one doubts that the world will never be the same or anything like the same again. This is known here as total war. ...

Bodo goes away at the end of the week on a ship. Roberta says that Harry is still so optimistic – based on the grounds that Hitler is having a final desperate fling. ...

Don't worry about us – I always was so resourceful and we won't be stuck and the minute the war is over I will tear for home. I'm dying to come as you can imagine, but not now when it means leaving L. high and dry. I would be miserable all the time and not able to enjoy anything – One's first duty is to one's husband and much as I hate not seeing you and Ginna, it would be worse not to see him when the urgency isn't terrific here for flight. I have weighed the subject carefully and in the long run it is better to risk it and stay here.

Nighty night and love
Helen.

---

[51] *Failure of a Mission: Berlin, 1927–1939* was written by Sir Nevile Henderson, British Ambassador to Germany when Neville Chamberlain became Prime Minister and who was in office for two and a half years. One reviewer, Robert Gale Woolbert, described Henderson as carrying out the disastrous policy of appeasement and accused him of revealing his own predilection for many Nazi theories, practices and personages, the book "illustrating the moral and intellectual dry rot that has come to paralyze such a wide section of Britain's ruling class" – *Capsule Review* (July 1940).

30th May
Mahee

Dear Ginna and Lloyd,

I feel that I should keep you reassured at this hopeless hour over here of our health and happiness. They're tough times, babe, and no mistake and what makes them so bad as that we all know that they're going to be worse before they're better! And sister, I mean worse!

You'd think with this pessimistic outlook that I'd be in Galway tonight sailing tomorrow or Saturday on the *Roosevelt* and I have nearly gone several times – the last time being about two hours ago, when I had just heard the six o'clock news.[52]

I go up and down like a see-saw, one minute thinking I must go and the next and usually thinking I wouldn't go for anything. Of all times to need it.

I have been reading *Days of our Years* which is of course, the most pacific propaganda I have yet read, up to my starting to read that, I had almost lost and forgotten my pacifist point of view in the last few weeks of furious and wonderful propaganda here since the change of Government. There was a speech of Herbert Morrison's one night last week, which would have made a proud British subject out of the most isolationist American.[53] What it is like even in Belfast now I don't know. Let alone England, but from the papers and radio 'feverish' is as good a word as any.

The weekly newspaper is the socialist and fairly highbrow *New Statesman* which I have subscribed to since war broke out.[54] It has always been violently anti-Chamberlain and reading last week's

---

[52] The day before this letter, over 33,000 Allied soldiers were evacuated from Dunkirk, during which three Royal Navy destroyers were sunk. The next day over 53,000 were evacuated, and over 68,000 on 31st May.

[53] Herbert Morrison (1888–1965) was a prominent Labour politician before he was appointed by the new Prime Minister, Churchill, on 12th May as Minister of Supply, responsible for supplying equipment to the armed forces. He gave a bullish speech on 8th May in the House of Commons criticising the government's conduct of the war, the immediate circumstance being the Norwegian and British battle against the Germans. "We insistently demand that this struggle be carried through to victory, with all vigour and capacity by the Ministers in command" (Hansard).

[54] *The New Statesman and Nation* was then edited by Kingsley Martin, on whose watch the magazine was at the time pacifist, isolationist, anti-imperialist and pro-Soviet Union.

number made my blood run cold. So does Mr. Churchill in his speeches and every time the news comes on we hold our breath.

The 5th Column party is the worst and everyone is suspected.[55] Percy and Doreen [Metcalfe] were here the night before last and [Percy] was very vehement and said that he would intern Mucki tomorrow.[56] I jumped on him for that, but it didn't shake his conviction. Apart from his worse than usual cracks at America which I was prepared for, he was very optimistic and cheerful, but he is definitely soured or cynical or something unpleasant. ... He is convinced that you can't beat people like the British and was very cheering – that being the day that Belgium gave in and my lowest ebb yet. Did I feel awful when I heard it on the 1 o'clock news and what made it worse, was that old Duff-Cooper in person came to the microphone to say that there was no cause for panic, however grave the situation!! Which was much worse than if he hadn't tried to cheer us up.

On the whole, people are as calm as cucumbers – outwardly anyway – not that I see any except our visitors – Auntie and Uncle Gus yesterday afternoon and Jack, Kay and Paddy last night.[57] Paddy thinking that the British almost deserve it for their blindness and lackadaisicalness in the face of Hitlerism – Kay wild against the 5th Column.[58] Taking car numbers and being generally suspicious. Marjorie Glendinning was over this morning to ask us to dinner next week and she said that a Canadian couple who have lived at White

[55] In the late 1930s and early years of the war, the phrase "fifth column" (originating in the Spanish Civil War) was popularly and loosely used to refer to those who supported the enemy without.

[56] Mucki, the nickname of Marion Klara Dorndorf, was the wife of Lavens Mackie, for whom see the letter of Boxing Day, 1939. Mucki was Jewish though Percy might not have known that, for the Dorndorfs had converted to Christianity. Mucki was born in Breslau, Germany (now Wroclaw, Poland) in 1909, the daughter of Hans and Grete Dorndorf; the family's Dorndorf shoe factory was of international renown and still trades under the family name although it was sold just before Hans' death in 1932. Mucki met Lavens in Czechoslovakia when he was on a business trip and they married in Breslau in September 1929 and they lived in a house called Rathfern, in Whiteabbey on the outskirts of Belfast. (I am indebted to Mucki's nieces, Rhoda Dorndorf and Diana von Sachsen for this information: pers. comm.) Mucki early became a member of Belfast society and became Chair of the Committee of the Association of Friends of the Royal Victoria Hospital.

[57] Kay Mackie and Paddy (Marie) Metcalfe, her widowed sister-in-law who was Herbert Bryson's sister.

[58] At this stage of the war there was widespread alarm about spies in the U.K., including spies among European refugees.

Rock for the past year and who moved to Armagh about a month ago have been interned for activities with the Free State.

I met them once at a party – he wrote political articles and she wrote books – time may tell whether they were 5th column! Elaine said on Sunday that a sculptor with a French wife whom we met there about a month ago are considered spies and all the kids in Comber shout "spy" after him!

... The people we know in France are all safe except Arthur Workman whose whereabouts is unknown.[59] The others had to leave all their things and run when the Belgians gave in and most of them are in England.[60]

Even apart from the horrors, life here is going to be so changed, so controlled and so expensive as far as luxuries go. Paper napkins, Kleenex, book wrappers etc are non-existent, cigarettes are 1/5 35 cents for 18 – petrol is 50 cents and getting scarcer daily – silk stockings and clothes will be rationed and life will be one hell of a mess any minute now apart from air-raids. England is being turned upside down and inside out. The news tonight says that they are taking down all the road signposts that may help the enemy. The 6000 refugees didn't come – I don't know why. ...

There was an air-raid warning practise this morning in Newtownards and Bertha and Molly were frantic – if anything does happen around here, I will knock them both unconscious and "carry on". Apart from the Germans and IRA getting frisky, I am sure that we are as safe as possible, but if that starts, Ulster won't be any healthier than the S. of England and you know how healthy that is!

Love,
Helen

P.S. Everyone hopes against hope that America will do something quickly – do you?

---

[59] On 22nd June 1940 (*Belfast News-Letter*, 24th June 1940), it was reported that Captain Arthur Workman of the Anti-Aircraft Brigade and who lived in Cultra, Co. Down (and was a member of a distinguished family), had been taken prisoner during the retreat towards Dunkirk. He was a stockbroker in civilian life and had fought in the Great War. Arthur's brother Jack Workman was married to Caroline and both were good friends of the Turtles'. Caroline was a Carr and cousin to Tommy and John Carr.
[60] Belgium surrendered to the Germans on 28th May.

2nd Jun.
Mahee

Dear Mother,

… The weather is breathtaking and yesterday and today have been all that June should be and then some. … Last night just before dinner, I walked up to the top of the hill where Ginna's Spinney is – now a cornfield with grass up to my hips nearly, waving in a gentle breeze and between the blue sea, the blue sky, the skylarks singing, the sun shining, the hawthorn white with bloom on every hedge, it reminded me exactly of that poem of Edna St.Vincent Millay's, called "God's world" which ends:

> Lord, I do fear
> Thou'st made the world too beautiful this year
> My soul is all but out of me – let fall
> No burning leaf; prithee, let no bird call

The garden is a picture – with half the length of the border a bloom with lupins, a laburnum tree showering "garden rain" (the German name for it) yellow poppies, orange wall flowers, pink and red painted daisies and everything else ready to burst into flower.

… I love to walk around this house at night – there is such a summery feel to it, tennis shoes on the bare floors, airy curtains or none, and of course the outdoors right there. Every night nearly when I am ready for bed, I just walk out of the bathroom and one step more out the front door and the night air, stars and smell of the sea always hit one so afresh and I like it all over again every night.

Janet left us today with Patrick and Rosemary who arrived after lunch yesterday. …

Patrick is so funny and was so cheerful about the war. He says that the Germans are no damned good – any of them at fighting especially.

Certainly the news is much better tonight, when we heard that 4/5 of the B. Expeditionary Force has been saved.[61] …

Gay and Zooks are so well and so brown and are having such a good time. We have a new baby goat and a new six weeks old kitten – both

---

[61] The Battle of France began on 10th May 1940 and ended when the British Expeditionary Force had to be evacuated; the operation went on through the middle of June. Over 11,000 BEF soldiers had died by that stage.

play with their own shadows and are a perpetual source of entertainment. ...

We got 4 big pats of butter from our cow today... Will write again soon – maybe tomorrow – Night. Night and love

Helen

7th Jun.
At Rottgers (Hairdresser) [Belfast]

Dear Mother,

"Here I am" having a day out – my first in six weeks and am I enjoying it! ... The weather is glorious – there hasn't been even a cloud in the sky for a week and it is really like June in Denver. ...

It always interests and amuses me to see the hot weather getups in town. People's summer clothes are of the 1922 vintage, except for young girls who manage to look right snappy. I am 1937 from my head to my feet – hat by Newsletter,[62] dress by Saks, shoes by Saks, quilted coat by you and 1938! ...

Molly [the cook] has lately started baking such good bread to use up our surplus milk... Everything we cook is made of gulls eggs and apart from the orange color, they are as good as hen's eggs. If you want to arouse sympathy in American breasts, you can say that your unfortunate Irish daughter is existing on seagull's eggs!

We have dozens crocked – the estimated price of eggs for the winter months from sixpence to a shilling each!

Harry was a ray of sunshine on leave from Mr. Churchill's private staff and as optimistic as he could be. He says that everyone in London is just mad cross at Hitler and not a bit scared – all they want is a gun and bullets. He says that "Winnie" sleeps three hours a night and one in the afternoon and works the rest of the time *unbelievably*.

... [Harry] is discretion itself about what he says and doesn't say. He says the war will be over a year from now – so you can count on seeing me a year and a week from now – if he is the prophet he thinks he is!

...

---

[62] presumably an allusion to the resource catalogue – the Newsletter – issued by the publisher Hat Life since 1872.

[8th Jun., Mahee]

This is a Saturday evening of our maidless weekend and the weather is still holding – not a cloud in the sky. We were saved today by a good breeze, but what it must be like in town I can't think – yesterday afternoon's shopping nearly killed me – the thermometer would only be around 80 degrees, but my dear the humidity! ...

I ... went to Roberta's for lunch – Harry was panting around in red linen shorts, a blue shirt and sandals and Bertie had on a nearly indecent sun suit – their garden was stifling. My day was nearly ruined by hearing on the 1 o'clock news that the *Washington* is calling at Galway next Wednesday to evacuate Americans for the last time until the War is over.[63] These boats coming nearly put me off my head trying to decide what is the best thing to do – whichever I do, I'll regret it probably – in my low moments, I nearly come and then I get over it again? ... There is just no doubt, that things are *bad* – as we took the maids to Comber this morning, men were taking down all the sign posts so that the invaders won't know where they're going. L. has joined a local defense unit here with drills and whatnot, but it is not connected with the army – more with the police. ...

We have had about three letters from you this week – one was opened by >>>>>> All British mail of every description is opened now, even *British Birds* – a magazine L. takes.

The radio for the past week has been devoted to stories of the heroism and wonder of the evacuation of Dunkirk. One man L. knows rowed in an open boat all the way. Jack Workman's brother is missing and since he was definitely seen at Dunkirk, he is pretty sure to be dead.[64] Harry said so many of them just drowned because of fatigue and that lots just waiting to be picked up couldn't make the effort to get into a boat when one did come! ...

[63] The 24,000 ton luxury liner SS *Washington* plied the New York-Hamburg route until Roosevelt's invoking of the U.S. Neutrality Act in 1939 made this illegal. The ship switched to a New York-Naples route until Italy declared war on Britain and France in June 1940. The ship was requisitioned as a troopship but resumed her commercial career after the war.

[64] Workman survived; his return after four years in a German prison camp was reported in the *Belfast Telegraph*, 19th September, 1944.

I have a copy of a cable that Marcia Mackie[65] sent to Vassar on their 75th anniversary. Quite a good one – I may send one to the Class of 1930 at Smith, which is running this year – I got a long and very amusing questionnaire to fill out for statistics, trying to find the average 1940 members of 1930 – How many children, income, maids, politics, cars, choosing husbands thus, wearing hair in the up-style etc. ...

Nighty night and love from Helen

P.S. Here is a copy of Marcia's cable: – she got it up with the help of Mr. Cook, her neighbour and the Vice Chancellor of Queen's who is so nice and such a brain and went to Harvard.[66]

Letter from Marcia:

To President Henry McCracken – Vassar.[67]

Warmest greetings for your 75th Anniversary from only alumna resident in Northern Ireland sent at the most critical moment in history stop. It is my earnest hope that Vassar's clarion voice will join with Couauts to appraise the issue and cherish freedom, if you would be free stop. Imbued with the free spirit of American education, I like all Vassar's graduates realise that if freedom dies in the old world it dies everywhere stop. Adherence to neutrality is not enough stop. It has already made serfs of 7 nations. Stop. To preserve liberty other

[65] Marcia Mackie (née Hopkins) was a Vassar alumna; she was the American wife of James Mackie (1895–1971, the eldest son of James Mackie and Elizabeth, née Pringle, whose brothers included Lavens and Jack; Jim Mackie became Chairman of Mackies in 1945.

[66] Sir David Keir (1895–1973) served as Vice-Chancellor of Queen's University, 1939–49. He was a visiting tutor at Harvard University 1923–24.

[67] Henry Noble MacCracken (President since 1915 of Vassar College, the prestigious women's college in New York State) was an internationalist and pacifist. He believed that education was the key to international peace and cooperation. In the 1930s there had been professors and visiting speakers who spoke favourably on campus of Germany and Hitler. MacCracken organised a scheme to welcome "displaced scholars", most of them Jews, to Vassar. However, he refrained from joining the forty college presidents who supported a boycott of the 1936 Olympic Games. The college under MacCracken did close ranks against Germany by the time of Germany's invasion of Poland on 1st September, 1939. Still, the college community favoured non-military intervention; MacCracken remained a pacifist and because of this fell out with President Roosevelt, a Vassar trustee. Once the United States entered the war in 1941, however, some Vassar faculty, male and female, went off to join the war effort and gradually the college as a whole put its shoulder to the wheel in a variety of ways. *Vassar Encyclopedia* (online): "Vassar in Wartime".

means must be found stop. Weltherrschaft[68] *threatens you and every other free country in the world stop. Would you take a perjurous word*[69] *as we have done in pursuit of peace stop. Take a warning from us here, who hoped the world loved peace as much as we stop. My love to Vassar and my message runs defend liberty while there is still time*

Marcia Hopkins Mackie – '27.

13th Jun.
Mahee

Dear Mother,

Just a quickie to let you know that we're doing fine still and enjoying ourselves enormously – we spent the day making hay up until about half an hour ago and it is now 11.15. [p.m.] ...

The news isn't good – I sent a little cable of propaganda to the Reunion of the 1930 class at Smith, inspired by Marcia's and saying

Chairman 1930 Class. Smith College. Northampton. Mass.

Greeting with a message from a member in Europe stop. Our reunion coincides with the gravest peril to both the old and new worlds stop. At this desperate hour I would urgently solicit all the help in your power to preserve liberty and the traditions which Smith stands for while there is yet time.

....

Love,
Helen

Tue. 18 Jun.
Mahee

Dear Mother,

... It is late of an evening, but not blackout time yet – midsummer coming up – it is ten to 11 and blackout isn't until 10 after. Lancelot is

[68] World domination.
[69] Perhaps an allusion to Hitler's discredited promises during agreements.

still out making hay and I have just lifted the kids. ... – a full moon is shining on the water – there is a yaller bowl of spicy carnations on the table and is all as cheery as if there were no war! We listened to "Winnie's" broadcast up in the hayfield and what with the sun setting and the stooks looking so peaceful ... it just plain didn't seem possible.[70] ...

Roberta rang up this morning to say that there are going to be boats going to America, so I may be there yet and sooner than you think – no particulars are known, but there will be a general exodus of kids to the dominions I'm pretty sure – the radio says that the plans are being formulated. She was going to ring up Harry tonight to consult. ...

Gay and Zooks are fine – Today we fed the ducks, played with the goat, bathed (throwing stones to Zoo) and generally got hot and sunburned – you wouldn't believe the weather unless you could see it! ...

Love,
Helen

6th Jul.
Mahee

Dear Mother,

Everyone is just waiting for the invasion, Blitzkrieg, Total War or whatever is going to happen and they are unbelievably calm and resigned. The country almost to a man realizes that it is now or never and if there is any hope for the future, Hitler will have to be stopped now.

We had an exciting night last week when the telephone rang at 2.30 and L. had to go out with the Local Defence Volunteers (L.D.V.) to

---

[70] What did not seem possible to Helen amidst the pastoral idyll she was living was the likely imminence of what Churchill called the Battle of Britain with an impending struggle between the German and British air forces. Churchill admitted and explained the immense setbacks in France and Norway in his speech to the House of Commons on 18th June, but dismissed panic and despair. He ended his speech with what was to become a famous piece of magniloquence with its answer to a thousand-year Reich: "Let us therefore brace ourselves to our duties, and so bear ourselves that, if the British Empire and its Commonwealth last for a thousand years, men will still say 'This was their finest hour'."

scan the skies for planes. Nothing happened but there was some definite information of parachutists and we were all assured that it was not a test but the real thing. The whole countryside was up all night ...

Janet Boyd and her three boys went, or is going on the *Washington*, but the rest of the Americans are staying. ... Bodo's ship was sunk day before yesterday but he is perfectly all right and safe in England.[71]

It is new pea, new potato, strawberry and raspberry time and everything is so good. Philip and Kathleen brought us bacon, sugar and butter but we are actually not short of any of them. Sugar is touch and go, but we don't ice cakes or make as many cakes and we use honey on porridge. We got 36 lbs of sugar extra for making jam and everyone this week gets 2 pounds more per ration book – 12 pounds for our household. We have made strawberry and raspberry jam.

I haven't been to town for two weeks and only three times this summer. Oh yes! Wednesday, I took Molly, Gay and Zooks up to have our pictures taken, the final thing ready to come to America. We all have our identity bracelets now – silver chains with a plain plate with our names and addresses and registration numbers on the other side. Gay was so thrilled with hers that she held her arm out in front of her the whole time and wouldn't use that hand. ... ·

The Free State as you know is still neutral (!!?!!) and there are no preparations at all for anything! Very different from the North which is full of troops, tank-traps, barricades, sand bags, and all the regalia of war!

Must go – write often.
Love,
Helen

8th Jul.
Mahee

Dear Ginna,

... I'm glad you're proud I stayed. I very nearly didn't and it was Lancelot's sense that kept me here through lots of unbalanced moments

---

[71] See the letter of 4th March, 1940.

on my part. I was all set to come twice – to the point of cabling that I was coming – but not quite.

Everyone here seems to be faced with the most appalling things to decide – whether to evacuate (self or children),[72] whether to join up, whether to move to the country, whether to close up a business, whether to keep maids, nurses etc and lots of personal problems that everyone seems to have. The only thing to do I've concluded is to make the best decision you can and then not regret it when something bad happens – in my case it is risking the kids for Lancelot's and my sake – so that we can stay together. ...

L. is thinking of abandoning stock-broking or only going occasionally and devoting more time to farming. We saw Phillip [sic] Bell on Sunday with his wife at Whiterock – farming hard days and doing architecture nights.[73] We will probably stay here for the winter and fire M. and B. and get a local maid. No one knows what to do because naturally no one can look farther ahead than the next meal.

Bodo is home – his ship was attacked by 15 German bombers at once. He is shaken badly according to Edie *via* Nancy Mitchell and won't talk about it – not much wonder![74]

[72] In May 1940 ten thousand children from the east and south-east coast of England were evacuated to Wales. These evacuations took place from target cities across the United Kingdom. On 7th July, 18,000 Belfast schoolchildren who had been registered by their parents left the city in 35 special trains and a fleet of buses for the country. They were billeted with friends, relatives or strangers. This being Northern Ireland, Catholic children had to go to Catholic homes, Protestant children to Protestant homes. See "The Evacuation Plans," *Belfast News-Letter*, 6th July, 1940.

[73] Philip Bell (1908–1982) was from a Northern Irish Quaker linen-manufacturing family. Trained as an architect at the Liverpool School of Architecture, he was a founder member of the Historic Buildings Council and of the Ulster Architectural Heritage Society. Hundreds of Bell architectural drawings are held by the Monuments and Buildings Record. He helped design the Armagh Planetarium, which is a matter of some happy note since it inspired his daughter Jocelyn's interest in the planets. Jocelyn Bell Burnell (b. 1943) went on to become a leading astrophysicist, discoverer of radio pulsars for which, it is widely believed, she should have won the Nobel Prize in Physics. See Paul Larmour, "Philip Bell, A Champion of the Modern Movement in Northern Ireland," *Architectural Research Quarterly* 17.1 (2013): 49–62; "Philip Bell Collection" in the Architectural Drawings Archive, Department for Communities (NI); Anne Hailes, "When life adds up to a big success story," *Irish News*, 14th October, 2013.

[74] See the letter of 4th March 1940. HMS *Foylebank*, an anti-aircraft ship, was attacked in Portland Harbour by German dive-bombers on 4th July, 1940. Two bombers were downed but roughly 22 bombs scored hits on the ship which sank the following day. Out of a crew of 298, 176 were killed and many more were wounded. One crewman was awarded a posthumous VC. Bodo Taggart had therefore a lucky escape. He told his son that as the ship was going down, he was dashing to his cabin to retrieve his naval issue binoculars and managed to save both them and himself: Redmond Taggart, pers. comm.

L. is very busy with his L.D.V. (Local Defence Volunteers) drilling etc and watching nights. All the papers are full of 'The Irish Danger' and if you join up in Eire it is to fight *any* invader – British or German! We are out of the rumour belt but I believe it's *awful* what he said that she said that she heard someone else say they had heard. I do hope this war or as it is openly called here by even the *nicest* people this bloody war won't keep us apart too long.

Love,
Helen

16 Jul.
Mahee

Dear Mother,

France is lost. In the *New Yorker* "Letter from London" this week the writer says that the British are either the stupidest people in the world or the bravest. I agree with her because their attitude is remarkable.[75] Everyone listens to people talking away about the coming Battle of Britain without turning a hair and as the fortifications go up all over town – tank traps, sand-bagged houses with Bren guns inside, air raid shelters every place and goodness knows what else in other places because I only know what is on the road from here to town, people just walk past unconcernedly. People with relations in England are being urged to come to England and the ones here are urging the English to come to Ireland and no one budges. Everything is so uncertain that no family wants to be separated if they can "stay together". Elaine on a bicycle with tea and bread for the men, the wobbliest, scariest-looking sight you ever saw. Raids in Wales day and night for two weeks. Dublin has lights, butter, sugar and petrol and life is really neutral. ...

[75] There being an understandable time-lag between the issue and receipt of a transatlantic magazine, it actually was in her cable of 22nd June (printed in the 29th June *New Yorker*) that Mollie Panter-Downes, having noted the fall of France on 17th June, wrote: "It would be difficult for an impartial observer to decide today whether the British are the bravest or merely the stupidest people in the world ... The individual Englishman seems to be singularly unimpressed by the fact that there is now nothing between him and the undivided attention of a war machine such as the world has never seen before".

Half of Bodo's ship were killed: 15 bombers made a dead set on them but it was fire that killed so many. Anxious times. It is terribly unreal even here on the edge of it and it is a good thing that it is because if we fully realized it I doubt if we could stand it. This place [Mahee] is soothing and restful to live in and it emanates peace – everyone who has been here this summer says so, so goodnight from an island of peace in the war zone!

Love and kisses from Helen x, Lancelot x, Gay x, & Julie x

25 Jul.
Mahee

Dear Mother,

L. has had to be out so much lately drilling for the Home Guard.

Every place is jammed with troops – Comber is full now and all the big houses have been taken and all the schools and public buildings are full.

We had one morning of excitement when 3 big flying boats spent the morning surveying and landing on the lough.

The war is no closer than ever. Huzza! I may go to Town tomorrow for a rest and change! L. is drinking buttermilk, the radio is playing, the weather is lousy, but we are enjoying ourselves despite everything and are as cool as cucumbers. Let 'em come!
Love,
Helen

27 July
Mahee

Dear Mother,

... Lancelot is out for the 5th night in succession with the Home Guard – tonight on parade at Newtownards. Last night I went along to Comber with a car full of black uniforms and guns and a trailer of about 12 more men in black with guns. We picked up everyone from here to Comber. ...

We hardly ever listen to the news any more – it is so dull compared to a month or two ago when we were afraid not to hear it. Alan[76] says that there is no comparison between Ireland and England for war atmosphere. The tension in Eng. never breaks and you can't budge for barbed wire, Bren guns, sand bags etc. Belfast is 50% war atmosphere compared to England, he says, and Mahee 0%. We might be any place but in the middle of a war for all we know.

I had such an interesting letter from Ginna today giving her viewpoint which is still pacifist – at which juncture we differ because it is as clear as a bell that Hitler has got to be fought, anything else spells doom for generations. I agree with all her theories about mass production producing dictators etc, but no appeasement will work for a minute with that gang. Now no one expects invasion and there is a decided lull. Hitler was supposed to invade on the 9th of July and be in London as conqueror on August 15th but he is behind this time.[77] Ginna also said that Lloyd heard that England will sue for peace in 8 weeks. I'll eat all my hats if she does until the last tool because you hear nothing but determined fight talk and everyone is prepared to give up everything rather than give in. It may be conceit or smugness or dumbness but it certainly is here and is something that will stump Hitler.

We have such good vegetables in the garden now – spinach, peas, beans, beets, carrots, cauliflower and lettuce. The gulls' eggs are still going strong and are a big help because eggs are 62¢ a dozen right this minute! We have 70 doz. crocked beside the gulls' eggs, because they are going to be from 12 to 25¢ each everyone says.

I laid in various supplies on Tuesday including soap, paper, woolen pants, nail-polish and we have plenty of everything around us including over ten tons of coal. As long as the Atlantic is kept open, I'm sure everything will be OK and I don't think Roosevelt will let his English fans down. Everyone here naturally thinks he is perfect. I still think America should *give* air-planes, guns, oil, ships and everything short of men to England for her own America's sake because it will pay her hands down to keep the war here.

Nighty night and love Helen

[76] Perhaps Alan Smiles: see below.
[77] The Battle of Britain began after 4th July, but although the Germans inflicted damage on coastal targets and shipping convoys in the English Channel (the Royal Navy destroyer *Codrington* was sunk the day Helen was writing), no invasion had taken place.

30 Jul.
Mahee

Dear Ginna and Lloyd,[78]

Arabella was here for the weekend and wanted me to go to the theatre which has opened for a short season so we went up yesterday morning and went to the Opera House last night to see *When We are Married* by J.B. Priestley – just fair.[79] The theatre was packed to the roof and I'll bet there weren't more than twenty native Belfast people in the audience. You can tell the new-comers a mile away because they are so smart! Every time I go to town I notice a) how crowded it is; b) how full of military of all kinds; c) how many wives and kids of military are here. Lorries, motor-bikes, camouflaged army cars of all kinds pour through the streets and the sidewalks are stiff with men in uniform. Also there are public shelters being put up every place. There are two huge ones in Donegall Place – one across from R[obinson] and Cleaver's and one outside the Carlton – just long brick, flat-roofed things like garages and they are hideous and look as if they would fall in if a bomb dropped... There are signs every place too – about keeping still, about saving for victory, about "Careless talk costs lives", about "Keep it dark", signs with arrows printing to Red Cross and Casualty centers and A.R.P. (air raid precaution) posts ...

About one-third of the shops and houses have their windows crisscrossed with tape and important public buildings are sandbagged and the ground floor windows bricked right up. ...

[78] "This letter was hacked to pieces by Examiner 4370", according to Helen's daughter Julie Mackie. The Ministry of Information was set up to control communication for the duration of the war. The MoI both issued and censored news. Newspapers were issued with guidance about what topics were subject to censorship. In the case of postal censorship, censors affixed a sticker to the exterior of the envelope, identifying the censor. Most of the mail censorship was apparently performed in Liverpool. It has also been claimed that the term "Examiner" was introduced to soften the impression given by the term "Censor" though much remains uncertain in the realm of wartime censorship in the UK. See the interview with Chris Miller reprinted online in 2007 from the January 2003 issue of *The Chronicle*, organ of the Great Britain Collectors Club; also Dr Henry Irving, "Chaos and Censorship in the Second World War," in a Gov.UK History of Government blog (12th September 2014; National Archives).

[79] "In the heart of Northern England, three respectable couples, married on the same day, at the same church, and by the same vicar, join to celebrate 25 years of blissful matrimony. Or so they think": blurb for an Oberon Books printing of this 1938 comedy.

I was at Rosie's, Eileen Bryson's, Roberta's and Maureen's and they all have super air raid shelters. ... outside walls, tin sheeting roofs plus sandbags under the ceiling and the equipment is a scream – all the same – including a bed, chairs, electric fire, a tap of drinking water, a john [chamberpot] behind a curtain, toys, books ... A.R.P. books, food (glucose, Bovril, tinned milk, canned goods, biscuits etc) candles, tools for digging out if necessary and they all have two entrances. Roberta has extra brick walls built into her cloakroom, steel girders etc and Maureen's is her wash house with sandbagged entrance – more amateurish. You can't imagine how ugly and bare and gloomy these shelters are and when you think that somewhere in England they are in them night after night for hours you can realize how dreadfully boring and uncomfortable it is. We are going to get under our bed with the kids if we have to, otherwise just stay in bed as it is extremely unlikely that there will be a real raid on Mahee but quite possible that someone might unload a bomb or two in his hurry home.

[31st Jul.]

This is the next morning and L. is still in bed and I am half-dead because we were up until 4 this morning calving a cow which ended in the tragic loss of both! It was a terrible performance and so unlucky that the first time we ever had it to do turned out to be the toughest case seen or heard of in years. The calf just plain couldn't be born – too big ... We had Johnny, Alec Johnson (a neighbour), a vet and L. all working from about 12 am, the vet arrived about 2 ... The calf was in back to front but the vet said that even if it had been straightforward, it would have been the same. ...[80] L. was so looking forward to raising a calf and having it for the children apart from the mama and her milk....

Lancelot is out every night with the Home Guard wearing a black uniform and a forage cap and looking pretty important. He has only Thursday night off this week – they drill, build sandbag huts, stop cars on the roads and shoot at targets and are generally being whipped into shape.

---

[80] Helen's graphic details have been omitted, though they are a reminder of the ruggedness of country life.

Will stop and give this to L. Write *soon* and *often*. We are all fine and dandy – no whooping cough, 2 maids and life is a song (almost).

Love,
Helen

1st Aug.
Mahee

Dear Ginna and Lloyd,

So many people we know are going to Donaghadee for August so I might take a day off and go there some day if we can raise the petrol. We still have about 25 gallons a month but it takes it all and more for L. to go to Town even a few days a month in the car. He goes every day of the week except Sat. and Sun. but will be home for two weeks this month to help with the harvest and he is working up to quitting the office for the duration and farming seriously – which plan is still uncertain and full of snags but it would be so nice for both of us. He loves farming and hates the office especially now when he does nothing but clerical work – government transfers etc, rather than real business.

John Carr is now in the fleet air arm and Roberta's nice brother Fred is shooting down Germans over the channel in a fighter that goes 360 m.p.h.[81] He shot his first one down about two weeks ago. Bodo is home again waiting to be called to another ship – it is the talk of the town how changed he is since his awful experience. He is gradually becoming normal but it was really a shock to see him when he first came home. The naval canteen that I used to work in is being killed with work now, from 7.30 a.m. until midnight. They work in three shifts and never breathe with the rush. Roberta stood and washed dishes without stopping for 2½ hours the last time she was there!

Cigarettes are 36 cents for 20 now! But everyone's nerves are so worn and torn that they go on regardless. Just now it is becoming noticeable for the first time that certain commodities have disappeared. American things stopped when war broke out, French things have

---

[81] On July 25, 1940, while attached to RAF 610 Squadron, Fred Gardiner was in a dogfight with a German fighter. His Spitfire was severely damaged and he himself wounded, but he managed to land the plane safely though it was a write-off.

stopped and of course everything from countries under Hitler has gone. Clothes are still as plentiful as ever and not exorbitant but it is strongly rumored that they, especially wool, will be rationed soon. Silk stockings have gone steadily up since war broke out and are limited in supply to the shops but not rationed and they will finally disappear. I still would like some slips sent because the cheapest of any worth buying here are 7.50 each – too much! I am going to buy a few years' supply of shoes for the children and some more for me although living here is easy on clothes – no stockings and always pants.[82]

We are having a new houseguest today – a voluntary farm hand, a schoolboy about 15 years old named Alan Smiles. He was dying to "dig for victory" on his holiday and Bodo told his parents that we needed hands so they came down last Sunday – pa, ma and 4 kids – and we arranged it. They are such a nice family and live across the street from the Carr's. This boy goes to Marlborough, one of the snappiest English public schools, and I will be so interested to observe him – he seems a dear, very boyish and nice – however I will give you a considered opinion later.[83]

Are my letters opened? Yours apart from about three right in the middle of the panic around when France gave up, aren't touched – and then they were opened by Examiner rather than Censor. Kathleen Scanlan told us about a letter Philip's niece wrote from Eng. that was completely cut out except for 'Dear Parents' and at the end, "and I could tell you a lot more if I had time. Love etc"! Bodo could never tell Edie a thing and always just talked about the tea he was going to have when his kettle boiled!

---

[82] This would have been un-British attire: women in slacks or pants were considered dangerously liberated in those days.

[83] Alan Smiles's mother Madeline was a Ewart, a famous name in Ulster linen production. Smiles joined the Royal Navy during the war and afterwards joined the Ewart firm before going to the United States where he died in 1996. Alan Smiles' father, Philip (b. 1890), was a director of Ewart & Son and became a Lt.-Commander in the RNVR during the war and was awarded an MBE in 1945. (See *Northern Whig*, 14th June 1945.) Philip was one of eleven children of William Holmes Smiles, who co-founded Belfast Ropeworks. One of Philip's brothers was (Sir) Walter Dorling Smiles (b. 1883), the Unionist MP who went down with the *Princess Victoria* that sank in 1953. Another brother was Alan Smiles (b. 1882) of the Royal Irish Rifles who was killed at the Somme. Philip Smiles' mother was half-sister to Mrs Beeton and his grandfather was Samuel Smiles. Two eminent Victorians in the ancestry of one east Belfast family.

Central City sounds so good.[84] I would love to spend the fall in Denver but nothing is a bit bad here yet, and things will change so slowly that we will wake up some day and find our lives completely different without our having realized it – in 2 or 3 years I should think this life will really be gone.

That's all I can think of now – I do wish you would write oftener. You don't know what red letter days they are when I hear from you all – meaning you and Mother because that's all I hear from. The day is too hot even to pick flowers so I will fling myself on the grass and read (or sleep.) We still are sleepy from our night before last 4 o'clock touch and yesterday there was a pall over the house as if a friend had died because of the poor cow. It was *awful* and such a complete waste and disappointment. I could have cried for L. who is so tender-hearted and he wanted to have a calf so much.

Love,
Helen

19th Aug.
Mahee

Dear Mother,

We had a real day out today. Lancelot is on a ten days 'working holiday' and today he, Eggy, Hilary and I went to a farm auction at Shane's Park, near Randalstown. It is the first time we have been any place but to Comber and Town since April! The military have taken over Shane's Park so the pheasant shooting is no more. ...

... Things are stirring up now in England but so far we have had no excitement here apart from every town and village and city simply crawling with soldiers. In walking a block in town you can count on seeing ten or twenty men in uniform just walking around shopping and one in ten cars you pass is either a military lorry or a staff car all

---

[84] Helen presumably refers to Central City, Colorado (about 35 miles from Denver), an historic mining settlement that sprang up in 1859 upon the discovery of gold. At the height of the rush, 10,000 prospectors flocked there. (In 2010, 663 persons lived there.) Ginna and Lloyd were perhaps visiting there on account of Central City Opera House which was a focal point during the summer festivals that began in the 1930s.

camouflaged meaning that they are painted khaki color with wavy black bands on the sides and tops. Comber is packed out with soldiers – Strandtown is seething with air force and in general you can't forget once you leave Mahee that "there's a war on". The last four words, "there's a war on", are a refrain here used in a comic way for an excuse for anything. Everyone is as flip as can be since the grim Battle of France and the daily slaughter of German airmen and planes is cheered wildly on all sides and regarded – and rightly – as a miracle.

We had one explosion about two days ago. I was awake after settling Zoo when at ten to one our bedroom windows rattled noticeably. There was no wind so I *knew* that a bomb or something had dropped someplace. At breakfast the next morning I stated positively that something had happened but L. and Jack Andrews pooh-poohed and said that it was a gust of wind – but I was proved right because everyone had heard it. There were many rumors and explanations but no official mention at all or even unofficial, the most prevalent and likely was that a German plane dropped a magnetic mine that either exploded in the air or in mud – that's the closest the war has come to us so far.

Eggy and Hilary were only here for the weekend – Eggy is going to work on airplanes at the Mackie foundry – the sale for painting has stopped except in the Free State and he wanted to do some war work and out of 3 choices chose that. He will be a factory worker from 8 am to 8 pm including Sundays and after his free, roving, outdoor life he expects that it will nearly kill him. He has been wandering around painting since he was 20.

Love,
Helen

23rd Aug.
Mahee

Dear Ginna and Lloyd,

The sea is grey despite the sun because big black clouds are hanging over it. My bathing suit and wrap are hanging over the bench, mute testimony to my Spartan before breakfast bathe. I don't do it every day.

Alan, our school boy, does and parks his on the bush outside his door. I don't think his suit ever dries and it is extra good to bathe in a clammy suit. He and Lancelot are out working – putting up the corn stooks that the wind blew down and I should be there helping – having done not a hand's turn on the entire harvest.

Alan is a rip-roaring success. He is one of the nicest boys I've ever met with incredibly easy manners for a boy of 16. He is not in the least self-conscious and plays tea parties with Gay, wipes Zoo's face, hands around tea at parties, plays golf with Johnny's boys, hangs up the blackout curtains for me, and talks with Lancelot – all with the same quiet, happy manner. He slaves all day with Johnny and Hansy and then rows around the bay or plays golf for exercise! I will be so sorry when our work situation which was hanging over us like a pall has been suddenly and miraculously cleared up. A Mrs Grainger who is staying with the Glendinnings to get a rest from her old, trying, ill husband heard that her husband has fired their two German Jewish refugee maids for nothing. They are a mother and a daughter and Mrs Grainger says that they are "sweet" and that she would do anything for the mother. They are Bavarian and she has had them a year; they never go out except once a week to Town; the Mother is a professional dressmaker, and the daughter looked after children when she first came to Belfast and they both come for £1 a week – *not* £1 each! The Mother is a good cook and they are both all that is conscientious and responsible and honest and they like being in the country! I am going to interview them on Monday but I have them as good as engaged. Mrs Grainger is a very nice and sensible woman – the kind you can believe about maids so everything seems lovely.

We certainly don't agree, you and I, on the situation because I am all for the U.S. sending everything they've got this minute to help England to stop Hitler. I was a pacifist and an isolationist up until May but now I have seen the light and realize that whatever the cost and that, sister, is going to be terrible, Hitler must be stopped or the world is lost for generations. ...

I am not a bit sorry not to be going back to Town – the blackout is so awful and now the streets are so messed up with barricades. No one has any petrol to go any place and lots of people have put their cars up. We have a good supply of petrol with our two cars, extra for farming and the tractor, but even so L. will find it hard to drive up and down every day in mid winter when he will always be in the dark – and the dark means black. We put on our pre-war headlight the other night for one second and were all nearly blinded. It is hard to describe to you how black everything is. They are so fussy now about lights every place, city and country, and we are really blacked out for the first time in our lives. ...

We have pretty many planes over practising and going places, but it is quiet compared to _____ _____ [censored] where they never cease. Betty told me that Roberta's nice brother Fred has been wounded in an air battle, but she didn't think very badly. Every time I heard an announcement about all those planes being down I wondered about him – he is so nice and so young.[85] The R.A.F. are talked of with reverence every place because they *are* so wonderful. Did you read Churchill's last speech?[86] I think he is so good – also Herbert Morrison, the minister of supply.

We had Mucki and her children down one day – her youngest brother Reiner [sic] is with her now. He has been interned but is free now but is not allowed to drive a car or have a bicycle.[87] Do you know that if you were staying here now you couldn't own a bicycle and would only be allowed to move in a 5 mile radius and have to report to the police every so often?

---

[85] This is an allusion to the 25th July dogfight over the English Channel. Fred was twenty-three.

[86] On 20th August, Churchill in his speech to the House of Commons had brought the nation up to date on the fortnight-old Battle of Britain being waged in the skies. He paid eloquent tribute to "the British airmen who, undaunted by odds, unwearied in their constant challenge and mortal danger, are turning the tide of the world war by their prowess and by their devotion," after which came the famous computation in the arithmetic of gratitude: "Never in the field of human conflict was so much owed by so many to so few".

[87] Rainer Dorndorf (1912–1986) left Germany via Paris in 1933 in advance of the terror (recent family conversion to Christianity would not have let German Jews off the Nazi hook) and after a spell in England, came to Northern Ireland where his sister Mucki was living. As a German national he was interned several times, in Crumlin Road (Belfast) gaol – where IRA prisoners assumed he was on their side and threw him cigarettes - and on the Isle of Man. Mucki used her contacts (and the stature of the Mackie family) to have him released. During the war he was living at Rathfern with his sister and her husband Lavens Mackie, later farming in County Down. He married a Belfast woman in 1948 and continued farming until in 1976 the couple retired to Spain. In am indebted to Rainer's daughters Rhoda Dorndorf and Diana von Sachsen for much of this information.

No one is allowed to go to England or Scotland for anything except wives of men in the forces or unless you can prove that your journey is of national importance. If you go for the duration you are allowed to go, but there is no way of getting back again. Mr and Mrs Taggart have gone. Bodo has gone to sea again. Armstrong Mitchell was home last week on leave. He is on the ground staff of some airport in Scotland. Esme is working hard with the soldiers' and sailors' and airmen's wives Association and some of her cases would make you squirm.[88]

I had better go to see if they need any help with the stooks again. It is quite fun stacking them because they are like dolls in Hawaiian skirts, four leaning against each other with the wheat kernels tasseling at the top.

My love to Lloyd
and to you

29th Aug.
Mahee
Dear Mother,

It is 1 o'clock and I am just hearing the news – these days not so good.[89] So far Belfast is untouched and if and when it starts here we will cable you occasionally so you needn't worry yet.

Bertha and Molly leave tomorrow morning and our two new ones – German Jewish refugees arrive with L. in the evening. They are Frau Noy and her daughter Trudy, a dressmaker and art student respectively. Trudy has looked after children and I have arranged for her to look after G. and J. every afternoon. They come for the same wages as M. and B: £3 each a month + insurance which is 1/3 each week each. They got less before but Mrs Noy did outside dressmaking. ...

---

[88] In 1944 Katie Pringle, wife of Kenneth Pringle, was the Chair of the Belfast Area Committee of the Soldiers', Sailors' and Airmen's Families' Association in which Esme Mitchell apparently worked in 1940. The Association was founded as the SSFA in 1885.

[89] "These days" probably refers to the sustained attacks by the German Luftwaffe on RAF airfields and aircraft factories in Britain between mid-August and early September. In the last week of August the RAF lost 200 fighter planes, the German air force 330. London itself was on red alert by the night of 28th–29th August.

[31st Aug.]

... Our refugees are here and so far so good. Their name is Neu, pronounced Noy, and the Mother is such a good cook. ...

[3rd Sept.]

We are having the loveliest spell of weather – just like we had in June and apart from our water being so short that no one can take a bath, all is rosy... It has been cloudy up to now but now the clouds are scattering and the sun is breaking through the mists and it is going to be boiling pretty soon – Huzza! There is no wind and the sun is sparkling on the water, the bees are buzzing, the birds are singing and you wouldn't believe that the war is a year old and that London had a seven hours' air raid last night![90] ...

In my poetic and wishful rather than realistic moments I think that it will be *so* nice and peaceful and good for my soul to stay here and in my tired and depressed and very realistic moments, I hanker for the fleshpots of Town which this winter will be limited to movies and quiet evenings with friends. I doubt if there will be many dances, but then again there may be more dances than ever on account of the vast hordes of troops that are stationed in every nook and cranny of Ulster. We actually had a camp of soldiers on Mahee for a few days last week and when I bicycled to the Beath's I kept meeting all the big army trucks pouring around the corners. ...

Harry ... was here last night. [He] is as usual very full of himself ... but he was terribly funny at times last night. He was trying to work up sympathy for himself and what *he* is going through with 6 and 7 air raids a day, during which no one takes shelter at all apparently because it would mean literally living in your shelter.[91] All our sympathy and inquiry was for Roberta's brother Fred who was shot in the foot over the channel, and realizing that something was happening to his machine, a Spitfire, he streaked for home and just as he got over land

[90] The United Kingdom and France declared war on Germany on 3rd September 1939. This continuation of the letter is clearly dated "Tuesday – 3 September" yet the policy of attacking London by air was not decided on until 6th September. Air raids against the capital began in the afternoon of 7th September. The first, daylight raid lasted 90 minutes, the second, night-time raid lasted over eight hours. No air raid is recorded for 2nd–3rd September.

[91] Helen must mean six or seven air raid warnings by siren, rather than actual raids.

at Dover his plane burst into flames starting with a terrible *phoof* of fire into his face burning off his eyebrows and eyelashes and involving getting his right hand terribly burned. He managed to push the roof back and get out backwards and fall off his plane and he fell through space with his burning plane falling beside him and his parachute unopened on his back. He had no feeling in his right hand and only pulled his parachute open at 150 feet off the ground (Harry says it must have been 300), but anyway just in the nick of time to break the fall. He was recorded as dead because the observers saw him fall and had him chalked off – "Parachute failed to open". Anyway some other observers sent ambulances and within 7 minutes of his landing he was in an ambulance and in another 7 minutes he was in a hospital and eventually he will be as good as new – hand, foot, face and all! His plane crashed within 50 feet of him and Harry said that Fred said that *would* have been the last straw after finally getting his parachute open to have had the plane land on top of him. He is the one hero that we know and are we proud! Roberta will get a gold caterpillar pin out of it because the parachute company presents a gold pin to everyone who genuinely saves his life by parachute... [92]

The maids are doing fine... And if Trudy and Mrs Neu turn out to be good with the children, I will stay nights in town with all my friends in turn to have a change during the winter ...

Mrs Neu came out of Germany a year ago on the 1st of Sept. and had to leave her Mother behind because her visa wasn't right and of course after the 3rd there was no hope of getting out, so she is still there. Mrs Neu says that she has to sew all the time so that she won't think. Trudy came the June before and they are both trying to get to America eventually. Trudy got everything of hers out including clothes for years to come because she had to spend all her money in Germany,

---

[92] On 12th August, Gardiner was again wounded and his Spitfire hit while engaging a German Bf-109 fighter, and again managed to survive. On 18th August, he was credited with downing a Bf-110 long-range fighter during an attack by 14 Spitfires on 50 German bombers and 50 escort fighters. Helen refers to an aerial engagement north of Dover on 25th August when Flying Officer Gardiner's Spitfire was hot and burst in to flames; he bailed out and was rescued in a stubble field by two soldiers. His flight entry was terse: "Shot down near Deal, parachute descent, aircraft destroyed". He spent a month in hospital and was awarded the DFC; nevertheless, he was listed as killed in action, an error that was discovered only after his death decades later.

but Mrs Neu only brought a small suitcase because she came in such a hurry. ...

Love,
Helen

14th Sept.
Mahee

Dear Ginna and
Lloyd,

Although it is 11.15 p.m., I am as wide awake as an owl and since Lancelot has just gone out to do his road patrol I might as well stay up and write to you – since I had a letter from you today.

Eggy and Hilary have just gone. Eggy was talking about Kiowa and I got downright homesick for the dry farms![93] Poor Eggie – this is his last weekend of freedom because on Monday he starts to work in an airplane factory. He painted a picture today and will paint every Sunday to keep his hand in. Lancelot has to stop cars about every tenth night for a spell. They have guns and wear their Home Guard uniform and inspect everyone's identity card. He goes to Ballydrain corner – four miles away.

It is the most heavenly night – cold and moonlit with no wind and if only the gas-light wasn't so hard and bright in this room it would be as pretty inside – nearly – as it is out. I don't quite know what we can do about this light because we have to have it to read or knit and candles aren't good enough for that – but the bright light on the white walls is awful.

Little by little we are making the house more livable for the winter. ...

We are having Calor gas put into all the bedrooms and are getting a new Esse stove. I don't know if you know what they are but they are super – the Swedes invented the idea and the Swedish stove is called Aga – the Esse is English and we think after seeing and hearing about both that it is better. ...

[93] Kiowa Indian country was originally western Montana, then the Rocky Mountain portions of Colorado, and finally the Southern Plains, including Oklahoma. Dry farming (non-irrigation cultivation of crops) was a practice of the Plains.

It is now nearly midnight – "midnight again!" – and I have turned on the radio to hear "And So To Bed" – ten minutes of reading of selections from good books and poetry and always so good – and such beautiful voices read them. I fell in love with one Frederick Allen the other night just hearing his voice.[94]...

Now the news is on. No invasion yet, thank goodness but since Churchill's speech on Wednesday night we are all ready for it.[95] People still bet that it won't happen and mostly hope that it will so that we can deliver the glancing blow to that man – I don't know what to hope – an invasion would be awful but it might shorten the war and everyone is certainly on his toes waiting – things are still really normal here with a few things going off the market and prices going up. ...

Here it is 12.30 so I will light 2 candles and go get in the bathtub and soak and brood until L. turns up –

Goodnight kids!

Love,
Helen

16th Sept.
Mahee

Dear Ginna and Lloyd,

It is pouring rain and has been most of today. I mended all morning and tidied drawers this afternoon and I feel so virtuous. Lancelot is home for a week and he has been weeding and thinning carrots all day. We have vegetables planted as far as the eye can see – 7 kinds of broccoli among them. ...

---

[94] Frederick Allen was a BBC announcer and radio actor; he later read the first BBC D-Day news bulletin at 8 a.m. 6th June 1944.

[95] Churchill's twelve-minute "Every man to his post" speech of 11th September was full of his customary frank disclosure of the war situation. He warned the British people that much rode on "the great air battle which is being fought between our fighters and the German air force", that "a heavy, full-scale invasion of this island is being prepared with all the usual German thoroughness and method", and that mastery in the air was crucial to Hitler's plans. The threat dwarfed in scale the Spanish Armada. No other British politician would likely have devised his inspired rhetorical stratagem: set the bar of defiance so high that the populace felt obliged to surmount it.

Another letter came from you today and there was one on Saturday – such a happy surprise. Certainly pacifism is common sense but not now – not with Hitler loose in Europe. We just heard today of the 185 down to 25 British with 10 British pilots safe – it is wonderful, isn't it[96] and Churchill's remark about "never in the history of conflict has so much been owed by so many to so few" was so good – don't you think his speeches are masterpieces? Goodness knows it must be pretty grim in London now. ...

Have only smoked 8 cigarettes today and it is now 5.30 – do you know why? It is because I have only 4 left!

Love,
Helen

21st Sept.
Mahee

Dear Mother,

... The weather lately has been as good as any we had all summer and now there is a nip in the air that reminds me of Colorado. When I think that it is over three years since I was home and nearly two since I saw you and Ginna I feel so sad and frustrated because there seems no immediate and sometimes no nearly immediate prospect of coming again. ...

We listen to the news every morning at 8 and these days it is pretty grim. I haven't been to the movies lately to see pictures of London but everyone says that it is frightful. Roberta told me the other day that twice Harry has had to lie on his face in Piccadilly while things crashed around him – and he such a dignified Lieutenant-Commander! The invasion plans must be badly upset by the bombing the ports have got

---

[96] Sunday 15th September saw a fierce, day-long battle in the skies over London and southern England. Up to 1500 fighters and bombers saw action. At close of hostilities, the British Air Ministry released a press statement claiming that between 175 and 185 German aircraft had been shot down. Churchill was told that there had been 183 kills for under 40 losses. But this is now regarded as an "overclaim" and one estimate of German losses is 56 with 28 RAF losses. Still, this significant British victory galvanized some quarters of American opinion in favour of military intervention. It also caused Hitler to shift tactics from daylight raids to night-time Blitzkriegs.

so I do hope that Germany will be wrecked as a war machine – it is the only hope for an early armistice and not a very likely thing either.

People who have been in air raids all say that the first one is the worst and that you get used to them. Nancy Mitchell is just home from visiting Charlie and was in a few. The first one made her sick she said, with fright I suppose and then she didn't mind the others so much though naturally they are far from enjoyable.

So far so good here – it still is the most peaceful spot imaginable and we don't even hear target practice. We get occasional planes passing over and looking businesslike and we often pass soldiers marching along singing but our lives otherwise are still peaceful and happy. ...

A week from today Arabella will be Mrs. Freeman and the excitement over the wedding is terrific. Our dresses are done and I am negotiating for a picture hat. ... Arabella is thrilled to death with the whole thing. They are going to Donegal for their honeymoon I think. ...

Love,
Helen

30th Sept.
Mahee

Dear Mother,

... There is no stock-broking now to speak of so L. and Jim [Barr] take turn about to have time off. ... I have converted Jim into a disciple of Louis McNeice the Ulster poet except that Louis doesn't live in Ulster now and is in America. I think I told Ginna to get one of his books – namely *Autumn Journal*. I am reading all the works of Katherine Mansfield lent me by a French girl who lives not far from here. She and her husband and baby are coming to lunch next Sunday.

Jack Mackie had an explanation about Hilary and Eggy not turning up [to lunch] – Hilary's elder brother committed suicide a few days ago – he had been wounded in the foot and heard the doctor say the he would never walk again so it must have unbalanced his mind because he began acting peculiarly and was found on a railway track having let a train run over him. He had a wife and little boy not much older than Gay. It is the most awful thing that can happen I think and Hilary can't go home because no one can go to England except to see a dying relative. ...

John Carr is in the Fleet Air Arm now and was in London for that bad night raid a few weeks ago. He says people stand and "rubber"[97] but they take care to keep "brave and close" to an air-raid shelter door. Everyone says the noise is the worst and with bombs dropping, screaming bomb screaming, and the terrific anti-aircraft barrage noise, no one can sleep a wink. ...

Everyone has been doing frenzied shopping because a new tax goes on everything tomorrow. No one is clear how it works but everyone knows that things are going to cost about 25% more. I have bought up everything that I can think of...

Have you read *A Good Home with Nice People*? It is about the maid problem and it quite good.[98] ... I will send this on the Clipper. ...

Love,
Helen

4th Oct.
Mahee

Dear Ginna,

... I am going to a big benefit bridge party this afternoon at Lady Glentoran's house near Comber.[99] It is called Ballyalloly and I don't know if you would remember it – a big new white house with a wonderful view? I am going to wear my new blue wool Jaeger dress with a white piqué collar, my fox cape and a new hat, a high crowned stiff black one with a bright red ribbon ending in two sticky-up tails at the back. ...

I bought the hat on Wednesday to go to [a friend] Mrs. McKee's for lunch and later to go to dinner and the theatre with Mr. Randolph[100]

---

[97] Presumably, rubber for rubberneck, American slang for gawp. "Brave and close" is an Ulsterism meaning "pretty close".

[98] This book by Josephine Lawrence was published in 1939.

[99] Hon. Emily Bingham, Lady Glentoran (d. 1957) married Herbert Dixon (1880–1950), created peer in 1939 (1st Baron Glentoran).

[100] Mrs McKee was in all likelihood Martha Gertrude McKee who lived with her sister Miss Edith Vint in Malone Avenue; they were the daughters of John Vint JP and Mrs McKee the widow of Rev. Dr. Ernest McKee (d. 1934). Mr Randolph was presumably John Randolph, U.S. consul in Belfast (see the letter of 14th April).

and it is really sweet and the first good hat I've had since Julie was born – and that it was only $7.50...

[5th Oct.]

Now it is Saturday same time, same place and everybody doing the same thing. ... We were having the Johnsons to lunch but they wired that they couldn't come. They are an art couple who live in a cottage between Newtownards and Comber on the shore. He is a sculptor and painter and she is French and literary. They are considered spies in Comber because they are so Bohemian and odd but they are quite nice![101]... Eggy and Hilary are coming too sometime during the day because Eggy will be painting this way. No one ever comes during the week but they pour in on Saturdays and Sundays petrol permitting. ...

No one knows what to think about the war. It looks so long and endless now. The spirit is as good as ever because no one would dream of giving in before Hitler is squashed but it looks discouragingly black and grim even when we win because there will be so much to do then and it will be such a tricky job trying to do the right think. ...

I am working up to writing something, what I don't know ... I might just do a paper on someone because my creative power seems nil.
We are having tinned (sausages) for lunch, the kids are so excited because they are real German frankfurters so eyes glistened my dear, glistened! ...

Love,
Helen.

---

[101] Nevill Johnson (1911–1999) was born in England, came to Belfast in the 1930s, and in 1949 moved to Dublin where he became part of the 1950s Dublin bohemian scene and a friend of Yeats's daughter, Anne. He was a painter, photographer and writer whose work has recently been rediscovered and championed. There was an exhibition of work across six decades in Newman House, University College Dublin in 2014. In 1984 he published his autobiography, *The Other Side of Six*. For Madame Johnson, see the letter of 27th March 1944.

9th Oct.
Mahee

Dear Mother,

… Last night there was such a storm that I had to get up to close our windows and even then the floor and desk were in puddles of rain. It was as bad this morning when we woke up with wild waves crashing against the wall and gate but by the time Gay, Julie and I went out for a "blow" the wind was dying and by 10 there wasn't a breath and it was warm and muggy. We walked along the shore and home by the fields and then took the pram to the shore again to blackberry. We have made blackberry and apple jelly which is so good, but these are just to eat. I thought how you would love them because they are just like the black raspberries you like so well. We all came on smeared from ear to ear with purple juice. …

I was in town all day yesterday doing more shopping before the 33% tax comes on to nearly everything on 21st October. …

I am going again on Friday to get Lancelot stocked up on underwear, pyjamas, socks and sweaters. The shops are doing a good business now because they certainly won't sell much after the 22nd… There is talk that there will be no knitting wool except in the Services colors . …

Cheese is the latest thing to disappear from the markets. You can't even get yellow cooking cheese, that is "New York Cream" to you and "Mousetrap" to Lancelot! Instead there is just one kind called "colonial" cheese, pale yellow with no taste. We have suddenly lost our extra butter and are down to 2 oz. per person per week and it is awful … Our tea ration is plenty for us. … We have plenty of meat and bacon and so we are alright.

I met Maureen yesterday at 1.30 and we went to see *Rebecca* which was so good – as you said. Did you notice that Rebecca's handwriting was exactly like Ginna's when she is in a hurry?[102] I saw Roberta and she said that Harry had been home for four days and was looking well although he says that he is scared to death dozens of times a day and that the scream of the screaming bombs seems to go right into your brain and that each one sounds as if it is coming straight at you.

---

[102] The Hitchcock movie version of Daphne du Maurier's 1938 novel *Rebecca* was released in 1940. Helen refers to the note in Rebecca's handwriting that Jack Favell (George Sanders) shows Maxim (Laurence Olivier) and that contradicts the idea of her suicide.

I had a card from Janet Boyd from Washington and she said that so far I have won on the staying here – she doesn't mention coming home and she has taken an apartment near her mother in Washington for the winter. ...

Jack Mackie, Philip Ware [sic][103] and Eggy and Hilary were here last Sunday, Jack to lunch and tea, Philip to lunch, tea and supper and Hilary and Eggy to tea and supper. Hilary told me all about her brother's suicide, so much that I had a nightmare about it that night. It was a terrible depression that caused him to do it. He was a nervous sort of person anyway and one that the war especially got down. Hilary goes on the same as ever but says she feels that she will never be the same again which she won't of course, and she says that she feels suddenly old. Eggy had painted a picture on his way to keep his hand in and Lancelot had been to a Church parade and drill and the police in Comber had been notified that a strange man was painting so he was told to ask him for his permit! Of course he didn't have one! It was quite a pretty picture. He has a beautiful exhibition on in Rodman's now, several of things around Mahee including one of our gate.

[10th Oct.]

This is Thursday and I am sitting out on a bench in the sunshine and it is as warm as Summer. We were blackberrying again this morning along the shore and it was divine. The sky was blue and the water so clear and the coloring of the trees so autumnal. ...

... so now it's bedtime and I can't think of any more news so

Goodnight and love,
Helen

It makes me *so sad* to think that it is nearly two years since we have seen each other however, I'm banking on the Neutrality Law being

[103] Philip Wayre MBE (1921–2014) is credited with helping to save the otter from extinction in England through the work of the Otter Trust which he set up in 1971 and which bred otters in captivity for release into the wild. He includes an account of a duck-hunting escapade on Strangford Lough with Lance in his book *Wind in the Reeds* (1965). He founded the Philip Wayre Wildlife Trust in 1994. See his obituary, *Daily Telegraph*, 10th July, 2014; and "Our Founder," on the Philip Wayre Upland Trust website.

revoked soon and I've seen that passage to and from England and America as well as trade etc. will be on much easier terms soon. H. We may be lucky and see each other sooner than we think, how I don't know but one never knows what will happen and meantime I'll send more Clipper letters more frequently – x x x

21 Oct.
Mahee

Dear Ginna and Lloyd,

... If you want to read a good book read "The Art of Reading" by Quiller-Couch. L. is reading the chapter on Children's reading now. The whole thing is a masterpiece and an inspiration.[104]

The thrashing machine arrived this evening so we are blocked in! Gay and Julie were so excited because it is such a huge thing just like a locomotive puffing smoke and fire. We are thrashing all day tomorrow – 2 men for breakfast at 7.30, 16 for lunch and 16 for tea!!! L. expects that we will have 10 tons of oats. Did I tell you that we have a new Ford Ferguson tractor plus all the implements.

We will have 20 acres ploughed this year so Mahee is beginning to look like a real farm. We have a silo made out of two old pig-houses at the bottom of the garden. We also have 32 tame wild ducks that live here and are always around and they look so pretty.

Trude [the art student Trudy Neu] had a friend staying with her over the weekend who is going to Buenos Aires as soon as she can via New York. She was such a nice girl, also a Jewish refugee whose family is already in B.A. All the Morovitzs [sic], (you remember Herbert), are in Canada.

I had lunch with Bodo and Edie on Thursday. Bodo has taken his father's death so hard and Mrs. Taggart has gone to England for good to live with her sisters. Bodo is still at home but is expecting to be called at any moment. They are coming down on Saturday if he is still here.
...

---

[104] *On the Art of Reading* (1920) began as series of lectures in the University of Cambridge, 1916–17, two of the lectures being on "Children's Reading". Quiller-Couch (1863–1944) was a novelist, critic and anthologist, editor of the influential *Oxford Book of English Verse* (1900). His pseudonym "Q" was a famous one.

I sent you "Autumn Journal" by Louis McNeice so I hope you like it. I have made Jim Barr an absolute fan and he has made 2 other fans!

...

[27th Oct. or 3rd Nov.]

The air raid warnings have started in Belfast – two Friday night and one last night for no apparent reason. We of course hear no warnings and so a shelter wouldn't be much use to us because we wouldn't know to go into it until things happened right beside us. This house is well constructed and there isn't much roofing to fall on us even if the house collapsed. I don't say that it would be enjoyable but it wouldn't necessarily kill us. I am going to have thick velvet curtains over G. and J.'s windows at night as well as the black ones to prevent glass blowing in if it does blow in. But rest assured that it would be bad luck if we are bombed here. Air-raid warnings if they continue will tend to keep people home nights because if you are out in the car you have to turn out the lights and stop and wait for the All-Clear. I must say that I'm thankful to be here away from the nervous excitement of the sirens and to escape sitting in a shelter nights. Bodo and Edith were in theirs twice on Friday night – baby, maid, dog and all! Luckily the warnings were both of short duration but is so upsetting for everyone and especially for children. It must also be upsetting for one's peace of mind generally to think every evening: "Well, I wonder what will happen tonight?" We've had over a year of not having to wonder. If we happen to be outdoors we can hear the sirens from Comber or Newtownards. We heard the All-Clear last night when we were out listening for enemy planes.

More later,
Love Helen.

Now on the eve of the Election people here are almost as worked up as if it was their own election and of course everyone here is 100% for Roosevelt ! I think the "Wilkie" buttons were the limit! We saw them in the Wilkie Number of "Life" (Magazine)...[105]

[105] Many Britons rooted for Roosevelt, but he was cautious about intervention though he later regretted promising not to send any American boys into any foreign wars. Willkie, a Wall Street businessman, himself advocated American support for the Allies but not military involvement; *Cont'd overleaf:*

[4th Nov.]

Darned if this isn't Monday week again – another sunny Day! They are worth noting in the winter time because this is winter alright now that it is November. Trude has the kids out for a walk and I am listening to the blaring radio playing music for the munitions factories. They have two half-hours a day of jazz for what Mr. Priestly [sic] called: "Hard work and high jinks"![106] Munitions factories work day and night and the day shift is 8–8. No joke and no Saturdays off! They started with no Saturdays *or* Sundays off but had to stop that.

Mrs. Neu is taking a bath in preparation for her week's holiday tomorrow. She always has a headache and occasionally is laid out with one, all because of worry that she has left her mother in Germany and over their situation as a whole, past, present and future. I feel terribly sorry for Trudy who bears the brunt of the work because Mrs. Neu only cooks and Trudy has hope and a cheerful philosophy but Mrs. Neu isn't interested in anything much and is a depressing companion for Trudy. However Mrs. Neu is intrinsically nicer and jollier than Trudy when she lets herself forget her troubles. Our food is as good as ever and with no mental effort on my part because I never need to say what pudding or lunch or soup we'll have but only have to order meat and staples.

We had the Scanlans here for the weekend arriving Thursday evening at 6 when we went to Arabella's to change for a dinner-dance at Thompson's restaurant.[107] In our party were A. and Gordon and the

---

[105] *Cont'd*: this left him free to accuse Roosevelt of secretly planning to take the U.S. into the war. There were numerous Willkie election buttons and they included allusions to Roosevelt's running for a third term: "No Man Is Good Three Times" and, perhaps the one Helen thought the limit, the tasteless "Third International Third Reich Third Term", a slogan hitting socialism, Fascism, and Roosevelt in one go.

[106] J.B. Priestley (1894–1984), the English writer, made morale-boosting radio broadcasts during the Battle of Britain and thereafter. It has been said that only Churchill was the more popular wartime broadcaster. When calling for more social justice, Priestley demanded "more flags and less red tape, hard work and high jinks." See James Curran and Jean Seaton, "Broadcasting and the Blitz" in *Power without Responsibility: The Press, Broadcasting, and New Media in Britain* (1981, 2003), p. 135.

[107] The venerable Thompson's restaurant in Donegall Place Belfast, dating from the mid-19th century, was spacious enough to accommodate dances and large meetings; it was the venue, too, for "smoking concerts": live musical performances for men-only audiences that smoked and conversed, a Victorian tradition that lasted until after the Second World War

Scanlans. We sat with Jack and Caroline Workman and Tommy and Stella Carr. It was such a good dance so we stayed until 2 when we repaired to A.'s to change and drink tea until about 3 before heading home. I got to bed at 5 the same time as the others but had to get up again at 8 to dress the children though went back again to bed until about 10. The Scanlans are so nice and we get along terribly well together. Philip has just bought a farm and so they were delighted to see ours. Philip though Irish, acts so English! He is fussy over food, clothes and things generally whilst Kathleen is so nice and so capable and is also very particular about things! I expect L. and I notice it more when we are so much the reverse. We are going to stay with them for a weekend in about 3 weeks. I love going to Dublin and their house is so nice and so warm. ...

There have been no more warnings or scares of air-raids since those two a fortnight ago so I hope it was all a mistake. ...

Kenneth Pringle came down to shoot with L. on Saturday and he and L. went out in the afternoon in a row boat and couldn't get back! They had to start drifting across to the other shore and just by luck drifted onto an island. Philip was watching them and saw the worst of it – Kathleen and I were out for a walk never dreaming that L had gone out because the wind was the worst I've ever been out in – we were literally blown along like leaves so we didn't hear about it until Philip came along saying that he had just rung up the [Whiterock] Yacht Club to send for them and by the time we ran up the hill to look they, L. and Kenneth were already on Gabbock Island.[108] The Yacht Club boat was out collecting 2 other people so we rang up all the towns around the Lough to get another boat with no success but just then we rang up the Club again and they said that the boat had started to the rescue and we saw it go past. We watched from the top of the hill with glasses and it was awful because the big rescue boat kept disappearing behind waves itself. L. said that he and Kenneth went down into hollows of water between waves when they could only see a little circle of sky and water all around them as high as the ceiling of a room!! They were only on the island about an hour and got home just at dark so all was well but I might easily have been a widdy! Percy and Doreen arrived for tea and stayed to dinner and the excitement was terrific. ...

[108] Gabbock Island is a small island on the opposite side of Strangford Lough to Mahee, off and to the south-west of Greyabbey.

It is late so I will wind this up and mail it before another week elapses. … Write often – I'll try to do better …

Love,
Helen

10th Nov.
Mahee

Dear Ginna,

We are sitting before a roaring fire and it so snug and comfortable in here and so wild and wintry outside. There is a lovely moon shining on the water that I stopped to look at on my way in to see "the girls" who are fast asleep. The nursery looks so sweet by candlelight and with the moon shining through the dotted Swiss curtains. There are four balloons on the floor and a few decorations up that we had for Julie's birthday party on Friday. …

Now it 8.45 and they are playing the National Anthems of the Allies. They do it every Sunday just before the News, it is such good propaganda. I like the French and Czecho-Slovakian ones the best. The Czech one is so sad and now of course we have Greece too![109] We don't have J. B. Priestly [sic] talking after the News any more which is such a pity because he was wonderful.[110] Everyone here is so glad that Roosevelt got in again. It was the big news item on Wednesday and before the Election too they talked so much about it. Too bad about Mr. Chamberlain.[111] He was so unpopular ever since the Spring and the time that people here realized how lackadaisical the war preparations had been. Everybody adores Mr. Churchill.

---

[109] The Italian Army invaded Greece on 28th October. The successful Greek counter-offensive was launched on 14th November, so Helen is writing as Greece is becoming one of the Allies by default and while the Greeks are organizing their campaign of armed resistance.

[110] Despite (or because of) Priestley's popularity, Churchill instructed the BBC to cancel the broadcasts on the grounds of Priestley's left-wing opinions. It was later claimed that Churchill's cabinet had fed him negative reports.

[111] Neville Chamberlain had resigned as Prime Minister on 10th May after the Allied debacle in Norway. He remained active and was a member of Churchill's wartime cabinet. He died on 9th November, 1940.

[11th Nov.]

This is Monday now and L. has gone to his L.D.V.[112] Trudy is fisselling[113]around in the kitchen and I should ask her in to sit since we are both alone and her light is bad but I don't like her well enough. She came in on Saturday night to show me some of her embroidery work, sewing and photographs of the toys she used to design in Germany. The toys were wonderful and her embroidery is too ... She painted Julie a sweet picture for her birthday of two little girls playing in big flowers and sort of a design of islands, sea and fields behind them suggesting Mahee rather than picturing it. It is in watercolors on greaseproof paper and is really lovely – very modern in style but fresh and alive looking and very graceful. ...

This is Armistice Day and I have had the radio on all day and have heard Lincoln's Gettysburg address twice. It all comes back to me from our record and if I heard it another twice I think I could say it. They played "A Hunt in the Black Forest" today too and it took me right back home.[114] If the radio isn't on the gramophone is and G. and J. love music and listen so well. Lately it has been the records from *Pinocchio* almost exclusively.[115]

... I still like living here despite the weather. I have enough to do with the children but not too much. Going to town once a week is enough of a change and I am always glad to come back. Having people for weekends is nice and makes me glad to have the peace and quiet when they go. I don't get half so tired or half so cross looking after the kids now. It was awful when I first started but now they are fairly independent. ... I wish you would take some interior pictures of your

---

112 The Local Defence Volunteers were formed in May 1940 and their name changed to the Home Guard two months later.

113 Helen is using an Ulster Scots verb describing the rustling sound of someone fussing.

114 "A Hunt in the Black Forest" by George Voelker Jr was a popular orchestral piece first recorded by Victor Records in 1907 in Philadelphia and again in 1926. The score includes a re-creation of a hunt with birds calling and hounds giving tongue.

115 *Pinocchio* is an animated Disney film of 1940, based on the children's novel, *The Adventures of Pinocchio* (1883) by Carlo Collodi. The film score was composed by Leigh Harline with lyrics by Ned Washington. The soundtrack was independently released and the most famous song was "When You Wish upon a Star". The Turtle family saw that movie and Disney's hit movie before it, *Snow White and the Seven Dwarfs* (1937), and were much taken by both.

and Ginna's houses and of yourselves to remind me how you look – two years is such a long time to be separated – and it looks like being at least three! And some pessimists think 20! However, I feel sure that it is a matter of months before the Neutrality Law will be repealed and we can go across on American boats. ...

Roberta's brother Fred is home for 3 weeks. His hand is healing up but Roberta says that he is so quiet and when he reads he heaves tremendous sighs. Most of his squadron have been killed.

Bodo is still at home on leave. T. McConnell is stationed here now – half on sick leave – he has lumbago, insomnia, strains in his back, nerves and I don't know what all – I hope that he doesn't take it out on Rosie.

I went to a Bridge and fork luncheon at Craigavad last Tuesday and won an 8/6 book token. I raced in and bought Louis McNeice's last book called *The Last Ditch*.[116] I am so "keen" on his poetry and have got Jim Barr just as enthusiastic as I am – it grows on you so – the poetry and whenever I haven't anything else to do I read it. I sent Ginna a book of his but it will probably take a long time to get there. ...

I have missed so many good movies – *Gone with the Wind* hasn't come here yet! It is rumored that it costs too much and Belfast won't pay! When it does come I'll take a day off and go all day!

Now it is 10.30 and I have been writing this since 8! L. hasn't come home yet so I may knit a spell. I can't listen to the radio any more because I have listened all day and am listened out! ...

Nighty-night and love,

Helen

21st Nov.

Dear Ginna and Lloyd,

This is the morning after the big storm and we have just been out to survey the damage which is only one tree blown down but what a tree

---

[116] *The Last Ditch* (1940) was the first volume of MacNeice's to follow *Autumn Journal* (1939) which was critically acclaimed. *The Last Ditch*, published by Cuala Press run by Lily and Lolly Yeats, sisters of W.B. Yeats, has been regarded by critics as an exploratory rather than fulfilled volume of verse.

– a huge willow. ... It was by the duck pond if you remember it near the shore and to the left from the house as you face the sea. Of all the storms we have had and there have been many, this was the worst.[117] It was on the side and back of the house so we didn't get anything of its full force but it blew down the curtains in our room and about 4.30 I shut ours and the nursery windows and L. got up and prowled around shutting banging doors, etc. The poor Neus thought that their window would come in and kept their heads under their eiderdowns to avoid flying glass!

Now the Lough looks wintery and peaceful and there is a yacht (aground) across from our window which must have blown from its Whiterock mooring chain and all, because it is quite stationary and right side up but marooned alright. ...

We haven't heard from you for weeks. I expect a lot of mail went down on the Jarvis Bay convoy – wasn't that pathetic?[118] ...

We are going to a dance tomorrow night at Craigavad with Eddie and Eileen Bryson – to dinner with them first and I will go to town with L. in the morning so I will have to put on my face today. I can't decide what to wear, all my evening dresses being three, four and five years old – all but my bridesmaid's dress which I may break down and wear. It is sweet, simple and girlish and I have reached the age of trying to look young! ... I am listening to the programs for schools. I listen every day and learn so much. Such good people talk, famous authors, musicians, playwrights, news commentators and such. The radio has improved so, at least the Home Service. All the light music, music-hall variety and dumb stuff is on another wave-length for the Forces. Do you ever listen to the BBC North American program? They should be good.

[117] Met Office records show that there were winds of up to 82mph registered at Aldergrove (N. Ireland) on 21st November, presumably in the early hours.

[118] HMS *Jervis Bay* was a British liner converted into an armed merchant cruiser; it became a convoy escort in May 1940. On 28th October 1940 it was the sole escort for a convoy of thirty-eight ships from six nations leaving Halifax, Nova Scotia for Liverpool. On 5th November the convoy was sighted by the German pocket battleship *Admiral Scheer*. The escort engaged the attacker but was sunk after twenty minutes of fighting, with 190 crew lost and 68 surviving. A lightly armed merchant ship, SS *Beaverford,* then engaged the battleship for four hours before the merchantman was sunk with all hands lost. The hostilities allowed the convoy to scatter and all but six of the thirty-eight ships to escape. (On the night of 9th April, 1945, after heavy wartime service, *Admiral Scheer* was in harbour at Kiel when an RAF bombing raid struck; after serious damage the pocket battleship capsized.)

We had Stella and Tommy Carr for the weekend and had such a good time with them. They are living at Newcastle and Tommy is still painting but not selling any since the Blitz or even since May when things got bad. Stella hates Newcastle because is so full of old people and she and Tommy both hanker so after their arty London life so that they just exist any place else rather than live there. They knew Louis MacNiece, Auden and all of the young arty intellectuals – painters, writers and others. They are going to the dance with the Brysons too[119]...

... There were German planes over N. Ireland the other night but there were no bombs dropped. However the sirens went but we don't hear them unless we happen to be outside.

I went to a coffee party at Mrs. Duffin's Monday morning after having my tooth pulled and saw everybody.[120] It was for the Maternity Hospital and Harry McMullan was there, home for a few days. I also saw Fred who has gone back now to fly again after being shot down in flames. He is the nicest person and it makes me feel so much worse about the whole thing to know a pilot. Harry said that they have linen on their blown-out windows and that they all work in overcoats. I felt so sorry for Roberta having two men leaving for such danger at once. L. talks frequently about joining up but I think it would be silly at this stage when the country is overflowing with army anyway.

This is evening now and we are parked before the fire. A piano recital by Schubert is just starting. Lancelot is reading the new *Readers Digest*. He said that the Glendinnings had 30 trees down and everyone along the road has several and that there were lots of trees over the road and that there were windows blown in at lots of places. ...

[119] *The Northern Whig* reported the dance (and the ladies' outfits, including Mrs Lancelot Turtle's) on 23rd November: it was held in the Royal Belfast Golf Club and was in aid of the Third Searchlight Regiment Royal Artillery Comforts Fund. Comfort funds provided gramophones, records, wireless sets, sports kits, games and pastimes for often isolated and lonely soldiers.

[120] Mrs Iva Duffin was married to Captain S.B. Duffin. They lived in Danesfort House, Belfast which had been built in 1864, as Clanwilliam House, for Samuel Barbour of the linen dynasty. It has been described as "one of the finest High-Victorian mansions in Ireland" (quoted in "Danesfort House", Lord Belmont in Northern Ireland website). It passed into the possession of the Duffins in 1883 after a Barbour daughter married Charles Duffin. In the 1940s it was sold to the tobacco giant, Gallaher Ltd, who later sold it to the Electricity Board for Northern Ireland. It is now the home of the United States Consul-General in Belfast. Captain Duffin moved to Rathmoyle House, an Edwardian country house on 120 acres in Helen's Bay, Co. Down.

People generally seem to me to be depressed about the length of the war through no one has any fears as to the outcome. Stella's father and sisters are still in London sleeping on their mattresses on the kitchen floor. A [news?] letter L. takes says that Hitler is trying for peace before Christmas by getting practically all the countries of Europe to accept his new order. ... two hopeful radio speakers thought that Russia might back Turkey against Germany in which event the jig would be up for Hitler. People generally say that America is doing all that she can but I think she could *give* the planes and guns instead of selling them.

Your chairmanship in the Red Cross sounds so important and makes my secluded life seem so selfish. I never do anything for anybody and it weighs on me sometimes. Living here it is hard to do much but I should do something – maybe we'll have some refugees one of these day and then my hands will be full. They aren't a bit full now because although I am busy off and on all day with Gay and Julie I have lots of time for sitting. I just counted up that we have had 36 house-guests since May! I still have Mr. Randolph the American Consul on my conscience so we must have him soon. ...

Our telephone is broken now since the storm and I hope they get it fixed soon because we want to go to Dublin to visit the Scanlans next weekend and I shouldn't like them to be cut off. I love going to Dublin better than anything and I am looking forward to the outing tremendously because I have only been away from the children one night since Easter and altogether not more than 8 days away from Gay since I came home from America 3 years ago! ...

I have just been listening to a propaganda play by Michael Arlen – it was good and only revealed its plot at the end and now it is nearly News time again.[121]

When I think it is two years today since I have clapped eyes on you it first seems impossible and next saddens me considerably. Here is Julie

[121] The play, *A Nightingale Sang in Berkeley Square*, was a Home Service dramatization of the story of the same name by Michael Arlen (1895–1956), born Dikran Kouyoumjian, the Armenian novelist, playwright and short storywriter. Arlen lived and worked in England until, shortly after the time the adaptation was broadcast, his loyalty to England was questioned while he was Civil Defence Public Relations Officer for East Midlands, and he left the country. The story was published in the collection *These Charming People* (1923, 1937). The adaptation was produced by Val Gielgud (brother of Sir John), a pioneer of radio drama. Eric Maschwitz, who wrote the words to the famous popular song with the story's title, confessed the title was "stolen" from Arlen's story.

a big girl to prove that the time has elapsed since you saw her a big-handed, big-footed, big-eyed ugly baby and so much has happened – your marriage, the war and general chaos. It will be so interesting when we finally do get together – I hope we won't be old crones! If the war is over by Christmas I will be on my way on the 26th but I think that if it isn't over a year from now it will be five or ten years!!! What do you think? I always think of G. and J. as being you and me over again although there lots of divergences in Gay – I'm sure I never was the problem she is but then she isn't so bad now and is nothing but jealous of Julie and very strong-willed about once a month or less so. ...

This letter is getting too dull so g'bye for now –

Love,
Helen

1st Dec.
Mahee

Dear Ginna and Lloyd,

... My heart isn't in my work with the kids any more because I have gone stale and I am tired of looking after them so I will renew my strength and vigor in Dublin. ...

The thing is that I have had too long a siege with the kids and too undiluted a life. I like looking after them but I need more outings and they are getting too dependent on me – to put it boldly I am ready to scream and yell. ...

There is no black-out in Dublin and no war atmosphere and no trouble yet so this is the time to go all-right.

[2nd Dec.]

Now it is Monday night and I'm not a bit frustrated or tired and am even pleasant and chatty to the maids – all because I spent a day in town! What's more I am going in again tomorrow and again the next day – both days with the kids it's true but it will be a change again. I only know when I go away from here how much I like it here.

Gus Turtle, with whom the story began

The photograph of Lancelot in RNVR uniform which he sent to Helen at Smith College in 1930

Mrs Ramsey and Ginna, Helen's mother and sister, in Denver

The cottage at Mahee Island, Strangford Lough

Helen with Lee (b. 1935–d.1936)

ABOVE: Frank Egginton, Natalie Starr (Helen's friend from Smith College), Helen and their tutor, the American novelist Mary Ellen Chase, mid-1930s

LEFT: Louis MacNeice

Herbert and
Catherine Synge Morawetz

Lavens Mackie, his wife Mucki and daughter Anita, and the Japanese ornithologist, Masauji Hachisuka

BACK ROW: Fred Gardiner, Roberta (Gardiner) McMullan, Jack Workman, Caroline Workman, Helen
FRONT ROW: Caroline Workman jnr., Peter McMullan, Jock Workman, Janet Webb, Julie and Gay

Collecting gulls' eggs at Mahee
FROM LEFT: Peter, Max, George and Charlotte Browne, Alan Smiles, Helen, Gay, Julie
and Belle Middleton

LEFT: Elaine and Jack
Andrews, with Helen,
and children Tom
Andrews, school friend
of Heather Andrews,
Heather, Gay and Julie

BELOW: Hay making at
Mahee, 1940
Helen, Alan Smiles, Julie,
Gay and Belle Middleton

Helen with Tom and Stella Carr, with Frank Egginton (hatless) at Mahee

Gay and Julie with Lancelot heading to Whiterock for tea in a trap

Sans Souci Park, Belfast
Arabella Freeman, Helen, Mrs Gus Turtle (Auntie), Gordon Freeman, Julie, Gay
and Mary Lee

88 Belmont Road, Belfast

Gay, Julie and Mary Lee with Ginna,
34 Malone Park, Belfast

Tom Carr portraits of Helen and
Helen with the three girls, Gay, Julie
and Mary Lee

T. Carr

I started Christmas shopping today and will continue tomorrow – in fact I will finish I should think. The toys are so few this year and so pathetic – Woolworths has hardly any. There isn't a tricycle in town, no Christmas tree decorations, no unbreakable tea sets and about one of everything you see. I'm perfectly sure that in a week there won't be a decent toy left in town. ...

I am so glad that you liked *Autumn Journal*. I will send you some more MacNeice for Christmas. I sent it because I liked it so well not for any emotional or mental reason. You always were one to find obscure meanings like the time you got so screw ball about Victor MacLaglan in *The Informer* and read some subtle point in his acting – do you remember?[122] I forget what it was but you were clear off all right. Louis MacNeice is in America now lecturing at Harvard – his son is parked in a country house in Ireland – Tommy and Stella know his ex-girl-friend and her husband (!!!) quite well and know Louis slightly and didn't think much of him and thought that the girl-friend was the limit! She is the one he talks about in *Autumn Journal* and she is now separated from her husband and she was wild when *A.J.* came out because he told how he fell out of love with her "dear against my judgment".[123] I have all his poetry books and the travel book, *I Crossed the Minch* and a personal essay called *Modern Poetry*. *A[utumn] Journal* got a very good write-up in *The New Yorker* during the summer. Louis gave a talk to the D.R.C. last winter and I liked him so well and I think his poetry is by far the best modern poetry I have read – As you said about Mrs. Lindbergh's book "it is right up my alley". As you can see I am completely sold on MacNeice and have never been so enthusiastic about anybody before. ... In one poem on Belfast describing the shops ... "harsh attempts at buyable beauty" – doesn't that hit off the lampshades to a T.?[124]

[122] *The Informer* (1935), an adaptation of Liam O'Flaherty's novel, was set during the Irish War of Independence and was directed by John Ford.

[123] Louis MacNeice in January 1940 left for the United States to take up a post at Cornell University (not Harvard), leaving his son Daniel in Ireland. In 1937 he had begun an affair with Nancy Coldstream who like her husband Bill was a painter. (She illustrated *I Crossed the Minch*.) The affair is one of the subjects of *Autumn Journal* (1939) in which he bids her adieu: "Thank you my dear – dear against my judgement". He resigned from Cornell and returned to London at the end of 1940.

[124] In one stanza of his poem "Belfast", MacNeice writes: "And in the marble stores rubber gloves like polyps/Cluster; celluloid, painted ware, glaring/Metal patents, parchment lampshades, harsh/Attempts at buyable beauty".

L. is out drilling tonight. It is so nice to leave town as the black-out and fog settle down and the trip seems nothing now and is so pretty. It is dark now in the morning until 9 and we have breakfast by firelight and candlelight and about 9.15 the sun rises opposite our window – a ball of fire except for about every other day when it slides up behind the clouds and sneaks out – like about noon. There hasn't been any real cold weather yet but today was raw as only Belfast can be. We both notice how much milder it is here than in town and the thick walls keep it much warmer than the thin Belmont Road walls sure did . ...

[4th Dec.]

Yesterday Gay, Julie and I went up with L. and a trailer-load of sheep before it was daylight meaning 9 o'clock but is a winter dawn all right and such a problem to dress for the day before dawn! If I put on my new high hat I feel such a fool and yet by afternoon I wish I had it so I just wear sport clothes to solve the situation. L. was so long at the market that we got out and luckily there was a public playground right there so G. and J. had the time of their young lives swinging, teeter tottering [see-sawing], riding on a communal rocking horse and a wonderful merry-go-round. It was just like when we were allowed to stop at Washington Park when we were little except that they had it all to themselves and that it was in the heart of the slums with wet cement instead of gravel underfoot and Gay fell twice (in her best coat) and got *black* dirty because the soot had made the puddles like ink. ...

Town depressed me so yesterday – and everyone agrees that we are well out of it. The openness of view here in all directions makes me nearly claustrophobic when I am in Belfast and it never was what you'd call enticing anyway – especially in December. ...

Merry Christmas!

And love,
Helen

11th Dec.
The Gables, Rathgar, Dublin.

Dear Mother,

Here I am in the midst of my holiday and having such a good time...

This house is so warm and bright and pretty that it reminds me of an American house and the atmosphere of Dublin is so un-British that it nearly feels like America too. And of course to see the lights and never to see any sign of war is heavenly after the dark, grim war-like North. Today is a lovely sunny day, but this whole week has been cold and rainy and I am glad to be away from Mahee.

I have seen three movies, been dancing, out to lunch, played bridge and at a dinner party so you can see that life is a giddy round and that I am having a real rest and change.

This house runs on oiled wheels because Kathleen is terribly efficient, has two super maids and a trained children's nurse so it is all easy and quiet and impressive. We have such good food so nicely served. Philip is very fussy about his food and his house and so it is exceptionally good.

[12th Dec.]

Now it is Thursday... The News just announced the death of Lord Lothian which is such a pity just at this time.[125] ...

On Sunday night Philip and Kathleen had to go out to dinner so I went to dinner with Mrs. Turtle who is staying at the Salt Hill Hotel about 8 miles out in a suburb. She had the funniest man to dinner – a real Dublin character and as crazy as a loon and he was a baronet too named Sir Valentine Grace.[126] He gave us dramatic readings in the gay

[125] Philip Kerr, 11th Marquess of Lothian (b. 1882) had been Private Secretary to Lloyd George and had helped draft the Treaty of Versailles of 1919 which he later came to regard as too harsh on Germany. Although he favoured appeasement of Germany in the 1930s, Lothian as British Ambassador to the United States from 1939 until he died was successful in his efforts to secure American support for Britain at war.

[126] Sir Valentine Grace (1877–1945) of Boley, Monkstown, 5th baronet, Captain, 4th Batt. Leinster Regt. On the website Dún Laoghaire (http://dunlaoghairecountty.ie) is recounted an urban legend involving a ghostly man's voice heard at night in 1977 singing "Danny Boy" and "Old Man River" among the houses of Rory O'Connor Park in Monkstown. Locals believed it was the voice of the baronet who had died some thirty years before. It was said he had ordered that no tree on his estate be harmed yet a large tree had been felled, awakening the baronet's shade. *Cont'd overleaf:*

ninety style and was just on his feet for the third time (in his shirt sleeves because his first two efforts had made him so hot) to give us his Wedding speech at one of his daughter's weddings when someone else came into the room. ...

Now there is an Irish jig on and it is real gay. We went to Bridget's and Maureen's dancing class yesterday and it was such fun – in the drawing room of such a pretty house in Foxrock, the fashionable suburb and such cute looking little girls and such a glamorous teacher in a red wool dress with a pleated skirt and red satin slippers. She was so graceful and all the kids were so clumsy. Last night we went to the Abbey Theatre to see a play about a nun who came to live with an ordinary family and changed them all. The acting was good but the play was poor[127] but the people were interesting in the audience – very Irish and bohemian looking. ...

I hate to go back to the blackout and war atmosphere but Christmas is less than two weeks away and that will be an excitement. ...

It is so funny here to see the newsreels – no mention of war and all pictures of America and Australia. The censorship is so strict in their effort to remain neutral and De Valera made such a good speech yesterday in reply to the intense British press attack on Eire (Eire rhymes with Sara) regarding the ports. A few people here think that Eire should join England but the I.R.A. is so troublesome and hate the English so that there would be terrible "troubles" both if England seized the ports and if Ireland gave them.

Philip is so Irish, that is nationalist in his point of view and thinks Eire is perfectly right not to help England. There are a few brick shelters in the streets and Philip helps the Red Cross to meet the refugees from England. Every ship load brings them in – so far only people with Irish

---

[126] *Cont'd*: One commenter identifies Grace as an actor and cites his appearance on September 9th 1929 at the Empire in Belfast in *General John Regan*, a 1913 comedy by George Birmingham. (When this play was staged in Westport, Co. Mayo, it provoked a notorious riot.) Another cites the 1920 British silent drama *Alwyn*, based on Theodore Watts-Dunton's novel of the same title and in which Valentine Grace is listed among the cast.

[127] Yet *Strange Guest* by the Irish novelist and playwright Francis Stuart was regarded as a surprise success when it played in the Abbey Theatre in December 1940; it was revived at the same theatre in 1946. By 1940, Stuart (1902–2000), who married Maud Gonne's daughter Iseult, had left for Germany to teach at Berlin University. He was later accused of having Nazi sympathies. The cast in 1940 included Ria Mooney and F.J. McCormick, well-known Irish actors, and the set designer was Anne Yeats, daughter of the poet.

connections or relations. One woman they met after the Coventry bombing was carrying a dead baby – she had seen her other 3 children blown to bits and was trying to keep this one safe and wouldn't let it go – she is now in the insane asylum and was cuckoo then when they met her – didn't know anything about anything.[128]

Now I am up in my bedroom – with a radiator behind this dressing table. Kathleen went to bed at 10 and Philip and I read until about 10.30 and then talked – he is a socialist and a pacifist and says he believes in anarchy as a form of government. He knows his history all right but is dead against England and all for Eire. ...

I hope this reaches you by Christmas and I send all best wishes for Christmas and the New Year. I think so much about home and wish and hope that my children can be as well brought up and have as happy a home life as we had. Do you remember how we used to sit under the Christmas tree in the hall and chew on those strings of candy beads? Have you still got the gold angel for the top of the tree? Even if we aren't together in person we can be at Christmas spiritually so like Tiny Tim said "God bless you all everyone".

Love and special Christmas kisses from Helen, Lancelot Gay and little tiny Zoo.

16th Dec
Mahee

Dear Mother,

It is the darkest week of the year and so gloomy in the mornings – it doesn't get light until after nine o'clock and now at nearly noon it is none too bright. However it isn't cold and it isn't raining which is something. ...

The North [of Ireland] couldn't have looked blacker and grimmer when I came home on Friday – full of soldiers, gloom and rain. Lancelot met me and then I did a little shopping and came down here alone because he had to go to a Home Guard meeting in Comber at 6 o'clock. Having been away from here made me see it with fresh eyes

---

[128] The most destructive bombing raid on Coventry carried out by the Luftwaffe was on the evening of 14th November.

and it looked terrible – the mud, the slop, the rain and the isolation all hit me forcibly and after the Scanlan's very smooth and luxurious house. The cottage looked so bare and bleak with no curtains or carpets to dress it up and not a flower! I always find that the little extra touches that I put on – just where the candles are, flowers, etc. are gone when I come home and it lacks an inviting, lived-in looked. ...

It was consoling to be here when the News announced yesterday morning that unidentified planes had been over Northern Ireland and that the anti-aircraft guns had been in action – we didn't hear anything but the Town people always have to decide when the siren goes whether to get their children up and go to a shelter – or whether to stay in bed. It would just make you wonder. No bombs were dropped. There is lots of speculation as to why we have escaped. Belfast is only supposed to have 1% of the industrial output of the British Isles so on that score it isn't very important.[129] Most people think that the Germans regard all Ireland as Eire or even if they don't, they are afraid of prejudicing southern Irish and American opinion if they attack N. Ireland. Anyway so far we have been lucky and can't be thankful enough. Everyone feels so cheered about the defeats the Italians are getting in Egypt and Libya.[130]

After I had seen the children on Friday I had to go back to Comber to get Lancelot. Of course it was raining *and* blowing *and* as dark as

---

[129] Although Belfast's industrial output was but a fraction of UK input, German intelligence as the war developed may have warned Hitler not to underestimate Belfast's importance and if so, the warning was justified. By 1945 Belfast shipyards had manufactured 140 warships and 123 merchant ships, and repaired or converted thousands more. Short & Harland produced 1200 Stirling bombers and 125 Sunderland Flying Boats. Munitions factories (including Mackies) produced 75 million shells while linen factories unrolled 200 million yards of cloth for the armed services. See "Northern Ireland and World War II" on the website Irish History Live: School of History and Anthropology, Queen's University Belfast. In addition, Harland & Wolff manufactured 10,000 field guns and 550 tanks while Sirocco Works made grenades, gun-mountings and radar equipment: see Jonathan Bardon, *Belfast: An Illustrated History*, pp. 235, 242–43.

[130] Italy declared war against Britain and France in June 1940. Mussolini's main objectives were to secure a seat at the eventual peace conference and to annex British and French colonial territories in North Africa. Italy invaded Egypt from Libya in mid-September but encountered fierce resistance from a numerically inferior British force. On 8th December an organized counter-offensive was launched and British, Indian and Australian soldiers drove the Italians out of Egypt back deep into Libya, taking tens of thousands of prisoners. Italian forces experienced fierce setbacks on 9th, 11th and 16th December, the day Helen was writing her letter.

pitch *and* the radiator cover of the Ford kept blowing loose and waving in front of the windshield. And I had to get out about four times in the dark and the rain and the wind to fix it and I could have screamed. I finally anchored it with a hairpin and calmed down by sitting in Comber square for ten or fifteen minutes thinking how awful the war is and how unfortunate the black-out is. It is so depressing apart from being so dangerous. Jack Andrews and L. finally turned up and Jack asked us up for supper. We arrived before Jack who had to go say goodbye to a cousin who was leaving for Egypt and Elaine wasn't too overcome when we arrived announcing that we had come to supper. …

Jack was telling us about his father's trip to London to see the King and Mr. Churchill and to present his credentials or whatever he had to do now that he is Prime Minister.[131] Jack said that his father said that the King was wonderful – so friendly and informal and nice – sitting alone in a small room in Buckingham Palace. The King said – "Come in Mr. Andrews, and tell me about your people – How are they? Etc." After about ten minutes Mr. A said: "Well, I suppose I'd better be going" and the King said "Not at all. You've come all this way to see me and I want to talk to you "so Mr. A. stayed another ten minutes and said again "Well I'd better go now" and again the King kept him for another ten. Mr. A. went to dinner with Mr. Churchill who was on the crest of the wave over the victories in Egypt and all during the meal reports kept coming in and he, Mr. C. was bouncing around like a schoolboy. …

I can't work up any enthusiasm about Christmas this year – nor can anybody. Hardly anybody is sending cards and no grownups are giving presents to each other. Gay is so excited about it because she can remember last year. When it comes close to the time I will probably be excited but so far it has left me cold. …

Must go so g'bye and love,
Helen

---

[131] John Miller Andrews (1871–1956) became Prime Minister on the death of Lord Craigavon (James Craig, hero of Ulster's resistance to Home Rule) on 24th November. Andrews had been a Northern Ireland M.P. since 1921, from the inception of the Northern Ireland state. His younger brother was Thomas, of *Titanic* fame. His son Jack (later Sir John Lawson) Andrews succeeded his father as M.P. for Mid-Down in 1953.

26th Dec.
Mahee

Dear Ginna and Lloyd,

There is the after-Christmas lull in the house as well as generally and it is evening and we are blacked in by the fire. L. is reading a play by Sean O'Casey that Jim Barr gave me for Christmas. Gay and Julie are in bed and we are going to have bacon and eggs for supper – eggs are going down in price now so we can eat them again without thinking "Here goes fourpence". The room is all decorated with holly and red candles and we have a Christmas tree with real candles on it by the fireplace on the window side. We have a holly wreath on the front door[132] and we have a new French door onto the porch. There is a red bow on the bathroom curtain rod and holly here, there, and everywhere. The mantelpiece is full of Christmas cards though we didn't get as many as usual and Gay's and Julie's mantelpiece is full too – they got about eighteen of their own – so popular! ...

[Jan. 1941]

Gay and Julie had a wonderful Christmas Gay was so excited and understood all about Santa Claus and couldn't hear enough about him. Zoo only understood indirectly but she takes in a lot and knew who came and who brought toys and what he looks like. ...

Julie, who didn't sleep a wink this morning is supposed to be sleeping in the guest-room but she is talking instead. John [Carr] left to go home to lunch. He is back here after the second frustrated attempt to get to the west Indies – Trinidad – he is going with the Fleet Air Arm and the second time he came home was Christmas eve after his ship had been bombed in the Liverpool blitzkrieg – He was under fire all night and now the ship is being repaired. He doesn't want to go a bit because he thinks that it too far from everything and the climate is too hot and too damp most of the time.[133] ...

Bodo was home for 10 days at Christmas and now he and Edith are in Scotland for 3 weeks before he goes off again. A young boy 21 whose mother I know, was blown up at sea on Boxing day – in made me feel

---

[132] A North American custom not an Irish one (until recently).
[133] See the letter of 15th February 1941 for what became of Lt John Carr.

so sad. He was their only son and their daughter is evacuated to Canada. However so far we only know about three people who have been killed. I pore morbidly over the death notices in *The Times* to see who has been killed "by enemy action" and occasionally I see a whole family wiped out, but surprisingly seldom – but, of course, not many people can afford death notices in *The Times*. I never read the newspapers because we hear it all on the radio and even then my mind wanders during most of the news.

Everyone is cheered up over the Italian flop in Greece and Egypt but everyone expects invasion "in the spring" which means from February on. The mere thought of it gives me chills and fever because I know how scared I would be. Everyone is saying that Hitler will probably do his worst to crush England this year – and the opinion on gas is divided between those who think it will come with the total war of the invasion and those who think that Hitler will only use gas if he sees that it is a question of one last fierce fling or failure. As long as we live here gas personally doesn't worry me, but I certainly wish this year were over. Not that I live in steady dread but I just feel that things are going to be a lot worse before they get better. I hardly ever think about the war *really* even when talking about it because if you realize it, it is hard to bear.

We danced the New Year in at Randalstown at an awful Red Cross dance that was so packed you could scarcely move. It was solid with Army from Generals down to the lowest soldiers and they were having the time of their lives. We went with Patrick and Rosemary and joined a huge and scattered party which never got organized. I didn't enjoy it but I was laid out with pains in my tummy and luckily it wasn't a good dance from my point of view so I didn't mind. ... We are going to another dance at Craigavad on Friday with Nancy and Dunsmuir Mitchell – Charlie is in Manchester hating every minute of it bombs or no bombs. He told Bodo that it was bad enough to live there but, By Gad, it was an insult to be bombed there! The Comber Hunt Ball is on the 15th and the Home Guard whist drive *and* dance (!!!) is on the 17th so you can see how giddy we are. I am beginning to think I had better get a new dress – not having had one since my bridesmaid's dress for nigh on to 3 years. Everyone wears sleeves at dances these days to match the dinner jackets of the non-uniformed men and I haven't got one...

[6 Jan.?]

Harry ... and Churchill are more than ever running the war and Harry lives in Berkeley Square now and is too, too utterly utter, to be amusing the way he used to be. ...

We have been reading *The Letters of Julian Bell* edited by his brother and I think you would like them. Julian was killed in 1937 in the Spanish war and was a son of Clive and Vanessa Bell and a nephew of Virginia Wolf (sic) – [he] called T.S. Eliot Tommy and knew everyone important and arty. There are some provocative open letters on different subjects too.[134] ...

What is the reaction to Lord Halifax as ambassador? Everyone was so exercised over it here and the general impression is that Roosevelt indicated that Lord H. would be O.K. although people here feel that he is too remote and above things but they think that his sincerity and religion will go down well in the middle west![135] Next to Churchill whom everyone idolizes Roosevelt is second and his fireside talk last Sunday was as eagerly anticipated and as fully reported here – or more so, than if it had been Churchill.[136] Nobody wants men from America but they do want everything else free and quickly and I think everything should be rushed over here p.d.q. [pretty damned quick] in American boats if need be. I will send you a 6 months subscription to the *New Statesman* which is offering a cheap subscription to get the British point of view around the world. It is a socialist weekly and we read it with great interest – they don't mince matters and usually have a grudge about something, but you'll see.

[134] Julian Bell's younger brother Quentin edited Julian Bell, *Essays, Poems and Letters* in 1908. Bell (1908–1937), though a pacifist, nevertheless decided upon active support for the Republican cause in the Spanish Civil War. He became an ambulance driver and was killed by a bomb at the Battle of Brunete.

[135] Lord Halifax was appointed to succeed Lord Lothian as British Ambassador to the United States. He had been Viceroy of India (1926–1931) and Foreign Secretary (1938–1940) during which time he was regarded (as was Lord Lothian) as an appeaser of Germany. He was allowed to remain prominent to encourage the notion of a Great Britain united against Hitler. The fact that he was 6'5" and aristocratic in bearing reinforced the impression of remoteness.

[136] This fireside chat of Roosevelt's was broadcast on Sunday, 29th December 1940. (Helen's reference to "last Sunday" rather than "yesterday", and the reference to Roosevelt's State of the Union below, suggests that she is writing her letter on Monday 6th January.) In his chat, Roosevelt said: "We have furnished the British great material support and we will furnish far more in the future".

It is hard for me to realize your married life your Red Cross work, music lessons and all and if you envy our "foreign household" I am full of envy for your American one and try to bring up my children as nearly as possible "the American way" – or the way we were "brung" up – instead of the starched nanny, nursery meals etc of old England. ...

I was just startled tonight to realize that Daddy has been dead for 5 years. I keep thinking of it as only one or two. I still am always in America in my dreams in our house even if the people are people from here that I am dreaming about and every now and then I have a really nostalgic nightmare of suppressed homesickness when I am just there for a day or two and have to come back or something. ...

The News was about Roosevelt's message to Congress[137], Bardia[138], Amy Johnson's disappearance[139] and a talk by Duff Cooper, the Minister of Information, about the victory over the Italians. The News lasted over ½ hour – usually it is about 15 minutes. ...

Oranges, apples and bananas are getting scarce – eating apples (good ones) are 35c. a pound. Oranges are about 5c. each and I don't think there are any bananas. There is also a shortage of hairpins. After buying in supplies of things during the summer I have used them – hairpins for one and am caught with about 4 and no Bobby pins!

Are you pole-axed? I am, so I will wait and add some more and mail this on Wednesday. I think I have a 2/6d stamp left so I will give this its due and send it on the Clipper. It makes me wild to think that your Christmas presents to us may be sunk and full of salt water now and the rag dolls for Gay and Zooksie. ... I forgot to make any New Years

---

[137] In his annual State of the Union message (6th January), FDR acknowledged fully the threat to world democracy from the tyranny of the Axis Powers. His message effectively renounced isolationism: "We must always be wary of those who with sounding brass and tinkling cymbal preach the 'ism' of appeasement." He pledged support to the Allies and to honour this the U.S. would step up its production of armaments.

[138] The Battle of Bardia in Libya was an episode in the Allied counter-offensive in North Africa. The Australian 6th Division played a major role in the defeat of the Italians on 3rd–5th January.

[139] Amy Johnson (b. 1903) was a pioneer English flyer who was the first woman to fly solo from Britain to Australia and also set records in flights from Britain to Moscow, Britain to South Africa, Britain to India. She joined the Air Transport Auxiliary in 1940. On 5th January 1941 she was forced to bail out over the Thames Estuary and in bad weather disappeared despite a rescue attempt by a ship whose commander dived into the water to save her and drowned. Her body was never found. It was claimed in some quarters that her plane had been shot down by friendly fire.

Resolutions – I should give up smoking but I can't work myself up to the high resolve required to make it tolerable. In case my mind fails me tomorrow goodnight now and love and a Happy New Year to you and Lloyd – my new in-law that I've never seen as such – and would so love to meet! *La vie* it seems to have been *comme ça* and for us so far downright agreeable.

Helen

1941

"Give us the tools, and we will finish
 the job"

SS Almeda Star is torpedoed, navy friend
 killed

Everyday changes wrought by the war

Incendiaries, bombs and land-mines
 dropped on Belfast

Fashion, food and gasbags in Dublin

"Churchill joins FDR for Washington Yule"

12th Jan.
Mahee

Dear Mother,

… Lancelot has a new job starting tomorrow and he has been studying it off and on since Friday afternoon when he got it and he only heard about it for the first time on Thursday. The job is in connection with the salvaging of stored food after air-raid damage and L's job is to arrange storage for it beforehand so that everything will go smoothly in moving it after the blitz. It is a Government job but not an army job although he will deal with army, police, A.R.P. etc. in making arrangements for the safe removal of the stores. L. was recommended for the job by Jack and Lavens Mackie who were asked by the food officer of Belfast if they knew of anyone fit for the job. It doesn't mean that L. will have to be out in the blitz but it does mean that the morning after his organization will have to be promptly put into action to avoid waste and stealing and being ruined by rain if exposed etc. He is clear wild about taking on the job and decided to do it with the minimum of encouragement from Jim Barr and only middling support from me. However, it is definitely a war job and a very important one and will settle the question of his joining anything else – it will also be for the duration and in Belfast so that is all in its favor also a salary of £500 a year which is probably lots more than could be made at stock-broking these days. On the other hand, it will be longer hours, harder work, a worrying responsibility and may mean moving to town, the last we hope to avoid if possible. In any case Gay, Julie and I will stay here because town isn't likely to be healthy this year and anyway there are no houses to be had at all what with the town packed with military and their wives and families. I told you didn't I, that there are 30 air force men in our old house? Anyway we will know more about it tomorrow when he goes to the new office and sees what's what. …

Now we have just had our usual Sunday night supper – cold roast beef and cauliflower salad. L. is studying again and we will have to forego our usual Sunday night occupation of listening to "Question

Time" from Dublin.[1] It is at 8.15 for ¾ hour and is always so good. The anthems of the Allies are always played at 8.45 in the BBC Home Service and I like the Greek and French ones best. The beginning of the Czecho-slovakian one always makes me feel so sad. There is a shortage now of dry batteries for radios and it will be a calamity if we can't get them soon. The meat ration is now 26c a week per person. So far we aren't rationed in meat at all except for kinds – sometimes no lamb, usually no liver etc. but we can get any amount any time. We and other people with cows are the only people who ever have cream because it is against the law to sell it. Hairpins are scarce, so are ribbons. I must have another good day shopping soon to buy things we need before they are all gone. We have been asked not to buy cheese unless we need it – that is unless we are miners or working men who really eat it for food and not just as an extra. Bacon is due to get scarce next winter because there is no feeding stuff for pigs. We are going to get a few hens soon – they will be my war work!

When L. came home on Thursday night and asked me how I would like to move back to town I got completely depressed at the thought of it which shows how much I like living here. It isn't every town but just Belfast which has no appeal for me whatsoever. There are no houses I like and no districts I like, not even the Malone Road which is the best but not nice. Some of the days lately here have been a dream – so calm and misty and the water looks so pretty and the sunrises and sunsets are a joy. ... But apart from the scenery it is the freedom I like – doing what I want any time I want and not bothered by people whom I don't care especially for but haven't the courage to say "No" to. The children are such good company and make me laugh so much and I like listening to the radio and generally I like being alone – I think I take after Daddy that way. ...

So far only the pinnies and bedroom slippers have come and from all reports the other things must be sunk. It makes me wild to think of rag dolls and presents for me and my children swimming around in the bottom of the sea but even at worst, what are presents compared to people but is only when your own things go that you get so cross. . . . It was announced in the papers that most of the November mail from

---

[1] *Question Time* was a popular quiz programme on Radió Éireann (which Radio Athlone had become in 1937).

America had sunk but you probably have had the dates announced too and can check up on it.

Gay is so crazy about Pinocchio ... Tonight just before she went to bed she was cutting things out of a magazine on the window-seat and talking away to a bull-dog (picture that she was cutting out) along with declarations of affection – that he was the nicest bull-dog she ever saw and so on. She said "and if you're unselfish some day you'll be a real bull-dog"! – all directly from the record of Pinocchio where the fairy touches him with her wand. ... She is always imagining things ... Belle told me that the other night when she was out of the room for a minute with Julie she went back to find Gay crying and when Belle asked her what was wrong she said "A big rat came out and hit me with a big stick"[2]...

There have been several air-raid warnings in Belfast lately but no one takes any notice – so far they have only been reconnaissance planes or taking photographs or goodness knows what. Everyone is prepared for Belfast's turn to have the blitz and can't understand why we have escaped.

[13th Jan.]

Now it is nearly midnight on Monday night. L. had to go out to a Home Guard rally in Comber at 11.30 and he may be out all night! That is the worst. He read about his new job all evening and I read *The New Yorker*, *The New Statesman* and 2 sorts of news letters we take on *The Situation*. Both news reports are convinced that Hitler will do or die against these Islands this year probably this spring. I must say I don't relish the prospect. The invasion talk is heard on all sides again – *The New Statesman* says February and tonight I read that the middle of January is rumoured which means the day after tomorrow! However, we've had these scares before and lived through it and meantime life goes on. There was no meat today in Comber or Newtownards and the butchers shops just closed. It is a hold-up preliminary to our being really rationed. Our household will get 5/10d. worth per week – about $1.40 and we'll take what we get and like it.

---

[2] Belle Middleton was the Turtles' wartime nanny; her sister Aggie, father Johnny and his wife, feature in the letters as trusted employed helpers at Mahee.

We can always shoot game and rabbits here and can fish so we are better off than most and we have vegetables planted as far as the eye can see! ...

... I shopped in town today and went to see the beginning of *The Great Dictator*; it is so good – I saw the middle and end last week. It is here for two weeks at two movies for propaganda purposes as much as for anything else. It is banned in Eire but special trains are being run North for people to come to see it![3]

... The Glendinnings are having 60 men billeted on them in their field right beside the house and they are wild but can't do anything. ...

Goodnight and love and kisses from us all.

Helen

21st Jan.
Mahee

Dear Mother,

Lancelot is home again having spent two nights at the Pringles because the roads weren't available for easy motoring. Today after a night of rain you can get through easily and although the snow has disappeared here because it is by the sea, there are still drifts piled at the sides of the roads. ...

The radio was a great boon to my five snowed-in days because there are lots of good programs especially for schools and for children – mine of course too young but I enjoy them when I have peace to listen. ... We listened to Roosevelt's inaugural address and later on in the evening there was such a good play by Allistaire [sic] Cooke on "The Office of President" giving highlights on other presidential bitternesses and troubles.[4] The English talks to schools are so good – given by good

---

[3] *The Great Dictator* (1940) was a serio-comic political satire written and directed by Charlie Chaplin and starring him as an Adolf Hitler parody and a persecuted Jewish barber. The fact that the film was banned in the Irish Republic while the authorities allowed trains to ferry picturegoers across the border to watch it typifies the split-mindedness of the southern Irish towards the War (the "Emergency" in their phrase).

[4] The Inauguration was broadcast by the BBC from Washington DC on the late afternoon of Monday, 20thJanuary. In the *Radio Times*, perhaps in a spirit of hopeful ingratiation given the war situation, the United States is described as "the world's greatest democracy". *Cont'd*

writers and London, Oxford and Cambridge professors. The music ones are also wonderful and the history ones are always plays very vividly presented. They are 20 minutes long each – 3 subjects from 11–12 and three from 2–3 every week day. I always try to listen to ones that interest me from 11–12 but from 2–3 I am usually hamstrung with the children. ...

[23rd Jan.]

... We have about 5 bunches of snowdrops in bloom and all the daffodils are sprouting so Spring is coming. I can hardly wait for it after this snow and slush and rain and cold. There are compensations though – for instance the divine dawn this morning. The sea was so calm and reflected the sky so perfectly that you would have sworn it was all sky and when the sun did come it was a blood red ball with a path across the water right to our gate. ...

Everyone from Churchill down, thinks that this year is going to decide things so if we live through this we will be O.K. I hope. The News is now on – mostly about the Italians in Africa because Tobruk has just fallen.[5]...

Gay's imagination is so terrific ... today she was looking at the moon and said that it, the moon, told her that it was coming to stay with us in the Summer. ...

Nighty-night and love,

Helen

---

[4] *Cont'd:* The cruciality of Roosevelt to the United States' decision to enter the war or stay neutral was presumably behind the broadcasting at 9.25pm of Cooke's 45-minute documentary drama *The Office of President: The Story of the First Citizen of the U.S.A.*

[5] The significant Libyan port of Tobruk fell to the Allies on 22nd January 1941. The Australian Army played a distinguished role in Operation Compass during the North African campaign.

7th Feb.
Mahee

Dear Ginna and Lloyd,

I have been trying to write to you for a week but I literally and honestly haven't had time because we have no maids! ...

It is a week tomorrow since Trude and Mrs. Neu left and for the first four days I never stopped – my energy and enthusiasm being at fever pitch and I house-cleaned as I went. ...

I am so busy time goes like THAT! and 1941 can't go by too quickly for me.

Just in the past 3 or 4 weeks food has been gradually disappearing – bananas, grapefruit, onions, spaghetti, jam and marmalade, oranges, lemons, chocolate, sweets of all kinds, biscuits, tinned things of all kinds of odd things, packets of jellies, etc. are going, going, gone. And the meat ration is 1/2d per person, 9d for children, butter 2 oz. a week, sugar 4 oz., tea 2 oz., bacon (about 2 strips each), margarine 4 oz., chickens are 8/- each – boiling fowl 6/-. You can only get a few kinds of candy, even offal is rationed (liver, lights, kidneys, etc.) Eggs are still nearly 4/- a dozen, cigarettes are noticeably poorer and are 1/5½ for 20 and you have to take the kind you can get – in fact the war has got here and the tension of the coming invasion or whatever "that man" [Hitler] is going to try, is creeping up day by day. They talk on the radio in thousands of millions but the new Budget will be a wheeker.[6]

However, despite all these snags we are as happy as kings with the garden full of snowdrops, Spring around the corner and the daylight until nearly 7 o'clock. Everyone is dying for Spring to come as they have never done before after the long, depressing winter and especially us with our first winter in the country nearly over. One of the big advantages of country life is this next-to-nature move that makes us appreciate every rag of sun, every bird that sings not to mention the bees and the trees.

[Love,
Helen]

---

[6] Helen has adopted a Northern Irish slang term, "wheeker", meaning awesome or terrific; the word was current until the late 1950s.

9th Feb.
Mahee

Dear Mother,

... It is a wonderful moonlit night and the waves sparkled so much in little diamonds of light that we had to go down to the wall to be sure that it was moonlight and not phosphorus. We have just listened to Churchill – I suppose you did too – and he is marvelous. The time was auspicious for him to speak to give us an idea of things and to buck us up for whatever is to come soon – if ever.[7] I gathered from your cable that you think that it is another crisis too. Anyway, I can't come home and wouldn't anyway so cheer up and don't worry about us. Rest assured that we are in as good a position as it is possible to be in and we are as happy as can be.

[15th Feb.]

Nearly a week has elapsed between Sunday since I started this and in between I have mailed you about a 16 page letter ordinary mail. I hope it makes the grade.

... Yesterday I went to town for a breather after the strain of flu and all and went to two movies with a little shopping in between. ... I called at the office for mail and Jim Barr told me that John Carr is "missing, presumed drowned". It made me feel so bad that I burst into tears on the spot to my and Jim's embarrassment. His, John's ship, was torpedoed on its way to the West Indies and only a few were saved –

---

[7] On 9th February, Churchill broadcast his famous "Give us the Tools" speech to the nation. He brought good news to his listeners: "...our affairs have prospered in several directions during the last four or five months, far better than most of us would have ventured to hope ... We have broken the back of the winter. The daylight grows". He noted the series of Allied victories in Libya, and although he cautioned that Hitler might attempt again an invasion of Britain ("In order to win the war Hitler must destroy Great Britain"), this time more prepared, he recounted his happy meeting in January with Wendell Willkie, chief Republican politician in the United States, and told his listeners what reply he would make to President Roosevelt who had sent a letter of introduction to the Prime Minister: "Give us the tools, and we will finish the job".

John not among them.[8] I told you I think, that his lot were bombed twice before they ever started – once in Liverpool and once some place else – anyway, John turned up here twice after he had said goodbye. The last time he was home he was here for a weekend and didn't want to go to Trinidad at all. I suspected because of a girl here some place but that was pure conjecture. There is a faint hope, of course that something may have picked him up but it is very faint and, according to Harry (so Roberta told me) who knows what the ship was and all about it, there is practically no hope. ... He has been in lots of danger ever since the war broke out and he said the time before this when he was home and came to see us that he had only one ambition: "to die of old age in bed".

Lancelot, believe it or not, is reading Fanny Farmer![9] He has just put the porridge in the bottom oven to cook all night – he thinks he has a flair for cooking but this is the second night in succession that he has put too much salt in it and had to make twice as much to even up. ... We are listening to such a good jazz band and it sounds so gay and pre-war. (L. has just found out that it takes 1 lb. Butter and 9 eggs for an English fruit cake and he is still shaken by it.) ...

Knox Cunningham was knocked down in England by a lorry when he was on his bike in the blackout and was nearly killed – he is all right now but had 3 transfusions and his lungs drained.[10] ...

Today was a lovely day – real springy. The movies I saw yesterday were *Foreign Correspondent* – British propaganda for the U.S.A. and pretty good but it needed humor and *My Favorite Wife* which was

---

[8] John Carr died when the ship he was travelling in was torpedoed by a German U-boat on 17th January, 1941. Lieutenant Carr was assigned to HMS *Goshawk*, a Royal Navy Air Station at Piarco in Trinidad. He was aboard SS *Almeda Star* of the Blue Star Line en route to Buenos Aires via Trinidad when it was attacked by U-96 about 350 miles west of the Outer Hebrides. *Almeda Star* sank leaving no survivors: 136 crew, 29 gunners and 194 passengers (including 21 officers and 121 ratings) were lost. Lt Carr was 33 years old; he is commemorated on the Lee-on-Solent Memorial in Hampshire and in Rockport School, Craigavad, County Down where he had been a pupil. See Barry Niblock, *Remembering their Sacrifice in the Second World War: The War Dead of North Down and Ards* (Antrim: Niblock, 2014), pp. 203–204.

[9] Fannie Farmer (1857–1915) was an American cook whose best-known book of recipes, *The Boston Cooking-School Cook Book* (1896), now known as *The Fannie Farmer Cookbook*, is still in print.

[10] For Knox Cunningham, see the letter of 27th September, 1939.

made for me by Cary Grant whom I adore.[11] But I don't like Irene Dunne. ...

[18th Feb.]

... There was a discussion on the food situation in the House of Lords today – Lord Woolton, the Minister of Food said that we will have to go back to the days of simpler living – the position regarding bread is strong but meat, eggs and cheese are the scarce things – especially cheese.[12] The meat ration is still 26c. a week per person with no prospect of a raise. The enemy has lost over 2,000,000 tons of shipping since the war started. The English losses have been low 20,000+ tons a week for the past several weeks bad enough. Goodness knows but nothing like the alarming figures before Christmas. The BBC is full of American news and Wendell Willkie was a huge success – also Harry Hopkins.[13] I heard a song over the radio today called "Thanks, Mr. Roosevelt" – have you heard it?[14] Mr. Herbert Morrison, the Minister of Home Security is my pet next to "Winnie" – he makes the best speeches and seems so nice. The first Lord of the Admiralty is now talking.[15] We are certainly being keyed up by all the radio speakers for "the supreme battle" – I hope it will soon be behind us instead of ahead of us but I repeat everyone is ready for everything. ...

[11] *Foreign Correspondent* (1940), a spy thriller set just before and just after the outbreak of the war, won Alfred Hitchcock a 1941 Academy Award nomination for Best Picture. Closing with the live broadcast to the United States of a bombing raid on London, the movie was intended to undermine American neutrality in favour of the Allies. Entirely different, *My Favorite Wife* was a 1940 "screwball" Hollywood marital comedy.

[12] The First Earl of Woolton (1883–1964) was Minister of Food 1940–43. By January 1941 the overseas food supply to Britain had fallen by half, no doubt inspiring his reassessment of British food habits. Meat, cheese, eggs and bacon were in short supply. By the summer of 1942, American and Canadian food supplies had alleviated the crisis.

[13] Harry Hopkins (1890–1946) was one of Roosevelt's close advisers. He helped devise and implement the Lend Lease programme by which the United States sent considerable aid to the Allies, including supplies of food.

[14] "Thanks Mr. Roosevelt" was performed by George Formby (1904–61) and included the words: "Thanks Mr. Roosevelt it's swell of you/For the way you're helping us to carry on/You'll see the British Empire smiling through/When these dark and stormy days are gone".

[15] A.V. Alexander, son of a blacksmith but later 1st Earl Alexander of Hillsborough (1885–1965), was the First Lord of the Admiralty, 1940–45 and again in 1945–46.

We got our new hen-house today and are getting 50 baby chicks in March – Wyandots and Light Sussex and Johnnie is getting Rhode Island Reds. Everyone keeps hens these days – That is about all the news I can drum up this time – our morale is so good.

Love,
Helen

12th Feb.
Mahee

Dear Mother,

The clerk in the Bank Buildings is so funny when you ask them for something they haven't got any more. He says: "That's just a memory!"

Coconut was one thing I wanted that was just a memory although you still get coconut candy. Varieties of candy are impossible to get and the shops are pathetic – sweet shops have about 3 kinds for sale and only about a pound altogether is allowed to any one person. ...

I had a letter from Kathleen Scanlan the other day – their position [in the Irish Free State] is far from rosy now! *No* petrol for private motoring, only ½ ton of coal a month and in cold weather they burn a ton every 12 days, bread restricted, also butter etc. It is generally thought that there is a good reason behind the lack of petrol in Eire[16] i.e. if there is an invasion the Germans won't have any petrol to seize and will have to bring their own if they want to be mobile at all. The Scanlans were just ready to build a summer house on their farm and it will be stopped automatically because of the shortage of timber, etc. but as Kathleen said, they have had 16 months of lavish living while we were rationed so they can't complain. Philip will be wild because he loves his luxuries and likes his life to move in a greased orbit with not one thing missing and he adores Eire so. ...

If we lived in town I would be always at canteens, sewing parties, etc. which thank goodness I'm not. The Naval canteen where I used to work is considered by everyone the finest canteen in the British Isles.

---

[16] The Irish Free State became Ireland (or Éire) with the 1937 Constitution and then in 1949 was renamed the Republic of Ireland.

It now has hot and cold showers and goodness knows what and the kitchens are redoubled again in size. The shifts are 5 hours in the afternoon and 5 to 6 hours at night – *hard menial work* – everyone I know who goes is killed. Roberta washed dishes the other day for 3 hours without lifting her head from the sink. ...

They are talking about Wendell Willkie on the radio – I saw him in the movies and saw what it was about him that won friends and influenced people all right. He has a most convincing, sincere manner although it may be a pose but it is good. Marcia Mackie got all worked up when she heard that he was coming to Eire and not Ulster and got Jack Mackie to ring up Jack Andrews to tell his father to invite Wendell to Ulster *at once* and then she wired to Willkie herself and offered him hospitality and said that he couldn't possibly understand the Irish Question by only going to Eire – but she got no reply![17]...

... I've made my mind up now to stay and come what may I'm staying. ... L. has to be in town in case of either Blitz or invasion but we have good neighbors and are at a dead end that no German would be likely to wander to – nothing to come for and he or they could be cut off and captured too easily. We could live for weeks by ourselves and have everything we need – meat, (rabbits, ducks, chickens) fish, milk, butter, wheat (we even have a grinding machine) vegetables, water, cod liver oil, Bemax,[18] Vitamin C tablets and Glucose D. Just remember how many millions of people there are in Great Britain, how many soldiers! What preparations have been and are being made and above all what spirit! Everyone is perfectly convinced that England will never be beaten and that alone will nearly save them.

---

[17] After the 1940 U.S. election, which he lost, Willkie became Roosevelt's informal envoy. He visited the U.K. in January 1941 and went across to Dublin where he tried to persuade Eamon de Valera to abandon neutrality but failed.

[18] Bemax was the trade name for a wheat-germ breakfast cereal made between 1927 and the mid-1970s. It claimed to be a rich source of vitamins B and E, copper, zinc and iron, and promised improved sleep, energy, appetite and nerves.

Stephen King-Hall who edits a weekly news-letter that L. takes doesn't think it is coming now anyway – he says that Hitler is going to the Balkans.[19] Isn't Churchill wonderful? Did you hear his last speech? ...

Goodnight and love,
Helen

1st Mar.
Mahee

Dear Mother,

It is just after lunch on Saturday afternoon. There are only three sounds in the house, the fast tick of the cuckoo clock, the slow tick of the grandfather clock and the steady puffing of the fire... It was a beautiful morning – sunny and warm but just at lunch time there was a blizzard and the snow is still lying in patches in the garden – although it has cleared up again. The snowdrops are nearly over, but the daffodils are in bud. ...

Yesterday Lancelot had to go to Lurgan to interview Philip Bell whom he wants to be an emergency salvage officer in case of a "blitzkrieg" here and so I went too. We went to lunch and it was like a field day – first going so far in the car with petrol paid for and supplied by the Food Office and secondly going out to lunch at a nice house. Philip has had neuralgia as a result of a cut on his arm for the past 8 weeks and can't go out. They have a household of ten – Philip and his wife, the other 3 Bells, a Czech refugee who helps garden and farm and a cousin of theirs who is a nephew of Philip Scanlan's who works in some mill and 3 maids. Mrs. Philip is nice and capable and quite good-looking although she wears glasses and goes wrong on her clothes though she tries hard. ... *Vogue* would have arrows pointing to the necklace and shoes and the query "What's wrong here?" Philip

---

[19] Stephen (later Sir Stephen) King-Hall (1893–1966) rose in the Royal Navy to become Commander in 1928. During the Second World War he served in the Ministry of Aircraft Production. He was the author of nineteen books on strategic policy and geopolitics, eight plays and two children's books. Helen may or may not have known that between 1897 and the 1920s his family lived in Quintin Castle, near Portaferry at the mouth of Strangford Lough into which Mahee Island juts. His younger sister Magdalen King-Hall (1904–71) became a well-known novelist.

was as rosy in the face as ever and we had a good lunch with all but two of the boys.

They are farming like mad as their war effort and L. heard some man in his club talking about them as a public scandal – 6 boys of military age not lifting a hand to join anything. ... [Philip] is quite bright and I warmed to him because I found out that he likes Louis MacNeice's poetry so we had a field day – he also hates *Punch* and seems to have an unusually broad outlook that belies his looks and his usual sailing talk. I could hardly wait to see their house ... but I could have cried with disappointment because it is British modern superimposed on Victorian and not a bit good. The best job in town in the modern style is Jack and Caroline Workman's house – especially the living room which rings the bell but Jack has everything made to order and to his design – even the furniture, carpet, fireplace *et al* and it is really finished and makes other efforts look just what they are...

The one o'clock news just announced that Bulgaria has joined the Axis and all of our newsletters are full of what caused the collapse of Bulgaria.[20] I pin my faith in Turkey and if it gives in I will be so disappointed.[21] The general feeling here about Hitler and his "Luftwaffe" and his invasion and his gas is "Let him come!" and get the darned thing over. March and April are supposed to be the crisis months so by the time you get this a month or so from now things will probably be at their height. However now life goes along just as usual and we are going to the Life Boat Ball with Mr. R. E. Workman on Thursday – Lancelot has to go to Liverpool Monday night to interview the Liverpool salvage officer who reported on the phone that he was "up to the eyes" so L. will see what he will have to do here (we hope not!) later. The planes are booked (out) so he will have to go by boat and will probably fly home on Wednesday. I hope Hitler's offensive won't start on Tuesday! The radio has just started to spout Welsh so I will have to turn it off! ...

One day just before Trudy and Mrs. Neu left I went to town by train from Comber and I tried to enumerate all the things that were different

---

[20] Bulgaria was neutral until Nazi Germany demanded it joined the Axis Powers and allow German troops to cross Bulgaria to attack Greece and thereby come to the aid of Italy whose invasion of Greece had failed.

[21] Turkey, however, despite overtures from both the Axis and Allied Powers, remained neutral until February 1945 when it entered the war on the Allied side.

because of the war – they were more than I thought – small things but it will give you an idea.

1 Living here in the winter to begin with – if you had told me even 2 years ago that I would be living at Mahee in Feb. with no maids and no nurse and *liking* it I would have died laughing.
2 Taking a train to go 5 miles when we have 2 cars.
3 No signs at stations to tell me where I was.
4 Lights blacked out in train.
5 Catching train from station to town – windows all criss-crossed with sticky paper to prevent splinters.
6 Half or about $^1/_3$ windows in town criss-crossed.
7 Air-raid shelters in front of rows of 'work-mans' houses on every street and all through the town in nearly every street.
8 Tram fares increased a penny
9 Tea party at Mrs. Carr's entire conversation about food and the lack of it (although plenty of food at tea including cakes, macaroons etc.)
10 Missed L. and had to take the train back to Comber.
11 Took 2 soldiers to the station who didn't know how to get there.
12 Blackout in train and outside
    ” ” in Comber to drive through.
13 Sherry party at Judge Andrews – practically every man in uniform because it was for the officers.
14 Home in blackout.
15 Lancelot on phone when I came in (not about me) but the big surprise was that the telephone was working!

Lancelot has to resign from the Home Guard because he has to be at the salvage work. He has a gas liaison officer attached to him now and we know lots about gas. ....

Nighty-night and love,
Helen

16th Mar.
Mahee

Dear Mother,

I seem to have been so busy lately the days slip by like magic and every Sunday it seems that it has just been a minute since the last Sunday. Today we listened to two summaries of Roosevelt's speech *and* the speech itself and the BBC was full of it all day.[22] On today's program too were the first plans for what to do in case of invasion so I expect it will be coming off pretty soon. The more wide-spread air raids and the heavy shipping losses show that we are working up to something. ...

L. has to go to Wales on Thursday to a conference – we are going to an L. D. V. [Home Guard] dance in Comber tomorrow night – otherwise no future engagements ...

Love,
Helen

9th Apr.
Mahee

Dear Ginna and Lloyd,

I only have about half an hour before going out to lunch – hippee! Hurray! but I will start anyway a much deserved letter to you – realizing that I haven't put pen to paper for a good month – shameful, but understandable if you knew the facts. The first reason was lassitude so terrific that I went to see Dr. Foster.[23] I knew already that I was

[22] On Saturday 15th March, 1941, President Roosevelt delivered a speech to White House correspondents on U.S. involvement in the European war. He fully acknowledged the threat of Nazism to democracies throughout the world and announced the end of efforts at appeasement with Germany and European dictators. He repudiated the idea that the United States was disunited and summoned Americans to the task of putting their country on a war footing. He reiterated the Four Freedoms he had spoken of some weeks before and which were to be defended at all costs – freedom of speech and worship and freedom from want and fear.

[23] Dr S.R. Foster MB practised at 17 University Square, Belfast. His elder son became Flight-Lieutenant Peter Foster and towards the end of the war was medical officer to a Spitfire Squadron in Burma. A younger son became Squadron-Leader John Watson Foster; in early 1945 he was awarded the DFC after he led three other pilots of his Mustang Squadron, 450 miles from base, against 15 Messerschmitt 109s off the coast of Norway and destroyed four of them. See *Belfast Telegraph* 6th April, 1945.

"worn out and nervous" – but my dead feeling couldn't be accounted for solely on "worn out and nervous" grounds. Well, Dr. Foster examined me from head to toe ... gave me some pills for the thyroid and a sedative for my nerves – advised a rest and/or change of occupation and now – only a week later I feel so much better – enough better to justify his diagnosis. Everyone is feeling run down after the long terrible black winter, terrible applying to weather and the nerves in my case are due to being shut up here too much with a) the kids b) the German maid c) no maids for the past two months d) the war which naturally affects everyone. ...

Night before last was the "Blitz". I slept through it despite a running commentary from Lancelot who was up from about 12–3 watching it from the top of the lane, was twice telephoned to – once xxxxxx [erased] and once xxxxx [erased] and I only became fully conscious of what had happened about 7 o'clock. It wasn't at all bad comparatively speaking – only about 8 bombs dropped and about 8 people killed, several fires and some damage and in town a terrible noise of gunfire, rattling windows and shaking house from about 12–4 off and on.[24] No one in town slept. I was in town all day yesterday and I wouldn't have missed that for anything. The people were so pleased and proud – it may sound funny but that is exactly what they are. Everybody talked about it – every salesman or woman, elevator girls and boys, all acquaintances neighbors everybody – so matey and delighted with themselves! L. was so amused when he was in Wales at hearing the different salvage officers shouting each other down about their respective blitzes – "my blitz" and "well now, in my blitz". Another term which is always used about the Germans is to describe them as "He" – "if he comes tonight" "when he came over – etc." he meaning Jerry rather than Hitler – why Germans are called Jerry I don't know – but it is a hangover from the last war.

---

[24] Helen may not have been in possession of the facts when she wrote this, though it indeed was not a major attack. "On the night of 7–8 April a small squadron of German bombers, led by a pathfinder Heinkel 111 ... raided Belfast, and completely destroyed the four-and-a-half acre Harland and Wolff fuselage factory, reduced a major timber yard to ashes, and delivered damaging blows to the docks. ... After returning to their bases in northern France, Luftwaffe bomber crews reported that Belfast's defences were 'inferior in quality, scanty and insufficient'. Sirens had sounded only after the first bombs had fallen": Jonathan Bardon, *A History of Ulster* (Belfast: Blackstaff Press, 1992), p. 564.

11th Apr.

Now it is Good Friday night and we are at home for the first time in 8 years! Last year we were in Co. Galway [it being] 1940. The year before in Paris (1939). The year before 1938 at Castlerock for gliding, 1937 you were over and we were in the South and West. 1936 we were in the Lake District and Scotland. 1935 the south of Ireland. 1934 south of Ireland and 1933 – Denver! I wonder where you are! ...

Easter Tuesday [15th]

I hope you missed the news of the bombs dropping on xxxxxx [erased – possibly Belfast].[25] For future occasions I will make the arrangement that we *won't* cable unless there is a casualty or damage so you won't be on pins and needles. I have come to the conclusion that the xxxxx [erased – possibly Belfast] people feel that it is better to be bombed than not to be noticed – at least as far as small raids go – and it was a very small raid – comparatively speaking. It is still the main topic of conversation every place with everyone still comparing notes and adding scraps of information – mostly rumour because everything is as hush-hush that no official statements as to damage, casualties etc. are given and we just have to put 2 and 2 together to get a composite picture and then no one knows because it is all rumor and gossip and "I hear" and "he said" and "she said *that*". ...

The Easter bunny came through our big window and filled [the children's] new party shoes with Easter eggs and a few presents – rubber balls on rubber bands, a toy iron for Gay and a little book for Julie and faces painted on hard boiled eggs by L. and a *sweet* little woven basket made by me! The Easter egg situation was serious because there are so few sweets anyplace. You are only allowed ¼lb. in most shops and half the shops haven't any! ...

Our household is a scream – some day I will write a book about housekeeping during the war in a remote country cottage ...

Gay collects the eggs every evening and we usually get from 10–16 – White Wyandot hens, 4 Banties and a Banty cock. We have over 40 lambs now, 12 bullocks, 2 cows, 3 Muskovy ducks, 32 wild ducks

[25] Helen is unbeknownst writing on a day which ended with a massive air raid on Belfast to which she refers in her next letter; she is referring here to the smaller raid on 7th–8th April.

(Mallard and mixed), bees – 2 hives and vegetables as far as the eye can see. Our purple flowering broccoli has just started and it is *so good*. We also have lots of onions, beets, peas, beans, carrots, potatoes, cabbages etc. all planted by L. who never stops working for a second. We are so well off for food compared to most people having our own butter and milk and vegetables and about 100lbs. of jam left and nobody else has any because it disappeared from the shops months ago and just now is being released for rationing ½ lb. per person per month.

Everyone realizes that we are coming into bad times but everyone is certain of ultimate victory. The meat ration is still a shilling a week per person and sixpence for children under 6. The cheese ration is 1oz. a week butter 4 oz. margarine 4 oz. or you can have 8 oz. butter or 8 oz. margarine, sweet biscuits are rare, bread is plentiful, oranges, lemons and bananas still are absent and have been for about 3 months. ...

You would be terribly proud of the British if you could see and hear them and have renewed faith in human nature when you hear what they smile about. Did you hear Halifax's speech? I thought it was *so good* it brought tears to my eyes about six times which Winnie and Honey Rosenfelt have so failed to do but of course they aren't that type[26]...

The news is now on 1 o'clock and it is always so long now because there are so many fronts, or theatres of war not to mention the Home Front. All those people from America are quoted at length and given great prominence in the news.

The Carrs had another communication from the Admiralty making it definite about John so there is no hope now. Their ship was attacked and torpedoed 2 days out of Liverpool and 3 hours after their S.O.S. there was help on the scene and there wasn't a sign of anything – not even a stick of wood. So the Admiralty thought that they might have got away but after about 6 weeks when they didn't turn up any place "the next of kin were informed". ... I saw Stella one day in town and

---

[26] Lord Halifax, British Ambassador to the United States, gave a speech to the English Speaking Union in New York on 15th April (Easter Tuesday), 1941. In it he acknowledged setbacks in North Africa and the Balkans but took heart from the resistance shown by the Greeks and Yugoslavians. A refrain in Halifax's speech is "with your help", and the speech is laced with a dignified gratitude that must have moved an American such a Helen, living in the United Kingdom. Halifax recognized more than once a comradeship between the U.S. and the U.K. that he believed was strengthened by the shared English language, a proposition appropriate to the occasion of his speech.

she told me about it – she said that Mrs. Carr has been wonderful but that Mr. Carr was nearly out of his mind for a week.

I have just helped Gay work her new jig-saw puzzle after lunch – it is of the King and Princess E. [Elizabeth] and Marg. Rose [Margaret] on horseback. Gay is much better at it than I am. We had such a killing conversation at lunch about "the spirit" meaning the soul. Gay was asking L. questions about Ben [Lance's golden retriever] whose picture hangs above the fireplace and asking if he was old and where he was now. So L. said that he was dead and buried at Mahee point. So Gay said "Yes, his shell" because I had told her how you buried the shells of dead people and their spirits went to heaven. So then today at lunch I asked Gay if she remembered where her spirit was and she pointed to her head and said "here" – Julie, of course, pointing simultaneously to her head and saying "here" although she had no idea what was going on. Then Gay with her finger on her scalp said "I feel my spirit, it's a bit wobbly!" ...

You say that you don't worry about us because Mother worries so much which is a scream – "Why should two worry" or "that lets me out" which is such common sense all except for one thing – why should she worry either? We don't worry a bit - nobody here does having long ago reached that stage in impersonality that you mention. Everybody thinks that if you're bombed you're bombed and that's all there is to it – which of course lets out the worse state of being half bombed but people really are amazing – I know you must hear all the time about the "morale" etc. but it is terrific – I often wonder if the Americans as a whole would be as good being more emotional and neurotic generally...

I will wind this up and mail it tonight. Give it to Mother and I will write her the sequel to it.

Love,
Helen

18th Apr.
Mahee

Dear Mother,[27]

This is the sequel or other half of the letter to Ginna and Lloyd that is meant for all of you although addressed to the Hughes and this to you. We have had no warm weather yet although May is only 2 weeks away and I am sitting bang in front of a roaring fire and it about noon. I have soup and another rice pudding in the oven and we are having cauliflower and raw turnip and carrot salad. ... We were at Mrs. Parker's at Whiterock to lunch and tea on Wednesday but the biggest party and the talk of the town is the party that Trude and Mrs. Neu and Louise Granger gave for their friends. I don't know how many were there most people say hundreds but I'm sure not more than dozens and I would say about fifty or sixty but it was such a super party and the noise and hubbub at it were so terrific that no one has been able to talk about anything since and that is 3 days ago now. They all brought presents some small and inexpensive but showy and sparkly and expensive big things – very bad taste we thought but there they're vulgar that way. We had been to see Jack and Kay just before the party started and just got home in time to dress and go out again. I put on my warmest clothes because you know how cold it is at Ginna's Spinney. Although we didn't enter into the real spirit of the party we had as good a view as anyone from our quiet corner in the sidelines and believe me it was some party.

They are terribly wealthy people who came and they just showed off in a disgusting manner and we got very tired of it and thought the party would never end – as it was it lasted from 10.30–5 although we came home and went to bed at about 2.45 and from what we heard people straggled home from about 4 on but the last to (go) was about 5. Neither Lancelot nor I like parties like that so we hope we never have to go to another. We were so fed up that at one point we just read

---

[27] On the night of 15th–16th April – three days before the letter – there was a massive air raid on Belfast by German bombers. (See the letter following for details of the deaths and damage.) Helen wanted to tell her mother and sister about it but feared her descriptions of what she and Lancelot witnessed from Mahee would be censored. So she attempted an "eye-witness" report in code. See the letter of 22nd May and the Afterword for a discussion of this letter. Billy Foulis (below) is unidentified.

in Ginna's Spinney or rather could have read. My old friend Frequency was my worst trouble and rather spoiled my evening. Julie wasn't there at all and Gay just dropped in for a few minutes complaining about the noise and then left again – Gay doesn't understand parties like that at all so I'm glad she didn't stay – she's really too young for all those people. We just stood around and smoked ourselves blue in the face and said "Gosh" at the wild array of people who turned up – it was fantastic and unbelievable and no parties at home can be compared to it so I can't describe it to you very well.

Do you remember how when Daddy got bored he used to go down to the basement and just touch it up a little? Well there were lots of those and whoppers too. The Scanlans and Billy Foulis and that man who used to slide down poles so fast from Liverpool and his wife who always wears a red hat came to see us the next day. They were a great help in cheering us up – everyone was amazed that the Scanlans came what with the family feud on but Lancelot saw them in town.

The most exciting part of the party for us was when those tweed people who gave you the green tweed got tight and were they lit up and did they make a racket! However they soon passed out cold but about fifteen of them were like Mr. Ritchie's back bone and you know how it was. …

The other half of this letter tells about the air raid – let me know if much is cut out so I will know what is allowed. I didn't mention any places so I hope you will get the drift. L. thinks you will think I have gone loopy over that party but we go out so seldom that it made a big impression on me.

Must go to bed.

Love,
Helen

27th Apr.
Mahee

Dear Ginna and Lloyd, and Mother,

We have lived here exactly one year today – and what a year! It has gone like a flash and is still going like a flash and believe me this year can't go too quickly for me believing as I do that if we live through this year we can live through anything. Personally speaking the war seems to have hit us with full force only this year beginning with L.'s war job, continuing with his earlier goings, later comings home and working Saturdays, getting into full swing with our domestic situation which coincided with the fairly sudden disappearance of all kinds of food from the shops, and culminating of course with the really bad blitz that we lived through about twelve days ago. It was the final push that pushed us straight into the war atmosphere with no doubt about it and no way out.[28] People are recovering now and you occasionally meet people who can talk about something else but not often. It changed a lot of things overnight apart from concrete damage – 1) no one will leave their families to take a holiday or for any reason but necessity in case *he* comes again. 2) All dances have been cancelled. 3) The canteen I used to work in is closed. 4) A general feeling of unreality and insecurity pervades. 5) We have evacuees! Six in all and seven on weekends. The only private one is Mary Morwood who is now Mrs. Rogers and who is having a baby in July and is afraid of losing it in a blitz. ...

Now it is 11.30 (midnight again) and I am clean and shining from a hot bath – Mary has just gone to the bathroom and L. is sitting here working on his reports smoking and swearing at Rock. We heard

[28] At 10.40pm on the evening of Easter Tuesday (15th April), air-raid sirens sounded in Belfast to warn of the approach of what proved to be 180 German bombers flying in formation over the Ards peninsula (not far from Mahee Island). Reaching Belfast, the bombers dropped flares then incendiaries, high-explosive bombs and parachute land-mines. There was massive loss of life, particularly in congested working-class districts, and tremendous material damage to narrow streets, York Street Spinning Mill (the largest in Europe) and the city's telephone exchange. The resulting fires required help (pumps and firemen) from Glasgow, Liverpool and Preston – and from Éire, whose neutral government authorized thirteen fire engines and 70 firemen to drive north from Dun Laoghaire, Dublin, Drogheda and Dundalk and which had to find their way through a blacked-out countryside and towns en route. (In the early hours of the morning, incendiaries and explosives were dropped on Newtownards aerodrome, a few miles from Mahee, and ten guards were killed.) In all, over 900 people are said to have died, exact numbers being difficult to ascertain in the confused aftermath. Thousands of residents, shocked and bewildered, evacuated their homes in Belfast for the countryside. See Jonathan Bardon, *A History of Ulster*, pp. 564–69.

Winnie's speech tonight which was what I predicted – a pep talk. His cracks about the killable and curable Germans were good.[29] ...

1st May

Now it is May Day – our 8th anniversary.... Gay and Julie are asleep with – what do you think? – a May basket hanging on their door full of primroses – made by me and *real* sweets. ... I hope that you got in touch with Lloyd or else failed to hear the news about Belfast whilst traveling because the American papers seem to have given it a prominent place according to cables received by Roberta and the Dolans from friends and relatives. I hope Lloyd got my cable because it was something to cable about – it told Mother about it in an open version and a disguised version – L. was afraid that she would think I had lost my mind as a result. As it was I was considerably unnerved and like most people I know my digestion didn't settle down for 2 or 3 days – just plain nervous indigestion and no appetite. Lots oopsed their cookies, most had frequency and generally a hectic time was had by all.[30] It was so bad that I thought if they came again the next night I just plain couldn't stand it – and with all this talk about morale you only know how *great* the Londoners are when you have been through one to think what they stood it night after night for weeks and are still standing it. Harry McMullan was buried for ½ hour the night after one "blizzard" as our evacuee Mother calls it. Harry incidentally oopsed his cookies every 2 hours for 4 days afterwards and still has a very weak memory – in fact he was just plain dazed and was walking down the strand at some early hour of the morning clad only in a

[29] Churchill's speech was broadcast by the BBC on 27th April and was another demonstration of Churchill's genius for morale-boosting eloquence. Although he recorded setbacks in Greece and Yugoslavia, he was buoyant in his forecasts, especially in the light of the growing energizing bond between the United States and the Commonwealth. He reported civilian British morale highest where Hitler had inflicted the most damage. He was wittily scathing about Mussolini: "this whipped jackal ... frisking up at the side of the German tiger with yelpings not only of appetite ... but even of triumph," and correctly foresaw the day when "this absurd impostor" would in the final reckoning be abandoned to "public justice". He ended in the hope of American commitment by quoting stanzas of a poem by Arthur Hugh Clough, then a little-known Victorian poet, with its closing line: "But westward, look, the land is bright".

[30] Many of those who experienced the Blitz suffered from shocks to the system: vomiting, diarrhoea, indigestion, nerves.

pyjama jacket – his only possession in the world and a blanket (borrowed) with tears of rage (or fright) pouring down his face. The bomb that got his house landed in his bedroom about 1 minute after he had left it running for the shelter bringing four storeys of brick, mortar and furniture down on a wardrobe which was on top of our Harry who was spread-eagled on the basement floor feeling, I'm sure just a little more fragile than he had ever felt in his life before. He rang up when he came home to recover and get clothes and he said that if anyone bangs a door or goes "boo" behind him he runs crying into the house and locks himself in a small room until somebody comes and tells him to come out that it is all right. ...

6th May

We have had two blitzes and 6 siren warnings in the last 78 hours. The night before last she started at 12.30 and went on until 5 and we went to bed about 3.30 – last night we slept through it. ... The casualties weren't so bad in this blitz but the damage was terrific.[31] ... There is not a window left in the center of town and over half the shopping and business district has disappeared. Tires are still burning, the town smells of smoke and there are no trains because there is no electricity – Cigarettes have nearly disappeared and you know how bad that is. ... The big red school for boys near where we used to live is gone – direct hit[32] ... Our part here was quiet compared to the last time. Gay and

[31] There were two attacks on Belfast on the nights of 4th–5th May and 5th–6th May. During the first, 100,000 incendiary bombs and then high explosives were dropped within three hours from around 200 German planes. The fatalities were fewer than during the Easter Tuesday raid (150 killed), but damage to the north, centre and east of the city was tremendous. Help to fight the resulting fires was required from local troops and from fire services in Britain and Éire. During his account of this attack, Barton notes that the South of Ireland's willingness to provide aid threatened to incur German anger by violating its neutrality. Harland & Wolff shipyard and other industrial sites were hit hard; Bardon records a 45% loss on ship construction: *Belfast: An Illustrated History*, p. 240. See also Brian Barton, *Northern Ireland in the Second World War* (Belfast: Ulster Historical Foundation, 1995), pp. 44–49. Herbert Morrison, the Home Secretary, sent a telegram of sympathy and support to Prime Minister Andrews.

[32] The pupils of Campbell College, a prestigious boys' school near where Helen and Lance had lived on the Belmont Road, were evacuated so that the building could house No. 24 General Hospital. On the night of 4th–5th May a bomb landed on the north-wing roof. See Keith Haines, *Images of Ireland: East Belfast* (Dublin: Nonesuch, 2009), p. 58.

Julie both slept through it – the windows rattled a bit but the doors didn't thump. I wasn't a bit scared I'm glad to say partly because I had to calm our evacuee Mother [Mrs Glover] down, she was "highsterical" but I gave her a good swig of my nerve sedative and she got better. Mary was as cool as a cucumber sitting knitting by candlelight. There was no spectacular display like the last time – just an ominous glow over the city and we knew that the fires were terrific. The street where we used to buy steamer tickets is gone. The shop where we whistled out the window once to L. when we were having morning coffee is gone. That good grocery shop – you know in the department store is gone. L.'s office is intact – the only building on the street without broken windows. I saw Austen Boyd wandering around with the other thousands early the morning after – the windows of his house are all gone and his office and store room gutted. ... We have people in tents in our fields and no one who can get out of town is staying in town.[33] You can't believe what a badly blitzed town looks like and from what we can hear ours is as bad as anybody's (regional pride) or worse (more regional pride).

This letter has been going on long enough. I will mail it and continue it in another one to Mother which I will hope you will interchange. Our household number 14 now and with no competent help behind me or beside me and not a cigarette in town I am wild!

Love,
Helen

6th May
Mahee

Dear Mother,

You'd never guess what we have in the house tonight! Of all things 5 evacuees! A mother and 4 children aged 8 mo., 9, 10, 12!

I picked them up walking along the road from Comber with their little bundles – just one family out of thousands that have been sleeping in the fields on the outskirts of the town and in the country for the past

---

[33] The Northern Ireland Ministry of Home Affairs later reported that by the end of May 1941, perhaps 220,000 people had temporarily fled from Belfast: Barton, p. 49.

two nights. This family was going to a tiny cottage which already had evacuees. I don't know how many and so I said that we had nobody and for them to come here – visible relief on their part and the cottage woman's part. These people weren't bombed out but are just scared out – they live in a slum area near xxxxxx [erased] and just wouldn't stay in town another night.[34] Not a single person on their street is living there any longer – they have just left their houses and fled and go back in the daytime. The roads out of town at 6 o'clock are jammed with cars stacked with prams, mattresses and all sorts of household equipment and most pathetic of all these little family groups which have been wandering around town with their little bags and parcels wrapped in newspaper ever since the blitz on Tuesday night. They break everybody's heart and I had been feeling awful that we had nobody. Roberta was supposed to come but she didn't turn up and we couldn't telephone so I went up to town yesterday to see it and her. She spent the night in her shelter fairly comfortably and isn't coming at the moment.

I asked a censor about what is allowed to be reported about a raid so I hope I can get an account over to you which is harmless and won't give away any secrets. The papers and the B.B.C. described it as a "vicious attack" and vicious is just the word for it.

Anything like the sound of the bombs dropping can't be translated into words – you have to hear it to get the full force of the awfulness of it. The paper says that the Germans say that there were hundreds of bombers over – our papers and B.B.C. don't say but we personally thought that there about as many as East ———- (not saying where!) ...

I was interested and excited at the beginning because we saw the first of it just as we arrived home ... The biggest surprise were the flares which come down on parachutes and hang about in the sky making everything literally as light as day for about 15 minutes each. ... I

[34] The Glovers lived in Mersey Street in industrial, working-class east Belfast. John Blake reports that after the air raids, "thousands of persons, who would not or could not be evacuated, refused to stay in Belfast at night"; there was, he writes, a "spontaneous and largely uncontrolled surge of people out of the city". Like the family Helen takes in, "Many of the refugees were drawn from that 'submerged tenth' of the population of Belfast whose condition the general public scarcely understands except in such times of emergency": John W. Blake, *Northern Ireland in the Second World War* (Belfast: Blackstaff Press, 2000), p. 241.

jumped behind a gate and said "My God!" for about the second time in my life and from about then on I didn't feel so good and was at stages like an aspen leaf. I came in to see how the kids were – Gay woke up when I went in or was awake and said that the wind was banging her window so that she couldn't sleep – I hung blankets on the blackout curtains and lined the sides of their beds with eiderdowns and put a pillow beside each of them on the corridor side in case the window blew in and told Gay to go to sleep – which she did.

Zooksie never woke up and Belle and Margaret slept through it all – how I don't know for the house shook, the windows rattled and worst of all were the awful whams at the door. Just as if a huge dog got up on its hind legs and gave a big push. We went to bed about 2.30 with the bombs still dropping and making that awful thud of a noise and actually went to sleep. The all clear didn't go until 5 and the siren blew at 10.30! We never hear either so it doesn't matter to us anyway.

The next day L. of course left early and I paced around the house in a completely distrait way – I couldn't get anybody on the phone so I went to the Glendinnings to see if I could phone Auntie. Their phone wouldn't work either and so I went to xxxxxxx [erased] Elaine's to find her in her p.'jamas having breakfast at 10 having got home from A.R.P. duty at 7 a.m. Nobody *knew* anything but rumors were rife ... I met Kay [Mackie] outside the P. Office and she had just come back from town and was able to give me first hand information. ... So I heard that the entire district where we used to live was all right except for a few incendiary bombs which they got out and the district where Arabella and Roberta live was all right but the worst district was the part we pass through on the way to Rosemary Webb's [35] and near where Lavens used to live. ... I went around with L. 2 mornings after to see the damaged area and it was just like all the pictures you see of other bombed areas whether in Spain, China or England and pretty depressing to see. The Hospital that I am on the committee of was hit and around L.'s office things are all right except for a few broken windows. The electricity never failed but the gas did and one big problem has been food in town in restaurants etc. I went to 5 on Thursday before I could get anything and then I got milk and biscuits.

[35] For Rosemary Webb, see the letter of 22nd May, 1939.

12th May

This is Monday morning and we still have our evacuees who are probably fairly permanent. ... Mrs. Turtle stuck the raid amazingly well – she was a wreck after the first one and in an awful state but somehow pulled herself together for the second. Gordon is an A.R.P. warden and has to be out in it and Arabella and the maid are left alone to fire-fight and do anything they have to. Everyone looked so tired and white and worried and sad after it – such a difference from the first raid which was small and made everyone feel proud and pleased as I told you.

I didn't recover for 48 hours as far as my tummy goes – nerves bad and digestion shot, no appetite etc. But more than anything it makes you realize what the Londoners stood night after night in the dead of winter – no one sees how they stood it at all. ...[36]

Gay and Julie are fine and are the only ones who are wholeheartedly enjoying the evacuees – Julie adores babies and this one is one that only its Mother could love being the image of its ma and it goes to bed at 10 p.m. and sleeps every night in the crook of its Mother's arm! It eats every 3 hours – a bottle of Farola and milk and water. Considering everything including its two nights on the hills it is healthy looking. The Mother carries it in a shawl and so does the little girl aged 11 ...

I am pretty sure they won't go back to their house in town which is still intact but they are too scared. They were all in the coalhole all night. ...

Love,
Helen

18th May

[P.S.] So sad to think the war will probably go on a year or two more – but if the U.S.A. comes in traveling won't be so restricted even if it continues dangerous for a while – sometimes I get wild because we

---

[36] By February 1941, for example, over 140 bombs had fallen in the neighbourhood of Whitehall alone where Harry McMullan and Dick Pim worked and on 16th April the Admiralty received three direct hits. See John Potter, *Pim and Churchill's Map Room* (2014), p. 13. On 10th–11th May, London suffered its most massive air raid when over 500 German planes bombed the capital for almost seven hours and caused many casualties (over 1400 dead) and damage.

can't see each other but usually I'm calm because worry and wildness won't help. What do you think of Lindbergh?[37] I'd like to know.

Also let me know if my reports of the blitzs [sic] are censored please. About half your letters are read by censors.

H.

22nd May
Mahee

Dear Mother,

... one or two things need clearing up.

A   There is no little Turtle on the way and the frequency is pure nerves – a common complaint during air-raids. I believe it's awful in the shelters – such a problem!

B   The party that I described supposedly given by Trude and Mrs. Neu was a subtly disguised version of the air-raid but I realize that it was too subtle. Lancelot upon reading it got hopelessly confused and was afraid you would think I had gone nuts because he said it was such balderdash. However since my undisguised letter got through I labored in vain – it wasn't one of my better efforts anyway but I did like the touch about the fire brigade from Liverpool as that man who slides down poles so fast and his wife who always wears a red hat!" Did you ever figure any of it out? I thought Ginna might have seen the light.

... Tommy Carr and Stella and Ann are coming tomorrow for the weekend and we have asked the Scanlans for the next weekend. The food problem is fairly acute where it comes to entertaining but everyone is in the same boat and our lack of a good cook doesn't show up amid the very plain cooking that all are forced to do. I bought the

[37] Charles Lindbergh delivered a speech to the America First Committee in New York City on 23rd April, 1941. He recommended American non-intervention unless it seemed likely that the United States could win the war. He claimed that England was losing the war and was seeking to drag America into a military quagmire. He argued for an isolationist Fortress America. Indeed, he claimed that it was the interventionists who were undermining democracy. He blamed the European democracies for their own defeat and said "I do not believe we should be too quick to criticize the actions of a belligerent nation". Incredibly, Germany is mentioned only once in his speech, when blaming France for foolishly declaring war on Hitler.

classic British cook-book – The Glasgow School of Cooking book[38] and made Queen o' Puddings yesterday and was it British or was it British. ...

Very luckily Gay doesn't know anything about planes dropping bombs and also very luckily we aren't near any anti-aircraft guns or she would be wild being awfully scary about guns and loud noises of any kind. ... Lots of children Gay's age are terrified and in town naturally they can't sleep through it because they have to be taken to shelters and there the guns are as near and so loud. When they are 6 and 7 they don't seem to mind it much and take great pride in *our* guns and *our* fighters and they are always told that that is what the noise is.

Bodo is in Egypt Edie has just discovered. He is 2nd gunnery officer on his ship which L. says is such a good and high position and is now a Lieutenant-Commander – so is Harry [McMullan] and so is Billy Stevens (sic).[39] ...

I went to see Doreen [Metcalfe] on Tuesday. Their baby looks mostly like Percy and is terribly cute – it is 8 months old now and has eyes exactly like pansies – streaky blue but not very big. ... Percy is in the naval reserve but with a permanent land job and so luckily here. He was nearly sent to Iceland and nearly to the Shetlands. Imagine being in Iceland in the winter with one hour or so of daylight!!! Somebody told me that the suicides in Iceland last winter among the troops stationed there were chronic. Tell Ginna that Helen Kirkpatrick who was in her class at Smith or maybe the year before is now in Iceland. She is the London correspondent for a Chicago paper and is a good friend of the Dolans.[40] I got a notice from Smith when her book came

---

[38] "*The Glasgow Cookery Book* – Centenary Edition, 2009 – A British/French cookbook with over 1000 tried and tested recipes that were used and developed as a textbook by The Glasgow and West of Scotland College of Domestic Science – fondly dubbed the Do. (or Dough) School by Glasgow citizens ... Its reputation for dependable and economical recipes ensured that its influence spread far beyond the walls of the Glasgow college": Amazon.co.uk. The Queen of Puddings is a British dessert from the 17th century consisting of breadcrumbs boiled with milk, the mixture then spread with jam and topped with a meringue.

[39] Belfast-born William Lawson (Billy) Stephens joined the Royal Naval Volunteer Reserve in 1930 and at the outbreak of the war joined the coastal forces: *The Independent*, 17th August, 1997.

[40] Major Francis J. Dolan and his family, including his daughters Margaret (Peggy) and Nell and son Temple, lived in Adelaide Park in the Malone district of Belfast. A Dubliner, Francis Dolan joined the British Army. At Queen Victoria's Diamond Jubilee celebrations, Major Dolan commanded the guard of honour at Westminster Bridge. *Contd':*

out – Mr. Chamberlain's Umbrella I think it was called.[41] ...

Every country district is the same as ours – packed with evacuees. We still have our 7 who show no signs of leaving... The kids don't go to school because it is too far – 4 miles and apparently beyond 3 miles they can't be made to go. ... We took Mrs. Glover to town on Tuesday so that she could get compensation for her curtains "that were blewed right out the windys" and she got £2.0.0. as a temporary loan for clothing and the curtains.

Herbert Bryson was called home from the army to help with the Social Welfare people – evacuation and all and the general chaos and lack of funds and lack of organization and lack of everything has him nearly crazy according to Rosemary whom I saw one day in town. Nobody needs to be told because it was so self-evident and every evening still at dusk people pour out of town and all horses and carts go every night. Right after the blitzes the confusion on the roads and the sights you saw were just like what we imagine France was this time last year. And it is far from straightened out. ...

... We never go to bed until after midnight these light nights because L. stays out until dark or after and then we sit a spell and there it is, midnight again. ...

It is this 2 hours daylight savings that throws us off and by mid-June it won't even be dark until midnight. I will go to the market and see what there is to buy and buy some cakes and things. You have to queue now for cakes (so many places have been blitzed) and also for cigarettes

[40] *Cont'd*: He went into business in London and Liverpool and came to Belfast where he rose to become President of the Belfast Wholesale Merchants' and Manufacturers' Association. His premises in downtown Belfast were destroyed in a German air-raid. He was a founder member of the Royal North of Ireland Yacht Club. See his obituary notice in the *Belfast News-Letter*, 14th January 1950.

[41] Helen Kirkpatrick (1909–1997) graduated from Smith College in 1931. She became a reporter in France for the *New York Herald Tribune*, and when she moved to the United Kingdom reported freelance for the *Manchester Guardian* and *Daily Telegraph*. She published two anti-appeasement books, the first being *This Terrible Peace* (1938), the second – not *Mr Chamberlain's Umbrella* (catchier title though it is) but *Under the British Umbrella: What the English are and How They Go to War* (1939). By 1941 Kirkpatrick had become a reporter for the *Chicago Daily News*. She achieved a scoop when the Duke of Windsor refused to be interviewed by her but was happy to interview *her*. In London she covered the Blitz and in June 1944 accompanied the invading American forces to the beaches of Normandy; later that year she rode into Paris with the liberating Free French Forces under the legendary General Leclerc. She was awarded the Medal of Freedom and the Legion of Honour.

(so sordid) and then you are doled out 20 if there are any in town. L. says that there are none in town today. ...

We are invited to the local Colonel's for tea on Sunday too so what with this and that we are downright gay!

Here comes L. clean as a pin and I haven't started the cocoa so

Goodnight and love
Helen

27th May
Mahee

Dear Mother,

Your air-mail letter came yesterday in 11 days, so things are definitely better. I wore my new hat yesterday to the D.R.C. and felt so snappy in it. ...

There is going to be a mock invasion of Mahee at the causeway tomorrow morning at 5 by the local troops. I hope the gunfire doesn't wake Gay up and I'm so glad we were told. ... They are going to throw a bridge over there at the Causeway. ...

It is just 1 o'clock now – time for the news – we will hear in a day or two whether there will be conscription here.

Big News – they've sunk the Bismark [sic]!!! We need good news at this stage and the loss of the Hood made everyone feel *awful* especially since so many went down on it.[42] Now they are talking about President Roosevelt's speech while everyone is going so agog about ————- so by tomorrow you may be our Allies – one more national anthem to play on Sunday night before the news – they now play Norway,

[42] At the Battle of Denmark Straits on 24th May, 1941, *Bismarck*, the largest German battleship, along with *Prinz Eugen*, attacked and sank the battlecruiser HMS *Hood* with the loss of over 1100 British lives. The Royal Navy pursued *Bismarck* and two days later she was torpedo-bombed by planes from the aircraft carrier HMS *Ark Royal* and engaged by four Royal Navy ships. Severely damaged, *Bismarck* was scuttled by its crew and sank with very heavy loss of German life. The sinking of *Bismarck* was regarded as a morale-boosting act of revenge at sea.

Belgium, Holland, France, Greece, Czecho-Slovakia, Poland, Yugo-Slavia – I think that that is all.[43]

Kathleen said in her letter that they [in the Irish Free State] are very short of tea, coffee and cocoa and of course there is no white bread and a minimum of petrol. Most cars around Dublin go on gas – you see a few here – they have huge things on the roof like a big blown up mattress and I think you can go about 50 miles on a bagful.[44]

It is only fair if they bring in Conscription here but it will be so hated by so many people.[45] I don't think L. would be conscripted because of the job he's got but otherwise he surely would be – it is from 18–40. Tommy Carr was so funny and so honest and said that he had run away from it once and couldn't bother to run away again because this war catches you wherever you go. Stella said that the Carrs are gradually getting over John's death but they still haven't touched his room and that Shirley is still heart-broken because she adored John so. ... We

[43] Roosevelt gave a radio address from the White House on the day of Helen's letter. He informed his fellow Americans that Germany had escalated the conflict into "a world war for world domination" and outlined likely scenarios were the Axis Powers to defeat Great Britain. Only "the epic resistance of Britain" at present prevented these scenarios achieving reality, which involved Hitler's military attention turning after the invasion of Britain to the Western Hemisphere. Short of a declaration of war, the speech committed the United States to full material support for the Allies and rapid transformation of the U.S.A. into a state of war readiness. The speech was a firm riposte to Lindbergh's the month before; without naming him, Roosevelt counts Lindbergh among those "sincere patriotic men and women" blind to "the ugly realities of international banditry and to the need to resist it at all costs": Franklin D. Roosevelt, "Radio Address Announcing an Unlimited National Emergency," 27th May, 1941.

[44] Gas-fuelled cars were developed during the Great War and reappeared during the Second World War. Uncompressed coal gas was one alternative to petrol and it was typically stored in a canvas bag or balloon riding on the car's roof.

[45] Conscription of eligible Northern Irishmen into the British armed forces was a highly controversial subject. Irish nationalists in Ulster were opposed to it, preferring to align their stance with the neutral Éire. Conscription would have added 48,000–53,000 men to the British forces and Churchill for one was for it. Ministers in the Northern Ireland parliament, led by J.M. Andrews, expressed their enthusiasm for conscription on 24th May, but they were Protestants and British loyalists. Helen when she writes appears to believe conscription is on the cards, but that same day the British government announced that conscription would not extend to Northern Ireland, aware of the resistance its implementation would generate in Northern Ireland and Éire. In any case, voluntary enlistment from both parts of Ireland was deemed sufficient to offset the serious political costs conscription would have levied. See Barton, *Northern Ireland in the Second World War*, pp. 52–54. Also Blake, *Northern Ireland in the Second World War*, pp. 194–200.

have new window boxes at the back with red geraniums and little by little the house is getting cuter and cuter. Write often and tell me all the gossip. The wife who wore the red hat was another fireman (weak) but I'm glad you figured out the letter.

Love,
Helen

1st Jun.
Mahee

Dear Mother,

I am writing this at the kitchen table after ten o'clock – it is really only 8 o'clock and the sun hasn't set yet. I am thankful to report that summer has come at last – day before yesterday and yesterday and today have been divine. They are the first warm days since last summer because it has been an appalling winter and a very cold spring. Last year on the first of June the Hawthorn hedges were in full bloom and this year they haven't even started. Everything is about a month late but it makes the hot days seem even more wonderful.

I bathed on Friday night just before supper and it made me feel fresh and young after a very hot tiring day of shopping town. I was buying food for the weekend because the Scanlans came Friday evening . ...

We managed awfully well on the weekend – the Scanlans unfortunately had to go back to Dublin last night after not even a 24 hour stay because of the bombing of Dublin Friday night. It completely ruined their stay because after we heard the news in the morning they were fairly anxious, although north Dublin was bombed and they live in south Dublin but they were wondering if their children had been scared.[46] We put a call through to Dublin and after about 4 hours got their house – only the eldest child had wakened and the others slept through it so they felt much better, but wouldn't have been happy to stay away anyway. ...

The latest here just announced today and a bolt from the blue to

---

[46] Around 2.a.m. on 31st May, German planes dropped four bombs on north Dublin, killing 28 people. Some thought that the raid was punishment for the aid Éire delivered to Belfast during the Blitz and a warning to it to keep out of the war. The Republic of Ireland received £327,000 compensation in 1958 from West Germany.

everyone is the clothes rationing. Luckily I have plenty of nearly everything and am congratulating myself on the tweed I bought at Newtownards the other day and the yards of Viyella I have for children's dresses and shirts for me. As I have lots of knitting wool which is rationed too ...

Nighty-night and love,
Helen

9th Jun.
Mahee

Dear Mother,

It is half-past eleven and we have just put on the light. L. is reading his book and I am as elated that we have a new cook and I don't know what to do. She has only been here about 5 hours but has already said that she will stay with us for years and years – middle-aged, good-looking, a Catholic, has been in two places – one 17 years and one 3 and she *seems* wonderful. After our winter of unrest it will be divine if she is good. She is what is called a "blitz-survivor" because she was in the bad district during the raid and her one aim was to get out of town. ... The Eggintons were here for the weekend ... Eggy ... hates working in a factory and is just living until the war is over when he will settle in Belmullet or New Mexico. ...

Elizabeth Morwood and a boy-friend were here camping for Saturday night. They hiked from Comber. She and Eggy would have had an argument if she had got started because Eggy was saying what a rotten lot of men work with him and that all they want is money and do as little work as they can although it is vital work and Eliz. is a Communist and takes the side of any working man regardless – however she has the sense to know that she gets too worked up so she didn't start. ...

Tommy Carr gave us the prettiest picture that he painted while he was here of the view to the right just outside our gate. It is so feathery and misty and pretty – a water color done with Gay's paints on just an old sheet torn out of a drawing book.[47]

---

[47] This painting still hangs in the Mahee cottage.

I have to do a paper for the D.R.C. for next Monday and I am *wild* – haven't even started. It will probably be on Louis MacNeice, but may be on *The Pleasures of Being Modern Minded*. ...

It is midnight again and you could read outside – it do beat all and are we dead in the morning! I lose myself on a rug outside in the afternoons. ...

Love and night-night,
Helen

20th June
Mahee

Dear Ginna,

... The political situation is quiet with all news bulletins pretty boring – talk about Germany and Russia and of course President Roosevelt and America movies in every news. Evelyn Laye is singing on the radio[48], L. is cutting the lawn, Mary is out for her walk, G. and J. are asleep looking like sunburnt angels, Josie (the new cook) is pottering in the kitchen and Belle is out. There you have our household in a nutshell. ...

Oh yes – another difficulty being cleared up is that our evacuees are leaving next week – back to a house in town in not a good area at all. It arose – the pending departure – because one evening I had a heart-to-heart talk with Mrs. Glover and told her that we would like them to pay for their coal. We have been supplying coal, potatoes, vegetables and milk for 2 months now and we have all to spare except coal which apart from being high-priced is rationed to the wholesaler and so we just can't buy as much as we would like. I also told Mrs. Glover that they shouldn't regard this arrangement as permanent because we have previous arrangements with Roberta if she is bombed out – but said that as far as we were concerned they could stay as long as they like if they paid for their coal and Roberta didn't have to come – but that it wasn't permanent and that it is such an unsuitable place for schools (4 miles) and shopping. So that must have brought them to their senses or sensibilities and they are going next week. ...

[48] Evelyn Laye (1900–1996) was an English actress who starred in stage musicals.

Last night we were out for dinner for the first time in weeks and came home without lights at midnight but tomorrow is the longest day and then back we go toward the awful black winters when it gets dark at 4.30. We were at the Poppers last night – he is a Czech and I think a Jew and she is English and I think a Jewess and they live in a lovely house which had no less than 21 windows broken during the first big blitz but no injuries or harm done otherwise.[49] All the houses in their neighborhood had most of the windows covered up with sheet iron or asbestos and the Poppers house is exhibit A of the idiosyncrasies of blast – no rhyme nor reason as to why the windows that blew in did blow in. ...

[End of letter mislaid]

28th Jun.
Mahee

Dear Ginna,

... I saw *The Philadelphia Story* twice last week and loved it[50] – it is pure escape for me to go to the movies and homesickness – not that I wish I were home now because I don't. I'm glad I stayed even if something pretty bad happens because I would be unhappy living in Denver now – worried sick about L. because I wouldn't know what it was like here and it is nothing to worry about when you're here.

The only thing that really would scare me stiff and I don't think it would affect us much here is invasion. It is not so much the danger of being killed but the awful insecurity and uncertainty – not knowing who was who and whether the radio was right and the general bedlam.

[49] The *London Gazette* of 19th September 1947 records the successful naturalization application of Thomas Frederick Popper originally from Czechoslovakia, an engineer in the linen industry and living in Ballysillan House, 614 Crumlin Road, Belfast. In the *Belfast News-Letter* of 26th March, 1946 there is a notice announcing an application for British naturalization received from Egon David Popper of Ballysillan House, 614 Crumlin Road. E.D. Popper was already one of the directors of the venerable William Ewart & Son Mill on the Crumlin Road. The Crumlin Road Presbyterian Church at 292 Crumlin Road was wrecked during the Easter Tuesday Blitz, perhaps occasioning the shattered windows of the Popper home. Egon David Popper died in 1985, aged 93.

[50] *Philadelphia Story* is the 1940 romantic comedy starring Cary Grant, Katharine Hepburn and James Stewart.

30th Jun. (morning)

Having seen a cloudless sky we, G.J. and I were all out in our swimsuits and would you believe it in half an hour the sky clouded completely over and we all had to put on sweaters. ...

Now as to politics – you say that war is the greatest crime of governments and that this particular war will not prove anything. I agree about it being the greatest crime and I think that the British Gov't. made as big a mess of policy as could have been made *but* at this stage with Hitler being what he is there is only one way to stop him and that is by beating him at war. You know that he and his gang are impossible to deal with and that if he wins, Europe will be plunged into such slavery and brutality that it will take generations of dark ages to see the light again. The fact that he is so powerful, destroys libraries, universities, brains in any form and people who could help lead the inevitable trend, means that he has got to be stopped and war is the only way. I know all your pacifist arguments because I argued on that side myself for 2 mo. of war. ... I know what you mean that £15,000,000 a day spent on war isn't getting mankind anyplace and that if it could be spent on social service or something beneficial instead of destructive it would be wonderful but until people are fighting for their lives they won't give up a darn thing. It's only in an air-raid that people realize that nothing counts but life – in other words that you can't take it with you and I know that you as a pacifist will say "but why take any life" but living under Hitler isn't living. I will be very interested to see Lindbergh's and Hutchin's speeches.[51] So far I am on the side of all aid for Britain including war much as I hate to think of America being in it because I am still 99 44/100 % American but I think that they can help end the war sooner and so lessen the tragedy – because sister is it tragic. I don't think the world will be settled for years and years or, as you say, until an economic democracy is reached, but the sooner Hitler is stopped the sooner the world can get going on a policy that if led by Britain and America won't be misled. Not that it will be perfect but anti-empire and all as you are, you must admit that living under England is better than living under Germany and don't

[51] Robert Maynard Hutchins (1899–1977) was a controversial educational philosopher who was director of the Yale Law School and then President of the University of Chicago. He opposed American involvement in the Second World War on the grounds that the United States was "morally unprepared".

misunderstand me I think England won't be boss any longer but America and England (America first). Another thing – even America could live in a world dominated everyplace by Hitler (which she can't because Hitler won't stop at America) it would be a very unhappy America because as long as this tragedy goes on you can't escape it no matter where you are – neutral or belligerent. As I said I held no brief for England up to last spring when Churchill came in but now they are fighting to rid the world of Hitler and admitting that every country is out for itself just as every individual is they mean well but the world this time – don't think I'm blinded by British propaganda – it isn't good enough.

Thems my sentiments and I think that the war will be over a year from this fall so get ready for an Irish invasion.

30th Jun. (afternoon)

I took [the evacuees] up to the train in Comber. They were sorry in a way to go but glad on the whole I think… we feel that we saved them from the 2nd blitz when their windows blew in and their ceilings fell so it was something. Also they eased our consciences during that time when we felt awful to have a house in a safe place with empty rooms.
…

A man on the radio just said that they need 30,000 women by August and 100,000 by Christmas – Women are conscripted in England now and nobody much has a maid. …

Lancelot has gone now to look after his bees – his latest craze. Had lunch and went to the movie with Auntie who is like somebody out of jail – just home from 2 weeks in Dublin where she had a wonderful time. Dublin is like that and I always feel a different person there – not repressed and inhibited like I do here. In fact Belfast and its people drive me crazy. When I am in Dublin I never want to come home. …

[Love,
Helen]

7th Aug.
Mahee

Dear Mother,

... Had ... arranged to go on a holiday with Maureen [Topping] ... At the last minute Julie got hives so I had to postpone going for a day but we finally got off and went to Dublin where we stayed at the Hibernian for a week.[52] I got along fine with Maureen and we giggled and giggled and both wanted to do the same things at the same time so all was well. She has been having a mental strain with Ken so was glad to get away. It was so hot in Dublin all the time and everyone wore summer dresses and no coats – it was just like Denver – or more like Northampton [MA] being very enervating. I bought 6 pairs of stockings and 3 Viyella shirts to wear with slacks and sent packages of food home and to Rosemary. ...

The news is on now with the Russian campaign taking first place – everyone is delighted about the war prospects and even the gloomiest people think it will be over in a year and the optimists say November!!![53]

We are having leg of lamb for lunch, peas, potatoes and tinned fruit that has been blitzed. The tins are all burnt and battered but the inside is good – L. got a chance to buy about 12 tins – all tinned goods practically has disappeared – certainly all fruit and all soup except Mock Turtle and Mulligatawny and the dull kinds. ...

12th Aug.

In Dublin Maureen and I saw 3 movies, went to the Gate Theatre, went to the Dail[54] and the Senate to hear Mr. De Valera who talked for an hour and was so nice. We shopped and ate and stared in amazement at

[52] The Royal Hibernian Hotel, Dawson Street was in 1941 the island's oldest hotel, going back to the early 1800s. In 1914 it was described as "the most fashionable first class hotel in Dublin": "The History of the Hibernian Hotel" – Arrow@DIT.

[53] Operation Barbarossa, the Nazi offensive against the Soviet Union, began on 22nd June, 1941. German success was swift in the first weeks and the Soviet counter-offensive did not get under way until that winter. Although Churchill pledged British support on the day the Nazi operation began, the optimism from today's vantage-point seems premature.

[54] The Irish parliament.

the style fashion and glamour on all sides . ... The things they haven't got in Eire are white flour, petrol, kerosene, coal and tea. You can't imagine how funny it is to have everything brown – bread, cakes, buns, sauces etc. and you get so tired of it and long for white bread and cake. The tea is as weak as water every place which suited me fine but kills the Irish – their ration is ½ oz. per person per week and the coffee and cocoa are scarce too. Half the cars had big gas balloons on top and the ration for a small car is 4 gallons a month of petrol. The times we cycled only about 2 private cars passed us going and coming although you see lots around in town in the daytime – but the bicycles are legion! When the lights change in the middle of Dublin at the foot of Grafton Street the bicycles start about 20 abreast – everybody cycles everywhere – glamour girls and all. There are signs up everyplace to conserve gas and electric power because they are so short owing to the coal shortage. Everyone says that all gas and electricity will be turned off this winter from 11 p.m. and the worst is that there are no candles and no lamp oil of any kind. Otherwise the food and other things are plentiful – all kinds of tinned fruits, dried fruits, onions, oranges, lemons and fresh summer fruits and of course the biggest treat for most people is cream – which is illegal here and has been since the first winter of the war.

The first night we were there we bought a box of strawberries each and I bought a tiny carton of cream and Maureen bought a shilling one but she couldn't finish it. We still haven't had a single tomato in this house this year – if you live in town you can nab them easily in the morning or profit by the "under-counter" trade – you never see them displayed but if you are in cahoots with the shop-keeper you get some slipped to you – the same goes on with everything scarce – cigarettes, strawberries, raspberries oranges and all. It is an awful racket and is known as the "black market" in its worst phases.

We went to the famous restaurant in Dublin called Jammets – it is terribly expensive and the food is supposed to be super and the people amusing. It has been going for about 100 years or so and looks something although it is small and conservative in décor – white tablecloths and an old-fashioned air of respectability. We also ate at

Michell's (sic), The Unicorn (run by Austrian refugees and so Continental) and here and there.[55]

We met a reporter friend of Maureen's in the Dail and it was he who got us passes in to hear De Valera – we feel so International or rather up in foreign affairs because it was a big debate about the emergency powers act and got very heated and wild. The reporter also took us to all the law courts including 3 police courts that were as good as a play. He took us to lunch at his house or rather flat and his wife had cooked the most super lunch. ...

We didn't hear the news at all and forgot that there was a war on. Eire didn't have the double summer time so they were an hour earlier than Ulster. Our time changed back last Sunday and we are so glad. We weren't in bed one night before midnight for 3 months, but now suddenly it is dark by about 9.30 and we have to black-out again after doing without it all summer. The searchlights were all practising last night and they are so pretty to watch. ...

Goodnight and love,
Helen

21st Aug.
Mahee

Dear Ginna and Lloyd, and Mother,

... The harvest is on now and what between feeding extra farm hands and soldiers who help us and having no cook my life is one long round of activity. ...

---

[55] Restaurant Jammet started by Michel and François Jammet was open between 1901 and 1967. The title of Frank McDonald's *Irish Times* article of 14th May, 2014 captures its reputation in its heyday: "Jammets: a Dublin treasure crowded with gourmets and wits". After the Second World War it was patronized by film actors because of the proximity of Ardmore Studios. Mitchell's bakery and café of Grafton Street, appointed confectioners to Her Majesty Queen Victoria in 1850, served customers from 1805 until the 1950s. It became Dublin's most fashionable premises in which to be seen. See "Mitchell's of Grafton Street," archiseek (online); and Rose Doyle, "Wine company keeps the spirit Alive for seven generations," *Irish Times*, 9th June 2004. The Unicorn is Dublin's oldest restaurant still open, starting up in 1938. It became an Italian restaurant and was owned for much of its life by Renato Sidoli, an immigrant from Bardi, Italy.

23rd Aug.

It is the most divine evening – sunny, warm and calm and I have just got Julie in and then listened to a very good radio talk on Home Life in Russia.[56] . ...

I have had such a busy day – I never drew breath until 5 o'clock. Aggie doesn't come on weekends so I had to go to Comber to buy lunch for 2 soldiers who came to help in the fields, get our weekly rations, collect our radio battery which was being charged and rush home to cook lunch. We had vegetable soup, sausages, 2 kinds of beans, potatoes, bread and butter and jam and tea. We haven't had a pudding for months. The grocer who married Annie, Johnny's second daughter, is such a live wire and gets us things that nobody else gets – today toffees 93 kinds, raisins, jellies, and mentholated spirits for a new lamp we've got. ...

One of the soldiers who was here today was in his house in London when it got a direct hit the front collapsed and the blast blew him out the back. ...

I have been reading two good books on the Film – *Footnotes to the Film* – a collection of articles by directors actors, scenery makers etc. and a French history of the Film translated.[57] If you get a chance to see *Quiet Wedding* don't miss it – it is English to the backbone and a scream.[58] Maureen and I saw it in Dublin and sat through it twice and giggled so much and so helplessly that we nearly had to go out. ...

[56] This interest in Russian domestic life reflected the fact that the Soviet Union was now an ally. "Family life in Russia" by Pearl Binder was broadcast on the BBC Home Service at 7.45pm, 23rd August. Binder (Lady Elwyn-Jones, 1904–1990) was a British writer, stained-glass artist, lithographer and book illustrator whose father, a Russian-Ukranian Jewish tailor, emigrated to the UK in 1890. See "Pearl Binder, artist & writer," *Spitalfields Life* (online magazine), 1st May 2010; see also "Pearl Binder," Wikipedia.

[57] Charles Davy edited *Footnotes to the Film: The Literature of the Cinema* (Lovat Dickson; Oxford University Press, 1937, rpt. 1970). Contributors to this work included Alfred Hitchcock on "Direction" and Robert Donat on "Film Acting".

[58] A British comedy of 1941 involving "premarital hanky-panky", *Quiet Wedding* was directed by Anthony Asquith from a screenplay by Terence Rattigan, based on a play of the same name by Esther McCracken and starring Margaret Lockwood and Derek Farr. According to the *New York Times*, which praised the film, production in London was interrupted five times by German bombs.

Did you read *The White Cliffs of Dover* by Alice Duer Miller?[59] Part of it or all of it was in *Life* and it was broadcast twice by Constance Cummings[60] and people here *loved* it – but then they love Dorothy Thompson too![61] She gives me *such* a pain ... The radio is quite good now and I listen to it practically all day every day. Maurice Shillington is in London now as "an assistant B.B.C. announcer".[62] ...

Jack Payne's band is playing "Song of India" now. The popular songs here now are "The Petals on the Daisies Tell Me So", "London Pride" (Noel Coward propaganda) "Mr. Brown of London Town (prop.)"[63] Apart from *The New Statesman* and *The New Yorker* which I read from cover to cover every week I hardly read anything – no time. With Gay away Julie won't leave my side all day and she is such a chatter box and has a new habit of saying "Why?" after everything I say – she doesn't really want to know but it just comes out as she draws breath. They just played "Pretty Little Busybody" and are starting "Ay Ay Ay Ay Ay I Like You Very Much" which they play at least 6 times

---

[59] Alice Duer Miller (1874–1942) was a New York-born poet and novelist whose best-selling verse-fiction *The White Cliffs* (1940) was credited with swaying American opinion towards intervention. The works ends: "But in a world in which England is finished and dead,/I do not wish to live". The book became a Hollywood movie in 1944 under the title of *The White Cliffs of Dover*. In earlier decades, Miller's satirical poems had furthered the cause of female suffrage.

[60] Constance Cummings (1910–2005) was an American-born British stage and screen actress.

[61] A 1939 issue of *Time* magazine recognized Thompson (1893–1961), the suffragist, journalist and radio broadcaster, as the most influential American woman after Eleanor Roosevelt. She became head of the *New York Post* Berlin bureau and in 1931 interviewed Hitler; the resulting book, *I Saw Hitler!* (1932) – in which she called him the archetypal "little man" – caused her to be expelled from Germany in 1934. Helen might have been annoyed by Thompson through her popular radio broadcasts in the late 1930s. Thompson's second husband was the American novelist Sinclair Lewis.

[62] See the letter of 4th December, 1939.

[63] Jack Payne (1899–1969), an English bandleader. "Song of India" was a song adapted from a 1896 Rimsky-Korsakov aria; Tommy Dorsey's 1937 instrumental (big band) version was immensely popular. Noel Coward wrote his patriotic song "London Pride" during the London Blitz in spring 1941; the perennial flower of the title ("London pride is a flower that's free") was known quickly to colonise the capital's bomb sites. "Mr. Brown of London Town", 1941 (by Reginald Arkell and Noel Gay), was a paean to the eponymous London Everyman who responded to the Blitz with true London grit; it was recorded by Carroll Gibbons and the Savoy Hotel Orpheans.

a day.[64] ...(here is "London Pride", I knew they would play it – described as "that grand number".)

[24th Aug.]

... We just had supper in the kitchen which is such a pretty room now and so clean and warm with our Esse cooker. We have the anthracite stove going in the bathroom again and it is *divine*. We have to black-out *again* about 9 o'clock – such a nuisance. We listened to Churchill who was as good as ever and seemed to be trying to make the *Americans* see the light.[65]

Have you seen it yet? The news of the 2000 mile bloody front of the Russo-German battle makes me clean sick. If Russia can't hold them for the winter we will have another panic here – bombing, invasion and all. ...

Despite my acid remarks on your political letters which were the result of an acid outlook on my part I would like you to continue giving me the lowdown on what America thinks. We saw Toby Spence at the Dolans. It is 2 years now since Kathleen and the boys sailed off to America – such a pity for him. I am always glad I didn't go last summer. ... but believe it or not I am more American than ever despite my "old world" wall paper. Have just decided that this room needs floor

---

[64] "Pretty Little Busybody" is a song of weightless charm unconnected to the reality surrounding its composition and recorded in 1941 both by Gracie Fields and the Joe Loss Orchestra. "I, Yi, Yi, Yi, Yi Like You Very Much" (1941, Warren and Gordon) was recorded both by The Andrews Sisters and Carmen Miranda.

[65] This letter, or portion of a letter, is undated and without a greeting but almost certainly the evening on which Helen wrote was the 24th August. That day Churchill broadcast to the nation about his waterborne meeting with President Roosevelt for three days in Placentia Bay, Newfoundland in early August. The meeting took place a couple of months after Hitler invaded Russia, a bloody campaign on which Churchill comments in his speech. President and Prime Minister, in Churchill's phrase, "flashed across the waters" several messages to the world, known formally as the Atlantic Charter, and Churchill succeeded in drawing the United States closer to war. The two leaders affirmed the wartime closeness of the United States and the British Empire; they agreed to avoid a Versailles-type exaction upon Germany when the latter was defeated; and they extended the spirit of hope to the conquered peoples: the Norwegians, the Czechs, the Poles, the French, the Dutch, the Belgians, the Yugoslavs, the Greeks. See "Winston Churchill: Broadcast Regarding his Meeting with Roosevelt", Jewish Virtual Library: A Project of AICE (online).

covering for the winter badly. Must go to bed now. Love to you and my in-law.

Helen

2nd Sept.
Mahee

Dear Mother,

… The Pims stopped by in their yacht on Sunday morning – Dick Pim is Churchill's aide-de-camp or private secretary or something important and both he and Harry were along on the meeting between Churchill and Roosevelt.[66] Marjorie and the 2 boys live in a suburb of London and had some bombing all right but nothing closer than ¼ mile away – close enough – goodness knows.

The two new maids are sisters – Nan and Eileen – Nan (Nanny to us) is about 26 and Eileen is 16 and has never been away from home before. Nan has been cook and nursemaid and seems so nice and so fond of children. I just hope it's true. If only they can get acquainted around the district I think they will like it. Nan was in the blitz in Belfast and doesn't want to go back there. The maid problem is the one big snag of living here – otherwise it is perfect – war or peace.

8th Sept.

How times flies! And my correspondence gets worse and worse and now I am suffering from an impacted wisdom tooth and radiating neuralgia. It isn't as bad as it sounds and my tooth will be coming out one of these days… I went to see Dr. Foster today and he sent me to the dentist who put a dressing on the erring tooth and if that doesn't help it I will have it out right away. I also went to the new movie *Target for Tonight*, a British propaganda film of a real bombing attack on Germany and it is *wonderful* – so well directed and so real.[67] It is bound

---

[66] For Dick Pim and Harry McMullan, see the letter of 21st September 1939.

[67] *Target for Tonight* is a lightly fictionalized 1941 British documentary, written and directed by Harry Watt. The film follows a Wellington bomber crew before and during a mission to destroy a German oil storage facility.

to be shown in America for propaganda purposes so be sure to see it – it will wring you out.

The maids are still doing nicely and seem to like it. Julie is so attached to me that I will have to stay out of the way until she gets over it. The maids are much more southern than northern both in their speech and temperament and they live on the border. ...

We have a new cow named "Bluebell" and have lots of butter again as well as having plenty of milk and being able to give the Brownes 3 quarts a day. The new cow gives 3 gallons in the morning and 6 quarts at night. That makes 3 cows we have and a calf. Elsie, Mary, Bluebell and Beulah are named after the Borden cow you know the one in the advertisement with the daisies round her neck.[68]

Our hens are laying so badly we barely get an egg a day from over 20! ... The ration is one egg per person per week. Our maids are playing the gramophone – now "Johnnie Pedlar" – do you know that? Both Gay and Julie are so musical and can sing quite well – and dance. I bought "I've Got Sixpence" the other day and they were so cute dancing hand in hand in the nursery.[69] ...

A friend of ours just flew home from America on a bomber – we don't know him well but he lives near here in the summer and is in the linen business and has been stuck in America for well over a year because there were no boats for passengers coming and if he came on the Clipper to Lisbon he couldn't get from Lisbon to London – only priority people can – ambassadors, govt. officials etc. so he finally wangled a seat in a bomber – he is in Ewarts who pulled strings and I think Dick Pim helped. Anyway his wife was wild because he couldn't come home so she will be delighted. ...

L.'s job has sort of died down until there is another blitz which we naturally fervently hope there won't be. He has to see about salvaging ship wrecked food now though so he has enough to do.

---

[68] The cartoon cow, Elsie, was adopted as a mascot on the advertisements of the Borden Dairy Company until the 1990s; the image was well-known in the United States and Canada.

[69] "Johnny Peddler" was recorded in 1940 by the Andrews Sisters, Geraldo and the Savoy Hotel orchestra, and Billy Cotton and his Band, and as "Johnny Pedlar" by Harry Roy and his Band. "I've Got Sixpence" was performed by the Phil Moore Four; this rollicking morale-booster of a song appears to have had its origins in folksong.

Matches are the latest thing to become scarce and oatmeal is nonexistent but cigarettes are more plentiful. ...

I haven't heard from either of you for *weeks* !!

Nighty-night and love,
Helen

1st Nov.
Mahee

Dear Ginna and Lloyd,

I will turn over a new leaf and try to do better since it is the beginning of a month. I owe everybody letters and seem to have such a little time to write which is surprising when you think that we have a cook and a nurse and lead a quiet country life. ...

It isn't light now until 8 and by the 21st of December it will be dark until 9 or 9.30 and by January even darker in the mornings but lighter in the evenings. One consolation is that we see the sun rise opposite our bedroom window every morning that it does rise and the cloud effects (there are practically always clouds) are divine. The winter here is even prettier to look at than the summer all due to the extraordinary lighting effects that are one of the chief charms of Ireland and some days are literally breathtaking and it is such a pleasure to drive and walk around. Eggy once said that people in the country pay more attention to the weather and it is so true. When we lived in Belfast I used to be surprised when people would say "how bad the weather has been lately" because unless it was icy I didn't notice the rain or the sun much but here I even know from which direction the wind is blowing every day and can see the point to the question "How does the East wind affect you?" which I thought so odd in 1933. In fact lots of the things I thought so odd in 1933 have become normal to me now – probably you would notice a greater change in me that I notice myself and as usual when we meet it will be downright exhilarating to compare notes and see the changes that the years and such utterly different environments have wrought.

For one thing I am not as repressed as I used to be here. Not that I was repressed with you but with the natives who are so repressed themselves and will always be foreigners to me and I to them. It is interesting to live among foreigners, but sort of sad in many ways. But I am convinced that people here on the whole enjoy themselves much more than Americans in their own quiet ways – 1. because they lead more ordered lives – which can of course be carried too far but which in most cases give a sort of perspective or frame to their lives. 2. because they enjoy nature so much more. 3. because they haven't the inbred characteristic of being "on the make" that Americans have – that is trying so hard to be richer, better etc. in the future that they can't enjoy the present 4. And finally because they have a better sense of values. However despite all of these things I would rather live in America because I think you are always happier in your own country. But if I had lived all these years in America I don't think I would have had as good an idea "of what I want" from life (I'm still pretty hazy but then my mind always was a hazy one and I only see things in a blurred sort of general way missing details for years, and then being struck all of a heap by some blinding revelation.

Two books that I think you would like very much for lots of little side lights are *Hudson River Bracketed* and the sequel – I forget the name but will put it in when I think of it.[70] They are by Edith Wharton who I have found very readable and interesting. I have read as many of her books as I can find, but there aren't many in the libraries here. She has a better idea of things than Willa Cather, I think, although she doesn't write such poetic prose. ...

Sometimes when I read *The New Statesman* or hear certain propaganda programs on the radio I feel an awful urge to rush out and help with the war effort because it is so very desperate. The general impression here is that no one will realize how critical our position is, but I with the rest keep hoping for a miracle before Total War is launched against what is repeatedly called "This Island Fortress."

I had one triumph this week – a huge pumpkin about 18 inches high and beautifully shaped. Mrs. Dolan told me that she had seen it so I rushed in and bought it and the kids love it. We took it to the party but brought it home again and G. and J. had it lighted in the nursery [for Halloween] for about ½ an hour after they went to bed.

[70] Edith Wharton (1862–1937) published *Hudson River Bracketed* (set in New York) in 1929 and it is regarded by some as unjustly neglected. The title refers to an architectural style originated by Alexander Jackson Davis. The sequel, *The Gods Arrive*, appeared in 1932.

I went to the canteen yesterday. It is fun but such hard work – the shift is from 1.30–5.30 and yesterday there were only 7 helpers instead of the usual 12 or 15 and we literally never drew breath. I was at the counter all the time serving tea, coffee, milk, sandwiches, buns, and selling cigarettes, soap handkerchiefs, shoe-laces, stamps, chocolate, tooth-paste etc and washing dishes in between as fast as I could. We got behind and got to the stage of having to wash a cup before we could put tea in it – it was frenzied. I was dead at the end of it. ...

The blackout is the thing that makes living in town so horrid and the streets and roads were practically empty at 10.30.[71] The trams stop at 10.30 and since nearly everybody goes everyplace by tram it isn't conducive to much social gaiety. Betty Haselden invited us to a dance last night at the Officers' Club but we couldn't go and I didn't care much.[72] I would love to go to a good dance, but ... I should think that the officers' club wouldn't be much fun though it would be interesting to see it. In London and most English towns I hear that the officers' clubs are glorified brothels but here they try to keep the floosies out but it is hard because all you need to get in is to be brought by an officer.

3rd Nov.

Now it is Monday morning and the thrasher [threshing machine] is here which means a cool 17 for lunch and tea!!! And I can sit down in the middle of it all with nothing to do – s'marvelous. The kids are parked in bed bribed to be good and the 17 will pour in for lunch at 12. I set the tables and generally whipped around. Mrs. Turtle is exercising in the drawing room and generally impeding the effort in every way that she can. What a woman! She is going home today and I can hardly wait. She has been here for 12 days and has fought every day of the 12 with someone – mostly L. because I leave the room on trumped up errands – argument on Socialism and I shook with rage. She is getting much worse – and has such a warped view point from living alone and puttering over herself all day. It is a pity that she is so unpleasant but she is. ...

---

[71] At the time of the letter, blackout was from 6.21pm until 7.55am.

[72] The Halloween Dance held at the Officers' Club, High Street Belfast, was in aid of the Ulster Hospital for Children.

Tell Mother that I'm not having a baby – she is always suspecting that I am but I'm not. I often wish I were and then sometimes I'm glad I'm not.

It is so too bad that we are so separated and life just streaming past us when we could be having such fun together. It is a damnable war and we don't know half of it. People here now have switched to the idea of a long war and the prospect is gloomy. I am thankful every day that I didn't come home last summer. The planes fly here all day and all night – L. is always hopping out of bed saying "That's a German plane" but it never is. ...

G.bye and love,
Helen

10th Nov.
Mahee

Dear Mother,

There has been a gale blowing for nearly 48 hours now right smack against the front of our house and we spend our entire time battling with the elements *inside* the house. Every single window leaks even the steel one in the dining room and in this, our new living room, it is like a bubbling spring to listen to and like a flood to deal with! We have towels, bathmats, tea towels, chamois and wash cloths on all the window sills and we have to renew them two or three times a day. The noise of the rain on the windows is deafening, the wind howls and roars in the trees and around the house the telephone rings and tinkles all the time but doesn't work and great gray waves with white tops crash against the wall all day because it has been raging since Saturday evening and this is Monday afternoon. ...

I listened to the radio and told the children a story at lunch-time that I had heard on the program for schools about a worm who felt so sorry for itself because it had no face, no legs, no arms, no hair and was so despised and gray – so God changed it into what it wanted to be – a monster 1,000,000 times as big as a worm and it wasn't happy either. Gay and Julie listened open-mouthed especially Gay who loves stories better than anything and she nearly cried over the worm's sad plight –

her face is so expressive. … It is only four now but so dark that I would need a light if I weren't near the window. Such a day!! – and I can't even call anybody up to condole and get sympathy. The wind and rain are just as bad as ever. The radio is playing away – an orchestral concert now. I have it on most all day and learn so much from it.

Alexander Woolcott [sic] gave the postscript to the news last night – and he was feebly amusing, but not good.[73] They usually have very good people to give that broadcast which everyone listens to. People are feeling that it is going to be a long war – I give it a year but then I'm an optimist. I think that Hitler finished himself by attacking Russia. The British are bombing Germany as hard as they can every night and everyone felt so bad about the 37 bombers that were lost on Friday night when the biggest air attack that was ever tried hit such bad weather.[74] …

The *New Yorker* English correspondent was in Belfast a few weeks ago and in the last one we got was her article "Letter from Belfast" – it is as good as all of her articles – the date is Sept. 27th if Ginna or someone you know takes the *New Yorker*.[75] …

Nanny has a beau among the soldiers at the Glendinnings so that is what makes her stay I should think. He is so nice looking and it seems pretty serious. She is quite attractive and a terrific hustler – when she works she goes full at it and accomplishes wonders. She also does what cooking organizing is done. She just came in with them and they are all playing in the kitchen. …

[73] Alexander Woollcott (1887–1943), the often acerbic theatre critic, essayist, editor and actor, was variously a reporter for the *New York Times*, radio broadcaster, and critic and commentator for the *New Yorker*. He was said to be the model for Sheridan Whiteside in the play, *The Man Who Came to Dinner* (1939).

[74] Oddly, Helen has got hold of morale-sapping numbers of lost planes. The apparent truth was bad enough. On 7th November, RAF Bomber Command carried out a large raid on Berlin, employing 160 bombers. Little damage was done to the city but over twenty planes were shot down or crashed. As a result, the Head of Bomber Command was dismissed and replaced by the later controversial Sir Arthur Travers "Bomber" Harris.

[75] Mollie Panter-Downes' "Letter from Belfast" (filed 21st September) notes the city's over-pitched loyalty to the monarchy and the United Kingdom, underlain with a fear that the U.K. will abandon Northern Ireland as part of a post-war settlement. She notes, too, the religiously based social compartmentalism of Ulster life and the seeming irony of enlistment in the British Army being more vigorous from neutral Éire than from loyal Ulster. Rationing is as in the U.K. but the contiguity of Éire has relieved the pressure on some goods. Not on gas (petrol), however, and she sees the cars with bags of coal-gas on top that Helen saw in Dublin.

I just said to Lancelot that it pays so to keep well because when I had 'flu and since I felt so depressed and then the war and everything gets you down so. Not that everybody isn't got down to the ground by it anyway, but if you feel well you can laugh it off which people are wonderful at doing. There are so many people like Edith, Barbara Glendinning, and others whose husbands are in the navy. Bodo has been away for nearly a year now and under fire and having an awful time – he is in the middle-east. Edith is so cheerful, but she doesn't sleep well and looks so thin and worried. Barbara's husband is home now but for months after he left she didn't hear a word and didn't know at all where he was. She has been with him for nearly two weeks now, but she is afraid that he has to go back to the same place after only a week's leave – the place is that country that Ginna used always to be reading novels about – you know those good classic novels by people with hard names to pronounce.[76] ...

Friday I struggled to town feeling punto to go to the Isaacs to lunch[77] and to buy Ann a wedding present. I had no intention of staying in town to go to Arabella's to dinner but in the end I did and had such a good time. ... Arabella had 10 people – us, Jack and Elaine, Eddie and Eileen Bryson, Jim Barr and an English girl named Judith Townley who is so nice. Gordon had brought a goose from the Free State and it was a hooping, hollering success. We played Lexicon afterward[78]. ... Arabella is such a good housekeeper and loves every minute of it – she spends most of her time doing it but she is good and a very easy jokey hostess. She is as happy as a lark and laughs so much. Getting married made a new person out of her. ...

Mrs. Carr, John's mother was there. Mrs. Glendinning says that Mrs. Carr looks so sad that it breaks her heart to see her. Mrs. Carr said that Tommy has just had an exhibition in London and that he got such a good criticism in the *London Times*. And now with the paper shortage and newspapers only about 2 pages each they must think he is good to have a criticism at all. ...

[76] Helen is – hardly subtly – alluding to the Soviet Union.

[77] For the Isaacs, see the letter of 15th November, 1939. Punto is a slang word meaning weird or shady but Helen's meaning is probably different: off-colour, perhaps.

[78] A card game based on, as the name suggests, the forming of words.

We haven't had any matches for over a week!!! And with gas and candles and cigarettes to light and the wind blowing our tapers out it is frantic. It is 8 o'clock and the wind is still roaring away, but the rain has stopped.

Love,
Helen

15th Dec.
Mahee

Dear Mother,

… We can hardly wait to get your letters to hear what you have to say about America entering the war. Our first inkling was a week yesterday – the fateful Sunday in fact – the 7th.[79] We went to Randalstown for the day – leaving here around 11 with a picnic lunch. We picked up Hilary and Eggy at their house and went on through the dark cloudy day and the rain. … We were using Eggy's petrol because we had our trailer to collect a wardrobe that Eggy had bought. … Hilary was as neat as a pin as usual – every hair in place and a hairnet on. Eggy was getting a cold and was glum and silent – he is so changed that you wouldn't know him … – very unhappy or else completely worn out.

Anyway we had tea and a good time with Rosemary [Bryson] where they had 3 turf fires blazing. It snowed there and we had to have the heat on about 3 and it was a terrible day. We had missed the 1 o'clock news but Rosemary said that Roosevelt had sent a message to the Emperor of Japan and that things looked bad. We missed the 6 o'clock news too but were "Johnnie on the spot" to hear the 9 o'clock news about the attack on Manila and Pearl Harbor. We got to bed about 11.45 but I got up again to hear the midnight news and heard the worst and realized that it was war this time all right. My feelings are mixed but I was mostly excited, pleased in a way but sad too to think that now America was at war and that you and Ginna and Lloyd and everybody are involved. We got up bright and early to hear the 8

[79] That day, Japan attacked Pearl Harbor in the Hawaiian Islands. The U.S.A declared war on the Empire of Japan as a result. President Roosevelt's broadcast speech to a joint session of Congress on 8th December is available online to see and hear.

o'clock news and talked so hard about it all the way into town that I had nervous indigestion in the middle of the morning and had to stop at a milk-bar to get some soup. Mrs. Glendinning rang up before we left about the party we were going to give together that night for the soldiers and she said "Did you hear the great news?" So that's how she felt. I had an appointment with the dentist at 10 and called in to see Roberta beforehand as she lives right across the Malone Road from where L. works now. She was sorry about it because she had hoped the war might be over in a year and now thinks it will be 2 or 3 anyway. My dentist said "Well, we're all together now" and was pleased. I saw Philsy Bell in the library[80] and he was sorry to see the war spread and felt depressed. I went to Janie McNeill's to lunch and we talked of nothing else – she was maliciously glad that America had to come in, but was sorry that it would mean not so many supplies for England and Russia.[81] When I say malicious I don't quite mean that – I mean that most people here were mad at America for not doing more sooner – though lately they have been better pleased with all the lend-lease stuff and lots thought genuinely that it would be more advantageous for England if America would stay out and be the arsenal – I definitely thought and know that America would never put her whole force into it until she was wholly in it and hoped that she would come in soon though now that it has happened I am sorry – in the way I said that I can't think of you living normal lives. At the D.R.C. in the afternoon I saw Auntie who didn't realize that America was at war with Japan and shortly after we got home at 7 she rang up in a great state of excitement having just listened to the President declaring war. We had to rush right out to the Glendinnings where we played Military Whist with about 30 soldiers from 7.30 to 11.30 and then they sang for about an hour and we didn't get home until 1. We heard the midnight news there and took our radio with us the next morning when we started for our tour of Ulster. I didn't think that Germany would come [invade] now at all

[80] For Philip Bell the architect see the letter of 8th July, 1940. The library is probably the Linen Hall Library where it has been reported Bell did much of his research: Anne Hailes, "When life adds up to a big success story", *Irish News*, 14th October, 2013.

[81] Janie McNeill was a member of the DRC and a friend of C.S. Lewis. Lewis dedicated *That Hideous Strength* (1945), published in the U.S. as *The Tortured Planet*, to Janie McNeill who was displeased: "'I hate it,' she told her friend Mary [Morwood] Rogers. 'I wish he'd dedicated any book other than this to me'.": Paul Simpson, *A Brief Guide to C.S. Lewis: From Mere Christianity to Narnia* (2013).

– we were in Enniskillen that night where we heard that the officers of the American Air Force had flown home on Monday and in Derry the next day we heard of the sinking of the *Prince of Wales* and the *Repulse*[82] and I listened to the President's fireside chat and realized from his tone that America was in a frenzy and a panic and from the papers which I pored over for the first time since Dunkirk I realized the same thing.[83] I still can't believe it – sirens in N.Y. and Boston, California blacked out and the whole business – as Raymond Gram Swing said in a wonderful broadcast Saturday night – the Americans felt as if a nightmare had come true. After his "American Commentary" on the radio there was a very stirring program "Salute to America" which I near bawled over and Auntie said that she did – I would have if I had been alone but Lancelot's male presence pulled me together. Last night they played American patriotic tunes before the 9 o'clock news because everybody, they said would like it to honor our new ally and I felt like the girl in the *White Cliffs of Dover*.[84] That's our story, what's yours. The sinking of the *Repulse* and *The Prince of Wales* nearly killed everybody here but it did stop people from making the cracks they started to make about how America had been caught napping and should have done better at defending herself. A few people did make the crack as I just piped up and said "what about England?"

We stopped to see Percy and Doreen and had lunch with them. It was Percy's one day a week off – he works the same hours something like Harry – 24 hours on 24 off so on – 48 off etc. Percy was surprisingly cheerful – usually he is very sour and bitter about the

---

[82] On 10th December, the battleship HMS *Prince of Wales* and battlecruiser HMS *Repulse*, part of a Royal Navy task force (Force Z) meant to deter Japanese military expansion, were sunk by torpedo bombers of the Japanese Imperial Navy near Singapore. Eight hundred and forty British sailors were lost.

[83] In his Fireside Chat of 9th December, Roosevelt did admit that "So far, the news has been all bad ... The casualty lists of these first few days will undoubtedly be large", but what Helen interprets as panic may well have been haste and American impatience (after years of ambivalence) to man the action stations.

[84] The girl is the American Susan Dunne, narrator of Duer Miller's narrative poem, "The White Cliffs", who visits England, falls in love with it, and falls in love with an Englishman and marries him. During the Great War she is unhappy at America's neutrality: "What could I do, but ache and long/That my country, peaceful, rich, and strong/Should come and do battle for England's sake/What could I do but long and ache". Then doughboys arrive in London: "At last – at last – like the dawn of a calm, fair day .../they came-/...And as the American flag went fluttering by/Englishmen uncovered, and I began to cry".

government and its mistakes – but he wasn't. He is a lieutenant now in the navy. ... Doreen is sweet but in local parlance "no crack". Percy wants to know if Ginna is still a pacifist and I assured him that I'm sure she isn't now – is she? ...

Zoo said the funniest thing today. She nearly bumped into the radio and said "I nearly fell into the radio and then I would be all newsy"!

... The news is on and it is going over the world place by place. California is in a state of emergency. Australia sounds jittery – they have been asked to forgo holidays. It will cramp Christmas all over the world. ...

Auntie is off on a toot to Dublin. ... It is funny to think that Eire, little Eire, is one of the few neutral places in the world!! They feel worse since America is in – there was an article in *The Irish Times* by the Minister of Home Security saying how serious their position is. ...

... I wish like anything that I could cook, sew, dress-make, remodel, dry-clean etc but I'm so heedless and unpractical that it is uphill work. You know me Ma, but as I often say and wish to go on record as saying if this war goes on for another two years our lives will be so different that we won't know ourselves. As it is so far we are perfectly happy and content and do you know I think we still will be, come what may, along material lines but then I always was a silver-lining looker for.

Must go to bed – Happy New Year,

love and kisses and many of them
Helen

21st Dec.[85]
Mahee

Dear Ginna and Lloyd,

I am sitting nearly on top of the fire writing by gaslight (dim) and waiting until 8 o'clock to turn on the radio to hear *No No Nanette*.[86]

[85] Unless Helen got her days confused (unlikely), this letter was written on Monday 22nd December when at 8pm the BBC Home Service broadcast the first Act of *No No Nanette*. On 21st (Sunday) at 8pm there was a "Christmas Tree Service" from a church crypt!

[86] *No No Nanette* is an American musical comedy of 1924, adapted from a 1919 Broadway play called *My Lady Friends*. It was a hit both on Broadway and in the London West End, opening in both in 1925.

Lancelot has gone to Newtownards to get two hives of bees and Gay and Julie are fast asleep dreaming about sugar plums and fairies and Santa Claus. We spent the entire day in town leaving here in pitch darkness at 8.30 and returning home in pitch darkness at 6.45. Gay and Julie were as good as gold – neither shed a tear or even whimpered which considering the long day, their quiet country lives, and the stresses and strains of Christmas shopping was pretty good. Not that we shopped all day, Oh dear no! But we did from 9.30–12.15. ...

G. and J. hadn't been in town since the summer practically so they were all agog to see the sights. We tried to find Santa Claus but he had had to go back to the North Pole because he ran out of presents to hand out. The toy situation is pretty pathetic – of course it's late in the day now, but this year's display was pretty terrible. ... We trimmed the tree yesterday and Gay's excitement was fever-pitch. She sang and gabbled and made up poetry and was literally beside herself. Our tree is small (nearly to the ceiling standing on a table) and as ugly as sin but it has so much hanging on it that it looks wonderful. We can't get candles but "it shimmers lovely" anyway. We have holly sprigs about the pictures in the *quaint* British custom and holly on the clocks and Gay used all the extra tinsel that the tree couldn't carry to decorate the nursery and their beds glisten and gleam and all in all we are having a riotous time. ...

Our hens have at last started to lay and we are giving eggs for Christmas presents and people love us as if we have given them pure gold.

23rd Dec.

This is Tuesday morning and only 9.30 and still too dark to do without a light. ...

We are actually going to a ball tonight – the first we have danced since last February. The Vailes asked us and are giving a fork supper first. The ball is an army officers' dance given by the Staffordshires the regiment that Colonel Vaile is head of and Jack and Elaine are going too. I am going to wear my new black dinner dress and my new Christmas present that I bought myself with some money that Auntie gave me augmented by my handsome husband. The present is a pair of aquamarine and gold and pearl clips, earrings or hair ornaments and they are sweet – antique and second hand and very cheap $12.50 for two and they look easily $12.50 each or more because they are old and good – and as I cheerily said to L. they will do for Gay and Julie when I'm gone. ...

The news was just announced this morning that Winnie is in Washington and guess who is with him no one but our old pal Harry. I stopped to see Roberta last Friday and asked her when Harry would be home and she said that he had rung her up from the Admiralty about a week before to say that he was going away for 6 or 8 weeks and that she wouldn't hear from him so she put two and two together and guessed that he had gone to America but she didn't think that Winnie had gone at this crucial stage in the war.[87] People do feel that things are pretty crucial now since the Japs have got so uppish. It was losing these two big battleships that nearly killed everybody here and as I told Mother it saved America's face for her un-preparedness. Everybody here is so mad at the isolationists who backed the plans for defending those islands, but it is easy afterward to see where you were wrong. Goodness knows England was just as blind. The ones I hand it to are the Russians who I honestly believe have won the war. I think that no matter how long it goes on the Russians have turned the tide and when you think of them fighting for 6 months on a 1500 mile front and pushing the Germans back again in the end it is terrific. They seem to be the only ones who understand total war. I do hope that you won't be so maddened by my cable that you won't write to tell me how you feel and think now. I'll bet a nickel that Kathleen Spence and her ma have moved inland from California.[88]

[87] Churchill's unannounced trip to the United States from the UK took ten days and he stayed three weeks, returning to England on 14th January, 1942. While in Washington DC he joined Roosevelt in a press conference on 23rd December, helped light the Washington Christmas tree, and on Boxing Day addressed a joint session of Congress. Together they planned a broad military strategy to defeat the enemy. Churchill had a five-day vacation in Florida and a trip to Ottawa to address the Canadian parliament before returning. See Dan Majors, "Christmas 1941: With world at war, Churchill joins FDR for Washington Yule," *Pittsburgh Post-Gazette*, 25th December 2011; Eric Trickey, "In the Darkest Days of World War II, Winston Churchill's Visit to the White House Brought Hope to Washington," 13th January 2017, Smithsonian.com.

[88] Helen knew her friend well. When the attack on Pearl Harbor happened in December 1941, Kathleen Spence was living in Seabright, a seaside town near Santa Cruz in California. Her mother bought her a house inland up in Spokane, Washington State, and she and her children lived in it until after Christmas 1942. Spence narrates these events in her unpublished autobiography written in 1983, pp. 87–88, kindly sent to me by Eleanor Grene.

Austen Boyd told L. that Janet wants to come home and bring the kids but he is against it. I get chills and fever when I think how very nearly I went too in 1940 and am so glad that I didn't although anything may happen yet, and I have no illusions about how much safer Denver is than Ireland, but you've got to risk something sometimes. The stories of the starving continent are nightmarish and even in England the food situation is only about half as good as it is here. This Christmas we got prunes, raisins, currants, 1 doz. oranges, a ham, and the Middletons gave us a turkey. In England the milk situation is so bad – 2 pts. a week for grownups. All babies under two get free cod liver oil and black currant juice which is a very wise move. I give G. and J. an ascorbic acid pill every day and they take an iron tonic. ... I have to go easy on eggs, but they look fine and are both big and fat and seem strong. Everybody says what a healthy place this is for them and I suppose it is. ...

Here comes a program called "Wise housekeeping" to which I always listen intently in an effort to improve mine but my heart isn't in it.[89] I am going to cook the turkey, though, probably Saturday. We are going to Auntie's for Christmas Day and to Arabella's on Boxing night if we can get Mrs. Middleton to come sit with G. and J. We only have 17 Christmas cards so far – no American ones yet – I didn't send any to America because as usual I waited too long and you can't buy pretty ones. Ours are a dull looking lot this year and the ones we sent were awful. I sent about 16 to children and 30 to grownups. We have quite a few service cards with just a crest of the regiment and Bodo sent us an airgraph one – done by photographing a card and then reducing it to about an inch square on a film and sending it airmail and then enlarging it again at this end.

The Glendinnings are having a worrying Christmas. Their son and 3 sons-in-law are in the services. Their son is in Ireland. Chris – Barbara's husband is at sea, Joan is stuck in India with 2 very young children and her husband has just gone to Singapore – of all places – and the baby's husband is in Malaya in the part where the fiercest fighting is going on – the baby is Mary who isn't 21 yet and was

---

[89] A weekly BBC Home Service "magazine programme for women in which all aspects of running a home in wartime will be discussed".

married nearly 2 years ago, had a four day honeymoon and off her husband went to Singapore[90]. ...

Our canteen was burned accidentally so until they get it all fixed up again we don't have to go. It was such bad luck because they just had it fixed up from the blitz when it was slightly damaged. I like to go to it though it is very hard work – 4 hours of frantic rushing. ...

Nanny has made Bobby and Jane [dolls] each a new dress and pixie cap and is making them wreaths and veils – probably something Papish! She has taught Zoo such a Papish prayer – something like this:

> As I lay down my head to sleep
> I pray the Lord my soul to keep
> If any evil happen me
> O Holy Mother watch o'er me.
> There are four corners round my bed
>   "   "   " saints   "   "   " head
> "Matt" and Mark and Luke and John
> God bless the bed that I lie on.[91] ...

Subtly and gradually England especially and Ireland incidentally have become so socialistic. Maids are gone in Eng. Big cars are out of sight, dukes and earls ride in Baby Austins or walk or take the train, anybody with a car gives lifts to anybody walking, there can be no ostentation of dress or food or entertaining and most noticeable of all is the spirit – no one gives a hoot about their lisle stockings – this all has exceptions but you maybe can see the drift. What is killing everyone is that here where there is no conscription workmen are getting fabulous wages while soldiers get their shilling a day, or whatever it is. Everybody thinks that all labor should be conscripted and they are beginning to do it in Eng. with the calling up of men and more people – in fact very soon in Eng. everybody will be a war-worker of some sort. ...

Gordon says that Eire is more jittery than ever since America has come in. They have no coal and no candles and no paraffin oil for

[90] The Glendinning son was Harden; Barbara Glendinning was married to Christopher Gotto RNVR (see the letter of 16th February 1943 for the Gotto family); Joan was married to Godfrey Vinycomb, Royal Indian Army Service; Mary was married to Humphrey Thomson RAMC.

[91] The editor (brought up Presbyterian in Belfast) said this prayer when a child on getting into bed, but without reference to the Holy Mother or to "saints": the Blessed Virgin was unsummoned and the saints were the less theologically problematic angels.

lamps and no petrol. The train services are awful and the passengers have to get out at peat bogs and help gather peat to stoke the engine. People sit with rugs around their shoulders and rugs over their knees but Dublin is as gay as ever! I might go for a toot there after Christmas. Jan. Feb and March are the worst months here. So far we have had no really cold weather. Today is so mild and the air is so soft and the light (no sun) makes all the colors so hazy and blurry – or is it just my astigmatism? ...

Do you know that I have been writing this letter all morning. I am just sitting here trying to make up news to keep me near the fire though I ran out pages ago.

Dunsmuir Mitchell has been invalided out of the Navy – he is farming at home living all alone in that big house.[92] We have asked him down for a weekend in January – also Alan Smiles, who is going into the Navy at the end of Jan. The Scanlans, the Carrs, and Maureen and Mark – there aren't enough weekends to go around but we can stretch some over into Feb. and March. ...

31st Dec.

Here I sit again of a Wednesday morning brooding on the end of one year and the birth of another. I said at the beginning of 1941 that if we could live through it we could live through anything and we sure lived through it but now I don't feel so desperate about 1942 and I should feel much worse. I fact I feel fine – after 6 maidless days during which I did a power of house clearing to my intense satisfaction I have all the nursery and kitchen drawers tidied and with labels on the outside. L. and I stayed up until midnight Christmas night cleaning the kitchen and all in all I impressed the maids terribly because the house was cleaner when they came back than when they went. ...

We are having the neighbors in to see the old year out and the new one in – fun and games sausage rolls, mince pies, chicken patties and cakes and turkey sandwiches, tea coffee sherry and whiskey. Arabella and Gordon gave us a bottle of sherry and we have a bottle of whiskey – also half a bottle of crème de menthe that we can trot out. Maybe

---

[92] Long after the war, in March 1973, Ernest Dunsmuir Mitchell of Carrowdore Castle was appointed Deputy Lieutenant for County Down: *Belfast Gazette*, 13th April, 1973.

we'll play the drawing game. A. and Gordon are going to the Grand Central dinner-dance. I'd better stop this one to you and write the rest to Mother – this is getting tiresomely long. I do wish we could see each other – sometimes the sadness of our separation sweeps over me but usually I don't think about it. But my eyes fill with tears when I hear the Americans in Congress cheering Churchill – he is superb.

Happy New year and love,
Helen

Do you remember 6 years ago tonight you and I hanging out of the Waldorf window in London bawling and drinking??

New Years Eve
Mahee

Dear Mother,

This is going to be a continuation of a long, long letter that I have just finished to Ginna so you can swap and thereby hear it all. ...

We had the best time at Auntie's on Christmas Day. Such a good dinner and the house looks 100% better and the atmosphere is 100% gayer and everybody loves to go there now. On Christmas Eve I was tired and couldn't work up any enthusiasm about being Santa Claus ... However after the news I got started and hung whole back seat full of holly around the house – Elaine had given it to me that afternoon and it made the kitchen and dining room especially too festive for words! ... We have a piece of ham hanging in the kitchen too so it has a real country look. Then we filled the stockings which were at the foot of their beds. We put an orange in the toe then paints, sweets, soap bubble pipes, soap, books, pencil boxes, crayons, and odds and ends and sticking out the top their old dolls, Bobbie and Jane . ...

Then we listened to Roosevelt and Churchill lighting the Christmas tree and then L. went to sleep and I milled around until 1, by that time full of the Christmas spirit. The next day, Christmas morning, I woke before the children so we were up when they saw their stockings and other presents. Then we had breakfast in the kitchen and slowly got ready for Auntie's. At Avalon ... we had a candlelight tea after Julie slept and Gay rested and then we came home and sung all the way home. Johnny had built us a beautiful big fire but by the time we had cleaned the house we hadn't much time to sit at it. The next day I just had the fires lighted and breakfast over when Joe, Isabel, Joey and Jamey and Miss Robson came for the day. However, as they walked in Aggie walked in so all was well. Isabel brought cold turkey and cake and butter and bread and milk and we supplied sausages, fried Spam, baked potatoes and plum pudding so we had a good lunch. They hunted rabbits with ferrets all afternoon and Miss Robson played with G. and J. and the Browne boys came to tea and right after tea I slapped G. and J. into bed and we went off to a dinner party at Arabella's. It was so nice too and she had Edith Taggart and some major as extra guests besides Auntie, Mrs. Turtle and us. Tomorrow night we have been asked to dinner at the Popper's. He is a Czech and the managing director of Ewarts and she is a Jewess of German origin. I think the Marshalls are going too. Mr. Marshall is director of the B.B.C. here and Mrs. Marshall is that American ex-chorus girl that you met at the Isaacs – she was my tap dancing teacher.[93] We hardly ever go out to dinner now but have had much more social life this year than last. However, we have only stayed in our room in town about 4 times – it is so depressing. L. says he always feels like a burglar and I feel that we are living in sin creeping into back-bedrooms late at night. ...

People here are so mad at Lindbergh and the isolationists. They think the world and all of Mr. Roosevelt – Johnny said that he would rather listen to Roosevelt than to Churchill. Johnnie and I had a talk about the war the other day and I ended up by saying "Well anyway 3/5th of the world is against Hitler or maybe it's 4/5th and Johnnie who always was an unbeatable battle said "I think it's 5/5th! ...

We had quite a good time at the one dance we went to. We were in the Colonel's party and there was a Brigadier General in our party who was so nice – his nephews are in Virginia – evacuees and his sister was married to a Czech minister in London.

Dance records are now 75c each and were 35c when war broke out. ... Bodo has been away a year yesterday. Temple Dolan was just home on embarkation leave – he is going east or middle east – no one knows. ...

---

[93] George Marshall OBE was the first station director of BBC Edinburgh then BBC Glasgow before arriving in Belfast in 1932 to become Regional Director of BBC Northern Ireland.

New Years Day 1942

This is 5.30 on New Years Day. L. had to work so it is like any other day... We had a surprisingly good New Year's Eve party here last night consisting of our neighbors – the Glendinnings and the Brownes. ... the supper was so good – chicken patties, sausage rolls, turkey sandwiches, home made muffin cakes, fruit cake and little mince pies and tea. Afterward we played the drawing game which they had never played and which they loved. We stopped at 12 for sherry and whiskey and sang Auld Lang Syne. In refilling the sherry glasses I got the whiskey bottle by mistake so the party went with a bang from then on – what did you do? ...

We are going to a dinner party tomorrow night. I will have my hair done at 10 and then I am going to two movies – *Sergeant York* and *Lady Hamilton*.[94] We will change, or at least I will at Arabella's and probably stay all night.

L. has to stay in town all next week-end where he works – eating, sleeping and all in a practice invasion exercise. You can imagine how mad he is to have his weekend ruined! ...

Now the kids are tucked in although the clock just struck 6 and the news is on. Zoo has the most beautiful eyes I have ever seen and she looked like a little door-mouse [sic] peeking out and her eyes sparkle so. Gay's eyes are more expressive and beautiful too but Zoo's are a dream. ...

Now I am going to pack and go to bed – ...

Nighty-night, Happy New Year and love,

Helen

---

[94] Howard Hawks' *Sergeant York*, starring Gary Cooper, was a 1941 movie treatment of the life of Alvin York, a much-decorated American soldier of the Great War. *Lady Hamilton*, aka *That Hamilton Woman*, was a black-and-white 1941 historical drama. Vivien Leigh played the married Lady Hamilton who became the mistress of Lord Nelson (Laurence Olivier). Nelson's struggle against Napoleon was intended to parallel England's struggle against Hitler. The Hungarian-British director Alexander Korda was suspected of running an intelligence-gathering operation in the United States aimed against German activists and American isolationists.

1942

Helen broadcasts on the BBC

The Turtles cope with crime

Helen meets her first regular American
    troops

Volunteering at the American Red

    Cross Club

Eleanor Roosevelt comes to town

Church bells celebrate victory at
    El Alamein

21 Jan.
Mahee

Dear Mother, Ginna and Lloyd,

Here comes the news preceded as always at 9 by Big Ben – They have the sloppiest song out about Big Ben but it certainly has a stabilizing effect in a tottering world.[1] The Far East news is still so bad but Russia is the hope of the world! I can even hear the Volga Boatman without wincing.[2] The *New Statesman* these days is more depressing than ever and that is saying a lot. I'm glad the Archbishop of Canterbury resigned – everybody thinks he is an awful old humbug – ever since the time Eddie [Edward VIII] abdicated and the Archbishop made such an awful speech about him.[3] ...

I am going to broadcast in the B.B.C. Home Service on the 18th of February at 9.45 a.m. on "Living in the Country". I have to make my own speech and read it – it will be 5 minutes long so if this letter gets to you before the 18th and you know anybody who can get the B.B.C. Home Service on their radios and feel like asking them to let you listen at 2 or 3 a.m. you can hear your baby talking away! I haven't thought yet what to say – it's supposed to be funny (!) and it's supposed to bring in that I'm an American (propaganda). I had to go have a voice test first at the B.B.C. which is like Buckingham Palace to get into it's all so Hush Hush and secretive and you are never left alone a minute in case you would bolt down the hall and disappear with all kinds of secret

---

[1] Helen possibly refers to "Big Ben is Saying Goodnight", composed by Alan Murray in 1932 and recorded by Ambrose and his Orchestra the same year, but more likely "When Big Ben Chimes", composed by Kennedy Russell and written by Helen Taylor in 1941.

[2] Glenn Miller and his Orchestra recorded "Song of the Volga Boatmen" in 1941.

[3] It is thought that Cosmo Gordon Lang (1864–1945) was the first Archbishop of Canterbury to resign voluntarily, which resignation he announced on 21st January, 1942. His opinion of the abdication crisis in 1936 and of the abdicated King was broadcast on 13th December and considered uncharitable. It provoked some anti-religious feeling in the United Kingdom.

information. Constance Higginson asked me to do it – she works there[4] and her sister who is a friend of Roberta's recommended me because she had heard that I read Louis MacNeice and hence must be well-read! I'll let you know if I get any Fan-Mail!!! The program is called "At Home Today" – Topical magazine Program and it is just a filler-in of time like gramophone records – you can imagine at 9.45 a.m. However, it's important to us! ...

We are going to Eggy's and Hilary's for supper tonight with no enthusiasm whatsoever – I have to go to the canteen this afternoon and am thinking of going later and going to see *Penny Serenade* first.[5] ...

Well – that's all folks,[6]

Love,
Helen

2nd Feb.
Ground Hog Day!
Mahee
Dear Mother,

We got home from Dublin last night at midnight and now it is 4 in the afternoon and it is *pouring*. ...

---

[4] The producer Constance Higginson of Craigavad, Co. Down began as an actress with the Group Theatre, Belfast and started in 1941 at the BBC (Northern Ireland) as an announcer and compère. In 1942 she became engaged to Prince Yurka (Yuri) Galitzine whose family came to England from Russia after the Great War, and married him in 1944. Constance was only the first of four wives of the remarkable prince (they divorced in 1951). Early in the war Galtzine served in Northern Ireland with the Royal Northumberland Fusiliers then in North Africa. In 1944 he was seconded to the Intelligence section of the Political Warfare Department of the Supreme Headquarters Allied Expeditionary Forces and became a war crimes investigator; towards the end of the war he was the first Allied officer to visit and report on a concentration camp first-hand. After the war he aided the SAS in hunting down Nazis. See Robin Saikia, "The Curious Case of Prince Yurka Galitzine," Foxley Books website; "The Prince Yuri Galitzine Prize", Rutland Local History and Record Society website; Michael Rhodes, "Prince Yuri Galitzine (1919–2002)", Google Groups Forum.

[5] *Penny Serenade* is a 1941 Hollywood happy-ending melodrama starring Cary Grant and Irene Dunne.

[6] The chirpy "That's all Folks!" ended Looney Tunes cinema cartoons.

The Scanlans invited us for any weekend ... We went to tea with Harry and Roberta Thursday afternoon to hear about Harry's trip to Washington with Winnie and was that something!! He stayed at the White House, has an autographed photo of Franklin and Elinor [sic], had a Cadillac and chauffeur and a plane and a pilot at his beck and call and if you remember Harry you will know that no one would have enjoyed it more or can make a better story out of it.[7] He bought Roberta 7 nightgowns, a housecoat, 4 pairs of shoes and different oddments of food – banana flakes, tomato flakes etc. He said that Mrs. Roosevelt is *so* nice and *so* bright and that the food in the White House was the best and the simplest that he had anyplace. He was at the Mayflower Hotel[8] when Winnie went to Canada and flew to Pittsburg (sic) and to Philadelphia to see Roberta's relations – a few of whom flew to Washington to see him. He isn't conceited about it for Harry is singularly non-spoiled. When he first got this job it went to his head but he has got over it and is very nice and amusing about it all and not a bit irritating. ... Well, after we left them we caught the train – Harry lent me *H.M. Pulham, Esq.* to read which kept me going on the train.[9] We got to Dublin and tried to get a taxi but because it was the end of the month no taxi had enough petrol to take us out to Rathgar which is only about as far out as the Belmont Road from Belfast – so we took a horse and cab – like they have in Central Park only much shabbier and with a candle lighted in the side lantern. It was a riot and Lancelot loved it – although Dublin is ½ blacked out not for A.R.P. but for the saving of fuel. The Scanlans were gone but the maid welcomed us and we sat and listened to the news and read and at 10 went up to see the new baby have her bottle. She is 5 months old and is sweet – named Vivienne Maeve – they all have such Irish names because Phillip is *so* Irish.

In the morning we got up for 9.30 breakfast and sat around until about 12 when L. and I went in on the train to Dublin and met

---

[7] See the letter of 23rd December 1941.

[8] The Mayflower Hotel has been in operation in the United States capital since 1925. Charles Lindbergh was honoured there in 1927, President Roosevelt wrote his Inaugural Address there in 1933, and Winston Churchill attended a state dinner there in 1945.

[9] A 1942 novel by John P. Marquand (1893–1960), a Pulitzer Prize-winning American fiction writer.

Sheelagh Bingham[10] for cocktails at the Hibernian then she came to lunch with us at the Unicorn, the Austrian restaurant and Phillip came too. ... Then L. went wandering to see bee equipment and I went home because it was raining and blowing and such an awful day. ... Then we had dinner and went to *The Great Lie* – Bette Davis still reminds us so of Ginna.[11]

Dublin has everything but tea, white flour and coal! The tea ration is ½ oz. per person per week which kills them. There is no white flour except smuggled in the black market at 1/- a pound! And there is no coal – the ration is ¼ of a ton a month or something awful and everybody burns turf which is very expensive – like everything else in Dublin. –

Saturday we got up late and went shopping again and to Mitchells in Grafton St. to see the style. In the afternoon we went to the Zoo with 3 of the 4 kids, came home for tea and then got ready for dinner and to go dancing at the Gresham. ... The Gresham was *packed* and *so* gay. We all drank too much and got very hilarious and it did us lots of good. Both Philly's and Rob take dancing lessons and Rob especially is such a wonderful dancer. They dance every Saturday night and often two other nights a week – can you imagine it? ... It beats the band. They all realize that they are living on top of a volcano, that they are crazy and that next winter may bring famine, war, or goodness knows what so their gaiety is too frenzied to be comfortable because every time they do anything they think that it is probably for the last time. We were glad to get home because there is something about all that life in the midst of so much war that is fantastic and not enjoyable. De Valera is in so deeply now that he can't do anything.

10th Feb.

This is much, much later – the 10th February to be exact and we are feeling so sad for the Glendinnings. Barbara just rang up to say that

---

[10] Sheila Bingham, a childhood friend of Lance's, was the daughter of Henry Bingham (b. 1881) of Annagh House, Co Mayo and Annie Frances, daughter of John Thompson of Windsor Park, Belfast (married 1906): see Bernard Burke and Andrew Charles Fox-Davies, *A Genealogical History* [also *Dictionary*] *of the Landed Gentry of Ireland* (1912), p. 44.

[11] Davis starred with George Brent and Mary Astor in this 1941 marital drama.

they had had a cable today that the husband of the youngest Glendinning, Mary, is feared dead in Malaya. They have all been worried sick since before Christmas and lately they have even been more worried because different people here began getting cables from their relatives from Singapore to say that they were all right but no word came from Humphrey and then in answer to a cable of inquiry they had a cable from a friend to say that there was no trace of him and now this one today which though not official is pretty definite.[12] Poor Mary! She was only 20 when she got married and had a 4 days honeymoon before Humphrey left – the only reason she got married was that there was a chance then – about 2 years ago – that she could go join him as his wife but right away that was changed and no wives were allowed to go. She is so pretty and gay and doesn't look a day over 15 and just to make it grimmer for the Glendinnings another daughter's husband is either in Singapore or Burma and she is stuck in India with two young children – the eldest is Zoo's age, and Barbara's husband is on the Atlantic fighting the Germans! So life is pretty grim for them. ...

The delay in writing incidentally was because I was working my broadcast which nearly had my hair gray and I'm sure it took as much out of Lancelot as it did out of me – having to hear it, advise and criticize. ...

11th Feb.

... Soap rationing started last Monday – we have a good supply that I have had since that critical summer of 1940 – mostly kitchen soap and we have about 3 doz. cakes of toilet soap. The scarce thing lately has been soap flakes. That makes practically everything but bread rationed – most tinned goods, barley, rice, semolina etc. are on a "points" system

---

[12] Mary Glendinning, youngest daughter of Helen and Lance's friends and Mahee neighbours, married Humphrey Thomson RAMC, formerly house surgeon in the Royal Victoria Hospital Belfast, in April 1940. *The Belfast Telegraph* of 12th February 1942 posted Captain Thomson RAMC as missing in action in Malaya and he was later reported dead. Humphrey's father was the distinguished physician from Hillsborough, Co. Down, William Thomson (1885–1950), Professor of Medicine at Queen's University Belfast. He became Deputy Lieutenant of Belfast and was knighted the year of his death. His obituary can be found on the Royal College of Physicians website under "Inspiring Physicians".

with tinned meat, tinned fish etc. Most people spend most of their day chasing food. We don't because shopping in Comber we take what we get.

21st Feb.

... Last Sunday when I got your cable about the frequency and short wave I got so excited to think that you might hear me that I chain smoked and had chills and fever and nervous indigestion. ... I knew that you would leave no stone unturned in trying – but if it is any consolation to you the thought that you might be listening to me made all the difference to me and made me be twice as good.

I finally got the darn thing written about 10 days ahead of time after great effort in spasmodic bursts. ... I was just told to write something funny about living in the country so you can see I had plenty of scope – much too much...

In the end it was a great success[13] ... My main faults were not enough expression and a tendency to race like mad. You know me Ma, I never was dramatic and if I try to be I sound so *affected*.

I wasn't scared until the morning when I had that sinking feeling, clammy hands, and other symptoms and when I started to read my heart beat so loudly that I nearly died but I recovered quickly and was as cool as a cucumber. I go into all these details because I know you will like to hear them and because it was such a big event in our quiet life. And although it isn't my place to say it there is nobody else to tell you (except Auntie) all our friends and acquaintances who heard have said that I was swell. ...

We are having trouble with the maids stealing little things so we are going to have to get rid of them – so far it isn't serious cigarettes is the only thing that we are positive about but various odd little things have been missing all along, but I think that they know that we are suspicious so that may stop them for a while. They keep their room locked which is a positive sign of guilt and have only been away from the house at the same time once since Christmas! Day before yesterday when I purposely sent Eileen on an errand while Nanny was out so that

[13] *At Home Today*, a twenty minute "Topical magazine programme", was broadcast on the BBC Home Service at 9.45a.m on Wednesday, 18th February. Helen's script is reproduced after this letter.

I could look through her room only to find both doors locked. L. had a quick look while I kept Eileen occupied later and couldn't find anything but his extra razor and a work-box and lots of thread but I could tell better if I could get in. It is so trying, but they always have bothered me but I just put up with a lot and tried not to let it get me because I knew how hard it is to replace them and I also know too well what it's like without anybody! ... They are playing "The White Cliffs of Dover" which I agree with Ginna is as wet as it can be [14] ... They are playing "Elmer's Tune" which I haven't heard before – it is good. I have "Rose A Day" on my brain and it's driving me crazy and Eileen who plays the mouth-organ as her only recreation! whistles it all day. [15]

Everybody was in the depths over the fall of Singapore and those 3 German ships getting away from Brest and the news is still awful. [16] I suppose the Spring offensive will be awful too. Churchill has had to take so much criticism lately but the changes in the Cabinet will do a lot to cheer people up. Raymond Gram Swing has good substance but his voice is so tiresome. There are so many funny stories going around about things the Americans have said about Ulster. I think the funniest is about the American who looked up at the barrage balloons and said "Why don't they cut the cables of a couple of those and let the damn place sink?" The other ones are all about Derry "I never saw a graveyard with traffic lights before". "We bury our dead back home"! and about Ireland "It would be all right if it had a roof." Also a story is going around "Where is the American navy?" and the answer is "It

[14] The soppy pre-War nostalgia of this 1941 song popularised by Vera Lynn in 1942 is balanced by the uncertain nature of the future: do the lyrics refer to "blue birds" (pilot uniforms)? or "bluebirds" (the American songbirds)?, the latter lending a cultural ambiguity to the song.

[15] "Elmer's Tune" is a song written in the 1920s but not orchestrated and recorded until 1941 by Glenn Miller and his Orchestra and by the Andrews Sisters. "Rose O'Day: The Filla-ga-dusha Song" was recorded in the UK in 1942 by Flanagan and Allen and in the United States by Kate Smith. It uses cod-Irish of an Irish-American stripe; given Irish neutrality, its popularity in the UK seems curious.

[16] Singapore Island, an important British military base, fell to the Japanese on 15th February. It was the largest British surrender in history – some 80,000 British, Indian and Australian soldiers were taken captive. The Fall of Singapore followed the successful Japanese invasion of Malaya. On 11th February, a squadron of ships from the German navy ran the British blockade of Brest, Brittany. They were belatedly if seriously engaged by the RAF and Royal Navy. Helen is referring to the battleships *Scharnhorst* and *Gneisenau* (which, though damaged, reached Germany on 13th February, both being destroyed in later action) and *Prinz Eugen*, a heavy cruiser that was soon after damaged in action off Norway.

is under contract to Metro-Goldwyn Mayer". I have seen a few Americans around town – looking so nice!!

I forgot to tell you that when we were in Enniskillen for one night we went to the American Technicians Dance[17] in the Town Hall next door to the hotel and had *real* Hot Dogs with American rolls – Hamburgers with Chili and cookies!! I knew it – Here is "Rose O'Day" (I just found out that it isn't Rose A Day). They play it all day. ...

Much love and many kisses,

Love,
Helen

LIVING IN THE COUNTRY

I want to tell you how to enjoy living in the country if you don't like animals, don't like crops, don't like hens and don't care. I like milk in bottles, water in taps, vegetables in shops and chickens on the table. Yet for two years I have lived on a farm surrounded by animals and crops, with milk in pans, water in wells and hens on the doorstep and love it. My point is that you can live in the country no matter what.

There has been a spate of books recently on this subject. As you look along the library shelves and read the titles, you begin to wonder if there is anyone left in the towns. "They moved to the Country". "He bought a Hilltop". "My Valley is Green", and "I bought a Mountain".

Now I have read all these books soberly and carefully and all these people love the country and their books are triumphant with cries of success in their great adventure. Of course going rural is always a roaring success otherwise there would have been no book. Also their praise is triumphant and if they will forgive me, smug, because I find with them that it is almost impossible not to feel self satisfaction

[17] In June 1941, several hundred civilian American "technicians" (in fact, military engineers) arrived in Northern Ireland "under conditions of some secrecy to begin work expanding harbor facilities on the River Foyle four miles below Londonderry." The engineers then helped create seaplane bases on Lough Erne. Such projects were completed when the United States formally entered the war in December. See Francis M. Carroll, "United States Armed Forces in Northern Ireland During World War II," *New Hibernia Review* 12:2 (2008): 18.

when friends incredulously ask "Do you mean to say you really like it, how do you stand it?"

How do I like the country? Let me count the ways.

1st: I like to look at it.

2nd: I like to work and sit in it as it makes me feel elemental.

3rd: I like it because it makes me feel poetic.

4th: I like it because I think there is some future in it.

I repeat my point, you can live in the country and like it and I have shown how I am similar to all the authors of all the books but now I will tell you how I am unique.

To begin with I'm an American with no inbred love of nature in my bones. Some Americans have it but mostly they haven't, but living in Ireland I felt a glimmer that there was something missing in me, something that kept me from being as enthusiastic as people around me in discussions of the apple crop, the potato blight and the turnip yield. To make it worse I have always lived in a big city. But living in Ireland I felt an awakening. I realised that either because I was who I was or because of my American city upbringing, I was missing something. On the strength of this I decided with a more than willing husband that we should buy a place in the country so that our children wouldn't grow up like me and could hold their own in agricultural conversation – we went one better than the authors who bought hills, valleys and mountains – we bought an island.

To be honest it is only half an island and to be perfectly honest it is only an island on the map because there is a bridge onto it, but we do have spells of high water when we are cut off from civilisation and even at low tide we are remote. 8 miles from a town, 4 miles from a bus and 3 fields, 2 gates and a mile of sea bottom road from our nearest neighbour and even after an unwary visitor has bounced his precious tires over the sea bottom, there is still a field to cross, two gates to open and shut and a cross turkey cock to meet. So all our visitors register some emotion – triumph at finding us at all, relief at finding their car not visibly damaged or hysteria if the turkey cock happened to be at the gate.

The house is a long low whitewashed cottage with blue windows and doors, a red tin roof and a riot of color inside. All the rooms are in a string like a train and they all face the sea. This strung out effect is invaluable on rainy days because my children can tricycle from end to end. Outside the lawn slopes down to the sea wall which has a blue gate in the middle of it that is downright quaint.

With this brief picture in your minds, you may be able to see why I get so much enjoyment out of looking. There is always the seascape varying enormously with the ebb and flow of the tide and within a stone's throw of the house. There are always gulls and other seabirds turning and flashing like jewels in the changing light.

To walk and sit in, there is shore and fields. I can feel elemental by leaning against the wind, rhapsodic by lying in the grass chewing a straw or merely Irish by walking in the rain on a soft day.

So we migrated for two summers to this whitewashed cottage overlooking the sea. I was still one of the majority of people who love the country in the summertime but scamper back to the city in the winter with rejoicing and relief.

However at the end of our second summer on the island in 1940, the cities didn't sound so healthy, so we stayed on and I was faced with what I had thought impossible – a winter in the country. At first I kept insisting that I liked it out of sheer bravado and for the smug satisfaction of surprising all my friends. Then one day when the Irish winter was at its worst – and I mean worst and we thought we might have to move back to town, to my own stupefaction my heart sank and I realised for the first time that I liked living in the country. I looked around in amazement. The rain was being lashed against the house by a 60 mile an hour wind, the ill-fitting window frames were gurgling and bubbling like springs and I didn't need to go out to know that the yard was ankle deep in mud.

What was it that made me want to stay? As nearly as I could figure it out, it was a rising in me of my pioneer ancestors. I felt like Daniel Boone, Scarlett O'Hara and Eliza crossing the ice all rolled into one. To put it plainly, I felt that I had at last come to grips with nature in the raw. Whether it is a blood red sunrise over the water opposite our windows or a walk along the shore at high tide when something as simple as a seagull lighting on the water or a lamb jump into the air with all four feet at once, I am as pleased as punch and wonder again and again where I've been all my life to miss such pleasures.

The Brains Trust recently in answer to the question "How can you cultivate the art of living?" came to the conclusion – or at least Professor Joad did – that as long as you keep a child-like eagerness for life in general you are doing all right and the simplest way to keep this zest seems to me to lie in living in the country.

22nd Feb.
Mahee

Dear Ginna and Lloyd,

... Tomorrow I am going to town. To lunch with Mrs. Stitt who has five children and to the D.R.C. at Arabella's. *Citizen Kane* and *Meet John Doe*[18] are both in town so I may have to go two other days – I am going Friday anyway and we are going to dinner at the Brysons – Eddie and Eileen. We were at Herbert and Rosemary's Friday before last. The Spence-Bryson agent from China was there and he had just come home from New York, but he wasn't as interesting as Harry – but then he, the agent wasn't staying in the White House and Harry was! ...

Our household is overshadowed at the moment by suspicion of the maids' honesty – an awful feeling. The minute I can replace them (and maybe before) we are going to have a showdown. The whole thing is wearing on the nerves and most unpleasant but I hope to get in my two cents worth before long. We had the winter out of them anyway and nothing vital is missing and they certainly are nothing to lose except that Nanny is quite good with the children but annoys me in lots of little ways. ...

We went to 3 dances in 5 days!! The most fun was in Dublin, the American Technicians dance in Enniskillen warmed the cockles of my heart and the only bright spot of the Comber Hunt Ball was my dance with a Canadian naval officer who was staying with the Glendinnings who was one of the best dancers I've ever seen and luckily it was a good fast one – We were asked to a dance at the new club called The

---

[18] If *Citizen Kane* (1941) needs no identification, *Meet John Doe*, as the title implies, does. It was, however, a successful 1941 Hollywood political comedy-drama directed by Frank Capra and starring Gary Cooper and Barbara Stanwyck.

Four Hundred[19] by Betty Harris but can't go and don't care much. ...

25th Feb.

We have been in an awful flap for a week and it is getting flappier every day – a case of us v. the maids whom we have now found to be part of a stealing and smuggling racket. The whole thing has me a nervous wreck – so I hope it ends soon – meantime until we catch them with the goods on them we have to bide our time. They are swiping stuff and posting it – registered post – to their mother who lives in Northern Ireland but right on the border. Three registered packages went last week! If they didn't register them there would be no way of checking but they do! I discovered this last week. We have been suspicious for some time but last Wednesday night 50 cigarettes that were in the cupboard Monday are gone. I asked about them but of course nothing was known of them. ... Then a letter came to Nan from her Ma which L. read – all about receiving the parcel, saying not to send any more for a while, that she had taken "the set" to so and so who said it was much too grand for them and some more talk about the border and the price somebody got for white flour – just as crooked as a dog's hind leg the whole pack – the mother is the receiver ... So now we are waiting for them to post one more parcel and we have arranged with the police in Comber to open it – then it will be sent and we will get a policeman to nab Ma at the other end. In the meantime we can try to find out what they have sent. So far the only jewelry missing is my aquamarine bar – one that A. gave me for being bridesmaid and the kids' baby pins that John Carr sent them. I have mentioned these but again no knowledge. Also my heavy tweed coat is gone ... I think they have been working on the attic including about 15 lbs. of bee sugar of Lancelot's. It is all very trying and I hope it ends soon in a triumph for us but unless you catch them with the goods they can lie their way out

---

[19] The Four Hundred Club in St Louis was said to allude to the number of people who really mattered in New York City in the late 19th century. The 400 Club on Chichester Street, Belfast was probably modelled on the 400 Club in Leicester Square, London which in the 1940s and 1950s catered to "the upper classes at night time" and during the war was frequented by members of the armed forces. A notice in the *Belfast Telegraph* on 29th December 1941 advertised dancing in the 400 Club from 9pm to 2am with the dress code "Uniform or Evening Dress", suggesting that the club catered to officers, gentlemen and their ladies.

of anything – even the most circumstantial evidence. L. is talking to detectives and having the time of his life. The worst is that they are fairly suspicious at the moment and it may take some time for them to break down and send another parcel. Ours as you can imagine is the world's easiest house to burgle – nothing locked – all our Belmont Road stuff – silver, linen clothes etc. put away in the attic and I never look at them – and you know me I would lose my head if it weren't tied on so it is very hard for me to be positive that I haven't lost something when it is missing. L. has copies of the letters and it is all high-powered detective work, intrigue and suspicion underneath and bland smiles on top ...

People are still telling me how much they liked my broadcast ... Arabella was thrilled and the prize comment is what A. said to me. She was talking it over with Rose, her maid afterward and A said "You know, Rose, Mrs. Turtle can't talk but her soul comes out on paper!" The Prime Minister [John Miller Andrews] congratulated me and lots of stray acquaintances heard it and thought it was good. This is all very conceited but I thought you would like to know! I forgot to tell Mother that I got 3 guineas for it – that's about $15 for 5 minutes – not bad! ... and Mrs. Marshall told me that "George" who is the director-general of the B.B.C. in Ulster was positively lyrical.[20] As I told Mother we were so sad to think of you all trying so hard and being so disappointed – I know how I would have felt if it had been one of you and I was trying to hear. ...

The Glendinnings have just heard that there is another son-in-law of theirs in Singapore – the daughter is in India. Mary is quite cheerful – the young one whose husband is lost in Malaya but periodically, her Mother says, she goes up-stairs and cries her eyes out. Saw part of *Citizen Kane* on Monday before the D.R.C. – will go again Friday I read such a terrific write-up in a highbrow magazine I take called *Horizon* but wasn't all that impressed[21].

---

[20] From 1932 until 1948, George Marshall was director of BBC Belfast where he installed a more powerful transmitter.

[21] The influential magazine *Horizon: A Review Literature and Art*, edited by the eminent critic Cyril Connolly, ran from 1940 until 1949.

1st Mar.

This is Sunday night and I have a streaming cold – eyes and nose pouring. No further developments in the maid situation except that they are leaving on the 15th – they gave notice after a discussion with me – so far I don't think they suspect that we know so we may get them. ...

I have been reading *The Hundredth Year* by Philip Guedalla which is *so* good – the year is 1936 and he makes such a wonderful case for Eddie Windsor and such a black one for old Baldwin.[22] I have just discovered Guedalla – he is so good and is sometimes on the radio and he is superb. I think that reading all of John Marquand's – *H.M. Pulham Esq.* (the best) *The Late George Apley* and *Wickford Point* – they are all very alike. The kids are fine. Saw *Meet John Doe* but *Citizen Kane* showed it up pretty much. Sorry this is such a mess both in form and content. Happy Anniversary! Fancy you having been married 2 years and we nearly nine!! It don't seem possible.

Love and Kisses,
Helen

1st Mar.
From somewhere
at sea
(From "Bodo" Taggart)[23]

Dear Helen,

I have seldom if ever received a more newsy, interesting and delightful letter than yours. I have read and re-read it and each time it has given me great pleasure. Please do send me another like it. The only reason I have not answered it before is a feeling that I could not send an adequate reply. You have preserved the dying art of letter writing, but have superimposed a modern brightness and interest and your own

---

[22] Philip Guedalla (1889–1944) was a London barrister, would-be Liberal Party parliamentarian, and prolific author of historical works. *The Hundredth Year* (1939) was a record of the year 1936.

[23] See the letters of 4th May 1939 and 4th March 1940.

independent thinking. Life here is full of luxuries compared with home. Edith wrote the other day and said that the egg situation was much easier. She could now get an egg once a week instead of once a month! I always have two eggs for breakfast, perhaps an omelette at lunch and maybe an egg savoury at night. There is a shortage, or was of wheat ashore, but that is over. The only other thing is meatless days ashore but that does not affect us. There are plenty of sweets and chocolates, no shortage of sugar, tea, jams and various conserves, silk stockings, underclothes, men and women's clothes hats etc. etc. toys, cameras, in fact everything, but they are all a wicked price. ...There is a *far better* collection of English books in the bookshops than Belfast could produce pre war. I just ache to spend about £12 in a lump of books. ... I recommend *An American Speaks* – Lawrence Hunt, *White Cliffs* – Alice Duer Miller and the following Guild Books (Penguin Type) *I Lost my Girlish Laughter* (one of the best and funniest books I have ever read) *McLeods Folly*, as a Portrait of an English Village ... *Corduroy* is excellent and would interest you for it is a man's first year on a farm. Also *English Justice*, a bit depressing but I feel true. ...[24]

The climate here[25] is supposed to be perfect, and on shore it would be, but in the hot weather, a steel ship gets like an oven. To ——— last summer my cabin was seldom lower than 90 deg. But we are lucky compared with those fighting in the far East. I am like most aching for home. I am not war-like, and wish only to be happily back in my job

---

[24] Lawrence Hunt's *An American Speaks* (1941) urged the United States to join Britain's cause in the Second World War. Jane Allen (a pseudonym for Silvia Schulman) published *I Lost My Girlish Laughter* in 1938: it was a controversial satirical novel inspired by Allen's experiences working in Hollywood under David O. Selznick. Orson Welles turned the book into a radio play. *McLeod's Folly* (1939), a novel by Louis Bromfield, was turned into a film in 1943 starring James Cagney. Adrian Bell's *Corduroy* (1930) was a best-selling account of life in the countryside by the London-born author and republished by Penguin in 1940. *English Justice* by "Solicitor" was first published in 1932 and revised as a Pelican Book in 1941.

[25] "Here" is somewhere in the Mediterranean. Bodo Taggart is recalling the evacuation of Crete in June 1941 in which HMS *Queen Elizabeth*, the dreadnought battleship on which he was serving, participated. German paratroopers invaded the Greek island on 21st May 1941; half of the Allied forces were evacuated by the Royal Navy. Taggart also witnessed, presumably from the decks of the *Queen Elizabeth*, the explosion following a torpedo attack by a German submarine, that destroyed the battleship HMS *Barham* at the cost of over 800 lives.

again with Edith and Elizabeth[26]. I have seen as much of the war, and more that I want. Coming here thro' the narrows was exciting enough, being at sea during Crete affair was also a bit too thrilling the sinking of the *Barham* which I saw, was our raids in harbour, and various other things, have given me as close a view as I want. Tho' as regards Air Raids in Harbour, those in Belfast and other places know more the horror than I do. In civilian life, one does one job, and if there is no work one relaxes. But naval and seafaring life involve spending hours doing absolutely nothing and yet being ... ready for instant action at any moment. I find that a strain and of course even in harbour whenever one is on board, one is liable for duty. ... and there is never any mental ease I find while on board. Of course the truth of the matter is that I am and always was bone lazy! I never thought I was courageous and now I know I am not! I am always scared stiff when things are happening. The worst is periods of waiting or periods when you in particular have nothing to do. When really busy, controlling the fire at the guns etc. it is not so bad, for your mind is occupied. But there is no doubt about it, I do not like being bombed!!

Edith keeps me fully informed about Elizabeth's doings and I am so sad that I have missed such a wonderful period in her life. The dawn of intelligence and character seems to me about the most fascinating period of a child's life, and I have missed that. A husband is not supposed to praise his wife, but I am going to break that rule with someone so understanding as you. I am so proud of her. ... In addition she has the terrific job of the W.V.S. housewives.[27] Her letters are full of travels, Lisburn Ballymena Holywood etc. etc. with a speech and encouragement and organization in each place. And she does have the wonderful gift of getting things done without offending people and creating rows. And then she is in this new Unionist Young Members,

[26] Taggart's wife and daughter. His wife Edith (Edie) Taggart was an active member of the Ulster Women's Unionist Council. Much later, in 1970 she was elected an Ulster Unionist Party member of the Northern Ireland Senate, only the second woman so elected; she served until the Senate was abolished in 1973.

[27] The Women's Voluntary Services, 1938–1966 (it became the Women's Royal Voluntary Services after 1966) was founded as a British women's nationwide voluntary service to recruit women into the Air Raid Precautions (ARP) and to distribute information to households about air attacks and means of neighbourhood self-protection. When war came, the WVS helped with the evacuation of civilians from endangered towns. During the Blitz WVS members helped provide food and drink to the bombed-out.

and is helping stir up things there. And with all that she remains a housewife ... How she manages to get the time I do not know. I am a truly lucky man in both my wife and daughter and I do so hope that I will be soon happily re-united to them. I consider that she is doing far better war work than I am. I am glad that Elizabeth and Julie and Gay are such friends and I hope that it will continue throughout their lives. A happy home life, simple pleasures and good friends are as much as anyone could ask for, and my separation has made me appreciate more the happy life that I had and hope will soon have again. Remember me to Lancelot. I am glad that he is getting such good value out of and making so many friends in his life at Mahee. I long to visit you again.

Yours affectionately,
Beaudeau

8th Mar.
Mahee

Dear Mother,

This seems to be the first day of Spring after three days of heavy snow – on one of which we were snowed in. ... The sun only shone yesterday morning for the first but today is glorious with blue skies, sunshine and fast melting snow. ... We will have lots of daffodils in bloom next Sunday – they are all in bud and we have hundreds and hundreds of narcissi too. ...

The maids gave notice last Sunday egged on by me and so far nothing has happened. No parcels have gone but we are going to have a policeman down before they go and we owe them £7.10.0 which we aren't going to pay until they crash through with some of the missing goods. The worst thing is 20 lbs. of sugar and lots of tea has gone, yards of elastic, thread, needles, tweezers, pins (3), honey, eggs, a necklace of Paddy's, little toys of the children's, towels and silverware – not real silver which is all here – but our ordinary Mahee silver. The atmosphere in the house is not good and I do the children all the time because Gay won't go near Nanny and Julie isn't keen. If they act nasty, which I think they will, we are going to get a search warrant for their mother's house.

19th Mar.

We have been maidless for ten days and this is the first evening I haven't been too pooped to write and you can just guess why I didn't write in the daytime! However 3 letters came from you today and one from Ginna so I am all bucked up to write and tell you the downright thrilling story of: "The Turtles Cope with Crime" or "Why our maids went to jail!" Before I start let me say that we are all bursting with health because I may not get around to it for several pages.

Well the maids were due to leave on Friday the 13th and on the Sunday before we stayed up until midnight making a list of things missing from the house which we gave to the police on Monday morning and told them to send it to Crossmaglen, the town where their Mother (the maids) live. L. told the police to tell the police in Crossmaglen not to do anything with the list until notified by him. His plan was to make a speech to Nan and Eileen on Thursday night saying that we had enough evidence to put them in jail, but that if they would return the stuff (we kept back £7.10.0. and their bicycle as security) we would keep it out of the hands of the police. The Comber police took the list and agreed to the plan. However Tuesday night the Comber police rang up to say that the Crossmaglen police had raided the Mother's house that day on receipt of the list and found it packed to the *roof* with our stuff – far more than we had listed – that they had Ma in jail and that they wanted to come down then and there to "lift" Nan and Eileen. L. told the constable that the next morning would do and my teeth chattered and my legs shook with nervous excitement. This, you must remember was after a month of detective work on our part, – opening letters, checking up with the Post Office, talking to police and detectives and meanwhile trying to pretend that all was as usual in the house and watching like hawks. I left them alone as usual but counted everything when I came home. They knew that we were suspicious because only two things disappeared in the 2 weeks that they were "under notice" (meaning about to go – they were 1 card of hair clips that you had sent and 1½ yds. of elastic that Eileen cut off a 3 yd. card that I left out on purpose. We had lines marked on the sugar and tea containers and they knew that I had counted the silver and linen. That night that the police rang up we had 2 farmer neighbors in so we had to wait until they went and then we went over to tell the

Brownes who were in bed but got up *wildly* excited. Their maid is a sister of ours and they had missed a few things but weren't sure how they were going to act – Mrs. Browne hadn't been feeling well and wasn't keen on being maidless but on hearing that the Mother's house was packed they decided that they didn't want a crook at any price so decided to have the police in there too – as yet our maids didn't know. The next morning I was wild! Zoo was in bed with a cold and I just sat and sewed with my eyes and ears peeled for the police. By 11 they hadn't come (our 'phone as usual wasn't working!!) so I went for Gay at school, tried to use the Glendinnings 'phone which was also out of order) and when I came home I found the police here – two!! Nan and Eileen hadn't admitted much, but weakly said that they had sent a few things home "because they didn't see the harm". The police and I searched their bags – which numbered 8 suitcases (!) but only found the elastic. Then the police went to interview the Browne's maid and left Nan and Eileen packing to go to jail. I talked to them quite pleasantly and asked them why they did it and if they thought we were blind – (as it happened we were – blind as bats) and Nanny just said she didn't know what came over her and that if she had only got to chapel oftener it wouldn't have happened etc. but Eileen said that she knew we knew. Neither one shed a tear or showed any emotion when they knew they were going to jail, but they acted a bit dazed. The Browne's maid didn't admit stealing anything so they left her and took ours away – Gay, Julie and I waving from the back-door!!! The same day a 4th sister in town was searched (instigated by L.) and a suitcase in her room was found packed with our things – jewelry, knitting wool, material, hair pins, lipsticks, slips, clothes etc and best of all a parcel addressed to the Mother from Nan with a letter in it. She had been afraid to send it because she knew her mail was being watched – the letter said "Dear Ma – here is yet another parcel – keep the things safely for me until I get home to sort them, don't send them to her beyond. What does Gertie need? (Gertie is sister Aged 6) How are her shoes? Does she need a coat? etc. etc. Love from Nan." Her parcel contained lots of my old summer clothes so when I got home I searched the attic and lo and behold half the things were gone – 4 evening dresses, slacks, shorts, summer blouses, the children's summer clothes (most of them) some baby clothes, and worst of all 4 suits of L.'s – also sheets, pillow cases, curtains, black out material, rags, shoes, towels, tablecloths, razor blades, a tweed coat, and I forget what else. When the stuff came from their Mother's house there were 74 items on the list and lots of the items were plural e.g. 10 napkins, 2 blouses, 3 dresses, 10 prs. stockings (holey) etc. We had 2 other houses searched in Crossmaglen – one "Her Beyond" who is Nan's Aunt and they found about 20 things there and also 2 houses in the Free State – one was Nan's sister who just got married and got some of our silver for a wedding present! – only one real silver thing – a sauce boat, but a muffin dish, divided sandwich plate and sugar bowl plated. Isn't it the limit?

22nd Mar.

Now it is Sunday and I have been fighting one day 'flu all day. The house is topsy-turvy, I have to go to court at 11 in the morning and we have a new nurse – temporary – coming home with L. tomorrow night!!! … tomorrow … I go to court and then come home to clean like mad for the new nurse who is another German, Jewish refugee. … She will have to live with us but in the summer we can always go out if we want. Her name is Trudy and we have never clapped eyes on her but both she and I can quit each other whenever we wish with no awkwardness.

We will be glad when the trial is over tomorrow. It is only at the "petty session" in Comber and there will be no jury. We purposely put the price of stuff low to avoid, if possible going to a higher court. We put the loss at £48 but is really closer to £100[28] but we have practically everything back already. The magistrate can give a sentence of 6 mo. in jail which they deserve but which we hope they don't get. They were in jail 3 days and their father bailed them out. I never did like them and wanted to get rid of them before Christmas but L. persuaded me to hang on saying that we wouldn't get anyone else in the winter and reminding me how awful it is without anyone in the cold, dark days so I weakly agreed. And kept out of their way as much as possible. The nanny one is the real crook – as smooth as glass and such a liar. She was a good worker while I was here but on the days I went to town she didn't do a thing and wasn't as nice as she could have been to the children.

[28] £100 in 1942 would have the buying power of over £4000 in 2020.

... The island of Mahee rocked with excitement and all of Comber knew it because it was in the local "Chronicle".[29] They will plead guilty in court so I shouldn't have to say much. But of all times to steal this is the worst with everything so scarce and so rationed. They stole so much food too that we will never get back – 24 pounds of sugar that L. had for his bees, tea, eggs, some tinned stuff and goodness knows what else. They stopped at nothing – pencils, pads of paper, thread, needles, pins, tape, elastic, lipstick, powder, hairpins, stockings, toys, gramophone records and children's books. ...

Ginna asked if many women wear uniform here – thousands do. Practically any and every young unmarried girl who didn't have to earn her living is either a "Wren (WRNS) Navy. An "At" (A.T.S – Auxiliary Transport Service) or a "Fanny" F.A.N.Y (Female Auxiliary Nursing Yeomanry?) or something + the Nurses, Red Cross, W.V.S. (Womens' Voluntary Service) etc.[30] The Wrens wear navy blue with Tricorn hat (the officers do) and their uniform is the nicest. The "ATs" and Fanny wear Khaki and look pretty awful on the whole and the nurses wear gray and red and look the worst of all. The American-born women here are going to be put in red cross uniform – gray coat and skirt, gray forage cap and red cross in white circle on the sleeve. I saw one – a nurse from Cal. [California] staying with E. Morwood and she looked so smart. All the women in England are conscripted from about 18–40 – that is why the maid problem is so acute. People here give us another year – Did I tell you that we advertised in 2 Irish (Dublin papers) for a Mother's help or Nursery Governess and from the *Irish Independent* we got over 60 replies! And from the *Irish Times* we got about 10. Some friends of ours, the Dormans, who live just outside Comber advertised for the same thing in the Belfast papers a month ago and do

---

[29] *The Newtownards Chronicle*, a reputable weekly established in 1873 and widely circulated in the Ards peninsula and around Strangford Lough.

[30] Wrens (members of the Women's Royal Naval Service) were the distaff branch of the Royal Navy, formed in 1917, disbanded in 1919 and re-formed in 1939. In 1944 there were 75,000 Wrens. The ATS was the women's branch of the British Army; at first a volunteer service, after 1941 unmarried women between twenty and thirty were called up. (But not in Northern Ireland.) They served abroad (some were at Dunkirk) but not in battle itself. FANY was the First Aid Nursing Yeomanry, founded in 1907 to provide assistance to civil and military authorities in emergencies. During the Second World War, emergencies included the invasion of Finland by Russia in 1939 and the military needs of Free Poles in the UK from 1940.

you know how many replies they got? None! An agency advertised for me and got one reply! It shows how acute the unemployment problem is in Eire or as Arabella says they are dying for tea. Their ration is ¼ ounce per week and ours is 2 or 4 oz. I forget which. We are always within our tea and sugar rations but our butter even mixed half and half with margarine only lasts about 5 days and then we are on marg. for 2 days but it is nearly as good as butter. If we had more puddings – apple sauce, cakes, rhubarb etc. our sugar ration wouldn't do. I am a whiz on Vegetable soup which we have in varied forms every day – the children like vegetables raw or in soup but leave them usually if they are boiled. I also am a whiz on Home made Cottage Cheese – on other things I'm no whiz. I've always had the feeling that given the time I would be *such* a good cook – especially on mixtures and the kind of cooking that you do throwing things across the kitchen into a bowl and then giving it a stir and slapping it into the oven. ... We get over 30 eggs every day now and sell them to the Gov't. Tomorrow is the collection day. G. and J. love to help collect them. ...

Thank you so much for the birthday present $25 turns into nearly $40 here – whoops dearie! I'll let you know what I blow it on. Much, much love and happy Easter.

Helen

Y'birthday!!
28th Mar.
Mahee

Dear Ginna and Lloyd,

Since you paid me the delicate compliment of writing to me on my birthday I likewise bows and sits down at 9.15 on this Saturday morning with the work done!!!! but we do have a German Jewish refugee temporary nurse who washed the dishes. ...

The German girl is 24 and is named Trudy – her real name seems unpronounceable in English and her last name is Schleimmer – she is waiting to get a nursery school job, is very quiet and nice ... is tall and big and slow and serious and is very gentle and patient and very nursery-schoolish with the children e.g. always explaining and reasoning and disciplining in an indirect way. ... We pay her £1 a week which is good pay but worth it – she hates to cook but helps with the dishes and sews and mends every time she sits down. ...

I am worn to a shadder with the fuss with our maids, no maids for two weeks, lack of sleep and spring fever but am taking Vitamin Tonic.

I have to do a paper for the D.R.C. on Robert Frost in about 3 weeks and I haven't even started and am so hampered because apart from his *Collected Poems* and a few Smith [College course] notes it will all have to come out of my head! Arabella is going to share the program with me – reading the poems – so if I get her to read a lot it will fill up time. ...

Monday was the Trial in Comber. ... It was a very informal court in Jack Andrews's mill – called a Petty Sessions and a magistrate came from Newcastle to be the judge. He was so nice and fatherly and talked to Nan and Eileen so wisely. Eileen who was lying to the bitter end said that she was 15½ having told the police about ten days before that she was 16½ (which was right). They pleaded guilty but had a solicitor with them to get Eileen off so Nan bore the brunt and got 4 months in jail without hard labor. For their defense they had a doctor's certificate to say that Nan was in a very delicate state of health and that if she was sent to jail she would spend all her time in the hospital and her other letters from former employers over a period of 12 years all but one of which praised her to the skies. The D.I. (District Inspector of Police) prosecutor for us and said that we had cut the price to about – we said that the value was £50 but it was well over £100 and that we weren't desirous of being hard on them but with all that the judge said that he had to send her to jail because 1) it was such a wicked thing for an older sister to lead a younger one so astray in her first job and 2) it wouldn't be fair to all the other maids who work away all their lives and never touch a thing. Which point of view eased our consciences for putting her in jail not that she didn't richly deserve it.

... after June there will be no pleasure motoring and everybody will have to lay up their cars – (Here is the King talking – time out). I wonder if you are listening too.[31] Now the news is on with Raymond

[31] King George VI must have broadcast his message on the BBC Home Service after *Saturday Social* at 8.15pm and the *News* at 9.00pm. Gram Swing gave the *American Commentary* at 9.20pm so we can date to the minute Helen's writing of this letter. The King's message has been described as one of encouragement to the Empire.

Gram Swing afterwards to give the regular Saturday Night American Commentary. Sometimes it is Elmer Davis who is better than Swing – we never hear Kaltenbourne [sic].[32]

It was so too bad that you didn't hear me broadcasting after trying so hard but it wasn't me putting on gramophone records – I don't know what the program before was because it was from London.[33] It would have been wonderful if you could have heard it. I found to my chagrin that my script which L. was supposed to have sent to you was still in his overcoat pocket but I will send it. I so hoped that I would get one genuine fan letter but I didn't. ...

Roberta is just home after staying about 6 weeks in London with Harry. She says that London is very gay and not a bit downhearted – lots to see and do and plenty of food in restaurants if you can pay for it! As the *New Statesman* said: "Never in a country facing starvation, has so much been eaten by so few". I take it that you know that statement of Churchill that this parodies as well as we do – that classic remark of his during the Battle of Britain about the RAF – "Never in the history of human conflict has so much been owed by so many to so few." (Swing is *so* dull to listen to but if you strain your attention it is usually worth it.) ...

The second hour of summer time comes on at Easter and it is *awful*. We never go to bed until midnight in the summer – the kids don't go to sleep until 9 and everything is haywire.

Here we go to bed so nighty-night. Many Happy returns.

Happy birthday and much, much love.

Helen

27th Apr.

It's terrible that 3 weeks have elapsed since I started this and I had it all sealed up to mail and then didn't – too Scotch to only send 2 sheets

---

[32] For Gram Swing see the letter of 2nd October 1939. In 1939, Elmer Davis (1890–1958), American author, journalist and broadcaster, became a news analyst at CBS replacing Hans von Kaltenborn (1878–1965) who had gone to Europe to report on political events there. Davis had a hugely popular audience for his nightly 5-minute newscast. In 1941 he was appointed by Roosevelt to be Director of the U.S. Office of War Information.

[33] The *Radio Times* for 18th February lists the New Georgian Trio in a programme running from 9.30am to 9.45am immediately before *At Home Today*.

when I could send 4! The cause of the long delay is that I've been so busy cooking and have had to write a paper on Robert Frost for the D.R.C. in any spare time I had! Now that is over and we are high and dry with no cook, no nurse, no nothing again. Trudy left yesterday morning after only being here 1 month – she was quite a help in a way and as nice as she could be but too lethargic to make me lament her loss wholeheartedly. ...

My paper at the D.R.C. was quite good – especially Robert Frost's poems that Arabella and I read. It lasted nearly an hour with reading by A., the paper, readings by A and I together (the dialogue poems – "Death of the Hired Man" and "The 100 Collars")[34] and reading by me. I wore the sailor dress that you sent, the hat you sent and knee length bright red campus socks that shook the D.R.C. to its foundations. ...

Things are getting scarcer and scarcer and more and more warlike here – not belligerently – but as far as rationing of nearly everything, so many things off the market, no petrol after June, coal rationed after June 1 and 66 2/3% tax on cosmetics, silk dresses, fur coats and all luxuries. Whiskey is now $7.50 a bottle and a Scotch and Soda is 3/- a glass – 75c. – if you can get it. All drink is practically non-existent – even beer and no pubs or even the Grand Central have anything but Guinness or Irish Whiskey. We have 3 bottles of whiskey stored for the Armistice ...

Billy Stephens is missing since the St Lazarre raid.[35] Everyone was

[34] "The Death of the Hired Man" may well have appealed to Helen not just because of its poignancy but because it concerns help on the farm, work, necessity, and in the end death. "A Hundred Collars", too, concerns farms; it shares improvised pondering with the more famous Frost poem, "Stopping by Woods". But "Collars" is complex and with a political edge (it is set around the time of William Taft's presidential campaign, 1908–9) and one wonders if the Americans in the audience caught the nuances. The bright red campus socks, an un-Frostlike touch, might have garnered more attention.

[35] The St Nazaire Raid was a British attack on the dry dock on the Loire estuary in German-occupied France. (Helen may have confused St Nazaire with Saint-Lazare, the Paris station.) Combined Royal Navy personnel and British Commandos carried out the operation on 28th March by means of small craft and an obsolete destroyer loaded with explosives which rammed and plugged the dock gates. There was fierce German resistance and many of the small craft were destroyed. The Commandos had to fight their way through the town to try to escape overland. On the British side 169 men were killed and 215 captured. Via Reuters, *The Northern Whig* carried a graphic eye-witness account of the raid in its 30th March edition. The writer makes no mention of prisoners and assumed that the Commandos were fighting their way to victory. The 2nd May issue told its readers that the raid's leader, the missing Lieut.-Col. A.C. Newman, had in fact been captured, so Helen would have had hopes that Billy Stephens would still turn up alive.

so disappointed that the India thing was such a flop[36] – otherwise just now the news is so good – at least we seem to be a little more offensive and something is holding Hitler's spring offensive up – if you want a really brilliant week to week reaction to the news the "Letter from London" in the *New Yorker* is it. She [Mollie Panter-Downes] is a genius for summing up public opinion. We got yours from Elmer Davis and Gram-Swing (who drives me crazy) but I would love to see a complete issue of the *Denver Post* occasionally – it is 3 years remember since I was there and I *drip* with nostalgia at anything American. The B.B.C. is plugging America for all they're worth and luckily I listen a lot. The programs for schools are magnificent. They are on for 20 minute periods for 2 hours every day – that is 3 from 11–12a.m. and 3 from 1–2p.m. They include geography, senior and junior English, senior and junior History, talks for 6th former current affairs, French, music, and stories for under 7's. The best people in their line in England are on (e.g. Louis MacNeice on poetry) and lots of professors from Oxford and Cambridge, journalists and authors and they are a dream as far as education made easy goes. Gay listens to the ones for under 7 and is fascinated...

The army had extensive maneuvers here the other day and had some cardboard figures up to shoot at and Gay and I were walking over to see what they were and Gay said "Maybe they're statues of Jesus". It is 10.45 and I just put the blackout up – it is pitch dark but I was just lazy about it. L. is out until dark every night now and won't be sitting a minute again until next winter. I have the feeling that we won't be here next winter but we may be. Must stop and write to a cook or two – Night-night and much love from all of us. ...

Love,
Helen

---

[36] A member of Churchill's cabinet, Sir Stafford Cripps travelled to India in late March in order to secure full Indian cooperation in the Allied war effort. However, despite the imminent threat to India from Japan, and despite Cripps' offer of Dominion status after the war, India declined to participate before full independence; India intended to mobilise in its own defence against Japan.

11th May
Mahee

Dear Ginna and Lloyd,

... Here I've gone and missed the news and now there is propaganda on for carrying gas masks – since Winnie's speech last night everyone seems to be gas-conscious.[37] People here are more optimistic than they have been since the beginning of the war because of 1) Hitler's speech,[38] 2) The delayed spring offensive[39] 3) The R.A.F. raids on Linbeck, Rostock etc.[40] 4) No raids to speak of here 5) The Coral Sea battle,[41] 6) The potential help from America 7) The repeated rumours of an [Allied] offensive on the Western front. All the optimists expect the war to be over this year and the pessimists say 1945 and they used to say 1950 or 1960. I think it will be over in the autumn of 1943 – and with luck before. Every day we expect the Russian front to spring into action again.

---

[37] In his 10th May broadcast, Churchill warned of the dangers of gas warfare and promised Britain would retaliate in kind were Germany to engage in it. Although in his speech he recalled the perilous days when Britain stood alone and the difficulty of military cooperation with Russia, he reminded listeners of the combined sea-power of the United States and Britain and ended optimistically... "tonight I gave you a message of good cheer".

[38] Helen may be alluding to the speech Hitler gave to the Reichstag on 26th April 1942 when he assumed even greater powers. It was a comprehensive overview of the war and its origins and full of defiance. Yet its very detail conveys a note of uncertainty; it fully recognises previous and present difficulties, including a past winter of unprecedented hardship on the Eastern front. Perhaps the Allies drew encouragement from the curiously human note the speech sounded.

[39] Hitler's spring offensive against Russia was hampered by RAF attacks in the west, by vigorous Red Army activity, and a variety of logistical difficulties: it was not expected now until the start of June.

[40] Helen is surely referring to Lübeck, a port on the shores of the Baltic Sea. It was attacked by RAF Bomber Command on 28th March 1942 and sustained heavy damage. Rostock in north Germany was an industrial and highly Nazi city and likewise was targeted by Bomber Command. Like Lübeck, Rostock was a cultural centre and such raids led Hitler to promise reprisal raids (the so-called Baedeker raids) against English cultural and tourist centres such as Bath, Norwich and York.

[41] The Japanese Navy and air and naval forces of the United States and Australia battled in the Coral Sea in the South Pacific off Australia on 4th– 8th May, 1942. The battle was initiated by the Japanese decision to invade New Guinea and the Solomon Islands. Both sides sustained heavy losses, but the United States the heavier losses. Even so, this was the first time the Japanese advance had been stalled, and the battle disrupted Japanese strategy.

Billy Stevens [sic] is a prisoner of war – he was missing for weeks after the St. Lazare [sic] raid. Osborne King is home on indefinite leave after being nearly burned to death off the coast of So. Africa – some explosion on his ship. He is all right but still very badly shaken I hear.[42] ... The Glendinnings still haven't heard any news of their 2 sons-in-law in Malaya. ...

After supper
same day:

Now it is after supper for which we had Kedgeree (rice, fish, eggs and margarine tossed in a pan) and it was quite good. ... The radio is playing "Milestones of Melody" by Geraldo and his band and tonight is Irving Berlin night and I am dripping with nostalgia for John Cooper and my other beaux ...

I am enormously cheered because I am going to town tomorrow ... I need new shoes, must buy some knitting wool (rumours that all wool is disappearing) linen practically has disappeared already. People like the Mackies were buying lots about a year or more ago and the prices even then were fearful. I have stopped using linen sheets except for visitors. ...

If there is any hope of no bombing next winter and we should know by then which way the cat will jump I think you will see us in a flat on the Malown (Malone)[43] ...

15th May

Now it is Friday night and this is our first day back here after three days on the skite.[44]

[42] It was later reported that in November 1944, Temporary Lieut. James Osborne King RNVR of Comber was awarded the DSC (Distinguished Service Cross) for "outstanding courage, resolution and skill while serving in light coastal craft in many successful engagements with the enemy". Adrian Hanna (ed.), Comber Historical Society: events 1942: www.comberhistory.com King later became Lieut. Commander DSC, DL RN. In 1947 Osborne King & Megran was begun and became a major commercial property consultancy firm based in Belfast (later simply Osborne King).

[43] Helen in her spelling is mimicking a posh accent since the Malone Road was the poshest neighbourhood in Belfast.

[44] "On the skite": an Ulsterism meaning hectic moving around or letting loose: "on the tear".

I got so desperate after writing to you – not that that made me desperate, but the confinement, the rain, the dishes and cooking and kids that I arranged to be out for 3 days and it did me a power of good because it poured all day today and I didn't even care ...

Wednesday we bought shoes for the children first then ice-cream cones and then took the train to Lisburn. We were on 2 trams and 1 train and I had a shopping basket and a suitcase *and* them to push on and off trams and trains. I once made the drastic error of going upstairs on the tram with them – it was glorious for them while we were up but coming down on a packed lurching tram down those twisty stairs with my usual shopping basket was awful. Luckily men especially are very helpful and lift them on and off and up and down and they are such cute children (!!!) that people rush to help. ...

17th May

It 11 now and not dark even yet. We are in the kitchen, L. is doing his bee things (folding sections for honey) it is raining and I must go.

When do you think the war will be over?

Love and kisses,
Helen

30th May
Mahee

Dear Mother,

It doesn't seem a bit like Decoration Day – partly because it is so cold and rainy – partly because I am just getting over 'flu or a bilious attack and mostly because I only heard it was Decoration Day on the radio.[45] However mentally speaking I am more in New York than on Mahee because 3 *New Yorker*s came in a bunch and I have been in bed for 3 days – I have read 2 from cover to cover since 3 o'clock today – it is

---

[45] Decoration Day was held annually in the United States on the last Monday of May. Between 1868 and 1970 it was observed on 30th May. It grew out of the custom of decorating soldiers' graves, a practice at least as old as Civil War days. As Helen's usage suggests, the name by which it is now known, Memorial Day, did not take hold until after World War Two.

now 10.30 and I am *steeped* in the idiom, the atmosphere and the liquor advertisements. The only other things I had to read were *New England: Indian Summer* by Van Wyck Brooks[46] and quite a good detective story.

I am listening to a program of opera music on gramophone records sitting in the kitchen in my green striped house coat my yaller satin bed jacket, my red nightgown and my cracking silver mules. Lancelot is out and about, Sadie has gone to bed and Gay and little tiny Zoo are sound asleep – bless their baby hearts. I have hardly seen them for over a week. Sadie came a week ago last Tuesday and on Thursday morning I left for 2 days and ½ in Cullybackey with Maureen and I had such a good time. She knows the whole American regiment that is stationed nearby [47] – the officers that is – and she had 2 in each evening to dinner – the nicest 4 of all and was I *thrilled*! Two were from Minneapolis – a Colonel Hougen and a Captain and 2 were from near Amalia [New Mexico] and they were all *so* nice. They are the first Americans I have met and after standing beside them in shops and walking by them in town you can imagine how glad I was to be able to talk to them at last. ... The Colonel Hougen was around 50 ... I am sure he is a big shot, but *so* casual.[48] He is a lawyer and was the one who defended the American soldier who shot the bus driver or did you hear about that.[49]

---

[46] Van Wyck Brooks' *New England: Indian Summer, 1865–1915* (1940) was a continuation of Brooks' history of American literature.

[47] The U.S. Army Corps (the 34th infantry division and the 1st armoured division) arrived in Northern Ireland in the early part of 1942. About a thousand American technicians had already been in the province since October 1941 (first arriving in June) and the first regular troops had disembarked in Belfast on 26th January 1942. It was a fluid deployment and it is difficult to pinpoint exactly where the soldiers whom Maureen knew may have been based. Toome (over 15 kilometres away from Cullybackey) was set up later in the year for U.S. airmen. See: John W. Blake, *Northern Ireland in the Second World War* (1956), p. 277 n.1 and Francis M. Carroll, *The American Presence in Ulster* (2005), p. 152.

[48] Lt. Col. John H. Hougen (1889-1978) was 53 years old. He had been a lawyer and had served in the Minnesota Legislature and was now with the 34th infantry division. The 34th went on to fight in several European theatres and returned to the United States in late October 1945 without those killed in battle (3,737) or missing in action (3,460). Hougen went on to write *The Story of the Famous 34th Infantry Division* (1949, rpr. 1979, 2012). He is buried in Arlington National Cemetery.

[49] On 17th April 1942, an American convoy was impeded at speed on the road from Limavady to Londonderry by a local bus empty save for the conductor. In the convoy were the army's Chief of Staff, General C. Marshall; Roosevelt's personal envoy, Harry Hopkins; the roving ambassador, Averell Harriman; and the commander of U.S. Forces in Northern Ireland, Major-General Hartle. *Cont'd*:

He also knew Ickes[50] and Frank Lloyd Wright and was such fun to talk to though he drank too much. ...

Our outlook has been changed somewhat by the fact that we are planning to go back to town next winter – other things being equal, of course – that is bombing and gas attacks – both of which sound more unlikely every day as we send over 1000 planes to bomb Germany and they send 10 back to bomb us.[51] I think their gig [sic] is up! ... The maid situation for the winter I have given up as hopeless. We went to Crossmaglen yesterday to get Nan and Eileen's mother and aunt jailed for receiving stolen goods. They got 1 month each and would have got more except for a sob-story lawyer that they had engaged. I wish you could have seen the town and the court!! The backward towns of the West of Ireland and Donegal were even better that Crossmaglen which is a border town in the mountains above Newry that exists on smuggling and rackets of all kinds. The Judge, the people and the courtroom were exactly like something you would read about and wouldn't believe but there it was and unbelievable even when you saw it. Nan was a wonder to be as smart as she was coming out of that environment but no wonder that she was dishonest because everybody in the town is. The court was packed with thugs all up for sugar and flour smuggling and everyone in the court would have been worth their weight in gold in Hollywood. There was no place to have lunch or even go to the john in the whole town but luckily we had some hard-boiled eggs and sandwiches with us. Nan is out of jail on the strength of her asthma and is home. The mother pleaded guilty and the aunt pleaded not guilty but the judge, who was so nice, said that he didn't believe a word she said! And she had just sworn to tell the truth, whole truth, nothing but - - - - so help her God!

On the way home we stopped in Newcastle to see Stella and Tommy. Tommy has an exhibition on in Dublin now. ...

[Incomplete ...]

[49] *Cont'd*: The rear armoured scout car attempted to rejoin the convoy ahead; as it drew abreast shots were fired, the bus crashed and the driver died of gunshots at the scene. This tragic episode is discussed in the Afterword.

[50] Harold L. Ickes (1874–1952) was an American politician and long-serving Secretary of the Interior (1933–1946) in the Roosevelt administration. Ickes is a character in the 1977 stage musical *Annie*.

[51] The first thousand-bomber raid was on Cologne on the night of 30th–31st May.

16th June
Mahee

Dear Mother and Ginna,

... Ginna's letter came too which made us feel as if we were hardly in the war at all compared to your excitements of everybody going, everybody's life being so upset and uncertain. Mahee is so peaceful, Lancelot hasn't had to go and so many of our friends are still at home that our lives aren't as upset as yours – English lives are but there being no conscription here makes such a difference.[52] I'm so glad that Lloyd got something he wanted and I do hope that he is too old to fly as a pilot – here all the pilots seem pretty young unless they are veterans of the last war or pilots in civil life. I know what a lost feeling I would have if L. went – goodness knows our lives are unsettled enough as far as plans go even now. I wait with baited [sic] breath to hear what next? Or what Ginna is going to do. The Women's army sounds quite good especially from our point of view if you could come over here!! That would be something. Is there any chance?

[*Down the side of the page*: Everybody always asks about you both too and what you think, etc. Everyone is so relieved that Ginna has stopped being an isolationist and a Lindberghite. I am doing my best to make hands across the sea.]

This past week I have met lots of Americans and have the bug out of my system now or at least my heart doesn't flutter every time I see one the way it used to. There are so many that it couldn't!

I went to two dances – one for enlisted men – American Red Cross Club and one at the officers' club. Both were quite dull from my point of view although it was fun to see and talk to so many Americans but I hate to dop around[53] with women without L. and there were no interesting or amusing or good dancing Americans to make it worth it, as well as the ever-present problem of how to get home. On Wed. night

---

[52] The Northern Ireland Prime Minister, Sir James Craig, had pressed Downing Street for conscription in 1939, but Northern Irish nationalists and the Eire government were fervently opposed; to avoid opening up another, domestic front in Ireland, conscription was shelved. Without it, voluntary enlistment levels, even in unionist Northern Ireland, after respectable activity at the start of the war, dipped embarrassingly by 1940. See Brian Barton, *Northern Ireland in the Second World War*, pp. 17–18.

[53] Helen seems to be using "dop" in the sense of "dap": to run or move quickly, to dip in and out of life.

the Brownes luckily brought me home – they having been out to dinner in town and Friday night I brought myself home arriving at 2.0 a.m. but it wasn't even pitch dark then! Lighting up time is past midnight now – we never get to bed until midnight or after and we are in a chronic state of sleepiness as a result. ...

Everybody including me is so impressed with you taking up Russian, Ginna – Elaine [Andrews] said "Isn't she wonderful?" Elaine has such a bee in her bonnet about Ulster's feeble war effort and feels it so that Jack [Andrews] is still running the mill and is only in the Home Guard. Jack's point is that all the people in Comber depend on the mill and that even though the flax situation is so trying and there is so little to spin he has to keep it open. I was so cheered up about the war until a day or two ago and now the Libyan and Russian fronts seem so critical.[54] I still think it can be over by autumn 1943 but hardly anyone else is so optimistic. ...

I was going to Dublin with Paddy Metcalfe last weekend but she was too ill to have any fun, and she went but stayed out at a hotel by her boys' school and saw them at their games etc. She wants me to go again on the 9th of July – but I'm not very enthusiastic about going though I always love Dublin. The train service in Eire now is a scream. The Cork-Dublin train took something like 19 hours the other day instead of 3 or 4. All the trains are started by lighting a fire of wood and then they put in bricks to get heated and then they get enough steam up to go about 20 miles at 20 mph and they then have to rake out all the bricks and start over again! That is true because there is *no* coal. They have 2 or 3 stagecoaches going and millions of bicycles and no private cars – doctors and priests and nuns and diplomats and a doctor can't give anyone a lift anyplace not even his own wife! Not even on a rainy day! ...

We are definitely going to town for the winter and I rang up Toby's mother who was in Dublin to put our name in for her house. She has it let furnished for £11 a month to an Army officer and had it let before to a Colonel for £15 a month so she should charge us £11 or £13 if the Army officer moves of course which I should think he would – and the Americans don't have wives so they won't want houses. Some of

---

[54] After the Italian Tenth Army was beaten in North Africa by British Commonwealth forces, Field Marshal Erwin Rommel was sent to retrieve the situation for the Axis powers. A series of battles ensued, to which Helen is alluding.

the Americans came on the ship that you came on right after Lee [Helen's son] died [in 1936] and some came on the ship that Ginna went home on right after Daddy [Lee Ramsey] died [in 1936] but everything they do is so hush-hush and if you ask them where they're stationed even if it is next door they say "Somewhere in Northern Ireland".

The Officers' Club was about 80% full of Americans on Friday. Rosie McConnell and Betty Haselden were hostesses that night and asked me to help entertain their Americans.[55] They had 3 in their party – one from Arkansas, one from Kentucky and one from N.Y. The southern accents of the Arkansas and K. ones nearly had me crazy and they were all hams – the Kentucky one was the best, but the other two were pains, the Arkansas one had a flashing gold tooth, kept saying he wasn't old enough to smoke and was generally fatuous. I danced with a Texas major who was a traveling salesman for paint and sort of fun to talk to but I only danced with one good dancer. ... Rosie and Betty had me partly to tell them what social level the Americans were and they had Goldie-Toothie spotted as the best – and I didn't want to run down their friends because they think they are so nice. *They are nice* too and friendly and came in a Peep or a Jeep – I suppose you see those around.[56] The town ["Belfast" erased by censor] is full of them. No soldiers have come to the town where Elaine is yet since the last ones moved on. I am dying for Americans to come but heard that the Americans wouldn't pass the water supply – said it was unsanitary – no wonder! There is no running water in the town and the householders have to go out to the corner and pump! ...

L. is losing his hair so fast that I have got him a tonic for it. It isn't very noticeable yet but his hair is both receding and thinning at an alarming rate and is about ½ gray. Mine is getting streaked with white hairs all through – none that you would notice yet unless you looked hard but it is sort of sad! In the last 2 or 3 months I have noticed my age so much not that I feel old but when I see how young the soldiers look and hear everyone I know talk about how old they feel and look

[55] Rosie McConnell, née Rosamund Reade, was the first wife of Terence McConnell; see the letter of 21st September, 1939.

[56] The origins of the name Jeep are unclear. Peep is sometimes regarded as a variant name for the same vehicle, but has also been defined as a Jeep in the service of an armoured division.

and how young so and so looks – it is just startling to realize that I have to think about it at all because when you're young you never do think about youth. ...

Our car only ever goes to Comber now and about 2 days of the week. ... You have no idea how it complicates things hanging around on trams and trains, carrying suitcases and shopping baskets, lifting children on and off, buying tickets with your hands full and generally pushing and crowding. We went to tea at Whiterock on Sunday in the pony and trap and it took us 1½ hours each way! It is about 9 miles but it was such fun. As Elaine says a trap makes everyone look so much of the "gentry". I drove the whole way but haven't gone alone yet, but it will be our only means of getting around the district after this month. ...

I have gone to the American Red Cross Club in the Plaza[57] a few times to help although the library hasn't opened yet – I am to help in the library but I have made beds and dillied around. It is so nice and is going to be terrific when it gets into full swing. I am going to the dentist on Fri. – and to see *H.F. Pulham Esq.* – did you read it? I loved it.[58] Here comes the sun so I must go lie in it to get my legs brown because I have no stockings without runs and refuse to paint my legs. Sorry this letter is so uninspired and scatterbrained ... I'm sleepy, the bees are buzzing and I want to get my head down – it is all so hard on my neck!

Much love to you both,
Helen

---

[57] In May 1942 the first of the many American Red Cross Clubs, which were to play a large role in Helen's wartime life, opened in the UK (in Londonderry). See David Reynolds, *Rich Relations: The American Occupation of Britain, 1942–1945* (London: HarperCollins, 1995), pp. 155, 157. The popular Plaza dancehall on Chichester Street in Belfast city centre was converted for American Red Cross Club use.

[58] Marquand's novel was made into a film in 1941, directed by King Vidor and starring Hedy Lamarr and Robert Young.

25th June
Mahee

Dear Mother and Ginna,

This is my idea of heaven – sitting outside in the sun – hot and nearly naked – rarely in the afternoon with nothing to do! ... When you think that in all June we have only had 2½ hot days you can see how wonderful a day like this must seem. There is just a little breeze which by supper time will probably be a cold wind but now it is divine. ...

This letter is supposed to be a birthday letter to you Mother. Happy, happy Birthday. How does it feel to be 63? It's a sad thought to think that I haven't been there in person to *say* Happy Birthday for 10 years or 11 – not since 1931 and I can't even send you a singing telegram. I must say that in June 1931 I never thought that I'd be sitting at Mahee surrounded by chickens, ducks and guinea hens and liking it. But as much as I like it the prospect of this winter here doesn't please me. It is not I who mind it, but the kids especially Gay, would be bored stiff – no children no school and from her point of view nothing to do. ... We have no visitors now except weekend visitors and neighbors and a week from today will mark the end of cars driving into our yard – it will be only our car, our tractor and our trap!

Now it is 5 o'clock and the last two hours I've been dozing and dreaming and getting sunburned ... I have 2 good books to read – both hooked from the American Red Cross Library where I work now and then and both things I've wanted to read. I have read most of one *The Family* by Nina Fedorova. It is so good and Ginna would like it because it about a Russian family in China but you both may have read it.[59] The other one is one of the new Thomas Wolfe books which I couldn't get very interested in the other day on the train.[60] We are on trains every day now – at least L. is and I am when I go to town. The journey has been complicated lately because they have been digging for an unexploded bomb on or near the line. All these bombs were known

[59] Nina Fedorova was the pen-name of Antonina Riasanovsky (1895–1985). *The Family*, about an aristocratic Russian family in exile in China in 1937, deservedly won the *Atlantic Monthly* fiction prize in 1940.

[60] This may have been *The Web and the Rock* (1939), *You Can't Go Home Again* (1940) or *The Hills Beyond* (1941), all published posthumously: Wolfe (b. 1900) died in 1938.

about but considered un-explodable after so many days and then the other day one blew up in London and killed 20 people so now they have to get them all up and some of them have sunk nearly to China[61]. ...

Now it is 10.30 and the sun is shining away still I was right about that cold wind. It is bitter outside. We chopped down thistles and nettles a while and then L. started to paint his beehive and I came in and sewed on a few buttons. Now it is 11 and we have just had cocoa and cake. I rang up Elaine to see when they can come down. She said that they would come once before the petrol vanishes forever! The cook answered the phone and said that Elaine was at Maxwell Court and that there was a party on tonight. Maxwell Court is Jack's father's house and I know who the party is for – [King] George and [Queen] Elizabeth whom Ginna and I went to see in London the year Gay was born.[62] They have been here a day or two although no press mention was made – Marcia went to lunch with them yesterday and so did Isabel but Elaine will be so interesting on the subject because her impressions are always so acute and so different from the usual opinion or rather the same better expressed. ...

Tomorrow I am going to town, to the Red Cross Club to the dentist and to the naval canteen. Last week sitting in that American Club surrounded by Americans with the windows open on a fairly hot day I felt, that I really was at home and I fairly purred with contentment ... I catalogued books for 2 hours in the morning and one in the afternoon and then took an American soldier with me to see *H. F. Pulham, Esq.* The soldier was at a loose end and was talking to me – such a nice boy from Albany, 29, a lawyer and a graduate of Hobart College, married but had only lived with his wife for 3 days – more fun to talk to than any I had met yet ... We would love to have some of them to stay but there is always that problem of getting them here... – they could come and go with L. if only their times suited. Auntie worked there yesterday and is going again tomorrow – she loves it too.

[61] After the Blitz, UXBs (unexploded bombs) were an ongoing menace in Britain, and bomb disposal teams suffered many casualties. In June 1942, a year-old bomb exploded in Gurney Street, south London, killing 12 and injuring 60.

[62] Maxwell Court is in Comber, not far from Mahee Island. The house is still in the hands of the Andrews family and currently occupied by Johnny Andrews, whose great-great uncle was Thomas Andrews of RMS *Titanic* fame and who keeps alive at the retail level his family's involvement in the linen industry.

The atmosphere is like a fresh breeze in the stiffness of Belfast and so different from the naval canteen where the sailors come – the sailors are scared to death of the "lady" canteen people and never talk except the very fresh ones but all the Americans are buddies with everybody and don't mean to be a bit fresh. ...

The news is *awful* these days. Everyone had been so buoyed up and now here we have plunged back into despair again over Tobruk and Sebastopol[63]. ...

Hope Lloyd likes his job, hope Ginna has a good one, hope the war will be over in 1943 and hope most of all that we can see each other soon and even when I say *soon* I know it means more than a year at least but you just can't think about that. ...

With a special big birthday kiss and much love from all of us to

Mother X
Mrs. Ramsey X
Grandma Bobbie X
Helen

13th July
Mahee

Dear Mother and Ginna,

... Monday night at 10 o'clock. L. is out chasing a swarm of bees, the kids are asleep looking like two baby angels and ... I have just eaten 2 raw young turnips and was it a mistake or was it a mistake. ... Mother's letter of June 29th arrived today saying that Ginna had been to Omaha and by now I hope you are a full fledged officer – if not, why not? I think it sounds so interesting – the getting around the country and of course I always hope you might even get as far as here but on second thoughts if the army got into a fight you would have to go too and that would definitely not be so good. ...

We are registered for groceries in Comber and the situation is that you can hardly buy even unrationed goods in a shop where you aren't

---

[63] Tobruk, Libya, a besieged British Army stronghold, was captured by Germany's Afrika Korps on 21st June. Sevastopol, on the Crimean peninsula, was to fall to the Germans on 1st July.

registered because they keep everything for their registered customers. However we do very well in Comber ... We are the proud possessors of 2½ doz. oranges this minute. Strawberries and raspberries are in now and peas, potatoes, lettuce, tomatoes etc. so housekeeping isn't so trying. We lead the simplest life possible as far as food goes and hardly miss a cook at all. ...

I am now being really reckless and am going to eat an orange – something I haven't done for about 2 years except sections of the kidwids, and the thought of how messy it's going to be has me nearly put off now! Here comes L. probably starving because he has been chasing that swarm of bees for hours with Harry – he said when he got them smoked out of the hole in the tree they swarmed on his neck!!! And is he stung. ...

Elaine and her children have been in Newcastle for a week – she will be home now. She told me all the inside talk about the King and Queen's visit because of course Jack's father and mother saw a lot of them.[64] The Queen apparently is a dream, has a wonderful type of make-up like enamel, but not too overdone, watches the King a lot to rush to the rescue if he gets tongue-tied. He apparently has a high nervous laugh but is otherwise all right. Most everybody saw them go by someplace although every plan was as secret as the grave and the papers could only announce their visit when they were safely back home

It wasn't them that Jack's father was entertaining the night I rang up Elaine but instead Mr. Wynant [sic] who was there for 2 or 3 days but had to fly back to London the afternoon of the dinner party so Elaine didn't see him but Mrs. Andrews thinks he is the most wonderful thing that ever walked. She fell madly in love with him and said he

---

[64] King George VI and Queen Elizabeth arrived in Belfast on 24th June aboard the cruiser HMS *Phoebe* for an unpublicised three-day visit that seems to have been thoroughly known about by the local people. After the first day spent on civic engagements, they visited an American military camp on their second day. They watched an infantry march-past and mechanised unit charge-past. They toured the camp in a Jeep, a new-fangled vehicle for the British. They were hosted by General Hartle, Commander, U.S. Forces and accompanied by John G. Winant, U.S. ambassador in London, and Herbert Morrison, British Home Secretary. After a day spent with the British army, they left on 26th June on a Royal Navy destroyer. Jack Andrews' father was the Northern Ireland P.M., John Miller Andrews.

talked all the time, knew everything about everything and spends alternate weekends with the Churchills and the Edens.[65]

Tommy and Stella Carr and their 2 daughters were here weekend before last. ... They are thinking of moving from Newcastle [Co. Down] because there are so many Americans there. Tommy said that he felt bad enough when Newcastle was full of English soldiers who had come so far to protect him but when they came 3,000 miles he couldn't face it. He still paints, teaches painting and is in the Home Guard but feels that he should be in uniform! He would be fairly hopeless and lost as a soldier but he may be driven by his conscience to be one yet. I was talking to Elaine on the 'phone this morning and she said how nice she thought the Americans were – Newcastle is seething with them and how sorry she felt for them and how disgusted they must be with the holiday tourists who aren't pulling their weight in the war. This is the "12th Week" which as you remember is a holiday all week.[66] Elaine is simply wild on the subject of no conscription in Ulster and the general lackadaisicalness of the people here compared to the people in England. She is nearly mental on the subject and would join up herself at the drop of a hat and leave her children if she dared. She takes the war very seriously or rather takes it to heart terribly and is unbalanced in some of her theories.

The news is on – so bad in Russia otherwise not terrible. The *New Statesman* these days is *terrible* – so depressing, so agin the government, so mad at everything and nothing but gloom on all sides. Everyone who reads it wonders why they do. ...

---

[65] The handsome John Gilbert Winant (1889–1947) from New York had been Republican Governor of New Hampshire before being appointed Ambassador to the Court of St James in 1941 and serving until 1946. He had succeeded the pro-appeasement Joseph P. Kennedy and was in great favour among the British, including Anthony Eden and Churchill with whose daughter Sarah he had an affair. After the war he was U.S. representative at UNESCO but retired soon after. Unable to adjust to the undramatic reality of retirement, the estrangement from his wife, and what he regarded as the disappointment of his career, he sank into depression and shot himself in 1947. On the day of his suicide, his book *Letter from Grosvenor Square* was published. He was the co-author also of *The Pursuit of Happiness in the Economic and Social World* (1946).

[66] The week-long public holiday in Northern Ireland straddling "the Twelfth", the commemoration of the victory of Protestant King William III over Catholic King James II in 1690 at the river Boyne in Ireland.

17th July

People are pretty downhearted about the war. ... My war effort is so feeble – 4 hours twice a month at the naval canteen and 4 a week about or more at the Red Cross Club but when I'm cook and live here what can one do? ... We had a mouse-hunt in the living room today. Gay danced around in the background screaming with excitement and babbling big words like "Helter Skelter" and I screamed twice when I was on my knees trying to clap a box onto it (it was only a baby) and it ran straight toward me. Gay screamed then because I screamed but Julie was disgusted and said in her deep voice "What are you making all that noise for?" Gay and I kept saying "There he is!" but Zoo indignantly kept protesting "It's a girl – don't say *he*, it's a girl"!

Helen

31st July
Mahee
Rabbit Rabbit[67]

Dear Mother and Ginna,

Ten o'clock of an evening and I am writing in the kitchen by the Esse cooker. I have just been in Newcastle for most of 2 days and one night staying with Tommy and Stella Carr. ... Newcastle is choc-a-block with Americans who whistle and yoo-hoo and say hello to every girl that passes. They sit around on the walls on the promenade waiting to see what happens and guess what? You've guessed it! Nothing ever does. So no wonder they catcall and whistle all the time. All the way home they were waving and calling from station platforms and wise-cracking with passengers and acting like little boys out of jail. Stella has met quite a lot of them and has only really liked one. Of the very few I have met I liked 3 or the 4 at Maureen's and I have met one in the canteen – Red Cross – who was such fun to talk to. I took him to a movie [see letter of 25th June] ... I had to leave before it was over so I didn't get

---

[67] "'Rabbit rabbit rabbit' is a superstition found in Britain and North America wherein a person says or repeats the words 'rabbits', 'rabbits' and/or 'white rabbits' aloud upon waking on the first day of a month, to ensure good luck for the rest of it." "Rabbit, rabbit, rabbit", Wikipedia.

a chance to ask him down but I would like to see him again. When we move to town we will have more chance to ask some in for meals – here it is hopeless getting them here and back in their brief time off.

On the whole my impressions of them are:

1 One and all they are desperately homesick.
2 They think Ireland is 50 years behind the times in everything.
3 They are interested in the blackout, blitzed buildings etc – but about Ireland and the Irish they are hardly curious – just think it is all too hopeless except that
4 They all think the scenery is *beautiful* – even better than back home, they admit, even if they come from Kansas!
5 They think the girls are terrible – dowdy etc.
6 None of them realized how bad our rations are and how very limited our purchasing power is – they are genuinely taken aback and dismayed – N.B. It has come on us gradually so we haven't the sudden shock that they get.
7 Most of them say that once they get home they are going to do all their traveling in the future in the U.S.A.
8 They never realized before how wonderful America is.
9 The "Irish question" has them beat (them and everybody else). They hear the Irish in Ulster say that they don't like the English yet can't understand why they hang on to England instead of going in with Eire.
10 They are all very careful about giving away any information and even if you know they live next door to you and ask them where they are stationed they say "Somewhere in Northern Ireland"!
11 None of them know that I am an American until I tell them – then they are stupefied and can't imagine (a) how I got here (b) how I have stuck it for 9 years.
12 They are universally friendly and so nice to talk to and not a bit fresh.
13 They fell on the Coco-Colas like drug addicts breathing in fervently and saying "My God! A real Coke" and each one told me how many months it was since he had had one.
14 They hate English cigarettes.
15 They think the British army hopelessly class-ridden or class-conscious.

My reactions are:

In a mass I *love* them all. My heart leaps with joy when I drive along behind a truck that says "U.S.A. left hand drive, no signals". I wave at all of them who wave to me. ...

12th Aug.

Now it is Wed the 12th and I am sitting by the first daytime fire that we have had for about 4 months – not that it is any colder or rainier than it has been but I have a wheeker of a cold. ... Lancelot and I ... are going to *Gone W. T. Wind* a week from Friday and are we thrilled. It is coming to the Ritz – 2 shows daily and 4/9 to book seats. The cheapest is 2/6. *Sullivans Travels* is here this week.[68] I will go on Friday if I have time. Our Naval Canteen is having a holiday for August so I get out of that – not that I've gone very regularly lately anyway what with having no help. The Red Cross one is fun although most of the helpers on the shifts I work with are pretty tough. The library part of it is more or less of a flop but I still go in and tidy the books and check out any that are taken out. The boys don't want the bother of books. ...

The food problem is sort of awkward. The American soldiers have oranges, apples, bananas, chocolate bars and white bread not to mention more meat, more everything and it is a bit difficult for people to understand why the precious shipping space is used for those things when English children scrape along with no fruit at all – that is no imported fruit. It nearly kills the soldiers, American, to eat English army food the difference in menus and cooking for one thing and the meagerness for another, but I suppose it is an insurmountable problem – one thing the Americans don't eat any British food and another if an army marches on its stomach they have to keep their "morale" up with food they like.

Our rations are getting tighter – biscuits are now rationed and candy, (3oz. a week) – it is 2 oz. now which is 5 caramels or 1 choc. bar and

[68] *Sullivan's Travels* (the title an echo of the satirical *Gulliver's Travels*) is a 1941 American satire written and directed by the inventive Preston Sturges and starring Joel McCrea and Veronica Lake. It pits filmic comedy against filmic social realism and plumps for the greater social value of comedy (implicitly, perhaps, in time of war).

you know what sweet eaters the people here are. I made some butterscotch and Pinoche with some pre-war brown sugar and it was so good.[69] For 2 or 3 weeks or more before anything starts to be rationed you can't buy it for love nor money anyplace and then the day the rationing starts the windows are stuffed with sweets and everybody gets their 2 oz.!!!

We still haven't a house in town and every night there are about 12 ads. for furnished houses on the Malone Road. I am getting worried because we don't want to stay here – L. would but I don't want to ...

18th Aug. or so!

This, I regret exceedingly to say is the 18th or so and here I haven't mailed this yet! It is our crowded household and always having people around to talk to. ... It was [a] heavenly morning but now a high wind has sprung up and it is getting unpleasant. There has been exactly one hot sunny day so far in August! Yesterday a howling gale blew all day and the kids were in the house all day banging doors.

Friday I went to town and was going to finish this at the hairdressers but had a manicure instead ... Then I went to the American Club but not for full time and in the afternoon saw *Sullivan's Travels* which was very disappointing after *The Lady Eve*.[70] I picked up Jim Barr at his office – I always leave my shopping basket and parcels there and he goes to Newcastle every weekend and we had to run like mad to catch the train. Jim and I after about 7 years of politeness to each other discovered that we have almost identical taste in literature – at least the same interests – and now we are buddies always loaning each other books and magazines. He wanted L. to come back to stock-broking but L. didn't – on account of no war effort there. L. has next week off and maybe the whole month of September. He applied for a month's leave without pay to get his harvest in. He needs a holiday terribly – the traveling every day is so wearing and you know L. – he never stops day or night. This year he spent so much time on his bees that the crops, vegetables, gardens, hens, duck, bantams etc. had to be squeezed into his leftover time from the bees. The double summer time kept it light

[69] Pinoche (a variant of penuche) is a fudge made of brown sugar, butter, milk or cream, and nuts.

[70] *The Lady Eve* (1941) was also directed by Preston Sturges and ranks high among the best films ever made. It stars Barbara Stanwyck and Henry Fonda.

until nearly midnight all summer and we always went to bed so late. I could sleep in the daytime but he never could. We are both thin, but well.

We had quite a good time in Newcastle. The house is so very attractive. It belongs to Jack [Workman]'s brother who is a prisoner of war in Germany and has been since Dunkirk.[71] The house is long and low and white and on the brow of a hill looking over a valley to the Mourne Mountains – not near the sea. ... their house in town has one wonderful modern room – it is all modern – but they went to town on one room helped by a London designer and it is a triumph for Belfast.[72] Jack is in some reserved occupation electrical engineer – all the boys and men L.'s age who aren't in the army will never go to dances or anyplace full of uniforms because they are so sensitive about not being in uniform when so many people are. ...

The news is now on with news of Churchill in Egypt and Russia and the announcement of the big landing at Dieppe which is "not an invasion!"[73] People expect something to happen before the Russian winter sets in – most people think something is all arranged or the Russians would be roaring for help. ...

Love and Kisses and more love,
Helen

22nd Aug.
Mahee

Dear Ginna,

... Yesterday we went to see *Gone with the Wind* and I loved it – enough to want to go again. The acting was all so good and the look of the places especially Scarlett and Rhett's house in Atlanta were so good. I was afraid that something would hold me back from seeing it – one of the children sick or even that I would sprain my ankle hopping

---

[71] See the letter of 8th June 1940. Although he was not heard from for a long time and presumed killed, Captain Arthur Workman "was taken prisoner during a retirement towards Dunkirk".

[72] According to Caroline Workman Anderson (pers. comm. to Julie Mackie), the cottage called Struan is still standing.

[73] The raid on Dieppe, France by Canadian and British forces on 19th August ended in defeat.

on or off a bus or tram and sister are we on buses and trams these days. ...

We have Americans in the town where Jack and Elaine live now and do they look out of place. I can't get over it yet that they are here in such quantities. I long to talk to all of them but haven't the nerve usually – they are too young and fresh and fresh means fresh except that when you do talk to them they aren't fresh. The dagos and wops[74] and colored ones are positively startling to behold in this subdued country – they don't go good – and do they look lost propping up the walls and killing time. Not that they don't work hard on maneuvres and things but in their spare time they seem so lost.

An ex-bar tender American soldier came to see me the other day. He was on a train from Newcastle that I was on once – drinking whiskey out of a bottle and offering me some ... and he came to see me the other day – by train to Comber, by bus to Ballydrain and then walking (5 miles!). ... He had about 2 inches of straight whiskey tossed back just after he came; he had left his bottle in the ditch some place along the way; he had about 2 inches more before supper and betwixt and between I heard his life story. ... Rosemary [Webb] can't "place" Americans at all – in fact no one here can – such a good write-up for democracy but everyone is so distressed at the awful type of girl they walk around town with – floosies of the worst sort. I'm not distressed particularly because I don't see what you can do about it – if the tough ones pick up tough girls you can't stop them – the thing to cut down on is drink which shocks everyone to the core. They stand in front of the City hall and tip a bottle up and you can imagine how *that* looks and *what* people think...

25th Aug.

... This last summer has been bad mentally. Lancelot was too engrossed in his bees and I had no outside interest to balance it. For a while I was interested in cooking but you know how soon that palls and there isn't anything here that interests me absorbingly I'm ashamed to say – crops, gardening etc. What I really need is a holiday so I am going in September to my first love – Dublin ...

---

[74] Period slang terms for Latino and Italian Americans respectively; by the late 1960s regarded as offensive.

1st Sept.

Now it is Sept. 1 and running true to Ramsey form I had a B.B. yesterday (in case you've forgotten Beauty Brigade). I suppose when we stop having occasional B.B.s we can safely say that middle age has *got* us. My B.B. consisted of oiling my parched scalp, egging my clogged pore face and then washing both. ...

The garden has such an autumnal look about it already and I love September in Ireland. There are usually lots of sunny days with that autumn feeling of going – going – gone that adds so much to their charm. Today is like that. Usually the blackberries are ripe soon and it is fun to pick them. ...

It is nearly hailing now and the Guinea hens are making a fearful noise. We have nearly 50 hens, looked after by Johnny and about 8 big ducks and 12 growing hens that we feed and about 10 baby bantams – looked after by us – mostly L. and Gay. We had 30 bantams about 4 cocks and 3 hens and 2 Muscovy ducks taken by a fox – it was so sad. We have 3 corrugated iron coops on the lawn which we brought up various families of ducks, Bantams and chickens in. We have all the eggs we want and sell the surplus to the gov't. for 3/- a dozen. You aren't allowed to sell or give away any eggs at all. Although we get plenty of food one does long for some things. Rosemary brought a small tin of tomato soup with her. We haven't been able to buy tomato soup for over a year or more and it tasted like nectar and ambrosia. When I think how you can go buy any kind of food you want – peanuts, nuts, bananas, saltines, corn on the cob, pineapple etc. it makes me wild. I do pretty well at the American canteen and just act like a glutton over tuna fish, grape jelly, pickles, cokes and white bread. I just thought of Chicken à la King too. We never have chicken – too expensive about $2.50 each and skinny at that. We never get steak either but we are having mushrooms and we do have our own tomatoes and apples are coming in. Compared to living in a town in England we are nearly as well off as you. They get 3 pints of milk a week, 1 egg a month or maybe it is 1 a week and have to buy vegetables which are scarce and expensive. And yet and rightly the Minister of Food, Lord

Woolton gets nothing but praise.[75] He has done wonders of fairness and distribution and nearly everything is rationed now so the rich aren't any better off than the poor except that they can eat out all the time (up to 5/- a meal) and can buy chickens and ducks. ... One thing I am sick of is margarine. But all in all we are doing splendidly and it makes housekeeping so simple and easy and no one expects anything.

... What a war! I remember so well 3 years ago today hearing on the 8 o'clock news that the situation had become very grave during the night and that the Germans had started bombing the Poles at daylight and then we knew that the worst was on us. But I must say I never thought that 3 years from then I would be sitting in the same room with my family still with me and life except for luxuries and petrol materially the same but my outlook must be radically advanced. ...

Now the news is on – the Germans haven't got Stalingrad yet – if only Russia can hold out until the winter again I think the war will be over by Christmas 1943 – if not – ! ... You are so lucky to know where Lloyd will be for the duration – I do hope he is in a safe job and that you like California better than you ever have before – enjoy the food for me!

Two good books about Belfast if you can get them are *Lost Fields* by Michael McLaverty and *An Ulsterwoman in England* by Nesca Robb.[76] I will be so interested to hear about your new surroundings and life so buck up and write often.

Love to you both,
Helen

---

[75] Lord Woolton, wartime UK Minister of Food, was indeed a popular figure despite overseeing rationing. He provided 650,000 schoolchildren with free meals and 3,500,000 with free milk. His name was given to a dish, Woolton pie, that was a mix of carrots, parsnips, potatoes and turnips in oatmeal and brown gravy topped with a pastry or potato crust.

[76] Michael McLaverty's novel *Lost Fields* appeared in 1942; there is a critical discussion of it in John Wilson Foster, *Forces and Themes in Ulster Fiction* (1974), pp. 40–41. Also in 1942 appeared the scholar Nesca A. Robb's *An Ulsterwoman in England, 1924–1941*. See Liam Harte, "Nesca A. Robb, *An Ulsterwoman in England, 1924-1941*" in *The Literature of the Irish in Britain* (2009).

13th Sept.
Mahee

Dear Mother,

After many trials we have made an offer for a house. ... I went to see it on Friday with the agent. It is in Sans Souci Park not very far up the Malone Road and is very well placed in a pretty lawn. It reminds me of a gay-ninety American mansion – ugly but dignified. ...

We quite realize that bombing may start again in which event we will rush back here – that is if English cities start to be heavily bombed again – depending entirely I think on what happens in Russia in the next 6 weeks. We heard a Russian Commentary tonight that would make your blood run cold. What it must be like to be living in Stalingrad I shudder to think.

14th Sept.

The war is getting everyone down sort of subtly. ... L. is so reasonable to talk to that he is my mainstay and prop in my despairing moments and he is just as glad to go to town for the winter as I am because the daily 38 miles of motoring and now 16 of motoring, 22 by train and being on 6 trams a day is *so* wearing – 2 trams to his office from the train, 2 home again and 1 each way for lunch compared to 5 minutes tram or walking night and morning if we get this Malone Road house. The American canteen is fun but we are too busy to get to know any of the boys well. I hope to entertain more Americans when we get to town – here it is impossible on account of transport ... I am a pretty good cook now – make wonderful sponge cakes, bake mackerel in milk to a turn, can make potatoes floury, make smooth white sauce, specialize in soups and "made-up dishes" and can face a stove with a confident gleam in my eye – if no enthusiasm!! ...

16th Sept.

Lancelot has increased his stocks of bees from 3 hives to 18, he has reared queens, caught swarms, fiddles with nuclei and there is *nothing* he doesn't know about bees. When we were in Newcastle for a weekend with Jack and Caroline Workman he took a test and became a "bee-master" and has something like a diploma saying that he is a bee-master. He always takes up every new hobby with such thoroughness that I have been a "bee-widow" all summer but having a husband with no hobby ... would be worse. We got around 80 sections of honey but next year we are going to be in the honey business. ... I sometimes go help swathed in a black bee veil and even in the middle of swarms etc. I wasn't stung once and neither were Gay and Julie. Once a swarm swarmed on L.'s neck!! But he had his veil on. He has been stung a lot but it doesn't affect him much. ...

Edith thinks that Bodo may be in America. He has left the Mediterranean, thank goodness, and is either in India or America – anyway E. got a cable to say "Arrived safely" but she has no idea where. Bodo is too honest to invent a code which most husbands and wives have to let the wives know where the husbands are.

Harry McMullan has been stationed in Belfast – he is coming home next Sunday and Roberta is so thrilled she nearly feels that the war is over. He is a Lt. Commander now I think and I don't know what he will be doing here. When you think that they have been separated for 3 years+ it is tough though he got fairly frequent leaves and Roberta used to go over for a month or so about twice a year. Roberta is a masterpiece of efficiency. She runs a huge house with one maid and a nurse – copes with a big garden and does more canteen work than anyone I know – about five 4-hour shifts a week – also knits, sews, cooks and never stops.

Betty Harris is back in her house in Holywood [Co. Down] after 2 years of floating around to her mother, kids at her mother-in-laws in Comber and ending with a few weeks in Rosie McConnell's gate lodge. Terence McConnell's father died so now Terence is Sir Terence and Rosie is Lady McConnell. Joy's mother is Lady Andrews now because the husband who is Lord Chief Justice was made a baronet and is now Sir James Andrews. Jack's father [John Miller Andrews] is considered simply hopeless as Prime Minister. Everybody likes him and realizes that he is doing his best ... Joy had a son about 3 weeks ago. Her husband is in a tank in Egypt and she hasn't heard from him yet. ...[77]

[77] For Sir Terence McConnell, see the letter of 21st September, 1939. The gate lodge was that belonging to the McConnell home, The Moat, Belfast. Like his grandfather, the first baronet, Terence was an estate agent. For Betty Harris and Joy Haselden see the letter of 17th August 1939. In London on 30th November 1940 Joy married Second Lieutenant Jeffery Adam Hepburn.

You ask what reader Gay could read in – she can read anything from *The Oxford Book of English Verse, Little Orphan(t) Annie* ... She can read Grimm's fairy *Tales, The Water Babies* and any of her *Reddy the Fox* books ... She is undoubtedly remarkably gifted along literary and poetic lines ...

In a way moving into town we will feel we are moving into the war – we will have to be so careful not to show a chink of light, rations are tighter and little oddments of food harder to get, constantly seeing soldiers and lorries and jeeps and peeps and breathing the war keyed up atmosphere of town. Everyone who comes here [Mahee] says that you forget all about the war. We usually listen to the news but never see a paper and the papers tend to make things worse. ...

The next [letter] will be from dear dirty Dublin where we will see lights, no soldiers, eat like mad and go gay. Thank goodness for Dublin to go to every 6 months. No holiday in Ulster is worth it – too grim everywhere but please goodness another year will see us all together again. Gosh! Is life maddening sometimes with you a-setting there and us a-setting here and no point.

Love and kisses,
Helen

20th Sept.
Shelbourne Hotel
Dublin

Dear Ginna and Lloyd,

It is only half-past nine of a rainy Sunday morning and we have been awake since 7.30! Lancelot has just left for home but I am staying until next Friday! ... It is because I have been trying for 6 months to come here and have been tied at home cooking fairly steadily. Now it is *divine* to be in a good hotel, eating good food with nothing to do but enjoy myself. We came on Thursday and I am going to the Scanlans tomorrow to stay until Friday thereby saving money and avoiding being alone in a hotel.

Auntie is at the Hibernian and has been for 2 weeks but is going home tomorrow. We tried to get in there but it was full – has been full for months. This hotel is the oldest and best in Dublin.[78] It is old-fashioned but nice and has a nice atmosphere. I think that all of Dublin has an 18th century atmosphere still and the quieter suburbs are incredible. We took a tram-ride out to Monkstown yesterday to visit Jonty Hannigan [sic] and his wife May, who is L.s first cousin. You remember Jonty, I'm sure. We were on top of the tram and could see into all the walled-in gardens and the general look and atmosphere and the people bicycling around in gay ninety hats – you know those straw gardening hats that British women wear – well with that and the lack of cars you would have sworn the date was 1913.

I was agreeably surprised in Jonty who is now very busy psychoanalyzing people. He says that he is wonderful. If only he were a little more humble or reticent you would have more faith in him.[79] Their house is so cuty and attractive in a seedy way – lovely pictures and photographs around but ragged loose covers. He talks all the time and is interesting and amusing but naïve and I feel superficial. May is quiet and nice and seems as happy as a lark with him. They have 5 daughters – we saw two – both *so* nice – the eldest and the youngest. Their house is a typical Dublin house with a flight of stairs up to the front door and a basement kitchen and is on such a quiet square with a big garden in the middle where people were playing tennis on grass courts. Dublin simply beats the band as to quietness and stand-still timelessness. There are no private cars except taxis and cars owned by doctors. There are a sprinkling of cabs, traps, donkey carts and carriages and millions of bicycles. It is like Amsterdam – even in thick traffic of buses, trams delivery vans etc. about 50 bicycles start out when the light goes green and do they whiz!

---

[78] The Shelbourne hotel opened its doors in 1824. Elizabeth Bowen wrote its biography: *The Shelbourne: A Centre in Dublin Life for More than a Century* (1951).

[79] Jonathan (Jonty) Hanaghan was an Englishman who was sent to Ireland in 1926 by Ernest Jones, Freud's friend and biographer. In 1942, the year of Helen's visit, Hanaghan, who was a pacifist and the first psychoanalyst to work in Ireland, founded the Irish Psycho-Analytical Association in Monkstown on the edge of Dublin. The IPAA combined Freudianism with Christianity. Whereas Helen found Jonty Hanaghan amusing but naive and superficial, his followers found him a "charismatic personality" and were impressed by "a kind of healing presence". Indeed, R. Cameron, the compiler of a book of Hanaghan's aphorisms after his death, *The Wisdom of Jonty* (Dublin: Runa Press, 1970), claimed that "the words of Jonathan Hanaghan were incarnational". See the Irish Psycho-Analytical Association website, and also Ross Skelton, "Jonathan Hanaghan: The Founder of Psychoanalysis in Ireland," *The Crane Bag* 7.2: 183–190.

The air is so soft and warm that it envelops you in an enervating mist and the 1st morning we were here I felt tired even down to my wrists. I'm so enervated sitting here that I don't want to do anything – even this letter is an effort and I felt exactly like writing letters when I started. If I had a good book to read, which I haven't, I would go to sleep over it. I am in "The Ladies Drawing Room" and am too distracted for anything because there is a mirror at the back of this desk in which I can watch my hands and you have no idea how it takes my mind off my work – or have you? I have on Peggy Sage Golden Sand nail polish and I think I'd look better without it. My nails look wider and squarer than I had thought and you will be glad to hear that I haven't bitten them for months – or smoked!!

Cigarettes are more or less rationed here to 10 a day and you have to call for your 10 every day in person and some days there just aren't any… They are plentiful now in the north since the price was put up to 2/- a packet. I occasionally buy some for L. and when I think that for 80 cigarettes I give out $2 it nearly kills me and I'm so thankful that I've given up. I haven't got much fatter either. I gained 5 pounds or so the first week but now am about the same at around 118.

There are only 2 trains a day now to Dublin and they are always packed. We came 1st class thus ensuring a seat, but even then sometimes if you leave it for lunch or anything you find a Mother and baby in it on your return. The Sunday night trains we hear, are awful and people stand the whole way.

I am listening to the European Service of the B.B.C. It is a Church service now… At home I listen often to church services – there is a 15 minute service every morning at 10.15. I still haven't faith – for instance I heard a most moving plea by an arch-bishop the other day on the radio for everyone in England to pray on their knees every day for the conquered peoples of Europe since that was the only way we could help them – that is we can't send food etc. but we can pray. He was so convincing and said he knew how shy people were about actively praying. I am shy all right but I still can't believe that praying for them is going to do them any good.

It makes me feel worse than ever now to be gadding around Dublin while Stalingrad is still being held so bravely and with such bloodiness. *The New Statesman* is *wild* because there is no second front and fears that even if Russia can hold and can win the Russians will never forgive us for not helping them more at this crisis. Time will tell us why we aren't ready because we obviously aren't or we would have attacked long ago. Meanwhile the lull in air-raids has everyone calm and peaceful again with all the evacuated people pouring back into town as transportation in country districts has become so bad.

Now the buses and trams have started – they only start at 10 on Sunday. L. shared a taxi with another man – otherwise he would have had to walk to the station – several miles away!

We have been twice to Jammets, the famous restaurant here. It is very expensive – you could easily pay £1 for a meal but we took the Scanlans Friday night and the bill was under £2.0.0. for 4 but 3 of us didn't have dessert – Philip had a peach melba 4/6 !!! and I nearly drooled when it came. The chef keeps screaming and fighting in the kitchen in French and there seem to be about 4 waiters, bus-boys etc. buzzing around every table and the food *is* good. I had been to the snack bar once with Maureen, but neither of us had ever been to the restaurant proper before. It is small and unpretentious with round tables and white tablecloths and a woman in a checked blouse sitting high up on a stool behind the cash box – very French!

In Dublin you can't buy bananas, margarine, dripping, bacon, radio batteries, anything to do with a bicycle, soap flakes, and I forget what else. Sugar, butter and tea are properly rationed with coupons – fuel is rationed too – coal that is and gas and electricity but you can buy peat and wood if you can pay for it. Their biggest hardship is tea – ½ oz. a week and as the Hannigans [sic] told us yesterday at tea time even if they had tea enough they couldn't have given us tea because they cook on gas and the gas is only turned on from 5.30–8.30 a.m. 11–1, 5–6 p.m. People who want to bake bake at 5.30 because that is the only time the pressure is strong enough! It sounds fairly easy but when you think of invalids and babies with bottles to be heated etc. it must have its trying moments. People were asked last year to cut down gas and light consumption by ½ or, I forget, but if their meter showed that they hadn't, their gas and elec. was cut off completely for several months.

When we come we try to smuggle – chocolate and candy – (L. went home stiff with thin bars) ribbons, cosmetics of all kinds (which are not only scarce with us but have a 66 % tax!! There is a good hair-tonic that I bought for L.'s baldness – Silvrikin it is called, and I only could buy one bottle in Belfast at 12/- and here the shops are full of it for 6/- a bottle. ...

We went to the Abbey Theatre Thursday night with Auntie and to Jammets to lunch with her yesterday. She is a wonder as to smartness, interest in dress, and aliveness but she depresses me. I feel somehow flattened out and dull around her and should *hate* to live with her. ... Jack and John Andrews came to stay with us in two bursts for shooting. ... [Jack] couldn't get over our coming to Dublin – he will *never* go any place except Comber and Whiterock – that's what's wrong with him. He is so Orange ... that I looked and looked for a really Papish postcard full of crosses and rosaries etc. to send to him ... but I couldn't find any bad enough.[80] ...

I have been writing for 2 hours so despite the rain I will take a walk around Stephens Green to admire the architecture – all pure 18th century – I am facing the Green now and our bedroom overlooks it and then go see Auntie for lunch. It is like a different world here even in peacetime but in war-time it is astounding. G'bye now and love to you both

Helen

The Gables, Rathgar
Dublin
24th Sept.

Dear Mother,

It is pouring rain and I am sitting in what they call "the lounge" at the Scanlans! ...

As usual I love being in Dublin and I love staying here although the house is a bit formal for my personal taste – when the gong goes everyone rushes to meals and it would put them out if you were very late. Philip still thinks that everything Irish is perfect including de Valera, neutrality and all. ...

There are no cars at all in Dublin except taxis, doctors and priests and the buses and trams at the rush hours are frantic. Not that it stops anyone from doing anything. When you get an invitation to a dance

---

[80] For Jack and Elaine Andrews, see the letter of 11th February 1939.

there is a little note at the bottom saying "changing room and bicycle park". Girls cycle to the dances in slacks, change into evening clothes and then cycle home. Taxis are a shilling a mile for long distance runs … and at the end of the month when taxis are low on petrol it is almost impossible to get one.

The food is still wonderful, there are still lights, no soldiers and no war atmosphere. The censorship is so strict that although there are headlines about the Stalingrad Battle both the German and English communiqués are given equal prominence and then the rest of the 4 sheeted paper is Irish local news – horseracing, theatres, movies, dances and of course Irish politics. …

Unluckily there are no good movies this week but we have been to the Abbey Theatre and to the Gaiety to see Jimmy O'Dea.[81] Dublin supports 3 small theatres – Abbey, Gate and Peacock, an opera house and 2 big theatres as well as more movies per population than any city in Europe.[82]

I feel the charm of the city and like Ireland so well that I feel I *must* have Irish ancestry – and then there is my untidiness (going out pinned up with safety-pins) … I have been reading such a good book here about an Irish family – the book is *Bowenscourt* by Elizabeth Bowen and is the history of an Anglo-Irish family and the influence their Irish country house had on them. One of the family names was Cole and I wondered where Daddy's brother got the name Cole – was that Irish? I would love to know if you can find out.[83] …

---

[81] James (Jimmy) O'Dea (1899–1965), a Dublin actor and comedian. Although he was a stage actor, he became most famous for his Variety and pantomime appearances. He also featured in several films, including *Darby O'Gill and the Little People* (1959).

[82] The three small theatres are still of great artistic significance. The original Abbey Theatre on Marlborough Street was active from 1904 until destroyed by fire in 1951. It was associated with W.B Yeats, Lady Gregory, John Millington Synge and Sean O'Casey. The Abbey Theatre Company opened the Peacock as an experimental theatre in 1927. A year later, Hilton Edwards and Micheál Mac Liammóir started the Gate Theatre which used the Peacock space until moving into the Rotunda Annex in 1930.

[83] Bowen's Court was built in County Cork in the 1770s by Henry Cole Bowen. The novelist Elizabeth (Dorothea Cole) Bowen was its biographer (*Bowen's Court*, 1942) and last owner who was compelled to sell it in 1959; shortly afterwards it was demolished.

Dublin is much warmer than Belfast and we hardly ever have a fire here on account of the acute fuel shortage. They are allowed a normal amount of electricity now because the river Shannon is in flood so there is hot water but all last summer and spring they only had hot water one day a week.[84]...

I met such a nice American at an Austrian restaurant the other night here. He is a special member of the legation and has only been here for 2 weeks having flown to Foynes [Co. Limerick] by Clipper. ... A whole row of Americans sat in front of us at the Abbey the other night. American soldiers in the North are not allowed to come to Dublin even in civilian dress and any soldier who came over in uniform British or American would be interned. However, the whole British army spends its leaves here in civilian clothes and everybody from the North who has a day or two's holiday comes here. The trains are *packed*.

Much love and kisses,
Helen

11th Oct.
41 Sans Souci Park
Belfast

Dear Mother,

I can't find my air-mail paper so I will make this narrow and small to try to tell you all about our new house. ... This is Sunday night and L. and I came up yesterday to get more or less settled before we bring the children up. We brought one trailer load yesterday and will bring the bicycles, tricycles and oddments on Tuesday morning. ... We have it until June 1, 1943 – or 8 months and we are very lucky indeed to get it even at £15 a month which is what we pay – but Sister is it a mansion! We have to black out 27 windows every night and compared to Mahee where we only black out about 10 that is something! Luckily the black out is good so we won't be troubled by the wardens. ... it is an exceedingly comfortable house to live in – solid, sunny and full of gas fires – 2 downstairs and 3 upstairs which is all very labor and coal

---

[84] The Shannon Hydro-electric Scheme was begun in the 1920s to harness the power of the River Shannon; it was completed in 1929.

saving even if we have to save gas too! The propaganda for fuel-saving on the radio and in the press is continuous – they are trying to get people to save enough voluntarily so that we won't have to have a complicated rationing scheme. Luckily there are lots of lamp plugs in the house but no power plugs – hence no vacuum cleaner. ...

Both Gay and Julie will go to nursery school at Richmond Lodge – in the same grounds as L.'s office, but in another building.[85] It is about 10 minutes walk up the Malone Road from here – all so handy. ...

[The letter ends immediately after a ground plan of the new house and a map of the neighbourhood in relation to Queen's University and the city centre.]

28th Oct.
Sans Souci

Dear Ginna and Lloyd and Mother,

... Now we are ensconced in town and enjoying every minute of it. You wouldn't think that Belfast could ever go to anybody's head – much less Belfast in war-time with a black-out, no cars, no maid, no parties but just plain city life. I beam as I jump from tram to tram with my shopping basket on my arm. We are 4 houses away from the Malone Road tram lines and sister, is it divine!!! We like living in what I please to call our "mustard colored mansion" and swallow the ornaments, pictures, bric-a-brac statues, Buddhas, and ornamental screens with a Giaconda like smile (whatever that is). L. is reading *Berlin Diary*[86] instead of doing his farm accounts and we are listening to the Bohemian comic opera "The Bartered Bride" which is being so well sung.[87] We have only been out two nights in nearly 3 weeks and I

[85] Richmond Lodge School was begun in 1879 and moved to the Malone Road in 1913. Originally formed for boy pupils and their sisters, it was girls' only by the time it amalgamated with Victoria College, Belfast in 1988. Both were regarded as prestigious seats of education.

[86] *Berlin Diary: The Journal of a Foreign Correspondent 1934–1941* (1941) by William L. Shirer (1904–1994) who later wrote *The Rise and Fall of the Third Reich* (1960).

[87] Smetana's *The Bartered Bride* staged by the BBC Theatre Chorus and Orchestra was broadcast (in commemoration of the Czechoslovakian National Day), on the Home Service at 8.05pm, 28th October.

went out to the theatre last Friday night with Katie Pringle while L. and Kenneth went to Mahee. I am not keen on leaving the children sleeping alone in town with only Sadie [the helper] in case of a blitz – not that I think there will be one being one of those optimistic people who think that Belfast's blitzes are over. However if they start blitzing England again in force we will cheese it back to Mahee. ... The first week we were here I hardly went out between cooking, sorting and getting settled. ... Oh *fabious* day! We are getting a cook on Saturday! ... One day we went to R[obinson] and Cleavers to lunch but it was so hot, crowded and slow that I decided I would rather cook at home. So many people eat out these days to eke out their rations that you have to go very early to avoid the crush and even then the food is lousy. The G[rand] Central is now described as an "upholstered sewer" since the soldiers bring their dubious girl friends there. I haven't been lately but we are going to go sight-seeing some night to see it. Our two night jaunts were to Arabella's on a pouring wet night, by tram of course, with a flash light to guide our faltering steps and sister, have you ever thought of the problem of one's hat blowing off in the black out? Well, mine did and the search was successful but fraught with adventures with wet slippery leaves, strange curbstones and you wouldn't know what! Arabella makes me scream with laughter and I laughed so much at her tonight on the 'phone that she thought that I had had a sherry – I haven't seen sherry except in Dublin for months. We have ½ a bottle Irish whiskey at Mahee and that is all. I don't know what is available these days because it is so scarce and expensive and we are so moderate that we just never drink anything. We had cocktails with ice at Harry and Roberta's where we went for our other evening out – such luxury. Harry has some job here now and works from 9 a.m. – 7 p.m. every day of the week including Sunday but he has Tuesday off when he and Bertie get the supper and entertain in a very lavish way – the maid's night out. ...

29th Oct.

Now it is Thursday morning – sunny and cold and I am in the nicest room in the house – the morning room cum nursery – the radio is playing "I'm dreaming of a white Christmas", the kids are at school,

Sadie is out for the day, we have not one but two maids coming, we are going to Simon Haselden's birthday party this afternoon and life is a song! ...

Gay and Julie love school. Julie is in the nursery school with 17 other little tykes from about 2½ to 5 years old. They mostly just play with prams, doll houses, sand piles and educational toys, have a rest and a drink of milk and are out of the way of their parents from 9.30 – 1. Gay is in what they call the kindergarten and does lessons as well as playing games. L. takes them both every morning because they are all in the same building – the Ministry of Food having taken over the school but half the school itself is evacuated to Port Ballintrae, a sea-coast town in Antrim so there is room for everybody. Sadie or I go get them because L. still lunches at his club both to save our food at home and because the food is better there and he sees his pals and buddies. ...

I haven't started regularly at the Red Cross canteen yet. I have been switched from the canteen to the library which Mrs. Dolan and I are supposed to be running. The whole Plaza is now taken over by the Club and it is all on a big and impressive scale. Marcia has some American Red Cross appointment and wears a uniform and runs the place as efficiently as anybody could.[88] ...

The egg ration is now 1 a month – I ask you! We are not registered because we have our own. Food is easier in town because you can get fish and odds and ends. I keep wondering what the cook will cook but she can always while away her time baking bread and scones and doing fancy things with potatoes. Our Mahee potatoes are so wonderful – having lived here now for 9½ years and hearing the talk I know a good potato when I see one. ...

Can you believe it is 4 years since we have clapped eyes on each other? I am getting gray and although I haven't bags under my eyes that swing in the wind I have circles that show even at the sides (they just came in these few hectic weeks in town *cooking and all*) and my throat looks crêpy! I laugh so over Ginna's letters for days after they

---

[88] Marcia (Mrs James) Mackie was according to one source, Director, and according to another source Assistant Director, of the American Red Cross Club in Belfast. At the end of the war she received an OBE: see *Belfast Gazette*, Friday 15th June, 1945. There is a Marcia Mackie Prize in nursing and midwifery at Queen's University, Belfast.

come even – that bit about not having to look pop-eyed to look awake had me in hysterics and G. and J. and L. all laughed too just at my laughing. I honestly think the war will be over about a year from now and then we can have a family reunion – I am still passing for a recently arrived American – nay tourist! – so my accent is not pure Belfast yet!!

Love and kisses to all.
Helen

5th Nov.
Sans Souci

Dear Mother and Ginna,

I have spent the morning on the telephone putting off Julie's birthday party from tomorrow to Armistice Day ... Edith [Taggart] was full of news – Bodo is in America near Richmond and was all set to come home but it was changed, but I hope it will come on again.[89] He hasn't been home for 2 years come Christmas. He loves America, thinks the food and hospitality are wonderful, thinks they drink astonishingly much, all the girls kiss him good-bye at the dances – married and single and he is buying lots of things.

Charlie Mitchell is back here again and is living at Rushmere, a boarding house until Nancy and the baby – now nearly 2 come over in

---

[89] In early 1941 when the Great War dreadnought battleship HMS *Queen Elizabeth* was refitted and was to rejoin the Mediterranean Fleet, Bodo Taggart was offered the position of assistant gunnery officer; en route the gunnery officer fell sick and Lieutenant Commander Taggart became gunnery officer: his job was to choose targets for the eight 15" guns aboard. In December 1941 in the shallow harbour of Alexandria, Italian frogmen attached limpet mines to *Queen Elizabeth* and HMS *Valiant*; though severely damaged, and nine sailors killed, the ships remained upright and maintained the illusion of seaworthiness; the frogmen were captured. In June 1942 after *pro tem* repairs on site, *Queen Elizabeth* steamed via the Suez Canal to Norfolk Virginia (near Richmond) to be comprehensively repaired. Bodo Taggart spent the rest of the war in the United States, save for a couple of trips back to Belfast. Now an expert on the subject, in New York he wrote the manual on the use of 15" guns and was promoted to Commander. After the war he resumed his architectural and engineering career and built his late father's Belfast firm into one of the two biggest firms in that line. I am grateful to Bodo's son Redmond for details of his father's naval career; see also "HMS *Queen Elizabeth* (1913)", Wikipedia.

February.[90] Charlie looks awful – Edith went to dinner with him last night at the G[rand] Central and was saying too how shocked she was. He is still jolly and funny but his face is so sunk in that he looks like somebody else. He has been in Birmingham for 2½ years living in a hotel and he hates the Northern English like poison – you remember the exaggerated, haw-haw army way he talks – he is a scream on the war – says that we will all starve, it will go on for ten more years and that any minute now the Germans will start eating the Frenchmen!! He is a Major and is in the pays corps – he was invalided out of the army before the war and feels awful that he isn't with his own old regiment. You feel the whole weight of the war when you talk to him, past, present and future because without being pessimistic in a down at the mouth way he is so fatalistic and hard-boiled and sort of doom-conscious – a lot of his attitude is personal – disappointment, thwarted ambition, and mediocre health. …

Everybody is so elated over the big success of the 8th Army announced today – the Germans are running in all directions!!![91] …

Edith is such a big shot in the W.V.S. She was out yesterday all day with 16 Americans looking over something and it sounded exactly like Mrs. Roosevelt's day – went all over a Liberator bomber,[92] had a special lunch-party with flowers on the table, a wonderful lunch with vitamin-pills passed too, a butler and goodness knows what. I was telling Elaine that as I came back to bed I felt that my life is so domestic and drab compared to the worldliness of Edith's. She is so active in politics too – a leading light in the Junior Unionist Movement, a public speaker and an organizer as well as a joiner![93] Elaine and I agreed that we just

[90] For Charlie Mitchell, see the letters of 12th September 1939 and 26th December 1940/[January 1941] where it is Manchester he is living in.

[91] The First Battle of El Alamein in Egypt had been waged during the month of July and ended in stalemate. The Second Battle began in late October. This time the British 8th Army (including Commonwealth soldiers), led by Lieutenant-General Bernard Montgomery (of Northern Irish descent) won the day when the German Afrika Korps, against Hitler's orders, retreated under cover of darkness. This Allied victory turned the tide of the war in North Africa.

[92] The Consolidated B-24 Liberator was an American bomber that entered RAF service in 1941. The plane proved effective in the campaign against German U-boats. The plane saw extensive combat for the duration of the war.

[93] For Edith Taggart, see the letter from her husband, Bodo Taggart to Helen (1st March, 1942). Edith Taggart, a prize-winning public speaker, vigorously campaigned for a greater youthful contribution to Ulster unionist politics, even to the extent of their fielding candidates for election to parliament. See *Larne Times* 29th January 1942.

aren't the type and she had just been dusting the stairs and was bound for the local church to play the organ in the pouring rain and she said "oh, this Irish rain! How I hate it!" It is a real November day – cold, dark and rainy with not a redeeming feature. ...

We feel so unsettled with no house of our own except Mahee which has definitely returned to the category of "summer cottage" now that G. and J. are of school age, and as petrol, tires and cars are gradually slipping away from us. We can always manage in a sort of way in the summer with a pony and trap and bikes but the winter living there is a thing of the past unless L. after the war becomes a farmer and the kids cycle 3 miles or 5 to the local school.

We were looking at our [home] movies last night of the past 3 summers and it is all so idyllic and heavenly looking – the sea so blue, the yachts so white, the flowers so bright, the children absolute dreams and the grownups so holiday looking lying around sun-bathing. ...

Must go hear the news about the big victory we have had – whoops dearie! I think he's licked – the big bo-hunk![94]

Now it is about 11.30 at night – L. is talking to Kenneth Pringle, I have been reading the *New Yorker* and fizzgigging around[95] having "had" the kids all afternoon and got the supper. ...

Betty Hazelden's [sic] party was terrific – 21 children and about 25 grownups. She is back in her own house at Holywood for the first time in 2 years or more and it was like a house-warming because she had only lived there for 6 months or so when she moved out. The house is a wonderful achievement for Ireland being "too, too, off white" and as nearly like *Vogue* as Ireland could achieve. Everything is pale and lovely and I felt just as crestfallen thinking of *my* party a week hence as I did do you remember the day? that I went to see Betty when Simon was born and you both waited out in the car and I came out to tell you how *wonderful* Betty looked lying in bed in a green moiré[96] bed-jacket and how *wonderful* the cradle was and how super it *all* was and how you both had to be held back from buying me a green moiré bed jacket

---

[94] Presumably Hitler. "Bohunk" is a North American disparaging slang word for someone of central European ethnicity (originally a portmanteau word from Bohemian + Hungarian) and in use at least until the 1970s.

[95] "Fizzgigging": another portmanteau coinage – gadding about or gallivanting, moving around frivolously: fizzing + whirling (as in a whirligig). Listed in Wiktionary as archaic and spelled "fizgigging".

[96] Moiré: a fabric with a wavy-water appearance (Merriam-Webster).

and putting bows all over me and the cradle. Well Betty's house, flowers, food and cake and all were positively breathtaking for this 4th winter of the war – maiden-hair fern around the birthday cake, pink frothy jellies with silver balls, chocolate covered cup cakes, rolled asparagus sandwiches and everything just perfection and when I heard that she hasn't even a maid – only a nurse I felt worse than ever. But she has her mother and her mother's maids and greenhouse behind her and her mother-in-law's flowers and a cake or two too and I sour grapsy thought "too much bad taste for war-time" and all the other consoling things. ...

7th Nov.
[Mahee]

This is Saturday morning instead of Friday and where are we but at Mahee. The sun is blazing, the fire is smoking and I am sitting on the window seat with the sun on my back and about as much energy as a clam! I didn't have a minute yesterday at the canteen and talked to so many American soldiers for so long – two for an hour each and then I took a rear-gunner shopping to buy some Carters Little Liver Pills – he had been in Ireland for 2 weeks and in Belfast half a day and he was a tough little cuss from Washington with not enough teeth to be anything but a rear-gunner and he was most amusing to talk to. He had been everywhere and done everything in America – placer mining at Cripple Creek, salmon fishing in the Pacific, fur trapping in Canada and was a real character. He said "God, this town hasn't got anything – no drug-stores, no barber shops etc." He couldn't get over the horse-traffic on the streets but admitted that the building looked solid "like San Francisco before the fire". We found a "drug store" and bought some paint to "touch up his gun sights" and I left him at Woolworths as happy as a lark. ...

Arriving here last night with L. was like really coming home. I can't tell you how heavenly it was to come in and find the house shining, 4 fires blazing, flowers on the table and the tea-kettle boiling and not a soul in sight. Aggie comes every Friday afternoon and does it and makes the beds, put bottles in and gives everything that little extra touch that just makes all the difference. We had a wonderful supper and then couldn't get our radio to work so had to go to the G'Dinnings where we stayed until 11.30 and lo! The tide was over the road and we had to walk home but it was a lovely, starry night and was fun. Must go cook some golden plover – George Browne [a neighbour] is coming to lunch.

3.30 p.m.

... Such a good concert has just finished in honor of Vaughan Williams's 70th birthday. Vaughan himself was there and the applause and fanfare were terrific.[97] Every Saturday there are such good concerts. The B.B.C. music for the Home Service is always so good and they seem to be having less and less light music and ballads. The B.B.C. is terribly maligned – Elaine thinks that if the war is lost it will be the B.B.C. that lost it. I think that apart from the suave smoothness of all the news announcers it is good on the whole. You can see the "changing face of Britain" reflected very clearly in the programs – there are so many discussion groups and non-B.B.C. accent speakers although it is far yet from being in the hands of the proletariat and still has that slick British attitude that can gloss nearly anything over with good diction and rhetoric. Did you read any of Douglas Reed's books – *Insanity Fair, Disgrace Abounding, A Prophet at Home* and *All Our Tomorrows*? The last two give quite a good, though very critical picture of England since 1940. You get tired of his everlasting complaining but on the whole he hits the nail on the head pretty often.[98]

I have our guest book out – we had 27 houseguests since January ... We had 29 last year and 36 the year before and only 11 in 1939 ... 24 in 1938 – the last year that American names appear and now it is nearly

---

[97] Vaughan William's 70th birthday was actually 12th October and between then and 16th October there were daily tribute concerts on the BBC Home Service; the last was broadcast on Saturday 7th November, 2.30pm–3.45pm: "'A Sea Symphony': from a concert in celebration of the composer's 70th birthday."

[98] These best-sellers listed by Helen were written before Reed (1895–1976, a London journalist, novelist and playwright) in the aftermath of the war questioned the magnitude of the Holocaust when his writings were construed as anti-Semitic and boycotted by publishers, booksellers and librarians. George Orwell, in reviewing a 1943 book, registered the anti-Semitism amidst the persuasive and well-written reportage. *Insanity Fair: A European Cavalcade* (1938) warned of Hitler's megalomania and the dangers of National Socialism; Reed opposed what he considered the appeasement of Munich.

1943!!! ... The Brysons had an American to dinner the other night and Nina who is nearly 4 asked her mother when she went to bed "What will the king be like?" And Eileen said "What king?" and Nina said "That merry king who is coming to dinner!" ...

Love and kisses,
Helen

[9th Nov.
Belfast]

Now I'm at Röttgers [hairdressers] but opened the letter to say that the cable for Julie's birthday arrived today and I'm so glad you got the record – I know just how breathless you must have been and I know how good it was so I'm as thrilled as you are that it arrived safely. We just had it made in time because now in town at school Gay and Julie both have already lost a lot of their nice accents and Gay says "och" every other sentence. They will probably have awful Belfast accents in a month. ... Now it is after supper – scrambled eggs and bacon, toast, jam and tea and everyone is so keyed up about the news! The whole atmosphere has changed and everyone feels that the tide has turned that Hitler's speech showed "the low, dull whining note of fear" more than ever, and that everything is definitely on the up and up.[99]

Mrs. Dolan just rang me up to tell me to be sure to stay on at the club because that dazzling smiler Mrs. F.D.R. is coming tomorrow.[100]

[99] On 8th November, Hitler gave a speech to senior Nazis in Munich (the "Stalingrad Speech") and unusually it was mostly delivered in his normal voice, rising familiarly only towards the end. On 30th September he gave a speech in Berlin. In both speeches, his needless detail can be interpreted as conveying a defiance tinged with uncertainty rather than his customary undiluted defiance. Helen is quoting Churchill from his speech in Edinburgh in October 1942 in which he claimed to detect a loss of heart among the Nazi leaders; the recurring note in their declarations was "the dull low whining note of fear".

[100] Eleanor Roosevelt arrived in Northern Ireland on Tuesday 10th November and visited Government House Hillsborough, the Red Cross Club in Belfast (where Helen helped out) and the Red Cross Club in Londonderry. During her visit she met Lady Montgomery, mother of the future Viscount Montgomery of Alamein. See Francis Carroll, The American Presence in Ulster, pp. 150–151. See also "Whirlwind Ulster tour by Mrs. Roosevelt," Northern Whig, 11th November. I believe that Helen was at Röttgers the hairdressers on Monday, 9th November and had heard, or read of, Hitler's Stalingrad speech of 8th November. Helen had also heard Mrs Roosevelt's BBC broadcast from Liverpool on 8th November on women's war work in the United Kingdom.

I will be very interested to see her. I suppose you heard her broadcast last night – she speaks so well and is certainly indefatigable in getting around and see things – The radio is playing "Yankee Doodle came to London Town". I wish I could see the headlines of the *Denver Post* today telling about the Americans in N. Africa[101]. The headlines of the [*Northern*] *Whig* today were all nothing but success in all parts of the world – after 3 years of Dunkirks, bombings, Tobruks, Hongkongs, and Singapores it is too wonderful at last to have a pincer movement of our own opening vista after vista of conquest and defeat for the Axis. ...

Eggie has another exhibition on at the moment. I rang up Hilary tonight to see whether they will come over some night but she sent word that she was cooking her husband's supper and would ring me back ... Eggie still works at munitions and has such long hours – you can imagine if she was cooking his supper at 8. He paints on weekends.

The town is always so crowded now and you can imagine trams and trains at the rush hour! I came home from Lisburn tonight on the 6 o'clock train ... The train was packed with war-workers. Jack Andrews's sister started work in a munitions factory today. Gay's ex-teacher Barbara is taking a course to be a radio-mechanic for the W.R.N.S ... I think in Eng. you never see anyone young who is not in uniform – here it is more than half uniforms and the houses all around us are full of Service people – in this district I mean – we have a houseful across the street. ...

People are so busy somehow in the daytime or they have got out of the habit or they haven't the heart or the blackout stops them or something but even the perennial goer-outers stay home. ... you can never get into any movie anyplace unless you go at 6 even at 3 in the afternoon they hang out the sign "Standing all parts". There haven't been many good movies since we came to town I saw *Roxie Hart* one day with Maureen and that is all.[102] People spend their days chasing food, doing war work and I don't know what but everyone has the same story that they never see anybody.

[101] Although the war in North Africa was largely a British and Commonwealth affair, Operation Torch in French North Africa, 8th–11th November, gave American forces a limited opportunity to engage with the Nazis; they won the naval Battle of Casablanca against the Vichy French and German enemy.

[102] Adapted from a 1926 play, *Chicago* by M.D. Watkins, *Roxie Hart* was a 1942 American comedy starring Ginger Rogers and directed by William Wellman.

... Do people still hate Roosevelt? One thing about this new offensive – it will keep Hitler busy with his planes a long way from here – I hope! People thing that the last gasp will be bad – gas and all but I hope that it will all collapse all over the continent at once and that the war will at least be over by Armistice Day 1943. What do you think toots? ...

Love again,
Helen

17 Nov.
Sans Souci

Dear Mother and Ginna,

How are you? I am fine. Which just shows that I am not specially inspired this afternoon but may work up to it. Just got an air-graph letter from Alan Smiles who is in South Africa – or was, on the 10th of October. An air-graph is a letter reduced to an inch size by photography and sent air mail and then put up again to normal size.[103]

... I am sitting at the gas fire in the dining room because we were at the Grand Central for dinner with Charlie Mitchell. L. is making candy for his bees from his blitzed sugar in the kitchen. The Grand Central has certainly gone down the hill fast. It was bad enough when the English troops were the only ones here but I regret to say, that since the Americans have come it has gone *much* lower – it is the girls they bring who are so *awful* – Ballymacarrot [sic] trying to look like the "Maloun" Road[104] and all so loud and tough. So much silver has been swiped in the G.C. that they only put down the cutlery for each course as you get it and no napkins. The food is just fair and pretty scanty for

[103] The British airgraph was jointly invented in the 1930s by Eastman Kodak, Imperial Airways and Pan-American Airways in order to reduce the weight of air-mail. The letter was written on a form, photographed, posted as a microfilm negative, transported by air, and at destination printed on photographic paper and delivered as an airgraph letter. The airgraph's small size, 2"x3", was limiting and when weight of air-mail became irrelevant on larger planes, the airgraph went out of fashion.

[104] Ballymacarrett is an east Belfast neighbourhood strongly working-class in Helen's day, a far cry from the affluent respectability of the Malone Road where Helen was living and pronounced "Maloun" by its posh inhabitants.

6/- dinner. The only drinks you can get are whiskey (Irish), beer and stout and gin sometimes.

Jack Andrews is talking to L. now – he just had a nasty accident on a Home Guard maneuver – fell over a bridge in the black-out into a 6 feet of water river and cut his head badly – was in a military hospital for a week but is all right again. ... luckily he wasn't knocked out at the time or he would have drowned because no one saw him. ...

Last night Caroline [Workman] got completely hysterical over a Peter Arno cartoon in the *New Yorker* and we got nearly as bad laughing at her.[105] It was the one, if you saw it, of a woman in a police barracks with her clothes all torn off saying "I want to report a tornado". L. had laughed for a good 5 minutes over it when he saw it but Caroline wheezed and chortled and choked until Harry [McMullan] told Jack that he would have to get her some tubes.[106] Harry is so amusing since he came home – he has mellowed or settled down or has seen the folly of keeping right up with Winnie and Co. or something but he is much nicer and of course has endless amusing anecdotes about 1) himself 2) Winnie 3) his trips with Winnie etc. and by the time it comes out of Harry it is a good story no matter how it started. He controls the shipping between here and England is pretty important in his own fragile way. ... Roberta is indefatigable and was knitting a fair isle sweater with 4 balls of wool at once!

... Friday is m'canteen day again. I go twice to the American Club now – two 4 hour shifts a week that is and don't go at all to the naval one – you can overdo this canteen business and I'm not keen on night shifts although a naval bus picks up and puts down the whole shift now at the junction. Eggy has an exhibition on in town now with several pictures of Mahee.[107] We haven't seen them for about 6 months. ...

Julie's party was such a success – 7 kids in all on the day and a row of Jack-o-Lanterns grinning on the mantelpiece that made the party. Our cook, who is a sour-puss and whom I don't like now *at all* rose to

---

[105] Peter Arno (born Curtis Arnoux Peters) drew cartoons for the *New Yorker* between 1925 and 1968; he created 99 front covers for the magazine, and gave it its distinctive visual style of illustration.

[106] Helen may written "tubes" in mistake for "zubes" – lozenges. "Zubes, Zubes, Zubes are good for your tubes" was one of its slogans.

[107] An exhibition of Frank Egginton's water colours of Irish scenery opened in Rodman's Art Gallery, Belfast on 2nd November.

the occasion well and made some good sandwiches and 2 good cakes and Elaine sent me 2 cakes and with scones and pancakes we had oceans of food. ...

Mrs. Roosevelt was at the Red Cross Club for 3 minutes last Tuesday – Auntie met her but I only gaped from the Library door – although it gave a list of all the Americans in the paper and said we all had been presented. The whole thing was funnier than you would believe and the funniest was Mrs. R. loping out of the Club with Marcia running behind her to say goodbye – half of the press couldn't keep up at all and only arrived at the club as Mrs. R. tore out. It was literally "Hello, boys" flashlight, flashlight "Goodbye, boys" and the 2 soldiers we had waked up just before she came into the library sat down again rolled over and went to sleep again and I doubt if they even knew who she was or what had happened. Anyway we all had the tea that was prepared for her but was it a riot!

The news is just too good to believe – nearly and when the church-bells rang on Sunday it was nearly as good as an armistice and my eyes filled with tears (although we only heard them over the radio at Mahee.)[108] We feel nearly 100% safe from bombing too which is a good thing – all the optimists (that's me, babe) give the war a year and even the pessimists only give it 2 or 3 now instead of the 7 or 10 that you might have heard 6 months ago. ...

We had Hilary and Eggy last Friday... Eggy seemed happier and doesn't work Sat. afternoons now so he has more time for painting but they lead an awfully war-torn life. He looks as if he had spent 2 or 2½ years in a factory (which he has) and says that if he ever went to the west of Ireland he just wouldn't come back – that he couldn't bear to start in again. When Hitler is licked he is going to quit and go to the west of Ireland and leave the rest to finish off the Japs without him. ...

There the news is over – no major changes anyplace. Germans being beaten on all fronts except the sea. I had better wind this long ramble up. I hope by the time this reaches you that you are full of the Christmas spirit even if you are by yourself. It is certainly sad that we are so far apart but the news is so cheering that it makes the future much brighter.

---

[108] Church bells rang out across Britain on Sunday 15th November in celebration of the Allied victory in the Second Battle of El Alamein.

I finish this off at Mahee.

Again Merry, Merry Christmas and Happy New Year and
Love from all of us.
Lancelot, Helen, Gay and Julie

5th Dec.
Mahee

Dear Ginna and Lloyd,

Merry Christmas! Do you think this letter will make it to you in about
15 days? If so – again Merry Christmas! And if not, Happy New Year!
I suppose that your surroundings are just about as different from
Mahee as could be. I hasten to say that we aren't living here but that
L. and I are just down for last night and today. This is the third time
that I have come down in the 8 weeks that we have been living in town
and each time I must say I marvel at the fact that we lived here for two
whole winters. It always seems now *so* far, so remote, so at the end of
the road away from it all and between the darkness, the rain, the wind,
the mud and the coldness of the house in the mornings, as I say, I
marvel. It is pouring this minute – a cold December rain and the wind
is also blowing – there is an embryo fire burning behind me but I have
on an angora sweater and my de Pinora swagger coat and my hands
are about as warm as a wet leaf.

   Despite all this I always experience a terrific exhilaration of spirit
when we come here. When we arrived on Friday night having ploughed
from town in the blackout – shopping in the blacked-out, jostling,
windy, wet streets of Comber and come into the warmth and coziness
of the cottage with 6 fires burning (to air it out) it looks so comfortable
and so compact and so clean and tidy – that I can't wipe the smile off
my face. It is the peacefulness of atmosphere that makes for a great
peacefulness of spirit. I can't settle at all the same way in town – I can't
concentrate on the radio programs or do anything for more than an
hour consecutively without ringing somebody up or going out shopping
or wondering what to do next. ... Can you believe that it is nearly
Christmas? It looks less than ever like it here with less than ever in the
shops to buy and what window displays there are all have their little

cards telling how many coupons below which pretty effectively discourages buying. ...

I went to a terrible charity matinee yesterday – it was a slick English comedy a la Noel Coward, done by amateurs who were pathetic.[109] The audience of Society with a capital S made me wonder quite a lot. I came home on the tram with Mrs. McElderry, a neighbor and member of the D.R.C. who has been to Oxford and is a brain[110] – she was saying that the people in the play are the kind that cause revolutions to be started. You know the kind who are so selfish and wrapped up in their own emotions and who say "But *Dar*ling!" but I wondered if the audience were much better on the whole – the ones who go to see and be seen. ... In the midst of war even if it was for books for the forces it was a complete waste of time. The longer I live the more I agin society. Here is the news on and am I glad I'm not in Italy! – daylight bombing raids in Naples.[111] Lancelot is fooling around with his bee candy and has re-lit the fire for me just as my feet are slowing becoming numb to the knees. It is so nice for me to hear the American commentators quoting so much and here on Thanksgiving Day almost all the programs were about America and Thanksgiving. You wouldn't have believed the interest that was taken here in the recent elections – front page news – commentaries and explanations on the radio and everybody asking me about it.[112]

---

[109] Helen may be referring to Coward's 1924 comedy *Easy Virtue* playing at the Grand Opera House, Belfast performed by the Savoy Players. "Due to restrictions on travel during the Second World War, the theatre presented weekly performances by the Savoy Players, a repertory company of actors who were performing in Ireland at the time. They famously performed for General Dwight Eisenhower when he visited the Grand Opera House with Field Marshal Montgomery in 1945": "History & Heritage," Grand Opera House website.

[110] Mrs McElderry's name and full identity are elusive. She was married to Robert Knox McElderry (1869–1949, born Ballymoney, Co. Antrim), who was Professor of Greek (1902–1916), then Ancient Classics (1916–1926) at Queen's College Galway (later University College Galway) before becoming Professor of Greek at Queen's University Belfast. See Kate Newmann, *Dictionary of Ulster Biography*. The McElderrys were a long-established Ballymoney family.

[111] American forces began bombing mainland Italy on 4th December, targeting Naples.

[112] The U.S. congressional election was on 3rd November, mid-way through the Democratic F.D. Roosevelt's third term as President. Despite Roosevelt's leadership in the middle of a war, the Republicans made gains.

The way the news has changed the atmosphere is astounding. When I was in Dublin in Sept. the editorial of the *Irish Times* said that if Stalingrad held for another week it would be a miracle but of course it wouldn't! Everybody was dreading the German onslaught on these little islands this winter as soon as the Germans finished with Stalingrad and the Russians and now look – Germans running out of Russia, Germans trying to run out of Africa and Italians running in all directions. We were so nervous about taking the children back to town but now we have them there for the night with never a thought. Since the African Campaign successes the news headlines are always repeated at the end of the news as well as at the beginning – as someone so truly said before that no one wanted to hear the bad news twice.

Maurice Shillington[113] announces quite a lot now but he isn't one of the regular news announcers who ever since the fall of France have announced their names as they read the news so in case of invasion we would know if there was a phony announcer. ...

In a magazine I take called *Horizon* (British) there was a long excerpt from an American book called *Air-Conditioned Nightmare* by Henry Miller. I think you would be very interested in the book.[114] I just read *The Moon is Down* while I waited outside a place in Cullybackey [Co. Antrim] for L. It was so good. When Holland was attacked I was still a pacifist and thought that they were crazy to resist at all when they were conquered in 2 days (or 3) and lost 200,000 men and I remember saying to Elaine how crazy I thought it was just for a word called "honour". She didn't say anything but just looked at me as if I were crazy and after you read *The Moon is Down* you can see that I was crazy. I found it out before I read *The Moon is Down* but it would have opened my eyes so I think there was a need for it to be written, if you can follow all that.[115] ...

[113] See the letter of 4th December, 1939.

[114] *The Air-Conditioned Nightmare* is an account of Miller's road-trip across America in 1940–41 after life in Paris. Draft chapters of what became a book published in 1945 appeared in various magazines. Miller developed something of a disgust for the United States during his long trip. At the time of Helen's letter, he was living near Hollywood. Miller had a reputation in France but his novels had been banned in the United States and Great Britain.

[115] *The Moon is Down* by John Steinbeck is set in a small European town occupied against its will by an unidentified army. It was published in the United States in 1942 but also illegally and secretly in Nazi-occupied France by a Resistance publisher, as well as in other occupied European countries. The novel was interpreted as encouraging resistance to German occupation.

Now lunch is over. Spam, cauliflowers, tea, bread and butter and L.'s blackberry jelly, which is so good. We are listening to a Philharmonic concert from the Albert Hall with Sir Henry Wood conducting – Wagner, Sibellius [sic] and Dvorak. It is still raining but has got lighter around the horizon. ... Now there is an Irish concerto by Moran about the coast of Kerry.[116]

I had dinner with Elizabeth Morwood and her husband, John Boyle, and her father the other night.[117] L. was in bed with a cold. Liz is as communistic as ever in a completely one-tracked humorless way. She is quite amusing but too one-sided for words. Her husband is big and fat and gross and coarse but handsome with such pretty brown eyes and curly brown hair. Colonel Morwood is surprisingly active in his mind and seems more up and coming than he used to under Mary's care which was a little too obviously the self-sacrificial sweet-tempered daughter. She is in England now with or near her husband who is an officer now. Bill [her brother] is some dramatic director in New York – something to do with Radio City and had an article or sketch in *The New Yorker* about a month ago which was poor. It out-New Yorkered the *New Yorker* in being about nothing – the good articles in the *N.Y.*

---

[116] The Royal Philharmonic Society Concert was broadcast on Saturday between 2.30pm and 4.25pm on the Home Service. The *Radio Times* listed the third offering as the *Violin Concerto* (1942) by Ernest John Moeran (1894–1950). Although born in London, Moeran became fascinated by the landscape of western Ireland (which he first encountered when on garrison duty with the Bedfordshire Regiment in 1917), particularly Kerry where he went to live and where he died. That landscape influenced his music greatly. Long neglected, Moeran's music is undergoing something of a revival.

[117] For Elizabeth Morwood, see the letter of 18th October, 1939. Morwood, who was educated at Girton College, Cambridge, married John (J.W.) Boyle (1914–1998), the Dublin-born Irish labour historian, and together they became a force in the Northern Ireland Labour Party. At the time of this letter, Boyle would have been teaching at Royal Belfast Academical Institution ("Inst"). The couple emigrated to Canada in the 1960s when Boyle was appointed Professor of History at the University of Guelph. There they became involved in the NDP, the Canadian labour party. Elizabeth died in 1995. See Francis Devine, "A Gentle Flowering: Elizabeth and John W. Boyle, Historians and Labour Activists," in *Essays in Irish Labour History: A Festschrift for Elizabeth and John W. Boyle*, eds. Francis Devine, Fintan Lane and Niamh Puirséil (Dublin: Irish Academic Press, 2008). Boyle is the author of *The Irish Labour Movement in the Nineteenth Century* (Washington D.C.: Catholic University of America, 1989).

seem to about nothing but have a subtle point but Bill's had no point.[118] Isabel Noble has had another daughter I think – I can't imagine her with a son, can you? The Irish concerto has a violin soloist which sort of spoils it for me – as you may remember I was never keen on the fiddle. ...

Merry, Merry Christmas and a Happy New Year.
Love to you both and kisses,
Helen

18th Dec.
Sans Souci

Dear Mother,

... With only a week to go until Christmas I am safe in telling you all the details about the coming little Turtle without spoiling your Christmas surprise – I hope. ... Aunt has been noble about keeping the secret though she disapproved heartily of the whole silence. However, I finally saw that she was right and that you would rather know and enjoy in anticipation your new grandchild. With only two months to go there is nothing to worry you and make you lie awake nights. I am as fine as a fiddle, as big as a house and as pleased as punch. ...

Goodness knows what rigors we will have in the post-war world but they will probably be plenty without a baby added. I would lots rather have another baby than do war work and it is much more important war work too with the population declining like anything. ...

I am going to The Park Nursing Home again and so will be handy for L. and the children to come to visit me.

I booked a room in August and was just in time. There is the most enormous crowd of babies being born – Dr. Foster says that it is always

[118] "A Moving Dilemma" by William Morwood, about house-moving and listening to the World Series on radio, reproduced perfectly that curious hybrid quality of many *New Yorker* cartoons and occasional pieces: the actuality of inconsequence and illusion of significance. William Garvin Morwood was born in India in 1909. When he returned to his mother's native country in the 1950s, he became a TV script-writer and editor in New York (See *Billboard* magazine, 2nd January 1954 which recorded his marriage to Minerva Ellis from Texas on 27th November 1953 in Tenafly, New Jersey.) In Helen's time he seems to have worked at NBC Radio City Studios. See "William Garvin Morwood", www.geni.com/people.

the same in wartime and half the women you see seem to be having babies.

We have a girl's name ready – Mary Lee – how do you like it? The Mary isn't for anyone but just goes well with Lee and we will call her by both names ...

Gay and Julie are thrilled to the core. Gay wants a boy "for a change" and Julie wants a girl because "I don't like those kinds of babies – boys". ...

I get 50 extra coupons for the baby before it is born and as soon as it is born it will have its own 60 coupons a year as well as orange juice, cod liver oil and a lot of other things supplied by the Gov't. The Ministry of Food gives expectant mothers priority in everything – if I needed it I could get extra eggs, milk, vitamins etc. but that is only necessary in England where the milk ration is 2 pts. of milk per person per week!! The egg ration is the same here as Eng. one per person per *month*! ...

Mrs. Turtle said that she would give us a new pram but I inquired today and there is a waiting list of 70 at Anderson and McAuley's for Utility prams which are £12 each. A pre-war pram I hear in Dublin is £30 or £40 so I will borrow Maureen's for town and use our own at Mahee – both re-painted and reupholstered or whatever they need. Maureen's is elegant and she doesn't want to sell it in case she ever has another baby. She would love one but then there is always Ken!! who is an uncertain quantity. ...

19th Dec.

... Edith rang up when we were at the theatre last night to say that Bodo is due home today after 2 years all but 10 days and he has been about 1½ years in the Mediterranean and about 3 months in America.

22nd Dec.

This is Tuesday morning – sunny and bright. ...

Last night we had 10 to dinner for Bodo – Bodo and Edith, Jack and Caroline, Arabella and Gordon and Eddie and Eileen Bryson. Johnny at Mahee gave us a turkey so we had it and I used my best long monogrammed table cloth. ...

Bodo finally held forth practically alone he came home on that ship you and Ginna came on the day before Christmas and had just about the same kind of a crossing. He was 3 months in America altogether but always expected to be leaving any minute so he never got far afield. He was mostly in Richmond and Norfolk, and was several times in Washington and 4 nights in N.Y. from where he sailed. There were as many 1000's on his ship coming over as I was old in 1921 if you can figure that out. ...

I got Gay's report today; here is what it said:

"Although Gay has only been with us for part of the term she has made good progress. She reads with fluency, expression and understanding and in this branch of the work is far beyond the average. She puts much thought into her writing, but individual letters still require careful practice. ...

Julie didn't get a report but it would have been an object of mortification for her parents, I'm afraid.

We are going to see *Mrs. Miniver* at 5.15 today. *Charley's Aunt* is on at the Opera House.[119] ...

Happy New Year and much love and kisses,
Helen

30th Dec.
Sans Souci

Dear Ginna, Lloyd and Mother,

... We stayed up on Christmas Eve until midnight – I was sewing up until the last minute and L. filled the stockings ...

We finally got G. and J. to bed with their slippers beside them and got to bed ourselves, as I said after 12. ... In their stockings they each

---

[119] *Mrs Miniver* is a 1942 morale-boosting American war drama directed by William Wyler and starring Greer Garson and Walter Pidgeon. Set in suburban London at the time of the Dunkirk evacuation and German fighter planes endangering civilian life, the film was warmly received and was credited with stirring American enthusiasm and sympathy for the Allied cause before U.S. entry into the conflict. In graphic contrast, *Charley's Aunt* is a perennial of the theatre: a three-act farce written by Brandon Thomas that was staged in London in 1892 and on Broadway the following year.

had an orange, the big lollypop that Mother sent, one of the walking toys that Mother sent, odd sweets scattered through, shiny money about 1/6 in all, a Woolworth cowboy hankie, a Woolworth bakelite brooch, paper doll sets, paper books, dolls' mittens, and their sweet ration ¾ of a lb. each.

Gay came into our room clutching her stocking at 4.30!!! L. got her back but about 5 I got up and found her playing with all her things so I got her down to sleep again. ... they both got underway around 8. ... I got G. and J. down to sleep after we heard the King – Gay was fit to be tied with tiredness and she slept and then felt better. ...

Yesterday we went to the "Monster Circus" at the Hippodrome in a party of 30+.[120] Elaine took us and besides her and her 3 there were Eddie and Eileen and their 3, Bodo and Edie and Elizabeth, Rosemary Bryson and her 4 (1 is an adopted Austrian Jew) and Paddy and her 3 and then little friends – also the Prime Minister [J.M. Andrews] and Morie (Jack's sister) and her little boy. Gay was beside herself with excitement and when we got off the tram she just stood and jumped up and down. The circus was long and dull but having the children made it fun and Gay laughed so at the juggling clown that people for about 6 rows looked around to smile at her. She gets as red as a turkey-cock and just loves it all. ... Julie never cracked a smile but looked at it all carefully and was very good considering her age and the fact that it was 2½ hours long. Every time the curtains went shut she asked in a loud voice when they would open the black-out again to everyone's great amusement. ...

It was in the morning paper that Dick Pim has been awarded the Order of the Crown of Yugoslavia for personal services to H.M. King Peter.[121]

Monday night I was at the Dolans for supper – Nell was home for a few days at Christmas. Bodo and Edie were there and Roberta and Harry and it was fairly painful because Harry, as usual, carried on a

[120] "Third Monster Xmas Circus. Spectacular Sensational Circus Acts. Lions, Horses, Ponies, Pigeons." *Belfast News-Letter* 11th December 1942. The Royal Hippodrome theatre in central Belfast was built in 1905 and demolished in 1998.

[121] For Dick Pim, see the letter of 21st September, 1939. "Captain R.P. Pim, R.N.V.R., who before the outbreak of war was an assistant secretary at the Northern Ireland Ministry of Home Affairs, has been appointed to the Order of the Crown of Yugoslavia for personal services to King Peter": *Belfast News-Letter* 30th December, 1942. In July 1942 Churchill asked Pim to look after King Peter who was only 17 and came to England after the Axis Powers overran his country.

Captain Richard (Dick) Pim with Churchill in the Map Room of the War Office

Fred Gardiner

Fred Gardiner (standing far right) with other
Spitfire pilots of 610 Squadron at RAF Hawkinge,
July 1940

Lancelot and Jack Andrews (front row, 6 and 9 from left)
with the Home Guard, in front of Andrews Memorial Hall,
Comber, Co. Down

Thibeaudeau (Bodo) Taggart

A gas bag, an alternative
power source for motor
vehicles, resurrected from
the Great War

The 'orgy of destruction' during the Belfast Blitz that Helen watched from a distant hillside
BELFAST TELEGRAPH

The military parade of American and British personnel outside Belfast City Hall on 25th January 1943, commemorating the arrival of U.S. troops one year before.

Julie as a juvenile mannequin at the Domestic Front Exhibition at Belfast City Hall 21st March 1944 showcasing outfits costing little or nothing. Lady Stronge, the Duchess of Abercorn, and Sir Crawford McCullagh, Lord Mayor are behind her.

'That Eisenhower smile': the General at Long Kesh airfield, Co. Down, 24th August 1945.
Captain Sir Basil Brooke follows him.
THE DEPUTY KEEPER OF THE PUBLIC RECORD OFFICE OF NORTHERN IRELAND (CAB/3/G/7)

Eleanor Roosevelt with a U.S. naval officer in Londonderry, November 1942

The American Red Cross Club in
Chichester Street Belfast in the
premises of the Plaza Ballroom

Marcia Mackie, Director of the American Red Cross in Northern Ireland and other attentive listeners

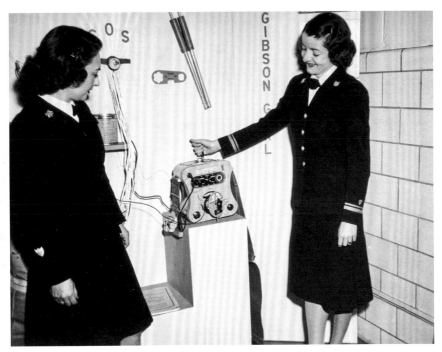

Ginna (right) in her WAVES (Women accepted for Volunteer Emergency Service) uniform

Guests at a dance in aid of the 3rd Searchlight Regiment Royal Artillery Comforts Fund,
Royal Belfast Golf Club, 29th March 1940. Helen with Captain Cyril Nicholson KC at far right.
Betty Shillington, the Marchioness of Dufferin and Major Michael Prynne are in the foreground, left.

Harry McMullan commentates on VE Day celebrations for the
BBC from the Reform Club overlooking Royal Avenue, Belfast.

Sisters Helen and Ginna
happily reunited in 1945

monologue quite a lot about Winston but people would rather have listened to Bodo. There is sort of professional jealousy between Bodo and Harry who are now both Lieutenant-Commanders. Harry has had much the more glamorous job but Bodo has been at sea all this time. ... At the last minute too Bodo broke a cup and saucer – a very beautiful dark blue valuable one at which point Mrs. Dolan very nearly swooned and the temperature dropped to about 30 degs and we all eased out. Harry and Roberta saw me home and H. apologized for being so "Winstonian" but said he couldn't bear the silences. ...

I was just listening to such a good mystery play and would you believe it just as they got to the solution the B.B.C. had technical trouble!!![122] And now there is a program located in Virginia.

Eight weeks from tonight we hope to have another little baby in the basket which is upstairs waiting to be trimmed. I have pink-flowered embroidered organdie and pink tiny polka-dotted silk – very transparent and lots of white organdie – and lots of blue ribbon. ...

You and Mother both left terrible gaps in your accounts of your trip in 1941 and I would love to see Daddy's and Mother's family tree. I could have sworn that there was a shanty Irish in me or anyway Irish – when I get to Dublin and points south I feel that my foot is on my native heath and my name is McGregor if you can follow the mixed metaphor. ...

I went to *This Above All* today with Maureen.[123] ... Maureen said she priced a hat trimmed with Beaver in R. and Cleaver's and the price was £26!!! They said that they sell them every day for £10 and £12. So many war workers are earning so much money and they buy anything at any price! Every day you hear fantastic stories and when I shopped around at Christmas and saw the junk and the price-tags attached I believed what David Anderson of Anderson and McAuleys told L. that although there were 8,000 sales recorded in A. and Mc. the day before Christmas there wasn't a thing worth buying in the shop.

[122] Helen was listening to a one-act mystery play, *Trial and Error*, written by L.A.G. Strong and broadcast at 9.20pm on the BBC Home Service. Strong, poet and playwright, was born in Devon but was proud of his Irish ancestry.

[123] *This Above All* (1942) is an American Second World War romance set in England. It is directed by Anatole Litvak and stars Tyrone Power and Joan Fontaine. It is a story of a love affair across the class barrier in a wartime military setting. The screenplay was written by R.C. Sherriff (author of the famous play *Journey's End*, 1928) from a 1941 novel by Eric Knight.

Things seem more controlled in England – second hand things anyway
but here the sky is the limit. The people I pity are brides and grooms
or people who have to buy necessities. ...

31st Dec.

Now the news is on – the Russians certainly have what it takes.[124]

Love and Happy New Year,
Helen

---

[124] On 29th December, General Erich von Manstein's troops had to retreat after his
failed attempt to relieve the German forces encircled at Stalingrad, leaving the
200,000-plus soldiers to an unhappy fate.

1943

Stalingrad is relieved after a four-month
  siege

Churchill, Roosevelt and De Gaulle confer
  in Casablanca

Helen's daughter Mary Lee is born

Lunch with the Countess of Antrim,
  sculptress

Friend's brother Fred, flying and fighting
  again

Helen undergoes operations to halt cancer

15th Jan.
Sans Souci

Dear Mother, Ginna and Lloyd,

... It sounds as if America is still living on its hump and we were like
that the first year of the war – we even had bananas! Now there is talk
of bread rationing with potatoes in the bread and wooden shoes! So
far it is just talk! ...

19th Jan.

Gay and I went to see Charlie Chaplin in *The Gold Rush* yesterday
which she liked and so did I but I only laughed once.[1] It is on at two
movies [cinemas] and one we couldn't even get into and at the other
one we had to stand inside for about ½ an hour – but then got a seat.
I may go to see Henry Fonda and Barbara Stanwick [sic] in *Good
Morning, Doctor* this afternoon – it is at the local movie [house] which
is just at the foot of Windsor Park on the Lisburn Road about 10
minutes away.[2] ...

There is a Living in Cities Exhibition on this week sponsored by
Queen's [University] and one of the leading English architects Clough
Williams-Ellis is giving a lecture tonight at Queen's. Tomorrow
afternoon Philip Bell is giving a lecture at the Museum – I am going to
both.[3] There is a prize plan competition out for the best plans for some
of the blitzed places – right around the Cathedral. There are blocks of
open spaces.

We were at Arabella's for dinner last night. Mrs. Turtle is going to
Dublin on Wednesday – great relief all round. She has got much worse
and we fought and fought about everything – no matter what subject

[1] A 1925 comedy with Charlie Chaplin in his Little Tramp character. On its 1942 re-
release, *The Gold Rush* won two Oscar nominations; Chaplin wrote, produced and
directed it.

[2] Directed by Wesley Ruggles and written by Dalton Trumbo, the 1941 romantic
drama played at the Majestic cinema among others in Belfast.

[3] On 20th January, the Northern Ireland Prime Minister opened the touring Living
in Cities exhibition at the Belfast Museum and Art Gallery (now the Ulster
Museum). Its theme was post-war town and county planning.

comes up she gets so unpleasant and has everyone arguing against her. The same thing happened when she came here to dinner on Friday. She brings out the worst in L. who automatically says something is black if she says it is white. ...

Bodo lent me *Excuse it Please* and I laughed so on Sunday morning in bed that it positively hurt me. It is by Cornelia Otis Skinner in case you don't know – quite an old book.[4] ...

Thursday I am going to lunch in town with Stella, tea with Mrs. McKee to meet Lady Rowan Hamilton and her son Hans whose eyes Arabella says are "loose in his head".[5] ...

On Saturday when we got home from Mahee Mother's Christmas card was here with the news that Ginna is about to be a WAVE. If it weren't for Christmas and Gay's birthday and Auntie's we couldn't have followed your movements but now we know you are home again but where Ginna is is still wrapped in mystery. I think the WAVES[6] sound much nicer than the army and I think Ginna will be happier doing something definite.

Now it is 1 o'clock and the news is on. It is all so good – Leningrad relieved,[7] Rommel still running and most things seem under control. It is sad to think that this will have to be a "bloody" year – a second front

---

[4] The extravagantly versatile Skinner (1899–1979) was born in Chicago. She acted in stage plays and radio drama, wrote and performed in historical monologues, published novels and autobiographies, and produced humorous pieces for the *New Yorker*. *Excuse It, Please!* (1936) is a collection of her essays.

[5] For Mrs McKee, see the letter of 4th October 1940; her son Lt Ian McKee was killed in Burma three months later while serving with the Royal Inniskilling Fusiliers. Lady Rowan-Hamilton (b. c1878) was the wife of Sir Sydney Orme Rowan-Hamilton (b. Newtownards in 1877), barrister (Chief Justice of Bermuda) and author. Their son Hans was 37 when Helen met him. Lady Rowan-Hamilton was the instigator in Ulster of the V for Victory Fund: "Its object is to provide bombers and similar equipment to bring us victory". A fund-raising Victory Bridge Party was held at Clandeboye, seat of the Dufferins, on 15th November, 1941. At this party the Marchioness of Dufferin's elder daughter, Lady Caroline Blackwood, later bohemian writer and wife to the artist Lucien Freud and poet Robert Lowell, sold Victory matches alongside her sister Lady Perdita while apparelled in "dainty frocks of white organdie". *Belfast News-Letter*, 17th November, 1942.

[6] The U.S. Naval Reserve (Women's Reserve), popularly referred to as WAVES: Women Accepted for Volunteer Emergency Service, and the volunteers as Waves.

[7] The siege of Leningrad by German troops lasted from 8th September, 1941 until Soviet troops managed to open a narrow land corridor to the city on 18th January, 1943.

seems necessary but the cost in men is an appalling prospect. Bodo was so interesting on Saturday telling about his adventures – including taking pictures of a ship being sunk right beside him and another being dive-bombed. He is hoping either for a research job (writing a book on gunnery or else teaching).[8] Here comes Gay and Sadie from school.

We are having vegetable soup, sausage pie and chocolate pudding for lunch – curried mutton for supper – Nancy Mitchell just rang up and we are going to a movie and then coming back here for tea – they just live up the road – 5 minutes away – their little boy was 3 on Gay's birthday and is as cute as a button. They have been trying for another for about 1½ years but so far with no success. I like Nancy so well and it is nice to have them so near.

Gay's hair is getting so long and I will have their pictures taken any minute now – speaking of mops Gay's takes the cake – nobody ever saw so much hair. At this point my hair looks like the Witch of Endor's – I am having a "perm" on Feb. 2nd – the last one won't do. ...

Love,
Helen

25th Jan.
Sans Souci

Dear Mother,

Goodness knows where Ginna is by now but you can forward this on to her. Lancelot is writing to you – this is the second letter he has started since the war – but he is a hopeless correspondent especially when he thinks I tell all the news.

3rd Feb.

Now it is Wednesday morning and I have just finished breakfast and have read all about Churchill and Roosevelt meeting in Africa which

---

[8] He succeeded in writing the book: see the letter of 4th March, 1940. For the ship that Taggart saw destroyed, see his letter of 1st March 1942 to Helen.

brings the time up to 11.30![9] I haven't been dressed for breakfast since about November. Unfortunately last week on Wed. I got 'flu which kept me in bed for 4 days and left me with an awful cough …

It is a rainy day but it isn't cold – the entire winter has been surprisingly warm which couldn't be luckier when we are all trying hard to save fuel. … We have been very comfortable indeed here even if the house isn't easy on the eye.

… Gay and I went to the unveiling of a stone to commemorate the anniversary of the landing of the A.E.F [American Expeditionary Force] in Belfast – a year ago yesterday. We only went by accident – we went to town to buy Mark a birthday present and got stuck in the crowds so we saw the parade and heard General Hartell's [sic] speech.[10] I hoisted Gay up onto the bonnet of an American army car so that she could see and talked to the driver who was such a nice boy from Virginia. Peeps and jeeps go flying up and down the Malone Road still but there are very few Americans in town. I miss talking to them now that I have stopped going to the club and am as mad as anything that no one I know has come over. Yesterday Gay and I had to get off the tram just where it had to stop owing to the ceremony and 2 Americans got off just in front of us and one said to the other "My congressman will hear about this!!!" They are all so full of fun and life compared to the more sober English troops.

Last Tuesday night L. and I went to a lecture at Queens by Mr. Clough Williams-Ellis who is an English architect and town planner who came over in connection with the Living In Cities Exhibition

[9] The Casablanca Conference to plan Allied strategy took place in French Morocco between 14th and 24th January, 1943. President Roosevelt and Prime Minister Churchill were joined by General Charles de Gaulle and Henri Giraud, leaders of the Free French forces. Premier Joseph Stalin did not attend, citing the battle for Stalingrad as his reason.

[10] The first regular U.S. soldiers actually set foot in Northern Ireland at Dufferin dock, Belfast on 26th January, 1942. Major-General Russel P. ("Scrappy") Hartle had been commander of the U.S.A. Northern Ireland Force from the start; see David Reynolds, *Rich Relations: The American Occupation of Britain, 1942–1945* (London: HarperCollins, 1995), pp. 90, 100. The commemorative stone was sculpted by Belfast stonemasons Purdy and Millard. The Governor of Northern Ireland (the Duke of Abercorn) and Major-General Hartle attended. There was a march-past of U.S. soldiers and marines while British and American troops lined the length of Donegall Square North. Helen had happened upon "The most brilliant military spectacle staged in the British Isles since the outbreak of World War II": https://www.ww2ni.com/belfast-city-hall.

which is now on at the Museum. He was wonderful – so funny and so witty and so spectacular to look at – he is nearly 60 I suppose and had on a green suit, polka-dot stock and a yellow under-waistcoat.[11] He said that the most beautiful city he has ever seen is Stockholm and so far he couldn't give Belfast second prize! (Roars of laughter.) However, he said that he hoped that after a while he would be able to come over here and say "What a city!" without being misunderstood. He has a town of his own in Wales – that he built that is called Port Merrion [sic] which is run as a hotel. Elaine has been and other people too say that it is a dream. He has written several quite good books for the layman about architecture and planning.

Philsy Bell is the leading architect on the committee for Belfast planning and is giving a lecture at 3.30 today. I saw him at the exhibition when I went the other day ... [I] rang up Elaine last night to ask her to lunch on Friday . Her life now is so dull ... John and Heather have both gone back to school[12] ... Comber is so deadly and Elaine's in-laws are stifling. Went to *Charlie's Aunt* with them one day and they wanted me to have tea and I got out of it – they are so sugary and vague and Oxford-groupy that I said I was too fidgety which was true. Elaine calls them the "rels" and is so funny about them. ... Heather is the prize of the family – John is so lazy but may be going through a phase – his only interests are birds, shooting, guns and more birds and he is extremely silent but so good looking the heavy black-browed masculine way. ... Heather is going to be a raving beauty – she has phenomenally big gray eyes and such a sweet face and is full of character and poetry and shyness and Gay adores her – she says that Heather is her best friend. ...

Last Friday just when I was in bed what if the thresher didn't loom up big and menacing at Mahee so L. and Mary (the cook) went down

Friday and stayed overnight – the thresher only arrived with us on Saturday so they had the usual 16 or so for lunch – and tea – Aggie came and helped and all went off with great gusto and I was thankful to have missed it. It is an ordeal at any time and now being so big I should have loathed it but would have had to supervise it from a chair anyway which I hate more than doing it myself. ... I think if L. could sell most of Mahee he would. His bees have superseded farming as a hobby and farming in war-time is anything but a hobby – there are so many restrictions and he has to plough so much and the labor problems are all so difficult. The petrol allowances that the few people who have cars have, have been cut to the bone and now the Glendinnings only get enough to go to the bus at Ballydrain instead of to Comber – the bus service is awful ... so what with one thing and another I shouldn't think we would be at Mahee for much more than a month this summer. ... After the baby comes I probably won't be able to go for weekend toots.

My English boy-friend Mr. Antrobus who was on the ship coming home from America the last time rang me up the other day.[13] He had just arrived from America in some convoy I think and was only in B'fast for a few hours. ... – he sounded so American and we got along as well as ever talking – by that time it was dark and he had to be on board again at 11 and had plans made with his ship-mates, I think, so I didn't see him. It was disappointing ... He said that he saw the real thing on the way over and he was as "scared as hell". He is still married to some half Spanish girl and she is parked on some farm outside San Francisco. He is about to join the English navy I think – I couldn't make out what he is now except an English volunteer. ...

I was so glad to get letters from home yesterday – 2 from Mother and one from Ginna – all from California. ... Ginna's letter made me laugh so hard – they always do – especially the part where after getting breakfast and getting Lloyd off she sat and wondered a while – such a Ramseyish thing to do. I just sit down and wonder about 10 times a

[13] Philip Antrobus (1907–1993) is identified in a letter of 7th August, 1937 written from SS *Larconia* on Helen's way back to Belfast from the U.S. In a 1940 letter Helen calls him her "beau of my last transatlantic trip home". He was from Worcester, England and emigrated to San Francisco to handle Lloyds of London insurance. He introduced kidnapping insurance coverage after the famous Lindbergh case in 1932. The girl he married was Cuban in the 1937 letter. His widow was called Mildred and may have been his second wife.

day – and it is so rare in Ulster where people "get on with things" and "carry on" until I'm tired!

I read *War and Peace* while I had 'flu. It is *so* good and is so popular here now that you can't buy, beg, borrow or steal it for love nor money. Jim Barr lent it to me. It is being broadcast in installments on the B.B.C. and after hearing last Sunday's L. liked it so well that he said if we have another daughter we will name her Natasha – not really![14] It is still Mary Lee for a girl and if I can persuade L. I will name it Tolliver if it is a boy – may change my mind yet. ...

Must to get dressed so I can quick go see Auntie, after lunch – we are having chicken! Hotcha!

Love,

Helen

12th Feb.

Sans Souci

Dear Mother and Ginna,

Am I excited or am I excited! First about Ginna being a WAVE and probably on her way to Northampton [Massachusetts] this minute and secondly because we just got a new cook – huzzas! She is "Temporary" for a month but it will tide us over the baby and give me a chance to find somebody else. Your cable came this morning and I rang up Auntie but she had already gone to town. I just read an account of the WAVES in the *Ladies Home Journal* showing pictures of Smith, Paradise Pond etc. and it nearly made me weep with nostalgia.[15] I haven't yet found out what an Ensign is but take it that it is a Lieutenant or sub– anyway. Anyway I am bursting to hear. After all the plans WAAC[16], radio expert, gray ladies[17], airplane mechanic and I forgot what else.

---

[14] In the translation of Louise and Aylmer Maude, Tolstoy's *War and Peace* was adapted for the BBC Home Service in eight hourly parts by Walter Peacock. Lancelot heard part 5 on Sunday 31st January at 3.30pm.

[15] Paradise Pond is a picturesque body of water with a spillway on the campus of Smith College, Northampton of which Helen was an alumna. It is said to have been so named in 1851 by the visiting Jenny Lind, "the Swedish Nightingale".

[16] Ginna must have contemplated joining the Women's Army Auxiliary Corps.

[17] Women of the the hospital corps of the American Red Cross volunteer services were called the Gray Ladies because of the colour of their uniform.

15th Feb.

Now it is Monday night ... L. is in bed with a cold, the new cook, named Edith, is in the kitchen and we have another cook engaged for March 1st named Bridget. I have been messing around all day tidying for the new cook, cleaning the stove, getting the lunch, fixing her room and all! Now I am thrown into a panic because I can't find Gay's ration book and can't remember whether or not I got it from the grocer on Saturday. I'm afraid that I did and now I only find Julie's in my bag – I got it to get a new vitamin page put in so that Julie can get free concentrated orange juice – I think that it is up to 5 that children can get it – also milk 7 pts a week for tuppence a pint. Gay may have a grown-up ration book – if it isn't green you can't use it but I am so absented minded that I forget if Winston, our grocer gave me one or two. We also have 30 clothing coupons among the four of us to be used before March 15th. ...

I am going to *Dangerous Moonlight* with Nancy Mitchell and her aunt tomorrow[18] and to a movie with Elaine on Friday – Probably Joan Crawford in *They All Kissed the Bride* – not that I like Joan Crawford! except in that take-off on the Oxford Group called Susan and God on the stage and I forget the name of the movie.[19] Saw *The Lady has Plans*[20] last week on my trip to town going the rounds of the registry offices and doing my last-minute shopping.

I feel fine. I have been feeling contractions for about 4 months and now and then yesterday and today I have sort of crampy sensations

---

[18] *Dangerous Moonlight* is a 1941 British film directed by Brian Desmond Hurst. A Polish composer, pianist and pilot volunteers for a Polish squadron of fighter pilots in England and is severely injured in the Battle of Britain. Helen was probably unaware that the director Hurst (1895–1986) was born Hans Hurst in a working-class street in Belfast several hundred yards from her Belmont Road home. After service in the Great War, Hurst moved to Hollywood. The most accomplished Irish film director of the twentieth century, Hurst released his most popular movie, *Scrooge (A Christmas Carol)* with Alistair Sim, in 1951.

[19] Crawford, who indeed divided picturegoers, donated her fee for the film to the American Red Cross. In the Hollywood comic drama, *Susan and God* (1940), written by Anita Loos, Crawford plays the title character who becomes a devotee of a new religious movement. The film adapted Rachel Crothers' successful Broadway play of 1937. Crothers had been provoked by Frank Buchman's "Oxford Group" which became "Moral Re-Armament" from 1938.

[20] A 1942 comic thriller with Ray Milland and Paulette Goddard and involving British government agents, Nazis, and criminals who steal the plans for a "radio-controlled torpedo". *The New York Times* called it a "thoroughly implausible tale".

that make me wonder hopefully but I am not counting on having it early though each night I hope that it will be tonight. If it is very late I will be *scatty* in the head. ... I haven't read anything but *The Denver Post*, *The New Yorker* and *War and Peace* since about November having got Fisher's *History of Europe* out of the Library having vowed not to take it back unread – maybe in the nursing home I can finish it – I think I am still at about Chapter III – Athens and Sparta.[21] ...

We have definitely decided on Penn for the boy's name – Lancelot Penn – and Mary Lee is still the choice for a girl but I sincerely trust you will have had a cable long, long before this reaches you. I did thank you for the baby book and fishy rattle, didn't I?

1943 looks as though it is going to be quite a year according to Winnie and Honey Rosenfelt. I suppose it has to come but I dread the news of the slaughter – Bodo was called back last Tuesday. I haven't heard where yet. ... The only Penn we ever knew was an acquaintance of L's named Penn Hughes ... Ginna may remember meeting him. I don't know how or why but one day I just thought of the name Penn – it is Quaker, it is American, it is plain and one syllabled which I prefer for a boy (with Turtle especially) and I hope you all like it. The other names we seriously considered were John and Patrick and Jonathan and I had a list of 12 or 15 "possibles" out of the book *What Shall We Name the Baby?*[22] ...

16th Feb.

Tuesday – Sitting up in our bedroom on our Victorian chaise lounge which has my heirloom coverlet on it. L. is still in bed solemnly reading a book by Cornelia Otis Skinner, it is a lovely sunny day the new cook is so nice and we are having ox-tail stew for lunch. ...

The Forces program is drooling out some bad jazz – in an article on fighting in the desert that Cecil Beaton wrote he said that all the allied

[21] H.A.L. Fisher (1965–1940), Oxford historian, Liberal M.P., was a cousin of Virginia Woolf's; his sister married Ralph Vaughan Williams. His 3-volume *A History of Europe* was published in 1935–36; Helen was probably reading the one-volume edition of 1942.

[22] Winthrop Ames edited *What Shall We Name the Baby?* in 1935. It listed 2500 boys' and girls' names with etymologies and meanings. Surprisingly, Ames (1870–1937) was an influential, and respected New York theatre manager, producer and director who was also a playwright and screen-writer.

soldiers listen to the German radio all the time because the music is so much better.[23] The B.B.C. home service is quite good but the Forces is terrible. Sans Souci Park looks so pretty this morning – this house sits out farther forward than any other house on this side and consequently gets all the sun. There is a Prunus tree coming into pink blossom in the next door garden. We have lots of crocuses in bloom but it is a poor garden for flowers. From where I sit in the bay window I face mountains and mountains are behind me. ... I like the handiness of the location – close to town, close to schools, close to Queen's where they have good lectures and concerts, close to the Museum – and near all our friends. ...

A singer that married a Gotto from Randalstown [Co. Antrim] is now on – he is one of the best tenors in England.[24] ...

Love again,
Helen

26th Feb.
Sans Souci

Dear Mother and Ginna,

I hope that this is "On the eve" of the event. I have just had my hair done when it didn't need it and had a "rich chestnut" rinse to encourage a red-haired child. ...

[23] *Horizon* magazine published two instalments of the Libyan diary of the famous photographer Cecil Beaton in January and February 1943. In the first, Beaton wrote: "The soldiers ... resent the poverty of the B.B.C. programmes in comparison to the richness of German light music." He went on: "We listen to the German radio for the quality of their music, which, relayed by the hour, is so much better than ours. We all listen to 'Lili Marleen'. ... This tune has become to Germany what 'Tipperary' was to us in the last war". (*Horizon*, 7: 21.)

[24] Henry Wendon (1900–1964) from Plymouth made his debut as an operatic tenor in *Aida* at the Old Vic Theatre in 1925. Thereafter he sang with Sadlers Wells Opera and Royal Opera House Covent Garden. He can be seen and heard in archived footage. There is a brief biography of him on the Opera Ireland website since he played Pinkerton in the 1947 mounting of *Madama Butterfly* in the Gaiety Theatre, Dublin: https://operainireland.wordpress.com/henry-wendon/ Wendon married Molly, the daughter of James Gotto and his wife in January 1931. In the 1930s he gave several recitals in Belfast and Londonderry. James P.C. Gotto (b. 1880) lived on the Malone Road in 1901, but by 1911, and having become a linen manufacturer, was living in Randalstown, County Antrim. See the Afterword for more on this remarkable family.

28th Feb.

Now it is Sunday, Ginna's anniversary and supposedly the baby's birthday and already frustration is creeping in on me. Julie was fine all day yesterday and is singing "God Save the King" loudly this morning and is going to get up this afternoon so that obstacle to my going has been removed. No obstacle remains now except the baby itself which is pretty formidable. L. is going to see a bee man who lives 40 minutes away by tram and I may go along on the top to see if that would help the situation. My natural aversion to tram rides for fun is still pretty dominant though especially with only a bee conversation at the end of it. ...

8th Mar.

Does history repeat itself or does it? Here I am just up after a whole week in bed with 'flu and no baby yet! It is only 8 days late and that isn't bad considering that it may be 3 weeks late yet! ... What a household our new maid walked into last Monday – me flat in bed with earache, 'flu, temp., sore throat, neuralgia – Gay and Julie both in bed and only Sadie to cope with the new maid. ...

Every day I look for a letter from Ensign Virginia giving us the low-down – we don't even know where she is. 6 *Denver Posts* came and I read them from cover to cover one day in bed and felt like a native again. I gave up *The History of Europe* I'm sorry to say and read 3 detective stories from the library and some more that Nancy lent me. I also read *Anna Karenina* and am about to get through *Don Quixote* and *Crime and Punishment* not to mention all of Dickens, Chekhov, and goodness knows what if the baby doesn't come soon! – and even if it does there is that long spell in the nursing home.

10th Mar.

This is Wednesday night – L. is up and went to work but shouldn't have and we are sitting in the nursery by the gas fire to save coal and are going to bed early – so we say but I'll bet dollars to doughnuts that it will be "midnight again". My day has been all at sixes and sevens – slept until 11 – rushed into town to the hairdresser only to find that they had made the appointment for tomorrow – so chagrinned [sic] that I went to another hairdresser who gave me a pep-talk on Russia but did my hair pretty well. Didn't get home until 2 – late for lunch – missed seeing G. and J. except for a second – they go to bed at 2 for an hour. Then I read *The Denver Post* – 6 of which arrived today ...

I rang the Park Nursing Home today to see if I needed to bring anything but my ration book and they are wild because there is hardly anyone in and 5 or 6 are due in and will probably all arrive together. I wish I could have it tonight – I am all ready now and am just killing time. ...

Too bad about the Ionides – Lancelot was just saying how much he disliked Margaret when she visited us.[25] I got a postcard from Janet Boyd from Montreal yesterday saying that she had just heard about the baby and was bringing me a doz. nappies – she is supposedly on the way now but no one seems very clear about it – Betty Carr is coming too. I forget if I ever told you that Betsy Barbour got married last spring and left her husband after 2 week-ends and came home – great speculation and gossip went on but the facts never came to light – she is back in London now in some war job. Isabel Noble said that the trouble with the Barbours was that they had no proper bringing up because their Mother died when Betsy was born.[26]

Bodo has some shore job in England – at least for the time being. Yesterday's paper said that in London anyone who thinks the war will be over later than November of this year is regarded as a gloomy pessimist.

Knox Cunningham was defeated by the Labour candidate – such a pity and such a blow to the Unionist party (Mr. Andrews's party) which is getting flayed with criticism on all sides now.[27] Edith is one of the

---

[25] What the problem was for the Ionides is unknown. For Margaret Ionides, see the letter of 22nd November, 1939; she visited the Turtles in 1933 or 1934.

[26] Elizabeth Barbour (1910–1973), daughter of J. Milne Barbour M.P, director of the world's largest linen-thread company, married Commander Hugh Chapman Maclean RN in Hanover Square, London on 3rd January 1942. See *Belfast News-Letter* 5th January 1942. Elizabeth Barbour's mother died in 1910, the year of Elizabeth's birth.

[27] For Knox Cunningham, see also the letter of 27th September, 1939. Sir Samuel Knox Cunningham QC (1909–1976) was a barrister, businessman, and politician. In 1943 he fought and lost the Belfast West by-election as a Unionist Party candidate. He became MP for South Antrim in 1955 and in 1959 was appointed Parliamentary Private Secretary to Prime Minster Harold Macmillan. *Cont'd:*

leading lights in the Junior Unionist party who are pretty hard on the old Unionists.[28] There is terrific dissatisfaction here with the Gov't but as Elaine always says Mr. A. would love to resign but there isn't anybody to take his place. ...

The Free State still seems to enjoy its neutrality – petrol, oil and fuel get scarcer by the minute with no stocks coming in at all. ... However Dublin is still gay and bright and warm and full of good food – for tourists anyway with lots of money. ...

The Denver Posts are a revelation to us with their advertisements for everything. Most of the shops now close at the lunch hours, all close at 5 and jewelers are hardly ever open – there is no new jewelry, they won't repair jewelry, and they don't want to sell what they've got – not that we want to buy it because there is a 66% tax on it!!

Love,
Helen

14th Mar.
Park Nursing Home
Wellington Park, Belfast

Dear Mother and Ginna,

"Here I am" sitting up in ½ the room I had when Lee was born – it has been made into 2 rooms and I am the corner one. L. is here reading *The New Statesman* and Mary Lee is asleep in the nursery upstairs with 4 other girls and 1 boy. There is a baby being born in the Labor Ward right this minute – the poor mama is groaning away.

Your cards came yesterday and I am glad your long wait is over – I know how you must have wondered what in the world was going on over here when she was so late. Luckily all around that she was – I was 4 days over 'flu and it was definite that G. and J. have whooping cough.

---

[27] *Cont'd*: There was dissatisfaction with John Miller Andrews' leadership on the Unionist back benches and the month after Helen's letter he was forced from office and replaced with Sir Basil Brooke.

[28] For Edith Taggart see the letter of 4th May 1939 and Bodo's letter to Helen of 1st March 1942. She was the niece of John Miller Andrews. The Junior Unionist Society, promoting the re-organisation of the Unionist Party, became the Ulster Young Unionist Council in 1946.

They both have it quite badly and Gay has 'flu too but they are over the worst.

Mary Lee started in earnest at 2 a.m. Thursday [11th March] with a bad pain every hour and middling pains every ½ hour. By breakfast time it was no worse but I rang up Dr. Foster who said to go in when they were coming every 15 minutes. ... by supper time they were nearly gone – the pains – except that every time I got up I had one. However, Dr. Foster rang up at 8 and said I'd better go and sleep at the home so we ordered a taxi for 10 and I took a bath and finished my packing. I felt that it would definitely come that night like Julie did and I felt if only I had felt good enough to walk all day the way I did before Julie was born it would be very speedy. ... Sure enough I just got into bed at 11 when I started having bad pains every 10 minutes. There were 3 of us all in labor at once – the first baby born was at 2.15 ... The other lady came off first around 4 ... Hers was a girl and the last thing I remember was Dr. Foster saying to me that they had run out of girls and the next I knew it was all over and I was able to find out that she weighed 7 pounds, had a cowl over her head (very lucky) and was the image of Gay. ... I shed a few tears of disappointment because it wasn't a boy but it was as much weakness and 'flu as real sorrow because I don't care terribly but I did like the name Penn and since we decided on that I wanted it to be a boy – Lancelot doesn't care a bit ... but just the same he would be pleased to have a son. Everybody else is crushed with sympathy for us because 3 girls are regarded nearly as a calamity. ...

15th Mar.

This is Monday morning and I feel as fresh as a daisy sitting up in my glamorous nightie and bed jacket. ... Mary Lee is getting prettier every day. As Nurse said she was no oil painting the first day... It was the easiest labor I've ever had ...

The *worst* is, of course, that Gay and Julie have such bad whooping cough. Julie has now reached the paroxysm stage and has terrible bouts[29] ... it is *maddening* that G. and J. can't come to see me and the

---

[29] Pertussis or whooping cough is a highly infectious bacterial disease that killed many children in the 1940s. The American pediatrician Leila Denmark (who lived to be 113) developed the first vaccine to combat it less than a decade before Helen's daughters became infected.

baby and they will go to Mahee for a week when they are able both to get the infection out of the baby's way and to give them bracing air to put them on their feet again. I'm not worried about them but it is bad luck having them both ill just now. ...

This room is full of daffodils – 4 enormous bunches and 1 doz. tulips and about 1 doz. Iris Stylosa from Mahee. ... It will be in the paper tomorrow about the baby. ... Arabella is giving a paper at the D.R.C. today on Lewis Carroll.

St. Patrick's Day

Today I really feel fine – everything is under control ... 6 more *Posts* came yesterday and the 1st one that I opened there was Ginna big as life and *twice* as handsome. Nurse O'Hara thinks you are too beautiful for words and rushed the paper out to show the Night Nurse.

This morning's paper had a rush of babies' births in it ...

I am only allowed little drinks and I spend my time thinking of cokes, grape-limeade and ginger ale with ice tinkling in it ...

The birds are all singing like mad. It is such a nice time to have a baby ... I said all along that I bet this baby would arrive on St. Patrick's Day and by gum! I was closer than anybody to it. Mary Lee isn't pretty in fact she is ugly ... She is getting more like L. and Julie and is very, very dark – the blackest baby in the home – against Nurse's uniform she looks like a negress. I had forgotten what fun it was to have a baby and what cute little noises they make – she looks like Churchill too! But as he says all babies do. ... I am enjoying myself hugely but miss you both terribly. I had an awful wave of homesickness yesterday when I think how indefinitely separated we are...

x x x x x! Helen

24th Mar.
Park Nursing Home

Dear Mother and Ginna,

Mary Lee and I are fine. She gained 4 ounces the first week and seems to be flourishing.

25th Mar.

... She slept all night last night and that made both of us sleep through the only air raid warning of the whole winter. The siren apparently went about 1.30 and the all clear was at 2. This morning no one talked of anything else – a few raiders dropped bombs in Scotland but nothing happened here. Everyone brought out all their old air-raid experiences and stories and the place hummed. One new mother got up to help move the babies who were already downstairs anyway ... Lancelot said the noise in Sans Souci Park was fearful with the fire brigade warming up ready for action. There is a National Fire Service Station [in Sans Souci Park] about as far from us as the Chase's house is from your house – it is in the Glendinning's old house – the prettiest in the Park - now ruined as you can imagine with fire engines, tin huts, cut trees, ruined floors etc. ...

The first visitor I had was Maureen who brought me an Afghan rug and daffodils and cherry blossoms. ... Stella brought me daffodils and a white matinee coat, Caroline Workman sent a dozen scarlet double tulips (a dream they were) ... Philip and Kathleen Scanlan sent the prettiest bunch of flowers I got and about the prettiest bunch I ever saw – a dozen pale pink tulips (like wax), a dozen double narcissi, and a dozen white daffodils with big yellow trumpet centers. ... Eliz. Morwood sent me tulips and daffodils, Silva Harrison sent daffodils, Molly McCleery sent polyanthus, Nancy Mitchell sent daffodils, L. brought me daffodils and narcissi and iris from Mahee, Janet Boyd sent big yellow narcissi with orange centers, Edith sent daffodils – I told you that Auntie sent tulips and Roberta brought daffodils. ...

The books all came and I read *The Apple in the Attic* before I gave it to Auntie. It was so good but I could have killed the husband.[30] ... We are saving the books for G. and J. for the Easter Bunny to bring. I was saving the paints and books and pencils, but they were a godsend to our poor sick children. The children's books are adorable – especially the *Gay A B C*. I have a *Gay Nursery Rhymes* illustrated by the same woman and love it. We are very lucky in having about 100 or more nice children's books – you know me and book buying and now I am glad I was so extravagant because you can't get anything and a 4 page cheap paint book is 2/6!!

[30] *The Apple in the Attic* (1942), by the Chicago novelist and playwright Mildred Jordan (1901–1982), is set among the Pennsylvania Dutch and is a story of a tense and strange marriage.

... Everybody loves her name which is very unusual here though I know it would sound quite usual with you. I don't care a bit now that it isn't a boy – if I ever really did – partly from a vestige of superstition connected with Lee and partly because little brothers aren't so desirable as big brothers – but I do know that when all my friends' sons are young men I will be green with envy. Everyone who comes or nearly everyone asks me if I am disappointed and I always say yes that I was. ...

My radio battery went pfut today – I haven't played it much anyway and my good resolutions about reading *Don Quixote* and Shakespeare went with the wind and I read trash consistently – the only goodish book was *Fame is the Spur* by Howard Spring who wrote *My Son, My Son*[31] – Oh yes and *Journey for Margaret* which was very good[32] and which I lent to Mrs. Webb thinking she was going home on Monday and darned if she didn't give it to her husband and he took it to Randalstown where it still is – a library book! ... Here comes Mary Lee for her 6 o'clock meal.

26th Mar.
Home – 5.30p.m.

I have just waked up from m'afternoon nap and had tea and re-read Ginna's letter from Smith [College] mailed March 9th – 11 days coming – not bad, not bad – as always I am *charmed* to get mail from home. Your job sounds fun and especially being in Northampton – when you say you got your permanent orders does it mean you will be in

[31] The Welsh novelist Howard Spring (1889–1965) published his most famous work, *Fame is the Spur* in 1940. It is the story of a working-class boy who becomes a socialist activist and then a career politician who is coopted by the class forces he fights. The novel has as background the rise of the British Labour party. It was made into a British film in 1947 and a BBC TV series in 1982.

[32] William Lindsay White's *Journey for Margaret* (1941) is an American war correspondent's experiences during the London Blitz and his desire, prompted by his wife, to adopt an English orphan. He adopts a three-year-old girl called Margaret in the book and returns to the U.S. In real life the orphan girl was Barbara and she grew up in New York, eventually inheriting the family editorship of the *Emporia* (Kansas) *Gazette*. White's father was William Allen White, "The Sage of Emporia", newspaper editor and leader of the Progressive movement in Kansas. See William Robbins, "Emporia Journal; Where Eloquence Seems a Birthright", *New York Times*, 20th October, 1988. White's story was made into a Hollywood drama (1942) starring Robert Young and Laraine Day.

Northampton for the duration or what? I got a shock when you said 11 years away from N-Hampton – but of course it is 13 since I have been there – one forgets how old one is getting despite my gray hairs which should remind me. Lancelot let his hair grow long because he didn't have time to get it cut and it was positively silvery and so pretty. Imagine you being the only coast guard officer in the station – what a responsibility to have thrust on you so suddenly but I'm sure your public will never know how your knees shake – if they do!
Ginna's birthday!

28th Mar.

A quiet Sunday afternoon – again I'm just awake from a nap, had tea and finished reading the newest *New Yorker* Feb 6 and such a good number. L. is out seeing a bee-man, Nurse is writing letters. Bridget is out and Mary Lee, bless her baby heart, is fast asleep. ...

29th Mar.

... They will be taking our gate and fence soon for scrap iron for bombs or guns or something. They were removing them in Wellington Park last week with a big blow-torch that showered golden sparks. I have just bought *A Time for Greatness* by Herbert Agar and *Education for a World Adrift* by Sir James Richard Livingstone who used to be Vice-chancellor of the University here and is now head of one of the Oxford colleges – he is mad on the Greeks and their way of life.[33]

We will take some photos soon of Mary Lee, this house and G. and J. in their best coats and Scotch caps. ... Lancelot is very proud and amused by his 3rd daughter. The biggest tragedy is that you can't see her and that we can't see you but I have sort of a sneaking suspicion

---

[33] Herbert Agar (1897–1980) was a Pulitzer Prize-winning journalist. *A Time for Greatness* (1942) was "a stirring call to the American people to seize the present and fleeting opportunity to lead the way to a better world where the 'explosive idea' of equality will become a reality": *Foreign Affairs* review, January 1943. The author of *Education for a World Adrift* was actually Sir Richard Winn Livingstone (1880–1960). Educated at Oxford, he was Vice-Chancellor of Queen's University, Belfast, 1924–1933, after which he returned to Oxford as President of Corpus Christi College. His short 1943 book was a defence of the liberal arts and classical culture in an age of specialization.

that Hitler will be beat this year and maybe the Japs next year and then we will have one hell of a reunion!! ...

With much love and many kisses,
Helen

8th April
Sans Souci

Dear Mother and Ginna,

It is mid-morning, I have just had my "elevenses" – tea, bread and butter and cake and am feeling wide awake though I am lazy enough to stay in bed. Mary Lee will be 4 weeks old tomorrow and I feel fine. ... Mary Lee is fine too. Tomorrow is her weighing day and from her goodness she should be 8 oz. heavier. ...

I went to *Desert Victory* with L. on Monday, *Suspicion* yesterday, and am going to *My Sister Eileen* today with Roberta and maybe to *Thunder Rock* tomorrow – making hay while the nurse is here.[34]...

Lancelot is back with Jim Barr again and I think it is a great relief to him. His other job was annoying and worrying although interesting in a way, but I think it took a lot out of him. He has an awful cough that has become chronic because of smoking. I haven't smoked for a year come Saturday thereby saving the large sum of £18 if I only smoked 10 a day and I often smoked more. Imagine that $100 and L. spends $200 a year on smoking. The new budget is coming out next week and people are afraid that cigarettes will go up to 2/6 or 63c a pack and you still get 2 packs for a quarter, don't you? ...

Yesterday I spent ¾ of an hour in Magee's choosing a picture with Mother's birthday money.[35] I have chosen two and Mr. Magee let me

---

[34] The Ministry of Information produced *Desert Victory*, a 1943 British account of the campaign led by Field Marshal Montgomery against General Rommel and his Afrika Korps. Despite winning a special Oscar the same year, it ruffled American feathers by underplaying the American contribution to the campaign. *Suspicion* (1941) was directed by Alfred Hitchcock and stars Cary Grant and Joan Fontaine who won an Oscar as Best Actress in 1941. *My Sister Eileen* (1942) is an American "screwball" comedy. In *Thunder Rock*, Michael Redgrave plays a campaigning journalist unable in the late 1930s to awaken his fellow Britons to the growing threat of Nazism.

[35] John Magee's art gallery in central Belfast dealt in the work of significant Irish artists, including William Conor and Paul Henry.

bring them both home to decide and now that I figure out my smoking savings darned if I don't think I'll keep them both! They are both originals – one a water color of Achill Island – pale, restful and as simple as A.B.C – modern and stylized and I have had my eye on it for months – a few cottages a boy and cliffs in the distance – the other is an oil painting of a bright bunch of flowers in a bowl. Pictures are the only things that there is no tax on – there is a high tax on frames but their pictures value is the same as pre-war whereas jewelry is 3 times the price it was. I don't know whether it is the Tryon gallery at Smith or my craze for color that makes me like pictures so well but I do.[36] We are going to buy one of Tommy Carr's for L.'s present to me for having Mary Lee – and for my birthday – instead of the pin – Tommy's are from £10 to £20, so Mr. Magee says. A Paul Henry original is £100 [37].

11th Apr.

Now it's Sunday and a sunny day. ... We are listening to the Brains Trust and the guest is Mayor Le Guardia and he is wonderful –so funny and so witty and he makes the English sound such stuffed shirts. At 7.30 I am going to listen to Transatlantic Broadcast – people to people. Today it is Times Square and the compère is Clifton Fadiman.[38] The Queen is going to broadcast at 9 – you will probably hear her[39] – Mother at 1 and Ginna at 3 – we now have 2 hours of daylight saving time and do I hate it. It isn't dark until nearly 10 and it is light at 7.

[36] Tryon Art Gallery at Smith College was established by Dwight William Tryon (1849-1925), an American landscape artist. He taught at Smith College between 1886 and 1923, there encouraging women artists, and founding the college art museum.

[37] Paul Henry (1877–1958), born in Belfast, is one of the most distinguished Irish artists, notably capturing west of Ireland landscapes in his paintings.

[38] This edition of the "Brains Trust" was broadcast at 4.15pm on the Forces Programme (which aired between February 1940 and February 1944). Fiorello H. La Guardia, Mayor of New York, was linked by telephone to the panel in the U.K., including Edith Summerskill MP and Quinton Hogg (later Lord Hailsham), M.P. "Transatlantic Call – People to People" was broadcast on the Home Service; "Times Square" was written and narrated by Clifton Fadiman, New York author and radio and television presenter.

[39] Queen Elizabeth said she wished briefly (for a little over two minutes) to play tribute to British women working to help win the war. The broadcast is available as an archive on britishpathe.com.

Did you see *Desert Victory*? It was so good and even better was the Russian documentary *One Day of War*.[40] I see in one of the 7 or 8 *Denver Post*s that came yesterday that it was on in Denver. ...

13th Apr.

It is just before lunch and such a lovely sunny day – Spring is about 2 months early this year and all the apple blossoms are out and the cherry trees and the laburnum is coming into bloom. ... Gay is so much happier than she was. Whether it is so long away from me or what I don't know but she is a different child. They are both *crazy* about the baby. Julie just giggles and giggles with pleasure and for 3 days after they got home they never left the baby's side when she was awake. They fight and argue about which one loves her most. Gay says that her little finger is no bigger than a dot and her prize remark, Gay's was, upon seeing me feed her "Isn't God wonderful to make you milk just like a goat". ...

14th Apr.

This is Wednesday and I am going to a movie with Maureen this afternoon – Bette Davis in *The Bride Came C.O.D.*[41] I always go to see Bette because she reminds me of Ginna and Henry Fonda reminds me of Lloyd. ...

Gay is reading *Little Women* for about the 3rd time. Sadie brought her *The Swiss Twins* and she read it in a few hours the same day. Just like her ma but I don't think I started so early – did I? I am thinking of getting them *The Book of Knowledge* – called here the *Children's Encyclopedia* and it is 12½ guineas I hear but worth it every time. Now the news is on about the newest offensive of the 8th Army – we hope the last battle in Tunisia. The morning paper said that people in London were so optimistic that they are talking about peace by

---

[40] *Day of War* (1942) was directed by Mikhail Slutsky who stationed 200 cameramen across the Soviet Union, capturing the war on 13th June, 1942. A shortened 1943 version (using footage from 160 cameramen) was called *One Day in the War* and was shown at a trade show in the Ritz cinema, Belfast on 2nd March 1943.

[41] This was a poorly received "screwball" comedy starring Bette Davis and James Cagney.

Christmas and the paper is full of hints and rumors about invading Europe this Spring. The announcer just said how grim and terrible the prospect is in N. Africa with the sole object to kill Germans and smash the German machine and to be prepared for terrible losses. If you have seen *Desert Victory* you will see what it is like. ...

The minute the war is over we will be on the first boat – me bursting with pride to show you my three beautiful daughters.

Love,
Helen

5th May
Sans Souci

Dear Mother and Ginna,

... Both Gay and Julie look fine – good color and sturdy looking. Julie still whoops when she coughs and they both get coughing fits when they run around the garden but neither of them spit any more. ...

... It is three months now that they have had it and I think nearly everybody in the school has had it too. ... I am an authority on w. cough now.

13th May

... We had snow on Monday and 2 or 3 days of the coldest weather of the winter but today is warm and spring-like. ... L. was at Mahee on Saturday but the wind and rain were so appalling the he couldn't bring any vegetables. Jack Andrews went with him. No one knows what to think about the change in Prime Ministers. ... The new cabinet has 2 ministers in it – both Presbyterian – I have met one who is pretty dumb. Sir Basil Brooke should be good I think[42]. Mr. Andrews was given an honor Companion of Honor and got a very fine letter of praise from

---

[42] Basil Brooke (1888–1973) was born at Colebrooke, his family seat in County Fermanagh and became 5th Baronet when his father died in 1907. His uncle was Field Marshal Alanbrooke. He remained Prime Minister of Northern Ireland until 1963 and during his tenure was ennobled as Viscount Brookeborough. His son Basil Julian, a Grenadier Guardsman, was killed in action in Spring, 1943. Brooke's Minister of Education was Very Rev. Professor Robert Corkey (1881–1966) and his Minister of Agriculture was Rev. Robert Moore (1886–1960).

Mr. Churchill but there is no escaping the fact that he was booted out. ... We went to the Grand Central to dinner and to see *In Which We Serve* to celebrate our wedding anniversary.[43] I can't believe that I have been married 10 years and have had 4 children. I feel as if I've been married about 3 and had no children – but about 6 o'clock tonight with my 3 on my hands I will feel like the old woman who lived in a shoe. Speaking of shoes – the situation is becoming fairly acute here now. I must stock up because they are going-going and children's shoes are also becoming extinct. The shoe shops closed for a week at Easter and close every week for 2 whole days and often they are shut other times because they have sold their quota.

Isn't Churchill wonderful? ... People are dreading the second front though they know it has to be done. Well girls, that's all for now. I will do better from now on because the baby is all right now I think and I have stopped worrying – Love to both of you and kisses

Helen

16th May
Sans Souci

I am sitting out in a deck chair in the sunshine trying to gather strength from my one day 'flu which I had yesterday and which has left me completely without energy. ...

4th Jun.

Fancy its being so much later – the 4th of June in fact and every day of June has been pouring wet – it is pouring this minute and I am in a heavy tweed suit and a wooly vest and am not a bit hot. ... Bridget is in the kitchen and I am in the drawing room listening to "Music While You Work" so I get up and do a little dance every once in a while. ...

Everything that you sent has arrived and we are so glad and grateful and thank you for *everything*... The candy was wonderful and came

---

[43] Noel Coward co-directed (with David Lean), wrote the screenplay and composed the score for, and co-starred in (alongside John Mills and Bernard Miles), this 1942 seagoing patriotic war film. The film succeeded at the box office and depicted what Bosley Crowther of the *New York Times* called "national fortitude".

just when our ration has run out. We used to have a store of candy always from trips to Dublin but now we are relying solely on our ration ¾ of a pound per person per month and it isn't much. ... I have started to eat candy for the first time in years – regularly that is and Gay and Julie have 2 pieces a day. ... A[rabella]. brought G. and J. each a small banana and I hadn't time to squash them up with sugar which would have been so much nicer but they like them anyway and had to be shown how to eat them and to be restrained from eating the skins. A ship-load or part of one came into Dublin and they were the first bananas we have had since the winter of 1939.

... I was going to *The Birth of a Baby Today* but stayed home to look after [Mary Lee] instead. This is the only city, so far, in Great Britain that men weren't allowed in to see it – wouldn't [it be] Belfast?![44] ...

Had lunch with Janet Boyd on Wednesday. She is so unrestful and the kind that cannot let any details slip by. ... She is so glad to be back – the flying boat that Leslie Howard was lost on was the same one that Janet flew on from Lisbon.[45] She looks old now but is just as attractive as ever in a boyish, Buster Brown way. – wears her hair short now at the back and curled on top.[46] I saw her two younger boys who are so attractive. Trevor boards at Rockport. Austen is a Captain in the army

[44] The *Northern Whig* newspaper reported on 27th March 1943 that the 1940 Belfast Corporation ban imposed on this 1938 American educational film about childbirth, using actors, was being lifted but only for women aged 18 or over. There was to be a fortnight's run in the Grosvenor Hall (not a public cinema) from the end of May. One assumes that Belfast Corporation was reflecting the pervasive influence of the Protestant and Catholic churches in Northern Ireland. Yet Belfast was not alone in reacting strongly to this film. Many states in the Union banned its showing; the Roman Catholic Legion of Decency in New York fought its exhibition. Even the issue of *Life* magazine that printed stills from the film was banned in several cities; the editor was arrested in the Bronx, though acquitted of the charge of obscenity. When the film was reissued in 1947, audience members were known to faint. See Notes on the film on the Turner Classic Movies website.

[45] The famous actor died when the KLM/BOAC DC-3 he was on flying from Lisbon to Bristol was shot down by German aircraft over the Bay of Biscay on 1st June, 1943. Seventeen died. The following day, an armed Short (Belfast) Sunderland Flying Boat searching the crash area was attacked by eight German fighters but managed three definite and three possible kills before crash-landing near Penzance. Some thought the Germans believed that Churchill was aboard the DC-3 flight. Others were of the opinion that the Germans knew of Howard's presence on board and killed him to demoralize Britain.

[46] Buster Brown, a mischievous boy, was an American comic strip hero created in 1902; he wore a page-boy haircut.

and is always at home being unfit for service too delicate I think – he is sort of a welfare officer.[47] She has a maid who is learning to cook but Janet still gets up at 6 or so to get through with her work. She went to a dance but said she isn't going to any more because she can't get up the next day! She apologized for every little flaw in the lunch, service etc. and it was all fine. She didn't rest a minute but I did. I went by train and came home by bus. Elsie McMullan was on the bus – she is a Wren (British equivalent to Wave) and works for Harry up at the Castle plotting ships.[48] Her husband is in the Army in England – they have no children. Her parents are going to Rosapenna for a holiday and they have to pay a £5.00 taxi fare now from Letterkenny to Rosapenna.[49] Petrol is so scarce now in Eire that not even doctors get any – except a tiny bit – for everything except an acute emergency they have to cycle. A tanker just came in the nick of time to save half of the buses from being stopped. It was going to take the Scanlans 2 days to go by bus to their farm 30 miles away. ...

Gay still is extremely jealous of Julie but I think is getting better. Julie still acts like a wild animal with excitement. ... At school when I go to collect them Julie runs at me like a charging bull and nearly knocks me flat. When I collect them they fight all the way home with each other and when Sadie calls for them they sedately prance home. If it weren't for cars whizzing up and down the Malone Road they could go alone ... There is so little traffic that cars go faster than ever – practically all military and the jeeps and the buses are the fastest of all.

---

[47] Austen T. Boyd was Assistant Command Welfare Officer, Northern Ireland for which he was later awarded an MBE. He was an active member of the Royal North of Ireland Yacht Club in Cultra and it was reported in 1943 that 174 members of this club were serving in the British armed forces: *Belfast News-Letter*, 10th May 1943.

[48] Elsie McMullan, no known relation to Harry McMullan, remains unidentified. One of the women whose experience Virginia Nicholson recounts in *Millions Like Us: Women's Lives in War and Peace 1939–1949* (2011) is a Wren who qualifies as a plotting officer and is transferred from Plymouth to Belfast near the end of 1942. "From her Operations Room in Belfast Castle she accurately tracked the merchant ships as they came up the Irish Sea from Liverpool and Glasgow, chivvied out to sea by their escorts of corvettes ... The Wrens in Belfast Castle learned to dread the signal which alerted them to a U-boat sighting or attack." (p. 161). Lt. Cdr Harry McMullan was in charge of this wartime operation.

[49] Elsie's parents were paying £229 (at today's rate) for a 31-kilometer taxi ride.

Poor Lavens had questions asked in the Imperial parliament about his hoarding of food. He wasn't prosecuted and questions were asked why not? With implications of bribery and corruption and mud slung generally. Then a question was asked in the local parliament with even more mud slung and they brought in how Mucki was a German which is quite beside the point but makes it so much worse-sounding.[50] It was the talk of the town and the whole thing is a pity – the fact remaining that they had an awful lot of food. The whole thing was a political ramp – Labour trying to put the Unionist Party on the spot.[51] Liz Morwood and her husband were here the other day for tea – they help edit a Communist paper called *Labour Progress* and are out and out Communists and trouble makers – pro-Irish, anti-English and agin everything.[52] They talk from soap boxes and are generally biased and completely impossible to talk to because they have that warped point of view that radicals and revolutionists have.

19th Jun.

… Yesterday a week ago Elinor [sic] Nicholson had me to meet the Countess of Antrim at lunch.[53] I went feeling fairly smart but as soon

---

[50] For Mucki, see the letter of 30th May 1940.

[51] It was, however, an independent Unionist MP (J.W. Nixon) who in Stormont alleged that Lavens Mackie had hoarded food, which contravened the Acquisition of Food (Excessive Quantities) Order, 1942. Rationed foodstuffs were not covered by the Order, but it was a criminal offence to hoard other foods until they became stale (e.g. bread) or unfit for human consumption, and it was alleged that the rice Mackie had hoarded (which he claimed was for turkey feed) was the offending foodstuff. J.W. Nixon claimed that it was Mackie's wealth and position that prevented prosecution. See Northern Ireland Parliamentary Debates, House of Commons Official Report (Unrevised), 26: 23, Tuesday June 8 1943, pp. 1012–1054.

[52] Actually, *Labour Progress* was published by the Northern Ireland Labour Party and it ran from 1941 to 1943. At a monthly meeting of the NILP Executive in 1943, the NILP rejected affiliation with the Communist Party of Ireland: see *Labour Progress* 3:1, p. 4 (August 1943). However, some members, including the political firebrand Jack Beattie (1886–1960), the Stormont Labour M.P (1925–1929) and Westminster Labour M.P. (1943–1955), were pro-Irish unification and to that extent anti-English.

[53] Angela Antrim, Countess of Antrim, née Sykes (1911–1984) and her husband, Randal MacDonnell, the 8th Earl of Antrim (1911–1977), moved to his family seat, Glenarm Castle, County Antrim, when war began. He was a Lieutenant-Commander in the Royal Navy, while she became active with the Women's Voluntary Service. Angela Antrim was a well-known sculptor. For Eleanor Nicholson, see the letter of 2nd October, 1939.

as I saw her or about an hour afterward I felt too hick for words – she was what one calls "terrifyingly smart". She is about my age with pale gold hair and a plain face and not ... a good figure, but her clothes were perfection. They were the kind that you don't notice for quite a long time because they are so unobtrusive. She had on a green tweed suit with a pleated skirt – such a beautiful tweed with soft colors of stripes and checks and a silk green striped blouse that didn't match and a powder blue felt hat that was perfect with it – stockings of exactly the right color and sport shoes – the whole thing was perfect with her hair and face. She is a Catholic – hence her friendship with Elinor and is so nice and unobtrusive. I was asking Rosemary about her and she said that she is an artist and a sculptress and so her wonderful color sense is explained. ...

20th Jun.

Now it is Sunday afternoon and Gay and Julie are being punished – I found them tricycling in the road and hauled them in Gay roaring like a dying cow. Julie is here in the nursery making birthday cakes out of plasticine and Gay is reading in bed. ...

The weather is so terrible here that everyone would gladly go anyplace else. Lancelot would cry about it if he were a girl because his bees are starving and not making honey and June is their big month. All winter he could hardly wait until June and now there are only 10 days to go. ...

I met Stella Carr in town one day and she came to a movie with me and then up here for tea. She had fled from Newcastle in a moment of pique and was just stomping the streets. The war has been unduly trying for them I think – and for Jack and Elaine – and for us when we lived at Mahee. Today is blowy and rainy – it is pouring now. I am trying to read *Black Lamb Gray Falcon* by Rebecca West all about Yugoslavia but it is a bit [*indecipherable*][54]. ...

[54] In his 2006 Introduction to a new edition of *Black Lamb and Grey Falcon: A Journey Through Yugoslavia* (2 vols., 1941), Geoff Dyer called it "a vast, ambitious and complex book".

Will address this to Ginna – the way you all flip around leaves us gaping, gasping and uncertain. I dream nights of being home – is it sad or is it sad?

Love,
Helen

26th July
Mahee

Dear Mother and Ginna,

As usual I have been awful in letting so long a gap grow between letters – now I am sitting in the bay window facing the sea, the tide is in and up to the gate, the sun is shining on the opposite shore but not here and it is a soft day.

… Gay and Julie are playing in the boathouse I think. They look fine too and cough much less than they did. They just run wild with the baby ducks, baby chickens, pet lamb, Guinea hens, 2 big pigs and themselves. I am so glad to be back that I never want to go to town, don't want to have any visitors, don't want to do anything but just sit. Life, she is a dream! The news that Mussolini had resigned came through late last night.[55] Maurice Shillington butted into a program to announce it[56] and we nearly hit the ceiling with excitement and rang up the Glendinnings and Jack and Elaine although it was 11.15 just to tell them. I'm such an optimist that any little encouragement like that sends me sky-rocketing off the deep end entirely and I can see myself stepping off the boat in New York followed by my three daughters – there, there and there! …

… we will probably stay here until nearly the end of September. … I never do a thing but the baby and I have only read two books in two weeks. The days just flow by and I don't know where they go. … The

[55] The war went badly for Italy from early 1942. Sicily was invaded by the Allies a fortnight before Helen's letter and the Allies bombed Rome a week before she wrote. Members of Mussolini's government rebelled against his leadership. King Victor Emannuel III summoned him to the palace and dismissed him; he was arrested and imprisoned as he left. Although he was later sprung from detention by German troops, he was a reduced figure thereafter. (Italy was to declare war on Germany in October of 1943.)

[56] For Maurice Shillington, see the letter of 4th December, 1939.

house is prettier than ever and I go from room to room enjoying it. ...
We have a whole mass of big white daisies and beautiful roses – pink
and golden. The border "makes a wonderful show" thanks mainly to
6 enormous mallow bushes which bloom for months – they are pinky
purple and like small hollyhocks massed on a bush. ...

They are now having bottled orange juice – free from the
government and sent from America under Lease Lend and gingerbread.
... The food problem is always with us but we manage by having meat
Saturday, Sunday and Monday; fish one or two days and bacon one or
two. We have cabbage nearly every day, new potatoes and quite good
puddings.

The two books I have read were both so good – *Cross Creek* by the
same woman who wrote *The Yearling* – autobiographical account of
the remote place she lives in Florida [57] – the other one is *Who are the
Americans?* by William Dwight Whitney – a masterpiece of information
about America for the English public. It is a small book published here
in a paper edition but it is superb. I read it twice without stopping –
Mr. Whitney from his name is American but from his book is sort of
dual British and American and is a lawyer.[58] I read another one first
Portrait by an Ally[59] – another explanatory book for the English about
America and I thought it was so good but this one makes it seem trifling
by comparison.

Most unluckily I have to have an operation on Thursday – a cist [sic]
has grown in my left breast and Professor Lowry is going to take it
out.[60] I found it by accident about 10 days ago when I was taking a

[57] Marjorie Kinnan Rawlings (1896–1953) won the Pulitzer fiction prize in 1939 for
The Yearling (1938). (It was adapted for the screen in 1946.) *Cross Creek*, an
autobiography, also set in Florida, was published in 1942. It too was made into a
film, in 1983.

[58] William Dwight Whitney (1899–1973) from Long Island, is not to be confused with
the Massachusetts philologist, William Dwight Whitney (1827–1894). *Who Are the
Americans?* (1941) was reissued in 1943.

[59] *American Close Up: Portrait of an Ally* (1943) was by the war correspondent and
prolific author, John Langdon-Davies (1897–1971). Among his many books are
A Short History of Women (1927), *Behind the Spanish Barricades* (1936), *A Short
History of the Future* (1936) and *Air Raid* (1938).

[60] This was Charles Gibson Lowry MD, D.Sc., FRCS (1880–1951), born in Limavady,
Co. Londonderry. In 1920 he was appointed Professor of Midwifery at Queen's
University Belfast and was Pro-Chancellor there 1949–51. He masterminded the
building of Belfast's Royal Maternity Hospital and co-founded the Royal College of
Obstetricians and Gynaecologists in London. His surgery was in University Square,
five doors up from Dr Foster's, and the Square was then called "the Harley Street of
Belfast". See "Charles Gibson Lowry," Wikipedia; R.W.M. Strain, "University
Square: A Sentimental Retrospect," *Ulster Medical Journal* 38:1 (1969): 17.

bath – hard little lump like a marble so as soon as Bridget came back I went to town to see Dr. Foster who said Cist – must come out and sent me to Lowry who said 2 Cists – must come out. It doesn't hurt at all and I don't expect ever will – but it is a nuisance to have to spend about a week in a nursing home in the Summer. I am quite excited about it – my only operation being tonsils and not worth mentioning. I have to go into the San Remo nursing home in University Street Wednesday night and will have it early on Thursday. ...

Edith rang up last night – Bodo is coming home on Saturday for a week's leave. He still doesn't know when he will go to America but I have given him a list of addresses and so you will probably see him, Ginna. He will be in New York most of the time and probably will go to Washington and Detroit. I like him as well as ever and he is so interesting to talk to because he is so intelligent and so well-balanced and has had such exciting times in this war. ...

I took time out there to hear the 1 o'clock news – the air offensive is unimaginable, it is so terrible. Again an optimist I believe that bombing alone can win the war but nobody here agrees with me. Fred Gardiner, Roberta's brother, is flying and fighting again – a Beaufighter and goes on intruder sweeps.[61] Rosemary Bryson's young brother was lost about a month ago. He was home on Thursday to see his new daughter – 2 days old, was called back on Friday, his father died suddenly on Friday night and when they tried to get in touch with him Saturday morning he was missing – lost Friday night. I only saw him once – he and his wife were staying at the Shelbourne [hotel] in Dublin when we were there last September and they had just had a son then – he looked and acted so much like Leslie Howard. Now his wife is left with a baby not even a year old and one a month old – he may turn up as a prisoner but being lost at night over the sea is bad. Did you see *The First of the Few*? It is so good.[62] I saw *Kingdom Harvest* on my day in town but thought it was much too far fetched and stagey to be

[61] The Bristol Beaufighter was developed during the Second World War by the Bristol Aeroplane Company. It was versatile, being used in night-time combat during the Battle of Britain, as a rocket-equipped ground-attack airplane, as a torpedo bomber, and, as Helen here notes, as an aerial reconnaissance aircraft.

[62] *The First of the Few* (re-titled *Spitfire* in the U.S.A.) is a 1942 docudrama produced and directed by Leslie Howard who also stars as the designer of the Spitfire fighter plane. The title alludes to Churchill's historic tribute to the Battle of Britain R.A.F. pilots.

real[63] – but I'm getting so high-brow in my choice of movies that I can hardly stand it – however I can still enjoy trash but can spot it miles away. ...

Auntie is in high spirits all the time now. ... She took my shift at the Red Cross Club today from 10–2 and on Fridays too. Last Monday a colored boy talked to me for the longest time mostly about his girl friends and dances – here!!! From his conversation and attitude he was as white as the driven snow. I finally had to cheese him off and, as it was I had to keep the conversation impersonal or he would have got fresh. It is such a mistake to have sent them here because they go to dances with white girls etc. and it makes the white Americans see red to see the black with the white and the fights are awful. One American the week before told me how he had quit some American club in England because colored boys were allowed and he just told them that it was O.K. by him if they wanted the colored boys but they could have *his* place.[64] The illegitimate babies left behind are legion – some black and some white and as the story goes twins – one white and one black. Propaganda on Venereal Disease appears every week in the press – even in the Belfast papers.[65] I wish I knew some Americans well enough to have them come to see us, but I don't. There has only been one I talked to that I really liked enormously and he was one of the first ones I met last summer – probably he is dead in North Africa by now – but he was so nice and such fun. I took him to a movie and was so sorry afterward because I would lots rather have talked to him. ... I am about to begin a study of Walt Whitman with an eye to a paper for the D.R. Circle and because I want to know about him.

[63] Possibly this was *The Harvest Shall Come*, a 1942 British documentary about agricultural work, directed by Max Anderson and starring John Slater. It was well received.

[64] The military's good conduct rules for American soldiers involved voluntary segregation at dances, parties and accommodation and mutual respect in unavoidably mixed locations (e.g. the American Red Cross Club). There was a race brawl outside an Antrim town public house on 30th September 1942 when U.S. military police clashed with American GIs: *Belfast News-Letter*, 2nd October, 1942. Tensions between black GIs and the white native population added a layer of complication. See David Reynolds, *Rich Relations: The American Occupation of Britain, 1942–1945*, pp. 221, 222, 228.

[65] For example, the *Northern Whig* for 21st May, 1943 carried in the classified ads a "Venereal Disease Warning". Readers were told that the number of V.D. cases had catapulted by 70% "under war-time conditions". Confidential advice and treatment were available at special clinics provided by local councils.

Arabella and Gordon are going south for 2 months early in August. We don't see them much. Arabella makes me laugh like anything but she is so dumb and talks such nonsense that it is hard to bear her for long although she means so well. ... Gordon continues to be a lamb – so dumb he can hardly stand but so nice and so funny. It is so interesting to see the difference between southern and northern Irish – Gordon is so very southern in outlook, temperament and speech. His stories about people and places down there are fascinating. He still complains about living here and Arabella has completely swung around and is *dying* to live in Dublin but she isn't dying enough to move. ...

I have started to smoke again too. Dumb isn't the word for it with cigarettes at 2/4 for 20 and after all my talk too! I think it was worrying over Mary Lee that brought the urge on. She is fine now and so I don't worry but the general strain of the war undermines everybody's nerves and keeps one keyed up. ...

Living here is so simple and so pleasant that it suits my lazy nature to the ground. The noise and confusion and hubbub of town life are far away and what do I care if I have no town shoes? And can't get an appointment to buy any? And that Gay and Julie need shoes too? And that I should be having a suit made for myself? ... how I do run on. I'll write you a big letter from the Nursing home.

Love,
Helen

5th August
17–21 Castle Place
Belfast
    [From Lancelot]

My dear Ginna

This letter brings bad news however I am thankful to say that I can end on a cheerful note so don't worry.

I think Helen told you in a recent letter that she had to have two little cists [sic] removed which was duly done last week on July 28th. It was a simple matter and she would have been home again in a week had everything been well. Unhappily upon examination of the offenders they did not prove negative and in order to nip in the bud a serious complaint it was necessary to remove her entire left breast without delay.

Accordingly this major operation was performed after a day's interval and I am now happy to relate that she is well out of the wood from the shock which left her in a very weak condition for a couple of days. ...

I need not relate how Helen has faced this ordeal for you know the metal she is made of as well as I do and I can tell you that an awful lot of other people know it too, both old and young.

Now I am most anxious that both you and your mother will not worry and I can assure you that Helen is in the best medical hands imaginable and has received the greatest care and attention. I have done quite enough worrying for us all and could not keep a meal down for days when I heard that she had to have a second operation. I am now quite cheerful about her so I hope you will be the same for you know that if anything I am almost a professional pessimist. ...

Gordon and Arabella go to Eire on Sunday for two months but their maid will be in the house until Thursday when I shall either move to the Club or fend for myself at Sans Souci Park.

I shall go to Mahee tonight to bring Gay and Julie to see Helen on Saturday and I think I shall bring them to town for a night before Arabella's house is closed so that Helen can see more of them. ...

I wish you could see all three as it nearly kills Helen that she can't show them off to you and your mother. Things are looking better however, and it may not be long now as the war tempo increases in the right direction. ...

Nothing gives Helen more pleasure than letters from home and so will you please write to her as often as you can find time.

I am sorry I can't beat a typewriter as I know you have trouble with my writing however I hope you can manage to make it out and I would underline *don't worry.*

I hope everything goes well with you and that you are not worn to a shadow with naval activity.

Affectionately,
Lancelot

13th Aug.
San Remo Nursing Home
Belfast

Dear Mother and Ginna,

I have been lazy about writing but feel it is high time to tell you all about "my operations"!! Ma! It was awful! The first one was nothing – just 2 little cists out with 2 little cuts about an inch long and I could read the next day and ate a good supper the next night and even smoked – however, I hadn't had nothin' yet as the 2nd operation proved – the first one was on Thursday, the 2nd on Saturday and from Saturday to Tuesday I felt terrible – was sick Saturday and Sunday and felt sick but wasn't Monday and Tuesday and only started to eat on Wednesday helped by a very bitter tonic that makes me eat like a horse. I even gnaw my bones – lamb chop and chicken – the food is swell – spiced peaches and pears and tinned apricots – omelets that are a dream and wonderful fillets of plaice.

Jack Andrews was here just now at lunch time and asked if I had heard from you, Mother, and I said a cable yesterday and he said "If she was here she would be proud of how you look". I feel fine and walked up to the hall to the john today and have sat up in a chair from 11–1 for the last 3 days.

I told you about the cists – well, the *worst* was that to everybody's surprise they were malignant – so right away they said that the breast must come off – so it did. It is a big operation – 2 hours and having had one of nearly 1 hour two days before I didn't stand it so well and had to have glucose and salt water dropped into my veins through a cut in my leg– the collapse if it was one was about as bad as when Gay was born – nothing like so bad when Lee was born. They gave me injections Saturday and Sunday nights so I felt no pain and kept the pain down in the day with Veganin (tablets like asperin [sic])[66] so I really didn't suffer but I felt terribly weak and sick …

Monday morning was my lowest ebb mentally – the injections have a lowering effect and I got the curse later in the day Monday – anyway Monday when I woke up was I weak!! And was I depressed!! And was I sick!!! … Well, you know me and my imagination – I had myself dead

---

[66] Veganin tablets contained paracetamol, caffeine and aspirin; the caffeine has since been replaced by codeine.

and buried, the funeral notice and several letters of sympathy written (all very flattering). I got the night nurse to go get Sister Sally – the assistant boss and I told her that somebody would have to do something that I was passing out – (and all the time, mind you pulse and temp. were fine) – she tried to talk me out of it but when I suggested brandy when she didn't take kindly to my suggestions of transfusions and something in my veins, she did get me some brandy and that bucked me up although it made me sicker but I kept it down, and in an hour I was able to joke with the nurses about myself and when L. came I was all right but, sister, so weak!!

Now it is 2 weeks tomorrow and I really feel fine – don't even take a nap after lunch and sleep like a top from 10 to 7 every morning and have I been spoiled – I always have 2 vases of flowers in my room –

… I personally am as optimistic as a June bug – I even take a warped pleasure in having had so *awful* a thing – cancer at my age is sensational *but* I am as sure as eggs is eggs that it is gone where the woodbine twineth and the wang doodle mourneth.[67] …

Nobody has yet admitted that it was cancer so maybe it wasn't but only the threat of it. I asked Mr. Purce, the surgeon who did it,[68] point blank if it was cancer and he said "that is what Prof. Lowry was afraid of" so I really don't think it was cancer but would have been if neglected. … So many people have had this operation – nearly everybody who comes to see me has an aunt or a grandmother or a cousin, who has had it – 10, 15 or 25 years ago and are all bouncing around still. Mrs. Turtle had it, so did Charlotte Browne's mother and it always means the threat of cancer. Prof. Lowry did the first op. and

---

[67] This favourite popular American saying of Helen's is of obscure origin. The 1894 edition of Brewer's *Dictionary of Phrase and Fable* quotes a correspondent: "*Gone where the woodbine twineth.* To the pawnbroker's, up the spout." Disappeared, like Helen's cancer, as she believes. The second part of the saying can be traced at least to the mid-19th century and William P. Brannan's parody sermon: "Where the lion roareth and the whangdoodle mourneth for her first-born" ("Whangdoodle" in Wiktionary.) The whangdoodle is a whimsical monster.

[68] This was G.R.B. (Barney) Purce (1891–1950) from Ballyclare, County Antrim and educated at Queen's University Belfast. During the Great War he was regimental medical officer to the 8th Btn, Royal Ulster Rifles. After the war he practised at the Ulster Volunteer Force Hospital, the Ulster Hospital for Children and Women, and the Royal Victoria Hospital. In 1948 he was elected President of the Association of Thoracic Surgeons of Great Britain and Ireland. His obituarist wrote that "'Barney' Purce had the qualities of greatness": *British Medical Journal*, 15th July, 1950.

helped with the 2nd. Mr. Purce is a wonderful surgeon and famous for doing this special operation. A lady next door to me had hers off yesterday morning and is doing fine.

15th Aug.

This is Sunday and I took a bath today and walked up and down the hall and had my lunch sitting up. Auntie is coming in to see me. Maureen lent me a little electric radio and I have about 40 books – all lent to me. ...

This Nursing Home is the best in town run by 3 sisters who are from Ballymena and so Ulster and so funny and their accents and idioms are a scream.[69] ... They have ice here and during the heat wave I had iced drinks all the time and Arabella lent me her electric fan – could you believe it in Ireland – for 3 days it was always summer at the roots of my hair – I hope you are as up on your ads as I am to get that subtle point![70] ... The first night my night nurse told me if I would take out my teeth she would wash them for me!!! And a few nights later the regular night nurse was just looking around to see that she had done everything before she left me for the night and said "you keep your teeth in at night, don't you?" so damming [sic] for Ireland.[71]

... As soon as my 3 week X-ray treatment period is over we are going on a spree to Dublin The X-ray is an added precaution and will start pretty soon I think – 10 treatments in 3 weeks then a rest and later some more. Mr. Lowry and Mr. Purce come about every 2 or 3 days – both of them are lambs. It didn't hurt a bit when the stitches came out – I haven't had time to count them but there 30 or 40 – I hope these details don't sound crude and shocking to you written down but you know my mind for wanting to know *all* about things and my idea is to tell you the worst so you won't have anything worse to imagine, but I know it sounds worse written than if I could tell it.

---

[69] The *Belfast Street Directory* for 1943 lists San Remo Nursing Home at 81 University Street with a Miss Crawford the owner or manager of the premises.

[70] Always summer at the roots of my hair: Presumably an American 1940s hair product jingle.

[71] Helen had her own teeth whereas back then lots of middle-aged British women did not; until a generation ago, the difference between American and British teeth was chasmic.

5.45 pm

Now it is Sunday at 5.45 and believe it or not we are listening to the Navaho Indians in Gallup, New Mexico.[72] After hearing this maybe some of the people here will believe me when I tell them that none of the people in New Mexico even know where England is. ... L. is here – he spent last night at Mahee and says they are all fine. He spent yesterday from before tea until 12.30 extracting honey – i.e. making honey in jars from honey in combs. He has a wonderful machine – sort of like an ice cream mixer + a beer barrel with a spout at the bottom that the strained honey runs out. ... He got about 300 lbs of honey altogether which isn't bad considering the rainy season. Are we popular or are we popular with our friends? Honey is 3/6 a jar to buy and is very scarce.

... The news is all so good maybe we can see each other before next August – high time too. Hope you got the snaps of Mary Lee. They are the image of her. L. is going to take a movie of Gay and Julie making Mary Lee smile – he says it is like a circus. Will write soon again don't worry that I will overdo, you know me – bone-lazy and with any excuse I just set and think or mostly just set.

Much love and kisses,
Helen

28th Aug.
Mahee

Dear Mother and Ginna,

It is after supper of a lovely day. The time changed a week ago so now it gets dark around 9. ... Can you believe it is 5 years since we have seen each other? It doesn't seem like it to me.

I feel fine. We came down on Friday afternoon and I stayed up for supper and was absolutely delighted to be home but after being away for 3 weeks I felt so detached and un-maternal. I wouldn't have known

---

[72] At 5.30pm on the BBC Forces Service (or Programme), "Transatlantic Call – People to People" went to Gallup, New Mexico for the annual Navajo powwow. The programme was co-written and co-produced by Alan Lomax, the famous American folklorist and collector.

Mary Lee if I had passed her on the street. ... We went on a picnic to the wheat field the next day where L. was cutting and I had to stop half-way and rest but I walked home all in one go. I stay in bed until lunch-time and then lie outside on a rug all afternoon and between the sea air and m'iron tonic I can feel the strength flowing back into me. I dressed myself today completely – the only thing I couldn't do before was fasten and unfasten my bra but I can do it now too. I even look pretty well – not too pale and fearsome.

... Sadie has been conscientiousness itself in looking after [Mary Lee] and I can just see that I'll never get Mary Lee back into my clutches again but I can spend more time with the other two. They have such a good time here and L. took them fishing this afternoon and they caught – or rather Gay caught – 3 mackerel herself and the excitement was beyond anything. I was sitting on the shore watching when they got the first and I thought that they would all go overboard. Apparently G. stood up when she felt the pull and tried to change places with Julie who wouldn't budge. ...

29th Aug.

Only 2 more nights here and then we are back to town for the winter to our great sorrow. I have only been here about 3 weeks altogether this summer and it seems like nothing. I feel better and better every day but still stay in bed until lunch time every day and just sit most of the afternoon. ... It is awful that I am so helpless but I can't take anything on while I am taking X-ray treatment – they are supposed to be so weakening. The weather is rotten. Every morning we wake up to hear it pounding on the roof and splashing in our French door. Friday morning was a dream so I just lay out in the sun all morning. G. and J. never leave me and are quite good on the whole. ... I hear Pop shooting his way home from the Brownes ... We were at the [Glendinnings] last night. Joan had just got a postcard from her husband – it was dated 14 months ago and said "I am really well". He is a prisoner in Japan but that was from Malaya. Their son [Harden] is in Sicily.

Ballywilliam[73]
4th Sept.

Now I've changed locale just for the day and am sitting in Elaine's living room – what a day! It is raining and blowing like November and looks as though it would never stop. ...

I heard yesterday that Marcia Mackie has just flown to America for a week! She is the director of the Red Cross Club here so managed it on the strength of that. Betty Shaw Carr works in the A[merican]. Red Cross Club in London; she is coming over today with Archie, her husband, on his ten day's leave.[74] I haven't seen her for years – she came home with Janet Boyd leaving her baby girl with her mother. I doubt if Toby Spence will bring Kathleen home with him – she is so scary and I can't say that I blame her with her little boys to think of. There was such a good program on the radio last night by Louis MacNeice on the 4th anniversary of the outbreak of war.[75]

To go back to that fascinating topic – my operation! Prof. Lowry came to bring me some books on Wednesday so I did a little plain and fancy pumping – I asked him when I would know whether I was cured and he said "We got it so very early that you need have not the slightest apprehension for the future". In other words I'm a cure now but they always give everyone these deep X-ray treatments as a precaution anyway. I have had six of the first course of 12 and am feeling quite good. ... Another thing I asked Prof. Lowry was whether Dr. Oliver Chance in Dublin who Mrs. Turtle heard was the best radiologist in Ireland could give me anything that they can't in Belfast and he said "No" that Chance was a good man but it is just as good here.[76] ...

[73] Jack and Elaine Andrews' house in the Townland of the same name near Comber, County Down.

[74] In July, 1943, Mrs Archie Carr is reported as an active member of the South Belfast War Hospitals' Supplies and Comforts Depot. "It would be difficult to name any hospital requirement or comfort for our soldiers it does not supply" – *Belfast News-Letter*, 22nd July.

[75] "Four Years at War" was broadcast on the BBC Home Service on 3rd September. The 45-min. programme was written by Louis MacNeice: "Story of what the men and women of Britain have endured and achieved since September 3, 1945".

[76] Oliver (Bill) Chance (b.1904) was a pioneer in radiotherapy and the founder of St Luke's Hospital, Dublin. His two brothers, Arthur (Duke) Chance and George Chance, were also distinguished medical men. Their father was Sir Arthur Chance, past President of the Royal College of Surgeons. The Chance family was living in Dublin when the Easter rebellion of 1916 took place and Sir Arthur's wife Eileen kept a vivid (and recently published) diary while her husband and son Arthur performed as surgeons at Castle Hospital during the rebellion.

Another thing I asked P. Lowry was where to get a false [breast] and he replied "Boots of Bond Street used to have lovely ones!" which I think is a riot. I went to the surgical supply people who are going to make me one to match the other – a gamgee sort of cotton wool covered with silk. ...

10th Sept.

Rushing downtown – many thanks for cabled money – I feel like a millionaire – still feel fine and everybody says I look the picture of health which I do –
 Love in haste
 Have to buy shoes for the kid-wids

Helen

24th Sept.
Sans Souci

Dear Ginna and Mother,

... I have an appointment to buy shoes next Monday – my street shoes are all so shabby – I've been trying to buy a pair since before M.L. was born. ... The shop windows are full of wooden-soled shoes and occasionally you hear a pair on the street clacking along. I am about to have 2 tweed suits made by a tailor – one purply blue and it is the most becoming color I can wear – like that taffeta evening dress I had when Gay was a baby and the other is dark and bricky rather than purply but much darker and redder than you usually mean by brick. ... The mesh stockings arrived just as my last pair ran and are the envy of all who see them. People now are all dowdy about the feet and legs – old shoes and lisle stockings or bare legs – how they bear it in this chilly weather beats me.

 Edith was here from 10–12.30 yesterday. Her baby is due in 2 weeks – Diana if a girl and Redmond if a boy. You can just tell now that she is having one – she wore her W.V.S. uniform up to a month ago. She had a cable from Bodo. He went over again on the same boat that you both came one Christmas. Marcia flew home by Clipper having gone by bomber. I haven't seen her for months. ...

I had a long and amusing telephone conversation with Harry the other night – in short bursts he is funnier than anyone I know and intersperses all his comments to male or female with dears, darlings and bless yous and "God bless" at the end – but he makes me laugh until I cry. He was very funny about Dick Pim who has got a lot of publicity lately. He went to America with Churchill and is now in a New York hospital having had an operation for sciatica.[77] Apparently Pres. Roosevelt arranged the whole thing according to the papers and Churchill visited Dick in N.Y. Harry said that Dick just saw a chance of getting a free operation on lease-lend and probably just said to Pres. Roosevelt "I have sciatica" and Pres. Roosevelt said "yes" or maybe just "um hm". Dick is known and famous for watching after Dick. When his sciatica was bad last winter he wangled a job at Gibralter [sic]. ...

We are going to Dublin some time in October for a week or more. I got a card from *The New Yorker* to say that I would now start getting it with the compliments of Ensign V. R. Hughes [Ginny] and I jumped for joy. I still read the *New Statesman* every week and have started reading poetry again because I went to a meeting of the Poetry Society last Sat. afternoon – not a soul I knew was there. They seemed to be mostly teachers and elocution teachers. A minister read a paper on Poetry in Translation and several women read poetry beautifully. It is mostly for reading poetry – but doesn't mean that I will have to read.[78]

... Here comes our lunch – *herrings*. We have fish every Tuesday and Friday. Eliz. Morwood brought me 2 lemons from Dublin and we made wonderful marmalade – L. made it mostly. He loves to make it but doesn't like me to tell people because he thinks it sounds sissy. He is fine – needs a holiday I think. ... Must go – I hear me daughters in the hall.

Much love and kisses
Helen

[77] For Dick Pim, see the letter of 21st September, 1939. Pim accompanied Churchill overseas to set up temporary map rooms for meetings with Roosevelt and later Stalin.

[78] The well-known Poetry Society began in London in 1909 as the Poetry Recital Society, and its Northern Ireland Centre in Belfast in 1943, to encourage poetry reading, speaking and making. In 1945, the Ulster poet John Hewitt lectured to the Society on Robert Frost: *Northern Whig*, 17th January.

4 Oct.
Sans Souci

Dear Mother and Ginna,

It is a wild October morning and I am having my eleven o'clock cup of tea in the nursery where I always sit in the morning when I am up.

I have done the laundry – ordered the lunch and now have the day – not to mention the week stretching before me. The question of what to eat is ever present and such a problem. We are having Spam today and curried beef for supper. Maybe I can get L. out this evening to the neighborhood movie to see *Casablanca*.

We went to Newcastle Friday night by train and came home yesterday Sunday by bus. It was a nice change and we had no rain – a lucky thing because we forgot our raincoats. The hotel has just re-opened after 2 years of being a clearing station for blitzed evacuees – as such it hardly ever functioned because there were no blitzes after it was ready.[79] There was a dance Saturday night which was quite gay – American technicians, a few soldiers British and American and the hotel residents – most of whom live on or off the Malone Road. We danced a few times – the band not being conducive to more. Tommy Carr came to dinner and danced once with me – Stella was in town for the weekend. We went to buy a picture from Tommy and decided to have him paint me and Gay and Julie instead. He has two or three very good portraits – one of Stella in a white blouse – and a red bow in her hair looking too French, Bohemian and ugly for anything – mouth too negroid and one of a girl in a yellow sweater – a lovely pose and one of his gardener with the dumbest blue eyes and open mouth. Tommy's style is impressionist and vague but he is very very good and according to Clive Bell and other critics he is one of the best young painters in England.[80] We may buy a picture that we liked of children on the sand at Newcastle with a pram with a sunshade on it. He has just sent most of his pictures to London to an exhibition there. Their house is so slap dash and so typical of the Bohemian life they lead. The dining room is also the studio and had pictures and frames stacked around the walls.

[79] The Slieve Donard Hotel, Newcastle, Co. Down was built by the Belfast and County Down Railway and opened in 1898. It is still in profitable operation.

[80] For Tom Carr, see the letter of 25th August, 1939. Clive Bell (1881–1964), the art critic, was married to Vanessa, Virginia Woolf's sister.

Ann was playing with friends and Tommy said Veronica was out in the garden eating stones. Sure enough there sat Veronica leaning against the sunny wall on a pile of stones looking at an art book. She is 2 and looks exactly like a tough boy with tight little curls only about ½ an inch long. She had on an old coat of Ann's that reached to her ankles and she is such a funny little thing. Tommy is so quiet and gentle and so nice. They are trying to find a house in town because they have no friends in Newcastle who are interested in the things he is interested in.

We went to Church yesterday and then to the Golf Club with Jim Barr for a drink before lunch. Jim reads the lesson in Church every Sunday and then goes to the Golf Club to recuperate. I sent him and Lancelot to a surrealist exhibition at the Museum last week which they enjoyed enormously. About 100 pictures there were all by one man who paints in all styles – chiefly Salvador Dali types. They were very interesting to see but Tommy says that the artist has nothing original to say. I took G. and J. to it and Gay was so funny – she wanted to know why they all looked so worried![81]

I feel much better after 10 days without any X-ray treatments. We went for two walks in Newcastle Saturday. The sea was a dream in the afternoon with the tide in and the sun making the waves silver as they rippled in. We went to see the Reverend Martin in the morning – a bee man who is over 80 and is so nice. He gave L. his bee-master's exam last summer.[82] Last night we made a cake with honey instead of sugar – L. and I.

Edith rang up to thank me for some magazines that I had sent through to a boy with T.B. and said that Bodo had taken Nat and an English naval commander's wife who is staying with Nat out to dinner.

[81] This was an exhibition of works by Colin Middleton (later RHA, RUA, MBE), the painter, since then highly regarded. The observation in the Wikipedia entry on Middleton (1910–1983) that his first solo exhibition was in 1944 in Dublin is contradicted by Helen's letter. In September 1943, the Ulster Museum and Art Gallery mounted 115 paintings by Middleton who later claimed: "… in the 1930's I was the only surrealist painter working in Ireland". See Ross's Auctioneers and Valuers website s.v. "Colin Middleton RHA RUA" and NIVAL (National Irish Visual Art History Library) database.

[82] Rev. William Martin (1859–1953) of Newcastle, Co. Down and Presbyterian Minister in Randalstown, Co. Antrim, was the first honorary co-president (with Lady Wickham from Comber) of the Ulster Beekeepers' Association, formed towards the end of 1942. David Wright, former Chairman of the UBKA: pers. comm.

It was the first time he had seen either Nat or the English girl and he thought that Nat was acting rather oddly and soon discovered that she was very drunk. He had quite a time keeping her on her feet and had to take her home right after dinner but then he and the English girl went out to the theatre, dancing and 2 night clubs and came home at 3! I told Edith to tell him to try Harriet next as an antidote!!!. Louise would be his best bet.[83] Bodo is at the Barbizon Plaza if you want to get in touch with him Ginna – Lt. Commander R. T. Taggart, R.N.V.R.[84] I told Bodo that Nat was intelligent and amusing but Bodo told Edie that he found her neither. Lancelot says that if Nat's drink went to her feet Bodo must have had quite a nice time. Edith is more or less in retirement now – her baby is due in about a week.

I tried to get Maureen and Nancy Mitchell to go with me this afternoon to see *The Magnificent Ambersons* but they are both going to the doctor.[85] Nancy has about 5 weeks to go and Maureen about 6.

A Russian girl has come to live across the street from us and she is having a baby in Nov. too – also Doreen so when I go to the Maternity Hospital I can just go from room to room – Maureen, the Russian and Doreen there and Nancy and Kathleen Morwood at the Park Nursing Home. ...

5th Oct.

I still take iron tonic and Vitamin pills and am getting fat and rosy. The first *New Yorker* came – huzzas but no letters for about 3 weeks. ...

Well, news is scarce but love is plentiful – much love and kisses.
Helen

---

[83] Natalie (Nat) Starr, Harriet and Louise were Smith College friends of Helen's. Natalie accompanied Mary Ellen Chase on Helen's teacher's visit to Cambridge to visit the Lindberghs before accompanying Chase on her visit to the Turtles in the 1930s. Natalie's family was in the diamond business.

[84] The former 38-storey, Art Deco Barbizon Plaza Hotel at Central Park South in New York is now called Trump Parc and owned by President Donald Trump.

[85] Director Orson Welles' second film was adapted from Booth Tarkington's 1918 novel.

24th–25th Oct.
Sans Souci

Dear Mother and Ginna,

It is Sunday night (the 24th) and we are sitting in truly British fashion one on each side of the fire and very nice too. We each have a lamp (not so British!) and the room is as disarrayed as ever. The radio is playing – a nice chorus singing "With a Song in my Heart" and there are *Denver Post*s and a *New Yorker* on the floor (Julie), and a yellow cardigan on L.'s chair (Julie), a blue one on my chair (Gay), a hat on the couch (me), a camera on the book case (L.). There is a sick bunch of golden rod behind L. and a dead bunch of chrysanthemums behind me. The room can look very nice when I pull it together and we have nice flowers. ...

29th Oct.

Our biggest excitement of the past few weeks is sitting for our portrait which Tommy Carr is doing. He has the drawing done and it is very good of all of us ... It is going to be huge – 36 x 40 and we have great hopes for a good one. ... I think it will be a very worthwhile thing because he is supposed to one of the best young painters in England and is in London now seeing about a show of his paintings which is at the best gallery in London ... It is going to be a pastel summery picture. ...

Nighty night and love
Helen

1st November
Sans Souci

Dear Mother,

... Lancelot is at the Stock Exchange dinner tonight given by Joe Cunningham's office to celebrate their centenary.[86] It is at the Grand

[86] For Joe (Josias) Cunningham, stockbroker and husband of Isobel (Mackie) Cunningham, see the letter of 27th September, 1939.

Central and he will be home in about an hour because it will have to stop before the trams stop running. We are having breakfast at 7.30 tomorrow morning and are going on the 8.30 train to Dublin. ... Gordon rang up lots of hotels before he finally got us rooms in some hotel on the quays. Eggie and Hilary rang up 12 hotels one Friday night 2 weeks ago and couldn't get in any and had to go out to Lucan about 12 miles out where Auntie had her fiasco holiday with Mrs. McKee. You would think that by November the rush would be over but it is as bad as ever and prices are sky high – for everything. People are worried about Dublin because although it is full of luxuries that we can't get, the necessities are scarce and wildly expensive. We have to take tea, sugar, and soap even to a hotel. I am all agog to get away from housekeeping for a while anyway. ...

L. had lunch today with Toby Spence who has just flown home from America. Kathleen isn't coming back until the war is over. I don't know what pull Toby used but it is very exceptional for a civilian to be allowed to go – Marcia was sent by the Red Cross but I doubt very much if just anybody can go – in fact I know they can't.

Harry says that the betting in naval circles is 2–1 that the European war will be over by April 1st. The Belfast papers are full of headlines about Germany cracking and the morale slipping etc. but no one believes it. We have just read such an interesting book called *Victorian Doctor* – a biography of Oscar Wilde's father and it is all about Dublin in the last century – you would like it.[87]

I have my name in at 3 agencies and will try in Dublin for a nurse. I interviewed one today and wrote to one. They are even scarcer than maids and get about 25/- (to) 30/- a week[88]. ... People are so desperate that they will pay anything for a hick from the wilds of Connemara or Donegal. The munitions and aircraft factories pay £4 and £5 a week for unskilled labor and the Americans pay £1.0.0 a day which hardly anyone can compete with and maids leave in shoals.

We are still hunting a house. There aren't any to be had except to buy at fantastic prices. Arabella expects to get £3,250 for hers and I think she might get nearly £3,000. ... I priced beds with Maureen the

---

[87] T.G. Wilson's biography, *Victorian Doctor: Being the Life of Sir William Wilde* was published in 1942. The life of Wilde Sr was full of cultural interest and professional scandal.

[88] That is, 25 shillings to 30 shillings (£1.05.0 to £1.10.0).

other day and the very cheapest was £35 per bed for a plain single bed – springs, mattress etc. There is a price control in England and brides can get permits for utility furniture but here things aren't so strictly watched and the prices at auctions are fantastic. ...

We were at the G.Dinnings on Saturday for tea and then went to a Hallowe'en party at the Dorman's and sister was it dull – I could have screamed with boredom. There were 2 Polish airmen there who were very amusing but they could hardly speak English – one of them had been in a Concentration camp and was nearly deaf. They both were married and their wives and children were in Poland – maybe! Hardin [sic] Glendinning is in Italy now and hates the Italians more every day, he says.[89] One of the Poles hates the French so and they both hate the Russians – what a world to straighten out!

... I will try to write you from Eire and tell you how the lights look and how the steaks taste. Dr. Foster told me to be sure to practice "lifting my elbow" in Dublin. Gordon owes me a bottle of champagne because Auntie didn't marry Doc. She still gets a girlish gleam in her eye when she talks about him and she is as happy as an elf in her new house. Must go finish my packing.

Goodnight and love,
Helen

4th Dec.
Sans Souci Park

Dear Mother,

... It is a raw, foggy horrible December day and I should be rushing out to join a fish queue but it is too cold yet so I am parked in the nursery with the gas fire hissing beside me and a bowl of water *most* hygienically absorbing the fumes or moistening the air or whatever you call it. The radio is playing a most divine Chopin piece and I have my hair tied up with a ribbon because I am short of hair-pins again. I have

[89] It was announced in the *Belfast News-Letter* of 26th August, 1944 that Major Harden Glendinning had been awarded the OBE for "gallantry and distinguished services" in Italy. In civilian life he was a stockbroker with William F. Coates & Co., Belfast, est. 1887. He died in 1990.

just talked to Joan Strachan[90] on the 'phone – we are going to a charity matinee this afternoon in aid of the Ulster Library for the Forces.[91] The papers are full of announcements of charity bazaars, my bag is full of raffle tickets, today and tomorrow are flag days for prisoners of war and every place you turn you are asked to "bring and buy" or just plain fork out. There never was a truer statement than that the whole of Belfast's social life is for some charity or another. However, this year I am delighted to go to sales and bazaars because it is our only hope of buying Christmas toys for G. and J. I have made the rounds of the toyshops about 3 times and you would have to see them to believe them – there is literally not one nice toy in town. In the first place there are hardly any and in the second what there are are junk, pure and simple, and in the 3rd place the prices are shocking. Maybe you will realize what it is like when I say that there isn't one single doll that isn't a rag doll! There are no trains, meccano, blocks, balls, marbles, paints, doll cradles, tea-sets, crayons, plasticine, no soldiers or little cars or mechanical toys and the situation is pathetic. I have bought two embroidery sets, two paper doll sets, 1 weaving set and 1 tiddlywinks and that is all. I am feverishly knitting Bobbie and Jane (the Didee dolls) new sets of clothes from a pattern that Roberta lent me – trust Roberta![92] Bobbie and Jane are still going strong – Bobbie is Gay's and has quite a lot of clothes made by Gay and me (Gay sews as well as I do) but poor Jane hasn't a stitch so she stays in bed with 'flu most of the time. Bobbie's eyes rattle in her head but Jane still has a china blue stare. ... The irony of it all is that Dublin is full of beautiful toys – export trade from England but the fuss of getting them through is hardly worth it. You have to pay duty and purchase tax and correspond at length with the Board of Trade in London . ...

[Julie] insists on being called Julie now instead of Zoo and it is a good thing. One whole day last week she was Louise and one day she was a mama. She was so indignant because Gay hit her and mamas shouldn't be hit. That day I told her to go in the nursery and play and

---

[90] Joan Strachan was the wife of William Strachan Jun., a director of Harland & Wolff shipyard.

[91] The Ulster Library Scheme for H.M. Forces, based in Belfast, sought donations of books and magazines for British soldiers overseas.

[92] Effanbee Doll Company of New York (founded 1910) introduced the realistic "drink and wet" Dydee (or Didee) doll in 1934 and it was in production until the 1950s.

she said "Mamas don't play they just walk around" and sailed in with her head in the air. She came home from school one day covered with scratches after having a fight with some little boy. They both have a bad Belfast intonation now and Gay says "och! no" and "och yes" – it is a pity but can't be helped. ...

Auntie is as cheerful as can be these days and has regained her happy outlook on life. She had her new ermine coat and hat on at the D.R.C. on Monday and it is terribly becoming as well as looking like Mrs. Gotrocks herself.[93] The paper at the D.R.C. was outstanding. It was by a Mrs. Forbes who is on the education board for the A.T.S. (women soldiers)[94]. She is a captain and every inch a woman in uniform – Her paper was on Chekhov the Russian playwright and short story writer and was it good! Her sidelights and background showed how really brilliant her brain is and since she lectures to the A.T.S. several nights a week her delivery was so good. She was a good friend of Isabel Noble's and used to get me down because she was too arty and intellectual for words but she has come down to earth and is definitely a whiz at her job. ...

[rest of letter lost]

15th Dec.
Sans Souci

Dear Mother and Ginna,

I'm afraid I have left this too late to wish you a merry Christmas but my intentions were so good. All last week I worked every evening, if I did anything, on my broadcast whittling it down. I only had about a week's notice before the script had to be in and the worst was to make it just 3½ minutes. My first effort took 5, reading fast which wasn't so hot but now my script is in, rehearsal Friday morning and it just takes a little over 3. ...

[93] In the American comedy film of 1931, *Honeymoon Lane*, Mrs Gotrocks was "a snooty rich dame"; in urban lingo, a Mr or Mrs Gotrocks is someone who acts as if he or she has lots of money to spend.

[94] Mrs Murray Forbes was Junior Commander of the Auxiliary Territorial Services, the women's branch of the British Army. In 1945 she managed the Ulster Library for the Forces when it was relocated to the Malone area and renamed the Northern Ireland Services Library: *Belfast Telegraph*, 17th December 1945.

Same evening:

> There is a band outside playing Christmas carols ... Our Christmas tree will be coming tomorrow or the next day – such a big one this year but not pretty. However when we get the ornaments on we hope it will make "a good show".
>
> I have had 3 treatments of my second course of X-ray. I will have either 9 or 12 and then I will be through. Now the Salvation Army Band is playing "Holy Night" – we thought of waking the kids but thought they would get too excited. I have got them some Christmas presents at vast expense – 2 rag dolls each and an oddment or two and some books. ...

17th Dec.

> Now it is Friday night – I had a treatment today and I can tell it – just a general pole-axedness – not bad but it makes me not want to run upstairs for anything or even bother to do anything much. They are supposed to be absolutely exhausting and make lots of people "frow up" but not me. ... Today I couldn't go straight to bed because Tommy was here painting from 12 – 4 (with) time out for lunch. The picture is sitting on our piano now and it is wonderful – so like me that it is uncanny in one of my cow-like dreamy moods – looking pleasantly into space. ... The whole household thinks it is a dream and Tommy is pleased with it too. He and Stella and their daughters are coming up to spend Christmas with the Carrs so it should be nearly finished shortly after Christmas. ...
>
> I rehearsed my broadcast today and only had to read it once – Ursula Eason, the programme director said it was "sweet".[95] I hope you can hear it without too much trouble but Ursula was very doubtful. Joan Isaacs[96] is an announcer now and is delighted. I think the B.B.C. would be such fun to work at. ...

[95] Ursula Eason (1901–1993) was born in London. She was appointed organizer for "Children's Hour" in Belfast in 1933. She pioneered television programmes for deaf children and it was she who transformed a quite ordinary series of five-minute programmes acquired from France into what became a cult classic, "The Magic Roundabout". See *Dictionary of Ulster Biography*, online.

[96] For Joan Isaacs, see the letter of 15th November, 1939. She was a stage and radio actress as well as announcer; in a BBC (NI) production of Richard Rowley's play, *Apollo in Mourne*, on Wednesday, 12th January 1938, she played a goddess. *Cont'd*

Lancelot, the big palooka, has turned the radio to the German propaganda program which is such trash.

Did I tell you to read *The Opinions of Oliver Alston* [sic] by Van Wyck Brooks – it is so good.[97] Haven't read anything else for weeks – except the *New Yorker*, the *Denver Post* and the *New Statesman*.

Charlie Mitchell has just arrived in Jamaica where Nancy hopes to join him as soon as she can – most likely after the war. Dunsmuir is in a nursing home struggling with his skin complaint (psoriasis). Hardin [sic] Glendinning is in Italy living in a palace with a priceless library. Stella is having the time of her life with the Americans – goes to 2 or 3 dances a week and Tommy says they might as well be living in America. ...

Played bridge Monday night with our octogenarian neighbors the Miss Macrorys who are a scream. They dress for dinner every night and are so up and coming especially the oldest one who wears a bright red wig. They had a Dr. Burnside there who was so "keen" that he panted all the time[98]. ...

We are toying with, and fighting about, buying the Willie Turtle house in Malone Park[99] which may be on the market after Christmas. It is a dilly in a way – red brick, bay windows but has been improved a lot since the Turtles were in it. It is big and has about an acre of garden which holds us back but we would get more money's worth out of it than out of a more modern house which are all awful – modern and hideous. ... – Life! She is a problem. Some nights (we) remind me

---

[96] *Cont'd:* She had a principal role in *The Middle Watch*, a comedy written by Stephen King-Hall and Ian Hay and performed in the Great Hall of Queen's University Belfast on 20th November 1941 with a cast drawn from the Royal Navy, British Army, WRNS and ATS: *Northern Whig*, 21st November, 1941. For Stephen King-Hall, see the letter of 12th February 1941.

[97] Helen had already recommended works by Van Wyck Brooks (1886–1963), American critic, historian and biographer. *The Opinions of Oliver Allston* (1941) is a wide-ranging expression of Brook's own critical philosophy.

[98] In all likelihood this was W. Massey Burnside MD, LRCP (Licentiate of the Royal College of Physicians) who lived on the Malone Road. He sometimes officiated at British Boxing Board of Control professional bouts.

[99] William H. Turtle, linen manufacturer and Lancelot's uncle, lived at 34 Malone Park in 1932.

exactly of the cartoon strip *Mr. and Mrs.* which always ended up in the dark with "and so far into the night".[100] We have been almost buying a house for 10 years and every road in town has on it a house that we nearly bought. Our Belmont Road house has just been sold for a huge price after the air force were in it for 3½ years wrecking it. I would love to see it now. Mr. McKelvey, a good local artist bought it.[101] ...

[The kids] are a very sturdy pair ... They both love to do everything – some children won't go here or won't go there but not ours who are rarin' to go everyplace. They go to Chapel every Sunday with nurse which would horrify anyone here who heard about it. They both sing so much and so well and Gay pounds the piano in all her spare time. Gay is still frantically jealous of Julie and they fight like Kilkenny cats all day but hate to be separated. Gay bosses Julie lamentably but Julie takes no notice most of the time. Must go to bed.

Happy New Year girls.

27th Dec.
Sans Souci

Dear Mother and Ginna,

... We had such a good time on Christmas Day. ... Our Christmas Day started around 7 – Julie was sitting up in bed with all her things back in her stocking (she woke up around 6 according to Nurse) except 3 – a knife, a magnifying glass and a pen holder and a pen. Gay had to be waked at 8.15 having had a good look at her things sometime during the night – I personally think just after we put them in at midnight – I am sure she knows that there ain't no Santa Claus but she won't let on. Julie however believes in him utterly. ... By using 2 apples and an orange we got their stockings full – new lisle stockings of mine – with gimcrack things – pencils, crayons, card games, little Santa Claus

---

[100] *Mr. and Mrs.* was a comic strip by the American artist Clare Briggs (1875–1930). The CBS radio series of the same name was broadcast from 1929 until 1930.

[101] Frank McKelvey (1895–1974) was a painter born in Belfast who became known chiefly for his landscapes and portraits. During his career he was regarded as on a par with Paul Henry. The re-numbered house is still standing.

lollypops, drawing books, other little books, tin baking dishes, Jello and a paper hat each, and I forget what else ... They are both riots and full of life. How I do get switched off on my kids! ...

[Love,
Helen]

1944

Helen's Christmas broadcast on the
  BBC

Irving Berlin dreams of a white
  Christmas in Belfast

D-Day and the balloon went up

Billy Stephens' escape from Colditz

A super-dooper Christmas

8th Jan.
Sans Souci

Dear Mother and Ginna,

Now it is the 8th of January and so much has happened that I will probably forget to tell it all. ... Tommy went back to Newcastle today so we can have a rest until next Thursday when Gay and I will go. He is painting 2 portraits – the small one is finished – it is the one he brought up from Newcastle every week and he was trying to paint the big one from it but it was too lifeless and now he is doing the big one from life too. He says it is the best big portrait he has done and I think he is making a special effort because Clive Bell gave him a write-up as a children's portrait painter and also because if it is good people here who see it will give him orders. ...

The really big item of news is that we have bought Lumeah in Malone Park and will be moving in May. ... It is a solid, dull-looking, dignified, typical good Belfast red brick house with a tennis-lawn to one side, a garden in front about as wide as the parking on Williams St. [Denver] and a bowling green and vegetable garden and fruit trees at the back. ... no glamour anyplace but a good family house in much the nicest and widest park in the Malone end – completely built up so that it can't be spoiled. We know a lot of the people in the Park – Morwoods, Isaacs, Jim Barr, Jack and Caroline Workman, Barcrofts[1], Bodo and Edith, Maureen's Mother and a few other acquaintances. ...

Edith told me that you both had had dinner with Bodo and that he said that you both looked so nice and were so nice and how smart Ginna looked in her uniform and how gay and witty and charming you both were – all lovely, lovely in fact. I'm so glad you saw him because

[1] Henry Barcroft FRS (1904–1998) was born in Cambridge where his father, Sir Joseph Barcroft FRS, from a Newry, Co. Down Quaker family, was Professor of Physiology at Cambridge University. Henry was himself Dunville Professor of Physiology at Queen's University Belfast, 1935–1948, before becoming Professor of Physiology at St Thomas's Hospital Medical School, London. He was the grandson of Sir Robert Ball (1840–1913), Astronomer Royal of Ireland, and great-grandson of the Irish naturalist Robert Ball (1802–1857), President of the Royal Geological Society of Ireland. For Jim Barr's mother, Mrs Ainsworth Barr CBE, see the letter of 21st February 1939.

when he comes home in Feb. we will get sort of first-hand news. Bodo has just been promoted to Commander – a "brass hat" he is now. He was one of 3 R.N.V.Rs [Royal Naval Volunteer Reserve] promoted – a great honor. ...

9th Jan.

Now it is Sunday night and Gay's birthday like Manfred's passed off quite quietly. Auntie and Julie came to tea and we had 7 big candles on a good cake iced with cocoa icing and Mary Lee sat up in her high chair gnawing a biscuit and was the life and soul of the party. ...

Holy Matrimony [2] was here a week or two ago but I didn't get there though I meant to. *Colonel Blimp* is here this week. [3] *This is the Army* is coming on Thursday for about 10 days – the original New York company – Gordon stood for four hours trying to book seats but had to give up. The crowds were so enormous that 18 policemen had to get their batons out. The next day the queue began to form at 4 a.m. It is so disappointing but the seats are nearly gone now. [4]

I'm sorry you didn't hear my broadcast but it was doubtful. I'll send you a copy of it. Not a great many people heard it but it made Benita Isaacs cry and several unexpected people told me it was good. ... and

---

[2] *Holy Matrimony* is a 1943 Hollywood comedy based on Arnold Bennett's novel, *Buried Alive* (1908) about a reclusive painter who exchanges his identity with his dead valet. The screenwriter Nunnally Johnson was nominated for an Academy Award but lost out to the writers of *Casablanca* (1942).

[3] *The Life and Death of Colonel Blimp* (1943) is an ambitious historical war film of sharply contemporary significance. It was written and directed by Michael Powell and Emeric Pressburger. The film borrowed its title from David Low's famous cartoon character who personifies British jingoism and ineffectual wind-baggery. Churchill was vehemently opposed to the film, seeing it as presenting a demoralizing image of the British soldier; the Ministry of War thus refused to release Laurence Olivier from war duty to star in the film; Powell and Pressburger engaged a lesser-known actor, Roger Livesey, to play the lead character. The film is nowadays regarded as a classic.

[4] Belfast was the only UK city outside London in which Irving Berlin's stage musical, *This is the Army*, played for more than one week. The musical opened with a gala performance in the Royal Opera House on Thursday, 13th January. Most of the cast were serving in the war. Berlin came to Belfast for rehearsals and was one of the performers, singing "I'm Dreaming of a White Christmas" and "Oh, How I Hate to Get Up in the Morning!" The *Northern Whig and Belfast Post* (14th January, 1944) thought the musical the best thing produced in Belfast for many a day.

Doug[5] wrote me a letter – I had written to him to tell him to listen. He said that the mention of Denver was music to his ears and that I had an exceptionally beautiful voice for an American. He said that he so often is so embarrassed for his fellow countrymen in discussions with English doctors because of their speech and choice of words. He is very busy but is coming over some time.

Lancelot is re-reading a lecture he has written on a disease that attacks bees – he belongs to a bee club. ...

Dr. Foster said that all the rest in the world wouldn't prevent the cancer returning if it was going to and said to go on leading a normal life and forget I ever had it – which I do. ... People still feel that they have to tell me how well I'm looking all the time and I feel fine – any tiredness is natural after so big an operation and after the X-ray treatments. I look young and so nice in the portrait despite my sprinkling of gray hairs. *Must* go to bed – it is midnight again – or nearly – Happy New Year – it will only really be happy for me completely if we meet but I don't think about it ... I think the war will be over by Easter – bombing will do it – to hell with their army.

Love,
Helen

12th Jan.
Sans Souci

Dear Ginna and Mother,

Here is my broadcast more or less as it was – they didn't give me a typed copy so I made it out from a few scratched up notes. Did I tell you I got £2.2.0 when income tax – £1.1.0 – comes off, ain't it awful[6]. I had a treatment today – my next to last and feel "feek" and "weeble" and my hair is more thatchy than usual because I washed it and left soap in the crown. I have on high heels – Cuban because I was at Edie's for tea and they make me so nervous. Gay was out today for the first – it was mild and she is still fine. She looks a bit peaked but otherwise

---

[5] Doug Moore, a Denver doctor friend of Helen's, stationed somewhere in England with the American forces.

[6] Helen would have been paid three guineas (three pounds, three shillings) for her broadcast.

there are no ill effects. She won't go back to school for another week or more. Julie is as lively as a cricket and as naughty as she can be – but so funny. At the end of lunch today we 3 got the giggles because I said the day was shockin'[7] – it reminded me of the time we went to work up in the attic. Serious as Gay is if there is a joke she laughs like a loon and can't stop. Did Auntie tell you that Julie said her combinations were semi-detached? They were so cute at the circus and Gay lives through everything so. After the lion taming act the ringleader asked if any lady in the audience would come up and *rassle* with the lion and Julie clung on to me and "Don't *you* go, Mummy" or did I tell you that Julie is back at school. Gay and I are going to pose tomorrow. I met such a nice English girl at Edie's today – she was telling us that she heard a story about General Montgomery. When the King was in Africa he, the King, was reviewing the troops with General Alexander and he said "What is General Montgomery like". General Alexander said "Oh, he's nice enough but I'm afraid he's after my job". The King said "Oh, I'm relieved to hear that I thought he was after mine!" Maybe Montgomery's conceit and publicity hunting aren't well enough known over there for you to get the point. ...

I am so glad you sent me those 6 new pairs of dotted Swiss curtains for Christmas – they will be so useful in our new house because we are terribly shy of curtains – thank you so much. ... Curtain material here is only obtainable by giving clothes coupons so the situation is impossible. ... However, after the war we will let fly with plastics or material made out of milk. ... Auntie is walking on air. The American Consul has asked her to a dinner party and to go to see *This is the Army*. Everybody in town is dying to go ... Something like this will set Auntie up for the whole spring. She has her hair up in curlers, is going to stay home tomorrow to give herself a facial and she is literally as excited as a bride. Tomorrow night where she is going is the opening night and a gala night with the Duke and Duchess going to be there *and all*.[8] I can hardly wait to hear about it. Must get L. his nightly drink of buttermilk and me some pop and then go to bed. Oh yes! Seats for

---

[7] An Ulster colloquialism.

[8] Attending the opening gala performance in the Grand Opera House of Irving Berlin's musical were the Duke of Abercorn (Governor of Northern Ireland) and the Duchess, the Prime Minster of Northern Ireland Sir Basil Brooke and Lady Brooke, and ranking American soldiers.

tomorrow night are £1 each and the paper said they could have sold out for £5 a seat. Maureen said in a tram today when an American got out the conductor told the whole tram that that was one of the actors from *This is the Army*. As our maid Kathleen would say "Isn't it awful". Meaning equally isn't it wonderful? Or Isn't it terrible. Awful is her one adjective.

Goodnight and love,
Helen

"A CHILDHOOD CHRISTMAS – AMERICAN"[9]

Whenever I half-shut my eyes and look at a candle-flame I think of Christmas and if by any chance I have a sprig of pine tree to smell at the same time I am instantly back in America and it is Christmas Eve. I am standing gazing at our lighted tree and whether I am 6 or 7 or 8 years old I never know because my memory blurs and I am any child at any Christmas tree with all the excitements rolled into one.

We lived in Colorado 2000 miles West of New York across the plains and prairie at the foot of the Rocky Mountains. We were very proud that our city of Denver was a mile high and we children believed that the sun on the snow dazzled our eyes more and that the stars seem closer because we were a mile nearer heaven. This was shortly after the last war before the electrically lighted outdoor Christmas trees and elaborate municipal decorations made all American cities like fairyland. But even then the decorations were something. Every house was gay with holly wreaths at the window, pine bough on the stairs and best of all the Christmas tree. This usually touched the ceiling and was hung with as much tinsel and as many shining ornaments as it could hold – hence the American expression "All dressed up like a Christmas Tree".

On Christmas Eve we hung up our stockings at the fireplace and sat waiting for bedtime. Our next door neighbor, a collaborator in the Christmas myth, always rang a string of sleigh bells out of her attic window and I'll never forget the fright we got the year they rang when we were still downstairs and we thought that Santa Claus was on our rooftop before we were even in bed.

---

[9] Helen's reminiscence was in the BBC Home Service programme, "At Home Today", broadcast at 9.30am, 20th December 1943.

Christmas morning was always the same at our house. It didn't matter which of the 3 children awoke first, our excited chatter and frantic struggling with long winter underwear and panty-waists soon roused the household. It was a strict law that we weren't to go downstairs until we were properly clothed and my father said so. We had to wait until he came up from the basement and made his annual remark that just as he was stoking the furnace he heard old Santa scrambling up the chimney. That was our cue and we dashed downstairs to the living room like a whirlwind to clutch our stockings and to try to open all the packages under the tree at once.[10] I suppose we ate breakfast but I have no recollection of it – my picture begins and ends on the living room floor where we spent the morning with our toys.

Our midday Christmas dinner was a family gathering with the usual Christmas fare. The highlights for us children being the turkey, cranberry sauce, candied sweet potatoes with marshmallows on top and ice cream and cake.

In the afternoon we sometimes went visiting or if the snow was tightly packed on the roads we were allowed as a special treat to tie our sleds behind the automobile for a ride – but whatever we did it was all enchanted because it was Christmas Day.

As we grew older our Christmases became gayer and more hectic – more shopping, more parties, more people and more fuss but the essential magic of Christmas for me is in my earlier years because as one of my own children says "Santa Claus is the magicest of all".

28th Jan.
Sans Souci

Dear Mother and Ginna,

... Now it is Friday night. I spent the day in bed with one day 'flu reading Edith Wharton's autobiography[11] and sleeping and now I am up by the fire feeling good but I would have a headache if I shook my head.

---

[10] Unlike their American counterparts, British children customarily receive their Christmas presents in stockings or pillow-cases slung at the foot of their beds.

[11] Wharton's *A Backward Glance* was published in 1934.

7th Feb.

… Just talked to Maureen – we are going to see *Now Voyager* or something with Bette Davis tomorrow – she still reminds me so much of Ginna that I never miss a picture – the last one I saw was *Watch on the Rhine* which I thought was superb.[12] I went to 3 in succession one week and an art lecture at the end – 3 days in succession I mean. I am so keen on pictures – always have been in a very inactive or unconscious way but now it has come to the surface. I went to 2 very good lectures at the Museum.[13] Our portrait has come to an unfortunate phase – Tommy is disappointed with the big one and thinks he will have to cut out the separate heads which are individually good but the ensemble is undoubtedly stiff. The small one is graceful and easy though it is nearly exactly like the big one but just a difference or two spoils it. We were all there yesterday to have L. take a photograph of us in a new position with me looking at the baby and Julie more relaxed and leaning against me. The trouble is that 4 of us present a nice problem of grouping that Tommy wasn't quite experienced enough to master or at least he wasn't careful enough about the positions and got so lost painting that he didn't notice that it was pretty stiff as a whole. Anyway it won't be lost because he can cut out the heads and the painting itself is charming and really 1st class. He is very proud of Gay's head which is the best. Anyway you stand a very good chance of getting some of them sent to you. I laughed so yesterday because the baby is 4 months older than when he started and her legs kept getting in everybody's way – they are twice as long as they were before. She has completely lost her shyness and chortled and

[12] *Now, Voyager* is a 1942 Hollywood movie with a screenplay based on the 1941 novel by Olive Higgins Prouty that took its title from Walt Whitman. Davis was nominated for an Oscar for Best Actress. *Watch on the Rhine* was released in 1943, adapted by Dashiell Hammett from the 1941 Broadway play by Lillian Hellman. Paul Lukas plays a German anti-Fascist activist. The film was nominated for a Best Picture Oscar.

[13] Helen may well have attended a lecture in Belfast Museum on 26th January by John Hewitt on "The Adventure of Subjectivity". Hewitt (1907–1987), who was an art curator in the Museum and who became a well-known poet and cultural figure in Northern Ireland, advanced the argument that artists were experimenting in dream, symbol and fantasy in reaction against technical progress and political and economic instability: *Belfast News-Letter*, 27th Jan, 1944. And she may have attended a lecture on "Science and the Preservation of Foodstuffs" on 19th January by A.J. Kidney [sic].

yoohooed[14] on the tram and at the Carrs. The whole town, at least all we know and some we hardly know are dying to see this portrait.

... There is the best dance band just going off the air – it had me nearly out of my shoes wiggling my toes. Now there is the entertainment for factory workers[15] – if you want quite a good picture of wartime England go to see the film *Millions Like Us*.[16] There is a revolution going on all right – very quietly but surely with no maids between about 15 and 60. ...

Love,
Helen

3rd Feb.
Mahee

Dear Ginna,

It is like old times being back at Mahee for a few days and it is so nice! We came on Tuesday for our last day of thrashing [threshing] and decided to stay until Saturday night. ... I have just done the fires, and looked at the kids and now the 9 o'clock news is on. ... They have just announced the death of Raymond Clapper.[17]

It is a wild and windy but moonlit night. We have had until today 5 days of May-like weather. Sunday was downright hot. We went to Dublin to May Hannigan's funeral. ... Do you remember Jonty?[18] ...

[14] Until around the 1960s when traffic drowned out voices, women shoppers would attract the attention of acquaintances on the other side of the road by hooting "Yo-ho" or "Yoo-hoo". Mary Lee is imitating the sound.

[15] Helen was listening to Charles Shadwell conducting the BBC Variety Orchestra (10.00am–10.30am) before the perennial "Music While You Work" for factory workers.

[16] *Millions Like Us* was made in 1943 and is a British docudrama portraying life in a wartime aircraft factory, many of the workers being women. Helen is alluding to the current and likely post-war scarcity of female domestic help in the light of the non-domestic jobs women have in wartime proven themselves capable of holding down.

[17] Raymond Clapper (b.1892) was killed in a plane crash on 1st February 1944. He was a Kansas-born journalist who became one of the most influential newspapermen in Washington DC. He was an FDR supporter and an early advocate of the United States taking up arms in aid of Europe attacked by Germany. He died when the plane he was in collided with another during the U.S. invasion of the Marshall Islands in the Pacific theatre.

[18] See the letter of 20th September 1942.

He is a psycho-analyst and a character. It was his wife May, Lancelot's first cousin who died suddenly on Thursday of a stroke. ... Jonty is such an egoist that it is hard to tell if there is anything to him or whether it is all blow. ...

15th Feb.

... Clothes are a big problem here now between prices of $80 to $100[19] for a suit – anything for a hat and upwards of $50 for a dress – not to mention the constant struggle with coupons. ... I am now pinning my hope to a prognosis in *Stars and Stripes* that says the war will end April 9th.[20] How is Ma? Does she get depressed and mad still and does she let you lead your own life? Do you think she is happy? Are you happy? ... If only we could see each other! I often think it is a pity that our letters are so remote and polite and so unrevealing. I only know that when I had my operation I longed for you so that I couldn't bring myself to mention your name and Lancelot had to say "If only Ginna were here – with her common sense". So that, far and all as you are away, we lean on the thought of you like on a pillar. ...

Love,
Helen

20th Feb.
Sans Souci

Dear Mother,

... We lost 79 bombers last night – the worst ever which is appalling but there must not be much left of Leipzig.[21]

---

[19] That is, £96 to £120. That is £4200 to £5300 at today's rate.

[20] *Stars and Stripes* is an American military newspaper published in the U.S but with a print run for service personnel overseas; it has been published in Europe continuously since 1942. An early editor, Harold Ross, founded the *New Yorker* magazine.

[21] The German city of Leipzig had been bombed heavily by the RAF in early December 1943, and sustained the loss of 1800 lives and many historic buildings. On 20th February 1944, 700 American and British bombers returned and dropped 2300 tons of explosives, killing almost 1000 people.

Auntie has a new picture and a new Persian rug that she wants me to come see. It is a shockin' cold day.

22rd Feb.

Now it is Tuesday and I am playing our new gramophone record "This is the Army" and do I love it. It is from the show with *Stage Door Canteen* on the other side – which is so sweet and so sad.[22] Stella is here – out shopping now – she is so gay and laughs so much and has such an American atmosphere about her – cartons of American cigarettes, an American officer's gloves and a misty look in her eye at the mention of Americans – she dances once or twice a week with one special one and about 4 come to their house all the time. Stella is as thin as ever and wears her hair up with a bow on top. She hasn't much to her – maybe more than I think – but she is so free from convention, repression and cattiness that she is very refreshing. ...

Had a letter from Doug this morning – he is tied up until nearly the end of March and then he is coming over – rain or shine he says invasion or no invasion. Everybody here is working up to a fever pitch of excitement over the terrific bombing and the impending invasion which everybody prays won't have to take place.

23rd Feb.

Now it is Wednesday and I just took Julie to have her first sun-ray treatment 2 minutes only. A friend of ours 5 minutes walk away has a sun-lamp – Betty Williams (one little boy Gavin aged 3) so in exchange for honey and an egg or two when our hens lay well we have struck an agreement – Julie will have 3 a week – and I may take Gay too – Treatments by a masseuse are 7/6 a time so we are saving over £1.0.0 a week. Kay Mackie has one too but the trip to Knock [a Belfast district] by tram and bus takes ¾ of an hour to an hour each way so this is much handier and another thing is that I don't want to be beholden to Kay because they have everything and wouldn't take money so we would just be "beholden" – such a good word that I got

---

[22] The 1943 American film *Stage Door Canteen* included musical numbers amidst the dramatic scenes set in a New York restaurant and nightclub for American and Allied servicemen. Many stars played cameo roles.

out of the movie *The Philadelphia Story*. Everybody whose children have had this – Roberta and Eileen and Rosemary Bryson swear that it improves their appetites and causes general improvement and gain in weight.[23] I am not going to let Julie go back full-time to school but only from 9.30–11 and then I will bring her home to sleep. She has been below par all winter – nothing bad and no one but a fusser like me would notice it so I hope this sun-lamp, more rest, more fresh air and a tonic will make her a big strongie again. ...

Fancy Ginna liking that poem "Pan and Syrinx" – I love it too and will send you all of his poems – I gave them to Jim Barr for Christmas. W. R. Rodgers is an Ulsterman – surprise! Surprise! A Presbyterian minister who lives near Portadown and whose wife, according to rumour is a dipsomaniac.[24]

28 Feb.

Now it is Monday morning. Ginna's 4th wedding anniversary and a lovely sunny day. ... I have just done the laundry and feel very virtuous – it really is the extent of my housekeeping. I am completely spoiled – I have breakfast in bed often ... Ma, it's awful, but in a furnished house in which now I haven't a crumb of interest because we are moving so soon – what can a girl do? ...

Stella left yesterday and she said she had a wonderful time. She is very alive and interested in everything and enjoys everything. ... We kept going most of the time – Monday – D. Room Circle (Stella's remark being "Where did they dig them all up?") ... Tuesday we went

---

[23] After World War Two, sun-ray therapy with ultra-violet lamps became even more prevalent, and was used to combat chest infections, tonsillitis, sore throats and acne and to develop sun-tans. It was discontinued in the 1960s when the connection between ultra-violet rays and skin cancer was established.

[24] W.R. Rodgers (1909–1969) was a Belfast-born poet who achieved a British and Irish reputation for poetry of great rhythmic vitality and energetic word-play. The first of two volumes, *Awake! And Other Poems* appeared in 1941 while Rodgers was a Presbyterian minister in Loughgall, Co. Armagh. His wife was then Dr Marie Harden Waddell, a general practitioner. Helen does her an injustice. Subject to depression, she was diagnosed as schizophrenic around the time of Helen's letter. She was the niece of Rutherford Mayne (Samuel Waddell), the Ulster playwright, and Helen Waddell the scholar and author of *Peter Abelard* (1933); Michael Longley calls her an unfulfilled writer in his Introduction to W.R. Rodgers, *Poems* (Gallery Press, 1993). Marie Rodgers died in 1953.

to a poor movie – *Flesh and Fantasy*[25] and Caroline and Paddy came to play bridge at night and Jack Workman later to talk to L. who was feeling seedy with his cold. He likes Stella so well too. She is so snappy on a shoestring and reminds me always of a fashion drawing in *Vogue* or *Harper's Bazaar* – with her odd face, big eyes, arched eyebrows, huge red mouth, and hanging hair or hair up and long red nails. Going about with her was like taking a freak around – she is stared at worse than Ginna ever was – because she is so very foreign looking and acting – she laughs all the time and is so animated and makes so many gestures that she makes everyone else look half dead. ...

Love in haste,
Helen

8th Mar.
Sans Souci

Dear Ginna,

Gambling on this letter making it in 20 days – Happy Birthday! To think that you are 32! But never to me. Even when I am 61 and you are 60 you will always seem young and fair I should think. ... We were in Dublin for it – my birthday so apart from being wished Happy Birthday at the dance the night before no notice was taken and it "passed quite quietly" just as well too because when one is 33 too much notice is sort of sad. ... Lunch at Philip's club – then *Holy Matrimony* (highlight of the whole trip), and had tea and got dressed for dinner – people arrived at 7 and I didn't start to dress until 10 to 7 and took a bath – rushing around wildly and unable to do a thing with my hair after a steamy bath – broke a tooth in a hard toffee whilst dressing and being tired kept wondering is it worth it? ... The dinner was good and with 2 enormous sherrys before it I bucked up but after dinner we had to go to the dance on the tram which I must say does at 32 take the gilt off the gingerbread ... the tram stopped outside the Gresham [Hotel] door but on a cold night, with no underwear on

---

[25] A 1943 American film, starring Edward G. Robinson, Barbara Stanwyck and Charles Boyer, that tells three separate supernatural tales. The *New York Times* agreed with Helen, thinking it "so much palaver".

hanging around street corners is no great shakes. The dance was so-so. There were among those present a coloured couple, a Jap, and a pair of midgets – nothing if not Cosmopolitan. There was one good dancer but I hit a slow fox-trot with him and couldn't follow him – however later, we did a waltzy and a quickstep (doesn't it take you back?) so it wasn't so bad. ...

There is still a great uncomfortableness about being in Dublin – any war picture is banned although the newspapers give war news from both sides – prices are scandalous – bacon nearly $1.00 (£1.30) butter and sugar all bought in the black market and made into cakes sold in cake shops – at wild prices. Chocolates are all around $1.50 a pound. The things that are cheaper are drink, cigarettes, cosmetics, jewelry and things without the terrific tax on them. Clothes are all expensive and they have no utility.[26] There is no coal at all for private use and petrol only for taxis and a little for doctors. ...

[*Letter unfinished?*]

17th Mar.
Sans Souci

Dear Mother and Ginna,

... This is Friday now – how time flies! It seems only a minute since last Sunday. Lancelot is reading his bee book, the fire made of coke (to save coal) is crackling and spitting and the radio is playing a concert. ...

The Irish news – the ban on travel to England was the talk of the town allright, allright.[27] The North has taken it so well, it seems to me – when you think that if L. were in the services in England he couldn't spend his leaves at home – I think it is the pink limit. Everyone thinks the South had it coming to them and also think that the Border should

---

[26] Utility "civilian clothing" was introduced by the British government in 1941 (hence the label CC41) to control prices, limit use of raw materials, and lessen labour required in production.

[27] Helen is parodying Ulster colloquial emphatic repetition.

be closed too but it would take so many people to guard it that it doesn't seem feasible.[28]

When we were in Dublin the Scanlans told us all about the big scare of invasion in the South the week before. The Army was standing by, there was explosive in the hedges ready to blow them up (Philip *saw* it) and the rumors were wild – a British invasion by sea was expected hourly and the border was supposed to be solid with American tanks ready to invade. By the weekend we were there it was all a joke (we hadn't heard anything about it) and the Sunday we left the man across the street told Phil very hush hush that the real reason was that the German and Jap Consuls were being threatened but none of us believed it! Eire was easing along so nicely that it looked as if she could sail right through the war with only minor difficulties but this travel ban is very hard to bear because it punishes so many people and the Irish ones are great ones for coming home.

… I was just planning next week with the aid of my engagement diary. Funny how you get so booked up so far ahead here that you have to keep a book to remember. I have kept them ever since we were married and I have them all and it is quite fun to look back on them. Next week I am trying to work in a trip to Newcastle to spend the night. Tommy wants me to come to finish the big portrait. The small one is hanging behind me – most people like it – the people who are more used to looking at pictures and who are more interested in them like it better than others. The ones not used to pictures don't think it is good enough of me – i.e. it doesn't flatter me but it is really exactly my expression. Everyone can see that it isn't good of Julie – it isn't a bit like her face – anyway we like it on the whole. …

Last Saturday we went by train to Portadown and then by taxi to Mullavilla where Norman is all packed up ready to go.[29] We bought –

---

[28] The Common Travel Area comprising the UK and the Republic of Ireland was suspended in 1939 at the outbreak of war with some travel restrictions imposed. Later, as a result of the neutral Irish government's refusal to expel diplomats of the Axis countries, the UK on 13th March 1944 suspended travel between the two islands. (Exceptions were made for Ulster boys and girls at English boarding schools.) Northern Irish citizens of the UK were incensed at immigration controls when they crossed to the mainland, and which were in place until 1952. The ban prevented Bodo Taggart's uncle, the vicar of Denby in England, from attending Bodo's father's funeral in Northern Ireland: *Belfast News-Letter*, 4th October, 1940.

[29] Norman Turtle's house and linen factory in County Armagh were called Mullavilla. He and wife Iris and his brother Herbert and American wife Katherine were preparing to move to the United States; an auction of textile machinery and mill furnishings was held in the spring of 1944.

provisionally – all the carpets out of Lumeah and all the net curtains, a white kitchen dresser and 2 kitchen tables, Katherine's American 4-poster mahogany bed (so nice!) not tall posters, also Katherine's day bed (American) – like a couch and it makes a double bed! . ... We hope to get to see the house in a week or so. ... – the problems that are going to beset us are *legion*.

Anyway if I go to Newcastle for Friday and Saturday Stella might find me a partner for the Saturday night dance among the Americans she knows – I am very curious to see her American beau – a captain from Illinois – a farmer. Which reminds me – about those plants which you want for beekeeping – they are called ANISE – HYSSOP and you can get the seed at 20 cents per packet from Mr. Melvin Pellett of Atlantic, Iowa.[30] Lancelot thinks that 3 or 4 packets will be enough and hopes you can get them. ...

Doug won't get over now. It was doubtful anyway because even before the ban soldiers weren't allowed to spend leaves in Ulster. I am so sorry because I was so looking forward to his visit. We had the nicest American boy here yesterday from New York – aged 22, married with a baby boy one year old. He came because he wanted to play with children – the Red Cross Club sent him and he was wonderful with the children. De Valera is now speaking in Irish – we will hear him in a minute in English – the big bo-hunk[31] ... This is St. Patrick's night and all the Americans are confined to barracks, I heard by listening in to a telephone conversation... Here is Dev. In English – he started 1500 years ago – like Hitler. Poor old Ireland – always in trouble. I used to think I would like to live in Dublin but after having this Irish nurse knowing Gordon and seeing the life the Scanlans live, I have changed my mind – they are too easy going even for me and you can't believe a word they say – this nurse and Gordon are so typical – they agree with everything and you never know where you are. They are so lacking in common sense but they are so funny and so crazy – but would get you down, I think, to see too much of them and all they care about is pleasure. Dev. is asking for men for the army! ...

---

[30] Anise hyssop is a North American flower rich in nectar and a great attractor of bees. Melvin Pellett belonged to an internationally known horticulturalist family.

[31] American derogatory slang for a man of central European descent, extended by Helen because of de Valera's height; she is presumably listening to Radio Eireann.

I am taking iron again getting into trim for this moving or as they say here "the flitting". ... I had [Dr Foster] look at my lymph ducts which are blocked again in my arm but it is the effect of the X-ray still working. He says that it is like the scar tissue on a deep burn that only heals 6 weeks later – the X-ray makes things inside contract as it heals.

I do feel much better lately – the iron helps because the X-ray goes for the red corpuscles and I didn't take it religiously enough while I was taking the treatment. ... My hair is in better shape too and looks quite cute. ...

Nighty-night and love,
Helen

21st Mar.
Sans Souci

Dear Mother,

Here is a picture that was in the paper of Julie being a Mannequin.[32] She was the only one whose picture was in though they took several. From left to right are Mrs. Atkinson [of the W.V.S], who described the dresses and told what they were made from and how much they cost – usually nothing, sometimes two pence or sixpence for thread or buttons. Next Lady Stronge[33] who is head of the W.V.S. [Women's Voluntary Services] in Northern Ireland and who takes life so seriously, next the Duchess of Abercorn[34] who made such a funny and witty

[32] The Domestic Front exhibition in Belfast City Hall was opened on 8th March by the Duchess of Abercorn and ran until 18th March. The exhibition displayed "methods of solving every imaginable wartime problem for the housewife", including clothing, feeding and heating the family: *Belfast News-Letter*, 2nd March. The photograph of Julie as a child model in front of the assorted dignitaries appeared in the *Belfast News-Letter* for 9th March 1944.

[33] Lady Stronge OBE was born Gladys Hall and in 1921 married Sir Norman Stronge (1894–1981), decorated veteran of the Great War. He was a sitting Unionist member of the Northern Ireland parliament between 1938 and 1969 and Speaker of the House, 1945–1969. On 21st January 1981, Stronge (aged 86) and his son James were murdered by the Provisional IRA while watching television at their home, Tynan Abbey, Co. Armagh, which was then burned to the ground.

[34] Lady Rosalind Bingham (1869–1958) became the Duchess of Abercorn when in 1894 she married James Hamilton, 3rd Duke, first Governor of Northern Ireland, 1922–1945. She was President of the National Federation of Women's Institutes of Northern Ireland.

speech and who is so nice and next the Lord Mayor Sir Crawford McCullagh.[35] . ... The next lap belongs to Lady Brooke wife of the Prime Minister[36] – Mr. Andrews was put out about a year ago. That day, the opening was fun but other days it was pretty much of a scramble and a mess but the children were always sweet and unselfconscious

The daffodils are all coming out in the gardens and look so sweet. That Charles of the Ritz is doing my skin so much good.[37] You can get creams etc. here but there is 100% tax on them. I shudder to think what Elizabeth Arden things are now. ... Ken [Topping] in his usual dogmatic way says that the Border will be closed any minute now. L. thinks it won't but even if it stays open I think the tourist traffic will fall off by leaps and bounds because everybody is so mad again. They could easily make you have a permit to travel but the consensus of opinion is that it would take too many soldiers to guard the Border effectively – 200 miles of mountainous border and in the town of Pettigo the border goes through the middle of the town and people wouldn't be allowed to cross the street![38] If we go to Dublin now we will have to say that we have to go to see Mrs. Turtle because going for fun would definitely be frowned on now. Not that it fizzes on Eire – St. Patrick's Night was the gayest ever with the trams solid with people in white ties etc. Now that I think of it I would like to live there – life is such a joke – and you don't have to drink and play cards all the time which they mostly do.

Nancy [Mitchell] was here for supper Saturday night. Charlie [Mitchell] loves Jamaica and has bought a car and a polo pony. He says that they have heard of the war there but only as a distant and dim

---

[35] Sir Crawford McCullagh (1868–1948, knighted in 1915) combined a successful business career with a career as Unionist politician (Stormont M.P. 1921–1928 and Lord Mayor of Belfast, 1915–1917; 1931–1942; 1943–1946).

[36] Lady Brooke (1897–1970) was born Cynthia Surgison and in 1919 married Sir Basil Brooke, later Prime Minister of Northern Ireland. During the war she was Senior Commandant of the Auxiliary Territorial Service (ATS).

[37] From 1926 Charles Jundt marketed his beauty products under the name of Charles of the Ritz [Hotel]; because of the high tax during the war, Helen appears to have got the products from Denver.

[38] The river Termon flows through the village of Pettigo and marks the border between County Donegal (in the Republic of Ireland) and County Fermanagh (in Northern Ireland); the Northern Irish section of the village is officially called Tullyhommon.

noise. Here is the news – the only place that the Germans aren't being licked hollow is Italy. No one understands Italy – the fighting, I mean! Am going to meet Mrs. Barr at 3 to hear Sir Richard Livingstone – Auntie is going too. ... Wednesday night L. is going to a bee meeting and Paddy [Metcalfe] and I are going to the Film society to see a French film with Raimu called *L'Etrange M. Somebody*.[39]

I still think the war will be over before the autumn but nobody else does. Did I tell you Roberta's brother got the D.F.C.?[40] We hardly ever see Roberta or Harry any more. Roberta is so busy ... and Harry is busy too and what entertaining they do seems to be naval. ...

Love and kisses,
Helen

27th Mar.
Sans Souci

Dear Ginna,

Just a quickie while I sit in the *sun*! We are having our 4th divine day – birds singing, flowers bursting into blossom, sun all day and never a cloud in the sky. Julie has just had her sun treatment and has gone for her rest. Mary Lee is talking away beside me in the pram – practising as Gay calls it. Today Auntie entertains the D.R.C. – 40 strong she thinks – it is Gordon and Arabella's last day in Belfast – their furniture went on Friday and they are going tomorrow but they won't move into their new house until after Easter. They are having it done up from head to toe. ... Gordon is the nicest man – much too good for this world and so dumb he can hardly get around – but so kind and he absolutely ruins Arabella and does everything she tells him to. ...

It sounds as if 1000 bombers were over Essen last night and only 9 missing.[41] Friday's loss of 73 was terrible.[42] When I see a newsreel I feel

---

[39] The much lauded *L'Étrange Monsieur Victor* is a 1938 French film by Jean Grémillon that stars the French screen and stage actor Raimu (Jules Auguste César Muraire) as the title character, and Madelaine Renaud.

[40] For Fred Gardiner, see the letters of 16th May, 1st August and 29th August 1940 and 26th July 1943.

[41] The industrial city of Essen in the Ruhr region of Germany was a prime bombing target for the Allies. On the night 26th–27th March 1944, 705 bombers were involved in the latest assault.

such a heel to be sitting here so happily and comfortably. ... G., J. and I went on a picnic on Saturday on the shores of the [River] Lagan - such fun it is and they fall into the spirit of a "toot"[43] so well and are so funny and so interested in everything. They ran barefoot along the tow path and had such a good time – so many adventures, Gay said and once when she had a handful of things – leaves, ferns etc she said that she had a handful of nature! We met the Johnsons and their 2 boys, Galway and Carol. Mrs. Johnson is French and her husband is English – a sculptor, an artist and in the brakes business for a living. Mrs. Johnson is such a mumper and a grumper. They are not very well off but she is a mumper anyway – hates the people here, hates Belfast because there is no culture, concerts etc. and couldn't understand how I could like it – because I do like it. ... [44]

5 Apr.

This is Wednesday April 5th – a cool, very damp day. I caught a cold in Newcastle over the weekend and still am all stuffed up with catarrah [sic] (never could spell it). Everybody has hanging on colds – Julie has catarrah too and Gay has a cough. The weather is lousy. It broke a week ago after 3 hot days like summer. The weekend in Newcastle was no fun because Tommy and Stella, as I told you, are about to separate and the atmosphere would kill you. Tommy never speaks to Stella and sometimes doesn't answer when she speaks to him. Stella is madly in

[42] *From previous page*: On the night of 24th–25th March, the RAF lost 72 planes (or 9% of the attacking force) in a bombing raid on Berlin. It was on this raid that an RAF rear gunner, Nicholas Alkemade, bailed out of his burning Lancaster without a parachute and survived a fall of 18,000 ft by landing on pine trees and soft snow; he suffered a sprained ankle; he was a prisoner of war much admired by his captors. Four of the seven-man Lancaster crew died. See "Nicholas Alkemade": Wikipedia; also www.warhistoryonline.com>nicholas-alkemade-the-raf-airman

[43] American word for a spree.

[44] For Nevill Johnson, see the letter of 5th October 1940. Madame Johnson was a music and French teacher, holding her classes at 11b Botanic Avenue. And, supplying the culture that she felt Belfast lacked, she sponsored an art exhibition in the same location later that year entitled "Salon des Independants". This showcased works by the emerging younger northern artists (born between 1910 and 1920) including Colin Middleton, George Campbell, Daniel (Dan) O'Neill, John Turner, Gerard (Gerry) Dillon, Markey (Marcus) Robinson and Tom Minton. See *Belfast News-Letter*, 3rd October, 1944. Several of these artists later established enduring reputations.

love with an American Captain who spends all his spare time with her.
We went dancing at the hotel Saturday night with him and his room-
mate, a very nice boy from Columbus married, 26, going to run a small
town newspaper when he goes home "and never cross the county line
again". They were both 10 mo. in Iceland first – I mean before they
came here also Scotland and England. … Stella's beau is a farmer from
Illinois, not a bit good looking, very dark with thick black eyebrows
and a huge wart on his cheek. He is as nice as he can be – reminded me
of Lloyd in his easy manner and his obvious popularity but not at all
in looks. If there weren't a war on I know Stella would run away with
him – as it is she wants to separate from Tommy but Tommy won't let
her. As soon as the Americans go she is going to get a job. The ban on
travel to England cramps her style badly because her mother was going
to get her a job in the American Red Cross Club in Bournemouth where
she works herself – Stella's mother aged 49 has been conscripted in
England!!! The situation in Newcastle is as you may guess fantastic –
Stella wearing her Captain's 2-bar on her collar – goes out with him
every chance she gets, Ann and Veronica love him, he is friendly to
Tommy if not exactly friends with him and Stella still shares a narrow
bed with Tommy! It beats all. I posed like mad in their freezing dining
room. Tommy talked and laughed with me – he never scintillates but
was more natural – but I can see how unhappy and embittered he is.
The marriage was a great mistake but I think Stella has tried harder
than Tommy to make it go. He gives terrible digs at the Americans in
general and under the circumstances I had to keep my answers back.
Time will tell what will happen but certainly their life together is as
unhappy a one as I've seen. Stella is light minded and scatterbrained
and only cares for a good time, her looks, clothes etc. but she is likable
and honest and a fairly good wife and mother – not fussy but not lazy.
They have a slatternly maid who cleans, but doesn't cook much, and
she takes the baby out in the afternoons – Ann is 8 and Veronica is 2½.
Tommy has no friends at all in Newcastle – 2 people come in to see his
pictures; he never goes out – paints all day and sits at home at night.
Stella's own mother ran off with another man leaving 3 little girls. I
can't quite see Stella on a farm near Chicago but she is adaptable and
gay and her beau, I know, will be a good kind husband – it is
mellerdrammer alright. That's enough about them. The portrait is

going to be very good – I am much prettier in it than in the small one and the pose is much prettier and makes this one look dumb – or at least insipid by comparison. ...

I still hope the *Stars and Stripes* man was right and that the war will be over on Easter Sunday! It just might yet. ...

Happy Easter

Love, girls –
Helen

11th Apr.
Mahee

Dear Muz and Gin,

Here I sit at 11.30 a.m. on the day we are leaving after our Easter Holiday with chaos all around me and cows bawling outside but I can't seem to get started to pack and organize – I always was one to wait until the last minute and I still am. I don't know what the commotion with cows is but the uproar is terrible. ...

Gay and Julie have had a wonderful time here this time. They are just getting to the age when they really appreciate Mahee – running wild, picking primroses in the woods, poking hens off nests to get their eggs, riding on the harrow and playing on the shore. ...

Bodo got home on Saturday – rang up yesterday at home to ask us to supper Wednesday – we rang him up and he says you look fine that Ginna has gained a lot, so Mother says but he couldn't see it. I will be so glad to see him and get indirect contact with you – the first in 5½ years. Too bad you didn't see more of him, but it's hard when you are both so busy. I am so fond of Bodo and quite like Edie too – but Bodo seems to me such a citizen of the world in the best sense of the word – so intelligent and so nice and so modest. I am so glad he got promoted to be a Commander instead of Harry – whom I like too but ... is so interested in Harry – and so Noel Cowardish. I don't know if you read the Competitions at the back of the *New Statesman*, Ginna, they are so good though usually too highbrow for ordinary people but there was such a funny one a month or so ago of famous last words of famous people – so good of Noel Coward, General Montgomery, Lady Astor and the Editor of the *N. Statesman and N[ation]*.[45] ...

[Love
Helen]

2nd May
34 Malone Park
Belfast

Dear Mother and Ginna,

We are actually installed – living in a confusion of carpet sewers and putter downers, carpenters, painters and plumbers but we love it madly already – in only 3 days. We moved from Mahee Thursday, from Sans Souci Friday and settled over the weekend. ...

I am in our bedroom – the whole downstairs is full of people – the bed isn't even made but I won't wait any longer to tell you all about it. One of the nicest things about it is its location i.e. the views from all the windows. ... To the left there is a lane and then trees lots of very tall ones to the next house which is as far away as the Troxdels from your house. To the right is our own garden – tennis court with a wide shrubbery border and then the Tobin's house a very French looking job – old fashioned and squarish with a yard and stable all enclosed. Their garden is on our side making their house 2 tennis courts+ away. ...

The weather has been hot and sunny and all the lime trees in the park – an avenue of them are just bursting into leaf – everything is a fresh yellow green and from our room lying in bed and from G. and J.'s room we just look into tossing tree tops – I always was a one for trees and I didn't realize until we moved in how very "treeful" we are and how very private. ...

The house itself is ugly – but pleasing if you can grasp that. ... as they say here – "a heartsome house". It has the biggest windows I ever saw. ... The house faces south with sun on the morning room, our bedroom and the kids' in the morning and evening (bay to west) except

---

[45] Noel Coward is reported to have said "Goodnight, my darlings, I'll see you tomorrow"; General Bernard Montgomery: "Well, now I must go to meet God and try to explain all those men I killed at Alamein"; Lady Astor: "Am I dying, or is this my birthday?" The editor of the *New Statesman* was Kingsley Martin.

the kids' and sun pouring into the drawing room and nursery all afternoon and until 9, 10, 11 o'clock in summer. ...

5th May

This is Friday night and our heat wave left us long ago and it is like winter. I haven't been warm for days. Lancelot is cutting the lawn in blue shirt sleeves – he had his hair cut today and says that over half the clippings were white and made him feel so old – I don't care how white it gets if only he could keep it – his hair is receding. ... On the couch beside me (sharing the heat of an electric stove) is the book of records from *Oklahoma* – and do you know how many arrived unbroken – I hate to tell you – the answer is 1 (one)! "I Can't Say No" and "Pore Jud is Dead" on the other side. Gay and Julie felt so sad about it for their own sakes and mine. It didn't seem to be insured but if it was, claim on it. ... Do you know what I carried home today from town? A basket full of lemons. A lot have come in from Spain and you can buy as many as you like for 6½ d. a pound – around 15c.

We are much more settled but my original enthusiasm has left me for padding around and working all day – I worked Fri., Sat., Sun., Mon., Tues., and Wed. and was I cross and tired yesterday. ... I stayed in bed all morning being the first morning I hadn't to get up and talk to workmen and read such a good book called *My American* by Stella Gibbons who wrote also *Cold Comfort Farm* and *Nightingale Wood* – a good novel writer.[46] We are at the dull part of the moving – now an orchestra is playing "A Shropshire Lad" by George Butterworth – it is so good.[47] The whole house is cleaned and straightened now with the usual little dumps of oddments – pictures, mirrors, lamps etc. ... We live in the morning room and it looks as though the Drawing Room will become an Entertaining room. I am always subconsciously trying to make it look American and more important feel American – the dining room and morning room running into each other helps the illusion. ...

[46] *My American* (1939) followed *Nightingale Wood* (1935), but neither novel by this English writer achieved the extraordinary success of Gibbons' first novel, *Cold Comfort Farm* (1932)

[47] The English composer George Butterworth (b. 1885) composed his A.E. Housman settings in 1911–1912. He won the MC in July 1916 at the Battle of the Somme and was shot dead by a sniper in August.

8th May

Again I was interrupted – now it is Monday afternoon and still chilly. …I have given Nursy notice which is a great relief to my mind – I gave her until July 1st to find another job. She is so nice but so hopeless and she is beginning to be worse than nobody because she bothers me. I would so much rather look after my own children but you have to be awfully healthy to do it without your nerves going to pieces. … Had a letter from Arabella; she loves her house and garden and Dublin despite the fuel restrictions – cooking is a nightmare on a turf range and all trams and buses stop at 9.30 but it doesn't fizz on the Dubliners. I don't think they are allowed any electric heaters or hot water and there isn't a single lump of coal for householders. …

Must mail this and go – more and more later so now much love,
Helen

11th May
Malone

Dear Mother and Ginna,

This time sitting in the sun in the drawing-room at the French desk and it reminds me so much of 88 Belmont Road – same desk, lamp, cigarette box and view into the garden. Today was glorious after 10 cool days when the sun never shone and I was never really warm. …

… Mary Lee ran a temp. of 99 – 100 degs Monday and Tuesday so I got Dr. Foster Wed. morning when starving and glucose didn't help – she had an infected tonsil – a germ, he said, so he put her on one of the sulphur drugs ½ a pill 4 times a day and her temp. was down in a few hours and she is fine today. It is the first she has had a temp. and I always get so panicky even when she is obviously only slightly ill – it is still a hangover from Lee who was only slightly ill too until the day he died.

… Just had to take time out to M.L. to change her and give her her 4th half pill – she is as lively as ever and giggled and giggled on the bed when I kept rolling her over – that deep base chuckle babies have when they are terribly amused.

… I just whizzed round the garden when I came out to put Gay's bike and Zoo's trike away and counted 57 rhododendron bushes. Now

I am sitting on the stoop and it is as warm as Denver and when you think it is around 9.30 [p.m.] that is sompn! I plucked 2 white lilacs to smell – if I shut my eyes I am in Cheesman Park.[48] ... L. is out doing a friend's bees – at this season I am positively widowed. The phone never stops with friends and strangers ringing up to ask advice. L. is about to take an exam. to become an expert bee master – a 3 hour paper and a practical exam. He went into bees with his usual thoroughness and knows all there is to know by now – so many people have them for the honey to help the jam and sugar ration. The birds are singing like mad and our local factory is buzzing like a buzzy saw. ...

... Julie is so bats about Dr. Foster and can't wipe the smile off her face when he is here. He is good with kids and such a comfort to their parents. All the mothers I know who have him lean on him so. A girl we know slightly, such a nice English girl named Elizabeth Edholm – married to a Swedish professor at Queens (also so nice) told me that her first reaction when she heard that they were moving to a job at London University was "But how can I leave Dr. Foster?".[49] Her 3rd baby, Mrs. Edholm's, was due today – she has two small daughters Brita and Corinna and they are dying for a boy. I am too now – although I love my daughters madly I think I will yearn (not actively) always for a son – I thought I wouldn't but I know I will. Little girls are much more interesting but big boys have some special appeal for women that is undeniably instinct. Mary Lee is quiet at last. She is so coy and roguish and knows she is being a devil when I get her up – she is so dark and vivid and animated. ...

I am still outside and it must be nearly 11 – we have each had a glass of real lemonade – divine. It will be dark soon now – we hardly black out at all and the move or "the flitting" as it is called here has certainly taken our mind off the news and the second front. When I see a convoy of Americans my heart constricts – I think that is the word – Stella was skin and bone weeks ago – she must be just bone and hair now because of her American beau and whether and when he may be going. I still hope it will be all over bar the shouting – done by bombing.

---

[48] An eighty-acre urban park in Denver.

[49] Elizabeth Edholm performed as a reader on BBC Northern Ireland; on 11th December 1941, she read poems by AE, James Joyce, W.B. Yeats and James Stephens between songs by Irish composers. Her husband Otto Edholm (1909–1985) was Lecturer in Physiology, Queen's University.

Fred Gardiner was written up the other day for being the leader of some outstanding "flak busting" raid over France.[50] He will be in Egypt by now I think. Dr. Foster has a Spitfire pilot son and another son a doctor with the R.A.F. in India[51]. ...

G'bye girls

Love and kisses,
Helen

11th Jun.
Malone

Dear Mother and Ginna,

It is a sleepy Sunday afternoon and we are all three writing letters. ... We had such a hectic and social week starting with last weekend when Gordon and Arabella came Saturday evening and stayed until Tuesday evening. They are fine and love Dublin and their house – there have been no trams there since Wednesday. The fuel problems are enormous – each household is allowed so many units of electricity and if you exceed them you are cut off entirely. Some days they couldn't even play their radios or have the ice-box on! We just heard the Barcarolle by Offenbach and it was divine. Now one of the most popular programs of the week is on "*Itma*" or "It's That Man Again" – we used to hate it but now can laugh at it occasionally.[52] ...

[50] The *Belfast News-Letter* of 29th April, 1944 reported that Squadron Leader Fred T. Gardiner led his squadron in a recent multi-squadron attack on a German convoy off the Frisian Islands. Five ships were damaged. Gardiner was awarded the DFC just before becoming wing commander at an RAF base in Egypt. After the war, unhappy at his country's economic prospects, he emigrated to British Columbia, Canada where he died in 2003. See Special to the Toronto *Globe and Mail* 29th Jan, 2004 and the *Times Colonist* (Victoria), obituary 5th November, 2003.

[51] See the letter of 9th April, 1941.

[52] "It's That Man Again" was a BBC comedy half-hour that aired from 1939 to 1949. The title borrowed a saying alluding to the frequency of Hitler's name being mentioned in the months leading to the outbreak of war. Tommy Handley was the main comedian on the show which was written by Ted Kavanagh. This programme and others were credited through humour with boosting the morale of the people during the war. Helen listened to "ITMA" on the General Forces Service, a BBC station that operated between 27th February 1944 and 31st December, 1946.

D. Day [6th June] was so exciting. We missed the first announcement at 9.30 a.m. but I was vaguely listening at 10.30 and when I heard an announcement that the King was broadcasting I was just beginning to wonder when L. rang up to say as they say here, that the balloon has gone up. Gordon came in a minute later, and then Arabella and they decided not to go on the 12 train but to wait until the 5.15 so that they could hear the news and also they had to get a permit to take a Paul Henry picture south. We listened at 12 and Arabella kept talking through the news until I could have screamed. ...

Last Monday at the D. R. Circle the program was original poetry by members anonymously read. Arabella came specially for it and gave two readings (reminiscent of her Mother's Day). A group of Irish poems (divine and beautifully done) and 2 readings from Shakespeare. If I don't look at her I love to hear her because her voice and her training are so good but her expressions bother me. I tried to write a poem and couldn't. Auntie wrote a very good and witty one about the D.R.C. – really good it was and I was very proud of her. The others were *wonderful*. It was the talk of the whole circle how good they were. Most members came prepared to be amused and as Mrs. Beath[53] put it "to smile and smirk" but again as Mrs. Beath said she was awed and staggered to think that she was sitting with people who could write like that and not know who they were. Arabella and Mrs. McDowell read then and I read about 6 to help out. I had a group of love poems – Three I found out later were by Mary Morwood and I wouldn't have believed it they were so good. Nancy Mitchell had 2 lovely ones – one called "The Escapist" and one about rain on the roof as she was going to sleep. She once made £20 writing poetry and used to write short stories that were published too. ...

We let Mahee for the month of June to a young honeymoon couple – a naval officer on leave and his wife. They have been married for a year but he has been abroad for 10 months so it is like a honeymoon. We went down a week ago Friday to get them settled in and they were so young and so in love and so sweet that we felt old and middle-aged beside them. Here comes the 9 o'clock news and Big Ben. ... We don't hear the American correspondent's report at all but the British ones are

[53] Mrs Beath, Vice-President of the Alpha Club in 1944 (Countess of Clanwilliam, President) was a frequent presence on public charitable occasions: see the letter of 10th May, 1939; she was now a widow.

very good – they are all together every evening after the 9 o'clock news in what is called the "War Report". Gay and J. were got up to hear the King on "Today" and they pray for the soldiers every night as the King told them.[54] ...

We had supper at Edie's Friday night – she is so busy with her kids, her W.V.S., her office and all and still entertains so much – a really efficient woman. Bodo is in England finishing his book. The sun is still blazing in at 9.30 – looking into the dining room from here looks so American. ...

12th Jun.

This is Monday morning. ... Getting up nearly kills me because it is after midnight every night that we get to bed. ...

I just wrote a letter to Stella whom we haven't seen for ages. I suppose her beau has gone and she will be in a state. Their household had an atmosphere of murder when I was last there so I suppose it's worse now. Our portrait hangs over the fireplace looking pretty terrific. Hardly anybody likes it because it doesn't flatter us at all but we like it still. ...

Love and kisses,
Helen

18th Jun.
Malone

Dear Ginna,

This really is a glorious June day after nearly 3 weeks of showery, cloudy weather. ... I am on the bench by the summer house in the corner of the garden and have just been looking across the tennis court (ahem!) to our tall red barracks of a house that is so different from the long low white house with shutters and Georgian windows that I

---

[54] King George VI broadcast to the nation, Empire, and the United States at 9.00pm on 6th June – D-Day. Towards the end, he said: "At this historic moment, surely not one of us is too busy, too young or too old to play a part in a nationwide, a worldwide vigil of prayer as the great crusade sets forth".

thought would be so nice – but the inside is and will continue to be more and more charming. ...

I tried so hard to write a poem for the last meeting of the D.R.C. ... I had 2 very good ideas – I know one was good because I heard the most beautiful poem on the radio by Frances Cornford with exactly my idea. Hers was called "Dusk in July" and it was about the light evenings and how late it was and how still but how light and it started off by saying very beautifully how it was dark in the heart of a rose in the garden and in the pool but light everywhere else even in the curtained rooms where the children were at last asleep with their hands open on the blankets. I am going to try to find it published someplace because it was so lovely and as I say exactly my idea because it is still light at midnight when we go to bed and so attractive to look out at the dusk and walk around the house.[55] The Venetian blinds make such pretty effects of light in the rooms. My other idea which I have still to work on is about the separate life our garden at Mahee seems to live when it is so much alone. I always think of it when we aren't there – so small and so peaceful and remote and yet so intimate and when I see it again I always feel again how it goes on its own way and is somehow all the more alive because it is so alone. It is the shape of it – the wall at the foot of the sloping lawn with the gate in the middle – bright blue and the 4 trees along the wall. Almost everybody senses its special charm that is so unstudied and so simple and natural. ...

We were at Mahee yesterday, another heavenly day – hot and sunny. The bride and groom were having breakfast outdoors at around 11 – he had just come off all night duty and was in pyjamas ready to go to bed outdoors and she was in a nightie and a housecoat and a super string of pearls. They are very young, very vague and very very newly weddish. When G. and J. and I started for the Glendinnings for tea she, the bride, was making mayonnaise with some very precious olive oil that her husband had brought from Egypt on purpose. She was dropping it in with an eyedropper and was about 1/8th down the cup after 30 minutes. When L. came to tea more than 2 hours later she was still wandering around with the bowl in her hands beating it and asking his advice on how to get it smooth!

[55] "Dusk in July" does not appear in the *Collected Poems* (1954) of the English poet Frances Cornford (1886–1960, mother of the Communist poet John Cornford) and which contains, according to her Preface, "all the poems I wish to preserve from my previously published work".

Stella came to tea on Wednesday – still madly in love with her American captain whom she goes to see about 3 times a week – she goes to Kilkeel because I suppose it was increasingly hard for all concerned when he came to her house. She is as open about the whole thing as a Shasta daisy and said that she would just go off with him if she could – she could but he, of course, being in the army couldn't run off with her. If you read about it in a book you would think it was too far-fetched to be true. ... Although she is a good but slap-dash mother she would apparently leave her kids without a backward look. ...

I wrote you a very frank and open letter the other day and then tore it up – it sounded awful. It is hard to tell you what I think, especially about myself. I think I am very wooly-minded but intelligent but not bright – intelligent meaning knowing what I want and not wasting my life on unimportant (to me) things like housekeeping and tidying. ... I am incurably social and still go to lots of things I hate – tea parties etc. – but I have successfully evaded much club, committee and "joiner" life which I really hate. I don't mind the American Red Cross Club – only because it is mainly talking to the boys and nothing to do with the other workers. ... I think our marriage is a great success though our minds only touch at so few points it is a wonder we get along so well – our interests as you know are so diverse but we think the same about people and our outlook is the same if not our minds – our point of view I mean. I really only enjoy conversation that is considered here high-brow but –

20th Jun.

Now it is Tuesday morning and I am still out – what I was just saying is that not many people here stimulate me but it is partly my own fault because over the course of years I have become pretty highbrow. ... Eileen Bryson just dropped by – home from a week in Dublin to thank me for having [daughter] Nina over while she was away. There are no trams at all in Dublin now and all buses stop at 9.30 p.m. She said the lighting was the worst though in the Gresham [Hotel] grill which is in the basement and is very snappily lighted usually, she said there wasn't a glimmer and you could hardly see your food and by their beds was a tiny light that strained your eyes to read by – but they dance and go on in Dublin no matter what. Eileen is so stiff and Ulster or maybe it's Comber ...

I do wish you could know my children – I honestly know that they are remarkable. They are all so good-looking and Gay is improving in every way by leaps and hounds – looks, disposition and amiability. ... She isn't naturally a happy child and isn't ever going to have an easy, happy life. She is very ambitious to do everything better than anybody and isn't very good with people – no tact. ...

About Julie I feel just like the mother in *Watch on the Rhine.*[56] I'm proud to have a daughter like her. It is because she was born with such a sweet nature ... L. adores the kids but hardly ever plays with them. He is always so busy with his bees or his farming or the garden and would work all his life away if left to himself and get odd. The war has changed him a lot mostly because he isn't in it. He tried to get in an A.A. [anti-aircraft] unit the first week of the war ... and wasn't taken – I don't know why but suspect his nerves or else his anything but winning manner under examination. Then the navy sent for him for an interview and he didn't go. I think he might have been much happier to go but I know he stayed because he couldn't bear to leave me and the children. There are enough men we know around who haven't gone so that isn't usually awkward but it has been sometimes. ... I doubt if the navy could have taken him because they are very strict about color-blindness but I was surprised when he didn't go to see. I hardly do anything myself so I can't say a word but I hate having to do evasive talk which I have to sometimes and it makes me very hesitant to entertain many Americans – not that I think it is very good policy to have the house full of men all the time anyway though I would have a lot more if I knew any.

I think I have become unconsciously very Europeanized – after all 1/3 of my life has been spent here but at the drop of a hat all my Red Indian (not to mention negro) blood comes flying back and I am aggressively American. I am still taken for something with the American army in shops and on the telephone but I am struck when I talk to Americans by the great gulf in the outlook between the 2 countries. ...

[56] In the movie, the Bette Davis character, Sara Muller, is proud of her son Joshua who when he turns eighteen decides to go to Germany in search of his anti-Fascist father who himself returned to Germany to assist a resistance fighter in trouble.

I often wonder if I would have been happier to marry an American – it would have been easier but not so interesting. L. couldn't be a better husband but our interests keep us separate even when we are both at home. ...

The war has changed everybody here so much – It is the silent revolution and there isn't much nonsense in the way of entertaining and society any more. Every time I look at Mother's picture I feel guilty and miserable. I can tell by her letters that she has never developed any philosophy and yet I try to bring up my children the way we were bought up – we had such a free and easy household and used to have such fun. I haven't quite yet got over the social ambition that was imbued in us (much more in me than in you) by Mother and the *Denver Post* and American life generally and was so well counteracted by Daddy's wonderful common sense.

We went to *Jane Eyre* last night – L., Maureen and I – coming home on the tram we talked to a boy who is just home on leave from the invasion – his job was finished and the organization is so wonderful and is going so like clockwork that he was given leave – he said that to see all those battleships lying there lousing off with no danger is terrific and he said that everything is going day by day exactly according to plan – e.g. on D day + 6 exactly what they planned to happen happened etc. We saw a good newsreel of Normandy – Churchill, Monty and all. *Jane Eyre* is a scream – so melodramatic but so good.[57] ...

Must mail this before anyone sees it. It is hard to break the reticence of years and as you say not satisfactory at all. But I agree with you that it isn't fair for me to ask you questions and not let on from this side. When we meet it will be divine.

As to being happy I think I am very happy – About once in every 2 months or so I have a cross, depressed day. If you were here or even near I would laugh more. I haven't had a good giggle for a long time. John Carr used to fill me with high spirits and a few other people do but not so much. L. makes me roar both with him and at him. Both he and Arabella have such a good sense of fun – Mrs. T. !?!? never really laughed in all her life. The great thing about L. is his tolerance and his complete lack of pettiness and his live and let live policy. I hardly ever

---

[57] This 1943 American movie adaptation of Charlotte Bronte's 1847 novel stars Orson Welles and Joan Fontaine; directed by Robert Stevenson, it was written by John Houseman and Aldous Huxley.

think much about you and Mother but if I do I long for you so it is nearly a pain – now for instance if you were here it would triple the enjoyment for me. L. hardly ever sits and talks – he is too restless and I don't do much but sit. I hope G. and J. and M. Lee don't marry foreigners and live far away if they are as good friends as we are.

Love
Helen

28th Jun.
Malone

Dear Mother,

Now I've sure gone and done it – Got German measles last week and not content with that I may have glandular fever – the measles were nothing – I had them for 3 days without knowing it – I had a rash on my arms neck and face but it was during a heat wave and I thought it was the sun! My only other symptom was rheumaticky pains and everybody I talked to had rheumatism too and said the heat brought it out. ... I have been in bed now 5 days and am going to get up today. I rang Dr. Foster up Monday to say what the heck again having heard of so much gland trouble and he said I should be getting better and that he would come take a blood test on Thursday to see if it was glandular fever.

30th Jun.

... I am up and a cure.[58] It is a lovely day – warm and windless...

Here comes the sun out – it is going to be another heatwave.

Tommy was here a minute this morning and is coming to sketch Julie and me this afternoon in an attempt to get the big portrait finished. Mary Lee looks tough today – she has a very determined face and chin and what a temper!

The main effect of this letter is to wish you Happy Birthday! To think that you are 65! And you only look about 50. I don't know how

---

[58] Helen was diagnosed with glandular fever, not German measles.

you do it. ... I am practically positive that we will see each other – you and I before you are 66 – I am practically positive.

3rd Jul.

I don't know what else I was so positive about now several days later. ... Letters came from you both today – yours in 14 days and Ginna's in 12 from N. York. I am so sorry about Morie's husband.[59] It only brings the war home to you when someone you know is killed in it or because of it. We still miss John Carr so much because we liked him so well and he used to drop in so often.[60] Tommy is nice too but not so gay as John was. ...

The war is zooming along so well that I have great hopes for you to come over soon. I certainly will come home as soon as possible but I should think you might be able to come over here sooner because the ships that take the boys home will presumably come back empty and the rush will all be from this side. The pilotless planes keep London at nearly constant alert.[61] We can tell pretty well by the radio programs which are cancelled – symphony concerts and dance bands from dance halls are usually given up and the announcer just says "We are sorry we are unable to give the published program but here are some gramophone records".

To think that tomorrow is the grand and glorious 4th. I don't get very homesick because I don't think about it much but when the time comes to think about *really* seeing you, I, like you will be ready to jump over the moon and kick over a couple of stars too.

I try to bring up our children just like we were brought up because we had such a happy childhood. I must try to see the *Sullivans* this week at the Classic[62] – my homesickness is so helped by the movies

---

[59] An American acquaintance, not to be confused with Nina Morie Crawford, the daughter of John Miller Andrews and sister of Jack Andrews.

[60] See the letter of 15th February, 1941.

[61] The V1 flying bomb (aka buzz bomb and doodlebug) was developed in Germany and launched repeatedly towards London in 1944 and 1945. The first strike was on 13th Jun 1944 so this was a new terror threat when Helen was writing this letter.

[62] *The Sullivans* (1944, later re-titled *The Fighting Sullivans*), directed by Lloyd Bacon and starring Thomas Mitchell and Anne Baxter, is the story of five brothers from Iowa who join the U.S. Navy after Pearl Harbor and ask to serve on the same ship, with tragic consequences. *Cont'd.*

and the Americans over here. I will be crushed when they all go – but you bet they won't. There was a story in the *New Statesman* the other day about an American soldier in England – the Englishman asked him why all the Americans were so cheerful and he said "because we know that when this is over we can go home and you have to stay on here". I have no birthday present for you but if you will blow yourself to something for $10 I will pay you back when the war is over.

There was such a wonderful American hill billy program on the B.B.C last Monday called *The Martins and the Coys* about the backwoods people in Kentucky – L. and I listened and loved it and Elaine rang up the minute it was over to say that she had been laughing and crying and *adored* it.[63] It reminded me of Central City Nights.[64] With this goes all my love and many, many happy returns when you are in the bosom of your family..

Love and kisses,
Helen

12th Jul.
Malone

Dear Mother,

Though it is 10.30pm I will quick scratch one off before we go to bed. We have had a busy day since 11 – Tommy came to paint us – the

---

[62] *Cont'd*: The real-life Sullivan brothers served aboard the light cruiser USS *Juneau* and all lost their lives when it was sunk by a Japanese submarine on 13th November 1942 at the Battle of Guadalcanal. Ten men out of 687 survived.

[63] *The Martins and the Coys*, which the *Radio Times* listing for 26th June 1944 announced as "A Mountain Ballad Opera", was a 55-minute programme produced in New York by Alan Lomax, the famous field-collector of folksongs and blues. The 16 traditional or topical songs were sung, composed or played by Woody Guthrie (then a merchant seaman), Burl Ives, Will Geer, Pete Seeger, Gilbert (Cisco) Houston, Sonny Terry, and the Almanac Singers. Elizabeth Lomax wrote the dialogue and her husband Alan arranged the music for a plot that is an adaptation of two legendary hillbilly feuds: between the Martins and the Tollivers and between the Hatfields and the McCoys. The families postpone their feud in order to join forces against Hitler.

[64] Possibly a reference to *Central City Nights*, a play staged in 1935 and listed in Orville Kurth Larson, *Scene Design in the American Theatre from 1915 to 1960* (Fayetteville: University of Arkansas Press, 1989), p. 297. For Central City, Colorado, see the letter of 1st August 1940.

portrait is still going on but is bound to be finished soon we all hope. He stayed until 1 and after lunch the 3 girls and I went for a picnic to Shaw's Bridge – it was a heavenly afternoon after a pouring morning ... the kids paddled in the River Lagan and Gay caught a minnow and a good time was had by all. This is the week of the "12th" and though they have given up the parade for the war the whole week is still a holiday.[65] *Snow White* is on at the Classic and the crowds are *terrible*. We tried one day at 12.40 and couldn't get in so we are going tomorrow at 11.30. ...

... We had supper with Hilary and Eggy last night. Hilary has been to a nerve specialist. She is exactly like Mrs. T in that she putters her life away fussing and worrying over trifles – e.g. she spent 2 hours the other evening getting paper straight in a drawer and let Eggie wait those 2 hours for his supper – the next day she had a tussle of an hour or two with some fringe on a rug.

Love,
Helen

21st Jul.
Cushendun

Dear Mother,

Gay, Julie and I are here for a week and are having the best weather of the summer. Cushendun [County Antrim] consists of 3 hotels and one street and it is a sweet little place.[66] There is a lovely sandy beach and the coast of Scotland is only 30 miles away and looks about 3 miles.

---

[65] The Orange Order volunteered to postpone the Twelfth of July annual parades for the duration of the war. It did not do so again until the coronavirus pandemic of 2020.

[66] Cushendun can be added to the list of Northern Irish villages and buildings designed by Clough Williams-Ellis. See the letter of 19th January, 1943. It was designed in the Cornish mode for Ronald McNeill (1864–1934), a Conservative politician born in Ulster; he was Sheriff of County Antrim and in 1927 was made Chancellor of the Duchy of Lancaster. That same year he became Baron Cushendun. As chief British representative at the League of Nations, he signed the Kellogg-Brian Pact the following year. Williams-Ellis designed a replacement building for McNeill's home, Glenmona House, which was burned by the IRA in 1922. The other buildings Williams-Ellis designed were in memory of Lord Cushendun's Cornish wife. The sermon Helen listened to seems ironically apt.

We are at the worst hotel but the only one I could get into. We only decided to come about a week ago and practically every hotel in Ireland is booked solidly for the summer, especially in the North because transport in the Free State is so difficult. Mary Morwood Rogers and her 3 year old Julian are here and her American sister-in-law Kathleen (James' wife) and her 2 year old son Bryan. We don't see them much all day but I sit with them in the evenings. Kathleen is very nice and level headed and Mary isn't bad. Her husband is in Italy now and Kathleen's is a doctor with the army in England.

23rd Jul.

This is Sunday and we all went to church. A sweet tiny little church on Lord Cushendun's estate – it was packed with practically everyone from the 3 hotels and the sermon was so good about thinking well before you start to build – counting the cost I mean. ...

There are about 40 people in our hotel – nothing to shout about but all very friendly. We have been out rowing twice – once I hired a boat and boatman and once the English father took his family and ours out fishing. We caught a fish to the children's intense joy but then Julie sat looking at it so sadly and said "Poor fish." They fished for minnows right in front of the hotel and caught two each with worms and pins. They have bathed all but two days and loved the waves. I have only read one book in a week which shows how much time I've had that book was [*So Little Time* by John P. Marquand].

[*Rest of letter lost*]

27th Jul.
Malone

Dear Mother and Ginna,

... We actually had a dinner party last night – 2 Queen's professors and their wives – Barcrofts and Edholms[67] and Nancy [Mitchell] and Edith

---

[67] Helen met the Queen's University lecturer Otto Edholm just after he had been appointed Professor of Physiology at Royal Veterinary College, London; he went on to become a leader in physiological research and the development of ergonomics in the UK. His obituary confirms Helen's impression of him: "a man of great charm": *Annals of Human Biology* 12.4 (1985).

[Taggart]. The table looked a dream with a low summery bowl of roses and delphiniums and *yellow* hollyhocks. We had soup, salmon and salad and potatoes and raspberry and red currant tart with some kind of ersatz cream. We finished up the ends of 2 bottles of whiskey and the conversation buzzed all evening. The Edholms are moving to England and I decided last night in a worn out mood that they are *too* charming …

Alan Smiles[68] is home after two years as a plain sailor in India, South Africa, Egypt, Malta and all around the Mediterranean with all kinds of action. Their ship was torpedoed once but only 3 people killed. He is home to get his commission and is nearly 20 and just the same and just as nice as ever. He came to see us the night we came home from Cushendun and the next day to see Gay and Julie. Julie was so excited to see him again that she acted like a lunatic – giggling and jumping around literally like crazy. …

We spent Tuesday evening with the Tobins, our next door neighbors who are so nice.[69] They are grandparents – in their sixties and Mrs. Tobin is a great friend of Elaine's – very English, Mrs. Tobin, and wears one of those English straw hats in the garden that are unmistakable. Apparently collects china and has it on top of a bookshelf in her drawing room so nicely arranged. Their 4 year old grandson is spending the summer with them – his mother just had a bad operation – she is Norwegian and a very nice girl. I haven't met their son who apparently used to be pompous but is vastly improved by his nice wife.

Bill Stephens is home having escaped from Switzerland through France to Spain dressed as a French labourer working for the Germans. His passport, papers and money and all were all arranged by British agents. He bought a cheap rucksack on the Riviera and it cost £25 and some meal he had at a station in France cost the equivalent of £10.[70]

---

[68] See the letter of 1st August, 1940.

[69] T.C. Tobin, Helen's next-door neighbour, was a naval architect. His article, "A method of determining natural periods of vibration of ships," published in the *Transactions of the Institution of Naval Architects* (1922), is cited as late as the 2nd edition of *Muckle's Naval Architecture* (1987, 2013).

[70] For Bill Stephens and the St Nazaire raid, see the letter of 27th April 1942. He was captured when the launch he was commanding was hit by defending fire and he and his men swam to shore. In Colditz Castle POW camp, Stephens and a Major Littledale soon hatched a plot to escape with two other prisoners. Having famously done so, Stephens reached Switzerland, then crossed France and made it over the Pyrenees into Spain. He was smuggled into Gibraltar and flown to Britain. *Cont'd:*

He is engaged, I think, to a divorced English girl with 2 children but he has been engaged so many times. I have bet L. a pound that the war will be over by Sept 3. ... The sun is struggling out. ...

We went twice during 12th Week to an amusement park on the edge of the Botanic Gardens and to *Snow White*. Gay and I went to see the first installment of *Why We Fight* at the Museum. Elaine saw the 2nd installment at a special show yesterday – an American film for the forces that you may have seen.[71] ... I read [Marquand's] *So Little Time* in Cushendun and enjoyed it but it just misses it. *H.F. Pulham, Esq.* was so much better I thought. Mary Morwood has written a book called *War Bride* based on her experiences trailing around England. I read it in manuscript and advised her that it was much too racy (polite word for dirty). It is quite well written in Mary's facetious style but just misses it too – like Mary herself! ...

Rest of letter in next installment – Hastily but lovingly yours
Helen

6th Aug.
Mahee

Dear Mother and Ginna,

We actually are at Mahee ... and it is simply heaven. We have had a whole week of glorious weather and have been here for 6 days. We are all getting as sunburned as if we were in Denver and the kids all look wonderful . ...

Edith rang up last night to say that Bodo is coming home on leave next Friday. She thinks he may be able to get out of the navy now and get established in a post-war planning in architecture before the rush starts. Apparently the navy is cluttered up with senior naval officers and they all expect to be released before the Jap war starts or to put it

[70] *Cont'd:* (See the Afterword.) For his part in the raid, Lt.-Cdr Stephens won the DSC. See *Northern Whig*, 17th March 1943. See Stephens' substantial obituary in the *Independent*, 17th August, 1997. Other details are revealed in "Colditz Escape: Tale of first British 'home run' revealed", BBC News website, 27th March, 2012.

[71] *Why We Fight* was a series of seven propaganda films (1942–1945) commissioned by the U.S. government and mostly directed by Frank Capra, rising, it has been said, to the challenge of Leni Riefenstahl's *Triumph of the Will* (1935).

better when the Hitler war is over. Harry [McMullan] is hoping to be pushed out too. ...

Mahee looks lovelier than ever ... The moon is full and is just like a big red ball rising over the water. ... We have a week old baby calf named Clover – Bluebell's daughter and we have lots of baby bantams as well as our usual tame wild ducks, guinea hens, donkey, pony, horse, cows and bullocks. ... "Framley Parsonage" is being broadcast now – it sounds like the last installment.[72] Our flowers consist of a few Shasta daisies, lots of big mallow bushes, roses, calendulas, poppies and a few shrubs. There are some red geraniums at the front door and my cactus plants are growing like mad in pots on the glass shelves on the porch.

I have taken a burst of energy for mending and patching – kids' pants and such – darning socks and being generally and unusually housewifely. It is much easier for me to work here than in town – always was. Now the news is on and Gay and Julie have just been in – such a funny conversation – Gay first saying "I despair, wait until you hear my story" – the story being how Julie was bothering her, Julie denying it all backwards and forwards. Gay is a scream because of the big bookish words she uses. She fed the bantys last night because she said they looked "so dejected". The other day when I was deciding whether to bring Mary Lee along to the Browne's for a walk Gay said "Do bring her because she hasn't been in sorcety much" – meaning society. I would have to write it down at the time to remember but her conversation is full of things like "I protest". She reads every minute that she isn't doing something – she has just started *Swiss Family Robinson* and knows *Rebecca* and *Little Women* nearly by heart. She reads *Tom Sawyer* and *Heidi* and at Cushendun I don't know what sort of books they were but I think English school books – because she began calling Julie a "duffer" and saying that people were so vulgar – and the way she rolls her eyes and her expressions make it even funnier and she is always so earnest – though when there is something funny no one laughs harder.

... The kids were at the Glendinnings for tea on Friday and they looked so sweet going across the fields in their summer dresses (blue with white tops that mother sent with the embroidered straps over the

---

[72] *Framley Parsonage* (1860) was the fourth novel in Anthony Trollope's Barsetshire Chronicles. This broadcast on Sunday 6th August, 8.30–9.00pm, corrects Helen's misdating of her letter to 7th August.

shoulders) sun hats and bare legs in sandals. I went to the top of the hill with them and they waved all the way to the gate. Joan and Mary [Webb – recent visitors][73] were told when they set out "Don't speak to any Americans!" – the British version of "only speak to women with children". The Londonderrys went by today in a big motor boat[74] – Julie very indignant and said "They shouldn't be out, should they?" because we don't even take out an outboard on account of petrol.

... I hope that you have [your] name down Mother, on a list for a priority passage over here the minute the war is over. As I said in my last letter we won't come until Ginna is a civilian again – according to Churchill the Jap war will be over sooner than he thought. The Webbs are such country girls, so unsophisticated and interested in crops and animals but they aren't a bit dumb – especially Mary. Their contact with the outside world is all through the radio. Now "Sunday Rhapsody" is on [9.35–10.35 pm] – Homage to Johann Strauss and will I love it. There is a little royal blue squat teapot of yaller daisies on this table and a huge jardinière yaller too of pink mallows on the hearth and a "summer bunch" in a red bowl on a side table and a pinky–purple bunch on the rug chest and 3 deadish hydrangeas in a green Wedgwood beer mug on the mantelpiece. The *Water Babies* is on the table and there is an assortment of binoculars, movie cameras, cartridges, beeswax and needles and thread sitting around. One leg of the couch has given way but the striped chair covers are as fresh and summery as ever. All the family's bathing suits and towels are hanging on the hedge. The bookcase has never been so neat in its life because Mrs. Turtle tidied it and no one has had time to untidy it. The Strauss program is as good as I thought – the announcer said of him "it was no small thing to make the world dance" and he was right. G. and J. are both going to be good dancers.

In haste now and with love!
Helen

---

[73] For the Webbs, see the letter of 22nd May, 1939.

[74] Charles, 7th Marquess of Londonderry (1878–1949), and his wife Edith, Marchioness (1878–1959) were both keen boaters. The Londonderrys' summer home, Mount Stewart (now a National Trust property), lies to the north-east of Mahee Island across Strangford Lough, about four miles away as the crow flies.

9th Aug.
Mahee

Dear Ginna,

... I spent the day in bed killing or at least fighting a cold and having an orgy of reading. The highlight was *The Bell for Adano* which I was so enthusiastic about at supper that L. is now reading it and when he voluntarily reads a novel it is indeed something.[75] The kettle is making such a funny whistling noise that L. thought somebody was playing an instrument. I have my wooden shoes off and my feet nearly in the oven – My big mistake was not wearing socks. ...

The *worst* is that come Friday we will have no maid for 2 weeks and 3 days – help! Kathleen went unexpectedly today to a dying father and goodness knows when she will be back – if ever and Margaret [nanny and maid] is going for her holiday on Friday! I am trying to get our ex-cook Bridget but if she can't come we are sunk! because Aggie is booked up for every day now and she used to save our lives.

15th Aug.

Less than a week later and a cook in the kitchen – Margaret went Friday morning with L. and Mary came Friday evening with L... Mary the new number is 70 if she is a day and looks and acts 90. Her feet "gave out" in a hostel of sorts and they haven't come back yet. She shuffles around and is the ticket for Mahee – seems as happy as a lark, never says an extra word and is a very good cook. She was with Uncle James Turtle for 5 years until he died and then she worked for Norman in Lumeah for 2 years. I got her from an agency here which can always produce somebody and we were lucky this time. Margaret will be back in 2 weeks. The kid-wids are all fine and as brown as Hawaiians (Irish version). I am listening to the Kentucky Minstrels – quite good.[76] Our radio is so temperamental that it takes about 5 minutes of trigger-finger

[75] John Hersey's *A Bell for Adano* (1944) won the Pulitzer Prize for the Novel in 1945. Set in Sicily after the Americans had occupied the island in 1943, the novel went far for American readers in vindicating their country's occupation of Italy. The novel was adapted as a Broadway play in 1945.

[76] Helen is writing between 8.15pm and 9.00pm when "Kentucky Minstrels" was broadcast on the BBC Home Service.

fiddling with to get anything but then it goes a dinger. We used to get mad at it and smack it but that didn't pay as it got older. ...

Today was lovely and sunny – the weather on the whole is lovely and I am nearly black m'self – in fact with my Charles of the Ritz Red pencil lipstick on that Mother sent I feel downright cute despite the fact that my hair is a wuzz because I washed it. I am about to knit babsa a cardigan – I haven't had a good go at knitting since I did outfits for G.'s and J.'s dolls Christmas before last ... I still have a very good supply of wool which now is all but impossible to buy – the shops' quota come in on the first of a month and lasts about half an hour and is 2 coupons an ounce. We are never at our wits' end for coupons like most people because of you and Mother and I never dream of buying a dress – my 2 new suits were my only burst in years and they were a desperation move. ...

I just rolled up a *New Yorker* for the Morwoods with an article in it by Bill Morwood who is now a private in the U.S. army. It is very *New Yorker*ish and neurotic but good. There has just been such a good Profile on Duke Ellington.[77]

... Now the 9 o'clock news is on with news of the 4th front in southern France.[78] I have bet L. that the war will be over on Sept. 3rd an optimist to the end – the usual belief here is that it will be over by Christmas.

Eggie and Hilary came about 10 on Friday night after my wearing day and stayed until Sunday night. Hilary has the makings of a Mrs. Turtle in her but is quite funny in a way. Eggie did 2 good paintings while he was here and is just the same as ever. They both have a lot to put up with. Hilary spends all her time titivating and puttering. ...

[77] For Bill Morwood, see the letter of 5th December, 1942. William Morwood's "Chain of Command", an army training short story published in the 24th June 1944 issue of the *New Yorker* is a more substantial piece than his earlier "A Moving Dilemma". The story concerns a neurotic private but is itself a studiedly unambitious affair, more episode than story. William Morwood died in Lane County, Oregon in May 1992. The 24th June issue contains a profile of Duke Ellington.

[78] Operation Dragoon, the Allied invasion of southern France, began on 15th August, 1944. It was intended to open up a new front in the war against Germany. The French captured the ports of Marseille and Toulon and French resistance against Nazi occupation intensified. The Allied operation was regarded as a strategic error by some, and the war continued beyond 3rd September 1944, Helen's hopes to the contrary (and as General Eisenhower was to caution people), yet Germany did withdraw from southern France with heavy casualties.

General Eisenhower has just given a dig at the people who measure the war in weeks! – so I'm a wishful thinker, am I. Hilary is now in the hands of a Faith-Healer for her nerves having given up a psychiatrist. I heard *Lady in the Dark* on the radio last night – not so hot.[79] …

Love and kisses – send this to Mama
Helen

1st Sept.
Mahee

Dear Mary Lou,[80]

I don't know whether it is because it is such a beautiful September morning or whether it is because my three daughters are all well, occupied and happy or because we have had a little *divarsion*[81] to break our five weeks of sitting on this island but my heart is tranquil, my nerves un-taut and life is a song for the first time in weeks. Not that life has been a husk but I was leading what I once heard described as a life of quiet desperation with only occasional bursts through of melody… Don't you find that most women are only unbalanced and neurotic with innumerable inexplicable ups and downs? I am as unstable as a May bug and mind you I am supposed to be "calm and sensible". There is still and will always be an other-worldliness about our Mahee garden and house that nearly everyone feels and remarks on – usually about how very peaceful it is here and how far away the war seems and it is always true. We have spent all the crises of the war here – declaration, and then from May 1940 until nearly Alamein – all such awful news – the summer of 1940 was indelible on anyone's mind in the British Isles (not to mention a *few* other places!) but even here

---

[79] The BBC Home Service broadcast the Kurt Weill play with music on the evening of 14th August. This radio adaptation was not of the 1941 stage production but of the 1944 American movie starring Ginger Rogers and Ray Milland. However, in the radio adaptation Gertrude Lawrence played the role she created in the Broadway production with music by Weill, lyrics by Ira Gershwin, direction by Moss Hart and co-starring Danny Kaye.

[80] For Mary Louise Gurd, see the letter of 29th April 1939.

[81] In this bubbly letter to her distant friend, Helen is imitating the southern Irish pronunciation.

the atmosphere was electric. The worst day for me here was when it was announced on the 1 o'clock news that Belgium had "given up" – the first indication of the real rot having set in. I was alone except for kids and maids and sister, did my heart sink and then flutter weakly when Duff-Cooper, then Minister of Information, came to the microphone to assure us in a most misguided way that "there was no cause for panic". Immediately panic seized us all. He was sort of a poetic Jonah – I remember him later going on about Paris and the chestnut trees – still on the wrong tack altogether. One of the highest points was also the 1 o'clock news bulletin that announced that Yugoslavia was not giving in as they said the day before – what a country! Did you read *Black Lamb – Gray Falcon*? I didn't read it all but it was good.[82] And only last week I burst into tears again at the 1 o'clock news when it was announced that Paris had been saved by the French.[83] I rushed in to tell Gay who being a very impressionable child started to cry too although it hardly means a thing to her. For you with a husband in Italy (at last hearing)[84] the war even at your distance is bound to be twice as poignant as it even is to us civilians and I never forget it. We in Ulster are curiously out of the war – even with blackout, rationing and bombing we still have no conscription and neutral Eire to go to anytime and some of their indifference seeps through no matter what. I have had a bet of several months standing with Lancelot that the war will be over by day after tomorrow – I doubt now whether it will be quite so soon but by the time you get this even the pessimists will expect it daily I should think.

If you could know the times I have thought of you and blessed you for all the things you sent us you would be amazed. ... I can't thank you enough ever for the cleanex [Kleenex tissues], the lipstick, the pink shawl, the green angora scarf, the colored tissue paper, the red skirt and sweater, the toys and whatnots as well as for the beautiful books that came later. What a girl! What a heart! What a friend!

[82] See the letter of 20th June, 1943. West's book is 1100 pages in length.

[83] The Allies advancing across France battled German resistance from 19th to 25th August. The French Forces of the Interior entered the city on 24th August and General Patton's U.S. Third Army the next day, when the German occupying army surrendered. General de Gaulle and the Free French marched triumphantly down the Champs-Elysées the same day.

[84] Fraser Gurd served with the Canadian Armed Forces, in the beginning as a junior surgeon.

I don't know whether Mother told you what a trying year we had last year – starting with Gay and Julie getting whooping cough in February just when Mary Lee was due – she was two weeks late luckily because I had 'flu and arrived easily ... Then when she was four months old I found a lump in my left breast which had to come out – turned out to be cancer so I had to have my breast off at once – a hell of an operation because they pared me down to the bone including the muscle of my arm. I was in a run-down, worn out condition to begin with which made me feaker and weebler than ever and after three weeks in a nursing home I could only totter out looking like a slug and feeling awful. I had to have two lots of X-ray treatments as a further precaution – 12 each time – and very lowering physically and mentally so I really just crawled around all winter – but come Spring I bounced back and though now I have no stamina I feel as good as ever and can look after the three girls without being utterly exhausted. The cancer never preyed on my mind as much as it might have because we got it so early and so many people I know of have had the same operation and have then lived to be nearly eighty. ...

[*rest of letter and date of despatch unknown.*]

7th Sept.
Malone

Dear Mama,

... Gay and Julie are so excited to think you are coming and have it all planned where you will sleep and what they will do. ... Gay and Julie have been brought up to believe that Denver is heaven and it has been backed up by all the nice things you send and have sent for so long.
We moved up on Tuesday – thankful to come because the weather has been shot to pieces Sunday it poured all day – Monday was a cloudburst with ducks swimming around haystacks in the fields honestly and the walls of Mahee started to wash away. It is pouring this minute but the sun is shining too – the kids will be coming home from school in ten minutes so I hope they don't get drowned. ...

Isn't it wonderful about no blackout? I had a bet on with L. that it would be lifted when the time changes a week from Sunday and Huzza!

I am right. I also had a bet that the war would be over by Sept 3rd but I lost that one. ...

We may go to see *Madame Curie*[85] tonight to see the newsreel of the liberation of Paris – wasn't it dramatic? ...

13th Sept.

Lancelot is thrilled with his Annise Hysop [sic] seed which arrived today he has it planted already and is reading about it this minute in his American bee magazine. He has his Expert Beemaster Certificate now, the only one of 4 who took the exam to pass and is going to take an all day exam on the 30th.

I read a good book – light called O *Western Wind* about English evacuees in America.[86] ...

Love and kisses,
Helen

10th Oct.
Malone

Dear Mother,

... I'll bet you are excited about Auntie. She was so excited the day she heard she could go that she nearly blew up. I am green with envy and would love to be coming too but having to say you are coming to live stops anybody who isn't foot-loose and fancy free. However, Auntie might as well go and enjoy herself... Mary Lee is singing "This is the Army"[87] around the corner in her pram. ...

The leaves are fluttering down from the lime trees in the park and there are bonfires every evening. I have the house full of Michelmas [sic] daisies and bronze chrysanthemums and hydrangeas – that's all

[85] This late 1943 "biopic" was directed by Mervyn LeRoy and starred Greer Garson and Walter Pidgeon; Aldous Huxley was an uncredited screenwriter.

[86] *Kirkus Reviews* described O *Western Wind* (1943) as a "High calibre woman's novel, with full emotional values sharpened up by intelligent writing ... This should find an audience". It was written by Honor Croome (1908–1960).

[87] "This is the Army, Mr Jones," a song from Irving Berlin's 1942 Broadway musical that was staged in Belfast in January.

we have. ... Must go now and get the Government orange juice and the chickens. Don't overdo getting ready for Auntie – she won't care if the nail heads on the basement steps aren't polished!

Love and kisses,

Helen

12th Oct.

Malone

Dear Mother,

Just a quick one while Lancelot is out at the bee meeting. ... I heard today that Mrs. Beath's second daughter's husband was killed at Arnhem – he was a glider pilot and was killed the first day. His widow is about 20 and has a baby daughter 9 months old. He, the husband, had won the Order of Stalin for something he did over a year ago – if they had ever gone to Russia they could have lived there free, never had to stand in queues or to pay on busses or trams – in fact all traveling free.[88]

I had a flight into high society last Saturday night – Mary Byers, who is living with her father now Sir Milne Barbour asked me out to dinner and to play bridge[89] – Lancelot wasn't asked because he doesn't play.

[88] The 1200 men-strong Glider Pilot Regiment of the British 1st Airborne Division played a risky role in the struggle with German defences in and around Arnhem in the Netherlands in September, 1944. The Germans were at first confused by the landing but then rallied to repel the British Army. If Mrs Beath's son-in-law (her daughter Jean's husband) was killed on the first day, that would have been 17th September; he was 24. Jean Beath married Captain Ralph Maltby from Essex whose mother was from Armagh and his uncle from Belfast. In April 1944, Captain Maltby had in April received the Soviet Order of Patriotic War after a mission in which sixteen officers flew over Germany to assess anti-aircraft defences and from which six officers did not return. See *Belfast News-Letter*, 13th April, 1944. Helen heard of Captain Maltby's death the day before it was reported in the *Northern Whig*, 13th October, 1944.

[89] Mary Byers, daughter of Sir Milne Barbour (1868–1951) was President of the Ladies' Guild (Co-operative movement). Chairman of the largest linen thread company in the world, Milne Barbour married a distant cousin from New Jersey (Eliza) who died in 1910. The Barbours lived in Conway House, Dunmurry on the outskirts of Belfast. Sometime after Milne Barbour's death, Conway became a hotel, then was bombed in the 1970s during the IRA campaign, repaired, and functioned as a hotel before being demolished. See Kathleen Rankin, *The Linen Houses of the Lagan Valley: The Story of their Families* (Belfast, 2002), pp. 54–55; "Milne Barbour", Wikipedia.

I went out on the bus and changed for dinner in Mary's room – my bag unpacked by a lady's maid, taken up by a butler – Ma! It was powerful. There were 8 for dinner – Pa, Mary, the housekeeper, Captain and Mrs. Duffin[90] whom I knew, an American naval officer and an English squadron leader. The dinner was so good and we were waited on by a butler and footman. I had 2 very dry Martinis before dinner which nearly knocked me backward because we never drink anything – nobody does because you can't get it – at least people we know who never did drink much, but I recovered shortly after dinner and enjoyed the bridge very much. The American was as smooth as glass – it was he who mixed the Martinis and had stayed with the McCleans in Colorado Springs (the Hope diamond ones) who had passed him onto the Weckbaughs for a few days because they weren't ready for him.[91] He had been to Central City too – he was from Washington. Sir Milne was a disappointment – too much like Adolf Menjou[92] and not much else. Mary is as gay and amusing as ever and drank so much seemingly with no effect. The house is a period piece if I ever saw one with a beautiful double drawing room reminding me of New York in 1900 (from impressions gained from the movie *Heaven Can Wait*)[93] it had rose satin brocade walls, banks of chrysanthemums, and blue-green curtains. The bedroom was chintzy and white woodworky with a huge dressing-room bathroom connected – no modern snap but lots of charm backed by a generation of wealth. I wore my one dinner dress – hadn't had it on for a year – now a rusty blacky with tarnished silver thread embroidery but my hair looked a dream. ...

I have just read a very good book called *The American Character* by an American anthropologist called Margaret Mead – good but

---

[90] For the Duffins, see the letter of 21st November 1940.

[91] Born in Denver, Evalyn Walsh McLean (1886–1947) was a mining heiress (daughter of Thomas Walsh, an Irish immigrant prospector who became a multimillionaire) who was the last private owner of the 45-carat Hope Diamond. See Wikipedia entry for Evalyn Walsh McLean. Ella Weckbaugh (1875–1971) was the daughter of John K. Mullen, one of Denver's most prominent businessmen and philanthropists of the late 19th century; she married Eugene Henry Weckbaugh and they lived in the locally famous Weckbaugh Mansion, built 1930–1933.

[92] There was indeed a physical resemblance between Milne Barbour and the American actor, Adolphe Menjou (1890–1963).

[93] The action of *Heaven Can Wait* (1943), an American comedy starring Gene Tierney and Don Ameche, begins in a wealthy neighborhood of Manhattan and continues between the 1880s and 1942.

deep[94]. The Nicholsons[95] and Tommy Carr were here on Monday night – Harry and Roberta wanted to come but wanted to come alone. Roberta is shy about her size according to Harry and Harry wants to come "when he can see the house and say My dear!" Tommy has finished a portrait of Julie which is a speaking likeness in her green velvet dress. I washed it – the dress – the other day most successfully – I am afraid to risk anything at the cleaners any more. I washed their blue velvet skirts too – now a program is on called *Appointment with Fear* but I don't think I can stand it – not sitting here alone, I can't – much as I like murder books. I only like the puzzle kind not the scary kind.[96] Our portrait is being changed again – Mary Lee brought from 8 months to 18 and looking so sweet. Gay has a new hair style and I look as though I am hearing voices – Tommy is very anxious to show it in London in his spring show so we may hear some professional criticism on it or even have it published. ...

Goodnight and love,
Helen

21st Oct.
Malone

Dear Ginna,

... It is Saturday night and I am alone in the house with 3 sleeping children. L. is at Mahee ... Gay went to a party this afternoon and I took Julie to a movie to compensate – such a mistake! It was a beautiful

---

[94] *The American Character* (1943) was the Penguin edition for the UK of the celebrated American social anthropologist's book, *And Keep Your Powder Dry: An Anthropologist Looks at America* (1942). Mead was the author of the influential monograph, *Coming of Age in Samoa* (1928).

[95] For the Nicholsons, see the letter of 2nd October, 1939.

[96] *Appointment with Fear* was a weekly late evening programme of horror and suspense stories on the BBC Home Service during the 1940s and 1950s. They were often written by the American writer John Dickson Carr (1906–1987), author of dozens of books of detective and mystery fiction. The storyteller was the Man in Black, played by the actor Valentine Dyall (1908–1985), one of the most distinctive radio voices of the day.

day and there we sat at *Clive of India* (of all things)[97] when we could have been pushing Mary Lee through the autumnal countryside – however I learned my lesson and we won't do it again.

Isn't it exciting about Auntie? ... She had the whole thing arranged one day before she even came home from town – American consul told her she could go ... and she had been to the police to file for an exit permit. I think she should have waited until we tried harder to get Mother over here but I suppose that is impossible. ... She cabled to Mother for a sick paper (Mother to be so sick she needs Auntie) and found the next day that that wouldn't do and that she must say she is going to America to reside which she promptly said she was, meaning all the time only to go for 6 months. It may be all right but it is rash... She may have trouble when she tries to come back here to claim her money because going to America to reside is fairly final and governments tend to become huffy if repudiated – I have experience of it – in 1937 I gave up my American passport because we weren't allowed both and I thought the British one would simplify traveling with L. and when I got it back in 1939 I had to answer some pretty pertinent questions about why I had given it up and Washington had to be cabled to before I got it back. The other and really rashest thing I think is going to live indefinitely with Mother when they have never been a rip-roaring success living together. When I say indefinitely I mean it – I doubt if American citizens will be allowed to travel for years and I honestly don't think Auntie will be allowed to come back for nearly a year after the Jap war. ... Maybe I have just been infected by British caution. ... Why is it that we are so wonderfully sensible? Do you think it is reaction from our excitable early atmosphere?

... I may be in a pessimistic mood and all may turn out as merry as a wedding bell. I would love to be coming – need I say but I naturally can't say that I am come to reside so it is impossible but if it were I would whip off tomorrow with Mary Lee on my back and Gay in one hand and Julie in the other. ...

...

[Love,
Helen]

[97] *Clive of India* is a 1935 American "biopic" of Major-General Robert, Lord Clive, starring Ronald Colman as Clive and Loretta Young as his wife Margaret Maskelyne.

9th Nov.
Malone

Dear Mary Lou,

Auntie may be coming to see you if she can when she lands in Montreal on her way to New York and then Denver. She doesn't know when or where she is sailing from but it will be any time now. She had to say she is going to America to reside to go at all and she may decide to stay – time will tell. ...

Our house is a cheerful muddle – I just live here. The cook more or less runs it. I work at the American Red Cross Club one day a week and the rest of the time mill around with the girls which I like better than any other work. ... We are quite social in a quiet way – film society last night, concert Saturday night Moisevich [sic][98], to see friends tonight dancing school this afternoon. Ulster is the most comfortable place in Europe to live I should think. We go to Dublin about twice a year and gorge. Dublin laughs everything off – they go to races in hearses and to balls on bikes but they always go. ...

I'm starting to get grey but feel skittish most of time. I read the *New Yorker* and the *New Statesman* weekly and fill up with *good* murders, *good* novels and deep sociological studies (not many). The thing I like best about living here is not have to keep up with Lizzie to the same extent that Americans do but contact with America always makes me feel twice as lively and fresh and happy – whether it is movies, soldiers or letters – there is no doubt that the people here are half-dead by comparison. I feel more American every year but subconsciously know I am becoming more European by exposure – however one day on American soil and it will drop off like a cloak I think. I never can imagine myself staying here or the girls young ladies here and Irish – they all look American and act it and have been brought up to think America is paradise backed up substantially by what comes to them from you and the family. The weather is lousy – hardly any summer and appalling winters but I am fairly indifferent and don't mind as

---

[98] Benno Moiseiwitsch (1890–1963) was a British classical pianist born in Odessa. In 1946 he was awarded a CBE for his contributions to the war effort, having performed prolifically for service personnel and charities. He performed at Queen's University on 11th November (Armistice Day) under the auspices of the British Music Society of Northern Ireland.

much as lots of natives. Our house is frigid – I am in front of the
nursery fire upstairs and have a nice view of mountains (mole-hills to
us) and the incomparable Irish skies. We have only been back and forth
to Mahee and Dublin for nigh onto six years and will I break loose the
minute I can.

I can recommend *The Death of the Heart* by Elizabeth Bowen,
Victorian Novelists by David Cecil[99]. Poetry by Frances Cornford,
Louis MacNeice and W.R. Rodgers – the last two both Ulstermen.
Have you ever any time to read? Or go to movies? Or are you too tired
nights to do anything but feebly listen to the radio. ... I have an awful
guilt complex about the war and how little we do – Lancelot tried both
army and navy and was turned down in 1939. He was in the Ministry
of Food for 2 years at the blitz time as salvage officer but now he
stockbrokes, farms and keeps bees. This letter has been written in a
wild rush but I have had a complex about it and you because I have
been so awful and you have been so grand. – To the day when we all
meet and with so much love and I can't say what thanks.

Helen

Fri. 24th Nov.
(American Red Cross Club, Belfast)

Dear Ginna,

Business is non-existent and there are no good magazines to read so I
will use my four hours of sitting here on a high stool for your benefit
(not all 4, you will be glad to hear.) My only boy this morning has been
an officer tying up a bundle of X-ray pictures – he did it so
professionally and was such fun to talk to – a young doctor from
Philadelphia who is thinking of marrying an Irish girl but who sees the
many pitfalls. I work here every Friday morning from 10–2, tidying the
room and sewing on buttons, stripes, flashes etc. It is very very quiet
today. Luckily the gramophone is right across the hall in the games

---

[99] *The Death of the Heart* (1938) by the Anglo-Irish writer Elizabeth Bowen
(1899–1973) is set in London and was later seen as reflecting the impact of pre-
war tensions on personal lives. Helen is presumably referring to Lord David Cecil's
Early Victorian Novelists: Essays in Revaluation (1934).

room so I hear what music there is but even that is spasmodic today – usually it is steady. I was here yesterday at a Thanksgiving Dinner – all the American women in town were scattered around the tables in the dining room – There were 2 dinners – one at 5.30 and one at 6.30. The one at 5.30 was orderly but gay but the 6.30 one had its disorderly groups who had killed the before dinner time in the pubs. I had two semi drunks beside me for the 6.30 one who were pretty funny – I asked one how long he had been here and he said "Long enough to get webbed feet." The other was a very attractive lady killer who pawed me from top to toe and whose remarks were punctuated with shouts to friends across the room "Hiya Bubber!" followed by loud and raucous laughter and a slap on the back for me. I stayed a while to watch the dance – jitterbug alternating with very slow dancing – the kind I hate but as was explained they have to rest. Can you jitterbug? I know that I am too old – but some of them made me green with envy they were having such a wonderful time – especially in a skipping rocking step. Most of the girls are as good as the boys and are they a wild looking lot and they try so hard with their clothes and hair.

Tonight we are going to a dance at the Officers' Club with the Nicholsons – some Hospital charity[100] – we haven't been to a dance for a year. ... I only have one dress – a black with silver embroidery – slightly tarnished and my hair is anything but soignée but maybe I can do something with it. I need a permanent but my hair is still in such bad condition I don't want to get one but my hand will be forced soon. ...

Stella is coming for the weekend – she leads a well nigh unbearable life for her in Newcastle. The American beau is with General Patton's army fighting hard.[101] I will have to park her out tonight – probably with the Smiths – an artist friend of Tommy's and his intense, neurotic wife[102]. ...

[100] The Committee of the Officers' Club (High Street, Belfast) organized a dance in aid of the Ulster Hospital for Children and Women on Friday, 24th November.

[101] The U.S. Third Army, led by General George Patton, had stalled during the draining Battle of Metz (in north-east France near the German border), and though the battle was won by mid-November, Patton was later criticized for lacking aggressiveness and decisiveness.

[102] Sidney Smith (1912–1982), son of a draper, was educated at Royal Belfast Academical Institution ("Inst") and attended evening classes at Belfast Art School, where he befriended fellow artist Dan O'Neill; he was a muralist as well as easel artist. This information courtesy of the Naughton Gallery in Belfast: "Sidney Smith", www.naughtongallery.com.

I took Gay and Julie and Mary Lee to see Lee's grave the other day – Mrs. Turtle had a plain headstone put up.[103] It didn't make me feel anything but mild regret. At very, very rare intervals of run downness and depression I am killed by it but having three others it is the greatest help possible. Sometimes when they are all together I try to picture Lee as a ten year old with them but it is too sad to think about so I don't – and having no other boys it is very hard to imagine anyway. ...

Lumeah in cold weather is a nightmare – like Avalon or worse. We sit in the Drawing Room which is huge and so hard to heat and never use the morning room at all. I don't know if I'll ever become very attached to it – at the moment it leaves me cold (pun) but maybe after the war I will get a burst of enthusiasm for it. I am so busy with the children when I'm home and it is too cold at night to do anything but sit in front of the fire.

The library is empty now. ...

I must write to Doug or he will be off home – he expects to be home for Christmas – he was so nice and such fun. Lancelot liked him enormously. We talked a lot about Lee who Doug thought was too bright for this world as an explanation of why he took so long to orient himself.[104] I often think of him when I am in here looking at all the boys. They all wring my heart especially the sleeping ones – the library is a favorite place for the ones who are just so tired or so bored or so lonely that they go to sleep. They are all so nice and so polite and so full of fun – and so young. ...

26th Nov.

Now it is Sunday morning and the coldest day yet – I am sitting nearly in the fire and I can still see my breath! ...

The dance was quite amusing mostly from a novelty point of view. ... It was the Officers' Club – a surprisingly nice place for Belfast but you could tell that we have been five years at war by the people – an indescribable lack of zest and the feeling that an old record was just going round and round. There was a wonderful young naval officer there who was one of the best dancers I ever saw and had one of the

[103] Helen's firstborn, Lee Turtle, was born on 11th January, 1935 and died on 8th December 1936.

[104] Helen's brother, Lee Ramsey Jr, died on 16th July, 1928, aged nineteen.

prettiest heads. I was green with envy of his partner who was a Wren in uniform. There weren't any very pretty dresses or girls.

Last night we went to a concert – Stella and I at Queens – a cellist who played a bad programme.[105] Gay and Julie are getting excited about Christmas and the toy situation is worse than ever. No more news so I will fire this off.

Love,
Helen

27th Nov.
Malone Park

Dear Mother and Auntie,

Auntie certainly left just in time – the weather is icy! ... Our house is like a big ice-berg. The only warm room is the kitchen. Last night Stella and I sat in our coats and L. in his dressing gown all evening. Stella came on Friday and is going Wednesday. I just tried to get tickets for *Boyd's Shop* at the Group Theatre and found that they are booked out for the whole week.[106] It has been running 5 or 4 weeks already. There are no good movies in town this week. The big red bag, the moccasins and tie arrived just this minute for which many, many thanks. The bag will be most useful and is so smart – I've seen lots of pictures of them in the American magazines lately. ... Stella is in town now buying me buttons and shopping generally. We are going to Kay Mackie's to tea and to Mucki's for supper both to meet Osborne King's new fiancée an English girl, the Honorable something. Osborne is Jimmy King, the late auctioneer's son. I haven't seen him since the war started. His picture

---

[105] On Saturday 25th November, Douglas Cameron (cello) and Eric Harrison (piano) played sonatas by Brahms, John Ireland and Rachmanninoff at Queen's University. Cameron (1902–1972) was a member of distinguished orchestras and quartets; Julian Lloyd Webber was his pupil. Eric Harrison taught at the Royal College of Music; in May 1944 he gave a recital in the Home Fleet Theatre, Scapa Flow, with the Royal Marine String and Wind Orchestra.

[106] When the Group Theatre came into being in 1940 as a result of several dramatic companies amalgamating for effective production, it found a large appetite in Northern Ireland for plays of local settings, themes and dialects. Although they staged established plays from farther afield, *Boyd's Shop* (1936) by St John Ervine (1883–1971), set in working- and lower-middle class east Belfast, not far from Helen's previous Belmont home, was a huge success.

was in the paper last week for winning the D.S.C.[107] He is in the navy and has been working off Holland in little ships. ...

Everybody I see asks about Auntie and says how brave she was. I figure that she is landing today or tomorrow and have half-looked for a cable since Saturday. I hope she wasn't frozen to death on the sea. ...[108]

[Love,
Helen]

Give yourselves – Mother, Auntie, Ginna and Aunt Ethel – each $10 for Christmas – I'll pay you back after the war! Merry Christmas, Girls!!!

25th Dec.
Malone

Dear Mother, Auntie and Ginna,

Your cable was telephoned this morning – the first we've heard that you joined forces and are in Denver – the last I heard was a letter from Mother who had flown to New York (up Gracie!)[109] and was meeting all the Montreal trains! But that was around the 27th of November. I'm glad to hear that Ginna is in New York too – Elizabeth City didn't sound so hot but it's always nice to see the country. ... Lancelot is joining films together and the three babes are fast asleep...

Thanks to the American mail they had a super-dooper Christmas. I got them 4 or 5 books each and made them each a white organdie drawstring bag decorated with green sequins (don't scream – they love it!) and a few odd knickknacks and the rest was all American.

[107] For Lieutenant James Osborne King, DSC, Royal Naval Volunteer Reserve, see the letter of 11th May 1942. His photograph appeared in a *Northern Whig* article of 23rd November entitled "Ulster hero in 'silent service' tradition". King, a keen point-to-point rider and yachtsman, was reluctant to discuss his naval feats with the reporter.

[108] In her letter of 14th November, Helen writes that she was told it takes about 15 days to cross the Atlantic in convoy so that her mother should expect Auntie to make landfall about 28th November.

[109] This might be a reference to Gracie Mansion, the home of the New York City Mayor, or a family joke.

... Norman and Willie, Emily, Amy and George came to dinner and stayed until 7.45 – fairly heavy going conversationally all day – lunch at 1.30 and tea at 5 – movies after tea.[110] Bob Hope is now on and is as funny as ever.[111] Julie believes so hard in Santa Claus that she wouldn't go into any room alone after 6 last night from nervousness and put some chocolate biscuits and milk out for him and drew a picture for him. I knew Gay knew about Santa so I asked her a day or two ago and she was thrilled to have a secret from Julie.

Bodo is home but he was out delivering presents on E[dith]'s bike. Our turkey was so good – we were supposed to have 2 American soldiers but the Red X rang up to say that none had come in to the club so none came. ...

I didn't give L. anything and he gave me 2 book tokens – making £3.0.0 of book tokens we got. The kids got books from nearly everybody who gives them presents ... I gave Jim Barr the new Louis MacNeice poetry book[112] – he hadn't heard of it and he gave me a £1.1.0 shopping token from R. [Robinson] and Cleavers ... Must beat it to bed – the radio is pounding away.

Night-night and love
Helen

29th Dec.
American Red Cross Club

Dear Mother, Auntie and Ginna,

Business is bad. There is dead silence here except for Auntie's pal Miss Gillespie who I hear scintillating in the hall and saying "Fine, Fine". ...

It is an icy day and so was yesterday – heavy frost like snow – seasonable but made for chilblains. ... I am going to meet L. and Tommy at Rodman's [art gallery] to see our finished – believe it or not

---

[110] Willie Turtle (1892–1972) was Lance Turtle's first cousin and married Emily Smith. Amy (b. 1927) and George (b. 1931) were their children.

[111] Hope was probably performing on "Command Performance" at 10.00pm on the General Forces service, recorded in the U.S.A. and relayed by the American Forces Network.

[112] Faber and Faber published MacNeice's *Springboard: Poems 1941–1944* in 1944.

– portrait which is being sent to London for an exhibition of all Tommy's paintings 40 some.[113] I am half afraid that he will crab it[114] in front of Tommy. Tonight L. is going to Mahee for the weekend and I am going to a buffet supper at Nancy's. ...

Yesterday we went to the circus which the children liked – we took Mrs. Grummitt and 3 of her 4 kids with us.[115] There was only one really good turn at the circus – a clown in baggy clothes who pretended he couldn't tight-rope walk and was really wonderful – you know the kind who is always teetering and falling but never does. ...

Will you send me Charles Graham's address please?[116] I want to send him a subscription to the *New Statesman* for a wedding present – a trifle late! I sent one to Mary Lou and will send her and Ginna Louis McNeice's new poems too – they are so good. Jim Barr was so pleased with his – he said it was the best present he got.

Amy Turtle who is 16 is so American – mad – knows all the slang and all the band-leaders and was so envious of the little jeeps the children have. ...

There was a wonderful movie at the film society the other night – made for the Americans – by some Americans and an English producer, showing and telling the Americans how to act in England and why the English are the way they are. I don't know what it was called but

[113] An exhibition of Tom Carr's paintings was held at the Leicester Galleries, London in March, 1945. "Conversation Piece", a portrait of the Turtle family, appears as plate 6 in Eamonn Mallie, *Tom Carr* (1989).

[114] Presumably Helen worries that Lancelot will criticise the painting.

[115] Mary was the wife of J.H. Grummitt, headmaster of the prestigious Royal Belfast Academical Institution 1940–1959 and a high-profile public figure. Before coming to Belfast in 1940, Grummitt had been principal of Victoria College School, Jersey until, twelve days before the Nazis invaded and occupied the island on 1st July, 1940, he escorted some Victoria pupils to Shrewsbury and then Bedford from where he was appointed to his post in Belfast. He became County Commissioner of the Boy Scouts. His wife Mary also led an active wartime public life. She was influential in the Women's Voluntary Services and was Commandant of the Girls' Training Corps in Northern Ireland. See J.S. Rowley, "Victoria College School: A Short History 1929–1956," h2g2 website; WikiVisual website; *Northern Whig*, 12th October 1940; *Belfast News-Letter*, 12th March. 1941.

[116] Charles Graham was a former Denver beau of Ginna's and her husband-to-be Lloyd's best friend. He visited Lance and Helen several times in the 1930s. Helen's daughter Julie visited Charles Graham's widow in Estes Park Colorado in 1991 where she learned of the Grahams' friendship with Clifford and Virginia (Foster) Durr, the civil rights activists. A lawyer, Clifford Durr (1899–1975) represented Rosa Parks in her epoch-making challenge to the constitutionality of the ordinance that legalised racial segregation on Montgomery (Alabama) buses.

Burgess Meredith was the G. I. and Bob Hope was in it for a scene explaining the money.

Mother would have appreciated that part because he threw all the pennies on the ground and said "you won't need those they just make you lop-sided". The whole movie made the Americans so lovable and the English so nice too. It was directed by Anthony Askwith [sic] , who is about the best English director.[117] I took G. and J. to a movie one rainy day last week to see *Once upon a time* about a caterpillar that danced to "Yessir, That's my Baby".[118]

... The library is empty now. Must stop because I have run out of news and I will skip in to lunch. I am so glad that Ginna is in New York – I think it would be so interesting because there is such a variety of things to do in your time off – don't let the squandering of money get you down – I was just reading about it in an old copy of *Life* which cited the Broadmoor and the Brown Palace – suites at the Broadmoor for $85 and $105 a day in constant demand.[119] As Daddy so rightly said "They're all crazy"!

On which note of wisdom I will cheese it to lunch.

Love and kisses,
Helen

---

[117] *A Welcome to Britain* (1943), a joint U.S.-U.K. government production, billed itself as "Britain for beginners ... or, Americans, at least." It was co-directed by the American movie actor Burgess Meredith and the British director Anthony Asquith (1902–1968, and son of H.H. Asquith, erstwhile Prime Minister of the U.K.), who later directed to acclaim *The Winslow Boy* (1948) and *The Browning Version* (1951). Bob Hope, born in England, appeared as himself in the film.

[118] In the American film *Once Upon a Time* (1944), Cary Grant plays a financially embarrassed showman trying to exploit for paying audiences a boy's dancing caterpillar.

[119] The Broadmoor Hotel, Colorado Springs, was built in 1918; the Brown Palace Hotel, Denver, was built in 1892; both are still in operation. $85 represents well over $1000 in today's money, $105 over $1500 (£1220).

1945

The biggest freeze since 1895

Ed Murrow's horrifying report from
    Buchenwald

"At 10.45 we heard that Hitler was dead"

The redoubtable Mrs Shipley, gatekeeper
    to America

Farewell to the American forces

Don't fence me in!

12th Jan.
American Red Cross Club

Dear Ginna,

I've been amused for 24 hours by your description of the Bradley girls having a fling in New York. When Mother said that Auntie had bought a mink coat I knew that she had busted wide open. I guess as you say, it's the unbeatable Battle – but I agree with you they both deserve it and they are a riot. I doubt in fact know that when you and I are closer to 70 than 60 – if we even hang on as long as that, that we won't have their spirit – we might but it will be so inarticulate by comparison that we will seem half dead. ...

Gay spends all her time reading – she always falls back on *Rebecca*, *Little Women, Tom Sawyer* and other classics which shows why they are classics. I read *Rebecca* about once a year myself and Gay has read them all scores of times. She has a nose for books like her Ma and is lazy like I am too. She is not naturally cheerful but maybe I wasn't always either though I am now...

The Club is quiet today. I have only sewed on one button for a boy who has been here for 2 years and is leaving today. I asked him if he was going home (foolish question) and he said "No the other way". I asked him if he was glad and he said "No". ...

Incidentally no *New Yorker*s have come for quite a spell and thank you for renewing the subscription it is a perennial joy to me. I am reading U.S. foreign policy by Walter Lippman[1][sic] and bought a good book with a book token – *The American Character* by D. W. Brogan[2] – very good – I read a good review of it in *The New Yorker*. Glad you like the *New Statesman* – it is too red for most people here and they are too agin everything with nothing constructive to put in its place.

[1] Walter Lippmann (1889–1974) was regarded as the most distinguished journalist of his generation. *U.S. Foreign Policy: Shield of the Republic* (1943) sold half a million copies in its first year. The book promoted the post-war policy of an Anglo-American-Soviet alliance to ensure security and prosperity.

[2] *The American Character* (1944) by the Scottish historian and broadcaster D.W. Brogan was one of many wartime books that attempted to explain the British and Americans to each other. Brogan's book, though, was said to be for an inquiring rather than popular readership.

I mostly skip the political articles but read the book reviews, movie reviews, essays, competitions etc. Here goes my last cigarette – I could only find 3 this morning and sitting in here with nothing to do I always smoke too much anyway. They are 2/4 for 20 which is ruinous. I usually don't smoke in the morning and do most of it at night. ...

We have just had a week of snow and ice and the feeling of our house is unbelievable. I told L. last night that if any American house was as cold they would think it was total war all right. There is a coke shortage and coal is scarce too – politics and miners. We have supper in the drawing room and breakfast in the kitchen rather than face the dining room. L. has chilblains but so far I haven't.

Our children are the only ones I know who haven't had either measles, chicken-pox or bad colds. ... Bringing up kids is certainly an uneasy business. Julie is our frailest one – easily tired and prone to colds and won't rest ever enough. Gay is the biggest worry though, with her temperament and her bouts of stuttering and sort of choleric disposition. ...

Now I've just had lunch and I'm dying to smoke – too late! I had lunch with Mary Byers who is as gay and giggly as ever. She says that Rollie, her husband [Major Roland Byers] is coming home in October from Burma ...

L. is going to a bee meeting tonight and I am having a girlish game of bridge with Mary and Kathleen Morwood, Peg Dolan and Ursula Dunsmuir – used to be Ursula Totten [sic] and lives in Malone park – husband in Italy. I like Nell better than Peg who is always anxious and trying to hide it. Nell is editor of a news-letter in London – a weekly or maybe monthly commentary on the news called *The White Hall Letter*. It costs £4.4.0 a year and is supposed to be very good and our Nell is the whole thing. There was an editor but he went to America.[3] Nell was telling me about her affairs in the real sense of the word. She is now trying to find somebody to marry but apparently not for love – she's had that. Peg's husband is in Cairo – he is the most over bearing

---

[3] Possibly an error for Mary and Elizabeth Morwood. For Peg and Nell Dolan, see the letter of 22nd May 1941. The commentary Nell edited, *White Hall Letter,* has yet to be located. Their mother Mrs Dolan and Helen were in charge of the library in the American Red Cross Club: see the letter of 29th Oct 1942. Margaret Temple (Peg) Dolan married Samuel Soames from Wiltshire. In January 1941, Ursula Totton married Robin Dunsmuir of the Argyll and Sutherland Highlanders. Her mother Norah was awarded an MBE chiefly for running the Ulster Library Scheme – see letter of 4th Dec 1943.

kind of Englishman good looking except wall-eyed and very intelligent but the kind of man you go out of your way to disagree with. Mary Morwood I can only stand rarely and she has such an objectionable little boy (it comes out so young) who runs to mama from Mary Lee saying "Aren't I mama's little sweetheart?" Just sewed on a button for a Nebraska boy who wouldn't care if it rained every day in Nebraska if he was only there. ...

Went to the Alpha-Club luncheon yesterday... The speaker was a glamour-boy B.B.C. announcer who was terribly good in a Harryish [McMullan] way.[4] There were 400 there – nearly anybody who was anybody or wants to be somebody. I had forgotten what a mass of Belfast women look like, I should say ladies, and sister are they a sour-puss lot. Do you remember those luncheons? People are smoking right and left – Sis, I'm clear wild. ...

I asked Nell Dolan about Anglo-American relations – her answer was the equivalent of "They stink". If I were the type I would worry nights about it but I compromise by reading and hearing everything I can on it and trying in such a small way to help. ...

Love and kisses,
Helen

28th Jan.
Malone

Dear Ginna – Mother and Auntie,

For once we really have something to write home about – even if it's only the weather but Sister you have no idea! When I tell you that the last spell like this was in 1895 and that Lough Neagh is frozen over you will appreciate that it is something.[5] It started a week ago Friday

---

4   A large crowd in the Carlton Hall, Belfast listened to Frederick Grisewood, in a talk entitled "Behind the Scenes in the BBC", speak entertainingly about life on the other side of the microphone. Freddie Grisewood (1888–1972) was for many years a distinguished British announcer and commentator. See *Belfast News-Letter*, 12th January, 1945.

5   Lough Neagh is the largest freshwater lake in Northern Ireland and the largest lake by area in the British Isles (151 square miles); five of Northern Ireland's six counties border it. The winter of 1894–95 brought severe cold; some scientists think it the culmination of the Little Ice Age; temperatures in the UK sank as low as -29C (-17F).

but only got into full stride with frozen pipes and frozen milk with the tops an inch off the bottle on ice on Monday and it has been like that every day getting colder every day. The lowest temp has been 7 deg above and it hasn't been above 32 degs the whole week. Nothing for Denver but you know the damp here – not to mention the coal shortage!!! The bedroom windows never become defrosted on the inside and only our scullery taps won't work – lots of people have not one drop of water running in their houses at all – johns not working etc. I have only found about three people who like it. I love it despite the fact that ten minutes upstairs leaves me wringing my hands and nearly crying with them. I had bad chilblains the first day or two but they have settled down now to red swollen itchy hands and not even burning feet. ...

Yesterday we went sledding on some big hills near the Lagan at the foot of Deramore Park – we borrowed Douglas Pringle's sleds [6] and he came with us. The hills are steeper than that 8th Avenue hill around Pennsylvania that was roped off. It took all my nerve for me to go down alone. Gay and Julie loved it and later went down alone too – so brave! Eddie Bryson and Jack Workman have been skiing all week –and Caroline [7] too – the snow is powdery and perfect for skiing. Eddie came to call on us Thursday night on skis – I was playing bridge up the park at the Tottons but L. was suitably impressed. Jack Workman has cracked a rib and some child aged 10 has fractured his skull and is described as "raving" in the hospital. Eileen and Eddie rescued him – apparently an awful episode – he didn't come to for four hours and now a week later he isn't properly to yet.

Lancelot and Kenneth [Pringle] went to Mahee yesterday, came home for supper and to bring some coal up in the trailer and then went back last night to shoot woodcock this morning – the snow has brought them to the sea. Mahee is frozen up – Johnny couldn't crack the ice on our water tank but the well doesn't freeze – some of the eggs froze and burst. Sis! It's awful and it shows no sign of thawing. The radio just said that some place in England it was 9 degs below and people are queuing for buckets of coal. Margaret [Helen's maid] says Eire is terrible – no coal and only damp turf – an awful lot of people just stay

---

[6] Douglas was Kenneth Pringle's brother.

[7] Eddie was Herbert Bryson's brother; his wife Eileen was Nina Andrews' daughter; for Jack and Caroline Workman, see the letter of 30th May 1940.

in bed and she said some houses she went to she just had to come out again. Her father is an engine driver on a train and so they have some coal. Lots of people here have no coal – only wood and turf.

Same evening

This is the evening – we went sledding again and it was much warmer – just before we left 2 pipes burst and flooded the scullery but Margaret's fiancé plumber came and fixed them temporarily. We can't have any hot water though. There were about 200 people out skiing, skating and tobogganing. ...

Isn't the news good? The Russians are only 95 miles from Berlin today.[8] ... The landscape all week has been a dream especially a few days when fog froze on the branches – Malone Park is all white packed snow but the Malone Road is brown. We have just had cocoa and cold roast beef sandwiches – really tasty and are going to bed soon – unwashed! To think of you sitting in New York – it still don't seem possible.

Love,
Helen

29th Jan.
Malone

Dear Mother and Auntie,

... Now it is after supper and I was just talking to Nancy [Mitchell] and asking her if she wanted Margaret's fiancé who is a plumber. I heard today that they had no water – scores of people haven't had a drop for a week – everything frozen solid – we had 2 burst pipes in the scullery yesterday but Johnny, the fiancé came and fixed them. One minute after I rang off Nancy rang up to say that everything had burst loose and the scullery, bathroom and cloakroom were knee deep in water. ... I enclose an editorial from *The Observer* yesterday and they are releasing plumbers from the army for "thaw leave". ... It is pouring now and the snow is a goner ...

8 The Soviet Red Army completed the occupation of Lithuania the day Helen is writing, and then crossed into Germany. By 31st January they were within 50 miles of Berlin.

Isn't the news good? ... Maybe the war will be over soon – the news is on now telling about the threat to Berlin – 90 miles away today. ... Kathleen Spence was booked to come home in March but Toby has told her not to come now on account of increased U-boat activity. Poor Kathleen! She literally missed the boat on the quiet time on the Atlantic if it was quiet? ... Poor Toby fell so much on his skis. Well, girls – I've shot my bolt but will write oftener – you do too so we won't feel so relation-less.

Love,
Helen

30th Jan.
Malone

Dear Mother and Auntie – (Send to Gin),

Just a quick one while we wait for supper to be ready – our cook isn't punctual – we are having woodcock tonight – the thaw started yesterday and nearly finished today – only our snowman is left in the garden – a little pile of snow. The dampness within is terrific – the cloakroom walls are running and all the mirrors are cloudy. It was lovely and warm today and very windy. I went to *The White Cliffs of Dover* with Maureen. It was better than I expected because I'd read half-hearted reviews.[9] Then I met the children at their dancing school at Shaftesbury Square and we bought them each a pair of Oxfords and Julie a new Burberry rain coat – the pride of her life and 12 coupons!! Then we had tea at the milk bar and then got an ice-cream at Woolworths and came home with L. When we got home we found that we had no water.

I washed my hands in our left-over tea and Lo and Behold on the 9 o'clock news they announced that the Northern Ireland water supply had had a serious breakdown so goodness knows when we will have any! L. and I just went out and collected the little pile of snow that was left – that and one pan full are all we have – can you imagine in Ireland?

---

[9] The 1944 MGM movie, *The White Cliffs of Dover*, was adapted from Alice Duer Miller's 1940 poem, *The White Cliffs*. See Helen's letter of 23rd August, 1941. The movie starred Irene Dunne, Roddy McDowall and Van Johnson and was a hit with cinemagoers. The ten year old Elizabeth Taylor was an uncredited actress in the film.

It is as mild as summer outdoors – I was out without a coat and not a bit cold. I am supposed to be lunching with Peg Dolan tomorrow but if there is no water none of the restaurants will be open. ... Mucki just rang up to borrow my infant feeding book – her old tartar of a nurse is going – it has been war between them for 6 months – the baby is 6 months old and Mucki is so busy with cows, turkeys, chickens and pigs that she leaves the baby entirely to the nurse. She is going to Scotland to buy cattle next week and then is going down to Ossie's wedding.[10] There is going to be wedding reception for 500 including the King, Queen and the princesses – if I can buy a *Tatler* I'll send you the pictures.

... We now have an egg crock and about 10 other vessels full of snow. Roberta thinks the schools will be closed because of sanitary arrangements. Harry has rung up the water works and they said that there had been so many bursts that they couldn't get pressure up for household supplies. We certainly have had 10 days of crises. The girl who did my hair yesterday had washed in her hot-water bottle water. ...

Old Hitler is going to speak in about half an hour – the big baboon. ... Now we are listening to Hitler who is working up to a frenzy. ...[11]

5th Feb.

The water situation is all right again for us though this morning's paper said that 10,000,000 gallons are still being lost daily with so many burst pipes not fixed. ... Gay wrote such a funny composition about it – the subject was "When the Thaw Came" and it ended: "We know a

---

[10] Lt Osborne King's wedding; see the letter of 27th November, 1944. In February 1945, he married Hon. Patricia White, WAAF, daughter of Lord and Lady Annaly of Longford.

[11] In his final radio address to the German nation, Hitler sought to galvanise Germans into heroic last-ditch resistance. The real enemy in his eyes was always "Jewish Asiatic bolshevism". The "bourgeois world" with its "unbridled economic liberalism" was always incapable of surviving, much less reversing, "the hurricane from Central Asia". England will not survive the hurricane either and will regret summoning help from "the steppes of Asia". Only National Socialism ("ideologically consolidated national communities") can defeat Soviet Russia, "the Kremlin Jews" and the "plutocratic-Bolshevist conspiracy". Hitler calls on the able-bodied, the sick and weak, city dwellers and country dwellers, women and girls, and especially the young, to fight to the last. What Helen hears as frenzy is a rising desperation in the voice of the Führer.

lady whose pipes burst and there was tremendous flood. She rang us up and said 'Listen' and we could hear the water running through the telephone." That was Nancy and it is true but more dramatically put than actual facts. ...

We took Edith to dinner at the Grosvenor Rooms Friday night and then went to the Group Theatre to see *Arms and the Man* – quite good.[12] Bodo is in hospital with a gland on his head and 'flu. He is definitely coming out of the Navy at the end of April, Edith thinks, but everybody thinks the war will be over by then anyway – 38 miles from Berlin this morning. Elaine thinks her baby will come early in April. Roberta's hasn't arrived yet. Our radio is busted but L. can bring one up from the office – this is no time to be without one. ... It is a lovely sunny day and the daffodils are in the shops. We haven't a flower in the house or garden and I miss them so much we have some pussy-willows and some variegated shrubs but that is all. ...

7th Feb.

We took Edith a goose today and went in a minute to shelter from a heavy shower ... Edith wasn't home but Ritchie her maid, told me that Percy [Metcalfe] is coming home next Monday Doreen heard yesterday. He has never seen Virginia who is about 15 months old – I have never seen her either. They think Percy will be a civilian again because his job is finished and he isn't trained for anything else. He is flying home and Edith who rang up is so afraid he will get pneumonia from the sudden change of climate – he has been in Sierra Leone – "the white man's grave" and has lost 14 pounds.[13]

---

[12] The plush Grosvenor Rooms restaurant in the Great Victoria Street station of the Great Northern Railway opened on 30th June, 1944, the centenary of the GNR. It was opened by the Governor of Northern Ireland the Duke of Abercorn, and among the guests were Lord Glenavy (Chairman GNR) and Sir Basil Brooke (nephew of Field Marshal Alanbrooke), the Prime Minister of Northern Ireland. See *Belfast Telegraph*, 30th June, 1944. George Bernard Shaw's relevantly titled play (first staged in 1894) was performed by the Ulster Group Theatre in Belfast.

[13] Sierra Leone was a colony of the British Empire in 1939 and so went to war alongside the mother country. Soldiers recruited in Sierra Leone fought in Burma alongside the British. The officers of the West African Frontier Force, set up to garrison west African colonies, were British.

... The news tonight announced that the Big 3 are meeting on the Black Sea and that the Russians are pouring over the Oder.[14] We read the best book last night called *Arnhem Lift* by an anonymous glider pilot. Jean Beath's husband was one of the paratroopers killed at Arnhem.[15] She has a job now at Oxford and her mother-in-law has the baby. ... We must go to bed because it has been "midnight again" for the last 2 nights. We just sit on and can't leave the fire though the cold weather has gone. ...

Nighty-night
Helen

8th Feb.
Malone

Dear Ginna,

Sitting by a nice fire at 11.30 in the morning with everything under control except I haven't told the cook what we would have for lunch yet. ... Margaret is doing as well as I knew she would with the kids – I told her so this morning. ... She is naturally good with children and so efficient. She is about 25 and very intelligent, looks sulky and will stand no nonsense about anything. She is engaged to Johnny Moffat an independent plumber but she has no notion of getting married and they have no money. Johnny is a nice-looking boy who I hope will be able to stand up to her. She has awful fights with him and gives him fits over the telephone. ....We are going to pay a sympathy call at the

[14] The Yalta Conference, attended by Roosevelt, Churchill and Stalin, was held in the Crimean peninsula city from 4th–11th February to discuss post-war arrangements in Europe. In January the Red Army crossed the Vistula and, under Marshal Zhukov, the Oder (both rivers flowing north into the Baltic Sea), a mere forty miles from Berlin. While Zhukov, having liberated Warsaw, tactically delayed the advance on Berlin, other Soviet forces continued west and on 27th January liberated the captives in Auschwitz concentration camp.

[15] See the letter of 12th October 1944. The author of *Arnhem Lift*, Louis Hagen (1916–2000), was a German Jew called Louis Levy whose family, having already run afoul of the Nazis, escaped from Germany in the mid-1930s. He enlisted in the British Army and flew in the Glider Pilot Regiment under the pseudonym of Lewis Haig. He fought in the Battle of Arnhem where he distinguished himself under fire. He later served in India, before which he wrote *Arnhem Lift* in a fortnight. After the war he became a much-travelled journalist and popular historian of Nazi Germany. *Arnhem Lift* was first published anonymously. See www.pegasusarchive.com.

Dolans tonight. Major Dolan is very ill in the Musgrave Clinic and Edith has got us to go with her tonight to cheer up Mrs. Dolan and Peg. Mrs. Dolan is in one of her down-in-the-mouth moods when she says she has no friends (her own fault) and the Major hasn't any (her fault too) but she blames it all on their religion.[16] Edith is always so good about sick people and does her duty nobly. ...

It is pouring rain and has been ever since the snow went. This really is the worst climate. We only have one torn umbrella for the whole house and the children have no galoshes, rubbers or boots. ...

We just read such a good book called *Arnhem Lift* – I will try to send it to you also Louis MacNeice's new poetry called *Spring-Board* . The B.B.C. has improved so much lately and they have such good programs of music, plays and features on a very high level. The Home Service is now serious on the whole and the Forces is mostly frivolous. If you take the *Radio Times* which we do and listen intelligently it is a great source of entertainment and pleasure.

Have you ever read *Middletown* and *Middletown in Transition*? They are sociological studies of a town in Ohio and the best books I know on American life and they are so depressing.[17] I read them years ago and would like to get my hands on them again. America as a whole is still one of my greatest interests especially in comparison to England. In *Horizon* this month there is a very outspoken article on American and English Nationalism by Bertrand Russell who was in America from 1938–1944 and who is so worried about how so many Americans hate England.[18] One thing that has dawned on me slowly and reluctantly is

[16] Major Dolan lived on until 1950. Presumably the Dolans were Roman Catholics living amidst predominantly Protestant neighbours and Mrs Dolan thought they were being informally boycotted. See the Afterword on the religious question in Northern Ireland.

[17] R.S. Lynd and H.M. Lynd, *Middletown: A Study in Contemporary American Culture* (1929) and *Middletown in Transition: A Study in Cultural Conflicts* (1937) were commercially successful sociological studies of a small mid-West town in Indiana (rather than Ohio) that revealed often invisible segregations in the population; they were much reprinted after the date of this letter.

[18] The philosopher Russell lived in the United States between 1938 and 1944, teaching in Chicago, Los Angeles and Philadelphia. His article on "British and American Nationalism" appeared in *Horizon*, January 1945, pp. 17–30. In it he candidly admits the hatred with which many Americans regard the English and attempts to offer explanations and solutions. If *Middletown* was an uncomfortable read for Helen as a citizen of a then modest mid-West town (Denver), Russell would have been an equally uncomfortable read for an American woman who quite likes the English and is living full-time among the British.

how much better English education is. I don't mean free education but paid schools and colleges. I know that I could have graduated from D.U. [University of Denver] and not known A.[19] – not Smith [College] of course which is wonderful and made us what we are today ...

Harry just rang up to say that Roberta just had another son –

At the Red+ Club: Now I am at the Red + – no business yet. I was just looking at a *Life* [magazine] which featured the teenage girls with their white bobby socks, moccasins and long pretty hair – how times have changed since we were at East[20] – marcelled and wuzzy[21] in our bull toed 3" heels – such a healthy change in 20 years – Gosh! 20 years! On people young enough and with a pretty color of hair I think that long straight hair is divine. My contemporaries' hair here is awful – still those tight rolls and bumpy "perms" – mine is bad now too – not a tight roll but a bumpy perm. I am letting it grow to wear it up – in desperation. You know how bad I always was with my hair which is so difficult. Just sewed a boy's glove – a boy from Chicago – the breezy type I like – then had coffee (which I still hate) with Mary Byers who is always so entertaining but fairly over-powering. She was saying what a pity it is that Jimmy King, Osborne's father, is dead and can't be at Ossey's wedding on Saturday because "he would make the Queen feel perfectly at home"! I see that *I'll meet you in St Louis* a new movie is based on 2115 [sic] Kensington a series of stories by Sally Benson that ran in the *New Yorker*. I loved them so because they got the flavor of American life as we lived it so well – hand-outs at Hallowe'en, conversations of the sisters, paper dolls, back yards and ash pits porches, watering the lawn and all those things that make me swoon with nostalgia.[22] I sent you *Arnhem Lift* and *Springboard* yesterday –

---

[19] Anything?

[20] Presumably East High School Denver, founded in 1875 and regarded as one of the top high schools in the United States (voted as such in 1957).

[21] A marcel is a soft wave in the hair achieved by a heated curling iron. Wuzzy presumably means wiry and curly.

[22] Sally Benson (1897–1972) was born in St Louis but became a short story writer in New York. She published 99 stories in the *New Yorker* between 1929 and 1941, some under the pen-same of Esther Evarts. *Meet Me in St. Louis* (1942) included eight vignettes that had appeared in the magazine under the title of *5135 Kensington*. Her title was taken from the movie *Meet Me in St. Louis* (1944) which though it had not been released was in the script stage. The movie starred Judy Garland and was directed by Vincente Minnelli who married Garland in 1945. 5135 Kensington Avenue, where Benson had lived, was demolished in 1994.

both so good. We are going to dinner tonight and to see *Western Approaches* with Nancy and Edith – Nancy is taking us to the movie and Edith to dinner.[23] The library is pretty full now. ... Lancelot has been nearly deaf all week in both ears from an accumulation of wax. He is going to Dr. Foster today to have it blown out – he had to once before and Arabella has to regularly – these waxy Turtles.

Just had a long session with Mrs. McGiffin, an American pal of Auntie's and such a good-hearted gossip but the kind that makes me dry-up like a clam.[24]

I read a synopsis of *When We were Young and Gay* in the *Readers Digest* and will certainly see the picture.[25] We went to *My Man Godfrey* one night this week. I remember you telling me how good it was in about 1935 or 1937 but it doesn't wear at all.[26] It shows too how movies have improved in the last ten years. Here come some American W.A.C.S – maybe because they are young or something – maybe because I've lived here too long – 12 impressionable years but I feel as remote from them as from the moon. I like American men so much better than American women. I went to *The White Cliffs of Dover* especially to see whether I was "sold on the English way of living" the way Irene Dunne was according to one review I saw. I am still wondering.

... I have hooked *Is Sex Necessary?* [1929] to take home. It is the only James Thurber I haven't read. I still can get hysterical reading *My life and Hard Times*[1933] and *Let Your Mind Alone!* [1937]. Nancy

[23] *Western Approaches* is a 1944 "docufiction" film (directed by Pat Jackson) which used real sailors rather than actors. It concerns a drifting lifeboat, a U-boat and a rescue ship. Although the Western Approaches is an area of the Atlantic Ocean lying to the west of Ireland and the west of north-west and south-west Britain, much of the action was filmed in the Irish Sea.

[24] Mrs McGiffin is listed in the Belfast street directory as head of house at 9 Malone Park in 1932, but a parenthetical note tells us that in 1943 the head of house is E.D. McGiffen [sic]. The latter may or may not be the American woman Helen knows.

[25] Helen must be referring to *Our Hearts Were Young and Gay*, a hugely popular 1942 book by Americans Cornelius Otis Skinner and Emily Kimbrough, recounting their European tour in the 1920s after college. It became an American comedy film in 1944. The historian Hugh Trevor-Roper discovered that the book was used as a codebook by German Intelligence.

[26] *My Man Godfrey* is a 1936 "screwball" comedy starring William Powell and Carole Lombard and directed by Gregory La Cava. It won six Academy Award nominations and its high reputation has held despite Helen's judgement.

was saying the other day that she felt beyond having an affair with anyone or even thinking of having a mild flirtation. I went through a stage like that but I have now passed into "the dangerous years". Not that I think I will but I think I could – but I wouldn't. I just thought this morning when L. and I came to town together how devoted we are. I went to the Classic to book seats for tonight and L. pattered along "just to see how you get on". He does the nicest things and is such an easy, ideal husband. Our lives are so uncomplicated by no personal relations strains. With Mrs. Turtle 100 miles away we are so free from bother.

Now I've just had lunch and a chat with such a nice boy – aged 40! and worried about getting a job when he gets home because of his age. This is such a good place to work if you want your faith in human nature bucked up. Not that I ever need mine bucked because it is boundless – hence my breezy optimism. I have been asked how to spell *Guiness* or is it *Guinness* and the date and have we a dictionary – which we haven't. If we had an extra one at home I'll bring it down. Two boys got the giggles at lunch and laughed so hard and so loudly that they had to go out. It was real too because everybody had to laugh too. ...

I have to go out and hunt oranges after I leave here. They come in every 2 months or so now but go like snow. ...

Here comes the navy in – they look about 15 years old with their hats on the back of their heads – awful sweet. ...

I look for peace in a month – do you? Even L. who is always pessimistic says 3 months. I must go to the American consul to see if there is a waiting list for passages over. Imagine Kathleen Spence having been in America since 1939. Our life before the war seems so far away – always in our big green Terraplane [27] and never on the trams but we had no peace of mind – what people now call the jittery thirties. Remember Lancelot every summer at Mahee saying "this is our last summer here". I have been putting drops in his ears every night while he lies on the bathroom floor – so little boyish and unselfconscious and always so funny. He is the nicest simplest person and I love to watch him move. I always loved the way Lloyd walked.

---

[27] The Terraplane was a make of car produced by Hudson Motor Company of Detroit between 1932 and 1938. In its quick acceleration and power, it was favoured by gangsters including John Dillinger and Baby Face Nelson.

That picture you sent of you and Lloyd dancing on your honeymoon is so attractive of you both – Lloyd looking the image of – now I can't remember – Oh yes – Henry Fonda. My mind gets woollier every day. I have been relieved now so will go – and high time too – what a letter!

Love and kisses
Helen

13th Feb.
Malone

Dear Mother and Auntie,

Just a quickie before I go to the Alpha Club to hear Joad[28]. I have about half an hour. It is raining as usual but there is no wind so I will wear my best hat – Dublin black sailor and carry our holey umbrella. ... Joad is so pompous but I hope he won't be too heavy. ... There are lots of oranges in again so I'll take my big basket with me to town and park it at L.'s office so I will look smart at the Alpha Club. ...

Joad was much better than I expected – in fact very nice and not a bit pompous. His talk was on "The Future of Civilization" and was pretty solemn but had its funny moments.[29] He was an hour late because his plane was delayed from London. Lancelot is talking to Percy who didn't know a week ago that he was even coming home. He sounds fine and is as pleased as punch with Virginia whom he had

---

[28] Unusually for a philosopher, C.E.M. Joad (1891–1953) was a household name in Great Britain. This prominent English thinker was the author of many books and numerous philosophical papers. He achieved his popular reputation through radio programmes, books of general appeal, and public lectures. His quirky participation was one of the reasons the BBC programme *The Brains Trust* (1940–49) had such high ratings. In February 1945 he toured Northern Ireland talking to the troops, but first he took part in a Brains Trust at RAF headquarters with a talk next day at the Alpha Club in the Carlton, in which he contrasted the optimism of the Victorians a century before with the sense of an ending felt today; we had misused science and technology and our spirituality was in retreat – only its revival could save us. See "Civilization's most serious danger", *Northern Whig*, 13th February 1945.

[29] At the start of the war Joad was in tendency left-wing, pacifist and civil libertarian while being opposed to the Marxist philosophy. As the war progressed, he abandoned pacifism and supported the British war effort. On the topic of the lecture Helen attended: Joad had published *The Story of Civilization* in 1931 and *For Civilization* in 1940, so it was a subject on which Joad had developing opinions.

never seen. I've never seen her either. Percy will be at home at least a month and will get petrol so we will probably see them. ...

It poured all day. Maureen and I went to a pretty bad movie – Spencer Tracy in the *Seventh Cross* and I didn't get home until supper time.[30] Eggie is coming tomorrow instead of today – still waiting for a plumber.

I was at Mahee on Saturday for the first since New Year's – the snowdrops are in bloom and look so sweet. Kenneth Pringle came along to get some potatoes – there aren't any in town – imagine a potato famine in Ireland and the week before no water! ...

The slips, pants, bras, nightie and girdle arrived today and are more welcome that the flowers in spring. They are all beautiful and will keep me going for years. ...

Here is the news on – Lancelot is going to take another expert bee exam on the 24th. He is studying hard every night for it, drawing all the insides and outsides of bees. ...

If you want to read a good book read *Arnhem Lift* – I sent it to Ginna and she can send it to you – good novels are *The Ballad and the Source* by Rosamund Lehmann[31] and I can't think of any others. I am reading a good book of criticism by Rebecca West[32] – either high brow or murder – that's me! ... Tell me all the news – I love to hear – even the smallest tidbits. I wear my hair up now and it looks much better. A communiqué was just announced from the "Big 3" whose meeting is

---

[30] *The Seventh Cross*, directed by Fred Zinnemann, is a 1944 war drama with Tracy playing a German prisoner who escapes with six others from a Nazi concentration camp in 1936. In the German novel which inspired the film, Tracy's character was a communist, but this allegiance was dropped from the American movie adaptation. Despite Helen's dismissal, the film was respectfully regarded and the co-star, Hume Cronyn, was nominated for an Oscar as Best Supporting Actor.

[31] Rosamund Lehmann (1901–1990) was a distinguished English novelist. *The Ballad and the Source* (1944) was acclaimed for its subtle portrayal of the relationship between a young girl and an elderly woman in Edwardian England.

[32] The book of criticism by West may have been *The Strange Necessity: Essays and Reviews* (1928) or *Ending in Earnest: A Literary Log* (1931).

just over.[33] I will hold this over to the morning in case I get a letter from you.

Night-night and love
Helen

18th Feb.
Malone

Dear Mother and Auntie and Ginna,

It is 12.15 and a lovely warm day. Gay and Julie have been dressing up in the garden playing house and now are cycling round the house like mad things. Eggie and L. are doing something to the bees I think. We have just been walking around the garden with Eggie getting him to give us his ideas on what he would do to liven it up – it is so dull. Eggie is always so full of good practical and artistic suggestions and as you know is interested in everything. He is staying with us indefinitely while Hilary is with her mother in England – her mother had a stroke but isn't too bad – up for two hours every day.

We have had a frantic 10 days or so of going out and rushing around so I stayed in bed all day yesterday to "let my soul catch up to me" – quotation from a story Joad told which he used as a symbol of what's wrong with the world – that it has gone too fast and hadn't stopped to let its soul catch up with it. I read two very good books – *Music in the Park* and *I'm a Stranger here Myself* – the first about a German spy in England and the second about life in the navy for ordinary sailors.[34] Last night I went to the last of the British Music Society concerts at

---

[33] The communiqué was released to the press on 12th February, 1945. Having declared that "Nazi Germany is doomed," the communiqué outlined the plans for a triple division of occupation of Germany, the complete disarming of Germany, the demand for German reparations, the convening of a United Nations conference, the liberation of all European states, and the establishment of a Polish Provisional Government of National Unity. See No. 1417, "Communiqué issued at the End of the Yalta Conference," Department of State, United States of America, Office of the Historian: Historical Documents, vol. II, 1945.

[34] *Music in the Park* (1942) is a novel by F.L. Green (1902–1953). *I'm a Stranger Here Myself* (1943) is a novel by Anthony Thorne.

Queens – a two piano recital by a newly married couple who were so obviously in love.[35] ...

Now I've just done a power of telephoning for the Red X. Mrs. Dolan is out of the picture and I have to do the juggling of times, get substitutes and all and I hate it. Major Dolan is a little better and is coming home with 2 nurses sometime but I don't think he will ever be up again. The Red X was so busy Friday that I hadn't time to write to you and I met the nicest boy – a Jew I think from New York. Marcia said the Queen wasn't at Ossie's wedding because "the girls had mumps" – the girls being the Princesses – such a homelike note.[36] ...

The D.R. Circle is tomorrow, paper by Miss Kyle on Virginia Woolf[37]. ...

Isn't the news good?[38] Even L. has a bet on that the war will be over by his birthday. Kathleen Spence is coming as soon as the war is over. We have a row of snowdrops in bloom but nothing else. ...

20th Feb.

Now it is George Washington's birthday and we have a new cook – I don't think a good cook but very pleasant and willing and a good cleaner. She has an American boy friend and went out in slacks last night[39] – goes out every night! ... Eggie is out painting and there is a big picture that he painted sitting on the couch – lovely but too pretty pretty for my taste. I would get tired of looking at it. I think he hasn't any soul in his painting. He is a very easy guest and very good company.

[35] Helen listened to a recital by Cyril Smith and Phyllis Selleck. They played Rachmaninoff, Schumann, Arnold Bax and Darius Milhaud. The music critic of the *Belfast News-Letter* declared it "a brilliant recital" (19th Feb.) Cyril Smith (1909–1974) was an English virtuoso concert pianist. He was an off-screen accompanist for Baird television broadcasts as early as 1935 and then joined the BBC where he met his future wife, Phyllis Selleck (1911–2007). Ralph Vaughan Williams and Lennox Berkeley composed pieces especially for them.

[36] Osborne King's wedding took place at the Chapel Royal, St James's Palace, Whitehall on 10th February. The reception was held in Admiralty House.

[37] Miss Kyle remains unidentified.

[38] Helen may be alluding to the Battle of Iowa Jima, the fierce contest between the Japanese Imperial Army and the U.S. Marines for the island south of Japan. After intensive bombardment from American warships, marines landed on the island on 19th February and the island was, somewhat prematurely, declared secure on 16th March.

[39] In the 1940s, slacks worn in public were regarded as daring attire for women; one suspects the influence of the American boyfriend.

... The news is on telling about the non-stop raid on Germany.[40] It can't be long now. ...

The D.R.C Monday was poor. Miss Kyle was too learned and it wasn't good. ...

The coal shortage is pretty acute. It is against the law for anybody to have more than ½ ton a month no matter how big the house or how cold the weather. The crocuses and snowdrops are all out and the birds are singing and spring is just around the corner. ...

[Helen]

6th Mar.
Malone

Dear Ginna,

... This is the 4th week that Eggie has been staying with us and what with a change of cooks and general turmoil I haven't had a really settled time at all. ...We stay up until midnight nearly every night – too late and enjoy having Eggie very much though there tends to be too much talk about the Mackies – inevitable because Eggie is so friendly with Jack and Kay and knows them all very well. Eggie gave me a lovely picture – I chose it from 3 – it is a snow scene and more like a design that his usually are – just a tree and 2 shadowy trees in the background. It is his £14.14.0 size so a very handsome present.[41] He paints about 3 days a week and works at Mackie's about 3 days. Hilary is in England with her Mother. I am pretty sure she is having a baby – at last. I hope it will improve her because she is so tiresome. Eggie couldn't be easier to talk to and to have around – so unfussy and natural. ...

Yesterday being m'birthday we went out to dinner and the theatre and I was in town for lunch with Stella and the D.R. Circle and my tap-dancing class in the morning – not home from 10.30 – 10.30 which I hate. I miss seeing my kids lots – I like Stella so well although she is so flighty – still in love with her American who is now in Germany still friendly with Tommy but not in the same bedroom and still blithe and

---

[40] Helen is likely referring to the British and American bombing raids on the city of Dresden between the 13th and 15th of February that caused such devastation as to provoke doubt as to their wisdom and morality.

[41] This painting, originally costing 14 guineas, is in the possession of Julie Mackie.

gay despite 6 years of living in Newcastle and hating it worse every month. The paper at the D.R.C. was by an Ulsterwoman [Nesca Robb] who is a distinguished Dr. of literature at Oxford – she wrote a very good book called *An Ulsterwoman in England* [1942] and her paper was on Walter de la Mare – a delight to listen to because she was so scholarly and brilliant – a visitor to the Circle – not a member.[42]

I have started to pose again for Toby Spence – he is trying to paint my portrait again – touching up the old one – I don't hold much hope that it will be good. If he started all over it would be better but he is so stubborn about suggestions and no one can tell him anything. It is pretty boring and tiring sitting upon a pedestal with a bright light glaring in my eyes but only a few sittings should do. Toby is crazy about painting but just hasn't got an artistic eye – though he has improved tremendously in 5 years in technique but he just lacks that something that I think I've got though I can't draw for nuts – the seeing eye I think they call it. ... Julie has it to a very marked degree already. Now it is after lunch and G. and J. have gone to rest and Mary Lee is playing around with me and is such a lamb saying "Deah! Deah! Deah! Mary Lee! Pick them up. Best girlie. Break the window. Pick them up" – and then lots of gabbling ... Here comes Eggie home again at only 3 o'clock. He must not have been in the mood. ... Now he is painting in his room and the kids are playing upstairs. It is raining away. ...

[Helen]

9th Mar.
Malone Park
Written fr. Red +

Dear Mother, Auntie and Ginna,

I have on my Red + apron for the first time and I feel efficiency + especially since I have got Stella Carr to work all day Monday thereby pushing out Mrs. Letcher who is the pink limit of unreasonableness and unpleasantness. I think people like Mrs. Letcher are bad for Anglo-

---

[42] Nesca Robb – see the letter of 1st September 1942 – received her doctorate from Oxford in 1932. Her family owned Robbs department store in Belfast, 1861–1973.

American relations.[43] I have been in charge of the Library since Major Dolan's illness and things have slipped mainly because the people have slipped. There was only one slip actually and that was Monday when no one came all day but there were no repercussions and it won't happen again. I now have Nancy extra to fill in gaps. She used to go Monday mornings but wants to tap dance so she can go other times. I may get Maureen to come too and between Maureen and Stella the glamour value of the library should zoom. Stella is so glad to get out of Newcastle for any reason any time and she loves Americans.

The town is full of grapefruit, lemons and marmalade oranges. We had our first grapefruit yesterday and they are divine. I have already eaten four. You can have as many as you like. The lemons will never be sold because no one has enough sugar.

… There is a boy sitting here who doesn't look a day over 16 but he must be more – it gave me quite a turn when I saw him. …

Stella came to supper after 8 hours at the Red X which she said she enjoyed. She was dizzy from looking at photographs of wives, mothers, babies and even twin brothers …

[Helen]

16th Mar.
Malone
Fr. Red + Club

Dear Mother and Auntie and Ginna,

It is about 12.30 or after and I've never drawn breath sewing, talking and tidying. The Club is fairly busy all the time now mostly on leave people over for a week from England – they all love it and the Club has got out such a good booklet called *Furlough Fun* with suggestions about what to do and where to go. I had a boy who had lost his eyesight in only eye over Berlin and another one gave me a candy bar – he had a 17 mo. old daughter whom he has never seen. Here comes the sun out. …

---

[43] Mrs Letcher may have been the widow of H.B. Letcher, manager of Scottish Provident who died in 1942 and whose son was H.J.O. Letcher, President of the Irish Linen Merchants' Association who worked in the New York offices of William Ewart & Son. See *Belfast Telegraph*, 8th July, 1942; 8th July 1944; 3rd March 1945.

The only real news item is that Tom Moore rang up last night and came out to see us. He is over here building a stereopticon (?) thing to assess bomb damage. His own invention and it sounds a pretty good thing.[44] He was pleasant enough but I never did take to him – and still don't. He isn't half as nice as Doug. He is curiously un-American being reserved and difficult and very quiet. He says he will come to see us again – he is his own boss and will stay here until he finishes the job but no one knows anything about it but him – no one knows what he is doing that is – it is no secret but just unfathomable. He looks the same as ever except much older and wears glasses all the time but he never had much charm or at least didn't show it for us. If he can get away we will take him to Mahee on Saturday. It is hard to imagine him the father of five – he seems so remote from it all. ...

Did I tell you Edie is having another baby in October? The idea is to have a son to play trains with Bodo. ...

I was going for my final pose with Toby but I put it off until Sunday night. ... If I have time today I will buy "My Guy's Come Back" such a good swing tune. The last one I bought was "Dance with a Dolly"[45]. ...

19th Mar.

Sorry to have kept this letter so long. Was tap-dancing this morning and I'm worn to a shred – dying for lunch to be ready – sausages. A rainy, dull day. Tom Moore came again yesterday and was much more human – in fact quite fun. He came around 4.30 – we had tea in the kitchen with the kids and then I parked them and then we had supper in the dining room – boiled eggs and grapefruit. After supper he and

---

[44] Thomas E. Moore, Doug's brother, was a Denver architect. During the war he served with the U.S. 8th Army Air Corps, and his architectural skills led him into photo intelligence. See "The architecture of Thomas E. Moore 1908–1970, the 1940s": https://temoore.ner/1940s/. Bomb damage assessment (BDA) reports were forwarded to senior airmen by intelligence specialists. Cameras were used for photo-reconnaissance before attacks and photo-interpretation after attacks. See Robert S. Ehlers, Jr., "BDA: Anglo-American Air Intelligence, Bomb Damage Assessment, and the Bombing Campaign against Germany, 1914–1945." Ph.D. dissertation, Ohio State University, 2005.

[45] "My Guy's Come Back" was a hit in 1945 for Benny Goodman and his Orchestra; it was covered in the U.K. by the Joe Loss Orchestra. "Dance with the Dolly (with the Hole in her Stocking)", 1940, was recorded by the Andrews Sisters who performed it in the movie, *Her Lucky Night* (1945).

L. came along to Toby's and criticized[46] the portrait and I sat for it. Tom left to catch the 11 bus to Langford Lodge[47] and L. stayed on until after 12 directing Toby's painting and improving the whole thing 100%. It is finished now and not too bad a likeness but not a good painting.[48] As L. says it seems to start out of the canvas at you. I always like to go to Toby's because they are all so funny there and we laughed and laughed. Toby takes all the candid criticism so well and so good-naturedly. Tom is coming again when he can. Stella is coming for the night tonight. I have asked the Isaacs up to play bridge and Maureen may come. Today is the D.R.C. – paper by Joan Isaacs on Katherine Mansfield. L.'s bee book came last Tuesday and he loves it – has been reading it ever since. Hilary came home last Sat. so Eggy didn't come again. ... Must mail this and go.

Love,
Helen

22rd Mar.
Malone

Dear Ginna,

It is a heavenly spring day – birds singing, lawn-mower mowing, daffodils in bloom and all. I have just had my hair done–up and look and feel like Marie Antoinette. I have been wearing it up but only in my own version more a char-lady's bun than a *Vogue* hair-do. I said to the hair-dresser "it's too high. I couldn't go out on the street like that" and she said "Do you know what I think, Mrs. Turtle?" And I said "No what" and she said "That you're letting people here get you

---

[46]Presumably Helen means "critiqued" rather than "adversely commented on".

[47] Langford Lodge on the shores of Lough Neagh near Crumlin had been an unfinished Royal Air Force base before it passed to the United States Army Air Force; it was readied by the U.S. technicians who preceded the American army, and opened on 15th August 1942, operated by Lockheed Overseas Corporation. See the website "Wartime NI": https://wartimeni.com/location/langford-lodge-crumlin-co-antrim/. The lodge was formerly a Georgian-style mansion and the home of the Pakenham family. Major Hercules Pakenham was killed in action in 1940. See "Langford Lodge", Lord Belmont website.

[48] This painting appears not to have passed into the Turtles' possession.

down". So I admitted it and said you couldn't help it and she agreed. ...

[Love
Helen]

Palm Sunday
25 Mar.
Malone

Dear Mother and Auntie and Ginna,

We are aimlessly sitting waiting for the water to heat for L. to take a bath – it is 10.30 so there is time to whip one off. ... Tom [Moore] went yesterday – he arrived here after 6 Thursday bringing a "Hospitality Ration" of 1 tin corn, 1 tin fruit salad, 2 tins salmon, 2 oranges and several candy bars and packets of chewing gum. ... He also brought me a book *A Yankee from Olympus*[49] and some *Saturday Evening Posts*. We liked him quite well but never got at all excited about him. He is so quiet that he seems to make no effort at all. ...

We went to tea at that packed milk bar and then came home and I got ready to go to dinner at the Barbour's in my new dinner dress. It fits like a glove and looks wonderful. There were only four of us and I was asked to make up a bridge table. Jack Colville, a bachelor stockbroker, was the other one and Mary and Sir Milne.[50] Jack called for me in a taxi and we had a wonderful dinner and played very serious bridge until 11.30. It wasn't much fun because Sir Milne has an over-awing or damping effect on a party and is much too serious about bridge. I had poor hands and lost every rubber but one but we were only playing for a penny so I only lost 1/8. Mary had on a lovely pale blue wool dinner dress embroidered with white beads – somebody in America had given it to her. She is quite subdued around her father and never smokes in front of him. ...

---

[49] *Yankee from Olympus: Justice Holmes and his Family* (1944) was written by Catherine Drinker Bowen (1897–1973). Oliver Wendell Holmes (1841–1935) was Acting Chief Justice of the U.S. Supreme Court and a much cited legal scholar.

[50] John Nicolson Colville (d. 1946) was President of the Belfast Stock Exchange and the Irish Lawn Tennis Association. He lived a few doors down from the Turtles: *Belfast Telegraph*, 19th Feb, 1946.

Tomorrow night we are going to a musical *Wild Violets*[51] and Tuesday to dinner at Nancy's – no other engagements this week. ... Stella was here Monday night for the night and I had Joan and Melanie Isaacs up to play bridge. Stella and Tommy are getting along fine now and I think Stella will stay with Tommy and not go off with her American captain. He is with Patton's army in Germany but I think Stella has seen the light. ...

[Love
Helen]

29th Mar.
Malone

Dear Ginna,

... Spring here is so heavenly to look at – the feathery willow trees and wonderful green buds and all the flowering almonds cherry and plum and apple trees but the snags are rain and chilliness – the latter always with us. ...

Now it is after lunch – chicken, leeks, potatoes and quite a good marmalade cakey pudding – all that + 2 Baur's chocolates[52], sitting by the fire, Geraldo and his orchestra and a screamingly funny conversation with G. and J. about the religious meaning of Easter – all that I repeat have raised my spirits to something nigh hilarious. The religious talk was a direct result of your remark that you wished we had been brought up in a more religious atmosphere. I wish we had too because I feel so lost about teaching them. ...

---

[51] *Wild Violets: A Musical Play* was first performed in England in 1932 at Drury Lane and published in 1937; the composer Robert Stolz also composed the popular *White Horse Inn* (1931). *Wild Violets* was staged in the Empire Theatre Belfast by the Belfast Amateur Operatic Society during the week of 26th–31st March. It was given a rousing review in the *Belfast News-Letter*, 27th March, 1945. The director Gwen Gracey MBE was a close friend of the legendary Mona Grey (1910–2009), Northern Ireland's first chief nursing officer who as well as introducing innovations in care wrote plays and pageants in order to raise funds for nursing facilities. These plays and pageants were mounted in the Empire Theatre by Gracey: see *Irish Times* 13th June, *Independent*, 4th August, 2009.

[52] The O.P. Baur Confectionery Company was established in 1872 in Denver by a recent German immigrant, Otto Baur.

I must tackle this religion seriously. They have prayers and hymns at school but nothing at home – occasionally prayers and little talks but not enough. Personally I'm a great believer in re-incarnation. A Miss Greeves in the D.R. Circle[53] has a theory that some people are old souls and some are new – on that theory I'm definitely new – not interested in anything old except anything that has to do with Southern Ireland and Western America. Do you remember how exciting the scenery and atmosphere was on that motor trip from Santa Fe when we were trying to get to the Mesa Verde?[54] Those two romantic periods of history fascinate me. England leaves me pretty cold historically and I'm too ignorant about other countries. It's the life in Ireland as it used to be and still is appeals to me terribly – in Eire that is – there is something about the countryside and the houses and the people and of course I love Dublin madly and feel so at home there. I could weep when we have to come home every time. It is raining so hard now that I may abandon my trip to town and try to nip in in the morning – must go order the rations now! Oh this mundane world that keeps interrupting my higher flights!

Alan Smiles was here this morning – home on about 5 days leave. He is stationed at Greenock now and is patrolling the Irish Sea. He is one of the most charming people I've ever known. He has been an ordinary seaman for four years or nearly 4. ... Alan was saying that he wants to be a farmer but expects he will have to work in town. He is 21 now – has a very intellectual father who is odd but pretends to be odder and a most efficient, pleasant Mother – the kind who cheerfully gets through more work at home and on committees than other people can do in 3 times the time. His 2 older sisters are WRNS – one married and one in France and his young brother – 18 or 19 is brilliant, odd, and asthmatic and is going to Cambridge in September. ...

[53] This could refer to Margaret Greeves, daughter of Captain and Mrs Greeves, prominent figures in the Ulster social scene, or to Miss Greeves (possibly the same) who was hon. treasurer of Queen Mary's Hostel, Belfast, or to Miss M.F. Greeves (again, perhaps one and the same), hon. secretary of the League of Nations Union (Belfast Branch).

[54] Since 1906, the Mesa Verde ("green table") has been in the Mesa Verde National Park, Colorado. It is known for its remarkable cliff-dwellings, built by the Ancient Puebloans between 900AD and 1350AD. The dwellings composed villages (or pueblos as the Spanish arrivals called them).

Good Friday –

Still chilly, still full of aspirin, still warding off a cold, still raining but Geraldo is still playing and it is like a tonic to an old horse. I should be packing and supervising and bustling but I am just sitting in a patch of sun like a cat on the window seat. ... We are going to Mahee in a little while. Geraldo is playing "Intermezzo" – it is an hour's program called "Dancing Through" giving snatches of dance tunes and I can't tell you what it does to me.[55] No, "Don't Fence Me In" isn't here yet but I am going to listen to a program tomorrow night of 10 hit tunes from the U.S.A. that it should be in.[56] ...
Here is the car – I must pack – Must go.

Love and kisses,
Helen

5th Apr.
Malone
fr. Red+ Club

[Dear Ginna,][57]

... Eggy painted 3 pictures at Mahee – all quite nice. The skies were lovely most of the days with big clouds scudding along and occasional showers. ...

Desmond Chambers whom you once met at the Nicholson's and the most brilliant barrister in town died in his sleep in bed with his wife Monday night. He was only 45 ... There was such a good appreciation

---

[55] Helen is writing between 1pm and 2pm as she listens to the General Forces Programme. Geraldo (Gerald Walcan Bright, 1904–1974) was a ubiquitous English band-leader of the time. "Intermezzo" (recorded by the Glenn Miller Orchestra among others) was the main theme of the 1939 Ingrid Bergman-Leslie Howard movie of the same name.

[56] Both Roy Rogers and Bing Crosby (the latter backed by the Andrews Sisters) recorded "Don't Fence Me In" in 1944. It is reported that 30 minutes after first hearing the song in the recording studio, Crosby laid down what proved to be a best-selling track. This cowboy hymn to the fenceless range (though composed by the urbane Cole Porter, with lyrics, however, by the Iowa-born Robert Fletcher) came to have at least a temporary symbolic force for Helen, tired perhaps of the constrictions of Northern Irish life.

[57] The beginning and ending of this letter missing.

of him in yesterday's paper I'm sure by Cyril Nicholson saying he was the Irishman of fable and story – gay, witty, gallant, generous, dashing etc.[58] His end was hastened by drink and his marriage was always a complete mystery – none of his friends had ever heard of the girl or knew when he courted her. ...

I have just read a biography of Alice Meynell by her daughter – you know the "Renouncement" she wrote "I must not think of thee" – she had 7 children too.[59]

The Marquess of Dufferin and Ava was killed in Burma yesterday. He was only 36 and had such a brilliant career in front of him ... married to a Guinness who is the talk of the town when she is here ...[60] I saw in *The Tatler* last week the picture of a girl who came to Mahee once with her husband in 1940 – he was interested in birds and was a pilot in the R.A.F. They were the most attractive pair – very young and very society and so nice. The girl is now married to a Marques [sic] and her husband is dead. She had a flat in Paris during the phony war and got out of France even after her husband. She had a baby with her and had so much gumption and sense for her years – she was only about 20 then. He was one of the very la de da Englishmen who give such a languid, sissy appearance and do such very tough things. They were the sort of people you can't forget – both so beautiful, so young and so nonchalant – they lived in some awful house in Newtownards [County Down].

---

[58] Helen is quoting the appreciation of J.D. Chambers KC that appeared in the *Northern Whig*, 4th April. The appreciation ends: "Like a comet he has passed across our sky". For Cyril Nicholson KC, see the letter of 2nd October 1939.

[59] Viola Meynell published *Alice Meynell* in 1929. Her versatile mother Alice (1847–1922) was an English poet, essayist, editor, critic and suffragist. She and her husband the writer Wilfrid (who both converted to Catholicism) had eight children. "I must not think of thee" is the opening clause of "Renouncement", a delicately woven sonnet whose theme is the release of chaste desire only in sleep: "I run, I run, I am gathered to thy heart".

[60] Basil Sheridan Blackwood, 4th Marquess of Dufferin and Ava (b. 1909), whose seat was Clandeboye, Co. Down, was serving with the Indian Field Broadcasting Unit in Burma and died on 25th March when a Japanese mortar shell found his unit. He was not yet 36. He was a close friend of the English poet, John Betjeman. In 1930, Basil had married his cousin, the flamboyant "Bright Young Thing", Maureen (née Guinness, 1907–1998).

I went to see Jane Villiers-Stewart[61] at the Park Nursing Home last Friday – she wasn't there – had been moved to the Maternity Hospital because of a breast complication. She was the young bride who with her husband rented Mahee last June – another attractive couple. It was pouring so Julie and I talked to Miss Strickland for a while and Miss Strickland told me that Jane lay there relaxing and enjoying it! Her first baby – and she didn't feel any pain. She had followed the instructions in a book about relaxing and believe it or not it worked. Her cousin did the same thing with her 5th daughter and Miss Strickland said she never saw anything like it. ... The most unexpected people do the most surprising things.

I have been asked to write a short story for the D.R.C. last meeting at the end of May. I love to write but never do and I don't think I'm a bit creative – only critical and I haven't an idea in my head. Reading about Alice Meynell has sort of inspired me to write something.

My favorite radio commentator was on last night – Wing-Commander Strachey of the R.A.F. He has the most ordered mind and the clearest way of putting things of any of them. He wrote some stories that were in *The New Yorker* several years ago and his wife came home from America with Janet Boyd – she writes too.[62] He said that it has taken 24 months of incessant . ...

[*rest of letter tantalisingly missing*]

[Love
Helen]

---

[61] Helen uses the correct spelling of the surname in the later letter of 20th May. Jane Fowler in 1943 married Michael Fitzmaurice (Mike) Villiers-Stuart RN (b.1911). Jane was an early convert to the Baha'i faith in 1953 and her children followed suit when the time came. See Jane Villiers-Stuart's son Garry's memoir in which he recalls growing up in Loughside house, Greenisland: "Growing up" and "Unconsciously becoming conscious", in "UK Baha'i Histories – Individual Stories": https://bahaihistoryuk.wordpress.com. Presumably Miss Strickland ran Park Nursing Home. While he was recovering from tuberculosis, Jane's brother Frank Fowler built a camp of wooden buildings on Mahee Island to lead a healthy, open-air existence. (Garry Villiers-Stuart: pers. comm.). Julie Mackie remembers Frank's camp as a marvellous play-ground for her and her pals.

[62] John Strachey (1901–1963) was an English politician and writer. He was elected as a Labour MP in 1929 but he moved leftwards towards Communism. When he lost his seat in 1931, he began writing and lecturing. During the war (by which time he had broken with Communism) he became an RAF wing commander and radio commentator. He was returned to Parliament in 1945 and was an unpopular Minister of Food because food rationing was maintained after the war. *Cont'd:*

13th Apr.
Malone
Fr. Red + Club

Dear Mother, Auntie and Ginna,

Everybody in here today is walking around with a paper in his hand looking sad. Everybody who hasn't a paper is trying to buy one. We heard about President Roosevelt last night on the midnight news and I nearly wept.[63] The few people I have talked to this morning ... have all felt so bad that they nearly cried and I got tears in my eyes talking about it. One [American] boy after reading the paper said "I guess his death will affect more people than anyone who ever has been" which puts it in a nutshell. I have heard several people here in the last year say that they thought he was a greater man than Churchill and you know what they think of their "Winnie". I don't know if you saw the photographs of the Yalta Conference, but if you did you will have seen how awful the President looked then – I never saw such a change in anybody and it made me very worried. ...

We had Peter and David McMullan to tea last Sunday. Peter came roaring in on his bike and whirled around the house three or four times before he could stop. Gay thinks and always has thought that Peter is wonderful and she is so skittish with him.[64] Both L. and I have an awful weakness for him too and nearly everything he says is funny. David is a nice, good looking little boy. Harry came to get them on Roberta's bike and came up to see Mary Lee who smiled and smirked and said "Hello Harry" and was generally captivating. Harry in his usual

---

[62] *Cont'd*: Among his books are *The Coming Struggle for Power* (1932) and *Theory and Practice of Socialism* (1936). Helen listened to Strachey's "War Commentary" on the Home Service just after the 9 o'clock News on 4th April. In 1933 he had married his second wife Celia Simpson, literary editor of the *Spectator* and to whom Helen is no doubt referring. Strachey's first wife was the Manhattan heiress Esther Murphy who with her brother Gerald frequented Paris with notable American expats; the Murphys inspired Scott Fitzgerald's *Tender is the Night* (1934); Esther is said to have been "almost famous".

[63] Tragically, President Roosevelt died when the end of the war was in sight. During a visit to his cottage in Warm Springs, Georgia for rest and recuperation, while signing documents and having his portrait painted, he suffered a fatal cerebral haemorrhage on 12th April.

[64] Sons of Harry and Roberta McMullan; see the letter of 16th May 1940 for Peter McMullan.

exaggerated way said "You're going to regret the day you had that one. If she goes on like this you will have to keep her in a cage when she grows up and let nobody see her but her mama". When we went downstairs I asked Harry to come to see the photographs of the kids and Peter came running in saying "Oh yes do see them. They are pure heaven! Absolutely pure heaven" which remark convulsed Gay and anything that I said was nice since she says "Pure heaven". Harry lent me *Some of My Best Friends are Soldiers* by Margaret Halsey which I have enjoyed more than I thought I would at the beginning of it. She still forces her laughs but she is a good racy writer with two good points – if you've read it you know that they are Jews and negroes.[65] I am reading it again because I skimmed through it so fast at the first go but I must absorb her points of argument. ...

Tommy came yesterday to finish our small portrait. He doesn't know if he will ever finish the big one because it will take so much more sitting that he doesn't know if we could bear it – especially the kids so he is finishing up the small one. He did me yesterday and improved me by 100% in about an hour. Now he is finished with me and is touching up the babes. He and Stella came over last night. Stella is such a vivid, vital person with such good sense although she is very frivolous and flirtatious but she amuses me a lot. ...

The Club is full today. I just sewed two pockets for an officer from Seattle who thinks Ireland is "pure heaven." They all do. He said he was afraid Roosevelt was a goner when he saw the Yalta pictures but he was afraid to give utterance to such a thought. There is a queue right out through the hall of new arrivals booking beds. Mrs. Cooke has been paging a boy called Carlos Commandos all morning. I saw Marcia in a District of Columbia car throwing in a back seat full of clothes to the cleaner this morning. Her children came home from school yesterday. Her teeth are blacker than ever. ...

I had a long heart to heart talk with a boy with a hangover today. He felt so nervous he couldn't even read or eat and he can't even wash his face or teeth without gagging. He was so funny about Mrs. Cooke paging Carlos Commandos and finally said "Jesus, I'm going to put her out of pain and tell her I'm Carlos Commandos".

---

[65] See the letter of 4th December 1939 for Helen's previous encounter with Halsey, who tackled anti-Semitism and anti-black prejudice in her books. *Some of My Best Friends are Soldiers* (1944) is subtitled *A Kind of Novel*.

14th Apr.

... Listened to the radio all evening last night about Honey Roosevelt. The Red + is having a memorial service at 11.30 tomorrow I must try and go. ...

Love,
Helen

20th Apr.
Malone
Fr. Red + Club

Here I set again – no business but several spells of talking and a present of a pack of Camels. We are having a divine spell of weather. I have on my new Easter bonnet with the white gardenia, my new dicky, my new pearl ear-bobs and do I feel ritzy! ... I have slipped so in clothes and outlook. That's Belfast for you but it has made its mark on me and I am shy about looking smart except in a tweed suit, flat-heeled British way. I am going to sell flags for the Maternity Hospital from 1–3 and then go up to the Maternity Hospital to see Elaine and her 5 day old son. She had it one day early with flying colors . ...

21st Apr.
Mahee

... SATURDAY: Now I am sitting in the porch at Mahee trying to keep warm but the sun only comes out "whiles" and it is pretty chilly. L. is working with his bees at the bottom of the garden and G. and J. are whooping it up outside with Peter and David McMullan who we brought with us for the day. Do you remember the day we sat on the window seat here 11 years ago and read *Les Miserables*? I mind it well! Our life before the war seems so long ago and so giddy. Now it is so staid and sober. We are so much the parents of children and act so middle-aged. My hat and dicky were a positive sensation in town yesterday. I felt so plush horsey but realized I looked and got used to being stared at by evening. As I went out of the Red + the doorman said "I thought you were going to a wedding" – which shows that that is the only time people here dress up. The forces news is now on – gunfire is heard in Berlin for the first time – hotcha! The indignation against the Germans is up to fever heat now since the liberation of the concentration camps. Even *The Times* has photographs that nearly make you sick and the radio reports are incredibly stark. The first one was by Ed Murrow from Buchenwald.[66] We were at the Brysons last Sunday night when we heard it and we were stunned with horror. I saw Joy on the street yesterday and she said that Adam, her husband,[67] is helping free these camps and throws up all the time. I sold flags for 2 hours and have got over my shyness and just nail the people so I sold an awful lot. ... The radio just announced that Ken Topping won the election yesterday – he is now a member of the local parliament at Stormont.[68] Maureen [Topping] has been making speeches right and left too and L. went to Larne on Thursday to help drive people to the polls. He got over 6,000 votes and his opponent only 2,000. Ken is the Unionist candidate and the other man was Labor. Ken will make such a good politician. He has such a good manner for strangers but we who know his home life sort of wonder.

I was surprised and very pleased at the universal sorrow felt here over President Roosevelt. Everybody was sick about it and the B.B.C. and the papers had nothing else on for days. Do you know much about Truman? Will he do? I went to a memorial service at the Red + and bawled like a baby. It was "Abide with Me" that did it. There was a big memorial service at the Cathedral here on Monday and a very impressive one at St. Paul's on Tuesday that I listened to over the radio. I have my feet propped in a child's wheel barrow and I am sitting amongst rubber boots, a watering can, a petrol tin, a decoy duck, a toy boat, a broken flower pot and seashells. The kids seem to be chasing the baby chickens who will probably never find their mother again. Peter and David are so funny – not the slightest bit shy. Peter keeps saying "I agree" and then David echoes "I agree absolutely". ...

---

[66] Edward R. Murrow's harrowing CBS radio report from Buchenwald concentration camp on 16th April, 1945 can be heard in full on YouTube.

[67] Joyce (Joy) Haselden married J.A.S. (Adam) Hepburn of the Tank Corps in 1940: *Northern Whig* 6th December 1940. For Joy Haselden, see the letter for 17th August, 1939.

[68] Colonel Topping (Walter William Buchanan Topping, known to his friends as Ken) went on to become the Minister of Home Affairs in the Stormont government 1956–59. See the letter of 21st February, 1939.

I am going to Dublin on Tuesday with Stella for two days. She hadn't anybody to go with so I said I'd go. I would much rather go with L. but he is so hard to budge. Stella talks and laughs a lot but is fairly amusing and I think it will be fun. Any change is good anyway – especially to Dublin. ...

Took G. and J. to see *It Happened Tomorrow* which they loved though they didn't understand it.[69] *Lady in the Dark*[70] and *Meet Me in St. Louis* are coming this week, but going to Dublin will stop me from going I'm afraid. Monday is the D.R. Circle at the Morwood's – I will dazzle them with my New York hat and it will dazzle Dublin too. ...

I'm so glad Lloyd is with you again in New York. You deserve a spell together. Edith is wild because she thought that Bodo would be out for good at the end of April and Lo! He got a new appointment the other day. They just plain won't let him go. He came home yesterday for a week's leave. He will stay in England I think which is something. Percy is still at home with no new appointment. I think the navy realizes Bodo's worth. The Prime Minister Sir Basil Brooke just lost his youngest son and his oldest one was killed two years ago and the middle one is fighting in Italy. Lady Brooke is lying in bed for a year to cure a T.B. spine.[71] L. gave her a bird box the other day so that she could watch the birds nesting. ... Marcia Mackie is trying to send her eldest daughter to Vassar in September. They will accept her if she passes the exam. for Cambridge but they still have to get an exit permit for her to leave the country.

---

[69] A newspaper that supernaturally prints tomorrow's news gives *It Happened Tomorrow*, a 1944 fantasy film, its plot. The film starred Dick Powell and Linda Darnell and won two Oscar nominations. The story on which it is based was borrowed from a one-act play, *The Jest of Hahahlaba* by the Irish fantasist, Lord Dunsany, published in 1928.

[70] The musical film *Lady in the Dark* (1944) stars Ginger Rogers and it was nominated for three Oscars. It was based on the 1941 Broadway musical of the same name, composed by Kurt Weill with lyrics by Ira Gershwin.

[71] Sir Basil Brooke, 1st Viscount Brookeborough, had three sons. Lieutenant Basil Brooke, Grenadier Guards, was killed in action in Tunisia in March 1943. It was reported in the newspapers of 19th April 1945 that a younger son, Lieutenant Henry Alan Brooke MC Tenth Hussars, was killed in action in Italy in April 1945; the middle son, John Brooke, Tenth Hussars, was also serving in Italy; he became 2nd Viscount Brookeborough. Lady Brooke died in 1970.

27th Apr.
Red + Club:

I didn't think I'd be here today but here I am again after three days in
Dublin wearing a new gold bracelet – not real gold but who can tell?
It was only 10/- and real gold ones exactly like it are £6 and up. I have
wanted one for years so you have no idea how satisfying it is for me to
have it on. Dublin was lovely. We went, Stella and I, at 9 o'clock
Tuesday and came back Thursday night at 10.30. With train fare,
shopping – hotel and all it cost about £8.8.0 just what Mother sent me
for my birthday. I bought L. a bow tie and a pound of sausages. … The
food is still wonderful and the town is flowing with drink of all kinds
– at pre-war prices or very nearly not bad anyway compared to this
and England. I got along very well with Stella who is gay and good
company. If I am tired her giggle bothers me but I didn't get tired, in
fact felt fine all the time. We went to the Abbey Theatre the first night
to see an Irish play *The Far Off Hills* by Lennox Robinson and the
second night to see *Death Takes a Holiday* at the Gate Theatre –
poorish play.[72] … We stayed at 2 hotels both unfashionable and cheap.
Dublin is always full now and you can't get into any good hotel without
reserving rooms far ahead, and it was especially full this week because
of the Punchestown races. We went to 2 picture galleries and one
picture exhibition, no movies. We were in the 3 best cocktail bars –
Shelbourne, Hibernian and Gresham where they have such good White
Ladies.[73] The clothes are still smart in the shops but look of very poor
quality. Had lunch with the Scanlans one day and with Arabella the
next and dinner at the Shelbourne with Arabella the night we went to
the Abbey. One player at the Abbey was about the best actor I ever saw
– he had a smallish, character part of a gloomy farmer who nobody
could cheer up – a roaring comedy part and he was so perfect that we
nearly went again the next night just to see him. Philip Scanlan says he

[72] *The Far-Off Hills* is a comedy by Lennox Robinson (1886–1958), an Anglo-Irish
dramatist who later became manager of the theatre that had played such a
significant role in the Irish Literary Revival. The "poorish play", *Death Takes a
Holiday*, was adapted into English in 1929 from a 1924 Italian play by Alberto
Casella. It became a Hollywood movie in 1934 starring Fredric March. The original
play is highly regarded.

[73] The White Lady cocktail, consisting of gin, Cointreau and lemon juice, was created
by Harry McElhone in 1919 in London before he had his own bar in Paris, the
famous Harry's New York Bar. Mixologists now add fresh egg white.

is the best actor in Ireland and I believe it. His name is F. J. McCormack.[74] Stella isn't so conspicuous in Dublin. When I walk around Belfast with her people practically stumble staring. She is full of fun and has a good disposition – got alone fine with Philip who said she was very stimulating – he argues so against England and Stella is a Londoner to her back bone. Philip is highly intelligent but with a stubborn blind spot about Eire which makes all of his arguments crazy. Kay, I think, disapproved of Stella's outrageous looks – too Bohemian and flashy and Carmen Miranda like for Kay who is so nice but so conservative. Arabella and Stella get along well – in fact Stella gets along with everybody – she is very unselfconscious and natural. Dublin is as crazy as ever with its 3 piece women's orchestras at the theatre. At the Gate the 3 pieces are in a little stage where the boxes would be and the lady violinist was 6 feet tall in a black dinner dress and size 9 or 10 ground gripper shoes that reached from front to back of her skirt. I pointed it out to Stella who took one glance and got completely hysterical and then I did too. Even by the second interval we couldn't look at the shoes without giggling hysterically – they turned up at the toes too.

The library is quiet today and I am going to cheese it at 1.20 and go to *Meet Me in St. Louis*. ...

The portraits we saw in the Dublin exhibition weren't good by comparison to Tommy's of us – they looked like stuffed people and 3 of the best portrait painters in Dublin were represented. I knew Tommy's was good but I didn't know how good until I saw those and those artists charge four or five times what Tommy does. I am eating fudge and chocolate peppermints like mad. ... I must get some darning because I'm in one of my driven moods when I can't sit and read. I must do something. I wish I felt like this oftener. I would get so much done. This room is so pretty in the evening with the sun shining in both front and side windows. A clarinet is playing "The Girl with the Flaxen hair" but I like that other one of his better – the name slips my waning

---

[74] F.J. McCormack (the stage name of Peter Judge, 1889–1947) was associated with the Abbey Theatre for thirty years and performed in around 500 productions. He was regarded by many as the greatest Irish actor of his generation and was especially praised for his roles in plays by Sean O'Casey. He appeared in several Hollywood movies.

mind but you know the one I mean "Au Clair de la Lune" – My mind came back.[75]

[Unfinished]

2nd May
Malone

Here we set still – waiting for the big announcement. The 6 o'clock news last night had me sure it would be today and then at 10.45 we heard that Hitler was dead and then this morning it doesn't seem so close.[76] Even so I wouldn't go out to have my hair done in case I would miss it. ... It must be soon – V.E. Day I mean, and I will put out the flag, take the kids and have a high old time.

I am not in a letter writing mood so I will pop this in the box – way overdue.

Peace will probably be old when you get this – I can't believe it, can you? It is so cold snow and frost for 5 days –

I wish I were in America for the peace. It won't mean quite so much but they will go lots wilder!!

Love and kisses and happy days,
Helen

3rd May
At Red + Club

Dear Mother and Auntie,

How near we are to V. Day you will know when you get this. I think it will be today or tomorrow. I am going straight from here to buy the biggest American flag I can find – our English one is at Mahee – we will get it on Saturday. I feel more excited outdoors and at home than I do in here – I suppose these boys think it will be so long before they

---

[75] Both compositions are by Claude Debussy.

[76] Hitler shot himself on 30th April 1945 inside the *Führerbunker* while his newly wedded wife Eva Braun ingested cyanide. Berlin surrendered to the Red Army on 2nd May.

are home anyway. Gay and Julie are worked up to fever pitch – they rush down to read the head lines every morning and have been very interested in the paper since they started guessing how many miles the Russians were from Berlin. ...

We are having a dinner party tonight – such a strain because we haven't had one for so long. We are having Mary Byers (an extra strain), Herbert and Rosemary Bryson, an AT [Auxiliary Territorial] named Lucy Rickman who went to college in America and whom we've never seen[77] and the Brysons are bringing a young midshipman who is staying with them. ... If it turns out to be V. Day I shouldn't think Mary or the Brysons will want to come. ...

A boy in here was trying to explain to me why all the soldiers are so indifferent to the exciting news. If they knew they could go home tomorrow it would mean something but as it is, they just live from day to day anyway. The Club is madly busy again – a long queue is waiting for bed bookings and the library is full. ...

6th May
Sunday night:

Still no V.E. Day but the radio says it will be before Thursday – got your letters from San Antonio and are glad you will be back in the U.S. for the big day. I bought my big flag and G. and J. are thrilled with it. It is on my bed waiting and Mary Lee loves it and says "Kissem Stars". ... Everybody has their flags ready – bunting, boutonnieres and all. There is going to be a 2 day holiday. We have our American flag and a Union Jack the same size to hang out from the balcony outside Gay's (the guest) room.

[77] Lucy Rickman (in 1945 a member of the Women's Auxiliary) had recently graduated from Swarthmore College, Pennsylvania. Her mother was Lydia Cooper Lewis of Philadelphia and her grandmother was Lucy Biddle Lewis, related to the famous Philadelphia Quaker family, the Biddles. Just before the Russian Revolution, Lucy's mother, a Quaker, had gone on a humanitarian mission in Russia with a Friends' Unit in which she met John Rickman, an English Quaker, Conscientious Objector, and well-known psychoanalyst and writer. (In the Second World War he joined the Royal Army Medical Corps.) Lucy herself remained a Quaker; in 1951 she married Bernard Baruch, a psychoanalyst, and became a psychiatric social worker. See Jamie Stiehm, "Bearing Witness in War and Peace," *Swarthmore College Bulletin* 2 (2015); Joanna Moorhead, interview with Lucy Rickman Baruch, *The Guardian* 25th April, 2014; see also Pearl King's Preface and Sylvia Payne's Foreword to John Rickman, *Selected Contributions to Psycho-Analysis* (1957, 2003).

We have only about 1/8 of a whiskey bottle to celebrate with but that will be enough. I am going to take the kids to town to see the flags and the excitement. Julie thinks that the devil wouldn't have Hitler in Hell so she can't think where he is! ...

... I can hardly settle to anything waiting for V.E. Day – though my fever pitch excitement has gone down since Tuesday. Our dinner party went swimmingly – ... The AT was nice – very intelligent and pretty tickled with herself and not a bit glamorous – American mother who was a Biddle from Philadelphie (6th cousin to the rich Biddles she says). We just talked and it was quite fun – though a relief to have it over entertaining "the rich Mary Byers" not being easy. Went to *Meet Me in St Louis* twice – took the kids the second time – they loved it. Will say nighty night and send much love and many whoops and hollers – especially hollers!

Helen x x x x x x

Dear Mother and Auntie, Ginna and Lloyd,

I should be in a hilarious and delirious frame of mind when I write this but I haven't been yet and won't be now – It seeped in too gradually and my high point was a week ago today when Churchill made a statement in the House and we knew then that it was all over but the shouting. The next night when Hitler's death was announced we felt wildly jubilant and I have been more or less teed up but never felt a wild rush of joy. I have just got myself some whiskey and barley water having had much too sober a celebration altogether. The day before V.E. Day I went to a movie with Nancy – *Casanova Brown* – the radio before I left said that it was expected hourly – I was all dressed up – Easter bonnet that Ginna sent – white gloves *and all*. When we came out of the movie after six – darned if all the flags weren't up and we were *wild* to think we had missed it – we bought a paper and sure enough it said that unconditional surrender had been signed but not a word about Mr. Churchill announcing it – and there were no crowds – people just walking around as usual.[78]

---

[78] Helen missed the announcement on account of a frothy romantic comedy. With some irony, *Casanova Brown* (1944), starring Gary Cooper and directed by Sam Wood, had been premiered in a part of France liberated by the Allies after D-Day.

Since I have started this letter I have said goodnight to the girls, Gay and Mary Lee with red, white and blue bows on. We are going to get G. and J. up at 10.15 and take them into town to see the lights and crowds if any but they don't know it. Well – Monday evening I told Nancy to come up to celebrate so up she came and at 9 o'clock still no official announcement except to say that the next day would be V.E. Day but no bands, no national anthems, it couldn't have been flatter. We started ringing up people to come celebrate i.e. drink and finally got the Tobins from next door who nearly leapt through the phone they were so pleased to come – this was about 10 o'clock. They are in their sixties but we gave them each a good stiff whiskey and we all drank and felt better but still not hilarious – much less delirious. We and Nancy had another after they went home and it all helped but was forced if you see what I mean – artificially stimulated. When I got home from the movie at 6 o'clock L. had our flags out looking wonderful and a little one sticking out from Mary Lee's balcony. They make me feel gayer than anything – especially the American one. On V.E. morning Nancy and [son] Donald came up and we went to have "elevenses" with Edith – Gay and Julie chose what they would wear because it was V. Day and wore big red, white and blue ribbons and waved flags and it was pretty gay. We went to town on the top of a tram to see the flags and they loved it – shouting "Oh boy" and screaming with delight. The weather both yesterday and today is divine – I am in a white dress now at 7 p.m., no fire, windows open and no cardigan and I am warm!! ...

18th May

Now it is Friday the 18th and the tumult and the shouting have died – the flags are down and things are the same as ever. Every day though the papers announce the end of another war time restriction – censorship, travel etc. I have been to the Consul and the travel permit office so far – both say all I need is a steamship ticket so I will bolt from here to McCalla's [travel agency] to see how that situation is – I haven't really much hope for an early sailing. It would be too good to be true, but my idea is to nip home before the army gets itself organized to travel. ...

Donald Mitchell ... and Nancy came with us to see the Victory Parade last Sunday. ... and we had the bright idea of coming here to the Red + to watch the parade – we sat on the upper deck of a double-decker bed up in the dormitory surrounded by G.I.s. We saw well and in comfort. The parade was 1½ hours late in starting . ...

EVENING:

... I went to McCalla's [travel agency] after the Red + and put my name on a list of "Prospective passengers". I asked if there were hundreds ahead of me and he said "Millions"! He could give me no idea in the world when sailing would be available but he thought not for many months. Have you started agitating at your end, Mother? Common sense seems to dictate that your chances Mother, are twice as good as ours because of the comparatively empty ships sailing eastward to Europe. I will start some wire pulling soon if I can – maybe some Red + racket – very dubious, of course seeing as how I'm just a day a week volunteer worker. The birds are singing and our garden is ablaze with rhododendrons and coming lupins. ... Travel restriction between England and Ulster has been lifted but I'm sure the accommodation will never meet the demand for months. However, it is nice for most people who have been hemmed in so long and have sisters and relatives in England. ...

Yesterday we went to Pixie Lindsay's birthday party at Holywood.[79] They live in the Pim Thompson's old house which is so beautiful and it was done up regardless just before the war when they were married.[80] Leslie's bedroom has quilted pink satin doors (mind you in Belfast!!!) and the same behind the beds all along the wall – Gay took one look

[79] Owing to illness Miss Pixie Lindsey [sic] was unable to appear as bridesmaid at Osborne King's wedding in London (*Belfast Telegraph* 12th February 1945). Pixie was the childhood nickname of Sarah Lindsay whose family lived in Lissue, an 1807 house near Lisburn that was given over partly to the Belfast Hospital for Sick Children during the war and wholly in 1947. Leslie is Pixie's mother.

[80] Coincidentally, J. Pim Thompson, formerly of Holywood, died in England on May 6th 1945, with his death reported in the *Belfast Telegraph* on the 12th. He was a Belfast stockbroker and the son of the head of a well-known linen firm. The newspapers called him a "leading Irish Freemason". There was a Pim Thompson Masonic Lodge 349.

and whispered to me "Are they rich?" and Nina [Bryson] said "Oh look Mummy, they have mattresses on their doors!" The whole house is too opulent for words with the drawing room stiff with photographs of the whole push[81] in their presentation gowns. Leslie, her 2 sisters-in-law, her ma-in-law and pa-in-law! It makes me tired – not sick but tired. Eileen [Bryson] and Edith were so funny about it coming home and Eileen began to worry about their new paint job on their dining-room – pale pink walls and a scarlet ceiling – I said reassuringly "but no satin" and Eileen with more humor than I've ever seen her show said "We could drape a little satin in someplace!"

You can imagine how we all smirked and preened during Mr. Churchill's speech when he praised Ulster so and gave such a slap to De Valera. People here are fit to be tied because De Valera went to condole with the German ambassador over Hitler's death. That was the last straw. I think Dev. is trying to make up by offering food to Europe (in tonight's news).[82]...

Mrs. Luke was telling me tonight about her celebrations – here on the night we had the Tobins over I took out a drink to Mrs. Luke in the kitchen – she said tonight "I was real tired and I thought I'll just enjoy this so I pretended I was in a big room full of people – (I have a great imagination you know) – and I lit a cigarette and drank the whiskey Mrs. Turtle, in 5 minutes my hands were *numb*, so I thought what will I do to get sober and I just went out and cleaned the front steps"!! We heard her out there and couldn't think who or what it was banging the brush around. *Yank* magazine today had such good articles

---

[81] The slang word "push" means "a group or gang": www.thefreedictionary.com.

[82] In his 13th May speech on BBC radio, Churchill said: "... had it not been for the loyalty and friendship of Northern Ireland, we should have been forced to come to close quarters with Mr de Valera or perish forever from the earth". For the duration of the war, Eamonn de Valera had closed Irish ports to Allied ships. Churchill seemed bitter in his references to Ireland, though said that the Irish war heroes on the Allied side (three of whom he named) erased the bitterness in his heart. An added provocation was the fact that on 2nd May de Valera signed the book of condolence on Hitler's death and visited the German Ambassador Hempel in Dublin. On 16th May, de Valera made a dignified reply to Churchill on Radio Éireann. On the 18th May in Dáil Éireann, de Valera offered to the needy peoples of the Continent supplies of food over the succeeding six months, including 20,000 head of cattle, 1500 draught horses, 16,000 cwt of bacon, 10,000,000 lbs of canned meat, etc. See Houses of the Oireachtas website, Dáil Éireann Debate, vol. 97, no. 7.

about V.E. Day in Paris and such good reporting on President Roosevelt's death.[83] Ginna's letter on it was as good as an article in the *New Statesman* – what a mind! What a mind! ...

At the D.R.C. on Monday at Maureen's ... Mary Morwood gave the paper – A Policy for Poetry – missed the boat as usual. ...

I forgot to mention that a basic petrol ration is starting again June 1st – and we will be able to go places and see things again – Hallelujah! Cars increased in price from 15–20% in one day! Lancelot is now earnestly sewing his bee veil onto his bee hat (I thread the needle) and give advice – he is a constant and unconscious RIOT! On which merry note I will beat it to bed. Ma! I sure write'em once I start.

Love and Kisses.
Helen

Sat. after V.E. Day
12th May
Mahee

[Dear Mother and Auntie,]

... The skylarks are singing and the sun is shining and it is nearly hot. We have had wonderful weather since V.E. Day. I am lying out at the back listening for Mary Lee to wake up. She looks adorable today in a short checked smock. ...

Mrs. D– , "Oh Mercy" to Auntie, asked me to give a joint picnic tea in our garden on the V.E. Day + 1 – i.e. she and I both ask friends to bring their own tea to our garden. I can't stand her but thought it was a good idea so we had 29 children in all and it was a roaring success. They went from 1½ to 13 and just milled around playing with the croquet mallets, bowls (balls), bikes, trikes and our toy car that Joe and Isobel gave us. G. and J. wore their stars and stripes skirts and had flags tied on their bikes and it was fun. That night we got them up at a quarter to 11 and dressed them and took them downtown in the car

---

[83] *Yank, The Army Weekly*, published by the United States military, began on 17th June 1942 and continued throughout the war. It was written by enlisted soldiers and not for public sale, so Helen most likely read it in the American Red Cross Club. The 11th May issue had articles on Roosevelt. See the website of *UNZ Review: An Alternative Media Selection*.

which we parked at the Technical [College] and walked to the City Hall which was flood-lit. The Ritz [cinema] was flood-lit in red, white and blue and the Hippodrome [cinema and auditorium] and [Great Northern Railway] station were lighted but the whole thing was tame. Donegall Place was solid with people and there were crowds milling around the City Hall – young toughs were dancing and singing but the whole thing was forced. We couldn't go out V.E. night … but you could hear the cheering from town out at our house and there were lots of bonfires etc. … Every single thing since the black-out was lifted has misfired. That was *so* tame and then the news of peace was expected for 10 days and even the news of the surrender was announced 24 hours before Churchill announced it. I never felt worked up enough to send you a cable – Ginna and Lloyd sent one saying simply Hallelujah! which was very cute of them. Yours came Thursday and I was delighted. Nancy felt she should send one to Charlie who is in the Walter Reid hospital in Washington but didn't feel elated enough either. If it hadn't been for the children's excitement we would have all been flatter than pancakes. Margaret thought that Churchill's announcement was more like the beginning of a war than the end – a very apt remark and the King was fairly dull. The B.B.C. did nobly V.E. night with programs – announcers outside Buckingham Palace etc. even New York we heard – I think London did go pretty wild – they have reason to. Everybody has flags flying and there are lots of American ones every place too. …

[incomplete]

20th May
Malone

Dear Mother and Auntie,

It is a perfect day for writing letters – a rainy Sunday – has been pouring since we woke up and is still pelting. …

LATER:

… It stopped raining just before 8 in time for me to whip out and pick some flowers and the room looks elegant with rhododendrons and lupins and some ragged little flowers in the Belleek horses on the mantelpiece. ...

Two good movies this week *Lady in the Window*[84][sic] and *Mrs. Parkington.*[85] L. is going on a Stock Exchange toot to Ballycastle tomorrow. G. and J. don't get a holiday. ... Eggy's father is over and we will have him to dinner after June 1st when Eggy can bring him in a car on his basic ration. I am trying hard to get a cook but they are increasingly scarce and expensive. Gay talks all the time about going to America and is starting to save her money already. ...

... Am reading *Left hand – Right Hand* by Osbert Sitwell – quite interesting autobiography.[86]

Helen

21st May

... The man in McCalla's and the exit permit man said that passengers shipping for the past 6–8 months has been nearly non-existent because the government just took the ships to take wounded soldiers home. He said he could give me no idea at all when I could go because anything might happen any time that would completely change the picture – for instance if they happened to send the *Queen Mary* or *Queen Eliz.* over with passengers we could all go but I can't see them letting any civilians over ahead of wounded men – nor should they. However, I will start pulling strings and see what can be done. ... Must go take my passport in to be renewed in case but don't keep on your toes – it will be sheer good luck and/or pull if I come within the next 6–8 months. Did I tell you that the man in McCalla's said that there were millions ahead of me and it doesn't make a bit of difference that I am an American citizen. But I will see what can be done in all directions.

Must go now.
Love Helen

---

[84] *The Woman in the Window* (1944) is a highly regarded Fritz Lang *film noir*. It stars Edward G. Robinson and Joan Bennett.

[85] Greer Garson and Walter Pidgeon star in this drama directed by Tay Garnett. It was nominated for two Oscars.

[86] *Left Hand, Right Hand* (1943–50) by Sir Osbert Sitwell is a 5-volume autobiography, the first volume of which Helen is reading, entitled *The Cruel Month.*

21st May
Malone

Dear Ginna and Lloyd,

I'm just in from being out or to be more Irish, I'm "just after coming in" which is about as misleading. I went to lunch at the Villiers-Stuarts to see Jane Villiers Stuart's new baby Sally. Jane is the one who lived at Mahee last June with her naval husband. They are both Southern Irish and as unlike people here as possible.[87] This was her father-in-law's house today – 300 years old and looking every inch of it. The whole place had that indescribably casual, broken-down air that you only get in Eire. Paint peeling, carpets fading and ragged, wonderful furniture, general untidiness akin to plain dirt, awful pictures on the walls – no attempt at any sort of style and the whole thing very comfortable. He is a widower so the place was a little more seedy than if a woman were around. He showed me his pedigree without blowing – descended from the Desmonds and Fitzgeralds and he really is somebody but slightly bats now on the subject of reincarnation. The whole lunch, conversation and atmosphere were incredibly non-material compared to the saving, thrifty, tidy, spick and span houses we usually go to. Theirs had gone a bit too far and it was a distinct shock. Jane wants to live in our house at Mahee permanently but I told her she couldn't. They may take it for June or maybe September or October. They are such a romantic out-of-the-world couple that they appeal to my imagination.

I tried to buy "My Guy Came Back" today – it is always sold out. I spotted it as a winner on the radio months ago before the shop had ever heard of it. I've heard "Don't Fence Me In" only once badly played – wouldn't have noticed the time but love the words.[88]...

---

[87] Jane was, in fact, Northern Irish but her husband Michael was, like her father-in-law, Horace Villiers-Stuart, born in Waterford, in the South. Sally later in life became Dr Susan Villiers-Stuart.

[88] "Oh give me land, lots of land, and the starry skies above/Don't fence me in./Let me ride through the wide open country that I love/Don't fence me in. ... I want to ride to the ridge where the West commences/Gaze at the moon til I lose my senses,/And I can't look at hobbles and I can't stand fences/Don't fence me in."

I am cross and hungry (no tea) Mrs. Luke is driving me crazy now too bothering me with questions, her cough and her forceful personality – overpowering it is I think – me, I just want peace and quiet. I am waiting for Stella to come and tonight we are going to *The Face in the Window*.[89] Somehow with my trip home remote and the war over here, there seems nothing to look forward to – kinda flat.

Love,
Helen

28th May
Malone

Dear Ginna,

Enclosed is a letter I started to Mother. I changed my mind about sending it because I thought her hopes would be raised too high and there are still a lot of bridges to cross – the facts are these:

I have been promised passage to and from via Montreal at any time practically on a Headline ship.[90] I could go in 3 weeks, at the end of June or the 2nd week in July.

I can't get an exit permit under existing rules – i.e. to visit a well mother is not sufficient reason for them to grant me a permit.

The permit office advises me to wait for a month when they think the existing regulations will be changed and anybody can go anyplace without an exit permit. That is all I would need would be the peace time requisites of a passport and a passage.

At the moment my American passport has expired but I can get it renewed at any time.

If I come to America on an American passport it will be taken from me the minute I arrive and I will not be able to get an exit permit from America.

---

[89] There was a 1939 British film, *The Face at the Window*, but Helen means *The Woman in the Window* (1944) which was playing at the Classic cinema in Belfast.

[90] The Headline Shipping Company of Belfast, also called the Ulster Steamship Company and G. Heyn & Sons, operated between 1877 and 1979.

I can give up my American passport and apply for a British passport if I like. I would rather retain my American one, if possible, but would change if that is the only solution.

The big stumbling block is a Mrs. Shipley of the Passport Division of the State Department at Washington who controls the exit permits[91]. ...

If Mother can't come soon within the next few months I will come. Too many years have passed already. ...

Would suggest that you ring up Katherine Turtle re Kathleen Spence.

Kathleen Spence is sitting in Montclair [New Jersey] trying to get an exit permit and Toby is wild over here. Katherine should have first hand information about Kathleen whose situation is approximately like mine as regards passports and British husbands. She has been in America nearly 6 years. ...

My chance on the Headline ship is only because Mr. Edmundsen arranged it – he is the head of the line[92] and if it is possible to go I can't let it dangle too long or it would be awkward since it is a personal favor. ...

The enclosed letter:

... I still think it would be fine if you could come here *Mother* – Mrs. Shipley permitting – I could probably get you over instead of me on a Headline ship sailing from Montreal. I asked Mary Byers all about it today. She went over in 1940 on a Headline ship with her daughter and Eliz. Edmundsen. There is no stewardess on board and there are

---

[91] The aptly named Mrs Shipley (1885–1966) was a famous, even notorious, national gatekeeper who was head of the Passport Division of the U.S. Department of Justice from 1928 until 1955. She warrants a two-and-a-half pages *Wikipedia* entry. She joined the State Department in 1914; when she became head of the Passport Division she had a staff of more than 70; by the end of the Second World War it had grown to 200. After the Neutrality Act of 1939 she reviewed each application personally and the number of passports issued fell from 75,000 to 2,000 per month. *Fortune* magazine called her "redoubtable" (1945) and *Time* magazine "the most unfirable, most feared and most admired career woman in Government" (1951). Helen and her family were subject to what was termed Mrs Shipley's "limitless discretion". "Ruth Shipley", *Wikipedia*.

[92] In a Board of Trade *Wreck Report* (HMSO, 1951) of an explosion aboard S.S. *Malin Head* in 1950, Walter Alexander Edmundson is listed as Manager, Head Line Buildings, Victoria Street, Belfast.

at most only 8 passengers but it is comfortable – food plain etc. but no hardships.

The consul refused to send the cable – said for us to approach Mrs. Shipley through a congressman. The consuls here are nice but they don't know A![93] Toby Spence says it's the Mrs. Shipleys of this world that are what's wrong. The current *New Statesman* holds out no hope any place. I hope you don't take it too seriously – life really isn't as bad as they think – in one competition they had for a slogan one of the entries was: "If you have tears prepare to shed them now!"

Have you any influential congressmen friends? I will run over and post this before I get you any more confused – did I say run? I mean skip. Have you heard the song about Sugar Candy?[94] Lancelot is groaning over it beside me – we live in suspense so I repeat:

Don't Fence me In![95]

The radio is playing "Don't Fence Me" which in the light of this letter I have adopted for my theme song. This is the second time today that I've heard it and only the 3rd time in my life but the bit about the cottonwood trees sure gets me, sister. The program just before this was based on such a nice rhyme. It was:

"Since singing is so good a thing
I wish all men would learn to sing"[96]

No particular news – weather rotten – when I really think about it I know that I am dying to come snags or no snags – if I can go and come back Sis, I'm half way there. There always was a crazy, wild, streak in us ... Sometimes I think I will write a book called "Life with Mother and Auntie" based on *Life with Father*.[97] They are just as funny. Now they are playing "My Guy Came Back" – I spotted that months ago – Sis, can I pick 'em. Can I pick boys too!?? The young naval officer

---

[93] Anything? Zilch?

[94] "Candy", sung by Johnny Mercer and Jo Stafford and the Pied Pipers, backed by Paul Weston and his orchestra, was a 1945 hit song.

[95] What follows seems once again to be addressed to Ginna.

[96] The 9.15pm programme on the BBC Home Service was entitled "Since Singing is So Good a Thing" and featured the BBC Chorus, BBC Singers and BBC Orchestra. Helen is now listening to "The Geraldo Music-Shop," treating listeners to "hit-tunes of today and tomorrow".

[97] Since the American film of that name was not released until 1947, Helen must be thinking of the 1939 play by Howard Lindsay and Russel Crouse or the 1935 volume of autobiographical stories by Clarence Day that the play adapted.

sailor that I picked out at a dance a few months ago as a dream was written up in today's paper as the head of a frigate group that had got 15 German submarines – he is a Lieut. Commander engaged to Peggy Duffin and famous in the navy – Sis, can I pick 'em?[98]...

G. and J. have been invited to a fancy dress party – Gay wants to go as a ballet girl and Julie wants to go as God!! ...

Don't forget when inquiring that we have our passage guaranteed – we could fix Mother's instead of mine the same way. Mrs. Shipley is hopeless to contact ... Janet Boyd tried to see Mrs. Shipley for 11 months and she was living in Washington! She then gave up, went to Montreal, wired Mrs. Shipley and got an immediate answer. Final thought:– Damn Mrs. Shipley! ...

Love and kisses, Tootsie
Helen

30th May
Malone

Dear Mother and Auntie,

The weather is terrible – rain every day nearly all day and no sun except in brief "bright intervals". I am at my desk in the drawing room listening to programs for Schools with half my attention this morning it is on "design". I heard such a good program the other night on

---

[98] The engagement between Lt.-Commander Raymond Hart and Margaret (Peggy) Duffin was announced in the *Belfast Telegraph* of 2nd June when readers were told that Lt.-Commander Hart commanded HMS *Vidette* (a V-class destroyer) when it sank a U-boat in 1943 during an Atlantic convoy attack and commanded HMS *Havelock* (an H-class destroyer) when it sank two U-boats in the Bay of Biscay in the same year. A group of six Belfast-based frigates was reported by the *Northern Whig* (28th May, 1945) and other newspapers to have had 15 recent submarine "kills" to its credit. The group scored a "hat-trick" during a single patrol; returning up Belfast Lough, the ships flew the Jolly Roger. Hart (1913–1999), DSC (1941), DSO (1945), CBE (1963), was born in Southampton. He had reached the rank of Commodore when he retired in 1963. This war hero played himself in the 1974 TV series, *The World at War* (see IMDb, online). His obituary appear in the *Independent*, 7th September 1999. See also "Raymond Hart", Wikipedia. The wedding was on 16th June: see *Belfast Telegraph*, 16th June. Peggy Duffin WRNS was in civilian life a champion horsewoman.

"Looking at Things."[99] In fact with selective listening – studying the *Radio Times* carefully at the beginning of the week I get an enormous amount of pleasure out of the radio and now they have started to have a weekly criticism in most papers and it is fun to see if they thought what I thought.

The first bowl of roses from the garden is on the desk and most of the rhododendrons are out now and the lupins and day lilies are all in full bloom so our garden is at its best. Now the Program for Schools is on "syncopation" – most of my education comes from these programs.[100] I bought the record "Don't Fence Me In" yesterday – it is brand new here. …

We were at the Dolans last night – Major Dolan is fine – was in town yesterday and apart from being a little shakier, is his usual gallant self. Mrs. Dolan weighs only 100 pounds but looks and acts better. Peg is going home to England in about 3 weeks. She has had an awful time here between her father's illness, no maids, no nurse + Mrs. Dolan! Temple is on his way home from India and since they haven't seen him for over 2 years they are walking on air. Peg's husband is being demobilized in August.[101]

The D.R. Circle on Monday was so good – It was the last meeting. Original poetry, stories and sketches. Mrs. McDowell read her own – a thing about an amateur concert and I laughed until I cried – it was one of the funniest things I've ever heard and I take off my hat to her. I had no idea she had it in her. Mrs. Waterhouse read one by Mrs. Bradshaw – wonderful and I read a short story written by Nancy – very good too. The poetry wasn't memorable at all except for one dedicated

[99] "The Arts" programme, BBC Home Service, 25th May, included "'Keep Your Eyes Open' – John Betjeman on looking at things". Betjeman was a poet with strong popular appeal and was later Poet Laureate from 1972 until his death in 1984. "Looking at Things" was an intermittent BBC radio series, independent of the Schools' programmes, that was broadcast for decades from the 1930s.

[100] "For the Schools" (Home Service, 11a.m. 30th May) contained a section on "Music and the Dance 6. – Syncopation: an important feature of modern dance music, and how it occurs in music of all kinds". Although these weekday radio programmes were meant to be broadcast in the classroom, British housewives and those at home through illness (men or unmarried working women) received a free education simply by tuning in.

[101] For Temple Dolan, see the letter of 22nd May 1941. Dolan is listed as a committee member of the Royal North of Ireland Yacht Club serving in H.M. Forces: *Belfast News-Letter*, 10th May 1943.

to the D.R.C. Committee by Miss Lewis which was very witty.[102]...

It is pouring. We are so glad they got old Haw-Haw – now Ribbentrop is the only one left.[103] I'm sure Hitler is dead but I don't think his body will ever be found. ...

Love and Kisses,
Helen

5th June
34 Malone

Dear Mother and Auntie,

It has been raining nearly steadily since V.E. Day and people are ready to scream. ... Mary Lee is washing with Margaret, Julie and Charles Barr are playing and I am in the dressed up drawing room – Dressed up because the Egginton family was here for supper last night Pa, Ma, Eggy, Hilary, Eggy's sister Bessie and her husband. I did some special flower arrangements because Mr. Egginton paints flowers a lot and he appreciated them. The room is so pretty with pretty flowers in it – mostly lupins and rhododendrons, some yellow lilies and some pink poppies. ...

Kathleen Spence started home last Wednesday so she should be here this week or next and I will have first hand information about how she got around Mrs. Shipley. You should know by then too if Mother can come. ... As soon as I talk to Kathleen I will see which passport to get and start about an exit permit – if I still need one by then.

[102] Mrs Waterhouse was Mary Waterhouse, the wife of Gilbert Waterhouse, Professor of German at Queen's University, Belfast. Gilbert Waterhouse (1888–1977) was an English-born scholar who taught at Queen's from 1933 until 1953 and lived at 92 Malone Road. In 1920 he had married Mary Woods. His papers are at the Institute of Modern Languages Research, University of London. Waterhouse was recruited by the Foreign Office, alongside other distinguished British professors, and a young Cambridge Fellow, Alan Turing, to work at Bletchley Park as a wartime codebreaker. See Michael Smith, *The Secrets of Station X: How the Bletchley Park Codebreakers Helped Win the War* (1998, 2011). Mrs Bradshaw is not definitively identified but Miss Lewis was probably Miss A.E. Lewis BA, headmistress of Princess Gardens School in Belfast.

[103] William Joyce, Lord Haw-Haw, was captured by British forces at Flensburg, near the Danish-German border on the 28th May. He was taken to London, tried for high treason at the Old Bailey, and hanged on 3rd January, 1946. Joachim von Ribbentrop was arrested near Hamburg on the 14th June by the Belgian SAS after Germany's surrender. He was tried for war crimes at Nuremberg, found guilty, and hanged on the 16th October, 1946.

Charles Barr is a year and a half younger than Julie and is the same height – he can read anything. He made a list of 79 people the other day. 70 flowers and 40 animals – he can write and spell!! – a prodigy. He is a very nice friendly little boy.[104] Hilary is pretty big now – 2 months to go. ... Mr. Egginton is a great wag but nothing like as charming as Eggy, I think.

Our new maid is so nice we only have her for 6 weeks, but she is pleasant, quiet, clean etc. and just goes ahead. Mrs. Luke bawled when she left and our sigh of relief nearly blew her out of the house. She is the kind you start by being amused by and then she drives you cuckoo. I have to go out in a few minutes to get our new ration books. James Stephens, the Irish poet, is giving a talk now on his poetry – he has such a brogue.[105]... I may take the kids to *The Constant Nymph* this afternoon at the Majestic.[106] It is such a bad day. We are going to dinner at Frazer and Vera's tonight at Newtownards.[107] It is so nice to be able to use our cars again after 3 years. The traffic is noticeably heavier and the curbs are packed solid in town.

... The papers are full of the local elections. Ken Topping has to fight the election again at Larne. He is sure to get in and it is just an awful

---

[104] Charles Barr is the nephew of Jim Barr, Lance Turtle's stockbroker partner. (See the letter of 30th September 1940.) It would have come as no surprise to Helen to learn that Charles Barr went on to have an illustrious career as a scholar. He conducted postgraduate research in Film Studies at London University in the 1960s and after a stint in educational television, was appointed as the first lecturer in Film Studies at the University of East Anglia in 1976. He retired in 2006 but then taught at Washington University, St Louis, and University College Dublin. Until recently he was Research Professor at St Mary's University, London. Among his books are *Ealing Studios* (1977), *English Hitchcock* (1999), and *Vertigo (BFI Film Classics)* (2012). Although his family then lived in England, Charles remembers being in Malone Park for V-E celebrations which included a bonfire and Hitler being burned in effigy. The editor had the pleasure of meeting Charles Barr on his recent visit to Belfast.

[105] Helen is writing at around 11.45am: on the BBC For the Schools programme at 11.40am was "A Poet speaks – James Stephens talks about his work" (for fourth-formers). Stephens (1880–1950) was a survivor from the great days of the Irish Literary Revival (c1890–c1925). His most famous prose work is *The Crock of Gold* (1912).

[106] *The Constant Nymph* is an American romantic drama starring Charles Boyer and Joan Fontaine (who was nominated for an Oscar for Best Actress).

[107] Vera's husband Fraser Mackie (1899–1981) was Jack Mackie's brother; he ran the Strand Spinning Company and also a mill in Lisburn: see Bernard Crossland (ed.), *The Lives of Great Engineers*, vol. 2, p. 85.

waste of time and money – but that's politics for you.[108] Margaret just said that Charles is an ideal companion for Julie. She has never seen her so quiet! Charles is reading to Julie now while Julie knits – such a romantic scene. I can hardly write for admiring my flowers as well as listening to James Stephens who is so good. ... Eggy's bachelor brother is a chess champion. He can play 16 people at once – he did in the Bahamas at some Fête that the Windsors gave and only 1 of the 16 beat him.[109]...

I expect to know next week if and when I am coming to America. In my mind's eye I think it will be the middle of July.

Goodbye girls
Love,
Helen

6th June
Malone

Dear Ginna and Lloyd,

The first summerish day there has been since around V.E. Day and the whole family is out enjoying it ... I am left all alone which is peaceful but sort of sad.

... I plan all the time to sail around the middle of July – based entirely on wishful thinking. Every day I wonder how I can bear to leave Mary Lee but I suppose I can. She won't miss us very much and I will have to have friends ask her out to tea a lot because she will miss having children around. ...

I went to see Stella yesterday and today. She had a miscarriage – not a very bad one – and is in a nursing home for 6 days – she pines for company and pins you down as to when. She has no regrets for the lost baby who was unintentional and she still hasn't made up her mind

---

[108] In the general election of 1945 Walter William Buchanan (Ken) Topping, Ulster Unionist Party, won 75% of the vote in Larne and cruised to victory. He won also in 1949, unopposed. The Larne constituency, which was an overwhelmingly safe Unionist Party seat, was abolished in 1973.

[109] The Duke of Windsor was Governor of the Bahamas between 1940 and 1945. Douglas Egginton was a noted chess player from Devon and won the Teignmouth Chess Club championship ten times between 1933 and 1957: www.teignmouthchessclub.com/archive

whether to stay with Tommy or marry her American beau who is now a major in Germany and may have to go to Japan. I pity Stella because her plight is acute. She really does love the American but doesn't want to leave her children and realizes what a good though difficult husband Tommy is. I have advised her to stick to Tommy and Stella's mother, who ran off from Stella's father leaving 3 daughters, has advised her to stick to Tommy but Stella is still havering and I'm sure if her American turned up here ready to take her she would go. She is flighty but a realist and likable because there is no humbug about her. I am very fond of Tommy too. Tommy has behaved so well through all this nightmare situation. ...

[unfinished]

12th June
34 Malone

Dear Mother,

... Kathleen Spence came home on Sunday and came here for tea yesterday – Monday. She looks exactly the same – a little more gray haired around the face but much more stylish than she used to look here.[110] The boys seem to be very nice – Ralph is 9½ and Stuart 7 and they are almost the same size. ... They sound as American as the flag and Toby just beams on them all and can hardly let the boys out of his sight.

Naturally I pumped Kathleen about how she got out – she was on an English passport and didn't have to have an exit permit but had to get a waver [sic] (whatever that is) from Mrs. Shipley. She says that a few American passports are being issued now if you have a good excuse to come. Mrs. Shipley is the person to write to about your passport and then you get in touch with the British Ministry of War Transport – 25 Broadway, and someone there nominates you for passage.

Lancelot and I discussed it and both think that it would be much better if you came here now, Mother. Traveling is still uncertain and hectic. Kathleen had a nightmare time of telephoning Mrs. Shipley and rushing around from place to place right up to 4.45 on the day before

[110] See the letter of 24th March, 1939.

she sailed! With all this uncertainty L. says positively that he won't let G. and J. go until things are more certain. ...

(I am listening to Eisenhower being given the Honorary Freedom of London)[111]. ...

Lancelot had the brain wave of me getting a letter from Dr. Foster or Lowry or both to say that I had had an operation for cancer and that you could come over that way on compassionate grounds. Kathleen suggested that if we could trump up a good illness Mrs. Shipley is forthcoming. ...

In case you begin to think I do need you because of cancer I make haste to assure you that I am fine and Dr. Foster says the cancer is as dead as Queen Anne – he looked at it the other day – but if we can use it to get you over we certainly will. Kathleen says there are 300,000 people trying to come. Her ship was almost entirely made up of evacuees – British children and it was an evacuee ship. ... (They are applauding Eisenhower like mad in London) – he has such a brilliant smile! ...

Eisenhower's speech was wonderful – I took time out to listen and he sounds a dream – if it was broadcast to America I'll bet there wasn't a dry eye in the country – mine certainly were wet. ... Lancelot has to write a letter to say that I have his permission to go.

So far here there is no ship that I know of that is taking people to America in big batches and without the Headline passage I literally couldn't come for months – maybe years – Kathleen came on the *Franconia* – 8 in a cabin – and only 2 stewardesses on her floor – it took 11 days.[112]

Elizabeth Morwood had a son last Thursday. They are going to call it Conor Edmund. When the nursing home – The Park – rang up John they said it was a girl so all the wires and telephone calls the Morwoods made had to be made all over again later when John came home from seeing Elizabeth who said it was a boy! When John congratulated E.

[111] The BBC Home Service broadcast at 12.05 pm "The presentation of the Honorary Freedom of the City of London to General of the Army DWIGHT D. EISENHOWER. G.C.B." The ceremony took place in the Guildhall, London.

[112] RMS *Franconia* operated as a Cunard liner between 1922 and 1956. During the war the ship was a troop carrier and at the Yalta Conference served as the headquarters ship for Churchill and the British delegation. Immediately after the war the ship carried returning troops and refugees across the Atlantic. It resumed passenger service in 1949.

on their daughter and she kept saying it was a boy he thought she was still dopey from the anaesthetic and he to soothe her down said "Well anyway, isn't it nice that we have a baby". But finally said he would go and see which it was – isn't that a riot? It must have been a rattled nurse. Liz had a fairly tough time – long and brought with instruments in the end but she is fine now.

G. and J. were so excited about the little Spence boys and them being so American. They played croquet and got along fine and Toby said that he hadn't seen his boys so well behaved for the whole time they had been home. They had to sit up all night crossing from Heysham. The travel restrictions are off between Ireland and England and the boats are crammed. Stella who was here for the night got up at 8 to go down and book a berth for 2 weeks from today.

We were at the Isaac's last night – Melanie is going to Iceland for a year – going to London today. We have rented Mahee for 3 weeks to the Villiers-Stuarts and their 10 week old baby. ...

The weather is appalling – cold and rainy. There hasn't been a good day since V.E. Day + 1.

Wilson is on at the Classic.[113] I must try to go – *Arsenic and Old Lace* is at the Ritz and I'd like to see it too.

Here comes the baker[114] – time out! – Got some chocolate wheaten biscuits. Food is very scarce now – meat ration cut to 1/- per person instead of 1/2. Tinned stuff is scarcer and more points needed – Europe being fed. However there are gooseberries in the garden and strawberries and raspberries coming on – it is an awful period for vegetables but peas are just in. ...

Love and kisses,
Helen

---

[113] *Wilson* was a 1944 movie portrait of President Woodrow Wilson (1913–1921), starring Alexander Knox as Wilson. It won six Oscars though flopped at the box office. Since Wilson was President when the Great War broke out, was a non-interventionist, yet presided over a nation that entered the conflict, there were parallels in the movie's story with events of the late 1930s and early 1940s.

[114] Breadservers who delivered their wares by vans were called bakers. The vans were horse-drawn in Belfast at least until the late 1940s.

15th June
Malone
Written from Red +

Dear Ginna,

I am trying not to be excited by the news that you may be having a baby but I can't help hoping. I wish you had gone into all the fascinating details now that there is no censorship but I assume that you didn't think it was fitten. I screamed and laughed over the remarks on the back of the pictures you sent. You look so important and just the same as ever to me. Lancelot said to tell you that you look just as young and pretty as ever. Julie's remarks were "Isn't she clean!" and "Has she any dandruff?" ...

Was just congratulating Marcia who has been awarded the O.B.E. (Order of the British Empire) in the King's birthday honors. She is one of the 3 women in Belfast to have it and is as proud as punch. It is the highest women's honor next to Dame and L. thinks that dame is only given to an unmarried woman or widow.[115] She certainly deserves it for running this place so well for 3 years. ...

Had Kathleen Spence over to tea on Monday to hear the low-down on getting out of America. From what she said a few American passports are being granted with a good excuse. Our plan prior to hearing about your baby was: to get Dr. Foster to write a letter saying that I had had an operation for cancer and it would be advisable for Mother to come to see me – a real racket because I am fine and at this point have no doubt that the cancer is gone where the woodbine twineth. I never read anything about cancer on purpose – it preyed on my mind enough anyway and you know my imagination – like wildfire. I have never felt as strong as I did before the operation but that is

---

[115] Dame is simply the feminine form of address for the honour of knighthood. The investiture for the 1945 King's birthday honours was held in Stormont, seat of the Northern Ireland parliament, and conducted by King George VI and Queen Elizabeth. Commander William Stephens (see the letter of 27th July, 1944) received the DSC and Bar and his mother, Mrs Lilian Stephens, the MBE. Marcia Mackie, who was director of the American Red Cross Club, was awarded the OBE. See: *Belfast News-Letter*, 19th July, 1945. On 6th August, 1945, Northern Ireland officially bade the American forces farewell at a dinner in the Red Cross Club. Mrs Mackie reminded the guests that the Belfast Club was the oldest in the European theatre of operations. See: *Northern Whig*, 7th August, 1945.

because my vitality was in a shockingly low state when I had it – so soon after Mary Lee and I worried a lot about her unnecessarily but I have been like that ever since the shock of Lee's death. However, I am as well as most people are here – the war has worn us down much more than we realize and Europe is a sick tired place – Ulster is the best place in Europe to be but the sobering effect of all these years is very noticeable – the Americans show it more than anybody – the G.I.'s I mean who have been here a few years are a different sort of people to the high-spirited, fresh breezy boys who arrived. But don't let me depress you unduly – it is just war. ...

16th June

... We will all try to come. I should think in Late August or September. I don't think L. could get out of the country until they stop making you have exit permits but as the man says that should be soon. I'm pretty sure we can all come on the Headline boat. I will go to the permit office on Thursday to see if the gal that applied got a permit. As you say Mrs. Shipley's cable does sound hopeful and Kathleen despite her trouble thought it was hopeful too. We still have to get out of this country though! But if all else fails I will try the cancer story.

... I really won't get worked up to fever pitch about coming until we have our tickets in our hands and exit permits and all – but I am in a helpless daze – unsettled and clear wild. You couldn't have had a baby at a more propitious time. When I think that G. and J. may go to Corona school I can hardly believe it.[116]... By the time we can get it all arranged I'm sure it will be August or later. We are having 3 G.I.'s to supper tonight – boys I met yesterday – I must whip out and pick some flowers. ... Went to *Wilson* last night and loved it. ...

[incomplete]

---

[116] The impressive Corona School on Corona Street in the Capitol Hill district of Denver was built in 1889. It was later renamed the Dora Moore Elementary School.

19th June
Malone

Dear Mother and Auntie,

Mother's letter came yesterday in 6 days – Good idea to send a doctor's letter. Lancelot now thinks he might be able to come too in which case we would all come! So cancel my last letter about your coming here and we will come there. L. will have to wait until the exit permit business is abolished and it may be August or September but we're coming. The reply from Mrs. Shipley to Ginna was non-committal but hopeful saying just to apply a month before I wanted to leave the U.S.A. As soon as your letter comes I will apply for an exit permit – don't fence me in! ...

This is the first nice June day and now after lunch even if it isn't so hot. Tonight the Smiles (Alan's parents) have asked us to the theatre to see the Princess Royal who is visiting Belfast for 4 days. We are going there to supper at 6.15 and then to the Empire at 7.30 in evening dress. It was very nice of them because the tickets are £1.1.0 each! The Princess is dining at the Milne Barbour's tonight.[117] ... Sunday we were all at Simmy for lunch – 14 to lunch.[118] Marcia and her 4 daughters + a friend, Jim, Jack and Kay and us. In the afternoon we looked at Ringdufferin their new estate – £11,000 worth – an old Georgian house in shocking disrepair but with lovely proportions and great possibilities – it has a lovely staircase, an Adam fireplace and lovely barns and outhouses.[119]...

Mrs. Turtle has invited us all to Hollybrook House[120] for two weeks starting July 12 – we are going to Dublin on July 7. ... In August we

[117] Mary, Princess Royal arrived in Northern Ireland on 19th June for a four-day visit. That evening she attended a gala performance at the Empire theatre in Victoria Square, Belfast. The Empire Theatre of Varieties opened in 1894, closed its doors in 1961 and was demolished in 1965.

[118] In the 1920s, Thomas (Tom) Mackie bought Simmy Island which is on the same side of Strangford Lough as Mahee Island. He built a house on the island for use by the sizeable Mackie clan.

[119] Ringdufferin House is south of Mahee Island. John Pringle (Jack) and Kathleen Mackie bought the house (built c1790–1800) and estate in 1944 but did not move in until the following year. A member of the Mackie family presently lives there.

[120] Hollybrook House, Co. Roscommon was built in the 1750s on the site of an earlier castle. It was owned in the 18th century by the Phibbs family, then by the ffolliott family. For some years last century it was run as a hotel, presumably when Mrs Turtle lived there as a paying guest.

will either go to Mahee or America – can you believe it? I can't until that permit + ticket and all are clutched in my perspiring hand. Sorry this is so hasty but I have to clean the car – gallop to the fair with the kids and be a glamour girl by 6.15 and it is about 3.30 now! Ma! Can I do it – You bet.

Love and X X X X
Helen

24th June
Malone

Dear Ginna and Lloyd,

Well I never did! The latest in the startling and swiftly following dramatic developments in the Thriller "Who is going to cross that ocean?" arrived today on the heels of a bombshell yesterday. I was lying quietly in bed yesterday with a little go of 'flu (better today, thanking you) when a letter from Mother written the 17th and one from Auntie written the 16th arrived announcing Auntie's departure for N.Y. on the 19th. ... that was surprise No. 1 in a story full of sudden turns and fancies or am I telling you? Tuesday – no Wed. last a cable arrived from Mother asking when we were coming – we cabled back Thursday – "Date uncertain because of British exit permit. Hope autumn." Which is the best we can do. Today a cable arrived from Mother saying "Both arrive N.Y. Monday passports pending. Sail when possible can't wait." NOW! What will Mother do when she finds out that you are having a baby? ...

We don't know if we are on our head or our heels, coming or going but I think it is the best for Mother to come now and we will come later. ...The *Queen Eliz.* sailed from Glasgow yesterday with 15,000 G.I.s aboard – shipping is still much tighter from east to west than west to east and will be for some time. I am thrilled that Mother is coming – but won't believe it until I get a cable that she has started – just like I can't believe we are going (are we?) until I have all the red tape in me mitt on the boat. Mother's and Auntie's letters gave me the impression that we were living in a slow-motion calm backwater and that they are whirling around somewhere about 6 feet off the ground – it don't sound like the same world to me. I am sitting out on a log against our garage in the sun and peace she is just flowing around me it really is "And what is so rare as a day in June?" first good day out of the past 30 – ...

Will you cable when Mother leaves and when and where she will land. We will be in the South and West of Ireland from July 8 but we will come by donkey turf, trains, taxi and jaunting car from the ends of the earth to meet 1, 2, or 3 – why not?

Keep us posted! We just can't keep up!

Love,
Helen

25th June
Malone

Dear Mother and Auntie and Ginna,

I am gradually beginning to realize that Mother is coming and the sun seems brighter already though I won't really blow my top – as they say – until I get a cable that you and Auntie have sailed. I think our mutual trying to get together has been very like the events working up to the end of the war – such starts and stops, uncertainties, frustrations, indecisions and general confusion – but now at last! Thank goodness! Mother has taken the bull or Mrs. Shipley by the horns and away she goes. This end is still dead end as far as exit permits go – still necessary and still strict. ... When the *Queen Eliz.* sailed last week the Head of the shipping company said that he thought the immense numbers of people on both sides of the Atlantic should be considered and that if he had the *Q.E.* he could have it ready for civilians in 6 mo. They first told us at the permit office that the restrictions would be off in a month but that is 6 weeks ago and no word of it yet. They can't let them off until there are some ships to take them. Since the restrictions have been off to England the ships are crammed to the railings and there is no hope of a berth unless you queue at 9 or before you want to go. London is apparently so crowded that you can hardly get along the streets. Barbara Gotto[121] says that if you are really trying to hurry someplace it is infuriating.

I hope to goodness you both come soon. You say maybe the middle of July that is nearly too good to be true but I can believe anything now – you seem so confident and it seems so simple. ...

Keep us posted, airmail letters from N.Y. come in 4 and 5 days. I hope ours are as fast. I could do with a good new girdle, please. Don't need another thing except always silk stockings. Come fast – when I hear you've started I will need to eat glucose all day every day to keep myself calm and collected – Ma! I can't believe it yet. If you need a cancer letter yet cable and we'll rush one over. Don't let anything hold you now. Lancelot said last night "I just like your Mother so well. I couldn't have been luckier with a mother-in-law and I don't know anybody I'd rather have to stay" and you know he means it because he is no gusher. The kids were speechless with surprise and excitement. I asked Julie what I should say to you today and she said to tell you she is going to give you her china pig.

We'll be seeing you ! ! ! ![122]

Even writing about it I feel a frenzy coming over me.

Love and kisses,
Helen

---

[121] Barbara was the wife of Sub-Lt Christopher Gotto; for the Gotto family, see the letter of 16th February, 1943; Barbara was a daughter of the Glendinnings of Reagh Island, near Mahee.

[122] An excited allusion, perhaps, to the recent hit song "I'll be Seeing You", recorded by both Billie Holiday and Bing Crosby in 1944 and sung in the 1944 movie, *I'll Be Seeing You*, starring Ginger Rogers and Joseph Cotten.

Postscript

It was a joyful reunion when in July 1945 Helen's mother and sister arrived in Belfast. Apart from closing the long gap of separation, another more serious objective was to tackle the post-war bureaucracy regarding civilians and travel.

Unknown to Helen but known to Lancelot, her cancer had returned and it was hoped that the more advanced treatment available in the United States would prevent it from spreading further.

As all the Atlantic flights to New York were for military personnel only, it seemed impossible for the entire family to travel. However, thanks to the thoughtful intervention of Dick Pim, transatlantic Clipper flights were arranged and that autumn and in relays the Turtles were on their way.

Helen's treatment in New York City began immediately. Her daughters went to Denver with their grandmother and to the school that Helen had been at, while their father returned to Belfast. Helen stayed in New York with Turtle cousins and Smith College friends until Christmas united the family in Denver. Early in 1946 Helen returned to New York to continue her treatment. Lancelot went back to Belfast in the belief that his family would be able to join him in the near future.

Throughout her ordeal Helen was optimistic about her recovery and her return to Belfast, as witnessed by the letters she wrote to her friends both in the North and South of Ireland all of whom had kept in touch with her.

Sadly this wasn't to be as Helen died in Denver in July 1946, aged 35.

Although Helen never returned to Belfast, her devoted friends were determined that somehow she would still be in their midst. So, together with Queen's University in Belfast, they endowed a scholarship for travel within North America which continues to this day. It is awarded to a candidate who would specifically continue Helen's example of friendship between the land of her birth and that of her adoption. Thus every year since 1949 the Helen Ramsey Scholarship is awarded and the memory of this remarkable and much loved person is celebrated.

On our return to Belfast in August 1946, my father had the unenviable task of coming to terms with his tragic loss as well as trying to get his daughters settled after their interrupted year. We were 9, 7 and 3.

Looking back, I think the reopening of the ice rink at the King's Hall at Balmoral (Belfast) was key for all of us. We could walk to it from Malone Park and did so every evening when our father got home from his office. We all joined the Skating Club where we learned to dance on ice, do figures of 8 as well as drags, jumps and spirals. We made new friends and before long were ready to perform in the first ice show since war had closed the rink. Even Mary Lee was steady enough to take part as a doll in one of the performances.

As you will have read in my mother's letters, my father always took up new interests with great enthusiasm and intensity and it was this characteristic that now came to his aid. He told me years later that Helen had encouraged him to learn how to play bridge as "single men were always in demand!" Eventually we all played and the cottage became the Las Vegas of Mahee as the Turtles, Webbs and Brownes gathered under the hissing Tilley lamps ready to take each other on. We played for "a penny a hundred" as if our lives depended on it and then we certainly thought they did.

The most important stabilising aspect to all our lives, however, was the arrival – a bit like Mary Poppins' – of Eleanor Browne from Oxford. "Brownie" (her army nickname, as we subsequently learned) had had a distinguished wartime career and had recently been demobilised along with a fellow officer who happened to be a friend of my father's. Morris Atkinson, who knew that we were all in need of a steadying presence at home, suggested that Brownie might consider leaving her current post-war position as Matron in a boy's prep school to give a helping hand. This she duly did on a very cold January day in the harsh winter of 1947 and said she could stay for three months. These three months became forty-nine years and our family is forever and gratefully in her debt.

JULIE TURTLE MACKIE

Afterword

Having met Lancelot Turtle on a visit to Northern Ireland in 1927, Helen Ramsey began her prolific letter-writing career when she returned to the United States and corresponded across the Atlantic with the young man she would marry in Denver Colorado six years later. When she returned to Northern Ireland as Mrs Lancelot Turtle in 1933, her transatlantic correspondence resumed with the recipients now being chiefly her mother and sister Ginna in Denver, Colorado.

The letters home were in the first instance extended bulletins about her new married and domestic life. They were faithful in their regularity, and if they were newsy and lengthy this stemmed in part, I think, from her homesickness while she nevertheless got on adapting briskly to marriage and to a new city, country and culture. Their length also reflected the cost and effort of transatlantic mail; the letters were often written over days before being sent by the next mail steamer to New York and thence Denver; this helps to give them their cumulative and miscellaneous effect that we associate with diaries and journals. Her mother and sister visited Helen and Lancelot at least three times and after those visits Helen in her letters could bring them up to date on the friends and relatives whom Ginna and her mother had met; the references are free and easy, gossipy and anecdotal. When children came along, the letters were reports on their development and doings; the letters were one means of keeping the Ramsey family united, especially after the death of Helen's father in 1935, and despite the 4,000 miles separation; the family team spirit is unusually pronounced and the closeness of the two sisters quite marked.

The frequency and detail of the letters she wrote (and the replies she received) helped Helen to maintain a dual life of the mind, in Northern Ireland and Denver, and despite her physical absence from her native country. Indeed, she claimed in 1939 even before the war that living in Ireland had generated "a rabid interest in America amounting almost to an obsession". The letters were an outlet for this rabid interest, but also a vivid demonstration of the ironies and attitude changes, the challenges and opportunities, the pains and pleasures of expatriation. The outbreak of war multiplied those challenges and pains, and although Helen was game about adapting to the circumstances of life in Belfast and the United Kingdom, the purpose of her letters home after September 1939 was surely a way of lessening her feeling of being marooned on the wrong side of the ocean for the duration of the war, with expatriation no longer voluntary but enforced. But as with all else in her life, rain or shine, Helen Turtle knuckled down and got on with it, exhibiting the resolve we associate with pioneer women.

And this quality in life of responding spiritedly to unavoidable circumstances was also her quality as a letter-writer. After her death, her Belfast friend Janie McNeill (friend also of C.S. Lewis) remembered the time Helen was asked in what period of history she would have chosen to live "and her answer 'Just right now' was illuminating, for she had that vivid interest in the present", and that interest animates the letters. Another friend, the architect Thibeaudeau (Bodo) Taggart caught that when as a serving officer he received a letter from her in 1942: "You have preserved the dying art of letter writing," he replied, "but have superimposed a modern brightness and interest and your own independent thinking".

Her letters record that she was on amber alert, as it were, to everything around her, and they themselves are often instant transcripts of the present and the eagerly anticipated future. "Now 'Sunday Rhapsody' is on – Homage to Johann Strauss, and will I love it," she writes, before word-painting a still-life to set the cottage scene and capture both the moment and (by a kind of descriptive shorthand) the family's varied interests, the lives of a gifted homemaker, a naturalist, and children at home in the outdoors: "There is a little royal blue squat teapot of yaller daisies on this table and a huge jardinière yaller too of pink mallows on the hearth and a 'summer bunch' in a red bowl on a side table and a pinky-purple bunch on the rug chest and 3 deadish hydrangeas in a green Wedgwood beer mug on the mantelpiece. The *Water Babies* is on the table and there is an assortment of binoculars, movie cameras, cartridges, beeswax and needles and thread sitting around. One leg of the couch has given way but the striped chair covers are as fresh and summery as ever. All the family's bathing suits and towels are hanging on the hedge. The bookcase has never been so neat in its life because Mrs. Turtle tidied it and no one has had time to untidy it. The Strauss program is as good as I thought – the announcer said of him 'it was no small thing to make the world dance' and he was right." It was one of the novelist Samuel Richardson's friends who asked him after he corrected his own letters: "shou'd they not appear extempore, and just as the thoughts flow'd at the time?" and Helen's do. And thanks to the BBC Genome project, we can often date the time to the nearest ten or even five minutes, since she often wrote her letters with half an ear cocked to the wireless, as the natives called it, which helps us re-create that immediacy.

At the same time, she was aware of what her mother and sister would find interesting. "I heard such a good talk on the radio the other day about writing letters," she tells them, "the whole point of which was to tell what *you* would want to know. I expect you would want to know all about Auntie. ..." On 3rd December 1936, in "the worst letter I've ever had to write", she knew that her mother and sister would want to know all the sad details of her little son Lee's sudden death the day before, and furnishes those details with a descriptive and narrative composure that I can only call noble. This Smith College graduate in English was a writer *manquée* but judged herself as critical rather than creative, which the letters surely go some way to dispute. Her letters lie mid-way between the Mass-Observation diaries British volunteers kept between 1937 and 1965 and the writings of those authors in the 1940s who championed the virtues of everyday life, as Marc Stears tells us in *Out of the Ordinary* (2020). (Though Helen's letters may also have been a kind of displacement activity, a substitute for the sterner task of attempting fiction.) She certainly could be critical in the sense of disparaging, often wittily so, being, as the Ulster saying has it, "pass-remarkable" about people. There is ginger in her friendship with Harry McMullan, Kathleen Spence and several others that adds spice to her anecdotes. But she was also self-critical in that way most Americans can be, comfortable as they are in their own skin. Both kinds of criticism are on display in the letter of 5th November 1942 when in a rich passage she heaps praise on her party hostess that then becomes fulsome, with its subtext of disapproval (is conspicuous consumption in wartime not bad taste? she asks), before Helen admits that her own sour grapes are a form of self-consolation.

All in all, Helen Turtle lived an examined life. She was aware that her own breezy optimism might skew reality; she sometimes felt guilty for not doing more in the war effort, even for living in Northern Ireland, a safer place than England, and for having at hand the literal fruits of country living during rationing such as crocks of gulls' eggs and wildfowl shot by Lancelot. She ponders motherhood and wifeliness, admits to finding raising children and running a home a challenge (even with help from nannies and maids), though also complaining of herself that "I am getting too wrapped up in my children". She reflects in one stocktaking letter on the state of her marriage and under what circumstances might she have an affair, before rejecting the possibility. Later, her friend Stella Carr, wife of the painter Tom Carr, acted out that very dramatic choice when the American soldiers in all their exotic yet cinematically familiar allure arrived in Northern Ireland. There is in the letters a strand of wistfulness, even a mild sense of captivity, as housewife, as mother, and as an educated woman seeking culture through the BBC, books and magazines, the theatre, cinema, the Drawing Room Circle but not, though this doesn't break surface as complaint, as a professional woman. (Just occasionally, the confining bell jar of her fellow Smith College alumna Sylvia Plath suggests itself.) She is infatuated with the poetry of Louis MacNeice who seems in the flesh to have embodied the culture she venerated.

The contrasting circumstances of Helen's life added lenses to her sight. The visits to the cottage on Mahee Island, then a remote corner of rural Ulster, meant that she was for most of the war an urban expatriate adapting to country life. Unlike her, Lancelot was at home equally in the city where he was a successful Belfast stockbroker, and in the country, on the shores or on the waters of Strangford Lough where he was a well-known ornithologist and shooter, in the days when one could be both a naturalist and a wildfowler. (Lancelot, glimpsed in the letters pursuing his own varied interests, is a quiet presence that still manages to exude a groundedness and reliability. There are sketches of his Turtle family background and his boyhood in his sister Arabella's memoir, *Ebb and Flow* (1971), printed by Dublin's famous Dolmen Press. Since Arabella (Cherry to her English friends) had apprenticed as an actress at the Old Vic, had been a touring dramatic recitalist in the 1930s, met royalty and the cream of English theatrical talent, and given talks to the Dublin Shakespeare Society, her memoir flows with anecdotes.)

But the most important source of Helen's multifocal vision of life came from her being an American in Europe, especially an American in Northern Ireland. Janie McNeill saw in Helen "that vitality and confidence which the new world gives to its children and which is one of their greatest contributions to the world of to-day". It would be hard to exaggerate the differences between Americans and Britons (especially Northern Irish Britons) before and during the war; it was like the difference between colour and sepia. Yet one of the revelations in these letters, for this writer at least, is the large number of Americans who were living happily in Belfast well before the war; there was even an Ulster Association of Southern California. Most of the Americans were middle- or upper middle-class women, many of them like Helen married to stockbrokers or directors of linen firms or captains of heavy industry; some of the couples had met on ocean cruises. More than a score of them were Helen's friends and acquaintances. They were on the whole energetic, competent and at ease in public life, oblivious to, or unheeding of, the restraints of class, religion or the sexual division of labour at work in pre-war Britain. Anne de Courcy tells us in *The Husband Hunters* (2017) that American heiresses came to Britain before the Great War in search of titled husbands – they "demand respect, even veneration, from their men whom they treated as equal". The self-possessed American women in Ulster formed a cohort between those heiresses in Edwardian Britain and the war brides to come and is an expatriate generation so far neglected by social historians; Helen drafted their first portrait.

The American women married chiefly into what has been called the linenocracy, shorthand for the professions and upper social class that grew at first out of the leaders of the linen industry in the Lagan Valley from the 18th century and then out of engineering, shipbuilding, finance and the law, and centred in Belfast. Helen's letters are peopled by members of such families as the Cowdys, Pringles, Glendinnings, Mackies, Cunninghams, Andrews, Barbours, Pims, Brysons, Workmans, Gottos and Duffins, some of whom combined distinction in industry with distinction in politics and social service and bore the late imprint of Plantation Ulster. There was a sense of social kinship; as we learn from Sean Barden's *Elm Park 1626–1954* (2004), this preparatory school in County Armagh was attended by many pupils from prominent families involved in linen-production or linen-making machinery, including the Andrews, Charley and Mackie families. The linenocracy, in its broadest sense, was predominantly Protestant; Northern Ireland itself in the 1930s was just under two-thirds Protestant, with Éire to its south over ninety percent

Catholic. Helen and Lancelot did have Catholic friends, including Eleanor Nicholson and her husband Captain Cyril Nicholson KC whose family owned Beech Hill country house, Co. Londonderry. It is true that the Catholics in Helen's letters are chiefly the maids or nannies recruited from the Free State, as Éire was popularly referred to. The religious populations in Ireland were to a degree self-segregating although in both jurisdictions there were also formal and informal mechanisms of sectarian exclusion. And the religious affiliations had their party-political correlation. Yet relations between middle-class and upper-class Catholics and Protestants were complex, with religion and social class vying for priority. In January 1931, for example, Mrs Dolan's daughters Nell and Peg attended a grand social affair in Bangor Castle organised by the North Down Women's Unionist Association, then part of the Northern Ireland political establishment that firmly ruled the province. In 1933 Peg married the son of a Protestant minister from Wiltshire. Major Dolan was a founder member of the Royal North of Ireland Yacht Club which seems to have been the port of choice for the linenocratic sailing fraternity. Major Dolan's obituarist is careful to say that Major Dolan had supported no political party, into which can be read a number of possibilities reflecting the nuances under the deceptive surface of an apparently simple state of segregation.

Despite any social segregation on religious grounds, the class and connection Helen married into had by commercial necessity, if for no other reason, a high centrifugal energy; the Turtles, for example, branched out into the United States, the Mackies into Europe. And Northern Ireland's major factories were inward magnets for European and American industrialists who needed the products and the lessons of Ulster's manufacturing expertise. The family of Helen's friend Herbert Morawetz (b.1915), the Czechoslovakian who came to work for Mackies, had a warm business relationship with the Belfast firm from the early 1930s and in 1935 Herbert, in preparation for heading up his family's textile factory, came to Belfast for a year to learn about the machinery that Mackies made for the factory back in Bohemia. He later returned as a refugee, escaping from the Nazis in 1939 in the nick of time via Poland. He and his family emigrated to Canada in December 1939. Between 1943 and 1945 his younger sister Sonja was a code-breaker at the Ottawa branch of the Bletchley Park Signals Intelligence. In 1951 Herbert moved to the United

States where he became a professor of chemistry at what is now the New York University School of Engineering. In 1974 he helped mastermind the defection to the West of Mikhail Baryshnikov. Herbert married Catherine Synge (b. 1923) whose father was the nephew of John Millington Synge, the Irish playwright; she was a distinguished mathematician at NYU. They both died in 2017, Herbert aged 102. (There is a 1986 oral interview with Morawetz in the archives of the Science History Institute.) The brother who came to lunch at the Turtles was probably John, who stayed in Belfast and appears in the Belfast newspapers after 1939 as a handy club tennis player; in 1944 he married Maureen McKee of Carrickfergus, whose father was a well-known builder, and took his bride to Canada in 1946. If not John, then it would have been Oskar (b. 1917) who followed his family to Canada in 1940 where he became a distinguished classical composer and was invested with the Order of Canada.

No less interesting a family were the Dorndorfs from Breslau, Germany (now Poland) whom we meet in Helen's letters in 1940. Marion Klara Dorndorf (b. 1909, Mucki to Helen and her other Northern Irish friends) told her niece Diana von Sachsen, née Dorndorf, that she met Lavens Mackie, whom she married in Breslau in 1929, while he was doing firm's business with the Morawetz factory in Bohemia. Her brother Heinz (b. 1905), sensing the danger from the growing Nazi party, left Germany for Australia via England and changed his name to Heinz Dunne. Another brother, Rainer (b. 1912), left for France, then England where he was a racing driver, competing in a 1938 Peugeot with Dorothy Patten, the famous race and test driver. When war broke out, he was interned on the Isle of Man. In 1940 he was released, probably on the recognizance of his sister Mucki and came to Belfast where he was briefly interned in Crumlin Road Gaol. IRA prisoners presumed he was anti-British (Irish republicans had courted German assistance since at least 1916) and threw him cigarettes. Again released, he joined Mucki and Lavens Mackie at Rathfern near Belfast. After the war Rainer continued racing a BMW and was well-known on the Irish circuits. He later married Georgina Russell from Belfast and farmed in County Wicklow and County Down before retiring to Spain. Mucki, it seems, had had several suitors before Lavens, probably including Fritz, the nephew of the Red Baron, the famous Great War German fighter pilot, Manfred von Richthofen; they remained friends and Mucki's niece Rhoda Dorndorf remembers that "Uncle Fritz" came to Northern Ireland in the 1960s to see the Mackies and visited the Dublin studio where *The Blue Max* (1966), in which the Red Baron features, was being filmed. In Northern Ireland Mucki became a rosette-winning breeder of Ayrshire cattle and supplied the Royal Victoria Hospital in Belfast with fresh milk during the war. (Her Scottish second husband was a Hereford cattle breeder.) Mucki's eldest child is Anita, first cousin of Helen's son-in-law, Paddy Mackie. Anita Mackie emigrated to the United States where she worked in Washington DC for the federal government, dispensing aid to seventeen countries (and possibly working for the CIA) before returning recently to rural Northern Ireland in her late eighties. Muckie celebrated her 104th birthday in March 2013, an occasion written up in the *Ulster Star*, a Lisburn, Co. Down newspaper; she died a month shy of her 105th birthday.

Helen's sociability inside her social set (and outside, once the American GIs arrived) means that her letters can be a kind of gazetteer. The family histories that we can draw from her letters disclose a significant layer of culture neglected on the whole by historians for whom families have not been primary data. They are all the more significant in Northern Ireland because a number of families were highly active and influential in industry, sport, and politics - northern equivalents, though not aristocratic, of the pre-Independence Southern Anglo-Irish in contemporary profile. To pursue the names in Helen's letters is to reveal an impressive web of kinship complicated by inter-marriage but also of family versatility. The war was an opportunity to multiply this versatility, though military service was often a family tradition in any case. In this regard, the Gotto family, into which the English opera singer Henry Wendon married, would repay study. This linen family included merchants, an Irish international rugby player, an Irish international hockey player, tennis players, golfers, cricketers, the Timber Controller of Northern Ireland at the time of Helen's 1943 letter, and serving sailors and soldiers. Captain Arthur Gotto of the Devonshire Regiment was cited for gallantry in 1943; his brother, Robert Vivian Gotto, became an RAF meteorologist during the war and later lectured in Zoology at Queen's University and was a member of the Irish Davis Cup tennis team, 1953–1961. Their daughter Priscilla, a competitive tennis-playing Captain in the Mechanised Transport Corps, was on her way home on 22nd November 1944 when the Flying Fortress she was travelling in (destination Langford Lodge, Co. Antrim) crashed in Shropshire killing her and six other passengers and crew.

Helen's letters chart her family's social gradient in Belfast from a modest rented house on the Belmont Road in east Belfast to the grander Sans Souci Park to ownership of a former Turtle residence in Malone Park in leafy south Belfast, perhaps the city's best address which in Helen's time housed a remarkable congestion of talent. And the Turtles employed domestic help, which from a 21st-century retrospect might wrongly imply an unusually privileged life. Their "good war" came instead from Lancelot's not being youthful or perfectly fit enough to be accepted when he tried to enlist, and from the family's access to a cottage in the country and by the sea. And in fact, until the Second World War, maids and nannies composed a very large employment sector. For several reasons, once war began there appeared "the servant problem" as domestic help became hard to find. The problem looms large in Helen's letters home, larger than my selection indicates. Moya Woodside, a psychiatric social worker in Belfast, wrote in her Mass-Observation diary in March 1940: "A tremendous scarcity of domestic servants is manifest. My mother, whose present girl is leaving, has had an advertisement in two papers every day for a week, and so far there has not been a single reply".[1] The sudden increase in "servantless homes" as *Harper's Bazaar* called the phenomenon in the United States in 1943 was taken by many as evidence that a social revolution was under way on the home front during the global conflict. Helen among others thought that Britain would become more democratic, even socialist, after the war. She foresaw the end of the servant class, as did the English novelist Margaret Kennedy in her wartime diary that became *Where Stands a Wingèd Sentry* (1941).

The domestic life of the Ulster linenocracy has not often been depicted, nor the linenocracy at play. And it has been lazily regarded as a philistine social class, merely sporty when it wasn't industrious. There would have been Ulster industrialists resembling Dickens's Josiah Bounderby, no doubt, but Helen's letters utterly discredit the distinguished Irish writer Sean O'Faolain's portrait of hell which masquerades as Belfast in *An Irish Journey* (1940). On the strength of a fleeting visit he writes of "the red factories and the grey buildings, and the ruthlessness with which the whole general rash of this stinking city was permitted to spread ... All the hates that blot the name of Ulster are germinated here. And what else could be

---

[1] Quoted in Mary Muldowney, "Woman in Wartime: The Mass-Observation Diary of Moya Woodside", *Irish Review*, summer 2010.

germinated here but the revenges of the heart against its own brutalization ... There is no aristocracy – no culture – no grace – no leisure worthy of the name. It all boils down to mixed grills, double whiskies, dividends, movies, and these strolling, homeless, hate driven poor". But Helen is a one-woman dismissal of this travesty. She takes omnivorous advantage of the plays, movies, lectures, concerts and recitals, magazines and journals (including the progressive London literary journal *Horizon* as well as her beloved *New Yorker*) on offer in Belfast. Her many books she seems to have bought but also borrowed from the city's venerable Linen Hall Library. She had a particular liking for women authors and I am personally grateful to her for introducing me to the neglected first-class writing of Nora Waln, Mary Bordern, Nina Fedorova and Silvia Schulman, which I have read with great pleasure. Helen's high metabolism, her serial and sometimes simultaneous attentions, increase the cultural inventory of her letters, to the profit of tomorrow's period historian.

She may have been an unusual woman but the liveliness of the Drawing Room Circle, for example, showed that other women of her class were as culturally aspirational. The DRC was the brainchild of the American Mary Morwood who graduated in literature from Stanford University. After graduation she was acting editor of the Californian magazine, *Overland Monthly* and had the distinction of accepting for publication Jack London's first short story to see print, "The White Silence". In Belfast she started the DRC in 1926. Like her fellow-American Helen, she was a rather indifferent housewife (no jam-making or pickling for them), relied on maids, but disliked drawing-room complaints about their deficiencies. She was something of a bluestocking and sat at her typewriter producing study-outlines for the women-only members. Her daughter Mary's girlhood recollections of the DRC meetings are among the Circle's papers in the Public Record Office of Northern Ireland.

Because of the blackout which meant a nightly domestic lockdown which we in 2021 can empathize with, reading became commoner during the war. R.M. Connolly, chairman of the Northern Ireland Branch of the Associated Booksellers of Great Britain and Ireland was quoted in the *Belfast News-Letter* in March 1944: "Since the war began books have entered into the lives of the public as never before and thousands are discovering the bookshops for the first time in their search for guidance on present and future problems". Helen was one of those who helped swell the readership of the *New Statesman* from 24,000 to 70,000 after war began.

Listeners to the BBC also multiplied. For Helen, the BBC's school programmes, like her reading, became part of her private Further Education syllabus, her curiosity being insatiable. Moreover, war demanded more news at decreasing intervals, and in turn Helen fed this news as report and comment into her letters to her Denver family, and as promptly as possible until they were war bulletins. The BBC nine o'clock News had 17 million listeners during the war, a huge fraction of the population and Helen became one of the addicted. But the Home Service (1939–1967) and General Forces Programme (1939–1945) also offered variety, drama, comedy, music (classical, popular, jazz), and documentary. The letters are a parade of the hit tunes of the day. Helen was aware of the criticisms being made of the BBC but grew to admire and rely on it. Her letters are a rich record of the BBC in the life of the nation in wartime. During blackout, petrol shortage and rationing, life shrank to its foreground (as it has for us during the Covid pandemic) and the wireless set became a domestic as well as local and national nerve centre. The family would listen as one and in wartime it was as though the family became the nation. When Helen's infant daughter Julie imagines falling into the radio and becoming "all newsy", she inadvertently, like another Alice, sees the set as a little vortex, the entrance to a larger different world.

The cinema, too, was a virtual escape from the constraints of wartime, usually to the exotic world of America which in Helen's case was home but now seen from afar. She was among the 32% of the British population that went at least weekly to the local picture-houses and her letters let us know just what that population in Belfast was watching on the screen: glamour and adventure, of course, but also newsreels of the war, and documentaries that combined entertainment with propaganda. Local picture-going helped raise and fortify the morale of the people; it helped unify the nation in a common pursuit, as the radio did the family.

When Sean O'Faolain published his caricature of Belfast, with its managerial class chiefly in his sights, the linenocracy were in fact at war, organising the production of the *matériel* by which Nazism could be beaten in the field, air and sea. Mackies, Short Brothers and Harland, Sirocco Works, Harland & Wolff and other engineering firms (as well as linen firms) produced, round the clock, ships, munitions, aeroplanes, or parts thereof, in an industrial contribution that compensated for the sometimes disappointing contribution of personnel in the absence of conscription in Northern Ireland. Helen's letters 1939–1945 are a useful rough chronicle of the progress of the war on the home front and the battlefront, from rumours of war through its declaration, the phoney war, blackout, rationing, the Battle of Britain, the Blitz, the decisive battles, the losses and deaths, and the final victory in Europe. The serial highlights are Winston Churchill's speeches to the nation she listened to on the BBC and which were the milestones that mattered most. The power of Churchill's language was a one-man reply to the visual panoply of Nazi strength conveyed in newsreels. His rhetorical power was concentrated through the intimate and yet collective medium of radio; each household listened alone and yet felt connected to the other households of the nation. Patriotism may have led Helen to believe that perhaps Roosevelt was an even greater man, and the poignancy of his early death may also have influenced her in this, but Helen's admiring letters have reminded me that Churchill was the irreplaceable standard-bearer in Britain's defeat of Hitler's Germany.

Because Helen knew personally some of those engaged in the war effort, either on the home front at the organisational level or as officers in the services, her detailed observations resemble but differ from those we find in the Mass-Observation diaries of the time, such as the diary published as *A Woman in Wartime London: The Diary of Kathleen Tipper 1941–1945* (2006). They also differ from, closer to home, the two world war diaries of the Voluntary Aid Detachment nurse Emma Duffin (1883–1979), born eight doors from what later would be Helen's doctor's surgery in University Square, Belfast and who in 1941 tended the casualties of the city's horrendous Blitz.[2] Helen watched the massive air-raid on Belfast on 15th April from some miles away, and aware of the censors wrote her report too cleverly in impromptu code as though recounting a party: the German flares, incendiary bombs and explosives were the "showy and sparkly" presents the partygoers brought; the German bomber pilots were the Turtles' German maids attending the "party"; the fire-brigades from the Free State whose arrival astonished the local citizens were the Scanlans turning up unexpectedly at the "party" (Philip Scanlan being a proud pro-neutrality Irish nationalist in Dublin), and the southern

---

[2] See *A Nurse in the Belfast Blitz: The Diary of Emma Duffin, 1939–42*, ed. Trevor Parkhill (2016).

firemen were the green tweed people. The account fails to be decoded at the Denver end, but the extended metaphor of a party to describe an air-raid obviously relays the strange euphoria that the sights and sounds of the Blitz generated in Helen. And this was not an unknown reaction. Charles Ritchie, the Canadian diplomat and lover of Elizabeth Bowen the Irish writer, in recording his experience of a London air-raid in October 1940 in his memoir *The Siren Years* (1974), found "there is an exhilaration in this orgy of destruction and in the danger", and for many Londoners the Blitz was indeed like a grotesque inversion of a party.

Capt. (soon to be Sir) Richard Pim and Lt.-Cdr Harry McMullan were among those Helen knew who wielded some real influence in the conduct of the war as members of Churchill's Map Room. It was Pim who told Churchill that Berlin had fallen. As his granddaughter Dede Pim tells it, Captain Pim received a message from President Roosevelt at 4 a.m. on 7th May 1945 that the Germans had surrendered. Churchill was sleeping at the time and his standing instructions were that he was not to be awakened unless Britain had been invaded. At 8 a.m. Pim accompanied by a butler went to the PM's bedroom. When Churchill read the message he said: "You have brought me very indifferent news every morning but you have redeemed yourself this morning, Pim. This is wonderful news".

Helen also knew, or knew the parents of, an assortment of those who turned out to be decorated war heroes, the most impressive of whom were her friend Roberta McMullan's brother, the indestructible Spitfire pilot, Fred Gardiner, and Lt.-Cdr Billy Stephens, though there were also Osborne King, Bodo Taggart, Raymond Hart and Helen's doctor's sons. My footnote to Billy Stephens did scant justice to the Ulsterman's extraordinary trials after the St Nazaire raid in 1942.

After capture Stephens and his men were taken to Stalag 133 for interrogation, then to Marlag prisoner of war camp. En route from Marlag to Colditz Castle POW camp, Stephens jumped from the train but was re-captured the next day and sent to Colditz with a week's isolation as welcome. Stephens and a Major Littledale and two other prisoners soon hatched a plot to escape. They got through a series of windows and evaded attention when the camp orchestra, conducted by Douglas Bader, the legendary Battle of Britain pilot, would stop playing, the signal that the sentry's back was turned. They dropped into a deep moat with knotted sheets and then scaled a ten-foot wall, after which they shook hands, split into two pairs and took their separate chances. Stephens and Littledale walked to Rochlitz station and caught a train to Chemnitz. They changed at Hoff, drank beer, then travelled on minor rail lines to Tübingen. After two days of walking they crossed the Swiss border under cover of darkness but were caught and interned. In June 1942 Stephens re-crossed the border and with forged papers made his way through France and over the Pyrenees to Spain where he was imprisoned once more. He managed by bribery to telephone the British embassy in Madrid which arranged to smuggle him in the boot of a car to Gibraltar and fly him to Britain. He may have been engaged to a divorced Englishwoman, as Helen was told, but he married a Swiss woman, Chou-chou de Meyer, who had sheltered him after he reached her country. Stephens' obituary in the *Independent*, 17th August 1997 described him as a handsome, fair-haired, blue-eyed daredevil.

At the start of the war Helen would have looked askance at those deemed war heroes, since she was a left-leaning pacifist. Her wartime letters chart her journey from military neutralism to interventionism, provoked by the emerging ruthlessness of Hitler's Germany and the onrush of German forces through Europe and towards the country in which she was now living. She dated her conversion to the British war effort to May 1940 when France fell. She was in advance of her sister back in the U.S. in this conversion because she was psychologically closer to the killing fields. In June 1942 she writes: "Everyone is so relieved that Ginna has stopped being an isolationist and a Lindberghite. I am doing my best to make hands across the sea". Before and after her conversion she took some of her cues from her fellow Smith College alumna and isolationist, Anne Morrow Lindbergh whose brother was a leader of the non-interventionist faction in American public life; but in May 1940 Anne herself came to believe that Germany must be stopped. Helen's journey was also her nation's and she is overjoyed when the U.S. throws off isolationism and pitches in. Other left-leaners in the United States followed suit. The folksingers who enthralled Helen in June 1944 in the "Mountain Ballad Opera" re-broadcast by the BBC, Will Geer, Woody Guthrie, and Pete Seeger were musical activists on the left who had agitated against American entry into the war. When the Nazis invaded the Soviet Union they literally and figuratively changed their tune and turned American patriots. The message of the opera was that left and right must end their feud, like the "Martins" and the "Coys", and get behind our boys. Helen, however, was the pacifist product of a liberal household and a liberal college and had urged her country to intervene precisely on grounds of defending liberty and long before the cancelling of the Molotov-Ribbentrop Pact and the invasion of the Soviet Union.

The social impact of intervention when American boots first stepped on to UK soil in Northern Ireland was epoch-making. It was the collision of two friendly but different cultures and Helen is highly attuned to the differences. Helen is overjoyed by the presence around her of her country's young men and their infectious vitality. Already she must have been among the liveliest of these American women expats: her restlessness, candour and openness are stereotypical American virtues. She loved dressing up, dining out or attending gala events: one can reconstruct her wardrobe over the years from the social columns of the *Belfast Telegraph*, *Northern Whig* and *Belfast News-Letter*. When the American troops arrive one realises what she had been missing. Like the American writer Margaret Halsey, she found the British repressed and must often have chafed against the respectability that too often dampened social life. With Americans on the scene her homesickness turned inside out to become exhilaration. She wore slacks, danced, and when the time came thought nothing of taking a lonesome American soldier to the movies, a woman confident and liberated unlike her Northern Irish sisters. In her thirties, she "trucked" and "jitterbugged", both dance crazes expressions of the black-inspired brio and exuberance that fed into the American psyche and gave the country its irrepressible confidence that Janie McNeill saw in Helen. Novelty in dance and music kept alive the promise of newness and a fresh start in what was still largely an immigrant America. The entrance of American popular culture into the UK in the 20th century had an electrifying effect. Helen was at home in the energy of this cultural infusion.

If Northern Irish life was just about adequate, life in Éire, especially in Dublin, was far more enlivening. The south of Ireland and the west of the United States were her favourite places, and she showed scant interest in England. Helen's portrait of wartime Dublin is a sharp-eyed and valuable one, noting as she does the odd ambiguous miscellany of rationing, blazing night-time illumination, censorship, crowded restaurants, crippling petrol shortage, unruly herds of daytime cyclists, laughter and high spirits. We are lucky, too, in having her introduce us to Jonty Hanaghan, married to Lancelot's cousin and Ireland's first psychoanalyst in a Catholic country in which the psychoanalyst was for many decades a *rara avis*. But Ireland being Ireland, nothing is quite what it seems. The Irish are so much more life-loving than their northern counterparts but will tell you anything. She grows a little disapproving of Ireland's neutrality and proud of Northern Ireland's engagement. She would have nodded in recognition to read what Donal Fallon wrote on the online group blog, "Come Here to Me: Dublin Life and Culture," in April 2017, especially given her adulation of the poet who came to the DRC: "The poet Louis MacNeice would remember being in Dublin on the day Hitler invaded Poland, and that in the pub 'the Dublin literati hardly mentioned the war but debated the correct versions of Dublin street songs. Dublin was hardly worried by the war … her old preoccupations were still preoccupations'."

But there was also a more pervasive ambiguity to Ireland's neutrality since there was a second smaller war going on, the IRA's ostensible war with Britain over the very existence of Northern Ireland. In May 1942 she meets and likes the colonel-lawyer who defended the America sergeant accused (in the first U.S. court-martial in war-time in the UK) of manslaughter by shooting dead the local bus-driver in April. Sergeant Clipsham's defence was that his deficient machine-gun went off accidentally and he was acquitted. What did not reach the newspaper reports was the certainty, as the historian Brian Barton sees it (in *Northern Ireland in the Second World War*), that the driver testified that he thought he was being cut off from his convoy in preparation for an IRA attack and shot pre-emptively who he thought was behaving like an enemy. Helen was not quite *au fait* with the darker politics of Ulster which after all can perplex even natives, and I for one am glad the politics did not dampen her great *joie de vivre*. It was her spiritedness, combined with wartime tensions, that so often kept her awake and attentive until it was "midnight again". Her canvas in the letters is the endless scope of every day and of the everyday, the sights and sounds of her whereabouts (and these can be in her thinking mind and feeling heart); this canvas she painted with verve, curiosity, and with a most attractive personality.

JOHN WILSON FOSTER

A NOTE ON THE TEXT

This selection from Helen Ramsey Turtle's handwritten letters retains something like sixty percent of the words she wrote home between January 1939 and June 1945. From Belfast she regularly wrote letters back to Denver after 1933 so that her daughter Julie is in possession of a large cache of correspondence which contains valuable observations of Northern Irish life as well as her experiences of marriage, motherhood and household management in a strange country in the third and fourth decades of the twentieth century. From her wartime letters I have omitted a great deal about Helen's young children, their activities and ailments, and the daily tasks of running a household; the domestic detail allowed her mother and sister to participate, as it were, in the growing family thousands of miles away. My footnotes are chiefly meant to draw out the social and cultural history embedded in Helen's letters. My selection was made from Mrs Joan Cowdy's transcription of the letters into Word documents. I have substituted italics for Helen's handwritten underlinings and also italicised the names of books, magazines, and films. Helen's American spellings and Americanisms have, of course, been kept. Ellipses indicate omissions.

JWF

Acknowledgements

As editor, I am grateful in the first instance to Mrs Eveleigh Brownlow of Portaferry, Co. Down for the lunch invitation that resulted in my meeting Mrs Julie Mackie and being introduced, at first by word of mouth, to her mother Helen's letters that she thought might be of interest, and which certainly proved to be the case. Julie herself has been an attentive custodian of both the letters and her mother's memory and has been of indispensable and knowledgeable help in checking the handwritten originals at my request, helping to identify many of her mother's relatives, friends and acquaintances who make their appearance in the letters, and on occasions contacting their descendants, some of them friends of long standing. She was helped in her task of identifying references and also establishing precise relationships by Caroline (Workman) Anderson, Charles Barr, Eveleigh Brownlow, Sue (Ewart) Cunningham, Sue Fetherston, Belinda (Cowdy) Haas, Simon Haselden, Sara Lindsay, Peter McMullan, Michael Nicholson, Dede Pim, Bunty Portig, Redmond and Diana Taggart, and Mark Topping. She is grateful to them, and to Ernie Cromie of the Ulster Aviation Society for his encouraging interest in the portrait of World War 2 in her mother's letters. From her childhood on Mahee, she remembers the Glendinning and Browne families, friends of her parents, and wishes to thank them for their neighbourly warmth over the years which continues to this day.

For my own part, it has been a pleasure being in contact with those related to members of what we might call Helen's cast – Redmond Taggart, Rhoda Dorndorf, Diana von Sachsen (née Dorndorf), Garry Villiers-Stuart, Barbara Grubb (née Villiers-Stuart), Mary Fleck (daughter of the Spitfire ace, Fred Gardiner), Alexandra Gardiner (Fred's stepdaughter), and Stuart Spence. It has been a special delight in corresponding with Daphne McMullan and her husband Peter McMullan of Nanaimo, British Columbia whose father Harry's presence enlivens many a scene recreated in the letters and who himself appears as a frisky and clever youngster, and in meeting in person the film historian Charles Barr, who also makes guest appearances as a gifted lad. For various kinds of help, I am also indebted to Martyn Anglesea (Ulster Museum), Marianna Apostolakis (Smith College), Rose Beetem (Denver Art Museum), Lorraine Bourke and Avril Loughlin (Public Record Office of Northern Ireland), Hannah Chandler (Official Papers Library, Bodleian Library, Oxford), the late Joan Cowdy, Daniel Calley, Dorothy Dunlop, Eleanor Grene, Elizabeth Gultekin (Central Library, Belfast), Susie Hill, Diarmuid Kennedy (McClay Library, Queen's University Belfast), Daniel J. Lawton (former U.S. Consul in Belfast), Liam Maguire (Queen's University Belfast), my wife Gail Malmo, Henry Patterson (University of Ulster), Mark Phelan (Queen's University Belfast), Des O'Rawe (Queen's University Belfast), David Wright, and Dominique Yupangco (University of British Columbia).